THE HISTORY
OF PROSTITUTION

ITS EXTENT, CAUSES AND EFFECTS
THROUGHOUT THE WORLD

by
WILLIAM W. SANGER, M.D.

RESIDENT PHYSICIAN, BLACKWELL'S ISLAND, NEW YORK CITY; MEMBER OF
THE AMERICAN ASSOCIATION FOR THE ADVANCEMENT OF SCIENCE;
LATE ONE OF THE PHYSICIANS TO THE MARINE HOSPITAL,
QUARANTINE, NEW YORK, ETC , ETC., ETC.

WITH NUMEROUS EDITORIAL NOTES
AND AN APPENDIX

"To such grievances as society cannot readily cure, it
usually forbids utterance on pain of its scorn; this scorn
being only a sort of tinseled cloak to its deformed weakness."   —CURRER BELL, *Shirley.*

Fredonia Books
Amsterdam, The Netherlands

The History of Prostitution:
Its Extent, Causes and Efects
Throughout the World

by
William W. Sanger, M. D.

ISBN: 1-58963-762-3

Copyright © 2002 by Fredonia Books

Reprinted from the 1897 edition

Fredonia Books
Amsterdam, the Netherlands
http://www.fredoniabooks.com

CONTENTS.

CHAPTER XVI.
HAMBURG.

CHAPTER XVII.
PRUSSIA.

CHAPTER XVIII.
LEIPZIG.

CHAPTER XIX.
DENMARK.

CHAPTER XX.
SWITZERLAND.

CHAPTER XXXIII.

NEW YORK.—STATISTICS.

CHAPTER XXXIV.

NEW YORK.—STATISTICS.

CHAPTER XXXV.

NEW YORK.—PROSTITUTES AND HOUSES OF PROSTITUTION.

CHAPTER XXXVI.

NEW YORK.—EXTENT, EFFECTS, AND COST OF PROSTITUTION.

CHAPTER XXXVII.

NEW YORK.—REMEDIAL MEASURES.

APPENDIX.

NEW YORK TODAY.

INTRODUCTION.

ARGUMENTS are unnecessary to prove the existence of prosti-· tution. The evil is so notorious that none can possibly gainsa it. But when its extent, its causes, or its effects are questioned a remarkable degree of ignorance or carelessness is manifested Few care to know the secret springs from which prostitution emanates; few are anxious to know how wide the stream ex tends; few have any desire to know the devastation it causes, Society has formally laid a prohibition on the subject, and he who presumes to argue that what affects one may injure all; he who believes that the malady in his neighbor's family to-day may visit his own to-morrow; he who dares to intimate that a vice which has blighted the happiness of one parent, and ruined the charac- ter of one daughter, may produce, must inevitably produce, the same sad results in another circle; in short, he who dares allude to the subject of prostitution in any other than a mysterious and whispered manner, must prepare to meet the frowns and censure of society.

Keen was the knowledge of human nature, acute the perception of worldly sentiment in the breast of an accomplished woman lately deceased, when she wrote, "To such grievances as society can not readily cure, it usually forbids utterance on pain of its scorn; this scorn being only a sort of tinseled cloak to its deformed weakness." How true the idea, many a man who has attempted to unveil a hidden crime, or probe a secret sorrow, but too well knows.

Not then to prove that prostitution exists, for that is so glar- ingly palpable that all must perforce concede it, but to ascertain its origin, progress, and end, is the object of these pages. The finger of scorn may be pointed at the labor; the self-righteous world may wrap itself in a mantle of prudery, and close its ears against sickening details; the complacent public may demur at an approach to sin and misery; the self-satisfied community may object to view wretchedness drawn from the obscurity of its hid-

B

ing-place to the full light of investigation: nevertheless, there is now existing a moral pestilence which creeps insidiously into the privacy of the domestic circle, and draws thence the myriads of its victims, and which saps the foundation of that holy confidence, the first, the most beautiful attraction of home. There is an ever-present physical danger, so fatally destructive that the world would recoil, as from the spring of a serpent, could they but appreciate its malignity; a malignity which is daily and hourly threatening every man, woman, and child in the community; which for hundreds of years has been slowly but steadily making its way onward, leaving a track marked with broken hopes, ruined frames, and sad recollections of stricken friends; and which now, in the full force of an impetus acquired and aggravated by concealment, almost defies opposition. There is a social wrong which forces upon the community vast expenditures for an object of which they are ignorant; which swells the public taxes and increases individual outlay for a vice which has hitherto been studiously kept in concealment. These reasons were sufficiently powerful to induce the necessary researches for the accomplishment of this work, and they are considered sufficient to justify its publication.

An unseen evil, of which only the effects are visible, is more frightful than one whose dimensions are apparent. No statesman would grapple with a political question until he knew its "form and pressure;" no philanthropist can satisfactorily encounter an unknown misery. Both may judge, to some slight extent, of the evil they can not see, but the one can not venture to remove it, nor the other to modify its woes until its power is fully known. This has so far been the case with prostitution. The world has studiously drawn a screen before it, and when the sufferings of its victims became so apparent that the vice was palpable, an additional mystery was thrown around it, and the people of the nineteenth century know it but as a sin with which they can not interfere. It has all the imagined force of a monster, because of its obscurity; all the virulence of an avenging fiend, because its true powers are hidden; and even those who suffered from its poison have been led to believe that its mysteries were so inscrutable as to defy all approach.

Hitherto reticence has been the policy. This position has been held too long, for it is false in principle and injurious in tendency. The day has arrived when the shroud must be removed; when the public safety imperiously demands an investigation into the matter; when those who regard it as a small wrong may have their attention directed to its real proportions; and when those who have viewed it as an unmanageable giant may be alike undeceived.

A small matter it decidedly is not: the eternal ruin of one misguided woman would effectually preclude such an opinion; the physical ruin of an impetuous man would prohibit such an estimate, and both these are among those daily consequences which call for an investigation. There is scarcely a person in the community who can not recall some circumstance he has known to support this assertion; for so wide-spread has been the baneful influence of prostitution, that there are comparatively few but have suffered, through friends or relatives, if not in their own persons.

Nor is it unmanageable, except when concealed. Stripped of the veil of secrecy which has enveloped it, there appears a vice arising from an inextinguishable natural impulse on the part of one sex, fostered by confiding weakness in the other; from social disabilities on one side, and social oppression on the other; from the wiles of the deceiver working upon unsuspecting credulity; and, finally, *from the stern necessity to live.*

It is a mere absurdity to assert that prostitution can ever be eradicated. Strenuous and well-directed efforts for this purpose have been made at different times. The whole power of the Church, where it possessed not merely a spiritual, but an actual secular arm, has been in vain directed against it. Nature defied the mandates of the clergy, and the threatened punishments of an after-life were futile to deter men from seeking, and women from granting, sinful pleasures in this world. Monarchs victorious in the field and unsurpassed in the council-chamber have bent all their energies of will, and brought all the aids of power to crush it out, but before these vice has not quailed. The guilty women have been banished, scourged, branded, executed; their partners have been subjected to the same punishment; held up to public opinion as immoral; denuded of their civil rights; have seen their offenses visited upon their families; have been led to the stake, the gibbet, and the block, and still prostitution exists. The teachings of morality and virtue have been powerless here. In some cases they restrain individuals; upon the aggregate they are inoperative. The researches of science have been unheeded. They have traced the physical results of vice, and have foreshadowed its course. They have demonstrated that the suffering parents of this generation will bequeath to their posterity a heritage of ruined powers; that the malady which illicit pleasure communicates is destructive to the hopes of man; that the human frame is perceptibly and regularly depreciating by the operation of this poison, and have shown that even the desire for health and long life, one of the most powerful motives that ever influences a human being, has been of no avail to stem the torrent.

But if history proves that prostitution can not be suppressed, it also demonstrates that it can be regulated, and directed into channels where its most injurious results can be encountered, and its dangerous tendencies either entirely arrested or materially weakened. This is the policy to which civilized communities are tending, and to aid the movement it is needful that the subject be examined, even at the risk of the world's contumely.

In some of the countries of Continental Europe the examination has been made, and the natural consequences of a searching and philosophical investigation are there seen in legislation, which aims not to dam a wild torrent, but to lead it where its rage may be harmlessly spent. When a mighty river overflows its banks, the uncontrollable flood works wide-spread ruin and devastation along its course; but the same river, confined to its natural channel, may be of immense service in carrying off a vast amount of filth and *debris* that otherwise would cause pestilence and death. In this Western hemisphere, and in the mother-country, Anglo-Saxon prudery has stood aloof from inquiring into a vice which every one admits to be offensive to the moral sense of the people, and has submitted to an accumulation of evils rather than seek to abate them, until the suffering and the wrong have become so boldly defined that they force themselves upon the public eye.

Assuredly it is high time to inaugurate a new line of action; to cast aside as unworthy those puerile doubts of propriety and expediency which have stood in the way of an onward progress. The very meaning of the word "propriety" supplies an argument in favor of the proposed course. Conventionally, it has been construed to mean an indefinite something which every person has moulded to suit his own predilections. Upon the same principle that a man who makes his living dishonestly would consider it a glaring impropriety to examine the laws of fraud, has the world decided it an outrage against propriety to inquire into a vice which many secretly practice, but all publicly condemn. Reasoning like this has been too often applied, and with too great an effect. Can there possibly be an impropriety in investigating a vice which threatens the purity and peace of the community, because in so doing unpleasant facts will be disclosed? Is there not a far more striking inconsistency in supinely allowing the same vice to exist and increase, without hinderance or examination?

Again: it must be conceded that the demands of propriety are universal. They are not restricted to any person or place, but press with equal force upon every member of the community in every possible situation. The common welfare is involved in their general application, and he well merits the good opinion of his fellow-men who points them to a case where propriety is outraged, and asks their aid to apply the remedy. In a word, *propriety* demands an exposure of all acts of *impropriety*, and the application of the needful cure.

Then the question arises, In what form shall the exposure be made? Truth admits of but one reply. It must be so explicit as to leave no doubt of its meaning; it must be so guarded as not to offend in its application. If the first of these rules is not observed, any disclosure will be worthless; if the remarks are vague, indefinite, or generalized, no good result can accrue. Take a simple illustration. It conveys no determinate idea to a benevolent man to say, "There is distress in a certain city;" but point him to the particular locality, and give him the precise circumstances, and his sympathy is at once aroused and effectively exerted. The same rule is equally applicable to a monster vice and to an individual hardship, and upon this principle have the disclosures of the following pages been based. The idea has been to particularize sufficiently to draw attention, but not enough to gratify a prurient inclination; to exhibit the evil in a truthful aspect, but not in a fascinating form. None can doubt the truth of Pope's well-known lines:

> " Vice is a monster of so frightful mien,
> As, to be hated, needs but to be seen ;
> Yet seen too oft, familiar with her face,
> We first endure, then pity, then embrace."

The endeavor should be to fulfill the imperative demands of propriety, without disturbing the conventional prejudices implied by the same word.

Then, as to expediency, or the fitness to effect some good end. It must be admitted that the mere fact of proving prostitution capable of control is a good object, and it is apparent that such proof can not be afforded while the vice remains a myth. Something must be known of its haunts and its customs ere any one can decide in what shape a supervisory power can be best applied. This knowledge must be obtained in defiance of deep-rooted prejudices. Commonplace objections about the danger of touching impure objects are best met by the remark that to the pure all things are pure. Though benevolence may at times lead its devotees through scenes where moral purity is shocked, and to neighborhoods where filth and obscenity vitiate the very air they breathe, there is no contamination to those whose motives are good. Inexpediency has been urged as often and as falsely as impropriety. In their application to this subject, both are perverted from their legitimate meaning; both are made subservient to a false taste, or a mawkish sensibility which fears to encounter an imaginary danger.

The safety of the community, so far as its sanitary condition is concerned, imperatively demands an inquiry like this. It is no longer necessary to prove that syphilitic taint is propagated by the direct agency of prostitution. That fact has been demonstrated years ago, and, reasoning from it, we rightly infer that the ravages of that poison can be checked by compelling abandoned women to certain judicious observances. One thing is absolutely certain, that the public health can not be endangered by the interference, and there is a moral certainty that it may be materially benefited. The value of this investigation, so far as relates to purely physical questions, consists in not merely pointing out where the evil is, but in showing to what extent it exists, and then contrasting the state of venereal disease, its rapid increase and augmenting virulence in this country, with its condition in those nations where similar investigations have resulted in practical measures.

Public safety imperatively demands this investigation as a means of tracing the habitual resorts of criminals. It is not necessary to inform any man conversant with city life that houses of ill fame are the common resort of the most abandoned of the male part of the community. There the assassin, against whose hand no life is secure, has a safe retreat. The burglar, who commits his depredations under cover of the shade of night; the swindler, who defrauds the honest trader by false representations; the counterfeiter, who earns a precarious living by his unholy trade—these hold there high carnival. There they meet to recount their exploits and divide the spoils; to devise new schemes of wickedness, or lay plans by which simple youths may be allured to vilest practices.

There is another phase of public safety which demands this investigation, namely, the preservation of female honor. Those who frequent these haunts of vice are forever employed in casting about snares to entrap the young, the unwary, or the friendless woman. They tempt her to minister to their libidinous desires, and swell the already overcrowded ranks of frailty. While these resorts are secret, there is every facility for such infamous conduct, with but slight probability of its detection, and still slighter opportunities for prevention. Thither, too, young men, and even boys, are inveigled by those who have grown old in vice, and there are they taught the horrid mysteries of unhallowed passion. Many a promising youth has left such haunts as these not only with a ruined constitution, but with loss of character and honor; many whose names swell the criminal records of the day date their first step in crime from the hour they entered a common brothel.

Again: Public safety demands this investigation because of the superior opportunities it will afford to reformatory measures. Start not at the supposition of reforming courtesans. There is hope even for them, for they are human beings, though depraved. Their hearts throb with the same sympathies that move the more favored of their sex. Their minds are susceptible to the same emotions as those of other females. Few of them become vile from natural instincts: poor victims of circumstances, many of them would gladly amend if the proper means were used at the proper time.

> " There is in every human heart
> Some not entirely barren part,
> Where flowers of richest scent may blow,
> And fruit in glorious sunlight grow."

This consummation can be achieved only when the pseudo-virtue of the world shall yield to true benevolence, and charity be indeed what it professes in name.

If public safety is thus urgent, private interest also has arguments in favor of investigating prostitution. No one need be told that public aid is required to give medical treatment to the unfortunate men and women tainted by this vice; nor need any one be assured that such aid, administered with every regard to economy, requires yearly a large portion of the taxes paid by individuals. It would be sheer folly to assert that any measures which can follow this inquiry will be efficacious in eradicating syphilis, but experience proves that an effective supervision would materially abate its influence, render it curable in a much shorter space of time, and reduce the expenses for each patient in a corresponding ratio.

Another large claim upon the public funds arises from the necessity of employing an extensive judicial and police organization to deal with the crime and the criminals generated and fostered in houses of ill fame. Nests of vice as they are now in their darkness and seclusion, it would be impossible to suppose a more fitting nursery for crime, or one whence more criminals would emanate. As with disease, so with crime. It can not be suppressed by placing its retreats under public notice, but it can be watched, and, once brought to the light of day, half its dangers and difficulties become surmountable.

Finally, private interest demands this investigation on mere private grounds—the individual and personal expenses caused by diseases contracted by debauchery. There is the money a working man must pay for his cure: this is his share of the loss. There is the unproductive time, and the loss of profits upon his labor: this is his employer's sacrifice. There is the deprivation of comforts and necessaries experienced by his family and dependents: this is their penalty. Society is thus involved in a general loss on account of an act of folly, or passion, or crime (call it which you please), committed in a concealed and secret haunt, and such loss could be saved by the intervention of proper means.

Common sense asks for a full investigation of all the evils attending prostitution. In the every-day affairs of life, any man who feels the pressure of a particular evil looks at once for its cause. He may be neither a philosopher nor a logician, and may never have heard of or read any of the luminous treatises which professedly simplify science, yet he knows very well that for every effect there must be some adequate cause, and for this he generally searches diligently till he can find and remove it. But here, in the city of New York, is a population who claim to be as intelligent as any on the Western continent, who have been for years suffering from the effects of a vice in purse and person; who have paid and are paying every year large sums of money on account of it; who witness every day some broken constitution or ruined character resulting from it, and who yet have never thought of seeking out the cause! Is it now too late to enlist your sympathies in the undertaking?

Hence we conclude that propriety, expediency, public safety, private interest, and common sense demand an investigation like this now submitted to the reader. And what is the argument brought forward to oppose it? The world's scorn—"this scorn being only a sort of tinseled cloak to its deformed weakness." But is not this scorn powerless against the array of favoring motives? Will it stand the test of comparison with any one of them, much less of all? Is not its influence lost when its real character is known? The reckless carelessness which has suffered a growing vice to increase and multiply, which has permitted a deadly Upas-tree to take root and blossom in the community until its poisonous exhalations threaten universal infection; which has, by its actual indifference, fostered vice, promoted seduction, perpetuated disease, and entailed death; shall this deformed weakness now raise its trembling hands, and exhibit its tottering frame, and lift its puny voice to forbid an examination into the sources of the danger? Has not the finger of this scorn too long forbid the search for truth? Has not the hour arrived when truth will speak trumpet-tongued, and when her voice must be heard?

Now the question will arise, Has the world's indifference produced these evils? Undoubtedly it has, and in the following manner: Laws have been placed upon the statute-book declaring prostitutes, and houses of prostitution, and all who live by such means, illegal and immoral. There the law yet stands. At uncertain intervals some poor and friendless woman is arrested as a vagrant, and, to appease the offended majesty of law, she is sent to prison, a scapegoat for five thousand of her class. It also sometimes happens that another woman equally guilty, but with money or influence, is arrested at the same time and for the same offense, and before she reaches the prison walls a legal quibble has been raised and she is free. Is there no culpable indifference in this? Houses of prostitution are proscribed by law. How many of them are ever indicted, or, if indicted, how many are suppressed? This, too, is owing to criminal neglect, and it is aggravated by the injurious effects arising from the mere circumstance of allowing a law to exist, and making no efforts to enforce it. The character of a people is judged, not by the laws that are made, but by the strictness with which those that do exist are enforced and observed. In regard to the first, there may be exhibited an acute perception of an existing evil, and a desire to reform it by legislation; but a second glance may reveal no wish to make this legislation effective. In the special matter of prostitution, the opinion is expressed elsewhere that prohibitory laws are worse than useless, and in the experience of New York City there is nothing to shake that opinion, notwithstanding the fact that the efforts made to enforce them are so "few and far between." Had existing laws been more vigorously enforced, their inefficiency would long since have been much better understood than it now is, and people would not have rested under the delusion that every thing necessary has been done.

There are yet other cases of culpable indifference. These same proscribed houses of prostitution are suffered to exist uncontrolled, and to spread disease and increase crime and vagrancy in all parts of the city. It has been generally conceded that they can not be suppressed. What effort has been made to hold in check their baneful influence? None—literally none. The statesman has looked on appalled at an evil of whose magnitude he could form no correct idea; the clergyman has hesitated to encounter those who he judged would not respectfully receive his admonitions; the masses of society have shrunk from considering a subject which was repugnant and distasteful. Is there no guilty indifference in this? There can be but one answer to this query; but one opinion as to the share this general apathy has had in fostering the evil.

To substitute for this apathy a healthy action is the object of this investigation. It is but the means to an end. In themselves, as mere matters of information, the facts and deductions presented in the following pages can do nothing but demonstrate the necessity of exertion; but of this necessity they do afford overwhelming demonstration.

Thus much for the general arguments as to the necessity of a work of this nature. There are other special and local causes which led to its accomplishment in the present form.

"The Governors of the Alms-House of the City and County of New York," or, as they are more generally known, "The Ten

Governors," is a body called into existence by an act of the State Legislature passed April 6, 1849, specially to take charge of the vagrant and pauper institutions of the city. The present members of the Board are the following well-known citizens :[1]

C. GODFREY GUNTHER, Esq., *President.*

ISAAC J. OLIVER, Esq., *Secretary.*

Washington Smith, Esq.[2] | Daniel F. Tiemann, Esq.
Anthony Dugro, Esq.[3] | Joseph S. Taylor, Esq.
Cornelius V. Anderson, Esq. | P. G. Moloney, Esq.
Isaac Townsend, Esq. | Benjamin F. Pinckney, Esq.

At the time these investigations commenced two other prominent men were also members of the organization, Hon. Edward C. West (now Surrogate of the city) and Simeon Draper, Esq. Both of these gentlemen had served as President of the Board of Governors with honor to themselves and satisfaction to their colleagues and the public; both took a lively interest in the projected inquiry, and to both am I indebted for much valuable assistance.

The act establishing the Board of Governors assigned to them, with their other duties, *the medical care of all persons who had contracted infectious diseases in the practice of debauchery, and who required charitable aid to restore them to health.* The result was that a very large number of persons, both male and female, chargeable to the citizens of New York through the medium of the institutions on Blackwell's Island, came under their cognizance, and they became convinced that some measures were necessary in connection therewith.

Individual members had held this opinion for some time before any official action was taken, and foremost among such was Governor Isaac Townsend. This gentleman was one of the originally appointed Governors, and has been connected with the Board by re-election ever since—a circumstance which made him perfectly acquainted with all the workings of the present system, and to him the public is indebted for the conception of this undertaking. For years has he labored to bring about this result, with an in-

---

[1] Since this introduction was written (1857) some changes have taken place in the constitution of the Board of Governors. The election of Mr. Tiemann to the Mayoralty caused a vacancy which is now filled by P. McElroy, Esq., and the resignation and subsequent death of Mr. Taylor has resulted in the election of William T. Pinkney, Esq.

[2] Now (1858) President of the Board.

[3] Now (1858) Secretary of the Board.

domitable energy and perseverance equaled only by his known benevolence and honesty of purpose. He frequently made the practicability of such a measure the subject of conversation with the gentleman who preceded me as Resident Physician of Black-well's Island, and, on my appointment (1853), the subject was again urged by him; nor could I be unaware of its importance. No official action was taken until the commencement of the year 1855. At that time Mr. Townsend was President of the Board, and one of his first acts in that capacity was to submit a list of in-terrogatories on the subject, which were adopted and transmitted to me. I transcribe them from the Minutes of the Board:

"At a meeting of the Board of Governors of the Alms-House, held Jan-uary 23, 1855, the following interrogatories were presented by the Presi-dent:

"1. What proportion of the inmates of the institutions on Blackwell's Island under your medical charge are, in your opinion, directly or indirectly suffering from syphilis?

"2. Are, or are not, the number of such inmates steadily on the increase?

"3. Do not patients in the different institutions, particularly in the Peni-tentiary Hospital, often leave before the disease is cured, so that they are liable to infect other persons after their departure?

"4. Are not the offspring of parents affected with constitutional syphilis subject to many diseases of like character, which cause them to become a charge upon the city for long periods of time, and often for life?

"5. What are your views in reference to the best means of checking and decreasing this disease, and what plan, in your opinion, could be adopted to relieve New York City of the enormous amount of misery and expense caused by syphilis?

"6. You will reply in full to the above queries at the earliest possible date.

"Resolved, That a copy of the above be sent to the Resident Physician, Blackwell's Island."

To reply to these questions, especially to the fifth, I discovered that it would be requisite to extend my investigations beyond the limits of the institutions on Blackwell's Island. This idea was communicated to President Townsend, who joined me in appre ciating the necessity of such a movement. He also was the means of interesting Mayor Wood and other officers of the city in the in-vestigation as subsequently carried on, while his continued exer-tions and earnest support aided me generally in the prosecution of the labor, and merit my most sincere and grateful acknowledg-ments.

The steps thus taken are fully detailed in the following letter to the Board of Governors, that letter, or preliminary report, having been called for in connection with the reports from the Medical Board of Bellevue Hospital, and from the Resident Physician of Randall's Island, which will be found, *in extenso*, in Chapter XXXVII. of this work:[1]

"Isaac Townsend, Esq., *President of the Board of Governors.*

"Dear Sir,—In reply to your letter asking for answers to certain interrogatories on the subject of prostitution and its diseases, I have to state that I am not prepared to report, nor can I do so for some considerable length of time to come.

"Had I confined myself to simply answering the queries propounded as regards the institutions under my medical charge, simply given you the gross numbers, with the percentages of those who have suffered or are now suffering from venereal disease, such reply could have been sent to you long ago. A report of this kind from this department would have been looked upon by the public at large as containing the history of nearly all the prostitution in the city, and particularly would a majority of the public have believed that nineteen twentieths of the disease resulting from prostitution found its home here. Such is not the fact. Great as is the number of prostitutes annually sent here, and enormous as is the number of cases of venereal disease yearly treated here, yet these compose but a small fraction of the sum total actually existing in this city. There are but few more prostitutes on the island than are to be found on the same number of acres in certain portions of the city ; and as for the venereal disease, why, gentlemen, the island has the advantage. It is the least dangerous locality.

"Believing these to be facts, I could not bring myself to think that any practical good would be accomplished by giving you the statistics of these institutions alone. It would have been merely doing what has been done before, and would have yielded no additional information for your guidance. But it appeared to me that the time had come when your attention might be solicited to the various facts attending the aggregate prostitution of the city ; for, despite all our prohibitory laws, it is a fact which can not be questioned or denied that this vice is attaining a position and extent in this community which can not be viewed without alarm. It has more than kept pace with the growth of our city. Unlike the vice of a few years since, it no longer confines itself to secrecy and darkness, but boldly strides through our most thronged and elegant thoroughfares, and there, in the broad light of the sun, it jostles the pure, the virtuous, and the good. It is in your

[1] To explain the apparent solecism of addressing a letter to President Townsend, detailing actions in which he had taken so important a part, it may be necessary to say that a standing order of the Board of Governors requires all official correspondence with them to be addressed to their President.

gay streets, and in your quiet, home-like streets; it is in your squares, and in your suburban retreats and summer resorts; it is in your theatres, your opera, your hotels; nay, it is even intruding itself into the private circles, and slowly but steadily extending its poison, known but to few, and entirely unsuspected by the majority of our citizens. The whole machinery of the law has been turned against these females without success; its only result having been a resolve, on their part, to confront society with the charge of harsh, cruel, and unjust treatment.

"From these considerations, I felt it my duty to obtain all the facts which could possibly be collected having any relation to the vice in question, assured that you were desirous of taking a comprehensive view of it; and hence the resolve, if possible, to trace to the fountain-head prostitution and its attendant diseases, so as to be enabled to bring the subject before you in a form which should exhibit it in its proper colors and dimensions.

"The first step in this investigation was to obtain ample and reliable information of the extent of the vice as it exists outside of these departments—a step which would have been beyond my power alone. From the bold and reformatory stand which his honor Mayor Wood had taken in regard to many matters connected with our city government, it was believed that he would render his assistance if convinced of the propriety and prospective usefulness of the investigation, and the result of an application by President Isaac Townsend to his honor fully justified the correctness of this supposition. He was found not only willing to aid in this great work, but fully alive to its necessity and importance. The plan adopted to forward the inquiry was to take a census of the city, so far as regards prostitution, including the number of houses of prostitution; the number of prostitutes; the causes which led them to become such; their ages, habits, birth-places, early history, education, religious instruction, occupation, etc., and which census is now being taken by the Chief of Police, George W. Matsell, Esq., and the Captains of Police.

"Simultaneously with this, inquiries are also being prosecuted concerning the extent of venereal disease in New York, which will afford interesting information. This, of course, will be done without individual exposure, nor will the report, when completed, assume the form of a guide-book by which persons can find houses of ill fame. I am desirous of obtaining the aggregate facts of the vice, and shall be cautious to take no steps toward gratifying a prurient curiosity or lacerating a rankling wound.

"When these facts are before you, they will be their own argument for the necessity of action.

"I do not trouble you on this occasion with any remarks upon the deadly nature of the venereal poison, but when you are informed as to the facilities for its diffusion will be the proper time to do so. Neither would it be consistent with this stage of the inquiry to enter into any discussion as to the plans that could be adopted in mitigation of the vice; for although prohibitory measures have failed to suppress, or even check it, yet, until its full extent is known, I do not imagine that you would deem it prudent to attempt to grapple a monster whose strength was not fully ascertained.

" You perceive that to obtain all the information necessary on this matter will be a work requiring both time and labor, and I respectfully ask your forbearance, with the assurance that I will lay the result of my inquiries before you at the earliest possible opportunity, and with the hope that the magnitude and importance of the subject will be an apology for the time to which it is necessarily protracted.

" I am, sir, yours, very respectfully,

" WILLIAM W. SANGER, *Resident Physician, Blackwell's Island.*"

To aid the police officers in the duty of taking the census alluded to above, a schedule of questions was prepared.[1] This was submitted to the Board of Governors by Governor Townsend, and a resolution was adopted at their meeting of October 23d, 1855, sanctioning the plan adopted, and authorizing him to have a sufficient number of copies printed. The mayor, the district attorney, the chief of police, and the captains of the several districts, willingly and zealously co-operated with Governor Townsend and myself, and every possible exertion was used to obtain accurate and extensive information. It became my duty to assist the officers in the execution of their task, and I am thus enabled to speak with certainty as to the authenticity of the statistics given, which were mainly collected *under my own observation.*

I gladly avail myself of the present opportunity to record my obligations for services rendered by his honor Fernando Wood, Mayor of the city of New York; George W. Matsell, Esq., Chief of Police; and to the Captains of Police in the different wards of the city, namely,

Capt. Michael Halpin,	1st ward.		Capt. Galen T. Porter,	12th ward.
" James Leonard,	2d "		" John E. Russell,	13th "
" James A. P. Hopkins,	3d "		" David Kissner,	14th "
" J. Murray Ditchett,	4th "		" George W. Dilks,	15th "
" Daniel Carpenter,	5th "		" John D. M'Kee,	16th "
" Joseph Dowling,	6th "		" J. W. Hartt,	17th "
" Edward Letts,	7th "		" George W. Walling,	18th "
" Charles S. Turnbull,	8th "		" Francis J. Twomey,	19th "
" Abraham Ackerman,	9th "		" Thomas Hannegan,	20th "
" George W. Norris,	10th "		" Francis C. Speight,	21st "
" Peter Squires,	11th "		" Daniel Witter,	22d "

[1] See Chapter XXXII. for these questions.

To Captains Halpin, Hopkins, Ditchett, Carpenter, Dowling, Letts, Turnbull, Kissner, and Dilks, in whose wards is found the greatest amount of prostitution, and upon whom fell the largest share of labor, I am more particularly indebted.

The necessary particulars were finally obtained, and are embodied in Chapters XXXII. to XXXVII. of this work, but there was still an important point to determine, namely, what had been done elsewhere, and what was the result of such action, to check prostitution and diminish the ravages of venereal disease. The Continent of Europe presented a field for this inquiry, and to it I turned for the information required, which is given in the various chapters devoted to the several countries in such a form as to show the measures which have been taken, the effect, and the causes which led to legislative interference, contrasted with those other parts of the world where, as yet, no remedial plans have been tried, notwithstanding the necessity which calls for them.

The reader is now in possession of the facts which led to this inquiry. Is it too much to ask his attention to the analysis and exhibition of prostitution as it is at the present time, he being well assured that no assertions will be made that are not supported by good authority, nor any conclusions drawn from doubtful premises?

So far as New York alone is concerned, the evil is known to a large portion of her citizens, although its ramifications are but very imperfectly understood; and the endeavor will be to present all possible information on the matter, and to give a truthful, unexaggerated picture of the depravity. Disagreeable as this must be from the nature of the task, it is hopeful from a belief that the result will tend to public good.

One of the most painfully interesting branches of the inquiry is that relating to the ages of the unfortunate women. Their number includes many who are but mere children; who but recently knelt at a mother's side, and in infantile accents breathed a prayer to the Almighty; who but recently sprang with eager, joyous bound to the returning footsteps of a father; who, in a happy and innocent home, have but recently given promise of a bright and virtuous life. Therein are also included many who were deprived by death of their natural protectors, and who, thus left unwatched and uncared for, have fallen before the destroyer ere yet the age of womanhood was reached.

The places of their birth form an interesting subject for consideration. In this land the frigid North and sunny South, the busy East and fertile West have each contributed their quota, while foreign countries have sent large numbers to swell the mournful aggregate.

The most useful portion of the subject will be found, it is imagined, in replies to the question, " What was the cause of your becoming a prostitute?" These tend to expose the concealed vices of mankind, and to prove that many of the unfortunate victims are " more sinned against than sinning." Among the reasons assigned for a deviation from the paths of virtue are some which tell of man's deceit; others, where the machinations employed to effect the purpose raise a blush for humanity; others, where a wife was sacrificed by the man who had sworn before God and in the presence of men to protect her through life; others, where parents have urged or commanded this course, and are now living on the proceeds of their children's shame, or where an abuse of parental authority has produced the same effect; and others still, where women, already depraved, have been the means of leading their fellow-women to disgrace. A bare allusion to these wrongs is sickening; but, while the gangrene of prostitution is rapidly extending through society, it becomes an imperative duty to examine its causes completely and impartially.

Another prolific source of female depravity will be exhibited by the several tables showing the description of employment pursued, and the wages received by women previous to their fall, and it will be a question for the political economist to decide how far mere business considerations should be an apology on the part of employers for a reduction in their rates of remuneration, and whether the saving of a small percentage on wages is not more than counterbalanced by the enormous amount of taxation enforced on the public at large to defray the expenses incurred on account of a system of vice which is the direct result, in many cases, of insufficient compensation for honest labor.

In conclusion, it must not be assumed that the information collected from two thousand women in New York City relates to *all* the prostitutes therein. The many difficulties surrounding the investigation, and especially the secrecy to which prohibitory laws have driven this class of persons, rendered the task impossible; but, from the best information that could be obtained of those whose knowledge of the vice was derived from actual experience, it is imagined that the replies represent about two fifths of the

C

total number.[1] They are presented with full confidence in their general authenticity, and may be very reasonably concluded to offer a fair average of the whole. They unquestionably exhibit an appalling amount of depravity and consequent wretchedness, with but very few redeeming features, and present mournful subjects for reflection to all classes, with forcible arguments for remedial measures. Without this end in prospect it would have been scarcely justifiable, at least in a moral point of view, to institute this inquiry or make these disclosures; but it certainly may be reasonably inferred that many will feel sufficient interest in the advance of virtue to aid in the mitigation of this enormous vice which threatens all social relations; which has already introduced physical suffering into so many families; and the influence of which, increasing in a direct ratio to its existence, will very probably extend its malignant poison, mental and bodily, into all ranks and classes of the community. The necessity for action is apparent, but its successful consummation must rest with the public at large, who have the bane exhibited before them in its actual power, and the necessity of an antidote demonstrated from positive facts, and not deduced from a mere arbitrary theory.

If some antidote be applied, even though a partial one, it will be a satisfaction to reflect that the investigations have not been profitless, nor the labor in vain.

[1] It is quite probable that the commercial and financial panic which commenced about the time these pages were nearly ready for the press, and continued throughout the winter of 1857–8, has added to the number of prostitutes in New York City, very likely as many as five hundred, or perhaps a thousand, but certainly not to the extent generally imagined. Allusions have been made elsewhere to the exaggerated estimates of the extent of this vice, and the opinions publicly expressed in regard to accessions to the ranks of prostitutes during the last few months generally seem to be of a similarly vague nature.

HISTORY OF PROSTITUTION.

[If the reader has not already perused the Introduction to this volume, he is advised to do so at once, as therein are stated the reasons which have called it forth, and extended it to the present dimensions.]

CHAPTER I.

THE JEWS.

Prostitution coeval with Society.—Prostitutes in the Eighteenth Century B.C.—
Tamar and Judah.—Legislation of Moses.—Syrian Women.—Rites of Moloch.
—Groves.—Social Condition of Jewish Harlots.—Description by Solomon.—The
Jews of Babylon.

OUR earliest acquaintance with the human race discloses some sort of society established. It also reveals the existence of a marriage tie, varying in stringency and incidental effects according to climate, morals, religion, or accident, but every where essentially subversive of a system of promiscuous intercourse. No nation, it is believed, has ever been reported by a trustworthy traveler, on sufficient evidence, to have held its women generally in common. Still there appear to have been in every age men who did not avail themselves of the marriage covenant, or who could not be bound by its stipulations, and their appetites created a demand for illegitimate pleasures, which female weakness supplied. This may be assumed to be the real origin of prostitution throughout the world, though in particular localities this first cause has been assisted by female avarice or passion, religious superstition, or a mistaken sense of hospitality.

Accordingly, prostitution is coeval with society. It stains the earliest mythological records. It is constantly assumed as an existing fact in Biblical history. We can trace it from the earliest twilight in which history dawns to the clear daylight of to-day, without a pause or a moment of obscurity.

Our most ancient historical record is believed to be the Books of Moses. According to them, it must be admitted that prostitutes were common among the Jews in the eighteenth century before Christ. When Tamar, the daughter-in-law of Judah, desired to defeat the cruel Jewish custom, and to bear children, notwithstanding her widowhood, she "put her widow's garments off from her, and covered her with a veil, and wrapped herself, and sat in an open place. . . . When Judah saw her he thought her a harlot, for she had covered her face."[1] The Genesiacal account thus shows that prostitutes, with covered faces, must have been common at the time. It is the more valuable, as it furnishes the particulars of the transaction. To keep up her disguise, Tamar demands a kid as her recompense. Judah agrees; and leaves his "signet, and his bracelets, and his staff" as a pledge for the kid. It appears to have been regarded as no dishonor to have commerce with a prostitute, for Judah sends his friend the Adullamite, a man of standing, to deliver the kid; but to defraud the unfortunate woman of her ill-gotten gain must have been considered shameful, for, when Judah learns that she has disappeared, he expresses alarm "lest we be shamed" for not having paid the stipulated price. It may also be noticed, as an illustration of the connection between prostitution and pure domestic morals, that when Judah learns that his daughter-in-law is pregnant, he instantly orders her to be burned for having "played the harlot."

Four centuries afterward it fell to the lot of Moses to legislate on the Jewish morals, no doubt sadly corrupted by their sojourn in Egypt. His command is formal and emphatic: "Do not prostitute thy daughter, lest the land fall to whoredom. . . . There shall be no whore of the daughters of Israel."[2] He was equally decided in his condemnation of worse practices, to which it would appear the Jews were much addicted.[3] He laid penalties on uncleanness of every kind, and on fornication; but it would appear that he rather confirmed than abrogated the customary right of a Jewish father to sell his daughter as a concubine.[4] With the practical view of improving the physical condition of the race, Moses guarded, by elaborate laws, against improper and corrupt unions. Adultery and rape he punished with death. The bride was bound, under pain of death by stoning, to prove to the satisfaction not only of her husband, but of the tribe, that she had been chaste to the day of her marriage.[5] A long list of relatives were specified among whom it was illegal to intermarry. Furthermore, Moses endeavored, with marked zeal, to check the prog-

[1] Gen. xxxviii. 11.   [2] Lev. xix. 29; Deut. xxiii. 17.
[3] Ex. xxii. 19; Lev. xviii. 23.   [4] Ex. xxi. 17.   [5] Deut. xxii. 17.

ress of disease among both sexes. Whether the maladies mentioned in Leviticus[1] were syphilitic in their nature, it were difficult to say. Modern medical science admits that, in hot climates, want of cleanliness and frequent amorous indulgence will generate phenomena similar to the "issue" so frequently mentioned by Moses. However this be, it is certain that both Jews and Jewesses were subject to diseases apparently similar to the common gonorrhœa; that these diseases were infectious; and that Moses, in reiterated injunctions, forbade all sexual intercourse, and almost all association, with persons thus afflicted. So earnest was his desire to eradicate the evil from the people, that he extended his prohibition to women during the period of their menstrual visitation.

Having done this much for the Jews, Moses appears to have connived at the intercourse of their young men with foreign prostitutes. He took an Ethiopian concubine himself. Syrian women, Moabites, Midianites, and other neighbors of the Jews—many of them, as it appears, young and lovely, but with debauched and vicious principles—established themselves as prostitutes in the land of Israel. For many years, until the time of Solomon, they were excluded from Jerusalem and the large cities. Driven to the highways for refuge, they lived in booths and tents, where they combined the trade of a peddler with the calling of a harlot. Unlike Tamar, they did not veil the face. Reclining within the tent, with no more clothing than the heat of the climate suggested, these dissolute girls invited the complaisance of passengers who stopped to refresh their thirst or replenish their wardrobe at their booth. So long as their practices violated no law of nature, the prudent legislator pursued a tolerant policy. Before long, however, abominable rites in honor of Moloch, Baal, or Belphegor, were formally established by the "strange women" and their male accomplices. Moloch, whose disgusting exactions we find in Phœnicia, and at Carthage also, demanded male worship. The belly of the god's statue was a furnace, in which a fierce fire was kindled and fed with animal sacrifice; around it the priests and their proselytes danced to the sound of music, sang wild songs, and debased themselves by practices of a disgusting and unnatural character. Nor was the worship of Baal less revolting. He too had his statues, in forms eminently calculated to excite the animal passions, and surrounded by cool groves in which the most shameless prostitution was carried on

[1] Lev. xv.

by all who would deposit an offering on the altars of the idol. It would even seem, from several passages in the Bible,[1] that the participators in these infamies were not invariably human beings. Against such enormities the wrath of Moses and his successors was aroused, on hygienic as well as moral and religious grounds. Participation in the rites of Moloch was punished with death.[2] Aaron's grandson did not hesitate to commit a double homicide to mark the Divine abhorrence of the daughters of Midian; and Moses himself, warned by the frightful progress of disease among the male Jews, struck at its roots by exterminating every female Midianite among his captives, save the virgins only.

An express command forbade the establishment of groves near the Jewish temples, evidently on account of the convenience such shady retreats afforded to prostitutes. Yet on various occasions in the history of Israel we find accounts of the destruction of such groves, and of the statues of the gods in whose honor human nature was defiled.[3] Solomon, whose wisdom was singularly alloyed with sensuality, not only set the example of inordinate lust, keeping, it is said, seven hundred wives and three hundred concubines, but repealed the wise restrictions of his predecessors in regard to prostitutes, allowing them to exercise their calling within the city of Jerusalem. They multiplied so fast that the prophets speak of them wandering on all the hills, and prostituting themselves under every tree, and at a later date they even invaded the Temple, and established their hideous rites in its courts. That noble edifice had become, in the time of Maccabees, a mere brothel *plenum scortantium cum meretricibus*.[4]

It is, however, apparent, notwithstanding the severe ordinances of the Jewish legislators, that prostitutes were a recognized class, laboring under no hopeless ban. Jephtha, the son of a prostitute, became none the less chief of Israel; and some commentators have contended that the retreat to which he condemned his daughter was simply the calling of her grandmother. Joshua's spies slept openly in the house of the harlot Rahab, whose service to Israel was faithfully requited by the amnesty granted to her family, and the honorable residence allotted to her in Judæa. Samson chose the house of a harlot to be his residence at Gaza; his fatal acquaintance with another harlot, Delilah, is the leading trait of his story. Even Solomon did not disdain to hear the

---

[1] Deut. xxiii. 18, etc.   [2] Ibid. xxiii. 18.
[3] Chron. xv. xvii. etc.   [4] Maccabees.

rival wranglings of a pair of harlots, and to adjudicate between them. Prostitution was in fact legally domiciled in Judæa at a very early period, and never lost the foothold it had gained. Of the manner in which it was carried on, an idea may be formed from the very vivid picture in Proverbs:[1]

" For at the window of my house,
  I looked through my casement,
  And beheld among the simple ones,
  I discerned among the youths,
  A young man void of understanding,
  Passing through the streets near her (the strange woman's) corner;
  And he went the way to her house,
  In the twilight, in the evening,
  In the black and dark night;
  And, behold, there met him a woman
  With the attire of a harlot, and subtile of heart.
  She is loud and stubborn;
  Her feet abide not in her house:
  Now she is without, now in the streets,
  And lieth in wait at every corner.
  So she caught him, and kissed him,
  And with an impudent face said unto him,
  I have peace-offerings with me;
  This day have I paid my vows.
  Therefore came I forth to meet thee,
  Diligently to seek thy face,
  And I have found thee.
  I have decked my bed with coverings of tapestry,
  With carved works, with linen of Egypt.
  I have perfumed my bed with myrrh,
  Aloes, and cinnamon.
  Come, let us take our fill of love until the morning:
  Let us solace ourselves with loves. * * *
  With her much fair speech she caused him to yield,
  With the flattering of her lips she forced him.
  He goeth after her straightway,
  As an ox goeth to the slaughter,
  Or as a fool to the correction of the stocks."

That prostitution continued to be practiced generally and openly until the destruction of the old Jewish nation, the language of the Biblical prophets does not permit us to doubt. It may be

[1] Ch. vii. 6, etc.

questioned whether it ever assumed more revoltingly public forms in any other country. The Babylonish conquest must have changed the parts, without altering the performance. At Babylon, the Jewish maidens, whose large, expressive eyes, voluptuous mouth, slender and graceful figure, with well-developed bust and limbs, were frequently the theme of ancient poets, peopled the houses of prostitution, and ministered to the lusts of the nobles. Nor even after the return to Jerusalem was the evil extirpated. It was to a prostitute that Christ uttered the memorable sentence, "Her sins are forgiven because she loved much."

CHAPTER II.

EGYPT, SYRIA, AND ASIA MINOR.

Egyptian Courtesans.—Festival of Bubastis.—Morals in Egypt.—Religious Prostitution in Chaldæa.—Babylonian Banquets.—Compulsory Prostitution in Phœnicia.—Persian Banquets.

BEFORE passing to the subject of prostitution in Greece, a glance at Egypt, and those nations of Asia which seem to have preceded Greece in civilization, may not be out of place.

Egypt was famous for her courtesans before the time of Herodotus. Egyptian blood runs warm; girls are nubile at ten. Under the Pharaohs, if ancient writers are to be believed, there existed a general laxity of moral principle, especially among young females.[1] Their religion was only too suggestive. The deities Isis and Osiris were the types of the sexes. A statue of the latter, a male image, made of gold, was carried by the maidens at festivals, and worshiped by the whole people. Nor were the rites of Isis more modest. "At the festival at Bubastis," says Herodotus, "men and women go thither in boats on the Nile, and when the boats approach a city they are run close to the shore. A frantic contest then begins between the women of the city and those in the boats, each abusing the other in the most opprobrious language, and the women in the boats conclude the performance by lascivious dances, in the most undisguised manner, in sight of the people, and to the sound of flutes and other musical instruments."[2] There is little reason to doubt that the temples, like those of Baal, were houses of prostitution on an extensive scale. Herodotus re-

---

[1] Ctesias, quoted by Athenæus, xiii. 10.   [2] Herodotus, ii. 60.

marks significantly that a law in Egypt forbade sexual intercourse within the walls of a temple, and exacted of both sexes that intercourse should be followed by ablution before the temple was entered.[1]

Where piety required such sacrifices, it is not surprising that public morals were loose. It was not considered wholly shameful for an Egyptian to make his living by the hire of his daughter's person, and a king is mentioned who resorted to this plan in order to discover a thief. Such was the astonishing appetite of the men, that young and beautiful women were never delivered to the embalmer until they had been dead some days, a miserable wretch having been detected in the act of defiling a recently-deceased virgin![2] Of course, in such a society, there was no disgrace in being a prostitute. The city of Naucratis owed its wealth and fame to the beauty of its courtesans, whose reputation spread throughout Europe, and was much celebrated in Greece. Rhadopis, a Thracian by birth, led the life of a prostitute in Egypt with such success, that she not only bought her own freedom from the slave-dealer who had taken her there on speculation, but, if the Egyptians are to be believed, built a pyramid with her savings. A large portion of her story is doubtless mythical, but enough remains to warrant the opinion that she was, though a prostitute, a wealthy and highly considered person.

In Chaldæa, too, religion at first connived at, and then commanded prostitution. Every Babylonian female was obliged by law to prostitute herself once in her life in the temple of the Chaldæan Venus, whose name was Mylitta.[3] Herodotus appears to have seen the park and grounds in which this singular sacrifice was made. They were constantly filled with women with strings bound round their hair. Once inside the place, no woman could leave it until she had paid her debt, and had deposited on the altar of the goddess the fee received from her lover. Some, who were plain, remained there as long as three years; but, as the grounds were always filled with a troop of voluptuaries in search of pleasure, the young, the beautiful, the high-born seldom needed to remain over a few minutes. This strange custom is mentioned by the prophet Baruch, who introduces one of the women reproaching her neighbor that she had not been deemed worthy of having her girdle of cord burst asunder by any man.[4] Similar statements are made by Strabo and other

[1] Herodotus, ii. 64.　　[2] Id. ii. 89.　　[3] Id. ii. 89.　　[4] Baruch, vi.

ancient writers. At the time of Alexander the Great the demoralization had reached a climax. Babylonian banquets were
scenes of unheard-of infamies. When the meal began, the women
sat modestly enough in presence of their fathers and husbands;
but, as the wine went round, they lost all restraint, threw off one
garment after another, and enacted scenes of glaring immodesty.
And these were the ladies of the best families.[1]

The Mylitta of Chaldæa became Astarte in Phœnicia, at Carthage, and in Syria. Nothing was changed but the name; the
voluptuous rites were identical. In addition to the forced prostitution in the temples, however, the Phœnicians and most of their
colonies maintained for many years the practice of requiring their
maidens to bestow their favors on any strangers who visited the
country. Commercial interest, no doubt, had some share in promoting so scandalous a custom. On the high shores of Phœnicia,
as at Carthage and in the island of Cyprus, the traveler sailing
past in his boat could see beautiful girls, arrayed in light garments, stretching inviting arms to him.

Originally the sum paid by the lover was offered to the goddess, but latterly the girls kept it, and it served to enhance their
value in the matrimonial market. In some places the girl was
free if she chose to abandon her hair to the goddess, but Lucian
notes that this was an uncommonly rare occurrence.

Very similar were the customs of the Lydians and their successors in empire, the early Persians. Their Venus was named
Mithra, in honor of whom festivals were given at which human
nature was horribly outraged. Fathers and daughters, sons and
mothers, husbands and wives sat together at the table, while
voluptuous dances and music inflamed their senses, and when
the wine had done its work, a promiscuous combat of sensuality
began which lasted all night. Details of such scenes must be left
to other works, and veiled in a learned tongue.[2]

[1] Quintus Curtius, v. 1.
[2] Macrobius, Sat. Conv. vii. Athenæus, xii. *passim;* Plutarch, Vit. Artaxerxes.

CHAPTER III.

GREECE.

Mythology.—Solonian Legislation.—Dicteria.—Pisistratidæ.—Lycurgus and Sparta.—Laws on Prostitution.—Case of Phryne.—Classes of Prostitutes.—Pornikon Telos.—Dress.—Hair of Prostitutes.—The Dicteriades of Athens.—Abode and Manners. — Appearance of Dicteria. —Laws regulating Dicteria. — Schools of Prostitution.—Loose Prostitutes.—Old Prostitutes.—Auletrides, or Flute-players. — Origin. — How hired. — Performances. — Anecdote of Arcadians. — Price of Flute-players.—Festival of Venus Periboa.—Venus Callipyge.—Lesbian Love.— Lamia.—Hetairæ.—Social Standing.—Venus and her Temples.—Charms of Hetairæ.—Thargelia.—Aspasia.—Hipparchia.—Bacchis.—Guathena and Guathenion.—Lais.—Phryne.—Pythionice.—Glycera.—Leontium.—Other Hetairæ. —Biographers of Prostitutes.—Philtres.

THE Greek mythology supposes obviously a relaxed state of public morals. What period in the history of the nation it may be assumed to reflect is, however, by no means certain. It is not reasonable to suppose that the Homeric poems were composed for immodest audiences, and it would perhaps be fairer to lay the blame of the mythological indecencies at the door of the age which polished and improved upon them, rather than of that which is entitled to the credit of their conception in the rough.

Our first reliable information regarding the morals of the Greek women, passing over, for the present, the legislation ascribed to Lycurgus, is found in the ordinances of Solon. Draco is supposed to have affixed the penalty of death indiscriminately to rape, seduction, and adultery. It has been conjectured that the safety-valve used at that time, ordinary prostitution being unknown, was a system of religious prostitution in the temples, borrowed from and analogous to the plan already described. This, however, is mere conjecture. Solon, while softening the rigors of the Draconian code, by law formally established houses of prostitution at Athens, and filled them with female slaves. They were called *Dicteria*, and the female tenants *Dicteriades*. Bought with the public money, and bound by law to satisfy the demands of all who visited them, they were in fact public servants, and their wretched gains were a legitimate source of revenue to the state. Prostitution became a state monopoly, and so profitable that, even in Solon's lifetime, a superb temple, dedicated to Venus the courtesan, was built out of the fund accruing from this source. The fee charged, however, appears to have been small.[1] In Solon's time, the Dicteriades were kept widely apart from the Athenian women of repute. They were not allowed to mix in religious ceremonies or to enter the temples. When they appeared in the streets they were obliged to wear a particular costume as a badge of infamy. They forfeited what rights of citizenship they may have possessed in virtue of their birth. A procurer or procuress who had been instrumental in introducing a free-born Athenian girl to the Dicterion incurred the penalty of death. Nor was the law content with branding with infamy prostitutes and their accomplices alone. Their children were bastards; that is to say, they could not inherit property, they could not associate with other youths, they could not acquire the right of citizenship without performing some signal act of bravery, they could not address the people in the public assemblies. Finally, to complete their ignominy, they were exempt from the sacred duty of maintaining their parents in old age.[2]

These regulations, for which Solon obtained the praise of Athenian philosophers,[3] were not long maintained in force. Tradition imputed to the profligacy of the Pisistratidæ a relaxation of the laws concerning prostitutes. It was believed that the sons of Pisistratus not only gave to the Dicteriades the freedom of the city, but allotted to them seats at banquets beside the most respectable matrons, and, on certain days each year, turned them into their father's beautiful gardens, and let loose upon them the whole petulance of the Athenian youth.[4] The law against procuresses was modified, a fine being substituted for death. "About the same time," says the scandalous Greek chronicle, "the death-penalty for adultery was also commuted for scourging."

Still, notwithstanding this falling off, it would appear that Athens was more moral than her neighbors, Corinth and Sparta. The former, then the most flourishing sea-port of Greece, was filled with a very low class of prostitutes. No laws regulated the subject. Any female who chose could open house for the accommodation of travelers and seamen, and, though Corinth was yet far

[1] Nicander, quoted by Athenæus, xiii. 25.
[2] Plutarch, Life of Solon: Lucian, Dialogues.
[3] Philemon, quoted by Athenæus, xiii. 25.
[4] Idomeneus, quoted by Athenæus, xii. 44.

from the proverbial celebrity it afterward obtained for its prostitutes, there is no doubt they bore a fearful proportion to the aggregate population of the port. At Sparta the case was different.
In the system of legislation which bears the name of Lycurgus,
the individual was sacrificed to the state; the female to the male.
Women were educated for the sole purpose of bearing robust children. Virgins were allowed to wrestle publicly with men. Girls
were habited in a robe open at the skirts, which only partially
concealed the person in walking, whence the Spartan women acquired an uncomplimentary name.[1] A Spartan husband was authorized to lend his wife to any handsome man for the purpose of
begetting children. That these laws, the skillfully contrived appeals to the sensual appetites, and the constant spectacle of nude
charms, must have led to a general profligacy among the female
sex, is quite obvious. Aristotle affirms positively that the Spartan women openly committed the grossest acts of debauchery.[2]
Hence it may be inferred that prostitutes by profession were unnecessary at Sparta, at all events until a late period of its history.

After the Persian wars, the subject of Athenian prostitution is
revealed in a clearer light. As a reaction from the looseness of
the age of the Pisistratidæ, the Solonian laws were reaffirmed and
their severity heightened. It has been imagined, from certain obscure passages in Greek authors, that the courtesans formed several corporations, each of which was responsible for the acts of all
its members. They were liable to vexatious prosecutions for such
acts as inciting men to commit crime, ruining thoughtless youths,
fomenting treason against the state, or committing impiety.
Against such charges it was rarely possible to establish a sound
defense. If the accuser was positive, the Areopagus, notoriously
biased against courtesans, unhesitatingly condemned the culprit to
death, or imposed on her corporation a heavy fine. In this way,
says an old author, the state frequently contrived to get back
from these women the money they obtained from their lovers.
Before the famous case of Phryne, they were wholly at the mercy
of their profligate associates. A man only needed to threaten an
accusation of impiety or the like to obtain a receipt in full. Phryne, so long the favorite of the Athenians, was thus accused of various vague offenses by a common informer named Euthias. Her
friend Bacchis fortunately persuaded Hyperides, the orator, to undertake her case, and he softened the judges by exhibiting her

---

[1] *Fainomerides.* See Plutarch, Life of Lycurgus. [2] Politics. ii. 7

marvelous beauty in a moment of affected passion. "Henceforth," says the hetaira Bacchis to Myrrhina, "our profits are secured by law."[1]

At this time, that is to say, at the height of Athenian prosperity, there were four classes of women who led dissolute lives at Athens. The highest in rank and repute were the *Hetairæ*, or kept women, who lived in the best part of the city, and exercised no small influence over the manners and even the politics of the state. Next came the *Auletrides*, or flute-players, who were dancers as well. They were usually foreigners, bearing some resemblance to the opera-dancers of the last century, and they combined the most unblushing debauchery with their special calling. The lowest class of prostitutes were the *Dicteriades*, already mentioned. They were originally bound to reside at the Piræus, the sea-port of Athens, some four miles from the city, and were forbidden to walk out by day, or to offend the eyes of the public by open indecency. Lastly came the *Concubines*, who were slaves owned by rich men with the knowledge and consent of their wives, serving equally the passions of their master and the caprices of their mistress. These all paid a tax to the state, called *Pornikon Telos*, which was farmed out to speculators, who levied it with proverbial harshness upon the unfortunate women. In the time of Pericles the revenue from this source was large.

All classes, too, wore garments of many colors. The law originally specified "flowered robes" as the costume of courtesans; but this leading to difficulties, a farther enactment prohibited prostitutes from wearing precious stuffs, such as scarlet or purple, or jewels. Thenceforth the custom, which appears to have been general throughout the Greek cities and colonies, prescribed cheap robes, with flowers or stripes of many colors embroidered or painted on them. To this a part of the women added garlands of roses. It was lawful in some cities for courtesans to wear light, transparent garments; but at Sparta, as may be imagined, the reverse was the rule, semi-nudity being the badge of virtuous women.[2]

Perhaps the most singular of the marks by which a Greek courtesan was known was her hair. It is said that no law prescribed the habit; if so, it must have been a sort of *esprit de corps* which

---

[1] Athenæus, xiii. 59; Alciphron's Letters.

[2] Athenæus, xiii. 20, *et sed.;* Suidas, Lex., Vo. Diagramma ; Æschylus c. Timarch. p. 134; St. Clement of Alexandria, Pædag. ii. 10; Becker, Charicles, i. 126; etc.

led all courtesans to dye their hair of a flaxen or blonde color. Allusions to this custom abound in the light literature of Greece. Frequently a flaxen wig was substituted for the dyed locks. At a very late period in the history of Greece, modest women followed the fashion of sporting golden hair. This forms one of the subjects of reprimand addressed to the women of Greece by the early Christian preachers.[1]

THE DICTERIADES, OR COMMON PROSTITUTES OF ATHENS.

This class approaches more nearly than any other to the prostitutes of our day, the main difference being that the former were bound by law to prostitute themselves when required to do so, on the payment of the fixed sum, and that they were not allowed to leave the state. Their home, as mentioned already, was properly at the port of Piræus. An open square in front of the citadel was their usual haunt. It was surrounded with booths, where petty trade or gambling was carried on by day. At nightfall the prostitutes swarmed into the square. Some were noisy and obscene; others quiet, and armed with affected modesty. When a man passed on his way from the port to the city, the troop assailed him. If he resisted, coarse abuse was lavished on him. If he yielded, there was the temple of Venus the Courtesan close by, and there was the wall of Themistocles, under the friendly shelter of either of which the bargain could be consummated. Were the customer nice, the great dicterion was not far distant, and a score or more of smaller rivals were even nearer at hand, as a well-known sign was there to testify.

The Dicteria were under the control of the municipal police. The door was open night and day, a bright curtain protecting the inmates from the eye of the passer-by; and in the better class of establishments, a fierce dog, chained in the vestibule, served as sentinel. At the curtain sat an old woman, often a Thessalian and a pretended witch, who received the money before admitting visitors. Originally the fee was an obolus[2]—about three cents; but this attempt to regulate the value of a variable merchandise was soon abandoned. Within, at night, the sounds of music, revelry, and dancing might be constantly heard. The visitor was not kept in suspense. The curtain passed, he was in full view of the dicteriades, standing, sitting, or lying about the room; some en-

[1] Pollux, Onom. ii. 30; x. 170; St. Clement of Alex. *loc. cit.*
[2] Philemon, quoted by Athenæus, xiii. 25.

gaged in smoothing their blonde hair, some in conversation, some anointing themselves with perfumery. The legal principle with regard to the dicteriades appears to have been that they should conceal nothing; no doubt in contrast to the irregular prostitutes, of whom something will be said presently. There was no rule, however, forbidding the wearing of garments in the dicterion, but the common practice appears to have been to dispense with them, or to wear a light scarf thrown over the person. This custom was observed by day as well as by night, and a visitor has described the girls in a large dicterion as standing in a row, in broad daylight, without any robes or covering.[1]

It seems that in later times any speculator had a right to set up a dicterion on paying the tax to the state. An Athenian forfeited his right of citizenship by so doing; but, as a popular establishment was very lucrative, avaricious men frequently em barked in the business under an assumed name. Comic writers have lashed these wretches severely. On paying the tax to the state regularly, the *pornobosceion*, or master of the house, acquired certain rights. The dicterion was an inviolable asylum, no husband being allowed to pursue his wife, or the wife her husband, or the creditor his debtor, within its walls. Public decency requires, says Demosthenes, that men shall not be exposed in houses of prostitution.[2] It was not, however, considered wholly shameful to frequent such places.

There appear to have been attached to these dicteria schools of prostitution, where young women were initiated into the most disgusting practices by females who had themselves acquired them in the same manner. Alexis vigorously describes the frauds taught in these places,[3] while there is a shocking significance in an expression of Athenæus—"You will be well satisfied with the performance of the women in the dicteria."[4]

Besides these regular dicteriades, there were at Athens, as there have been in every large city, a number of women who exercised the calling of prostitutes, without properly belonging to any of the recognized classes. They were sometimes called free dicteriades, sometimes she-wolves, and also cheap hetairæ. Some were native Athenians who had been seduced and abandoned,

---

[1] Xenarchus and Eubulus, quoted by Athenæus, xiii. 25
[2] Demosthenes against Neæra.
[3] Alexis, quoted by Athenæus, xiii. 23.
[4] Athenæus xiii. 26.

and who, led by stings of conscience and idleness to pursue their career, had still an invincible repugnance to adopt the flowered robe and yellow hair of the regular courtesan. They roamed the Piræus, and even the streets of Athens, after dark, eking out a miserable subsistence by the hardest of trades, and haunting the dark recesses of old houses or the shade of trees. Others, again, were old hetairæ whose charms had faded, and who sought a scanty subsistence where they were not known, and shrank from encountering the eye of a lover where the friendly shade of night would not hide the ravages of time. Others were the servants of hotels and taverns, who were always expected to serve the caprices of visitors.

All of these led a most miserable life. Now and then we hear of one or two of them meeting a rich and inexperienced traveler, after which the heroine of the exploit naturally ascended to the rank of hetaira; but, in general, their customers were the lowest of the port people—sailors, fishermen, farm-servants. Their price was a meal, a fish, a handful of fruit, or a bottle of wine. One poor creature, who belonged to no class in particular, but acquired some celebrity by being kept by the orator Ithatocles, was named Didrachma because she offered her favors to the public generally for two drachmas, about thirty-five cents.[1]

Perhaps the most curious fact in reference to these prostitutes is the singular predominance of old women among them. It appears to have been adopted as an invariable rule for this sort of courtesans to paint their faces with a thick ointment, and it is even said that the great painters of Greece did not disdain to beguile their leisure hours by thus improving upon nature.[2] Of course, under this disguise, it was impossible to distinguish a young face from an old one. An aged prostitute thus bedizened would place herself at an open window with a sprig of myrtle in her hand, with which she would beckon to people in the street. When a customer was found, a servant would open the door and conduct him in silence to the chamber of her mistress. Before entering he paid the sum demanded, when he found himself in a room lighted only by a feeble glimmer passing through the curtain, which now hung down over the window. In such a twilight the most venerable old woman could not be distinguished from a Venus.[3]

[1] See Lucian. Dialogue of Courtesans, *passim.*
[2] Letters of Alciphron, 46.   [3] Lucian, *loc. cit.*

THE AULETRIDES, OR FLUTE-PLAYERS.

Female flute-players were a common accompaniment to an Athenian banquet. The flute, which in modern times is played by men, was rarely seen in male hands in Greece. Though the fable ascribed its invention to the god Pan, and its development to the mythical king Midas, it was monopolized at a very early period by women, who consoled themselves for the ravages it wrought in their beauty by the power of fascination it imparted among a people intensely musical. Flute-playing soon became an essential rite in the service of certain deities. Ceres was invariably worshiped to the sound of the flute. And when the Athenians had once tried the experiment of listening to flute-players after dinner, they never would dine in company without them.

Thebes appears to have been the native city of the earliest famous flute-players,[1] but before long the superior beauty of the Asiatic girls—Ionians and Phrygians—drove their Theban rivals out of the field. Dancing was combined with flute-playing, and in this art the Asiatics bore the palm from the world. During the golden days of Greece, numbers of beautiful girls were every year imported into Athens from Miletus and the other Ionic ports in Asia Minor, just as in more modern times a similar trade was carried on between Trebizond and Constantinople.

An Athenian hired his flute-players as a modern European noble hires his band. They charged so much for their musical performances, reserving the right of accepting presents in the course of the evening. Some were singers as well as performers. At each course a new air was played, increasing in tenderness and expression as the wine circulated. It is stated that the sounds of a good flute-concert excited people to such a state of phrensy that they would take off their rings and jeweled ornaments to throw them to the performers: those who have witnessed a triumphant operatic soirée can readily believe the statement. But the fair artists did not wholly rely on their music for their success. The performer danced while she played, accompanying every note with a harmonious movement of the body. There is no doubt these dances were in the highest degree immoral and lascivious. Athenæus tells a story of an embassy from Arcadia waiting upon King Antigonus, and being invited to dinner. After the hunger

---

[1] Anthology, ed. Jacobs, ii. 633.

of the venerable guests was appeased, Phrygian flute-players were introduced. They were draped in semi-transparent veils, arranged with much coquetry. At the given signal they began to play and dance, balancing themselves alternately on each foot, and gradually increasing the rapidity of their movements. As the performance went on, the dancers uncovered their heads, then their busts; lastly, they threw the veils aside altogether, and stood before the wondering embassadors with only a short tunic around the loins. In this state they danced so indecently that the aged Arcadians, excited beyond control, forgot where they were, and rushed upon them. The king laughed; the courtiers were shocked at such ill-breeding, but the dancers discharged the sacred duty of hospitality.[1]

A flute-player who had achieved a success of this kind was enabled to conclude a lucrative bargain for other performances. We find allusions to fees as high as two talents (say $2500) and fifty pieces of gold,[2] though these were evidently unusual charges. Many of the most fashionable flute-players were slaves who had been brought to Greece by speculators. They were commonly sold by auction at the dinner-table, when their owner judged that the enthusiasm of the guests had attained the highest point. An anecdote is told of one of the most esteemed names in Greek philosophy in reference to this strange custom. He was dining with a party of young men, when a youthful flute-player was introduced. She crept to the philosopher's feet, and seemed to shelter herself from insult under the shadow of his venerable beard; but he, a disciple of Zeno, spurned her, and burst forth into a strain of moralizing. Piqued by the affront, the girl rose, and played and danced with inimitable grace and pruriency. At the close of the performance her owner put her up to auction, and one of the first bidders was the philosopher. She was adjudged to another, however, and the white-haired sage so far forgot his principles as to engage in a fierce conflict with the victor for the possession of the prize.[3] Hand to hand battles on these occasions were common in the best society at Athens, and a flute-player in fashion made a boast of the riots she had caused.[4] Of the fortunes realized by successful artists in this line, an idea may be formed from the gorgeous presents made to the Delphian oracle by flute-players, and from the fact that the finest houses at Al-

[1] Athenæus, xiii. 86.   [2] Letters of Alciphron, 34.
[3] Athenæus, xiii. 86.   [4] Antiphanes, quoted in Athenæus. xiii. 51.

exandria were inscribed with the names of famous Greek auletrides.[1]

As might be inferred from the character of their dances, the
auletrides were capable of every infamy. Constantly breathing
an atmosphere of debauchery, and accustomed to the daily spectacle of nudities, they naturally attained a pitch of amorous exaltation of which we, at the present day, can hardly form an idea.
They kept a cherished festival in honor of Venus Peribasia, which
was originally established by Cypselus of Corinth. At that ceremony all the great flute-players of Greece assembled to celebrate
their calling. Men were not usually allowed to be present, a
regulation prompted perhaps by modesty, as the judgment of
Paris was renewed at the festival, and prizes were awarded for
every description of beauty. The ceremony was often mentioned
as the Callipygian games; and a sketch of a scene which took
place at one of these reunions, contained in a letter from a famous
flute-player, justifies the appellation. The banquet lasted from
dark till dawn, with wines, perfumes, delicate viands, songs, and
music. An after-scene was a dispute between two of the guests
as to their respective beauty. A trial was demanded by the
company, and a long and graphic account is given of the exhibition, but modern tastes will not allow us to transcribe the details.[2]

A knowledge of these scandalous scenes, it may be briefly
observed, would be worse than useless, were it not that they
illustrate the life of Greek courtesans; and, being performed
under the sanction of religion and the law, they throw no inconsiderable light on the real character of Greek society. Their
value may be best apprehended by trying to realize what the
effect would be if similar scenes occurred annually in some public
edifice in our large cities, under the auspices of the police, with
the approval of the clergy, and with the full knowledge of the
best female society.

It has been suggested that these festivals were originated by,
or gave rise to, those enormous aberrations of the Greek female
mind known to the ancients as Lesbian love. There is, no doubt,
grave reason to believe something of the kind. Indeed, Lucian
affirms that, while avarice prompted common pleasures, taste and
feeling inclined the flute-payers toward their own sex. On so
repulsive a theme it is unnecessary to enlarge.

[1] Theopompus, Dicæarchus, etc. quoted by Athenæus, xiii. 67.
[2] Letters of Alciphron, 44.

GREECE. 53

Many flute-players seem to have been susceptible of lasting affections. In the remains we have of the erotic works of the Greeks, several names are mentioned as those of successful flute-players whose gains were consumed by exacting lovers. It does not appear that they often, or ever, married. The most famous of all the flute-players was Lamia, who, after being the delight of Alexandria and of King Ptolemy for some fifteen or twenty years, was taken with the city by Demetrius of Macedon, and raised to the rank of his mistress. She was forty years of age at this time, yet her skill was such that she ruled despotically her dissolute lover, and left a memorable name in Greek history. The ancients asserted that she owed her name, Lamia, which means a sort of vampire or bloodsucker, to the most loathsome depravities. Her power was so great that, when Demetrius levied a tax of some $250,000 on the city of Athens, he gave the whole to her, to buy her soap, as he said. The Athenians revenged themselves by saying that Lamia's person must be very dirty, since she needed so much soap to wash it. But they soon found it to their interest to build a temple in her honor, and deify her under the name of Venus Lamia.[1]

THE HETAIRÆ, OR KEPT WOMEN.

The Hetairæ were by far the most important class of women in Greece. They filled so large a place in society that virtuous females were entirely thrown into the shade, and it must have been quite possible for a chaste Athenian girl, endowed with ambition, to look up to them, and covet their splendid infamy. An Athenian matron was expected to live at home. She was not allowed to be present at the games or the theatres; she was bound, when she appeared in public, to be veiled, and to hasten whither she was going without delay; she received no education, and could not share the elevated thoughts or ideas of her husband; she had no right to claim any warmth of affection from him, though he possessed entire control over her.[2]

Now, to judge of the position into which this social system thrust the female sex, one must glance at the mythology, or, to speak more correctly, at the religious faith of the Greek people. It has been conjectured that they derived their idea of Venus from the East. However this be, Venus was certainly one of the

---

[1] Plutarch, Life of Demetrius, 16, 19, 24–27; Athenæus, xiii. 39.
[2] Demosthenes against Neræa, p. 1386; Becker, Charicles, ii. 215.

earliest goddesses to whom their homage was paid. Solon erected opposite his dicterion a temple to Venus Pandemos, or the
public Venus. In that temple were two statues: one of the goddess, the other of a nymph, Pitho, who presided over persuasion;
and the attitudes and execution of the statues were such that they
explained the character without inscription. At this temple a
festival was held on the fourth of each month, to which all the
men of Athens were invited. But Venus Pandemos soon made
way for newer and more barefaced rivals. Twenty temples were
raised in various cities of Greece to Venus the Courtesan. In one
author we find allusion made to Venus Mucheia, or the Venus of
houses of ill-fame. Another celebrates Venus Castnia, or the goddess of indecency. Others honor Venus Scotia, the patroness
of darkness; and Venus Derceto, the guardian deity of street-
walkers. More famous still was Venus Divaricatrix, whose sur-
name, derived, it is said by a father of the Church, a *divaricatis
cruribus*,[1] must be left in a learned tongue. And still more re-
nowned was Venus Callipyge, whose statue is at this day one of
the choice ornaments of one of the best European collections of
antiquities. It owed its charm to the marvelous beauty of the
limbs, and was understood to have been designed from two Syra-
cusan sisters, whose extraordinary symmetry in this particular
had been noticed by a countryman who surprised them while
bathing. All these Venuses had temples, and sacrifices, and
priestesses. Their worship was naturally analogous to their name,
and consistent with their history. Their devotees were every
man in Greece. Yet it was in this society, trained to such spectacles, and nurtured in such a creed, that matrons and maidens
were taught to lead a life of purity, seclusion, and self-sacrifice.

The consequence was obvious. While ignorance and forcible
restraint prevented the women from generally breaking loose, the
men grew more and more addicted to the society of hetairæ, and
more liable to regard their wives as mere articles of furniture.
Nor was the anomaly without effect upon the kept women. They
alone of their sex saw the plays of Alexander and Aristophanes;
they alone had the *entrée* of the studio of Phidias and Apelles;
they alone heard Socrates reason, and discussed politics with
Pericles; they alone shared in the intellectual movement of
Greece. No women but hetairæ drove through the streets with
uncovered face and gorgeous apparel. None but they mingled in

---

[1] St. Clement of Alex.: Hortat. Address, 97.

the assemblages of great men at the Pnyx or the Stoa. None but they could gather round them of an evening the choicest spirits of the day, and elicit, in the freedom of unrestrained inter-course, wit and wisdom, flashing fancy and burning eloquence. What wonder that the Hetairæ should have filled so prominent a part in Greek society! And how small a compensation to virtu-ous women to know that their rivals could not stand by the altar when sacrifice was offered; could not give birth to a citizen!

There are many reasons besides these why the contest was un-equal. Tradition reported several occasions on which hetairæ had rendered signal service to the state. Leæna, for instance, the mistress of Harmodius, had bitten off her tongue rather than re-veal the names of her fellow-conspirators. Recollections like these more than nullified the nominal brand of the law. Again, every wise legislator saw the necessity of encouraging any form of rational intercourse, in order to arrest the startling progress which the most degrading of enormities was making in Greece. When Alcibiades was openly courted by the first philosophers and statesmen, it was virtue to applaud Aspasia. And besides, it can not be questioned, in view of the Greek memoirs we possess, that many of the leading hetairæ were women of remarkable mind, as well as unusual attractions. Indeed, the leading trait in their history is their intellectuality, as contrasted with other class-es of dissolute women in antiquity.[1] That trait can be best illus-trated by referring to the lives of a few of the more celebrated hetairæ.

A Milesian prostitute, named Thargelia, accompanied Xerxes on his invasion of Greece. Some idea may be formed of the po-sition in society occupied by prostitutes from the fact that Xerxes employed this woman as negotiator with the court of Thessaly, just as in later times modern ministers have used duchesses. Thargelia married the King of Thessaly.

Fired by her success, another Milesian girl, named Aspasia, es-tablished herself at Athens. She set up a house of prostitution, and peopled it with the most lovely girls of the Ionic cities. But wherein she differed from her rivals and predecessors was the prominence she gave to intellect in her establishment. She lec-tured publicly, among her girls and their visitors, on rhetoric and philosophy, and with such marked ability that she counted among her patrons and lovers the first men of Greece, including Socrates,

[1] Grote's History of Greece, vi. 100.

Alcibiades, and Pericles. The last divorced his wife in order to marry her, and was accused of allowing her to govern Athens, then at the height of its power and prosperity. She is said to have incited the war against Samos; and the principal cause of that against Megara was believed to have been the rape, by citizens of Megara, of two of Aspasia's girls. What a wonderful light these facts throw on Greek society!

Enraged beyond control at her success, the virtuous women of Athens rose against her. She was publicly insulted at the theatre; was attacked in the street; and, as a last resort, was accused of impiety before the Areopagus. Pericles, then in the decline of his power, and unable to save his friends Phidias and Anaxagoras, appeared as her advocate. But on such an occasion his eloquence failed him. He could only seize his beloved wife in his arms, press her to his breast, and burst into tears in presence of the court. The appeal succeeded; possibly the judges made allowance for popular prejudice; at all events, Aspasia was acquitted and restored to society. She lived to be the delight of a flour merchant, under whose roof her lectures on philosophy were continued with undiminished success to the day of her death.[1]

Her friend, and the inheritor of her mantle, Hipparchia, led an equally remarkable life. She was an Athenian by birth, and of good family, but, having heard the Cynic Crates speak, she declared to her parents that nothing would restrain her from yielding herself to him. She kept her word, and became the philosopher's mistress, in spite of his dirt, his poverty, and his grossness. She is reported to have acquired great reputation as a practical professor of the cynic philosophy. Having engaged one day in a fierce discussion with a somewhat brutal philosopher of a rival sect, the latter, by way of answer to a question she put, violently exposed her person before the whole assembly. " Well," said she, coolly, " what does that prove?" This woman was one of the most voluminous and esteemed authors of her day.[2]

Bacchis, the mistress of the orator Hyperides, illustrates the character of the Athenian kept woman from another point of view. She was extremely beautiful, and gifted with a sweet disposition. One of her early admirers had presented her with a necklace of enormous value. The first ladies of Athens, and even foreign

---

[1] Plutarch, Life of Pericles, 24, 32, etc. ; Demosthenes against Neræa, p 1350; Aristophanes, Acharm. 497, etc.; Athenæus, xiii. 25-56.
[2] Diogenes Laert. vi. 96.

women of rank, coveted the precious trinket in vain. She was in the height of her fame and charms when she heard the orator Hyperides plead. Smitten on the spot, she became his mistress, and observed a fidelity toward him which was neither usual with her class, nor reciprocated by her lover. On one occasion, a rival announced that the price of her complaisance would be the possession of the necklace of Bacchis. The lover had the meanness to ask for it, and Bacchis gave it without a word. Again: when all Athens knew that she was the mistress of Hyperides, an officious friend came to tell her that her lover was at that moment making love to another woman. Bacchis received the announcement tranquilly. "What do you intend to do?" asked her visitor, with impetuosity. "To wait for him," was the meek answer. She died very young, and her lover partially atoned for his ill treatment by pronouncing a splendid oration over her remains. Very few passages in Greek literature are marked by such eloquent tenderness and genuine feeling as this fragment of Hyperides.[1]

Gnathena, and her heir and successor, Gnathenion, were famous in their day as wits; the biography of the first was written in verse by the poet Machon.[2] She began life as the mistress of the comic poet Dyphiles, but soon abandoned him to keep a sort of *table d'hôte* for the wit and fashion of Athens. The "best society" gathered around her board, and at the close of the meal she sold herself by auction. Athenæus has chronicled a number of her witty and sarcastic sayings, adding that the grace of her elocution imparted a singular charm to every thing she said. Her protegée, Gnathenion, grew up in time to receive the mantle which age was wresting from the shoulders of Gnathena. An anecdote is preserved which throws some light upon the profits of the calling of hetairæ. At the temple of Venus, Gnathena and her protegée met an old Persian satrap, richly clothed in purple, who was struck with the beauty of the latter, and demanded her price. Gnathena answered, a thousand drachmas (about two hundred dollars). The satrap exclaimed at such extortion, and offered five hundred, observing that he would return again. "At your age," maliciously retorted Gnathena, "once is too much," and turned on her heel. In her old age it appears that Gnathena was reduced to the disgraceful calling which the Greeks termed *hippopornos*.[3]

[1] Athenæus, xiii. 56, 66, etc. ; Alciphron's Letters, 30.
[2] Athenæus. xiii. 39, etc.   [3] Id. xiii. 43. 47.

But the fame of these hetairæ is eclipsed by that of the only two kept women who can rank with Aspasia—Lais and Phryne. Lais was a Sicilian by birth. Like the Empress Catharine of Russia, she was taken prisoner when her native city was captured, and sold as a slave. The painter Apelles saw her carrying water from a well, and, struck with the beauty of her figure, he bought her, and trained her in his own house. This, again, is a striking picture. Fancy a leading modern painter deliberately training a prostitute! It is to be presumed that Apelles gathered round him the best society in Greece. Lais, when her education was complete, was as remarkable for wit and information as for her matchless figure and lovely face. Her master freed her, and established her at Corinth, then in the height of its prosperity, and the largest commercial emporium of Greece.

Corinth and the Corinthian prostitutes deserve particular notice. It appears that almost every house in the place was, in fact, a house of prostitution. There were regular schools where the art of debauchery was taught, and frequent importations of young girls from Lesbos, Phœnicia, and the Ægean Islands supplied them with pupils. Ancient erotic writers are full of allusions to the danger of visiting Corinth; the proverb, *Non cuivis homini contingit adire Corinthum*, which most moderns have erroneously conceived to refer to Lais alone, was, in fact, an adage justified by the experience of merchants and sailors. It would be incor-rect, however, to compare Corinth with modern sea-ports, where the natural demands of sailors require a cheap supply of women. The first-class hetairæ of Corinth charged as high as a talent (say $1000) for a single night's company, and $200 appears to have been no unusual fee. For the common sailors, the commercial shrewdness of the Corinthians had established a temple to Venus, containing a thousand young slaves, who were obliged to prosti-tute themselves for a single obolus (a cent).[1]

It was in this metropolis of prostitution that Lais commenced business. She soon rose to the first rank in her trade. Her capriciousness gave additional value to her charms. Even money could not purchase her when it was her whim not to yield. She refused $2000 from the orator Demosthenes, who had actually turned his property into money to lay it at her feet; but she yielded gratuitously to the muddy, ragged cynic Diogenes, and

---

[1] Plato, De Rep. iii. p. 404; Aristoph. Plut. 149; Müller, Dor. ii. 10, 7; Strabo, viii. 6, 211.

graciously shared the patrimony of the philosopher Aristippus. To the latter, who occupied no mean rank in Greek society, a remark was made to the effect that he ought to debar his mistress from promiscuous intercourse for his own sake. He replied phlegmatically, "Would you object to live in a house or sail in a ship because others had just preceded you in the one or the other?" Xenocrates, the disciple of Plato, resisted Lais successfully. She had made a wager that she would overcome his stoical coldness. Rushing into his house one evening in affected terror, she besought an asylum, as she said thieves had chased her. The philosopher sternly bade her fear nothing. She sat silent till Xenocrates went to bed; then, throwing off her dress, and revealing all her wonderful beauty, she placed herself at his side. He gruffly submitted to this encroachment. Growing bolder, she threw her arms round him, caressed him, and exhausted her arts of fascination, but Xenocrates remained unmoved. "I wagered," she cried, "to rouse a man, not a statue;" and, springing from the couch, she resumed her dress and disappeared.

The people of Corinth desired to possess her statue, and, having spent her money in embellishing the city, perhaps she was entitled to this mark of respect. Myron, the sculptor, was deputed to model her charms. He was old and gray; but so fascinating was her beauty, that at his second visit he laid at her feet all the savings of his life. The haughty courtesan spurned him. He went away, placed himself in the hands of a skillful perfumer, had his hair and beard dyed, and his appearance rejuvenated. Then he renewed his suit. "My poor friend," said Lais, with a bitter smile, "you are asking what I refused yesterday to your father."

In old age Lais had leisure to repent of her caprices. She had spent her money as fast as she made it, and she retained her calling long after her charms had vanished. Epicrates has drawn a melancholy picture of a drunken old woman wandering over the quay at Corinth, and seeking to sell for three cents what had once been considered cheap at a thousand dollars. Such was the end of Lais.[1]

Phryne was more fortunate. She husbanded her attractions with judgment, and to the close of her long life retained her rank and her value. Her wealth was such that, when Alexander destroyed Thebes, she offered to rebuild the city at her own ex-

---

[1] Diogenes Laert. ii. 84; St. Clement of Alex. Strom. iii. 47; Pausanias, ii. 2, 4; Ausonius, Epig. 17; Athenæus, xiii. 26, 54. et.

pense, provided the Thebans would commemorate the fact by an inscription. They refused. She had counted among her lovers the most famous men of the day, among whom were the orator Hyperides, whose successful defense of his mistress has already been mentioned; the painter Apelles, and the sculptor Praxiteles. It was to her that the latter gave his crowning work—his Cupid. He and Apelles were both privileged to admire and reproduce her nude charms, a privilege rigorously denied even to the most opulent of her lovers.

Phryne was a prodigious favorite with the Athenian people. She played a conspicuous part in the festival of Neptune and Venus. At a certain point in the ceremony she appeared on the steps of the temple at the sea-side in her usual dress, and slowly disrobed herself in the presence of the crowd. She next advanced to the water-side, plunged into the waves, and offered sacrifice to Neptune. Returning like a sea-nymph, drying her hair from which the water dripped over her exquisite limbs, she paused for a moment before the crowd, which shouted in a phrensy of en-thusiasm as the fair priestess vanished into a cell in the temple.[1]

Other famous hetairæ achieved political and literary distinction. When Alexander the Great undertook his Asiatic expedition, his treasurer, Harpalus, a sort of Crœsus in his way, accompanied him, surrounded by the most lovely women the court of Macedon could afford. Rewarded for his fidelity by the governorship of Babylon, and still farther enriched by the spoils of that lucrative office, Harpalus sent to Athens for the most skillful and lovely hetairæ of the day. Pythionice was sent him. She was not in the bloom of youth. Some years before she had been the familiar of young Athenians of fashion; she was now the staid mistress of two brothers, sons of an opulent corn-merchant. But her tal-ents were undeniable. She arrived at Babylon, and was installed in the palace; began to rule over the province, and governed Harpalus, it is said, with sternness and vigor. In the midst of her glory she suddenly died; poisoned, no doubt, by some one of the hundred fair ones whom she had supplanted in the governor's affections. Harpalus, inconsolable for her loss, expended a large portion of the contents of his treasury in burying her and com-memorating her fame. No queen of Babylon was ever consigned to the grave with the pomp, or the show, or the ostentatious afflic-

---

[1] Ælian, V. H. ix. 32; Alciphron's Letters, i. 31; Jacobs, Alt. Mus iii. 18, 36, etc.; Athenæus, xiii. 59. etc.

tion which did honor to the memory of the Athenian prostitute.
Her tomb cost $50,000; and historians, admiring, in after ages,
its splendor and its size, inquired, with mock wonder, whether the
bones of a Miltiades, or a Cimon, or a Pericles lay under the pile!

Harpalus found consolation in the arms of a Greek garland-
weaver named Glycera, for aught we know the poisoner of Pythionice. She, too, became Queen of Babylon, issued her decrees,
held her court, submitted to be worshiped, and saw her statue of
bronze, as large as life, erected in the Babylonian temples. She
was a woman of a masculine mind in a feminine body. When
Alexander returned from the East, breathing vengeance against
faithless servants, she compelled her lover to fly with her to At-
tica, where she raised, by her eloquence, her money, and her address, an army of six thousand men to oppose the hero of Macedon. It is said that she purchased, at what price we know not,
the silence of Demosthenes; she certainly bribed the Athenian
people with large donations of corn. But she could not bribe or
persuade her wretched lover to be sensible; his folly soon roused
the Athenians against him, and he was exiled with his mistress.
In this exile, one of his attendants cut the throat of the venerable
lover, and Glycera, left a widow, returned to Athens to pursue her
calling as a hetaira. She was no longer young, and needed the
aid of the dealer in cosmetics; but her prestige as the ex-mistress
of Babylon procured her a certain celebrity, and she soon obtained
a position in the society of Athens. Out of a crowd of admirers
who attached themselves to her court, she chose two to be, as the
French would say, her *amants de cœur*. One was the painter Pausias; the other the comic poet Menander. The former achieved
one of his most brilliant triumphs by painting the portrait of his
mistress. But, whether his temper was not congenial to hers, or
his rival inspired an exclusive affection, Glycera soon discarded
Pausias, and became the mistress of the poet alone. Menander,
we are led to believe, was a man of a harsh, crabbed disposition;
the haughty Glycera was the only one whom his *boutades* never
irritated, who bore with all his ill temper. When he was successful, she heightened his joy; when his plays were ill received, and
he returned from the theatre in low spirits, she consoled him, and
endured the keenest affronts without murmuring. Her amiability
had its reward. From being one of the most dissolute men of
Athens, Menander became solidly attached and faithful to Glycera
and, so soon was her Babylonish career forgotten, she descended

to posterity in the Athenian heart inseparably coupled with the dearest of their comic writers.[1]

Another famous hetaira was Leontium, who succeeded her mistress Philenis in the affections of the philosopher Epicurus. She is said to have borne him a daughter, who was born in the shade of a grove in his garden; but, whether she put her own construction upon the Epicurean philosophy, or did not really love the gray-headed teacher, she was far from practicing the fidelity which was due to so distinguished a lover. She figures in the letters of Alciphron as the tender friend of several younger fashionables; and she has been accused, with what truth it is hard to say, of attempting a compromise between the doctrines of Epicurus and those of Diogenes. However this be, Leontium was undoubtedly a woman of rare ability and remarkable taste. She composed several works; among others, one against Theophrastus, which excited the wonder and admiration of so good a judge as Cicero. She survived her old protector, and died in obscurity.[2]

Something more might be said of Archeanassa, to whose wrinkles Plato did not disdain to compose an amorous epigram; of Theoris, a beautiful girl, who preferred the glorious old age of Sophocles to the ardent youth of Demosthenes, and whom the vindictive orator punished by having her condemned to death; of Archippa, the last mistress and sole heir of Sophocles; of Theodote, the disciple of Socrates, under whose counsels she carried on her business as a courtesan, and whose death may be ascribed, in some part, to the spite caused by Theodote's rejection of Aristophanes; and of others who figure largely in every reliable history of intellectual Greece. But we must stop.

In most of the nations to which reference must be made in the ensuing pages of this volume, prostitutes have figured as pariahs; in Greece they were an aristocracy, exercising a palpable influence over the national policy and social life, and mingling conspicuously in the great march of the Greek intellect. No less than eleven authors of repute have employed their talents as historiographers of courtesans at Athens. Their works have not reached us entire, having fallen victims to the chaste scruples of the clergy of the Middle Ages; but enough remains in the quotations of Athenæus, Alciphron's Letters, Lucian, Diogenes Laertius, Aristophanes, Aristænetus, and others, to enable us to form a far more

[1] Pausanias, i. 37, 5; Athenæus, xiii. 45, etc.; Diod. xvii. 108; Arr. *ap*. *Phot*. 70.
[2] Diogenes Laert. x. 4: Athenæus, xiii. 29; Cicero, de Nat. Deor. i. 33.

accurate idea of the Athenian hetairæ than we can obtain of the prostitutes of the last generation.

Into the arts practiced by the graduates of the Corinthian academies it is hardly possible to enter, at least in a modern tongue. Even the Greeks were obliged to invent verbs to designate the monstrosities practiced by the Lesbian and Phœnician women. Demosthenes, pleading successfully against the courtesan Neæra, describes her as having seven young girls in her house, whom she knew well how to train for their calling, as was proved by the re peated sales of their virginity. One may form an idea of the shocking depravity of the reigning taste from the sneers which were lavished upon Phryne and Bacchis, who steadily adhered to natural pleasures.

The use of philtres, or charms (of which more will be said in the ensuing chapter on Roman prostitution), was common in Greece. Retired courtesans often combined the manufacture of these supposed charms with the business of a midwife. They made potions which excited love and potions which destroyed it; charms to turn love into hate, and others to convert hate into love. That the efficacy of the latter must have been a matter of pure faith need not be demonstrated, though the belief in them was general and profound. The former are well known in the pharmacopœia, and from the accounts given of their effects, there is no reason to doubt that they were successfully employed in Greece, as well by jealous husbands and suspicious fathers as by ardent lovers. A case is mentioned by no less an authority than Aristotle, of a woman who contrived to administer an amorous potion to her lover, who died of it. The woman was tried for murder; but, it being satisfactorily proved that her intention was not to cause death, but to revive an extinct love, she was acquitted. Other cases are mentioned in which the philtres produced madness instead of love. Similar accidents have attended the exhibition of cantharides in modern times.

CHAPTER IV.

ROME.

Laws governing Prostitution.—Floralian Games.—Registration of Prostitutes.—
Purity of Morals.—Julian Law.—Ædiles.—Classes of Prostitutes.—Loose Prosti-
tutes.—Various Classes of lewd Women.—Meretrices.—Dancing Girls.—Bawds.
—Male Prostitutes.—Houses of Prostitution.—Lupanaria.—Cells of Prostitutes.
—Houses of Assignation. — Fornices. — Circus. — Baths. — Taverns. — Bakers'
Shops.—Squares and Thoroughfares.—Habits and Manners of Prostitutes.—So-
cial standing.—Dress.—Rate of Hire.—Virgins in Roman Brothels.—Kept Wom-
en.—Roman Poets.—Ovid.—Martial.—Roman Society.—Social Corruption.—
Conversation.—Pictures and Sculptures.—Theatricals.—Baths.—Religious In-
decencies.—Marriage Feasts.—Emperors.—Secret Diseases.—Celsus.—Roman
Faculty.—Archiatii.

LAWS GOVERNING PROSTITUTION.

OUR earliest acquaintance with the Roman laws governing prostitution dates from the reign of the Emperor Augustus, but there
is abundant evidence to show that prostitutes were common in
the city of Rome at the time when authentic history begins.

It does not appear that religious prostitution was ever domiciled
in Italy, though in later times the festivals in honor of certain deities were scandalously loose, and, to judge from the Etruscan
paintings, the morals of the indigenous Italians must have beer
disgustingly depraved.

In the comedies of Plautus, which are among the oldest works
of Roman literature which have reached us, the prostitute (*mere-
trix*) and the bawd (*leno*) figure conspicuously. They were thus,
evidently, in the third century before Christ, well-known characters in Roman society. When the Floralian Games were instituted we have no means of knowing (no credit whatever must be
placed in the puerile stories of Lactantius about the courtesans
Acca Laurentia and Flora[1]); but it is certain that the chief attraction of these infamous celebrations was the appearance of prostitutes on the stage in a state of nudity, and their lascivious dances
in the presence of the people ;[2] and there is evidence, in the story
that the performance was suspended during the presence of the
stern moralist Cato, that they had been long practiced before his
time.[3] Indeed, it would not be presuming too far to decide, with-

[1] Lactant. i. 20.   [2] Martial, i. 1; Seneca, Epist. 96.   [3] Val. Max. ii. 10, 8.

out other evidence, that prostitution must have become a fixed fact at Rome very shortly after the Romans began to mix freely with the Greek colonists at Tarentum and the other Greek cities in Italy, that is to say, about the beginning of the third century before Christ.

We learn from Tacitus[1] that from time immemorial prostitutes had been required to register themselves in the office of the ædile. The ceremony appears to have been very similar to that now imposed by law on French prostitutes. The woman designing to become a prostitute presented herself before the ædile, gave her age, place of birth, and real name, with the one she assumed if she adopted a pseudonyme.[2] The public officer, if she was young or apparently respectable, did his best to combat her resolution. Failing in this, he issued to her a license—*licentia stupri*, ascertained the sum which she was to demand from her customers, and entered her name in his roll. It might be inferred from a law of Justinian[3] that a prostitute was bound to take an oath, on obtaining her license, to discharge the duties of her calling to the end of her life; for the law in question very properly decided that an oath so obviously at war with good morals was not binding. However this was, the prostitute once inscribed incurred the taint of infamy which nothing could wipe off. Repentance was impossible, even when she married and became the mother of legitimate children; the fatal inscription was still there to bear witness of her infamy.[4] In Rome, as in so many other countries, the principle of the law was to close the door to reform, and to render vice hopeless.

There is every reason to suppose that these regulations were in force at a very early period of the Republic. Of the further rules established under the imperial regime we shall speak presently. Meanwhile, it may be observed that there is ground for hoping that, at the best age of the Republic, the public morals were not generally corrupt. The old stories of Lucretia and Virginia would have had no point among a demoralized people. All who are familiar with Roman history will remember the fierce contest waged by Cato the Censor against the jewels, fine dresses, and carriages of the Roman ladies,[5] an indication that graver delinquencies did not call for official interference. This same Cato, after the death of his first wife, cohabited with a female slave; but,

---

[1] Annal. lib. ii. 85. [2] Plautus, Pænulus. [3] Nov. 5.
[4] See Tabl. Heracl. i. 123. [5] Plutarch, Vita Catonis
L·

though concubinage was recognized by the Roman law, and would seem to have involved no disgrace at a later period, the intrigue no sooner became known than the old censor married a second wife to avoid scandal.[1]   A similar inference may be drawn from the strange story told by Livy of the Bacchanalian mysteries introduced into Rome by foreigners about the beginning of the second century before Christ. It is not easy, at this late day, to discover what is true and what false in the statement he gives; but there is no reasonable doubt that young persons of both sexes, under the impulse of sensuality, had established societies for the purpose, among others, of satisfying depraved instincts.   To what extent the mania had extended it is not possible to judge; the numbers given by the Latin writers are not very trustworthy. But we may learn how strong was the moral sentiment of the Roman people from the very stringent decree which the senate issued on motion of the Consul Postumius, and from the indiscriminate executions of parties implicated in the mysterious rites.[2]

Other evidences of the purity of Roman morals might be found, if they were wanting, in the remarkable fidelity with which the Vestals observed their oaths; in the tone of the speeches of the statesmen of the time; in the high character sustained by such matrons as the mother of the Gracchi; and, finally, in the legislation of Augustus, which professed rather to affirm and improve the old laws than to introduce new principles.

As we approach the Christian era the picture gradually darkens.   Civil wars are usually fatal to private virtue: it is not to be doubted that the age of Sylla and Clodius was by no means a moral one.   Sylla, the dictator, openly led a life of scandalous debauchery; Clodius, the all-powerful tribune, is accused by Cicero of having seduced his three sisters.[3] Soldiers who had made a campaign in profligate Greece or voluptuous Asia naturally brought home with them a taste for the pleasures they had learned to enjoy abroad.   Scipio's baths were dark: through narrow apertures just light enough was admitted to spare the modesty of the bathers; but into the baths which were erected in the later years of the Republic the light shone as into a chamber.[4]   Even Sylla, debauched as he was, did not think it safe to abdicate pow-

---

[1] Livy, xxxiv. 1, et seq.
[2] Livy, xxxix. 8–19.   See also St. August. De Civ. Dei, vii. 21.
[3] Cicero, ad Fam. i. 9.
[4] Val. Max. ii. 1, 7; Cicero, de Off. 1, 35.

er without legislative effort to purify the morals he had so largely contributed to corrupt by his example.[1]

Of the Augustan age, and the two or three centuries which
followed, we are enabled to form a close and comprehensive idea.
Our information ceases to be meagre; on some points, indeed, it
is only too abundant.

The object of the Julian laws was to preserve the Roman blood
from corruption, and still farther to degrade prostitutes. These
aims were partially attained by prohibiting the intermarriage of
citizens with the relatives or descendants of prostitutes; by exposing adulterers to severe penalties, and declaring the tolerant
husband an accomplice; by laying penalties on bachelors and
married men without children; by prohibiting the daughters of
equestrians from becoming prostitutes.[2] Tiberius, from his infamous retreat at Capreæ, sanctioned a decree of the senate which
enhanced the severity of the laws against adultery. By this decree it was made a penal offense for a matron of any class to play
the harlot, and her lover, the owner of the house where they met,
and all persons who connived at the adultery, were declared
equally culpable. It seems to have been not uncommon for
certain married women to inscribe themselves on the ædile's list
as prostitutes, and to occupy a room at the houses of ill fame.
This was pronounced a penal offense; and every encouragement
was held out, both to husbands and to common informers, to
prosecute.[3]

In other respects the republican legislation is believed to have
been unaltered by the emperors. The formality of inscription,
its accompanying infamy, the consequences of the act remained
the same. Prostitutes carried on their trade under the ædile's
eye. He patrolled the streets, and entered the houses of ill fame
at all hours of the day and night. He saw that they were closed
between daybreak and three in the afternoon. In case of brawls,
he arrested and punished the disturbers of the peace. He punished by fine and scourging the omission of a brothel-keeper to
inscribe every female in his house. He insisted on prostitutes
wearing the garments prescribed by law, and dyeing their hair
blue or yellow. On the other hand, he could not break into a
house without being habited in the insignia of his office, and being

[1] Plutarch, Vit. Syllæ, 85.
[2] Lex Jul. et Pap. Popp.; Lex Jul. de Adult.; Dig. 35, tit. 1, § 63; Gaius, ii. 113.
[3] See Dig. 48, tit. 5.

accompanied by his lictors. When the ædile Hostilius attempted to break open the door of the prostitute Mamilia, on his return from a gay dinner, the latter drove him off with stones, and was sustained by the courts.[1] The ædile was bound also, on complaint laid by a prostitute, to sentence any customer of hers to pay the sum due to her according to law.[2]

CLASSES OF PROSTITUTES.

It was the duty of the ædile to arrest, punish, and drive out of the city all loose prostitutes who were not inscribed on his book. This regulation was practically a dead letter. At no time in the history of the empire did there cease to be a large and well-known class of prostitutes who were not recorded. They were distinguished from the registered prostitutes (*meretrices*) by the name of *prostibulæ*.[3] They paid no tax to the state, while their registered rivals contributed largely to the municipal treasury; and, if they ran greater risks, and incurred more nominal infamy than the latter, they more frequently contrived to rise from their unhappy condition.

We have no means of judging of the number of prostitutes exercising their calling at Rome, Capua, and the other Italian cities during the first years of the Christian era. During Trajan's reign the police were enabled to count thirty-two thousand in Rome alone, but this number obviously fell short of the truth. One is appalled at the great variety of classes into which the *prostibulæ*, or unregistered prostitutes were divided. Such were the *Delicatæ*, corresponding to the kept-women, or French *lorettes*, whose charms enabled them to exact large sums from their visitors;[4] the *Famosæ*, who belonged to respectable families, and took to evil courses through lust or avarice;[5] the *Doris*, who were remarkable for their beauty of form, and disdained the use of clothing;[6] the *Lupæ*, or she-wolves, who haunted the groves and commons, and were distinguished by a particular cry in imitation of a wolf;[7] the *Ælicariæ*, or bakers' girls, who sold small cakes for sacrifice to Venus and Priapus, in the form of the male and female organs of generation;[8] the *Bustuariæ*, whose home was the burial-ground, and who occasionally officiated as mourners at funerals;[9]

---

[1] Aulus Gell. quoting Ateius Capito.
[2] Pierrugues, Gloss. Erot. For the duties of the ædiles, see Schubert, de Rom. Ædilibus, liv. 4.   [3] See Plautus, *passim*.   [4] Suetonius.   [5] Cicero
[6] Ausonius.   [7] Plaut. Panulus.   [8] Cic. pro Cælio.   [9] Juvenal.

the *Copœ*, servant-girls at inns and taverns, who were invariably prostitutes;[1] the *Noctiluœ*, or night-walkers; the *Blitidœ*, a very low class of women, who derived the name from *blitum*, a cheap and unwholesome beverage drunk in the lowest holes;[2] the *Dioboboares*, wretched outcasts, whose price was two oboli (say two cents);[3] the *Forariœ*, country girls who lurked about country roads; the *Gallinœ*, who were thieves as well as prostitutes; the *Quadrantariœ*, seemingly the lowest class of all, whose fee was less than any copper coin now current.[4] In contradistinction to these, the *meretrices* assumed an air of respectability, and were often called *bonæ meretrices*.[5]

Another and a distinct class of prostitutes were the female dancers, who were eagerly sought after, and more numerous than at Athens. They were Ionians, Lesbians, Syrians, Egyptians, Nubians (negresses), Indians, but the most famous were Spaniards. Their dances were of the same character as those of the Greek flute-players; the erotic poets of Rome have not shrunk from celebrating the astonishing depravity of their performances.[6]

Horace faintly deplored the progress which the Ionic dances— *Ionice motus* — were making even among the Roman virgins.[7] These prostitutes carried on their calling in defiance of law. If detected, they were liable to be whipped and driven out of the city;[8] but as their customers belonged to the wealthier classes, they rarely suffered the penalty of their conduct.

Apart, again, from all these was the large class of persons who traded in prostitutes. The proper name for these wretches was *Leno* (bawd), which was of both sexes, though usually represented on the stage as a beardless man with shaven head. Under this name quite a number of varieties were included, such as the *Lupanarii*, or keepers of regular houses of ill fame; the *Adductores* and *Perductores*, pimps; *Conciliatrices* and *Ancillulæ*, women who negotiated immoral transactions, and others. Then, as almost every baker, tavern-keeper, bath-house-keeper, barber, and perfumer combined the *lenocinium*, or trade in prostitutes, with his other calling, their various names, *tonsor*, *unguentarius*, *balnearius*, &c., became synonymous with *leno*. This miserable class was regarded with the greatest loathing at Rome.[9]

---

[1] Juvenal. [2] Suidas. [3] Plautus, Cistellaria. [4] Suetonius. [5] Martial.
[6] Plaut. Panulus. Juvenal says,
"*Ad terram tremulo descendant clune puellæ.*"
[7] Horace, Od. iii. 6, 21. [8] See Schubert, *loc. cit.*
[9] Terence, Adelph. 1; Catullus, etc.

This hasty classification of the Roman prostitutes would be incomplete without some notice, however brief, of male prostitutes. Fortunately, the progress of good morals has divested this repulsive theme of its importance; the object of this work can be obtained without entering into details on a branch of the subject which in this country is not likely to require fresh legislative notice. But the reader would form an imperfect idea of the state of morals at Rome were he left in ignorance of the fact that the number of male prostitutes was probably full as large as that of females; that, as in Greece, the degrading phenomenon involved very little disgrace; that all the Roman authors allude to it as a matter of course; that the leading men of the empire were known to be addicted to such habits; that the ædile abstained from interference, save where a Roman youth suffered violence; and that, to judge from the language of the writers of the first, second, and third centuries of the Christian era, the Romans, like some Asiatic races, appeared to give the preference to unnatural lusts.[1]

HOUSES OF PROSTITUTION.

Having examined the laws which governed prostitution at Rome, and the classes into which prostitutes were divided, it is now requisite to glance at the establishments in which prostitution was carried on.

M. Dufour and others have followed Publius Victor and Sextus Rufus in supposing that during the Augustine age there were forty-six first-class houses of ill fame at Rome, and a much larger number of establishments where prostitution was carried on without the supervision of the ædile. As it is now generally admitted that the works bearing the name of Publius Victor and Sextus Rufus are forgeries of comparatively recent date, the statement loses all claim to credit, and we are left without statistical information as to the number of houses of prostitution at Rome.[2]

Registered prostitutes were to be found in the establishments called Lupanaria. These differed from the Greek Dicteria in being of various classes, from the well-provided house of the Peace ward to the filthy dens of the Esquiline and Suburran wards; and farther, in the wide range of prices exacted by the keepers of the various houses. It is inferred from the results of the excava-

---

[1] Rom. i. 26, 27, and all Latin poets, *passim.*
[2] See Bunsen, Beschreibung der Stadt Rome, 1830, i. 173.

tions at Pompeii, and some meagre hints thrown out by Latin authors, that the lupanaria at Rome were small in size. The most prosperous were built like good Roman houses, with a square court-yard, sometimes with a fountain playing in the middle. Upon this yard opened the cells of the prostitutes. In smaller establishments the cells opened upon a hall or porch, which seemingly was used as a reception-room. The cells were dark closets, illuminated at night by a small bronze lamp. Sometimes they contained a bed, but as often a few cushions, or a mere mat, with a dirty counterpane, constituted their whole furniture. Over the door of each cell hung a tablet, with the name of the prostitute who occupied it, and the price she set on her favors; on the other side with the word *occupata*. When a prostitute received a visitor in her cell, she turned the tablet round to warn intruders that she was engaged.[1] Over the door of the house a suggestive image was either painted, or represented in stone or marble: one of these signs may be seen to this day in Pompeii. Within, similar indecent sculptures abounded. Bronze ornaments of this style hung round the necks of the courtesans; the lamps were in the same shape, and so were a variety of other utensils. The walls were covered with appropriate frescoes. In the best-ordered establishments, it is understood that scenes from the mythology were the usual subjects of these artistic decorations; but we have evidence enough at Pompeii to show that gross indecency, not poetical effect, was the main object sought by painters in these works.

Regular houses of prostitution, *lupanaria*, were of two kinds: establishments owned and managed by a bawd, who supplied the cells with slaves or hired prostitutes, and establishments where the bawd merely let his cells to prostitutes for a given sum. In the former case the bawd was the principal, in the latter the women. There is reason to suppose that the former were the more respectable. Petronius alludes to a house where so much was paid for the use of a cell, and the sum was an *as*, less than two cents.[2] Messalina evidently betook herself to one of these establishments, which, for clearness' sake, we may call assignation houses; and as it appears she was paid in copper (*æra poposcit*), it is safe to infer that the house was of slender respectability.

The best houses were abundantly supplied with servants and luxuries. A swarm of pimps and runners sought custom for them

[1] Plautus, *Asinaria;* Martial, Ep. *passim.*   [2] Petronius, Satyricon, i. 28.

in every part of the city. Women—*ancillæ ornatrices*—were in readiness to repair with skill the ravages which amorous conflicts caused in the toilets of the prostitutes. Boys—*bacariones*—attended at the door of the cell with water for ablution. Servants, who bore the inconsistent title of *aquarii*, were ready to supply wine and other refreshments to customers. And not a few of the lupinaria kept a cashier, called *villicus*, whose business it was to discuss bargains with visitors, and to receive the money before turning the tablet.

Under many public and some of the best private houses at Rome were arches, the tops of which were only a few feet above the level of the street. These arches, dark and deserted, became a refuge for prostitutes. Their name, *fornices*, at last became synonymous with *lupanar*, and we have borrowed from it our generic word fornication.[1] There is reason to believe that there were several score of arches of this character, and used for this purpose, under the great circus and other theatres at Rome,[2] besides those under dwelling-houses and stores. The want of fresh air was severely felt in these vile abodes. Frequent allusions to the stench exhaled from the mouth of a fornix are made in the Roman authors.[3]

Establishments of a lower character still were the *pergulæ*, in which the girls occupied a balcony above the street; the *stabula*, where no cells were used, and promiscuous intercourse took place openly;[4] the *turturilla*, or pigeon-houses;[5] the *casauria*, or suburb houses of the very lowest stamp.

The clearest picture of a Roman house of ill fame is that given in the famous passage of Juvenal, which may be allowed to remain in the original. The female, it need hardly be added, was Messalina:

> "Dormire virum quum senserat uxor,
> Ausa Palatino tegetem præferre cubili,
> Sumere nocturnas meretrix Augusta cucullos,
> Linquebat comite ancilla non amplius una,
> Sed *nigrum flavo crinem abscondente galero*,
> Intravit calidum veteri centone lupanar,
> Et *cellam vacuam* atque suam. Tunc nuda capillis
> Constitit auratis, titulum mentita Lyciscæ,

[1] Hor. Sat. i. 2, 30; Juv. Sat. iii. 156; Suet. Jul. 49.
[2] Prudentius, in Agn; Boulenger, Cirque, etc.
[3] *Olenti in fornice*, Hor. *Redolet fuligmura fornicis*, Mart.   [4] Plautus.   [5] Id.

Ostendit que tuum, generose Britannice, ventrem.
Excepit blanda intrantes, atque *œra poposcit*,
Et resupina jacens multorum absorbuit ictus.
Mox lenone suas jam dimittente puellas,
Tristris abit, et quod potuit, tamen ultima cellam
Clausit, adhuc ardens rigidæ tentigine vulvæ,
Et lassata viris necdum satiata recessit;
Obscurrisque genis turpis fumoque lucernæ
.Fœda lupanaris tulit ad pulvinar adorem."[1]

The passages in italics contain useful information; we shall allude to some of them hereafter. Meanwhile, it is evident from the line *mox lenone*, etc., that, at a certain hour of the night, the keepers of houses of ill fame were in the habit of closing their establishments and sending their girls home. The law required them to close at daybreak, but probably a much earlier hour may have suited their interest.

Allusion has already been made to the fornices under the circus. It is well understood that prostitutes were great frequenters of the spectacles, and that in the arched fornices underneath the seats and the stage they were always ready to satisfy the passions which the comedies and pantomimes only too frequently aroused.[2] This was one formidable rival to the regular lupinaria.

The baths were another. In the early Roman baths, darkness, or, at best, a faint twilight reigned; and, besides, not only were the sexes separated, but old and young men were not allowed to bathe together.[3] But after Sylla's wars, though there were separate *sudaria* and *tepidaria* for the sexes, they could meet freely in the corridors and chambers, and any immorality short of actual prostitution could take place.[4] Men and women, girls and boys, mixed together in a state of perfect nudity, and in such close proximity that contact could hardly be avoided. Such an assemblage would obviously be a place of resort for dealers in prostitutes in search of merchandise. At a later period, cells were attached to the bath-houses, and young men and women kept on the premises, partly as bath attendants and partly as prostitutes. After the bath, the bathers, male and female, were rubbed down, kneaded, and anointed by these attendants. It would appear that women submitted to have this indecent service performed for them by

[1] Juvenal, ii. Sat. vi. 116.
[2] Cyprian, Ep. 103; Boulenger, De Circe Rom.; Arnob.; Tertullian.
[3] Seneca, Ep. 86; Val. Max. ii. 1, 7.   [4] Plin. H. N. 33, 54.

men, and that health was not always the object sought, even by the Roman matrons.[1] Several emperors endeavored to remedy these frightful immoralities. Hadrian forbade the intermixture of men and women in the public baths.[2] Similar enactments were made by Marcus Aurelius and Alexander Severus; but Helioga-balus is said to have delighted in uniting the sexes, even in the wash-room. As early as the Augustan era, however, the baths were regarded as little better than houses of prostitution under a respectable name.[3]

Taverns or houses of entertainment were also in some measure brothels. The law regarded all servants waiting upon travelers at inns or taverns as prostitutes.[4] It would appear, also, that butchers', bakers', and barbers' shops were open to a suspicion of being used for purposes of prostitution. The plebeian ædiles constantly made it their business to visit these in search of unregistered prostitutes, though, as might be expected from the number of delinquents and the very incomplete municipal police system of Rome, with very little success. The bakers' establishments, which generally included a flour-mill, were haunted by a low class of prostitutes to whom allusion has already been made. In the cellar where the mill stood cells were often constructed, and the ædiles knew well that all who entered there did not go to buy bread.[5]

Finally, prostitution to a very large extent was carried on in the open air. The shades of certain statues and temples, such as those of Marsyas, Pan, Priapus, Venus, etc., were common resorts for prostitutes. It is said that Julia, the daughter of the Emperor Augustus, prostituted herself under the shade of a statue of Marsyas. Similar haunts of abandoned women were the arches of aqueducts, the porticoes of temples, the cavities in walls, etc. Even the streets in the poorer wards of the city appear to have been infested by the very lowest class of prostitutes, whose natural favors had long ceased to be merchantable.[6] It must be borne in mind

---

[1] "Callidus et cristæ digitos impressit aliptes."—Juvenal, ii. Sat. vi.
[2] Spartianus, Hadrian, c. 1.   See Ovid, Ars Amat.
[4] Ulpian, liv. xxiii. De rit. nupt. ; Jul. Paulus, Dig. ; Cicero.
[5] Martial, xvi. 222.
[6]   Lesbia nostra, Lesbia illa,
      Illa Lesbia, quam Catullus unam,
      Plus quam se atque suas amavit omnes,
      Nunc in quadriviis et angiportis
      Glubit magnanimos Remi nepotes.
                            CATULLUS. Carm. 58.

that the streets of Rome were not lighted, and that profound darkness reigned when the moon was clouded over.

HABITS AND MANNERS OF PROSTITUTES.

A grand distinction between Roman and Greek prostitution lies in the manner in which commerce with prostitutes was viewed in the two communities. At Athens there was nothing disgraceful in frequenting the dicterion or keeping an hetaira. At Rome, on the contrary, a married man who visited a house of ill fame was an *adulter*, and liable to the penalties of adultery. An habitual frequenter of such places was a *mœchus* or *scortator*, both of which were terms of scathing reproach. When Cicero wishes to overwhelm Catiline, he says his followers are *scortatores*.[1] Until the lowest age of Roman degradation, moreover, no man of any character entered a house of ill fame without hiding his face with the skirt of his dress. Even Caligula and Heliogabalus concealed their faces when they visited the women of the town.[2]

The law prescribed with care the dress of Roman prostitutes, on the principle that they were to be distinguished in all things from honest women. Thus they were not allowed to wear the chaste *stola* which concealed the form, or the *vitta* or fillet with which Roman ladies bound their hair, or to wear shoes (*soccus*), or jewels, or purple robes. These were the insignia of virtue. Prostitutes wore the *toga* like men; their hair, dyed yellow or red, or filled with golden spangles, was dressed in some Asiatic fashion. They wore sandals with gilt thongs tying over the instep, and their dress was directed to be of flowered material. In practice, however, these rules were not strictly observed. Courtesans wore jewels and purple robes,[3] and not a few boldly concealed their profligacy under the *stola*. Others, seeking rather to avoid than to court misapprehension as to their calling, wore the green toga proudly, and over it the sort of jacket called *amiculum*, which, like the white sheet of baronial times, was the badge of adultery. Others, again, preferred the silk and gauze dresses of the East (*sericœ vestes*), which, according to the expression of a classical writer, "seemed invented to exhibit more conspicuously what they were intended to hide."[4] Robes of Tyre were likewise

[1] Cicero in Cat.   [2] Lampridius, Script. Hist. Aug. *Elagabalus.*
[3] Martial, Ep. i. 36, 8; ii. 39; vi. 64, 4.   See Becker's Gallus, i. 321.
[4] See also Seneca.

in use, whose texture may be inferred from the name of "textile vapor" (*ventus textilis*) which they received.

The law strictly prohibited the use of vehicles of any kind to courtesans. This also was frequently infringed. Under several emperors prostitutes were seen in open litters in the most public parts of Rome, and others in litters which closed with curtains, and served the purpose of a bed-chamber.[1] A law of Domitian imposed heavy penalties on a courtesan who was seen in a litter.

In the lupanar, of course, rules regarding costume were unheeded. Prostitutes retained their hair black, but as to the rest of their person they were governed by their own taste. Nudity appears to have been quite common, if not the rule. Petronius describes his hero walking in the street, and seeing from thence naked prostitutes at the doors of the lupanaria.[2] Some covered their busts with golden stuffs, others veiled their faces.

It has already been mentioned that the rate of remuneration exacted by the prostitutes was fixed by themselves, though apparently announced to the ædile. It is impossible to form any idea of the average amount of this charge. The lowest classes, as has been mentioned, sold their miserable favors for about two tenths of a cent; another large class were satisfied with two cents. The only direct light that is thrown on this branch of the subject flows from an obscure passage in the strange romance entitled "Apollonius of Tyre," which is supposed to have been written by a Christian named Symposius. In that work the capture of a virgin named Tarsia by a bawd is described. The bawd orders a sign or advertisement to be hung out, inscribed, "He who deflours Tarsia shall pay half a pound, afterward she shall be at the public service for a gold piece." The half pound has been assumed by commentators to mean half a Roman pound of silver, and to have been worth $30; the gold piece, according to the best computation, was about equivalent to $4. But whether these figures can be regarded as an average admits of doubt, even supposing our estimate of the value of the sums mentioned in the ancient work to be accurate.

The allusion to Tarsia suggests some notice of the practice of the Roman bawds when they had secured a virgin. It will be found faithfully described in that old English play, "Pericles, Prince of Tyre," which is sometimes bound up with Shakspeare's

---

[1] Seneca, Ep. 80, 110; Suet. Jul. 43; Claud. 28; Domit. 8.
[2] Petron. Satyr. i. 26

works. When a bawd had purchased a virgin as a slave, or when, as sometimes happened under the later emperors, a virgin was handed to him to be prostituted as a punishment for crime, the door of his house was adorned with twigs of laurel; a lamp of unusual size was hung out at night, and a tablet exhibited somewhat similar to the one quoted above, stating that a virgin had been received, and enumerating her charms with cruel gross-ness.[1] When a purchaser had been found and a bargain struck, the unfortunate girl, often a mere child, was surrendered to his brutality, and the wretch issued from the cell afterward, to be himself crowned with laurel by the slaves of the establishment.

Thus far of common prostitutes. Though the Romans had no loose women who could compare in point of standing, influence, or intellect with the Greek hetairæ, their highest class of prostitutes, the *famosæ* or *delicatæ*, were very far above the unfortunate creatures just described. They were not inscribed in the ædile's rolls; they haunted no lupanar, or tavern, or baker's stall; they were not seen lurking about shady spots at night; they wore no distinguishing costume. It was in broad daylight, at the theatre. in the streets, in the Via Sacra, which was the favorite resort of fashionable Rome, that they were to be found, and there they were only to be distinguished from virtuous matrons by the superior elegance of their dress, and the swarm of admirers by whom they were surrounded. Indeed, under the later emperors, the distinction, outward or inward, between these prostitutes and the Roman matrons appears to have been very slight indeed.[2] They were surrounded or followed by slaves of either sex, a favorite waiting-maid being the most usual attendant.[3] Their meaning glances are frequently the subject of caustic allusions in the Roman poets.[4] Many of them were foreigners, and expressed themselves by signs from ignorance of the Latin tongue.

These women were usually the mistresses of rich men, though not necessarily faithful to their lovers. We possess no such biographies of them as we have of the Greek hetairæ, nor is there any reason to suppose that their lives ever formed the theme of serious works, though the Roman erotic library was rich. What little we know of them we glean mostly from the verses of Horace, Tibullus, Ovid, Propertius, Catullus, Martial, and from such works

[1] Juvenal, Sat. vi.; Tertullian, De exhort. cast. 45.   [2] Juvenal, Sat. vi.
[3] Petronius, ii. 352.   [4] Plautus, Miles; Apuleius, ii. 27.

as the Satyricon of Petronius, and the novel of Apuleius, and that little is hardly worth the knowing.

The first five poets mentioned—Catullus, Horace, Propertius. Ovid, and Tibullus—devoted no small portion of their time and talent to the celebration of their mistresses. But beyond their names, Lydia, Chloe, Lalage, Lesbia, Cynthia, Delia, Neæra, Corinna, &c., we are taught nothing about them but what might have been taken for granted, that they were occasionally beautiful, lascivious, extravagant, often faithless and heartless. From passages in Ovid, and also in one or two of the others, it may be inferred that it was not uncommon for these great prostitutes to have a nominal husband, who undertook the duty of negotiating their immoral bargains (leno maritus).

The only really useful information we derive from these erotic effusions relates to the poets themselves. All the five we have mentioned moved in the best society at Rome. Some of them, like Horace, saw their fame culminate during their lifetime; others filled important stations under government. Ovid was intimate with the Emperor Augustus, and his exile is supposed to have been caused by some improper discoveries he made with regard to the emperor's relations with his daughter. Yet it is quite evident that all these persons habitually lived with prostitutes, felt no shame on that account, and recorded unblushingly the charms and exploits of their mistresses in verses intended to be read indiscriminately by the Roman youths.

Between Ovid and Martial the distance is immense. Half a century divided them in point of time; whole ages in tone. During the Augustan era, the language of poets, though much freer than would be tolerated to-day, was not invariably coarse. No gross expressions are used by the poets of that day in addressing their mistresses, and even common prostitutes are addressed with epithets which a modern lover might apply to his betrothed. But Martial knows no decency. It may safely be said that his epigrams ought never again to be translated into a modern tongue. Expressions designating the most loathsome depravities, and which, happily, have no equivalent, and need none, in our language, abound in his pages. Pictures of the most revolting pruriency succeed each other rapidly. In a word, such language is used and such scenes depicted as would involve the expulsion of their utterer from any house of ill fame in modern times. Yet Martial enjoyed high favor under government. He was enabled to procure the naturalization of many of his Spanish friends. He possessed a country and a town house, both probably gifts from the emperor. His works, even in his lifetime, were carefully sought after, not only in Rome, but in Gaul, Spain, and the other provinces. Upon the character and life of courtesans in his day he throws but little light. The women whose hideous depravity he celebrates must have been well known at Rome; their names must have been familiar to the ears of Roman society. But this feature of Roman civilization, the notoriety of prostitutes and of their vile arts, properly belongs to another division of the subject.

ROMAN SOCIETY.

It was often said by the ancients that the more prostitutes there were, the safer would be virtuous women. "Well done," said the moralist to a youth entering a house of ill fame; "so shalt thou spare matrons and maidens." As this idea rests upon a slender substratum of plausibility, it may be as well to expose its fallacy, which can be done very completely by a glance at Roman society under the emperors.

Even allowing for poetical exaggeration, it may safely be said that there is no modern society, perhaps there has never existed any since the fall of Rome, to which Juvenal's famous satire on women can be applied.[1] Independently of the unnatural lusts which were so unblushingly avowed, the picture drawn by the Roman surpasses modern credibility. That it was faithful to nature and fact, there is, unhappily, too much reason to believe. The causes must be sought in various directions.

Two marked distinctions between modern and ancient society may at once be noticed. In no modern civilized society is it allowable to present immodest images to the eye, or to utter immodest words in the ear of females or youth. At Rome the contrary was the rule. The walls of respectable houses were covered with paintings, of which one hardly dares in our times to mention the subjects. Lascivious frescoes and lewd sculptures, such as would be seized in any modern country by the police, filled the halls of the most virtuous Roman citizens and nobles.[2] Ingenuity had been taxed to the utmost to reproduce certain indecent objects under new forms.[3] Nor was common indecency adequate

---

[1] Juvenal, Sat. vi.
[2] Propertius, ii. 6; Suet. Tib. 43, and Vit. Hor.; Pliny, xxxv. 37.
[3] See the collection at the Museo Borbonice at Naples, etc.

to supply the depraved taste of the Romans. Such groups as satyrs and nymphs, Leda and the swan, Pasiphæ and the bull, satyrs and she-goats, were abundant. Some of them have been found, and exhibit a wonderful artistic skill. All of these were daily exposed to the eyes of children and young girls, who, as Propertius says, were not allowed to remain novices in any infamy.

Again, though a Horace would use polite expressions in addressing Tyndaris or Lalage, the Latin tongue was much freer than any modern one. There is not a Latin author of the best age in whose writings the coarsest words can not be found. The comedies were frightfully obscene, both in ideas and expressions. A youth or a maiden could not begin to acquire instruction without meeting words of the grossest meaning. The convenient adage, *Charta non erubescit*, was invented to hide the pruriency of authors, and one of the worst puts in the wretched plea that, " though his page is lewd, his life is pure." It is quite certain that, whatever might have been the effect on the poet, his readers could not but be demoralized by the lewdness of his verses.

Add to these causes of immorality the baths, and a fair case in support of Juvenal will be already made out. A young Roman girl, with warm southern blood in her veins, who could gaze on the unveiled pictures of the loves of Venus, read the shameful epigrams of Martial, or the burning love-songs of Catullus, go to the baths and see the nudity of scores of men and women, be touched herself by a hundred lewd hands, as well as those of the bathers who rubbed her dry and kneaded her limbs—a young girl who could withstand such experiences and remain virtuous would need, indeed, to be a miracle of principle and strength of mind.

But even then religion and law remained to assail her. She could not walk through the streets of Rome without seeing temples raised to the honor of Venus, that Venus who was the mother of Rome, as the patroness of illicit pleasures. In every field and in many a square, statues of Priapus, whose enormous indecency was his chief characteristic, presented themselves to view, often surrounded by pious matrons in quest of favor from the god. Once a year, at the Lupercalia, she saw young men running naked through the streets, armed with thongs with which they struck every woman they saw; and she noticed that matrons courted this flagellation as a means of becoming prolific. What she may have known of the Dionysia or Saturnalia, the wild games in honor of Bacchus, and of those other dissolute festivals known as the eves of Venus, which were kept in April, it is not easy to say, but there is no reason to believe that these lewd scenes were intended only for the vicious, or that they were kept a secret.

When her marriage approached the remains of her modesty were effectually destroyed. Before marriage she was led to the statue of Mutinus, a nude sitting figure, and made to sit on his knee,[1] *ut ejus pudicitiam prius deus delibasse videtur.* This usage was so deeply rooted among the Romans that, when Augustus destroyed the temple of Mutinus in the Velian ward in consequence of the immoralities to which it gave rise, a dozen others soon rose to take its place. On the marriage night, statuettes of the deities *Subigus* and *Prema* hung over the nuptial bed—*ut subacta a sponso viro non se commoveat quum premitur ;*[2] and in the morning the jealous husband exacted, by measuring the neck of his bride, proof to his superstitious mind that she had yielded him her virginity.[3]

In the older age of the republic it was not considered decent for women to recline on couches at table as men did. This, however, soon became quite common. Men and women lay together on the same couch so close that hardly room for eating was left. And this was the custom not only with women of loose morals, but with the most respectable matrons. At the feast of Trimalchio, which is the best recital of a Roman dinner we have, the wife of the host and the wife of Habinus both appeared before the guests. Habinus amused them by seizing his host's wife by the feet and throwing her forward so that her dress flew up and exposed her knees, and Trimalchio himself did not blush to show his preference for a giton in the presence of the company, and to throw a cup at his wife's head when her jealousy led her to remonstrate.[4] The voyage of the hero of the Satyricon furnishes other pictures of the intensely depraved feeling which pervaded Roman society. The author does not seem to admit the possibility of virtue's existence; all his men and women are equally vicious and shameless. The open spectacle of the most hideous

---

[1] Mutinus, cujus immanibus pudendis horrentique fascino vestras inequitare matrones. . . . . Arnobius, v. 132. See also St. Augustine and Lactantius.

[2] August. De Civ. Dei.   [3] Catullus, Epithalam. ; Arnobius, *loc. cit.*

[4] Petron. Satyr. ii. 68.

debauchery only provokes a laugh. If a man declines to accede
to the propositions which the women are the first to make, it must
be because he is a disciple of the *aversa Venus*, and whole cities
are depicted as joining in the hue and cry after the lost *frater* of
a noted debauchee.

The *commessationes*, which Cicero enumerates among the symptoms of corruption in his time, had become of universal usage.
It was for them that the cooks of Rome exhausted their art in
devising the dishes which have puzzled modern gastronomists;
for them that the rare old wines of Italy were stowed away in
cellars; for them that Egyptian and Ionian dancing-girls stripped
themselves, or donned the *nebula linea*.[1] No English words can
picture the monstrosities which are calmly narrated in the pages
of Petronius and Martial. Well might Juvenal cry, "Vice has
culminated."[2]

It is perhaps difficult to conceive how it could have been otherwise, considering the examples set by the emperors. It requires
no small research to discover a single character in the long list
that was not stained by the grossest habits. Julius Cæsar, "the
bald adulterer," was commonly said to be "husband of all men's
wives."[3] Augustus, whose youth had been so dissolute as to suggest a most contemptuous epigram, employed men in his old age
to procure matrons and maidens, whom these purveyors of imperial lust examined as though they had been horses at a public
sale.[4] The amours of Tiberius in his retreat at Capreæ can not be
described. It will suffice to say there was no invention of infamy
which he did not patronise; that no young person of any charms
was safe from his lust. More than one senator felt that safety required he should remove his handsome wife or pretty daughter
from Rome, for Tiberius was ever ready to avenge obstacles with
death. The sad fate of the beautiful Mallonia, who stabbed herself during a lawsuit which the emperor had instituted against her
because she refused to comply with his beastly demands, gives a
picture of the age.[5] Caligula, who made some changes in the tax
levied on prostitutes, and established a brothel in the palace, commenced life by debauching his sisters, and ended it by giving grand
dinners, during which he would remove from the room any lady
he pleased, and, after spending a few minutes with her in private,

[1] Petron. Satyr. ii. 70, etc.   [2] Juvenal, Sat. vi.   [3] Suetonius, Jul. 51.
[4] Videsne ut cinædus urbano digito temperat?   Suet. Aug. 68, etc.
[5] Suetonius, Tiberius, 42.

return and give an account of the interview for the amusement of the company.[1] Messalina so far eclipsed Claudius in depravity that the " profuse debauches" of the former appear, by contrast, almost moderate and virtuous.[2]

Nero surpassed his predecessors in cynic recklessness. He was an habitual frequenter of houses of prostitution. He dined in public at the great circus among a crowd of prostitutes. He founded, on the shore of the Gulf of Naples, houses of prostitution, and filled them with females, whose dissolute habits were their recommendation to his notice. The brief sketch of his journeys given by Tacitus, and the allusions to his minister of pleasures, Tigellinus, leave no room for doubting that he was a monster of depravity.[3]

Passing over a coarse Galba, a profligate Otho, a beastly Vitellius, a mean Vespasian, and a dissolute Titus, Domitian revived the age of Nero. He seduced his brother's daughter, and carried her away from her husband, bathed habitually in company with a band of prostitutes, and set an example of hideous vice while enacting severe laws against debauchery. After another interval, Commodus converted the palace into a house of prostitution. He kept in his pay three hundred girls of great beauty, and as many youths, and revived his dull senses by the sight of pleasures he could no longer share. Like Nero, he violated his sisters; like him, he assumed the dress and functions of a female, and gratified the court with the spectacle of his marriage to one of his freedmen. Finally, Elagabalus, whom the historian could only compare to a wild beast, surpassed even the most audacious infamies of his predecessors. It was his pride to have been able to teach even the most expert courtesans of Rome something more than they knew; his pleasure to wallow among them naked, and to pull down into the sink of bestiality in which he lived the first officers of the empire.

When such was the example set by men in high places, there is no need of inquiring farther into the condition of the public morals. A censor like Tacitus might indignantly reprove, but a Martial—and he was, no doubt, a better exponent of public and social life than the stern historian—would only laugh, and copy the model before him. It may safely be asserted that there does not exist in any modern language a piece of writing which indicates

---

[1] Suetonius, Caligula, 24.

[2] _d. Clɜ꜀dius, 26; Juvenal, Sat. vi.

[3] Tacitus. Ann. xv. 37–40.

so hopelessly depraved a state of morals as Martial's epigram on his wife.

SECRET DISEASES AT ROME.

At what period, and where, venereal diseases first made their appearance, is a matter of doubt. It was long the opinion of the faculty that they were of modern origin, and that Europe had derived them from America, where the sailors of Columbus had first contracted them. This opinion does not appear to rest on any solid basis, and is now generally rejected. The fact is, that the venereal disease prevailed extensively in Europe in the fifteenth century; but the presumption, from an imposing mass of circumstantial evidence, is that it has afflicted humanity from the beginning of history.

Still, it is strange that Greek and Latin authors do not mention it. There is a passage in Juvenal in which allusion is made to a disgusting disease, which appears to bear resemblance to venereal disease. Epigrams of Martial hint at something of the same kind. Celsus describes several diseases of the generative organs, but none of these authors ascribe the diseases they mention to venereal intercourse.

Celsus prefaces what he says on the subject of this class of maladies with an apology. Nothing but a sense of duty has led him to allude to matters so delicate; but he feels that he ought not to allow his country to lose the benefit of his experience, and he conceives it to be "desirable to disseminate among the people some medical principles with regard to a class of diseases which are never revealed to any one."

After this apology, he proceeds to speak of a disease which he calls *inflammatio colis*, which seems to have borne a striking analogy to the modern *Phymosis*. It has been supposed that the *Elephantiasis*, which he describes at length, was also of a syphilitic character; and the symptoms detailed by Aretous, who wrote in the latter half of the first century, certainly remind the reader of secondary syphilis; but the best opinion of to-day appears to be that the diseases are distinct and unconnected.

Women afflicted with secret diseases were called *aucunnuentæ*, which explains itself. They prayed to Juno Fluonia for relief, and used the *aster atticus* by way of medicine. The Greek term for this herb being *Bonbornion*, which the Romans converted into *Bubonium*, that word came to be applied to the disease for which it was given, whether in the case of females or males. Modern science has obtained thence the term Bubo. The Romans said of a female who communicated a disease to a man, *Hœc te imbubinat*.[1]

We find, moreover, in the later writers, allusions to the *morbus campanus*, the *clazomenœ*, the *rubigo*, etc., which were all secret diseases of a type, if not syphilitic, strongly resembling it. It must be admitted, however, that no passage in the ancient writers directly ascribes these diseases to commerce with prostitutes.

Roman doctors declined to treat secret diseases. They were called by the generic term *morbus indecens*, and it was considered unbecoming to confess to them or to treat them. Rich men owned a slave doctor who was in the confidence of the family, and to whom such delicate secrets would naturally be confided. But the mass of the people were restrained by shame from communicating their misfortunes; as was the case among the Jews, the unhappy patient was driven to seclusion as the only remedy. However cruel and senseless this practice may have been as regarded the sufferer, it was of service to the people, as it prevented, in some degree, the spread of contagion.

Up to the period of the civil wars, and perhaps as late as the Christian era, the only physicians at Rome were drug-sellers, enchanters, and midwives. The standing of the former may be inferred from a passage in Horace, where he classes them with the lowest outcasts of Roman society.[2] The enchanters (*sagœ*) made philtres to produce or impede the sensual appetite. They were execrated, and even so amorous a poet as Ovid felt bound to warn young girls against the evil effects of the aphrodisiacs they concocted.[3] Midwives also made philtres, and are often confounded with the *sagœ*. The healing science of the three classes must have been small.

About the reign of Augustus, Greek physicians began to settle at Rome. They possessed much theory, and some practical experience, as the Treatise of Celsus shows, and soon became an important class in Roman society. It was not, however, till the reign of Nero, that an office of public physician was created. Under that emperor, a Greek named Andromachus was appointed *archiater*, or court physician, and *archiatii populares* were soon afterward appointed for the people. They were allowed to receive money from the rich, but they were bound, in consideration

---

[1] Scaliger. [2] Horace, Sat. i. 2, 1. [3] Ovid, Remed. Amor.

of various privileges bestowed on their office, to treat the poor gratuitously. They were stationed in every city in the empire. Rome had fourteen, besides those attached to the Vestals, the Gymnasia, and the court; other large cities had ten, and so on, down to the small towns which had one or two.[1] From the duties and privileges of the *archiatii*, it would appear they were subject to the ædiles.

It may seem almost superfluous to add that no careful medical reader of the history of Rome under the empire can doubt but the archiatii filled no sinecure, and that a large proportion of the diseases they treated were directly traceable to prostitution.

CHAPTER V.

THE EARLY CHRISTIAN ERA.

Christian Teachers preach Chastity.—Horrible Punishment of Christian Virgins.—
Persecution of Women.—Conversion of Prostitutes.—The Gnostics.—The Ascetics.—Conventual Life.—Opinion of the Fathers on Prostitution.—Tax on Prostitutes.—Punishment of Prostitutes under the Greek Emperors.

PERHAPS the most marked originality of the Christian doctrine was the stress it laid on chastity. It has been well remarked that even the most austere of the pagan moralists recommended chastity on *economical* grounds alone. The apostles exacted it as a moral and religious duty. They preached against lewdness as fervently as against heathenism. Not one of the epistles contained in the New Testament but inveighs, in the strongest language, against the vices classed under the generic head of luxury. Nor can it be doubted that, under divine Providence, the obvious merit of this feature in the new religion exercised a large influence in rallying the better class of minds to its support.

From the first, the Christian communities made a just boast of the purity of their morals. Their adversaries met them on this ground at great disadvantage. It was notorious that the college of Vestals had been sustained with great difficulty. Latterly, it had been found necessary to supply vacancies with children, and even under these circumstances, the number of Vestals buried alive bore but a very small proportion to the number who had incurred this dread penalty. Nor could it be denied that the chastity

[1] Dig. 27, 1, 6; Cod. Theodos. xiii. 3. De Medic. et profess.

of the Roman virgins was, at best, but partial, the purest among them being accustomed to unchaste language and unchaste sights. The Christian congregations, on the contrary, contained numbers of virgins who had devoted themselves to celibacy for the love of Christ. They were modest in their dress, decorous in their manners, chaste in their speech.[1] They refused to attend the theatres; lived frugally and temperately; allowed no dancers at their banquets; used no perfumes, and abstained generally from every practice which could endanger their rigorous continence.[2] Marriage among the Christians was a holy institution, whose sole end was the procreation of children. It was not to be used, as was the case too often among the heathen, as a cloak for immoralities. Christ, they said, permitted marriage, but did not permit luxury.[3] The early fathers imposed severe penitences on fornication, adultery, and other varieties of sensuality.

Persecution aided the Church in the great work of purifying public morals, by forcing it to keep in view the Christian distinction between moral and physical guilt. At what time it became usual to condemn Christian virgins to the brothel it is difficult to discover. The practice may have arisen from the hideous custom which enjoined the violation of Roman maidens before execution, if the existence of such a custom can be assumed on the authority of so loose a chronicler as Suetonius.[4] However this be, this horrible refinement of brutality was in use in the time of Marcus Aurelius.[5] Virgins were seized and required to sacrifice to idols. Refusing, they were dragged, often naked, through the streets to a brothel, and there abandoned to the lubricity of the populace. The piety of the early Christians prompted the belief that on many conspicuous occasions the Almighty had interfered to protect his chosen children in this dire calamity.[6] St. Agnes, having refused to sacrifice to Vesta, was said to have been stripped naked by the order of the prefect; but, no sooner had her garments fallen, than her hair grew miraculously, and enveloped her as in a shroud. Dragged to the brothel, a wonderful light shone from her body, and the by-standers, appalled at the sight, instead of offering her violence, fell at her knees, till, at last, the prefect's son, bolder and more reckless than the others, advanced to consummate her sentence, and was struck dead at her feet by a thunderbolt.[7] Theo-

[1] Ambrosius, De Virg. lib. i.   Prudentius in Symmach.; Basil, Inter. 17, resp.

[2] Cyprian, De Pudici. etc.   [3] Clem. Pædag. ii. 10.   [4] Sueton. Vit. Tiber.

[5] Tertul. Apol.   [6] Basil, De vera Virgin. 52.   [7] Ambros. Epist. iv. ep. 34.

dora, a noble lady of Alexandria, was equally undaunted and equally faithful to her creed. The judge allowed her three days to deliberate, warning her of the consequences of obstinacy. She was firm, and was led into a house of prostitution. There, in the midst of debauched persons of both sexes, she prayed to God for help, and the sight of the half-naked virgin bent in fervent prayer struck awe into the minds of the people. At last a soldier declared that he would fulfill the judgment. Thrust into a cell with Theodora, he confessed that he was a Christian, dressed her in his clothes, and enabled her to escape. He was seized and executed; but the Christian virgin, refusing to purchase her safety at such a price, gave herself up, and died with him.[1] Similar stories are contained in several of the Christian fathers.[2]

There is, unhappily, no reason to doubt that in many instances the brutal mandate of the pagan judges was rigorously executed, and that the faith of many Christian virgins was assailed through the channel of their virtue. This appears to have been frequently the case during the persecution of Diocletian, when we hear of Christian women being suspended naked by one foot, and tortured in other savage and infernal ways. The practice led to the clear enunciation of the important doctrine of moral chastity, already stated by Christ himself in the Gospel. The Romans could not conceive a chaste soul in a body that had endured pollution, and hence for Lucretia there was no resource but the poniard. It was left for St. Augustin, St. Jerome, and the other fathers, to assert boldly that the crime lay in the intention and not in the act; that a chaste heart might inhabit a body which brutal force had soiled; and that the Christian virgins whom an infamous judge had sentenced to the brothel were none the less acceptable servants of God.[3]

The only retaliation attempted by the early Christians was the conversion of prostitutes. The works of the fathers contain many narratives of remarkable conversions of this character, and a learned Jesuit once compiled a voluminous work on the subject. The Egyptian Mary was the type of the class. She confessed to Zosimus that she had spent seventeen years in the practice of prostitution at Alexandria. Her heart being opened, she took ship for Jerusalem, paid her passage by exercising her calling on board, and expiated her sins by a life of penitence in the woods of Ju-

[1] Ambrose, Epist. iv. 34.

[2] See Ruinart, Actes ii. 196; also Palladius, Vit. Patr. cap. 148, etc.

[3] August. contr. Jul. l. iv.; id. ep. 122, and the other fathers.

dæa. She lived, the legend said, forty-seven years in the woods, naked and alone, without seeing a man. A chapel was built at Paris during the Middle Ages in her honor. The painted windows, representing her in the exercise of her calling on shipboard, were in existence at a very late period.[1]

In revenge for the victories of the Christians, the pagans accused them of committing the grossest immoralities. For many centuries the early Christian congregations met under circumstances of great difficulty, in secret hiding-places, in catacombs. Their religious rites were performed mysteriously. Lights were often extinguished to foil the object of spies and informers. These peculiarities served as the pretext for many obvious calumnies. It was commonly believed, even by men of the calibre of Tacitus, that the Christian rites bore strong resemblances to those rites of Isis which, at an early period of Roman history, had created such alarm and horror at Rome. Nor were these calumnies confined to the heathen. In the third and fourth centuries, when sectarian rivalries menaced the destruction of the Church, similar accusations were freely bandied. That they were wholly unfounded in every case seems difficult to believe, in the face of the clear statements of such writers as Epiphanes. What the precise doctrines of the various sects called Adamites, Cainites, Nicolaites, and some subdivisions of Gnostics, may have been, it were perhaps superfluous now to inquire ; but it seems not unreasonable to suppose that, in some instances, men of depraved instincts may have availed themselves of the cloak of Christianity to conceal the gratification of sensual habits; or, on the other hand, that minds in a state of religious exaltation may have stumbled upon impurities in the search for the state of nature. In comparatively late times we have seen, in America as well as Savoy, a few persons of weak minds give way to religious enthusiasm in a manner that warred with public decency. Similar aberrations may have been more frequent during the seething era which preceded the establishment of Christianity, and prostitution, in some shape or other, may have again become a religious rite in certain deluded or knavish sects. Nor was it unnatural, unjust though it certainly was, for the heathen to charge Christianity at large with the vices of those of its followers who worshiped in a state of nudity, and accompanied prayer with promiscuous intercourse.[2]

[1] Reynaud, Act. Sanct.
[2] Ignat. Ep. ad Trall. et ad Philad. ; Clement. Strom. 3; Epiphan. Hær. 27; Theodor. Hæret. i. 5.

Even in the bosom of the true Church practices would break out from time to time which jarred sadly with the moral theory of the Apostles. Many persons of both sexes, under the influence of religious enthusiasm, sought relief for their troubled souls in solitude, and unwisely attempted to mortify the flesh by practices which too often sharpened the appetites. One only needs to read the eloquent effusions of St. Jerome to become satisfied that the course of life adopted by many early Christian recluses, of both sexes, must have led unwittingly to moral aberrations. Young men and young women, devoting themselves to a life of seclusion in the woods, living like wild beasts, without clothing and without shame, would naturally revive the system of religious prostitution in a more or less modified shape. On the other hand, in many parts of Europe, Christian churches thought it not unsafe to accept the legacies of the heathen religions in the shapes of idols, forms, and ceremonies. Saints succeeded to the honors of gods; dances in honor of Venus became dances in honor of the Virgin; statues which were originally intended to represent heathen deities were saved from destruction by being adopted as fair representations of Christian saints. Until very recent times there existed, in various parts of Europe, statues of Priapus, under the name of some saint, retaining the indecency of the idol, and associated with the belief of some simple women that the image possessed the power assigned it in mythology. In processions, during the third and fourth centuries, sacred virgins were seen to wear round their necks the obscene symbol of the old worship, and in places the holy bread retained the shape of the Roman *coliphia* and *siligines*. St. John Chrysostom complains that in places he designates, women were baptized in a state of nature, without even being permitted to veil their sex.[1] A majority of Christian teachers, unwilling to deprive the masses of a superstitious convenience afforded them by paganism, allowed them to pray to certain saints not only for fertility, but for the removal of impotence from husbands and lovers.[2]

To these immoral features must be added occasional instances of looseness in conventual life. The preamble of various edicts in France and elsewhere leaves no room to doubt that, in several instances, immoral persons had assumed the religious garb, and collected themselves together in religious communities for the purpose of gratifying sensuality.

[1] Letter to Innocent I.   [2] Calvin, Tr. Relig.

These were the aids Christianity afforded to prostitution in its various forms. They are a mere trifle in comparison with the obstacles it threw in its way. Independently of the effect produced by the moral teaching of St. Paul and the Apostles, the rising power of the Church was vigorously exerted to modify the legislation both of the Eastern and Western empires on the subject of sexual depravities.

The fathers did not uniformly proscribe prostitution. Saint Augustin said, "Suppress prostitution, and capricious lusts will overthrow society."[1] Jerome recognized prostitution, and argued that, as Mary Magdalene had been saved, so might any prostitute who repented.[2] The canons of the apostles excluded from the ministry all persons who were convicted of having commerce with prostitutes, and excommunicated those who were guilty of rape, but they passed no general sentence on prostitutes.[3] But the apostolic constitution branded as sinful any sexual intercourse *quœ non adhibetur ad generationem filiorum sed tota ad voluptatem spectat.*[4] The same principle is asserted in various passages of the work; wine being denounced as a provocation to impurity, and the faithful are warned against the society of lewd persons (*scortatores*). The Council of Elvira pronounced the penalty of excommunication against bawds and prostitutes, but it expressly commanded priests to receive at the communion-table prostitutes who had married Christians.[5] St. Augustin conceived that no church should admit prostitutes to the altar till they had abandoned the calling.[6] A similar doctrine was expressed by the Council of Toledo. At a later period, as we advance in mediæval history, we find the councils recognizing prostitution, and prostitutes as a class. In 1431, at the Council of Basle, a holy father presented a paper on the subject of prostitution, in which it was implied to be the only safeguard of good morals. A century later, the Council of Milan took especial pains to identify prostitutes as a class. They were to wear a distinctive dress, with no ornaments of gold, silver, or silk; to reside in places expressly designated by the bishops, at a distance from cathedrals; to avoid taverns and hostelries. The execution of the decree was intrusted to the bishops and the civil magistrates.[7]

---

[1] Tr. Ord. lib. ii. c. 12.
[2] Ep. ad Furiam, ad Fabiolam.   See also Lactantius, lib. vi. cap. 23.
[3] Can. 61, 77.   [4] Constit. lib. viii. c. 7.   [5] Canons 12, 44.
[6] Lib. de fid. et oper. c. xi.   [7] Const. Milan, tit. 65, de meret. et lenon.

The *vectigal* or tax paid by all persons subsisting by prostitution was exacted by the emperors, from Caligula to Theodosius. It was usually collected every five years. Zosimus accuses Constantine of having enlarged and remodeled the tax, but apparently without foundation. The early Christians made it a subject of reproach to the emperors.[1] In consequence of their assaults, Theodosius abandoned that portion of the law which laid a tax on bawds, leaving the tax on prostitutes. The latter was levied as rigorously as ever. A contemporary writer describes the imperial agents hunting for prostitutes in taverns and houses of prostitution, and forcing them to purchase, by payment of the tax, the right of pursuing their calling.[2] At length, in the fifth century, prostitution and the tax on prostitutes, or *chrysarguron*, were formally abolished by the Emperor Anastasius I., and the records and rolls of the collectors burned. It is said that some time afterward, the emperor gave out that he had repented of what he had done, and desired to see the *chrysarguron* re-established. The announcement gave great joy to the debauchees, and numbers of persons prepared to avail themselves of the re-enactment of the law. The emperor let it be known that he desired to have matters placed, so far as could be, on their old footing, and would therefore desire to collect as many as possible of the old rolls and records. They were gathered together at all parts, and laid at the imperial feet. Notice was then given to the people to meet at the circus on a given day; when they were all assembled, the whole collection of documents was burned, amid the frantic applause of the populace.[3]

It has been asserted, however, that the *chrysarguron* was revived subsequently, and was levied under Justinian. That legislator altered the old Roman laws regarding prostitution, and relieved prostitutes from the ineffaceable ban of infamy which the republican jurisprudence had laid on them. He permitted the marriage of citizens with prostitutes, and encouraged it by his example. His own wife, the Empress Theodora, had been a ballet-dancer and a prostitute. When she attained the imperial dignity, her first thought was of her old companions. She built a magnificent palace-prison on the south shore of the Bosphorus, and in one night caused five hundred prostitutes in Constantinople to be seized and conveyed thither. They were kindly treated; their every wish was gratified; but no man entered their asylum. The ex

Justin, Apol. pro Christ.   [2] Evagrius, Hist. Eccl. liv. 3, c. 39.   [3] Id. ib.

FRANCE DURING THE MIDDLE AGES.

periment was a complete failure. Most of the girls committed suicide in their despair, and the remainder soon died of *ennui* and
vexation.

Theodosius had laid heavy penalties on brothel-keepers;[1] Justinian reiterated them, and increased their weight. The seizure
and prostitution of a girl he punished with death. He who connived at the prostitution of females was to be expelled from the
city where he lived, and any person harboring him was to be fined
one hundred gold pieces. Whatever legislation could effect to
uproot the system of procurers and public prostitution, Justinian
did;[2] but his laws contain no trace of any harsh policy toward
prostitutes. Those unfortunate creatures he regarded with an indulgent humanity, which, for the sake of human nature, one may
perhaps ascribe to the kindly sympathy of the empress.

CHAPTER VI.

FRANCE.—HISTORY DURING THE MIDDLE AGES.

Morals in Gaul.—Gyncecea.—Capitulary of Charlemagne.—Morals in the Middle
Ages.—Edict of 1254.—Decree of 1358, re-establishing Prostitu⁺ion.—Roi des
Ribauds. — Ordinance of Philip abolishing Prostitution.—Sumptuary Laws.—
Punishment of Procuresses. — Templars.—The Provinces.—Prohibition in the
North.—Licensed Brothels at Toulouse, Montpellier, and Avignon.—Penalties
South. — Effect of Chivalry. — Literature. — Erotic Vocabulary.— Incubes and
Succubes. — Sorcery. — The Sabat. — Flagellants.—Adamites.—Jour des Inno-
cents.—Wedding Ceremonies.—Preachers of the Day.

THE Roman accounts of the Gauls represent them as leading
virtuous lives. *Severa matrimonia* is the expression of the histo
rian. This would appear to apply more particularly to the wom-
en than the men. As is usually the case among semi-civilized
nations, the Gauls, Germans, Franks, and most of the aboriginal
nations of Northern Europe imposed upon the women obligations
of chastity which they did not always accept for themselves.
Adultery, and, in certain cases, fornication, they punished capital-
ly; but, if the early ecclesiastical writers are to be believed, these
rude warriors were addicted to coarse debaucheries, in which intoxicating liquors and promiscuous intercourse with females played a prominent part. The feasts which followed victories in the
field, or commemorated national anniversaries, bore some resemblance to the Roman *commessationes*, though, of course, they lacked

[1] Cod. Theod. lib. xv. tit. 8, De lenon.   [2] Novel. i4, col. 1, tit. 1, De lenon.

the refinement and the wit which occasionally strove to redeem those disgraceful banquets.   So far as the females were concerned, there is no doubt the Roman writers judged correctly.   Whether the severity of the climate tempered the ardor of northern sensuality, or the harshness of the law kept the passions in check, the female population of Gaul, from the time of the Roman conquest for at least two or three centuries, was undoubtedly virtuous. Prostitution was comparatively unknown.   An old law or usage directed that prostitutes should be stoned, but we do not hear of this law being carried into effect.

Simultaneously with the consolidation of the kingdom of the Franks, we note that concubinage was an established institution, recognized by the law and sanctioned by the Church.   All the Frank chiefs who could afford the luxury kept harems, or, as they were called in that day, *gynecea*, peopled by young girls who ministered to their pleasures.   The plan, as it appears, bore some resemblance to that which is at present in use in Turkey and some other Mohammedan countries.   The chief had one lawful and proper wife, a sort of *sultana valide*, and other wives whose matrimonial rights were less clearly defined, but still whose condition was not necessarily disreputable.   How the people lived we are not so well qualified to say, but no doubt prostitution prevailed to some extent among them, though in all probability the public morals were purer than they became toward the tenth and eleventh centuries.

Perhaps the first authentic legislative notice of prostitution in France is to be found in the Capitularies of Charlemagne.   That monarch, who seems to have seen no mischief in the system of *gynecea*, was severe upon common prostitution.   He directed vulgar prostitutes to be scourged, and a like penalty to be inflicted on all who harbored them, kept houses of debauch, or lent their assistance to prostitutes or debauchees.   In other words, Charlemagne treated the same act as a crime among the poor, and as an excusable habit among the rich.

Our information regarding society in the Middle Ages is necessarily obscure and scanty, but we have enough to learn that immorality prevailed to an alarming degree during the tenth, eleventh, twelfth, and thirteenth centuries.   Probably the rich men who had their *gynecea* were the most virtuous class in the nation. Most of the kings set an example of loose intercourse with the ladies of the court.   The armies of the time were noted for the ravages they committed among the female population of the countries where they were quartered. Both of these classes seem to have yielded the palm of debauchery to the clergy. It is a fact well known to antiquaries, though visual evidence of it is becoming scarce, that most of the great works of Gothic architecture which date from this period were profusely adorned with lewd sculptures whose subjects were taken from the religious orders. In one place a monk was represented in carnal connection with a female devotee. In others were seen an abbot engaged with nuns, a naked nun worried by monkeys, youthful penitents undergoing flagellation at the hands of their confessor, lady abbesses offering hospitality to well-proportioned strangers, etc., etc. These obscene works of art formerly encumbered the doors, windows, arches, and niches of many of the finest Gothic cathedrals in France. Modesty has lately insisted on their removal, but many of the works themselves have been rescued from destruction by the zeal of antiquaries, and it is believed some have still escaped the iconoclastic hand of the modern Church. When such was the condition of the clergy, and such the notoriety of that condition, it would be unjustifiable to expect purity of morals among the people.

Louis VIII. made an effort to regulate prostitution. It proved fruitless, and it was left to the next king of the same name, Louis IX., to make the first serious endeavor to check the progress of the evil in France. His edict, which dates from 1254, directed that all prostitutes, and persons making a living indirectly out of prostitution, such as brothel-keepers and procurers, should be forthwith exiled from the kingdom. It was partially put in force. A large number of unfortunate females were seized, and imprisoned or sent across the frontier. Severe punishments were inflicted on those who returned to the city of Paris after their expulsion. A panic seized the customers of brothels, and for a few months public decency was restored. But the inevitable consequences of the arbitrary decree of the king soon began to be felt. Though the officers of justice had forcibly confined in establishments resembling Magdalen hospitals a large proportion of the most notorious prostitutes, and exiled many more, others arose to take their places. *A clandestine traffic succeeded to the former open debauchery,* and in the dark the evils of the disease were necessarily aggravated. More than that, as has usually been the case when prostitution has been violently and suddenly suppressed, the number of virtuous women became less, and corruption invaded the family circle. Tradesmen complained that since the passage of the ordinance they found it impossible to guard the virtue of their wives and daughters against the enterprises of the military and the students.

At last, complaints of the evil effects of the ordinance became so general and so pressing that, after a lapse of two years, it was repealed. A new royal decree re-established prostitution under rules which, though not particularly enlightened or humane, still placed it on a sounder footing than it had occupied before the royal attention had been directed to the subject. Prostitutes were forbidden to live in certain parts of the city of Paris, were not allowed to wear jewelry or fine stuffs, and were placed under the direct supervision of a police magistrate, whose official or popular title was *Le roi des ribauds* (the king of ribaldry). The duties of this officer appear to have been analogous to those of the Roman ædiles who had charge of prostitution. He was empowered to arrest and confine females who infringed the law, either in their dress, their domicil, or their behavior. It was afterward urged against the maintenance of the office of *Roi des ribauds* that it was usually filled by reckless, depraved men, who discharged its duties more in view of their private interests and the gratification of their sensuality than from regard to the public morals. Instances of gross tyranny were proved against them, and, in the absence of evidence to show that their appointment had been beneficial to the public, but little regret was felt when the office was abolished by Francis I.

To return to Louis IX. In his old age he repented of what he had done, and returned to the spirit of his early ordinance. In his instructions to his son and successor, he adjured him to remove from his country the shameful stain of prostitution, and indicated plainly enough that the best mode of attaining that end would be by re-enacting the ordinance of 1254. Philip dutifully fulfilled his father's request. Prostitution was again declared a legal misdemeanor, and a formidable array of penalties was again brought to bear against offending females and their accomplices. But, like many a legislative act in more modern times, Philip's ordinance was too obviously at variance with public policy and popular sentiment to be carried into effect. It was quietly allowed to remain a dead letter, and, with probably few exceptions, the prostitutes of Paris pursued their calling unmolested.

A few years afterward, its nullification was authoritatively sanctioned by fresh sumptuary laws. A royal edict directed courtesans to wear a shoulder-knot of a particular color as a badge of their calling. The whole force of the government was rallied to enforce this rule, and also those which had been enacted by Louis IX. The records of the court contain innumerable reports of the arrests of prostitutes for violating these enactments. When they had taken up their abode in a prohibited street, they were imprisoned and dislodged; when their offense was wearing unlawful garments or jewelry, the forbidden objects were seized and sold, the constable apparently sharing the proceeds of the sale. Pimps and procurers were dealt with more severely. As usual, the statute-book contained a variety of conflicting enactments on this subject, and menaced them with all kinds of penalties, from burning alive to fine and imprisonment. It appears beyond a doubt that, during the thirteenth and fourteenth centuries, several notorious procuresses were burned alive at Paris. Others were put in the pillory; were scourged, and had their ears cropped; while many of the richer class escaped with a fine. There are records of cases in which the procuress was exposed naked to the insults of the mob for a whole day, and toward evening the hair on her body was burned off with a flaming torch. Others again were chased through the city in a state of nudity, and pelted with stones. These barbarous penalties appear to have been very much to the taste of the people. Procuresses have always been an odious class, and it is not surprising to find that the punishment of a notorious wretch of the class was observed as a joyous holiday by the populace of the French capital. On the other hand, the prostitutes themselves were often subjects of public sympathy.

Peculiar reasons operated at this period to produce a favorable sentiment with regard to prostitutes. The horrible depravities of the Templars were becoming known. Society was horror-struck at the symptom of a revival of the worst vice of the ancients. There have been, as is known, ingenious and eloquent efforts made, in comparatively recent times, to throw a veil over the corruptions of the Templars, and to prove that they fell victims to royal jealousy, but the argument is not sustained by the facts. Documents on whose authenticity and credibility no possible suspicion can be cast, establish incontrovertibly that the sect of the Templars was tainted with unnatural vices, and that one of the chief secrets of its maintenance was the facility it afforded to de-

G

based men for the gratification of monstrous propensities. That
this was the opinion which prevailed in Paris at the time of
the outburst which finally led to the suppression of the order,
there is no room to question. It is easy to understand how
the horror such discoveries must have awakened would lead
men to entertain more lenient views with regard to a vice which
had at least the merit of being in conformity with natural instinct.

Thus far of Paris only. During the Middle Ages, as is well
known, most of the provinces of France were self-governing communities, which administered their own affairs, and received no
police regulations from the crown. A complete examination of
the subject throughout France would therefore involve as many
histories as there were provinces. Our space, of course, forbids
any thing of the kind, and we can only glance at leading divisions.

Most of the northern people had adopted, partly from the old
Germanic constitutions and partly from the Roman law, severe
provisions against prostitution, but they were nowhere, apparently, put in force. Occasionally a notorious brothel-keeper or
professional procuress was severely punished, but prostitutes were
rarely molested. In the north and west of France, indeed, toleration was obviously the natural policy, for we are not led to believe that in that section of country the evil was ever carried to
great excess. In Normandy, Brittany, Picardy, and the great
northern and western provinces, a virtuous simplicity was the rule
of life among the peasants, and even the cities did not present any
striking contrast. In many provinces, usage, not fortified by the
text of any custom, allowed the seigneur to levy toll upon prostitutes exercising their calling within the limits of his jurisdiction.
Some old titles and records refer to this practice. One sets down
the tax paid by each prostitute at four *deniers* to the seigneur.
Others intimate that the tax may be paid in money or in kind, at
the option of the seigneur. In many seigniories this singular tax
was regarded with the contempt it deserved.

In the south of France we meet with a different spectacle.
There prostitution had long been a deeply-seated feature of society. The warm passions of the southerners required a vent,
and, in the absence of some safety-valve, it was obvious to all that
the ungovernable lusts of the men would soon kindle the inflam-
mable passions of the dark southern women. Public houses of

prostitution were therefore established in three of the largest cities of the south—Toulouse, Avignon, and Montpellier.

That of Toulouse was established by royal charter, which declared that the profits of the enterprise should be shared equally by the city and the University. The building appropriated for the purpose was large and commodious, bearing the name of the *Grand Abbaye*. In it were lodged not only the resident prostitutes of the city, but any loose women who traveled that way, and desired to exercise their impure calling. It would appear that they received a salary from the city, and that the fees exacted from the customers were divided between the two public bodies to which the enterprise was granted. They were obliged to wear white scarfs and white ribbons or cords on one of their arms, as a badge of their calling.

When the unfortunate monarch Charles VI. visited Toulouse, the prostitutes of the Abbaye met him in a body, and presented an address. The king received them graciously, and promised to grant them whatever largess they should request. They begged to be released from the duty of wearing the white badges, and the king, faithful to his promise, granted the boon. A royal declaration specially exempted them from the old rule.[1] But the people of Toulouse, no doubt irritated by the want of some distinguishing mark between their wives and daughters and the "foolish women," by common consent mobbed the prostitutes who availed themselves of the king's ordinance. None of them could venture to appear in public without being liable to insult, and even bodily injury. Resolutely bent on carrying their point, the women shut themselves up in the Abbaye, and did their best to keep customers at a distance. Their calculation was just; the city and the University soon felt the effects of the diminution of visitors at the Abbaye. The corporation appealed to the king; and when, during the disorders which distracted France at that time, Charles VII. visited Toulouse, a formal petition was presented to him by the *capitones*, praying that he would take such steps as his wisdom might seem fit to mediate between the prostitutes and the people, and restore to the Abbaye its former prosperity. The king acted with energy. He denounced the assailants of the prostitutes in the severest language, and planted his own royal *fleurs de lis* over the door of the Abbaye as a protection to the occupants.[2] But the people did not respect the royal arms any more than they did

[1] Ordonn. des Rois de France, vii. 327.   [2] Ibid. xiii. 75.

the "foolish women." On the contrary, assaults on the Abbaye became more numerous than ever. The prostitutes complained incessantly of having suffered violence at the hands of wild youths who refused to pay for their pleasures; and the civic authorities proving incompetent to check the disorder, the prostitutes found themselves compelled to seek refuge in a new part of the city, where, it is to be presumed, they enlisted adequate support among their own individual acquaintances. For a hundred years they inhabited their new domicil in peace and quiet. The University then dislodging them in order to occupy the spot, the city built them a new abbaye beyond the precincts of the respectable wards. It was called the *Chateau vert*, and its fame and profits equaled that of the old abbaye.

About the middle of the sixteenth century the city yielded to the scruples of some moralists of the day, and ceded the revenues of the Chateau vert to the hospitals; but the grant being made on condition that the hospitals should receive and cure all females attacked by venereal disease, it was found, after six years' trial, that it cost more than it yielded. The hospitals surrendered the chateau to the city. It happened, just at this time, that many eminent philosophers and economists were advocating a return to the old ecclesiastical policy of suppressing prostitution altogether. After a discussion which lasted several years, the city of Toulouse adopted these views, and closed the Chateau vert. A magistrate, high in authority, left on record his protest against this course, founded on the scenes of immorality he had himself witnessed in the suburbs, and the country in the neighborhood of Toulouse; but the city authorities adhered to their opinion, and contented themselves with arresting some of the most shameless of the free prostitutes.[1] From that time forth, prostitution at Toulouse was subject to the same rules as in the rest of France.

The history of prostitution at Montpellier was analogous. At an early period, the monopoly which the crown had granted to the city being farmed out to individuals, fell into the hands of two bankers, in whose family it remained for several generations. During their tenure, a brothel was established in the city by a speculator of the day, but the holders of the monopoly prosecuted him, and obtained a perpetual injunction restraining him from lodging or harboring prostitutes.

At Avignon prostitution was legalized by Jane of Naples just

[1] Ann. de la Ville de Toulouse, par Lafaille, ii. 189, 199, 280.

before the cession of the city to the Pope.   The ordinance establishing a public brothel seems to have been drawn with care, and, though doubts have lately been thrown on its authenticity, they are not so well founded as to justify its rejection.   Prostitutes were ordered to live in the brothel.   They were bound to wear a red shoulder-knot as a badge of their calling.   The brothel was to be visited weekly by the bailli and a "barber," the latter of whom was to examine the girls, and confine separately all who seemed infected.   No Jew was allowed to enter the brothel on any pretext.   Its doors were to be closed on saints' days, and special regulations guarded against the prevalence of scenes of riot and disorder.[1]

This ordinance seems to have remained in force during the whole occupation of Avignon by the Popes, and its penalties were occasionally inflicted on offenders.   But if Petrarch and other contemporary writers are to be believed, the city was none the less a refuge for debauchees, and a scandal to Christendom. Petrarch complains that it was far more depraved than old Rome, and a popular proverb confirms, at least in part, his opinion.[2]

There were, however, in some southern provinces, severe laws against prostitution, although some of the penalties seem to have been framed as much with the view of stimulating as of repressing the passions.   In one or two cities we find accounts of prostitutes and their customers being forced to walk naked through the streets by way of expiation.   In others, the punishment of the iron cage was inflicted on pimps and procuresses.   When a procuress had rendered herself particularly obnoxious, she was seized, stripped naked, and dragged in the midst of a great crowd to the water's side.   There she was thrust into an iron cage, in which she was forced to kneel.   When the cage door was closed, she was thrown into the river, and allowed to remain under water long enough to produce temporary suffocation.   This shocking punishment was repeated several times.

A potent influence over the morals of the southern people, the higher classes at least, was exercised by the institution of chivalry. It was of the essence of that institution to promote spiritual at the expense of sensual gratification.   The chevalier adored his mis-

[1] Astruc, *De morb. vener.*

"Sur le pont d'Avignon
Tout le monde y passe."

The bridge was a haunt of prostitutes.

tress in secret for years, without even venturing to breathe her name. For years he carried a scarf or a ribbon in her honor through battle-scenes and dangers of every kind, happy when, after a lustrum spent in sighs and hopes, the charmer condescended to reward his fidelity with a gracious smile. It is evident that sexual intercourse must have been rare among people who set so high a value on the merest compliments and slightest tokens of affection; nor can there be any question but the effect of chivalry was to impart a high tone to the feelings and language of society, and to soften the manners of all who came within its influence.

If, on the other hand, we glance at the literature which flourished in France during the period of the revival of learning, we can not but infer that the morals of the people at large were not pure. During the thirteenth, fourteenth, and fifteenth centuries, the standard reading of the educated classes among the French was the celebrated *Roman de la Rose*, a work of remarkable talent, but, at the same time, distinguished by a cynic vein of philosophy and a singular obscenity of language. No portion of that work was wholly free from lewd expressions, and it would be impossible to quote fifty lines of it to-day in a modern language. The doctrine of the author with regard to women was insulting and cynical.[1] They were uniformly depicted as being restrained only by legal difficulties from giving way to the loosest passions; and all men, in like manner, were painted as seducers, adulterers, and violators of young girls. Such was the reading of the best society in France. The *Roman de la Rose* was to them what Shakspeare is to us.

Nor was it alone of its kind. Of the works which that age has bequeathed to us, nearly all are tainted with the same grossness of language and pruriency of idea. All, or nearly all, breathe the air of the brothel. It was rather a matter of boasting than of shame with the authors. Villon and Regnier seem to plume themselves on their familiarity with scenes of debauch, and their extensive acquaintance among the prostitute class. The best of their works are descriptions of episodes of dissipation; their most lively sketches have prostitutes, or their fortunes, or their diseases, for the themes. They seemed to fancy they were imitating Horace when they borrowed his most odious blemishes. Some of them were actors as well as poets, and used the machinery of the

---

" Toutes estes, serez, ou fûtes,
De faict ou de volonté, putes."—*Roman de la Rose.*

stage to disseminate their lewd compositions. Though it was still unusual, or even unlawful, for women to appear on the stage in their time, the boys who played female parts were well drilled to the business, and the performances which delighted the towns and villages of France fell but little short, in point of grossness, of the theatrical enormities of the imperial era at Rome.

One may form some idea of the popularity of erotic literature at this period in France from the amazing vocabulary of erotic terms which is gathered from the works of Rabelais, Beroald de Verville, Regnier, Brantome, and their contemporaries. There was not a form of lewdness for which an appropriate name had not been invented; and as to the ordinary acts and instruments of prostitution, a dictionary of synonyms might have been compiled without embracing all of them. Monsieur Dufour, in his conscientious work, fills a couple of pages with the mere words that were employed to express the act of fornication.

Many events likewise indicate a loose state of morals. The history of the *incubes* and *succubes*, filling some space in every treatise on demonology, is a most curious feature of the morals of the day. The existence of demons who made a practice of assailing the virtue of girls and boys was admitted by some of the fathers of the Church,[1] who quoted the words of Genesis in support of the singular doctrine. They were of two kinds: *incubi*, from the Latin *incubare*, male demons who assailed the chastity of girls; and *succubæ*, female demons who robbed boys of their innocence. The old chronicles are full of accounts of the mischievous deeds of these evil spirits. As might be expected, the *incubi* were more numerous and more enterprising than the *succubæ*. For one boy who confessed that a female demon had attacked him in his sleep, and compelled him to minister to her sensuality, there were a score of girls who furnished very tolerable evidence of having yielded their virginity to creatures of the male gender, who, they were satisfied, could be none other than devils. The ecclesiastical writers of the period have preserved a number of scandalous stories of the kind, which were so well credited that Pope Innocent VIII. felt impelled to issue a bull on the subject, and provide the faithful with an efficacious formula of exorcism.

Females, most of whom appeared to be nuns, confessed that they had been subject to the scandalous visits of the demons for long periods of time, and that neither fasting, nor prayer, nor

---

[1] St. August. *per cont.*; St. John Chrysost. Hom. 22, sup. Gene.

spiritual exercise could release them from the hated plague. Some girls were brought to admit a similar intercourse, and were burnt at the stake as partakers of the nature of sorceresses.[1] Married women made similar confessions. They stated that they were able to affirm that intercourse with demons was extremely painful; that their frigid nature, combined with their monstrous proportions, rendered their society a severe affliction, independently of the sin. It was noticed that the women, married or single, who applied to the ecclesiastical authorities for relief from this curious form of torment were almost invariably young and pretty.

In the year 1637 a public discussion took place at Paris on the question, Whether there exist *succubæ* and *incubi*, and whether they can procreate their species? The discussion was long and elaborate. It was conducted by a body of learned doctors, in presence of a large audience, composed partly of ladies; and while the judgment of the tribunal appeared to be in the negative, it was not so emphatic as to settle the question.[2] Even a century later, when one of the royal physicians undertook to explode the theory of lewd demons, and to prove that girls had endeavored to conceal their intercourse with lovers by attributing to them a devilish character, the public was not convinced, and the *incubi* were not left without believers. The laws still pronounced the penalty of death against all persons, male or female, who had commerce with demons.

Another practice which was brought to a close about the same time was entitled "*Le sabat des sorciers*," the witches' vigil. It appears that, at the earliest times of which we have any record, the inhabitants of France and Germany were in the habit of frequenting nocturnal assemblies in which witchcraft was believed or pretended to occupy a prominent place. In the thirteenth century they were denounced by Pope Gregory IX.,[3] who was satisfied that the devil had to do with them, and that their prime object was the gratification of sensuality. His bull did not attain its object. The witches' meetings were still held, or believed to have been held throughout the fourteenth, fifteenth, and part of the sixteenth centuries. The popular belief was that the persons in league with witches anointed their bodies with magical oint-

---

[1] Bodin, Demonomanie.

[2] Recueil general des questions traictées es Conferences du Bureau d'Adresse. Paris, 1656.   [3] Hist. Ecclesiast. Henry XVII. 53.

ment, bestrode a broom, and were forthwith carried through the air to the place of meeting; that Satan was present at the ceremony in the form of a huge he-goat, and received the homage of the witches and their proselytes; that songs and dances followed next in order, and that the whole performance was closed with a scene of promiscuous debauchery.[1] The Inquisition took the matter in hand, and obtained affidavits from several females averring that they had had commerce with demons on these occasions, and relating with singular crudity the peculiar sensations they experienced.[2] On the strength of this evidence prosecutions were instituted, and many persons were condemned and executed.

It has been usual in modern times to regard the persecution of the witches as a proof of the barbarous intolerance of the ancient Church; but, in truth, a careful examination of the evidence leaves no room for doubting that witchcraft was only the cloak of real vices. Most of the persons who were burned in France as sorcerers had really used the popular belief in magic to hide their own debaucheries, and had succeeded in depraving large numbers of youth of both sexes. It was stated by a theological writer of the time of Francis I., that in his day there were one hundred thousand persons sold to Satan in France.[3] Allowing for some exaggeration, it must still be inferred from this statement that this form of prostitution had assumed alarming proportions. Nor is there any good reason for doubting but priests and other persons of lewd propensities turned the simplicity of the village girls to account in very many instances, and richly earned the severe penalty that was inflicted upon them by the arm of the Church. The vigil, or *sabat*, disappears from history during the sixteenth century. That it had been for some time before its extinction a haunt of debauchees and a fertile source of prostitution, the writers on demonology and the old chroniclers establish incontrovertibly.

Other aids to prostitution were obtained from the very ranks of the Church. During the Middle Ages numbers of strange sects appeared, many of which relied for success on the favor they allowed to sensuality. At the present day it is not easy to determine what proportion of the stories that are in print respecting many of these sects were the fruit of sectarian jealousy on the part of their rivals; some of them were doubtless calumniated, but there

[1] Bodin, Demonomanie. [2] Nicolas Renny.
[3] Pere Crespet, De la Haine de Satan.

are others about whose character and practices there is no room for controversy.   The Flagellants, for instance, who counted eight hundred thousand proselytes in France in the fourteenth century, were unquestionably depraved.   They marched in procession, men and women together, through the cities of France, each member of the society using the whip freely on the bare back of the person before him; and at night they assembled in country places, and proceeded to more serious flagellations.   The opinion of learned persons ascribed erotic effects to these flagellations, it being said, apparently with truth, that when the flagellants had excited their senses by their discipline, they gave way to frantic debauchery.   However this be, it is plain that the spectacle of naked men and women marching in procession and scourging one another can not but have been provocative of prostitution.[1]

Another similar sect was the Adamites, who argued that nudity was the law of nature, and that clothes were an abomination in the sight of God.   It is said that, at first, the Adamites insisted on nudity only during their religious exercises, and that their proselytes stripped themselves within the place of worship; but one, Picard, who became a leading authority in the sect, took the ground that their principles should be carried out boldly in the face of the world.   He and his followers, male and female, accordingly appeared in the streets in the costume in which they were born.   The Inquisition very properly laid hands on them, punished some, and exiled the others.[2]

Again: if we pass from individual accidents to the state of society at large, we shall find many features that can not have been aids to virtue.   Allusion has already been made to the obscene character of much of the early poetry of France, and to the excessive grossness of those works especially which obtained, and perhaps deserved, the widest popularity.   Many of the customs of the day were equally adverse to sound morals.   To cite one by way of example: On the *Jour des Innocents*, which fell on the 28th of December, men were allowed to invade the bed-chambers of girls, and, if they could find them in bed, to administer the chastisement which used to be common in schools.   Hence arose the proverbial expression, *Donner les innocents à quelqu'un*, which meant to birch a person on the bare skin.   No doubt the old chroniclers were justified in saying that when the girl was worth

---

[1] Boileau, Hist. des Flagellants; Pic de la Mirandole, Tr. contre les Astrolopies, liv. iii. ch. 27.   [2] Bayle's Dictionary, Vo. *Picard.*

the trouble, the invader of the chamber was not satisfied with inflicting a chastisement.[1]

Marriages were attended with ceremonies far grosser than any that were practiced in Rome. It was not only decorous, it was fashionable, both for men and women, to spy out the bed-chamber of the newly-wedded couple, and the fortunate man or girl who had contrived to see the interior of the room through a chink in the wall or a hole in the door was loudly applauded when the result of his or her discoveries was made known.[2] The invention of bridal chambers is therefore not original in America, as some have supposed.

Strange to say, neither the lewdness of the poets nor the grossness of the social habits of the times strikes one as more singular than the tone of the sermons which were delivered in Paris at the same period. One of the most famous preachers of the day was Maillard, who rose to eminence under Louis XI. His sermons on the luxury and corruptions of the times were very popular. We find him cursing the "burgesses" who, for the sake of gain, let their houses to prostitutes: "*Vultis vivere de posterioribus meretricum*," he cries, indignantly. He denounces with extraordinary virulence the "crimes of impudicity which are committed in churches," and which "the pillars and nave would denounce, if they had eyes and a voice." He did not spare his congregation. Turning fiercely to the women who sat before him, he apostrophized them: "Dicatis, vos, mulieres, posuistis, posuistis filias ad peccandum? vos, mulieres, per vestros traitus impudiæ, provocastis alios ad peccandum? Et vos, maquerellæ, quid dicitis?" He thunders against this latter class, the procuresses, who ought, he says, to be burned at the stake, especially when, as is often the case, they are both the mothers and the venders of their daughters. Words fail him to denounce the intercourse of abandoned women with ecclesiastics; he invokes the divine wrath upon those of his congregation *quæ dant corpus curialibus, monachis, presbyteris.* Both he and other famous preachers of the day pronounced maledictions upon lewd convents, which some of them say are mere seraglios for the bishops and monks, where every abomination is practiced.

It was estimated that at this time, say the fifteenth century,

---

[1] Lenglet, Dufresnoy sur Marot, iii. 97; Richelet's Dict.

[2] Brantome, in his Dames Galantes, describing a marriage, says, " *Chacun estoit a l'escontes. a l'accoustumée.*"

when Paris was comparatively a small city, it contained five to
six thousand prostitutes, who were said by an Italian to be far
more beautiful and attractive than any prostitutes he had seen
elsewhere.

CHAPTER VII.

FRANCE.—HISTORY FROM THE MIDDLE AGES TO LOUIS XIII.

The Court.—Louis IX. to Charles V.—Charles VI.—Agnes Sorel.—Louis XI.—
Charles VIII.—Louis XII.—Francis I.—La Belle Feronniere.—Henry II.—Di-
ana de Poictiers.—Lewd Books and Pictures.—Catharine of Medicis.—Margaret.
—Henry IV.—Mademoiselle de Entragues.—Henry III.—Mignons.—Influence
of the Ligue.—Indecency of Dress.—Theatricals.—Ordinance of 1560.—Police
Regulations.

THE memoranda we have already given will enable the reader
to form an idea of the state of society at large. It remains to say
something of the court, which, in some respects, was France.

From Louis IX. to Charles V. inclusive, it is said that the kings
of France set no example of debauchery, and that the court rather encouraged virtue than vice. When the sisters-in-law of Philip
the Handsome scandalized Paris by their loose life in the Tour de
Nesle, into which they were said to make a practice of inveigling
students, whom they assassinated when their lubricity was satiated, the king had them brought to punishment and dealt with as
though the popular scandal was well founded in fact. When
Charles VI. ascended the throne the scene changed. This unfortunate monarch was not only himself weak and depraved, but his
wife, Isabel of Bavaria, was more vicious still. The pair encouraged every practice that could shock modesty or outrage decency.
The queen lived almost openly with her lover, the Duke of Orleans. The king, so long as he retained his reason, was a leading
actor in the scandalous masquerades of the court, and narrowly escaped losing his life on one occasion when he disguised himself
as a devil, and danced immodestly before the ladies of the court.
Round his loins, as round those of his fellow-demons, a sort of
girdle of tow had been fastened, and all the masqueraders were
chained together. In the midst of their dances, some foolish person threw a lighted torch at them. Their girdles took fire, and
all were burned to death except the king, whom the Duchess of
Berri saved by courageously raising her skirts and throwing them
over the burning monarch.

Charles had had many mistresses in his youth. When he went mad, the physicians directed the queen to refuse to discharge her conjugal duty. Charles had enough of his former nature left to resent this privation. He even employed force, and succeeded at last in compelling his wife to resume her place in the royal couch. She contrived, however, to defraud him by hiring a pretty girl to take her place. It is said Charles never detected the fraud. His wife, meanwhile, gave the reins to her loose passions, and was known to have had at least a score of lovers.

A very striking picture of the manners of the time is afforded by the story of Agnes Sorel. She was, as is known, the mistress of Charles VII., a lady of good family, and, otherwise than as the king's mistress, of spotless reputation. Her influence over the king she used for the best of purposes. It was she who roused him to make the efforts which eventually expelled the foreigner from France. Her private character was laudable : she was amiable, generous, kind, and true ; yet when she visited Paris in company with the king, the crowd followed her whenever she appeared in the streets, insulting her, and calling her a prostitute in the grossest terms. The king lived with her eighteen years, but never ventured to acknowledge her publicly as his mistress. Of the four daughters she bore him, three only were legitimated by his successor.

Louis XI. had a seraglio and a colony of bastards before he became king, nor did he alter his mode of life when he assumed control of the kingdom. His favorites were usually chosen from the lowest class of his subjects, many of whom had gone through an apprenticeship for the king's service in the houses of prostitution of the capital. Louis never pretended to bear them any affection ; he used them as he used the men of letters who composed for his diversion the lewd tales which have reached us.

Charles VIII. appears to have been more virtuous than his predecessors, though, of course, he did not pique himself upon any conjugal fidelity. A story is told which reflects credit upon his character. It is said that during his campaign in Italy, when he retired to his chamber one evening, he found there a young girl of marvelous beauty in a state of complete déshabillé. She was kneeling and in tears when the king entered. On Charles inquiring the cause of her sorrow, she confessed that her parents had sold her to the king's valet for the use of his majesty, and conjured Charles to spare her. The king was touched by her distress. He inquired into the facts, and, finding that they were as she stated, and, farther, that she was betrothed to a youth of the neighborhood, he sent for him and married the young couple forthwith.

It appears certain that Charles's death was caused by his indiscreet commerce with the sex. All the chroniclers state that he fell a victim to the indulgence of his passions, being frail of body and of feeble constitution.

The court of Louis XII. was purer than that of his predecessors, owing to the austere virtue of the queen. Louis himself had shared the profligacies of his family in his youth, but, on becoming king, he allowed his wife to regulate his household according to her principles. For the first time for many years, say the old chroniclers, prostitution was banished from court.

We shall have something to say of Francis I. in connection with syphilis, of which he was a conspicuous and an early victim. At the age of eighteen his mother stated that he had been punished where he sinned. The misfortune did not operate as a warning. His life was notoriously dissolute at a time when profligacy was so much the rule that it was hardly likely to be noticed. Brantome asserts positively[1] that his expedition to Italy was prompted by the desire to make acquaintance with a courtesan of Milan whose charms Admiral Bonnivet had extolled. Previous to his time, it seems, there had always been attached to the court a body of prostitutes for the use of the courtiers. Francis suppressed this body, and actually invited the ladies of the court to take their place. Brantome reviews this policy, and while he praises it in view of the "joyous pastimes" to which it led, he is bound to acknowledge that it produced the greatest immorality ever known in France. The ladies of the town followed the example of those of the court, and but little was wanting but that every woman in France became a prostitute.

It was the custom during this reign for the king to invite all his courtiers and their wives and daughters to lodge at the royal palaces from time to time. The ladies had apartments by themselves, and to each room the king had a key. We are assured that the husbands, fathers, and brothers of ladies who refused to submit to the royal demands had but little chance of retaining their offices. If they had been guilty of maladministration or peculation, as was the case with most of them, they could hope

Vies des Hommes Illust. : Bonnivet.

for pardon only through the complaisance of their female relatives. The story of M. de St. Vallier, who was reprieved on the scaffold in payment for the favors which his daughter, the beautiful Diana of Poictiers, had granted to the king, is too well known to need repetition here.

It was the boast of Francis that he had always respected the honor of the ladies of the court, and the boast was just, from his point of view. His visits to his mistresses were always made in a mysterious manner, and at night. Even to the Duchess of Etampes, who was his acknowledged mistress and procuress for a period of nearly twenty years, he never behaved in public in a manner to compromise her reputation. In private he was not so scrupulous. When this lady's husband disturbed the king one evening, Francis drew his sword on him, and threatened to kill him instantly if he dared to reveal what every one knew, or to punish the wife at whose adultery he had connived for years. His idea seems to have been that words alone constituted the sin of debauchery. On one occasion he took all the ladies of the court to see the royal deer in the rutting season; but when a gentleman ventured a very obvious pleasantry on the scene, he exiled him from court for life.

His death has been frequently described. Some writers imply, by their silence, doubts of the authenticity of the story of *La Belle Ferronnière;* but it rests on very tolerable evidence. This lady, who was uncommonly beautiful, was the wife of a lawyer or a merchant (the authorities do not agree on the point). The king solicited her favors, but, strange to say, was met with a positive refusal. On consultation with the court lawyers, however, Francis was informed that he could, by the exercise of his royal prerogative, enjoy the company of any woman he pleased, and the Ferronnière was accordingly notified that the king commanded her to yield to his desires. She confided the order to her husband, who, on reflection, counseled her to submit. Meanwhile Ferronnière himself used his best endeavors to catch a syphilitic disease, which he communicated to his wife. She gave it to the king, who died of it after much suffering.

Henry II. had the merit of fidelity, not to his wife, but to his mistress. The latter was the famous Diana de Poictiers, whose successful intercession with Francis I. on her father's behalf has been already noticed. Brantome asserts that she did not emulate the constancy of her royal lover, saying that in her youth she had "obliged many persons." He tells a story which, if true, reflects credit on the temper of the king. Visiting his mistress one day, he surprised her in the company of a courtier named Brissac, who had only time to hide himself under the bed. After spending some moments with Diana, the king asked for some refreshments. Some boxes of confectionery were brought him, and in the midst of his meal he took a box and threw it under the bed, saying, "Halloo, Brissac, every body must live!" Diana lost no portion of her lover's heart in consequence of her infidelities. This she owed in some degree to her extraordinary beauty, which she preserved so late in life that it was commonly reported she was in the habit of using soap made of liquid gold. Henry was proud of his mistress, and never concealed their liaison. He had his arms interwoven with hers on many public buildings and pieces of plate. He used constantly to ride through the streets with the beautiful Diana on his crupper; and he showed her so marked a preference over his wife that judicious courtiers never made the mistake of courting the latter.

But the orderly life of the king was not imitated by the court. According to Brantome and Sauval, the excesses of the age of Francis were aggravated under Henry. It was rare, says the former, that ladies presented their virginity to their husbands; and husbands who objected to the intimacy of their wives with "kings, princes, noblemen, and others of the court," were eschewed from society. A woman was held to be virtuous because she begged her lover to wait till she was married to gratify his desires; married women who retained their love for the same *galant* for several years were considered models of purity. Brantome intimates distinctly that ordinary debauchery fell short of the desires of the courtiers; incest, sodomy, and similar enormities could alone satiate the passions of the old debauchees of the day.

The same writer partially explains the spread of vice by saying that within the last half century the ladies of France had acquired the arts of Italy; nor is it doubtful that with the Medicis many of the monstrous vices which have been peculiar to Italy ever since the age of Imperial Rome were imported into France. We hear of all kinds of instruments of debauchery; of lewd books and lewd pictures; of indecent sculptures and bronzes being sold without let or hinderance in the stores of Paris. It was the age of Aretino; and besides that famous or infamous writer, a number of other Italians had competed for the prize of lewdness in composition.   Poets, painters, sculptors, seemed to try how far art could be prostituted.   Cellini, Leonardo da Vinci, Giulio Romano, Nicollo dell' Abate, and, indeed, almost all their contemporaries, debased their genius by the execution of indecent works.   Many of these found their way to Paris.   When Pope Clement VII. undertook to prosecute the authors of indecent works, whether in letters or art, most of the compositions that were endangered by his bull were transported to France.   Brantome alludes to many of them as being quite common in his time.   He describes, for instance, a silver goblet on which the most indecent scenes were graven, and which a nobleman of the court always obliged the ladies who visited him to use at table.   Other noblemen had their rooms painted in fresco in similar taste.   It is stated that Anne of Austria caused three hundred thousand écus worth of frescoes of this kind to be removed from the ceilings of the palace at Fontainebleau.[1]   But in the reign of Henry II. it does not appear that any one was ever prosecuted for dealing in this kind of merchandise.

During the three following reigns, it was Catharine of Medicis who gave the tone to the court, and really ruled the kingdom. All historians concur in stating that she used prostitution as the mainspring of her policy.   She had a court of sometimes two to three hundred ladies of honor, whom she employed to worm out the secrets of the politicians of the day.   They were known as the Queen's Flying Squadron, and it appears they performed their duties successfully; of course, at the cost of whatever virtue or decency the court still retained.   Brantome is still our authority for asserting that they introduced a new feature of debauchery; they took the initiative in affairs of this kind, and instead of yielding to the entreaties of lovers, it was they who pressed their lovers to meet them half way.   He likewise informs us that they aided the establishment in France of other vices which had hitherto been peculiar to Southern and Eastern climates, by the revival of practices which had been common among the *hetairæ* of Athens.

It has been asserted that Catharine willfully tutored her children in habits of debauchery, in order to divert their minds from politics, and retain control over the kingdom, but this scandal does not appear to rest on authentic evidence.   It is unquestionable, however, that Charles IX., the author of the massacre of St. Bar-

[1] Sauval, Amours des rois de France; from which work many of the facts in the text throughout this chapter are drawn.

tholomew, lived in incestuous intercourse with his sister Margaret,
and there seems no reason to doubt the truth of the story that
Catharine more than once entertained the king and court at a
banquet at which nude females served as waiters.

Perhaps the best idea of the morals of the time can be obtained
from the adventures of the Margaret just mentioned, who married
Henry IV., King of Navarre, and afterward King of France. It
is said that at the age of eleven she had two lovers, both of whom
claimed to have robbed her of her virtue. Marrying the King of
Navarre, she found means to leave her husband and reside at
Paris, whose air suited her better than the country. Here her
debaucheries were a common theme of scandal, her lovers being
counted by the score. Happening at last to give birth to a child
which mysteriously disappeared, her brother Henry III. sent her
to her husband in a quasi-disgrace. Henry of Navarre refused to
cohabit with her. The king vainly endeavored to reconcile the
couple. With more zeal than tact, he used as an argument with
his cousin that the mother of the King of Navarre had not herself led an irreproachable life. At this Henry burst into a laugh,
and remarked to the envoy that the king was very compliment-
ary in his letters, his majesty having in the first described the
vices of the wife, and in the second alluded to the frailties of the
mother.

He persisted in refusing to receive Margaret, and she took refuge in the little town of Agen, but no sooner began to lead her
usual life there than the people rose and expelled her. She found
a second refuge in the fortress of Usson, and there she lived
twenty years in a sort of prison which she converted into a
brothel. She was debarred from the society of men of fashion
and courtiers, but for her purposes, servants, secretaries, musicians,
and even the peasants of the neighborhood answered as well, and
of these there was no lack. Returning to Paris in her old age,
she did not alter her course of life. She became outwardly devout, and established a nunnery and monastery near her hotel;
the latter, the people said, in order to have monks always at hand;
but the list of her lovers remained undiminished to the very verge
of her death.[1]

Nor did her husband present any striking contrast to his wife,
though he reflected so severely upon her in the work published
under the title *Le divorce Satirique*. Bayle remarks that, had he

---

[1] Le divorce Satirique.

not expended so large a portion of his energy in the pursuit of sensual pleasures, he would have been one of the greatest heroes of history.[1] He was profuse and indiscriminate in his attachments; duchess or farmer's daughter, it was all the same to him. He changed his mistress once a month at least. As an exception to this rule, his affection for Gabrielle d'Estrées, a very lovely creature, whom he shared with the Marquis of Bellegarde, and who bore him, or them, three children, lasted several years. He was not faithful to her, and made no secret of his infidelities, but he loved her passionately. On one occasion he left his army in the midst of a campaign, disguised himself as a peasant, and traveled through the enemy's country to meet her. He once went to see her, but was stopped at the door with the announcement that Bellegarde was with her. His first impulse was one of rage. Drawing his sword, he rushed toward the door, but stopped half way, and saying, "No, it would make her angry," he returned home. Gabrielle was a very beautiful and charming person. She was in the habit of having herself painted in a state of perfect nudity, with her children playing around her.

When she died, Henry proposed to replace her by Mademoiselle D'Entragues, whose beauty had made some sensation at court. Negotiations were opened with the lady, who dutifully placed the matter in the hands of her family, and father, mother, and brothers began to treat with the king for the prostitution of their daughter and sister. They asked a hundred thousand crowns. The king thought the sum large, and offered fifty thousand, but the family refusing to give way, he acceded to their demands. They then added that they would like to have a promise of marriage, conditioned upon the lady's bearing a male child within a year. To this likewise Henry agreed, in spite of Sully's remonstrances; and Mdlle. D'Entragues became the acknowledged mistress of the king. It need not be added that the promise of marriage was never fulfilled.

Some time afterward Henry fell in love with a young lady who was betrothed to Marshal Bassompierre. As ardent as ever, he sent for the marshal, explained his feelings, and ordered Bassompierre to renounce his claims. The marshal obeyed, and Henry married the lady (who was a Montmorency) to the Prince of Condé. The marriage was hardly over before the king opened negotiations with the bride. It will be scarcely credited that the

[1] Bayle's Dictionary, Vo. Henry IV.

emissary he employed was the mother of the Prince of Condé, who left no means untried to effect the dishonor of her son. The prince, of less complacent temper than most other courtiers, refused to allow his wife to become the king's mistress. He removed her from France, and, just as Henry was about to send after her, the assassin Ravaillac freed Condé from the danger.

The disorders of Henry III., the predecessor of the King of Navarre, are shamefully notorious. There was a time during his reign when, for the same reason which induced the establishment of *Dicteria* at Athens, prostitution almost seemed a desirable institution at Paris. In his youth he had been a famous seducer of the ladies of honor. An anecdote of his life at this period not only reveals the tone of the court, but happily shows that depravity was not so universal as might be imagined. When Henry was chosen King of Poland, he was anxious to settle his mistress, Mdlle. de Chateauneuf, by finding her a husband. He applied to a courtier, the Provost of Paris, M. de Nantonillet, but received the scathing reply that "M. de Nantonillet would not marry a prostitute till the king had established brothels in the Louvre."

It is best, perhaps, to throw a veil over the later stories of Henry III., his *mignons*, and the frightful infamies that were practiced in Paris in his time. They may be divined from the fact that Brantome mentions some orgies in which the king and a party of friends, male and female, stripped themselves naked, and tried to place themselves on a level with the brute creation, as rather redeeming instances of his sensuality.

We shall take occasion hereafter to follow the history of the court from Louis XIII. to modern times. Meanwhile, some features of society bearing on prostitution in the age we have sketched must be briefly noted.

It is asserted by all the chroniclers that the influence of the League (*Ligue*) was most pernicious. A sort of religious enthusiasm seems to have been kindled by the sectarian strife of the period, and practices which purported to be religious, but were only immoral, were encouraged by the highest authorities. Religious fanaticism ruled throughout France. Men and women walked naked in processions which were led by the curates. As was natural at an age of civil war, violence was freely used toward females by both of the contending armies. At every city that was taken, either by the Leaguers or the Huguenots, all the women, married and single, were violated by the soldiery; such, at least, is the statement of a contemporary historian. Moreover, in the general confusion, no proper police was enforced either at Paris or elsewhere, and the windows of print-shops teemed with lewd pictures, which no one, says the historian, thought of having seized. It was, in fact, a period of anarchy. The *Moyen de parvenir*, by Beroalde de Venille, which has reached us, affords some criterion of the popular literature of the day. Aretino, text and plates, was much in vogue; and Sanchez and Benedicti left their lay rivals far behind in the composition of works which may contend for the palm of lewdness with Martial or Petronius.[1]

Throughout the Middle Ages, and, indeed, up to the middle of the seventeenth century, great complaint was made by the clergy of the indecency of the dress of the people of France. About the thirteenth century it became fashionable to adorn the toe of the shoe or boot with an ornament in metal; either a lion's claw, or an eagle's beak, or something of that kind. Some immodest person ventured to substitute a sexual image in bronze for the usual appendage, and the fashion soon became general. Women even adopted it, and all the best society of Paris soon exhibited the indecency on their feet. The king forbade their use by royal edicts,[2] and a special bull was fulminated against them by Pope Urban V.,[3] but the monstrous shoes held their ground against both, and were only disused when fashion set in a different direction. The *Braguette* was another enormity of the same character. Originally, it is said, the working-classes invented the idea of a small bag hanging between the knees in which a knife or other utensil could be carried. The fashion was adopted about the beginning of the fifteenth century by men of rank, and became immediately of an immodest nature. All the arts of fashion were called into requisition to give the *braguettes* the most novel and remarkable appearance, and every possible means was used to render them at once disgustingly indecent and extravagantly rich. They were attached to the dress with gay-colored ribbons, and, when the wearer was a rich man, were adorned with jewels and lace. At the time Montaigne wrote, *braguettes* had almost gone out of vogue: they were worn only by old men, who, in the language of the essayist, "make public parade of what can not decently be mentioned." Women, on their side, invented hoops, bustles, and low-necked

[1] De Matrimonio, Le Somme des Peches.   [2] Charles V. 17th Octob. 1367.
[3] A.D. 1365

dresses. The libraries contain a large collection of works written by moralists and preachers of the time against these " indecent abuses" of the ladies. As they are all in use at the present time, we may perhaps conclude that the old French moralists were un-necessarily alarmed; but it is likely that the form of the bustle was by no means as modest as that of modern crinoline skirts, and that the fashion of ladies' drawers had not yet come in. Such, at least, is the inference from some of the criticisms they provoked. The exposure of the breasts was checked for a time under Louis XIV., but the reform was evanescent, and the custom against which churchmen thundered in the sixteenth century survives to-day.

Some allusion has already been made to the theatre. Theatri-cals were forbidden by the early French kings, at the instigation of the Church, but the prohibition was evaded by the performance of scenes from the Gospel dramatized. From the remains of these Moralities it would appear that they were always coarse and often immoral. The devil always played a prominent part, and would have been inconsistent had he not outraged decency. Under Henry III. women began to appear on the stage, and farces very broad in ideas and language began to be played instead of the old Moralities. We are led to believe that nothing was too scan-dalous to be represented on the stage; in fact, the idea seems to have been to crowd as much sensuality and vice into the farces as possible. Scarcely any incident of life was too indecent to be either portrayed or described, and if the latter, the description was given in the most undisguised language. It is altogether impossible to transcribe scenes of this nature. Enough to say that women were made to go through the pains of childbirth on the stage; husband and wife went to bed in presence of the public; and when modesty prompted the retirement of actors for causes still more indecent, a colleague rarely failed to explain why they had retired and what they were doing behind the curtain. Many of La Fontaine's most *grivois* stories were taken from farces which were once acted with copious pantomime before the ladies of Paris. Even as late as the reign of Henry IV., plays of this character were commonly acted at Paris at the Hotel de Bourgogne. It was usual for the star actor to speak a prologue or an interlude, which was invariably recommended by its indecency. We have some of the titles of these prologues, and they were generally of the same character as the one on the question, *Uter vir an mulier se magis delectet in copulatione.*

Of the number of regular prostitutes exercising their calling in France during the fifteenth and sixteenth centuries no correct estimate can be made. It was undoubtedly large. During the religious wars, a writer on the side of Protestantism undertook to draw up a statement of the number of prostitutes and lewd women whose vices were chargeable to the clergy. His estimate is, of course, open to suspicion, as being a sectarian performance; but, allowing for great exaggeration, it will still appear alarming. He calculates that there were at that time one million of women, more or less, who led habitually lewd lives, and ministered to the passions of the clergy. These were independent of the married women who were led into adultery, and of the pimps and procuresses who were in clerical pay.[1]

To return to the laws regulating prostitution, it appears that a serious effort was made to put it down under the sovereignty of Catharine of Medicis. An ordinance of Charles IX., dated 1560, prohibited the opening or keeping of any brothel or house of reception for prostitutes in Paris. For a short period it seems that the practice was actually suppressed, and the consequence is said to have been a large increase of secret debauchery. A few years after the passage of the ordinance, a Huguenot clergyman named Cayet proposed to re-establish public brothels in the interest of the public morals, but the authorities of his Church assailed him so vehemently that his scheme fell to the ground without having had the benefit of a public discussion, and he was himself driven to join the Romanists. In 1588 an ordinance of Henry III. reaffirmed the ordinance of 1560, and alleged that the magistrates of the city had connived at the establishment of brothels. Ordinances of the provost followed in the same strain, and all prostitutes were required to leave Paris within twenty-four hours. An ordinance dated 1635 was still more rigorous. It condemned all men concerned in the " traffic of prostitution" to the galleys for life, and all women and girls to be "whipped, shaved, and banished for life, without any formal trial." As might be imagined, this ordinance was alternately disregarded and made to serve the purposes of private malice. Men who wished to revenge themselves on their mistresses accused them of being prostitutes; but *it does not appear that the actual supply was ever seriously diminished.*

[1] Cabinet du Roi de France. Paris. 1581.

CHAPTER VIII.

FRANCE.—HISTORY FROM LOUIS XIII. TO THE PRESENT DAY.

Exile of Prostitutes.—Measures of Louis XIV.—Laws of 1684 and 1713.—Police
Regulations.—Ordinance of 1778.—Republican Legislation.—Frightful state of
Paris.—Efforts to pass a general Law.—The Court.—Louis XIII.—The Medicis.
— Louis XIV.—La Vallière.—Montespan.—Maintenon.—Literature of the Day.
—Feudal Rights.—The Regency.—Duchess of Berri.—Claudine du Tencin.—
Louis XV.—Madame de Pompadour.—Dubarry.—Parc aux Cerfs.—Louis XVI.
—Philippe Egalité.—Subsequent Sovereigns.—Literature. — Lewd Novels and
Pictures.—Tendency of Philosophy.—The Church.

WE have thus sketched the history of prostitution in France
from the commencement of the French nation to the reign of Louis
XIII. This chapter will complete the subject to the present day.

The ordinance of 1560, prohibiting prostitution in any shape,
and granting twenty-four hours only to prostitutes and their accomplices to evacuate Paris, remained in force till late in the eighteenth century. Though, so far as the general traffic went, it was
a dead letter, it enabled the police authorities to imprison or exile
unruly prostitutes from time to time, and was the basis of the
high-handed measure by which the colonists of Canada were first
supplied with wives direct from the Paris stews. It also enabled
noblemen and officials connected with government to avenge
themselves upon unfaithful mistresses, and to exercise a conven·
ient sort of tyranny over the pretty *ling*ères and sewing-girls of
the metropolis.

In 1684 Louis XIV. made some alteration in the laws governing prostitution. He provided prisons for the detention of prostitutes, and armed the lieutenant of police with authority to correct them; and he drew a broad line of distinction between dissolute women who were not actually upon the town and the class
of prostitutes proper.

A farther police regulation on the subject was made in 1713.
By that measure a sort of regularity was introduced into the procedure against courtesans and lewd women. They were definitely
divided into two classes: women who led dissolute lives without
being precisely prostitutes, and prostitutes proper. The police
were authorized to interfere against both on complaint of any per·

son who charged them with outraging public decency. In the case of prostitutes the proceeding was summary. The culprit was summoned, condemned on slight evidence, and sentenced either to exile, imprisonment, or, more rarely, to a whipping or the loss of her hair. With regard to dissolute women who were not regular prostitutes, the authorities proceeded more cautiously. They were entitled to all the privileges of other accused persons, sentences rendered against them being subject to appeal; and, when found guilty, the penalty inflicted was usually a fine. Occasionally, the houses where they had carried on their calling were closed, the furniture was thrown out of the window, and a crier proclaimed their disgrace throughout the city.

Monsieur Parent-Duchatelet, who had the patience to read all the records of proceedings against prostitutes in the city of Paris from 1724 to 1788, *infers* the law from these instances of its application, and concludes: (1.) That, notwithstanding the ordinance of 1560, brothels were licensed by the police. (2.) That prostitutes were never troubled except on complaint of a responsible person. (3.) That brothels were disorderly; that riots, rows, and murders not unfrequently occurred within their walls or in their neighborhood. (4.) That the punishment was left to the discretion of the magistrate. (5.) That the penalties inflicted were lighter toward the close of the period examined. (6.) That certain streets in Paris were wholly occupied by prostitutes.[1]

Probably with a view to enlarge the discretion of the magistrates, a new ordinance was passed in 1778, renewing, in peremptory language, the prohibitive provisions of the enactment of 1560. This ordinance, which bears the name, and probably emanated from the office of Lenoir, the police magistrate, declares that no public woman shall hereafter try to catch (*raccrocher*) men on the wharves or boulevards, or in the streets or squares of Paris, under penalty of being shaved, whipped, and imprisoned; that no householder shall let his house, or any part thereof, to prostitutes, under penalty of five hundred francs fine, and that boarding-house keepers shall allow no men and women to sleep together without seeing their marriage contract.

The most curious feature in connection with this ordinance was the fact that it was not intended or held to interfere with established brothels, which the government continued to license as before. It was intended to affect private prostitutes only. We

---

[1] Parent-Duchatelet, De la Prostitution dans la Ville de Paris, ii. 473.

may judge of its success from the general statement that, soon
after its passage, the streets and squares were thronged with prostitutes.   No woman or modest person could walk the garden of
the Tuileries at night.   Lewd women showed themselves at their
windows in a state of nudity, and shocked public decency still
more glaringly by their postures in the streets.   It was, in fact,
so complete a failure, that two years after its establishment it was
practically repealed by a new police regulation.

In 1791, the whole body of the legislation of the monarchy was
abolished, and in its stead the republican Legislature enacted a
code which was the only law in force in France.   That code making no reference to prostitution, it was inferred by lawyers that
women had a natural right to prostitute their bodies if they chose,
and accordingly the traffic became open and free.   The consequence of this was a tremendous development of the vice.   Prostitutes established themselves in every street, and monopolized
every public place.   Paris became scarcely habitable for modest
women.   An outcry against this monstrous state of things reached the Executive Directory in 1796, and that body sent a message
to the Council of Five Hundred, begging them to legislate on the
subject.   The message was clear and able, calling upon the council to define " prostitute," and suggesting that " reiterated offenses
legally proved, public notoriety, or arrest in the act," appeared to
constitute proof of prostitution.   It seemed to call for penalties,
in the shape of imprisonment, on women exercising this calling.
But neither this suggestion, nor a subsequent project of the same
character was ever carried into effect.   Napoleon swept the Palais
Royal of the prostitutes who had made it their head-quarters, and
broke up some of the greatest brothels by harassing their inmates
in various ways, but he made no law on the subject.

In 1811, M. Pasquier, Prefect of Police, drafted a bill for the
regulation of prostitutes, but it never went into effect, and the imperial ordinance drawn by the prefect has been lost.   Five years
later, M. Anglis, Prefect of Police under Louis XVIII., attempted
the same thing with no better success, the law officers of the
crown seeming to have supposed that the general provisions of
the articles of the code on public decency and " outrages upon
public morality" covered the particular case of prostitution.   The
last efforts that were made in France to obtain a law for the regulation of prostitution were in 1819 and 1822, when the ministry
seriously thought of settling the whole matter by a royal declara-

tion.   These endeavors had the same fate as the former ones, leading to no result.

A general impression has prevailed of late years that the moral sense of the public would be shocked by any legislative act licensing so great a sin as prostitution; and as the government has assumed, without constitutional warrant, the control and regulation of prostitutes, and has exercised as full authority as it could have done had there been a law on the subject, the deficiency has hardly been felt.   A conscientious official has occasionally experienced qualms of conscience at acting without legal warrant; the government has sometimes been frightened by a menace of resistance from some bold lawyer, but no trouble has ever actually arisen, and custom now gives to the police regulations the force of law.

We shall review these regulations in another place; meanwhile a glance must be cast upon the progress of morality in France during the seventeenth, eighteenth, and nineteenth centuries.

The gallantry which distinguished the court of Henry IV. became more refined, though not less criminal, under Louis XIII. Adultery and seduction were every-day matters in the circles which educated Mary, Queen of Scots, and developed the wit of the author of Grammont's Memoirs.   Every lady was presumed to have a lover; every man of fashion more than one mistress. Richelieu boasted that no lady could reject him when he chose to throw the handkerchief, and Mazarin was accused of intrigues with the queen herself.   Louis did not blush to visit his mistresses at the head of his guards, and in all the pomp of royalty; and, as an instance of their influence over him, it has been stated that it was at the request of Mademoiselle de la Fayette that he consented to visit his wife nine months before the birth of Louis XIV.

A race of women had sprung up, under the teaching of the Medicis, who combined political skill with licentious propensities, and conducted state and amorous intrigues with equal ardor and success.   The ladies who surrounded Anne of Austria and Mary of Medicis, and that brilliant circle which has been described in the Memoirs of Madame de Longueville and Madame de Sablé, were undoubtedly as dissipated as they were refined; their virtues were in inverse proportion to their wit.   Paris no longer witnessed the Louvre converted into a royal preserve, or detestable debauchees haunting its dark passages; but there reigned throughout the

court an air of polished sensuality, which, in point of fact, must
have been at least equally prejudicial to good morals.

Louis XIV. imbibed the spirit of the age during his minority.
Royal mistresses had become a recognized institution, fathers and
husbands rather courting than dreading dishonor at the hands of
the king. After having dispensed his favors with some impar-
tiality among the ladies of the court, he discovered, apparently to
his surprise, that one of them, a charming girl, named Louise de la
Vallière, really loved him. The only person who showed much
annoyance at the warmth with which the king entered upon this
new liaison was the Duchess of Orleans, Henrietta of England,
the king's sister-in-law, who seems to have expected that she
would be the fortunate recipient of whatever crumbs might fall
from the royal table. She was unable, however, to divert Louis
from his purpose; La Vallière became his mistress, and bore him
two children. When he grew tired of her, as he did soon after
the birth of her second child, she retired into a convent, and expiated her fault by thirty years' austere penitence.

The king then turned his attention to a lady of noble rank, the
wife of the Marquis of Montespan, and in a business manner exiled the marquis to his estate, and lived with his wife. A woman
otherwise virtuous, proud, and queenly, she lived with the king
for fourteen years, and bore him eight children. These children
were openly legitimated by Louis, and were married by him to
members of the royal family. He even contemplated securing the
throne to them, though they were thus doubly adulterine.

The last mistress of Louis XIV. was the famous Madame de
Maintenon, the widow of the poet Scarron; a person of remarkable abilities, and old enough to have recovered from the passions
which were said to have disturbed her youth. She was introduced to the king as the governess of his illegitimate children, and
by her arts contrived not only to wean the king's heart from his
mistress, but even to alienate the children from their mother.
For thirty-five years she wielded supreme control over Louis's
mind; and whatever may be said of her early life, and however
harsh a judgment must be formed of her political measures, it
must be allowed that, in general, her influence was exercised for
the good of religion and morality. Under her direction the court
became positively devout. Intrigues were concealed, not ostentatiously paraded before the public eye; and the ladies by whom
she was surrounded were obliged to lead at least outwardly deco-

rous lives. She might not be able to check the monstrous practices of the Duke of Orleans; but much of the looseness of the
court she could, and really did bring to an end. Her royal lover,
who at first piqued himself upon rising as far above obligations
of fidelity to his mistresses as he considered himself superior to
political obligations to his people, resigned himself to the spiritual
direction of the marquise, and allowed old age to assert its rights
in condemning him to virtue. All things considered, the last
twenty years of Louis XIV.'s reign was perhaps the most moral
in the whole history of the monarchy.

This is well illustrated in the history of the literature of the
day. The leading philosophers, writers, and poets of the age of
Louis XIV. forbore to shock decency, and may be read to-day as
safely as any modern work. Preachers—Bossuet, Massillon, Bour-
daloue—exercised a potent influence over the tone of letters and
society. Corneille, Racine, and their contemporaries provided the
stage with a repertory that could never bring a blush to the cheek.
Even Molière, who did occasionally let slip a joke of questionable
propriety, for the pit's sake, seems a daring innovator when he is
contrasted with his predecessors. Decency is, in fact, one of the
most striking characteristics of the literature of the age.

We may also date from the reign of Louis XIV. the final extinction of many of the old feudal rights which were at war with
morality. Horrible as it may seem, there were parts of France
where the custom allowed the seigneur to debauch the daughter
of his vassal without obstacle or penalty. In some provinces it is
said to have been customary for the seigneur to enjoy the first
night of every girl married within his manor. In others, the peculiar authority of the seigneur over the serfs who were attached
to the glebe was held to endow him with the right of using the
bodies of their wives and daughters as he saw fit. No written
custom justified these monstrous privileges, but frequent allusions
to them in the old French writers show that in certain parts they
were sanctioned by usage. Louis XIV. made it his especial business to break down the privileges of the nobility, and it was no
doubt to the general police regulations he made for the government of the kingdom at large that the extinction of these rights
was mainly due.

With the Regency the scene changes. The Duke of Orleans
had long been one of the most depraved men in France. So long
as Louis XIV. lived he had perforce observed a certain outward

decorum; but the death of the monarch, and the duke's high-handed seizure of the regency, enabled him to give free scope to his propensities. He resided in the Palais Royal, and gave suppers there almost every evening to a select circle of roués and fast women, among whom Madame de Parabère long held the place of honor. The company not unfrequently varied the entertainment by the performance of charades and tableaux, among which the judgment of Paris was a favorite of the regent. The conversation of the guests was so gross as to shock all but the initiated, and when they separated they were generally all intoxicated.[1]

The most startling and horrible feature of these entertainments was the fact that the regent's daughter, the Duchess of Berri, was almost always present. Her life was a romance. Married while a child to the Duc de Berri, by her passionate temper and her levities she was the bane of her husband's life. She embraced the infidel and licentious doctrines of the age in company with her father, and the pair were so fond of each other that the most horrible suspicions began to gain ground. They were dispelled for a time by the discovery of an intrigue between the duchess and her chamberlain, which so provoked the duke that he seized his wife by the hair and beat her. On his death, which occurred soon afterward, she gave the reins to her passion, and set an example of scandal. At the Luxembourg, where she had apartments, she exhibited the state of a queen, and lover succeeded lover with startling rapidity. At last she seems to have fallen in love with an officer of her guards, named Riom, whose only merit was youth. He subdued her. She became as docile and submissive to him as she had been intractable and haughty with her former lovers, and all Paris was talking of the transformation. After about a year of this *liaison*, she gave birth to a child. During the pains of childbirth she was not expected to live, and the curate of St. Sulpice was sent for in all haste to administer the extreme unction. The ecclesiastic happened to be a rigid champion of morality, and he refused to administer the rite till Riom had been dismissed from the Luxembourg. The duchess would not consent to part with her lover, and for many hours this strange conflict went on by the bedside of the failing woman. The curate was obstinate, however, and no sacrament was administered; but the duchess recovering, the regent used his authority, and sent Riom to join

[1] See Taylor's House of Orleans, vol. i. and Memoires de la Duchesse d'Orleans, *passim*.

his regiment. It killed his daughter. She invited her father to sup with her, and used all her eloquence to persuade him to let her marry Riom; but the regent remaining firm, she withdrew to her chamber, took to her bed, and died two days afterward.

In alluding to the regent's mistresses, a word should be said of the famous Claudine du Tencin, whose adventures shed a flood of light on the morals of the day. She was a pretty girl, of respectable, if not noble family, living in a distant province. To escape from a marriage that was forced on her, she took refuge in a convent. Instead, however, of suiting her habits to her place of residence, she contrived to alter the mode of life at the convent so as to meet her desires, and it became famous for the gayety of its social entertainments and the liveliness of its inmates. One of the gentlemen who were allowed to share its hospitality was the poet Destouches. He was smitten with the pretty Claudine, who acknowledged the charm of his accomplishments, and, after a few months' intimacy, gave birth to a male child, who became the mathematician and philosopher D'Alembert.

Claudine had a brother, an abbé, a man of considerable cunning, and no principle whatever. He persuaded his sister to go to Paris and seek her fortune. He obtained an introduction for her to the regent, and Claudine contrived to produce such an impression that she was soon installed as titular mistress. This did not last long, however. One day, venturing to remonstrate with the regent on his loose mode of life, his habitual drunkenness, etc., her lover lost patience with her, and suddenly summoned a crowd of his courtiers from the ante-chamber to witness the déshabillé and listen to the sermons of madame. In revenge, Claudine rushed out and became the mistress of the prime minister, Cardinal Dubois. Her brother, the abbé, got a bishopric for his share in the transaction.

At the death of Dubois, Madame du Tencin gave him as successor the Duke of Richelieu, the most famous lady-killer of the court. But she was growing old, and ambition had more attractions for her than love. She became an authoress, wrote religious works and novels, patronized letters, and brought out Montesquieu's Spirit of Laws. Her salons became the most fashionable in Paris. It was not a little singular that she should have been the head of one literary clique, and her son, D'Alembert, the chief of another—neither positively jealous of the other, yet living on terms of cold reserve.

Louis XV. trod in the steps of his great-grandfather and the regent. His amours attracted no attention, being evanescent and trifling, till he quarreled with the queen, and bestowed the title of mistress on the Countess of Mailly. This lady had four sisters, three of whom had reached womanhood. They were jealous of their sister's success, and solicited a share of the royal favor. The monarch graciously granted their prayer, and admitted all four into an associate *liaison*. He was much hurt when the fifth, at the age of sixteen, declined an interest in this delectable partnership. Falling ill soon afterward, he allowed his confessor to frighten him into parting with the sisters, and when he got well replaced them by the wife of the subfarmer of the finances, Madame le Normand d'Etoiles. He created her Marquise de Pompadour, and compelled the court to recognize her. Happily for him, she was a person of moderate taste and habits. She patronized letters, was the friend of Voltaire, and seems to have employed her influence over the king for his advantage and that of the public. It is recorded, as an instance of the heartlessness of the king, that when she died he stood at a window to watch her funeral pass, and noticing that it was a rainy day, observed, with a smile, " that the marquise had bad weather for her long journey."

Her successor was Madame Dubarry, a common prostitute, fished out of the Paris stews in consequence of her skill in debauchery. Her real name was Vanbernier; but, in order to present her at court, a nobleman of the name of Dubarry was persuaded to marry her. It was under her reign that the *Parc aux Cerfs* (in which Madame de Pompadour was said to have had a hand), reached its highest point of celebrity and eclat. This was a royal seraglio filled with the most beautiful girls that could be bought or stolen. The monstrous old debauchee who filled the throne of France had a weakness for very young girls, fifteen being the age at which he preferred his mistresses. Under the skillful directions of Dubarry, a host of pimps and purveyors searched France for young girls to suit the king's fancy. Where negotiations could not be effected, the prerogative was stretched, and the police authorities judiciously blinded; but we are led to believe that it was seldom necessary to resort to these violent measures, and that French fathers of that day seldom made difficulties except about the sum to be paid. That the king was liberal may be inferred from the sum which this seraglio cost him—not less than one hundred millions of francs. It was a large, handsomely furnished building at Versailles, giving every woman her separate apartments. The king rarely visited each one more than three or four times; but, on the occasion of his first visit, he prided himself on observing the etiquette of a husband. He insisted on the poor child whom he was about to ruin kneeling down by the bedside, and saying her prayers in his presence. It need hardly be observed that the Parc aux Cerfs was the great reservoir from whence the brothels of the time derived their supply of recruits. After a residence of a few weeks or months, in case they became pregnant, the poor children were thrown out upon the world, and ruin was a necessity.

The last monarch of the old French line, the unfortunate Louis XVI., forms a bright contrast to his predecessors. His education had been severe, his principles were naturally strict. Placed upon the throne after the Revolution had become inevitable, his whole attention was devoted to the business of reigning, and attempting reforms which came quite too late. Neither he nor his wife ever gave rise to merited scandal.

The profligate character of the court was, however, sustained by the Orleans family and their connections. Philippe Egalité was a true descendant of the regent. On the very eve of the Revolution he indulged in orgies that were closely imitated from those of the Palais Royal.

Our sketch of the immoralities of the French court naturally ends here. Though the period of the Directory was marked by a general looseness in the best French society, and both Napoleon and Louis XVIII. set no example of conjugal fidelity to their subjects, yet vice was not exhibited so openly under them as it had been under former kings, and the laws of decency were not actually set at defiance. Their frailties were private matters, into which it is scarcely the duty of the historian to intrude. The same may be said of Charles X. and Louis Philippe. The former had, in his youth, been a sharer of many of the excesses of the Orleans family, but at the time he became king he was an old man, and could afford to lead a decent life. Louis Philippe had never afforded a theme for scandal, and as king he set an example of rigorous morality.

If we turn back now to the period of the Regency, we shall find letters sympathizing in the most marked manner with the court. Under the regime of severe etiquette and decency established by Louis XIV., authors respected the ear of innocence; under the brutal sway of the regent, and the lewd influence of the satyr Louis

I

XV., the old prostitution of literature was revived. Thus we find that the most successful authors of the day, such as Voltaire, handled themes grossly immoral in themselves, and rendered still more offensive by their mode of treatment. The most popular novel of the eighteenth century—Manon Lescaut—the work, by the way, of an abbé, is the narrative of the adventures of a prostitute. Of all the romance writers of that age, no one was more widely popular or more generally read than Crebillon *fils*, whose works would almost fall into the hands of the police at the present time. Diderot, Mirabeau, Montesquieu, and, with few exceptions, all the most eminent men of France, prostituted their genius to the composition of erotic works which were widely read by women as well as men. Of the light poetry of the eighteenth century very little is fit for modern reading, the poets being, as a general rule, either dull or depraved. Nor were the arts behindhand. Frescoes differing but little from those which had adorned Fontainebleau under Francis I. again covered the walls of rich men's houses; and the most fortunate painters of the day were those who could best outrage decency without positively suggesting the brothel. Lewd books and pictures were freely sold in Paris during the Regency, the reign of Louis XV., and the Revolutionary period. Napoleon burned all he could find, but there still remained enough to supply the demand almost ever since.

It should be noticed in connection with the state of morals in France during the second half of the eighteenth century, that the tendency of the philosophical doctrines which were then current was to undermine the respect paid to marriage and chastity. The former, being a sacrament, was assailed as part of the ecclesiastical system; the latter was conceived to be at war with the natural, and, therefore, the proper passions of mankind. Several of the philosophers left it to be inferred from their writings, or stated broadly, that promiscuous intercourse, or, at all events, unlimited facilities of divorce, were the natural destiny of the human race, and that the restrictions which have been imposed on sensual gratification had no warrant in reason or sound ethics. These foolish notions brought forth fruits after their kind. Under the Directory, prostitutes were received into certain societies, and ladies of fashion became prostitutes. Even under the Empire it was not unusual for a lady to request her husband to pay her a visit, as it was well, perhaps, to avoid questions of legitimacy arising at any future period.

There was one branch of society in which morality had made great progress during the century : that was the Church. It still contained cardinals like Dubois, and bishops and abbés like Du Tencin, but the vast body of the country clergy led pure moral lives. This point is placed beyond a doubt by the silence of the parties opposed to the hierarchy when the Revolution broke out, and they were so disposed to assail the priesthood on every vulnerable point. It may be broadly stated that the vices which had infected the whole body of the clergy during the sixteenth century had disappeared by the eighteenth ; despite the law of celibacy, the country curates were, as a rule, moral, austere, virtuous men.

CHAPTER IX.

FRANCE.—SYPHILIS.

First recorded Appearance in Europe.—Description by Fracastor.—Conduct of the Faculty.—First Hospitals in Paris.—Shocking Condition of the Sick.—New Syphilitic Hospital.—Plan of Treatment.—Establishment of the Salpétrière.—Bicêtre. —Capuchins.—Hospital du Midi.—Reforms there.—Visiting Physicians.—Dispensary.--Statistics of Disease.—Progress and Condition of Disease.

IT properly belongs to this chapter to allude to the rise and progress of the diseases termed syphilitic.

Whether they were of ancient date—whether the "shameful diseases" which have been mentioned in the chapter devoted to prostitution at Rome were the same as the modern syphilis—may be decided by the reader. It will suffice here to say that, throughout the Middle Ages, a species of disease, termed sometimes leprosy, sometimes *pudendagra*, appears to have prevailed in France as in other European countries, and to have chosen for its chief seat the organs of generation. It was not, however, till the close of the fifteenth century that public attention began to be generally directed to the subject of sexual disease.

We shall briefly enumerate the earliest notices of its appearance. When Charles VIII. entered Naples in 1495, he found the city suffering from a plague (syphilis) to which the prejudice of the natives gave the name of "French malady." Italy, said the writers of the day, was attacked simultaneously by the French army and this new disease.[1] Most of the Italian writers accuse

[1] Nicolas Leoniceno, De Morbo Gallico, and others.

the French of its introduction.   Benevenis, however, says they got it from the Spaniards, and Guicciardini candidly admits that his countrymen were the real propagators of the malady.   German physicians likewise traced its origin to Naples, and placed it about the year 1493,[1] ascribing it to an untoward planetary conjunction.   The disease appeared at Barcelona in 1493, and in other parts of Spain in the following year.[2]   But sixty years before, in 1430, public regulations had been made in London to prevent the admission of persons attacked with a disease very similar to syphilis into houses of prostitution, and requiring the police to keep constant watch over such as should show symptoms of this *infirmitas nefanda*.[3]   The first authentic allusion to the disease in France is the ordinance of the Parliament of Paris, dated 1497, ordering all persons attacked by the " large pox" to vacate the city within twenty-four hours, and not to return till they were cured ;   providing a sort of hospital for those who can not move ; and appointing agents to bestow four *sols parisis* on the exiles to pay for their journey.[4]   This ordinance alludes to the disease having been prevalent for two years.

It may therefore be taken for granted that, whether syphilitic diseases had existed before or not, they prevailed to a very alarming extent throughout Europe at the close of the fifteenth century.

To prevent misconception, it may be as well to give the diagnostic signs of the " French malady" as furnished by Fracastor : " The patients were in low spirits, and broken down ; their faces were pale.   Most of them had chancres upon the organs of generation.   These chancres were obstinate ; when cured in one place they reappeared in another, and the work was never ended.   Pustules with a hard surface appeared upon the skin, generally on the head first.   On first appearing they were small, but gradually increased to the size of an acorn, which they resembled in shape. In some cases they were dry, in others humid ; some were livid, others white and pale, others again hard and reddish.   They burst after a few days, and discharged an incredible quantity of vile fetid humor.   When they began to suppurate they became true phagedænic ulcers, consuming both flesh and bone.   When they attacked the upper part of the body they gave rise to malign fluxions, which gnawed away the palate, or the windpipe, or the

---

[1] Ulrich de Hutton, De Morbi Gallici curatione.
[2] Roderic Dias, Contra las Bubas.   [3] W. Beckett, Phil. Trans. vol. xxx.
[4] Registres du Parlement de Paris, 1497.

throat, or the tonsils. Some patients lost their lips, others the nose, others the eyes, others the whole organs of generation. Many were troubled with moist tumors on the limbs, which grew as large as eggs or small loaves. When they burst, a white and mucilaginous liquor exuded from them. They were usually found on the legs and arms. Some were ulcerated, others again remained callous to the last. And, as if this was not enough, the patients suffered terrible pains, especially at night, not only in the articulations, but in the limbs and nerves. Some sufferers, however, had pustules without pains, others pains without pustules; but, in most cases, both occurred together. The patients were languid, had no appetite, desired to remain constantly in bed. The face and legs swelled. Some had a slight fever, but this was rare; others had severe headaches for which no remedy could be found."[1]

At first, it seems, the faculty, strangely misapprehending its duties, refused to treat patients assailed by this new plague. As at Rome, they were left to the tender mercies of quacks, barbers, and old women. About the beginning of the sixteenth century, however, the extent of the mischief provoked sympathy from the physicians, and one or two treatises appeared on the subject. Sudorifics seem to have been the chief agent employed. Large use was made of holy wood (the wood of the lignum-vitæ-tree), which was imported from America for the purpose. It was doses of holy wood, in decoction, which are said to have saved the life of the great Erasmus.

After the passage of the law of 1497, a house in the Faubourg St. Germain was appropriated to the reception of the victims of syphilis; but there is no reason to believe that any attempt was made to treat them there. They were left to die, or to quack themselves. Eighteen years after, in 1505, the house in question being too small for the numbers of the sick, and it being clearly shown that syphilis was not contagious except by sexual intercourse or positive peculiar contact with the person afflicted, a new decree of Parliament appropriated funds for the construction of " a hospital for persons attacked by the large pox (*les grands vérolés*)," and directed that they should be properly cared for.[2] This decree was never carried into effect. Thirty years afterward the condition of the sick was far worse than it had ever been, they being left to die in the streets. A new decree, in 1535, appointed commissioners to choose a locality for a hospital; and, notwithstanding some oppo-

---

[1] Jerome Fracastor, De Morb. Contag. [2] Registres du Parlement de Paris, 1505.

sition from the religious authorities, they performed their task.
A small hospital was appropriated to syphilitic patients, and persons suffering from itch, epilepsy, and St. Vitus's dance.   It was
soon filled, and several patients were thrust into the same bed.
Owing to mismanagement on the part of the directors, it was short
of linen, lint, and medicine.   The Parliament interfered, but without success ; and, in despair, the unfortunate sufferers contrived to
effect an entrance into the hospital general, the Hotel Dieu.   They
were soon admitted on the same terms as other sufferers ; but, as
the establishment was far too small to accommodate all who sought
refuge there, they were thrust four and five together into the same
bed, and persons with syphilitic diseases lay by the side of men in
contagious fevers, and others with broken legs and arms.

The Parliament interfered a second time.   The municipal officers of Paris were assembled, and called upon to provide a hospital for venereal cases ; but for many years the strenuous opposition of the Hotel Dieu neutralized all the efforts that were made.
It was not till 1614 that the project of the Parliament was realized, and a syphilitic hospital actually opened.

Up to this time, that is to say, for a period of a century and a
quarter, persons attacked by venereal disease were left to the care
of Providence.   Males could, with some exertion, occasionally obtain admission to the Hotel Dieu, where they often contracted new
diseases without getting rid of the old ; but of females, not a word
had yet been spoken.   No one in that hundred and twenty-five
years had ever raised a voice to plead on behalf of the prostitutes ;
it never seems to have occurred, even to the Parliament which had
so much sympathy for the *pauvres vérolés*, that the women likewise deserved pity and attention.

We possess no information with regard to the treatment used
in this new hospital.   It is certain, however, that, in obedience to
the law of its foundation, patients were soundly whipped when
they entered and when they left it, by way of punishing them for
having contracted the disease.   In 1675 the managers of the hospital declared that this practice deterred many sick persons from
coming forward and confessing their condition ; but it prevailed,
apparently, for a quarter of a century afterward.

About the middle of the seventeenth century, under the reign
of Louis XIV., a hospital prison, named the Salpétrière, was established for the reception of prostitutes ; but, by a strange inconsistency, in 1658 it was closed to women suffering from syphilis

(*femmes gatées*), and physicians were directed to examine all women "who showed symptoms of syphilis on the face." A few years' experience showed the fallacy of this system. Diseased women were confined in the place; should they not be treated there? The physicians thought they should, and accordingly, though in violation of the rules of the establishment, a small room was appropriated to this class of patients. It appears that at this time a prostitute found some difficulty in obtaining admission to the Salpétrière; it being not unusual for unfortunate creatures to have themselves arrested for vagabondage, and to submit voluntarily to the whipping which the ethics of the day required in the case of females as well as males, in order to obtain medical treatment. It will be seen that our New York system can not claim the merit of originality. Prostitutes, in fact, flocked to the Salpétrière in such numbers that the room furnished by the connivance of the authorities was soon far too small to accommodate them. The hospital managers declared to the royal government that medical treatment was out of the question in so crowded an apartment, and that a putrid fever might be expected if better accommodations were not provided. In reply, the government placed at their disposal a ward in the hospital of Bicêtre.

This was in 1691. For nearly a hundred years afterward the severe cases of venereal disease were sent to Bicêtre, the milder ones kept at Salpétrière. Both establishments were a disgrace to humanity. The patients were cheated of the food allowed them, and supplied with cheap broth and cheese in its stead. No baths, and but few medicines were at their command. Their ward was filthy, close, and in ruin. Patients were often obliged to wait so long for medical attendance that their maladies became incurable. The air in which they lived was pestiferous, and no one could visit the hospital without being shocked at its aspect.[1] Medical men who saw the place expressed amazement that so many persons should exist in so small a room. Eight women slept in a bed, and in the room appropriated to those whose turn for treatment had not come, the patients slept by gangs, one half sleeping from 8 P.M. to 1 A.M., and the remainder from 1 A.M. to 7 A.M. The floor was covered with dirt and filth, and the windows were nailed down, for fear of their being broken if opened. There was but little linen, and that was in rags, and abominably dirty. One

[1] Cullerier: Report of Chirurgien Mareschal; Report of M. de Breteuil to the Government; Parent-Duchatelet. ii. 180.

hundred persons only were treated at a time, fifty men and fifty women. A new batch was admitted to treatment every two months, and, as the hospital always contained from three to four hundred sufferers, some cases remained six or eight months without any treatment whatever. Many died before they reached the hands of the doctors. The diet was the same for all. Those who had not been admitted to treatment were supplied with coarse bread, cheese, rancid butter, and (very seldom) a little meat. The surgeons of Bicêtre usually made fortunes in a short time.[1]

If any thing farther were needed to characterize the hospital of Bicêtre in the eighteenth century, it would be the rules in virtue of which no diseased person could claim admission until a complete year had elapsed from the time of their first application, and every diseased person was turned out, whether ill or well, after six weeks' treatment. It was stated to M. Parent-Duchatelet that the average mortality was one hundred women and sixty men per annum.[2]

In 1787, Dr. Cullerier was appointed surgeon in charge of syphilitic cases at Bicêtre. He commenced his administration by denouncing the state of things he found there, and it is mainly from the *memoires* he addressed to the government that the preceding facts have been obtained. His representations seem to have met with but little success. In 1789, however, the bulk of the prisoners at Bicêtre were set free, and he immediately availed himself of the increased room to accommodate his patients.

The reform was so slight, or rather so vast a reform was needed, that the moment the attention of the republican government was drawn to the subject, it removed the syphilitic cases from the hospital of Bicêtre to the hospital of the Capuchins. That establishment was enlarged, and named the Hospital of the South (l'Hôpital du Midi). Gardens and baths were provided; ample wards permitted the classification of diseases; the food was of the best kind, and sufficient in quantity. This immense step was the work of the republican authorities.

It was, however, only the first of a series of reforms. Originally, men and women of all grades were admitted promiscuously. This led to grave inconveniences. The decorum of the hospital was frequently disturbed by the conduct of some of the men with regard to the prostitutes in the adjoining wards. To obviate this, a new hospital was set apart, under the reign of Charles X., for

---

[1] Cullerier : Parent-Duchatelet, ii. 184.   [2] Parent-Duchatelet, ii. 186.

the reception of male patients only. It is the Hospital de Lourcine.

A still more serious trouble arose from the mixture of prostitutes with other women who, from the infidelity of their husbands, hereditary disease, or other causes, found themselves infected with syphilis. For some time complaints had been made on this head, but an accident, which occurred in 1828, compelled the authorities to act. The daughter of a professional nurse, residing in the vicinity of Paris, caught syphilis from a child her mother was nursing, who had inherited the disease. It took the shape of a virulent chancre on the palate, and the girl was sent to the Hospital du Midi for treatment. She found herself thrust among the vilest prostitutes, whose language and sentiments shocked her so terribly that she insisted on leaving the hospital at once. The physician on duty declined to grant her request, whereupon the poor girl contrived to get into the yard, and threw herself into a well. She was drowned, and on an autopsy of her corpse it appeared that she was a virgin. This dreadful incident aroused the public mind. Hitherto the disposal of the prostitutes had been a subject of dispute between the administration of the hospital and that of the city, each wishing to thrust them upon the other. The government now interfered, and special accommodation was provided for prostitutes at the prison of Saint Lazare. The Hospital du Midi was devoted exclusively to such women as were not inscribed on the rolls of the police.

Before these distributions took place, when men and women were indiscriminately received at the Hospital du Midi, the average annual admissions, from 1804 to 1814, were 2700; from 1822 to 1828 it exceeded an average of 3100. Twenty years ago the mortality was said to be less than two per cent.; it was ten per cent. at Bicêtre.

At the Hospital du Midi, diseased persons who do not desire admission to the hospital are treated outside, all the medicines they require being furnished them free of charge.

It would appear, from stray allusions in various old ordinances, that some sort of medical office had been established in the eighteenth century by the government, for the purpose of affording gratuitous advice to prostitutes, and denouncing those who were diseased; but there exists no positive evidence of any such establishment or office. It was not till 1803 that a regulation was made by the prefect of police, requiring all public women to submit to be visited by a physician appointed by him. The plan was a bad one, as the physician was paid by fees which he was authorized to exact; and it was rendered worse in practice by the dishonesty of the man chosen for the office, one Coulon. This individual made money and neglected his duties. The system was altered in 1810, and a dispensary established, with a strong medical staff, who were directed to visit all the prostitutes in Paris. This institution is still in existence; it will be further noticed in the next chapter.

When the dispensary was established, its medical officers were directed to offer to prostitutes the choice of being treated at home or going to the hospital. Almost all chose the former. The physicians then undertook to decide themselves which should go to the hospital and which remain in their houses. The results of their experience, and the policy it compelled them to adopt, are shown in the following table, which was compiled by Parent-Duchatelet:

Year.	Treated at home.	Year.	Treated at home.	Year.	Treated at home.
1812	276	1817	123	1821	27
1813	300	1818	No report.	1824	27
1814	296	1819	25	1825	7
1815	No report.	1820	19	1826	4
1816	"				

The system of treating prostitutes at home was, in fact, given up. It was found they could not be compelled to take the medicines given them; and that, though laboring under the most severe disease, they would not abstain from the exercise of their calling.

The tables prepared by the sanitary office, or dispensary, at Paris, afford a clear view of the extent and progress of disease in that city. Of those which are furnished by M. Parent-Duchatelet, we shall take a few of the most striking. The following gives the aggregate disease for a period of twenty years:

Years.	Average Patients.	Total. Patients.	Years.	Average Patients.	Total. Patients.
1812	51	612	1826	93	1116
1813	79	948	1827	Report missing.	
1814	102	1224	1828	104	1248
1815	Report missing.		1829	99	1188
1816	88	1056	1830	91	1092
1817	76	912	1831	110	1320
1818	68	816	1832	78	936
1819	58	696			17376
1820	62	744	Add approximate estimate for three years wanting }		3250
1821	55	660			
1822	Report missing.		Total diseased in twenty years }		20626[1]
1823	69	828			
1824	84	1008			
1825	81	972			

[1] Parent-Duchatelet. ii. 124.

Other tables, apparently drawn with care, show that the proportion of disease to prostitutes varies widely in different years. In 1828 it was six per cent., that is to say, six out of every hundred prostitutes were diseased; but in 1832 it was barely three per cent. Four or five per cent. would seem a tolerably fair average.[1]

From another table compiled by the same author we gather that, during a period of eighteen years, January was found the most fatal month for prostitutes; next came August and September; while February, April, May, and July seemed seasons less favorable to disease. M. Duchatelet, however, candidly admits that he can trace the operation of no law here, and inclines to the belief that the variation is wholly due to chance.[2]

CHAPTER X.

FRANCE.—PRESENT REGULATIONS.

Number of Prostitutes in Paris.—Their Nativity, Parentage, Education, Age, etc.—Causes of Prostitution.—Rules concerning tolerated Houses.—Maisons de Passe.—Windows.—Keepers.—Formalities upon granting Licenses.—Recruits.—Pimps.—Profits of Prostitution.—Inscription.—Interrogatories.—Nativity, how ascertained.—Obstacles.—Principles of Inscription.—Age at which Inscription is made.—Radiation.—Provisional Radiation.—Statistics of Radiation.—Classes of Prostitutes.—Visit to the Dispensary.—Visiting Physicians.—Punishment.—Offenses.—Prison Discipline.—Saint Denis.—Tax on Prostitutes.—Inspectors.—Bon Pasteur Asylum.—(Note: Duchatelet's Bill for the Repression of Prostitution.)

IT remains to describe the state and system of prostitution at Paris at the present day. The vast importance of the subject will doubtless justify the length at which it must be treated.

It was usual, during the last century, to estimate the number of prostitutes in Paris at twenty-five or thirty thousand. Even as late as 1810, the number was said by good authority to be not less than eighteen thousand.[3] The police rolls show that these calculations were wide of the mark. According to them, the average number of prostitutes inscribed had risen, from about 1900 in 1814, to 3558 in 1832, the last year of which we have any record. Assuming that the number at present is 4500, or thereabouts, which would suppose an increase equal to that noted before 1832, the

---

[1] Parent-Duchatelet, ii. 130.   [2] Id. ii. 138.
[3] MSS. Reports quoted by Parent-Duchatelet, i. 30; Restif de la Bretonne; *Pornographe*.

prostitutes are one to every two hundred and fifty of the total population. Of these the city of Paris furnishes rather more than one third. The remainder come from the departments; those bordering on Paris being the most fruitful of prostitutes, and the north being largely in excess of production over the south.

The vast majority of these prostitutes are the children of operatives and mechanics. Of 828 fathers, there were

Weavers	19	Liquor-sellers	22
Peddlers	12	Smiths	23
Masons and Tilers	28	Grocers and Fruit-sellers	18
Water-carriers	11	Soldiers, on pensions	30
Stage and Carriage Drivers	35	Clock-makers and Jewelers	16
Shoemakers	50	Barbers and Hair-dressers	16
Farmers and Gardeners	31	Persons without trade or calling	64
Servants	23	Tailors	22
Individuals employed in Foundries, etc.	18	Plasterers, Pavers, etc.	21
Day-laborers	113	Coopers	11
Carpenters	31	Painters, Glaziers, and Printers	25

Whereas there were only

Surgeons, Physicians, and Lawyers	4
Teachers	3
Musicians	9

The inference drawn by M. Parent-Duchatelet from this is, that brothels are supplied from the classes of domestics and factory-girls; and that girls not bred to work rarely find their way into them. Rather more than one third of the fathers of these prostitutes were unable to sign their names.

Of the prostitutes born at Paris, about one fourth were illegitimate; of those born in the departments, one eighth were illegitimate.

Rather more than half the Paris prostitutes could not write their names; a degree of ignorance which argues very remarkable neglect on the part of parents, for at Paris every one may learn to write gratuitously, and a person who can not write will always experience difficulty in obtaining employment.

Nearly half the prostitutes were between the ages of twenty and twenty-six inclusive. One declared herself, or was proved to be, only twelve years old; thirty-four were over fifty; two were over sixty. On reference to the rolls of inscription, it appeared that the bulk of the prostitutes registered themselves between the ages of eighteen and twenty-two; but thirty-four were inscribed before the age of fourteen, which may be assumed to be the period of puberty in France, and a few after passing fifty.

The following table shows the number of years during which the Paris prostitutes had exercised their calling at the time the inquiry was made:

Time	Number of Prostitutes.	Time.	Number of Prostitutes.
1 year and under..................	439	From 12 to 13 years..............	99
From 1 to 2 years..............	590	" 13 to 14 "	98
" 2 to 3 "	440	" 14 to 15 "	107
" 3 to 4 "	485	" 15 to 16 "	80
" 4 to 5 "	294	" 16 to 17 "	19
" 5 to 6 "	139	" 17 to 18 "	14
" 6 to 7 "	150	" 18 to 19 "	17
" 7 to 8 "	143	" 19 to 20 "	4
" 8 to 9 "	96	" 20 to 21 "	—
" 9 to 10 "	100	" 21 to 22 "	1
" 10 to 11 "	109	" 22 to 23 "	—
" 11 to 12 "	93		

M. Duchatelet made careful inquiries into the causes of prostitution. He admits that, the difficulty of obtaining trustworthy information on this head being very great, many errors may have found their way into his calculations. He gives them, however, for what they may be worth.

Want..	1441
Expulsion from home, or desertion of parents...........................	1255
Desire to support old and infirm parents	37
" " " younger brothers and sisters, or nephews and nieces	29
Widows with families to support...	23
Girls from the country, to support themselves	280
" " " " brought to Paris by soldiers, clerks, students, etc..	404
Servants seduced by masters and abandoned	289
Concubines abandoned by their lovers......................................	1425
Total......................	5183

It appears that there were in Paris, in 1832, two hundred and twenty "tolerated houses"—that is to say, brothels. The rules regarding these are numerous. They can not be established in certain localities, such as the Boulevards, or other great thoroughfares. They must not be within one hundred yards of a church, or within fifty or sixty yards of a school, whether for boys or girls; of a palace or other public building, or of a large boarding-house. The proprietor of the house must have given his consent before the house can be used as a brothel. Two houses can not be established side by side, much less can they have the same entry. As a general rule, a preference is given to small, narrow streets, especially *culs de sac*, and to places where brothels have been established before.

With regard to the interior of these houses, they must contain a room for each girl; on no account are two prostitutes allowed to occupy the same room, much less the same bed. Each room must, moreover, be amply provided with utensils, soap, and water, for ablution. No house of prostitution can have back or side doors, or in any way communicate with the adjoining buildings. No house can contain dark closets, or dark passages, or concealed hiding-places. In none of them can any trade or traffic be carried on.

With regard to the class of houses called *maisons de passe* (assignation houses), the police authorities require that in every such house two regular prostitutes, inscribed on the police rolls, shall live permanently. The object of this rule is to obtain a control and supervision over these houses. Before it was adopted the police was often embarrassed by denials of its authority to invade them. It is found that the prostitutes, being naturally hostile to the mistresses of the houses, will act as agents of the police in the event of any scandalous proceedings.

The windows of houses of prostitution must be roughed, as also must those of rooms where individual prostitutes live. They can only be partially opened. These regulations were made in consequence of the shocking scenes that were witnessed at the windows of brothels after the Revolution, naked women being the least of the scandals that used to be exposed.

No one can keep a house of prostitution in Paris without an authorization from the police. Men are never permitted to keep establishments of the kind. A woman who desires to open a house must apply in writing to the Prefect of Police. On receipt of her application, reference is made to the Commissary of Police of the ward to ascertain her character. If she has been condemned for crime or misdemeanor, her request is rarely granted. If she stands in the police books as a woman requiring supervision, she can not succeed. Nor can she obtain a license, under ordinary circumstances, *unless she has been a prostitute herself.* The reason of this regulation is obvious; no one but a prostitute understands the business thoroughly; and as the position of brothel-keeper is found to be the most demoralizing station in the world, it has been the policy of the Paris police to throw impediments in the way of persons not wholly depraved devoting themselves to so dangerous a calling. Furthermore, the applicant must have reached a certain age. She must also be of sober habits, and apparently possessed of sufficient force of character to be able to command a house full of prostitutes. She must possess a sum of money sufficient to guarantee her against immediate failure, and she must own the furniture in the house she wishes to keep.

When all these conditions are fulfilled, the applicant receives a pass-book, in which the number of girls she is allowed to keep is specified. In this book she is bound to enter the name of every prostitute she receives, whether as a boarder or a transient lodger; her age, the date of her entry into her house, the date of her inspection by a physician, and the date of her departure from the house. A printed form in the beginning of the pass-book reminds the mistress of the house that she is bound, under heavy penalties, to inscribe on the police rolls every girl she receives within twenty-four hours of her arrival.

In the event of the neglect of these rules by the keepers of houses of prostitution, the license is revoked. It is understood that the police enforce this regulation with due rigor.

Much has been said and written about the manner in which the keepers of houses of prostitution obtain recruits. M. Parent-Duchatelet, whose sources of information were the best, gives it as his opinion that most of the prostitutes are obtained from the hospitals, especially the Hospital du Midi, where female venereal diseases are treated. It appears that this hospital and others are haunted by old women who have been prostitutes, and who, in their old age, eke out a livelihood by enticing others into the same calling. They soon discover the antecedents and disposition of every young girl they find in hospitals; and if she be pretty or engaging, she must either have much principle or careful friends to rescue her from the clutches of the old hags. While she lies ill on a bed of pain, the latter are constantly with her, and gain her friendship. They know the devices that are needed to impose on her simplicity, and not unfrequently are enabled to strengthen their promises by small donations in money, or a weekly stipend during her convalescence. For a pretty girl as much as fifty francs will be paid by a brothel-keeper. As the girls in France, with few exceptions, come to Paris to be cured when they have contracted disease from association with lovers, it seems quite likely that, as M. Parent-Duchatelet supposes, these hospitals are a fruitful source of prostitutes.

Other brothel-keepers have female agents in the country towns, who send them girls. One well-known woman, who kept for many years one of the largest establishments in France, employed a traveling clerk with a large salary. Some obtain boarders from

their own province or native city; others, who have followed a
trade, get recruits from the acquaintances they made at the work-
shop.   Latterly, it would seem, pimps have carried on their trade
with unusual boldness and success.   Some time since it was noticed that an uncommon number of girls arrived at Paris from
Rheims.   They all came provided with the name and address of
the houses to which they were destined, and drove there from the
stage-office.   Information was sent to the police authorities of
Rheims, and on their arrival the girls were sent back again.   The
design of the authorities was baffled for a while by the cunning
of the pimps, who sent their recruits round by other roads; but
the police finally triumphed by refusing, for a year or two, to inscribe any prostitutes from Rheims.

It is notorious, however, that the same traffic is carried on at the
present day to an alarming extent between London and Paris,
London and Brussels, and other large cities in the neighborhood.
Several societies have been formed, and the police have made
great exertions to suppress the trade, but without any particular
success.

It is understood that the prostitutes of Paris receive nothing for
their "labors" but their board, lodging, and dress.   The latter is
often expensive.   In first-class houses it will exceed five hundred
francs, which in female attire will go as far at Paris as five hundred dollars will in New York.   The whole of the fees exacted from
visitors goes to the mistress, and the girls are reluctantly permitted to retain the presents they sometimes receive from their lovers.   They are usually in debt to the mistress, who, having no
other means of retaining them under her control, hastens to advance them money for jewelry, carriages, fine eating, and expensive wines.   No written contract binds them to remain where they
are; they may leave when they please, if they can pay their debts;
and the obligation they incur for the latter is one of honor only,
and can not be enforced in the courts.

Houses of prostitution, when well conducted, are very profitable in Paris.   It is estimated that the net profits accruing from
each girl ought to be ten francs or more per day.   Many keepers
of houses have retired with from ten to twenty-five thousand francs
a year, and have married their daughters well.   The good-will of
a popular house has been sold for sixty thousand francs (twelve
thousand dollars).

We now come to the great feature of the Paris system: the inscription of prostitutes in a department of the Prefecture of Police, called the *Bureau des Mœurs*. It seems that some sort of inscription was in use before the Revolution, but no law referring to it, or records of the rolls, can be found. Various systems were employed during the Republic and the Empire. The one now in use was adopted in 1816, and amended by a police regulation of 1828.

Prostitutes are inscribed either

1. On their own request;
2. On the requisition of the mistress of a house; or,
3. On the report of the inspector of prostitutes.

When a girl appears before the bureau under any of these circumstances, she is asked the following questions, the answers being taken down in writing:

1. Her name, age, birth-place, trade, and residence?
2. Whether she is a widow, wife, or spinster?
3. Whether her father and mother are living, and what their calling was or is?
4. Whether she lives with them, and if not, when and how she left them?
5. Whether she has had children, and where they are?
6. How long she has been at Paris?
7. Whether any one has a right to claim her?
8. Whether she has ever been arrested, and if yes, how often, and for what offenses?
9. Whether she has ever been a prostitute before, and for what period of time?
10. Whether she has, or has had, venereal disease?
11. Whether she has received any education?
12. What her motive is in inscribing herself?

The answers to these inquiries suggest others, which are put at the discretion of the officials. Their practice is so great that they are rarely deceived by the women; M. Parent-Duchatelet affirms that they could tell an old prostitute merely by the way she sat down.

The interrogatory over, the girl is taken by an inspector to the Dispensary and examined, and the physician on duty reports the result, which is added to the inquiry. Meanwhile, the police registers have been consulted, and if the girl has been an old offender, or is known to the police, she is now identified.

If the girl has her baptismal certificate (*extrait de naissance*) with

K

her, she is forthwith inscribed, and registered among the public women of Paris. As prostitutes rarely possess this document, however, a provisional inscription is usually effected, and a direct application is made to the mayor of the city or *commune* where she was born for the certificate. This application varies according to the age of the girl. If she is of age it is simply a demand for the "*extrait de naissance* of —— ——, who says she is a native of your city or *commune*." If, on the contrary, she is a minor, the application states that "a girl who calls herself —— ——, and says she was born at ——, has applied for inscription in this office. I desire you to ascertain the position of her family, and what means they propose to take in case they desire to secure the return of this young girl."

It often happens that the family implore the intervention of the police; in that case the girl is sent back to the place whence she came. In many cases the family decline to interfere, and then the girl is duly inscribed on the register. She signs a document, in which she states that, "being duly acquainted with the sanitary regulations established by the Prefecture for Public Women, she declares that she will submit to them, will allow herself to be visited periodically by the physicians of the Dispensary, and will conform in all respects to the rules in force."

Of course this procedure is occasionally delayed by falsehoods uttered by the women. It often used to happen that the mayors would report that no person of the name given had been born at the time fixed in their city or commune. In that case the girl was recalled, and made to understand that truth was better policy than falsehood. Girls rarely held out longer than a fortnight or so, and, at the present time, the number of false declarations is very small indeed. They seem satisfied that the police are an omniscient machine which can not be deceived.

When the girl is brought to the office either by a brothel-keeper or an inspector, the proceeding is slightly varied. In the latter case she has been arrested for indulging in clandestine prostitution, but she almost invariably denies the fact, and pleads her innocence. The rule, in this case, is to admonish her and let her go. It is not till the third or fourth offense has been committed that she is inscribed. When the mistress of a house brings a girl to the office, interrogatories similar to the above are put to her. If she has relations or friends at Paris, they are sent for and consulted. When the girl appears evidently lost, she is duly inscribed; but if she shows any signs of shame or contrition, she is often sent home by the office at the public expense. It need hardly be said that when a girl is found diseased she is sent to hospital and her inscription held over. It occasionally happens that virgins present themselves at the office and desire to be inscribed; in their case the officials use compulsion to rescue them from infamy.

In a word, the Paris system with regard to inscriptions is to inscribe no girl with regard to whom it is not manifest that she will carry on the calling of a prostitute whether she be inscribed or not.

From the following table, prepared by M. Parent-Duchatelet from the records of a series of years, it appears that the mistresses of houses inscribe over one third of the total prostitutes:

Girls inscribed at their own request		7388
" " by mistresses of houses		4436
" " by inspectors		720
Total		12544

The age at which girls can be inscribed has varied under different administrators. Under one it was seventeen, under his successor eighteen, under the next twenty-one years; but now the general rule is that no girl should be inscribed under the age of sixteen. Exceptions to this rule are made in the case of younger girls—of thirteen, fourteen, or fifteen, who lead a life of prostitution, and are frequently attacked by disease. From a regard to public health, they are inscribed notwithstanding their age.

Only second in importance to the subject of inscription is that of "radiation," the obliteration of an inscription. This is the process by which a prostitute takes leave of her calling, throws off the control of the police, and regains her civil rights. At Rome, as has been shown already, no such formality as radiation was known to the law; *once a prostitute, always a prostitute*, was the Roman rule. This system did not long sustain the test of a Christian examination.

The policy of the French *Bureau des Mœurs* on this head is governed by two very simple maxims: 1st. The amendment of prostitutes ought to be encouraged as much as possible; 2d. But no prostitute should be released from the supervision of the police and the visits of the Dispensary physicians until there is reasonable ground for believing that her repentance and alteration of life are sincere and likely to be permanent.

A person desiring to have her name struck from the rolls of

public women must make a written application, specifying her reasons for desiring to change her mode of life, and indicating the means of support on which she is henceforth to rely. In three cases the demand is granted forthwith: 1st. When the girl *proves* that she is about to marry; 2d. When she produces the certificate of a physician that she is attacked by an organic disease which renders it impossible for her to continue the calling of a prostitute; and, 3d. When she has gone to live with her relations, and produces evidence of her late good behavior.

In all other cases the office awards a "provisional radiation." For a period of time, which varies, according to circumstances, from three months to a year, the girl is still under the supervision of the police, such supervision being obviously secret and discreet. When the girl passes triumphantly through this period of probation, her name is definitely struck from the roll of prostitutes.

When a girl, after having her name thus struck out, desires to be inscribed afresh, her request is granted without delay or inquiry, it being wisely supposed that she has repented of her decision. A re-inscription also takes place when a girl, after radiation, is found in a house of prostitution even as a servant.

A prostitute is struck from the rolls by authority of the office when she has disappeared, and no trace of her has been found for three months.

M. Parent Duchatelet gives the following table of radiations, which, taken in connection with the table already given of the number of prostitutes registered, shows the movement of reform:

Years.	Women struck off the Rolls of Prostitutes			Years.	Women struck off the Rolls of Prostitutes		
	At their own request.	In consequence of absence.	Total.		At their own request.	In consequence of absence.	Total.
1817	485	575	1060	Bt. forw'd	4096	5650	9746
1818	477	582	1059	1826	486	554	1040
1819	469	571	1040	1827	490	542	1032
1820	415	716	1131	1828	572	415	987
1821	433	733	1166	1829	298	536	834
1822	417	739	1156	1830	334	502	836
1823	502	605	1107	1831	284	452	736
1824	442	602	1044	1832	449	718	1167
1825	456	527	983		7009	9369	16378
	4096	5650	9746				

Once inscribed, prostitutes are divided into three classes:

1st. Those who live in a licensed or "tolerated" brothel.

2d. Those who live alone in furnished rooms.

3d. Those who live in rooms which they furnish, and outwardly bear no mark of infamy.

In the eye of the law there is no difference between the three classes; all are equally subject to police and medical supervision. Every girl that is inscribed receives a card bearing her name, and the number of her page in the register; a blank column of this card is left to be filled by a memorandum of the date of each visit by the physicians of the Dispensary.

But the three classes differ in respect of the place where they are visited. The Dispensary physicians visit the inmates of brothels in the houses where they live; all other prostitutes visit them at the Dispensary. Yet another visit is made by the Dispensary physicians to the Dépôt, or Lock-up, at the Prefecture of Police; as there are always a certain number of prostitutes arrested for drunkenness or disorderly conduct every night, it was thought well to seize the opportunity of their confinement to inquire into the state of their health.

All houses of prostitution are visited by the Dispensary physicians once a week; the hour of the visit is known beforehand, and every girl must be present and pass inspection. The examination is private; the result is noted in a "folio" kept by the physician, and a corresponding memorandum is made in the pass-book of the house and on the card of the prostitute. When disease is detected, the mistress of the house is notified, and cautioned not to allow the girl diseased to receive any visitors. That afternoon, or the next morning, she comes or is brought to the Dispensary, where she undergoes a second examination, and, if the result is the same as at the first, she is forthwith sent to Saint Lazare for treatment.

Free prostitutes, that is to say, those who live in lodgings or rooms furnished by themselves, are bound to visit the Dispensary, and submit to examination once a fortnight. They choose the time and day themselves, but more than a fortnight must not elapse between the visits.

It appears, from tables published by M. Parent-Duchatelet, that these rules are strictly enforced. Free prostitutes are visited nearly thirty times a year, and prostitutes in tolerated houses more than fifty times. We have alluded elsewhere to the results of the visits.

Experience has proved that the only safe method of punishment for prostitutes is imprisonment. Formerly they were whipped, and at a later date their hair was cut off; but the humane spirit of modern legislation has rejected both these punishments as unduly cruel. At the present day, offenses against the rules concerning prostitution (*delits de prostitution*) are punished by imprisonment; misdemeanors and crimes provided against by the code being within the cognizance of the ordinary courts in the case of prostitutes as well as other persons.

Delits de prostitution have been divided by the *Bureau des Mœurs* into two classes, slight offenses and grave offenses; slight offenses are:

1. To appear in forbidden places.
2. To appear at forbidden hours.
3. To get drunk, and lie down in doorways, streets, or other thoroughfares.
4. To demand admittance to guard-houses.
5. To walk through the streets in daylight in such a way as to attract the notice of people passing.
6. To rap on the windows of their rooms.
7. To absent themselves from the medical inspection.
8. To beg.
9. To remain more than twenty-four hours in their house, after having been pronounced diseased by the physician.
10. To escape from the Hospital or Dispensary.
11. To go out of doors with bare head or neck.
12. To remain in Paris after having been ordered to leave, and presented with a passport.

This class of offenses is punished by imprisonment for not less than a fortnight or more than three months. One month is the usual term.

A prostitute is held to be guilty of grave offenses when she

1. Insults outrageously the visiting physician.
2. Fails to visit the Dispensary.
3. Continues to prostitute herself after being pronounced diseased.
4. Uses obscene language in public.
5. Appears naked at her window.
6. Assails men with violence, and endeavors to drag them to her home.

These offenses are punished by imprisonment for not less than three months, and not more than a year, rarely more than six months. The time is fixed in these cases with reference to the former character of the prostitute.

When a prostitute is arrested she is taken to the Prefecture of Police, where there is a room specially appropriated to her class. She is tried within forty-eight, usually within twenty-four hours of her arrival. When condemned, she is conveyed in a close carriage or van to the prison.

The prison at Paris usually contains from four hundred and fifty to six hundred inmates. They are all obliged to work. A few are generally found incapable, either from idiocy, blindness, or incorrigible obstinacy, of performing even the simplest work. These are lodged in a department called "the ward of the imbeciles." The others are allowed to choose their work; the bulk naturally take to sewing. They are paid a small sum for what they do, partly as they proceed with the work, and the balance when they leave the prison. Industrious girls receive, from the money coming to them, from five to eight *sous* daily. That this, added to the ample food supplied by the prison, suffices for their wants, is proved by the frequent purchases they make of flowers and other superfluities. Formerly, prostitutes in prison were not expected to work, and at this period fights and disturbances were of constant occurrence. Now the discipline is excellent and the prisoners orderly. The only penalty for disobedience of rules or misconduct is close confinement in the *cachot*.

M. Parent-Duchatelet admits that the prison discipline is so gentle that the punishment has no terrors for prostitutes. It is quite common to find girls who have been thirty times condemned to imprisonment. He recommends the use of the tread-mill as a corrective.

His experience led him to question the utility of nuns and priests in the prostitutes' prison. He does not think they do any good, and inclines to the belief that the counsels and visits of married women, who look rather to the moral than religious reform of the women, would be productive of more benefit.

The old practice in France was to admit visitors to the prostitutes' prison at certain hours and in a certain room, but this was found to be productive of great evils. The scenes in the visitors' room were outrageous, and a new system was accordingly adopted. No one was allowed to visit a prostitute but a *bona fide* relation, and even such a one was required to obtain a written permit from the Prefecture of Police.

A certain number of prostitutes are sent every year to the prison of St. Denis. These are those who, from physical or mental infirmities, such as recto-vaginal fistula, cancer, incurable organic disease, idiocy, etc., are incapacitated from pursuing their calling, and run risk of starvation. Not more than eight or ten of these are sent to St. Denis in the course of the year. The mortality among them there is not less than twenty-five per cent. per annum.[1]

Until a few years ago, a tax was levied on the Paris prostitutes for the support of the Dispensary. Each mistress of a house paid twelve francs per month; each girl living alone, three francs per month. A fine of two francs was also laid on all prostitutes who were behind their time in visiting the Dispensary. The product of these various taxes amounted to from seventy five to ninety thousand francs per annum. The system was abolished on the ground of its immorality. A popular notion is said to have prevailed that the police received half a million or more from the tax on prostitution, and attacks on the administration in consequence were incessant. The police authorities gave way at last, and the municipal council of the city undertook to defray the cost of the Dispensary for the future. Similar taxes appear to have existed at Lyons, Strasbourg, and other cities.[2]

Allusion has been made to inspectors. At the time M. Parent-Duchatelet wrote there were ten inspectors, who had each charge of one tenth of the city. Their business was to see that the regulations governing prostitutes were carried out. They arrested offending women, and transferred them to the Prefecture of Police. In case of resistance, they summoned the aid of the ordinary police of the ward. They were not allowed themselves to use violence either to arrest or drag a girl to prison. They were usually picked men of good character. Their salary was twelve hundred francs a year, besides handsome presents.[3]

In conclusion, a word must be said of the establishment called the *Bon Pasteur*. It is a Magdalen Asylum established many years ago by some benevolent ladies, and now mainly supported by an annual vote from the city of Paris, and an allowance from the hospitals. It receives prostitutes who desire to reform; feeds, clothes, and instructs them; provides them with places when they desire to leave, or with work when they wish to remain in the establishment. The rule is that no prostitute can be received under eighteen or over twenty-five years of age. Beyond these limits it has been found that the humane efforts of the directresses of the establishment have rarely led to any result. No compulsion is used in any case by the managers. Girls are free to leave as they are free to come. So long as they remain, however, they must conform to the rules of the establishment, which are strict

---

[1] Parent-Duchatelet. ii. 273.   [2] Id. ii. 398.   [3] Id. ii. 403.

without being monastic. The average admissions to the asylum for the first twelve years of its existence were twenty per annum. The mortality among the residents was very large, being equal to twenty per cent. on the t tal number during the twelve years. Of the whole number (two hundred and forty-five), forty were dismissed for insubordination twenty-seven left of their own accord, and probably returned to heir old courses, and fifteen were returned to the police. The remainder were either restored to their families, or placed in situations in the hospitals or elsewhere.

Small as these numbers appear in comparison with the large army of prostitutes exercising their calling at Paris, it is not at all doubtful but the establishment is a useful one. No one can help but concur with M. Parent-Duchatelet when he observes that, "did it not exist, it would be necessary to create it."

NOTE.—As M. Parent-Duchatelet has written the best, we might almost say the only philosophical work on prostitution extant, it may be useful to subjoin the text of the statute which he proposed to regulate the subject of prostitution.

LAW RELATIVE TO THE REPRESSION OF PROSTITUTION.

Art. 1. The duty of repressing prostitution, whether with provocation on the public highway or otherwise, is intrusted at Paris to the Prefect of Police, and in all the other *communes* of France to the mayors respectively.

Art. 2. A discretionary authority over all persons engaged in public prostitution is vested in these functionaries, within the scope of their powers.

Art. 3. Shall constitute evidence of public prostitution either, 1st, direct provocation thereto on the public highway; 2d, public notoriety; or, 3d, legal proof adduced after accusation and trial.

Art. 4. The Prefect of Police at Paris, and the mayors in the other *communes*, shall make any and all regulations which they may deem suitable for the repression of prostitution, and such regulations shall bear upon all those who encourage prostitution as a trade—lodgers, inn-keepers and tavern-keepers, landlords and tenants.

Art. 5. The Dispensary at Paris for the superintendence of women of the town is placed on the same footing as the public health establishments. Other similar dispensaries may be established wherever they are needed.

Art. 6. A full report of the proceedings of these dispensaries shall be forwarded annually to the Minister of the Interior.

M. Duchatelet conceived this short law to be adequate for the purpose. It may be presumed that he took for granted that the mayors of the *com-*

munes would never attempt to carry out original views of their own on the subject; he doubtless gave them credit for sufficient self-abnegnation to adopt, without question, the elaborate and sensible plan which experience has taught the authorities of Paris. How far this assumption was justifiable appears uncertain, in view of the fact that at Lyons and Strasbourg, the prostitutional system has always differed from that of the capital. In both those cities a tax has been levied on prostitutes till a very late period; at Lyons it was exacted, it is believed, in 1842.

CHAPTER XI.

ITALY.

Decline of Public Morals.—Papal Court.—Nepotism.—John XXII.—Sextus IV. —Alexander VI.—Effect of the Reformation.—Poem of Fracastoro.—Benvenuto Cellini.—Beatrice Cenci.—Laws of Naples.—Pragmatic Law of 1470.—Court of Prostitutes.—Bull of Clement II.—Prostitution in Lombardy and Piedmont. —Clerical Statute.—Modern Italy.—Laws of Rome.—Public Hospitals.—Lazaroni of Naples.—Italian Manners as depicted by Lord Byron.—Foundling Hospitals.—True Character of Italian People.

BIRTH-PLACE of modern art and literature, dowered with the fatal heritage of beauty, Italy, in the varied passages of her career among the nations, has been as remarkable for the vice and sensuality of her children as she has been eminent for their talents and acquirements.

The heart of the historical student thrills with respectful sympathy over the sorrows and ennobling virtues of her patriots in all ages, or his intellect is captivated with enthusiastic admiration and reverence in considering the monuments of resplendent genius given to mankind by her sons. Let him turn the page, and his soul recoils in disgust and deepest horror from the narrative of corruption the most abandoned, ambition the most unscrupulous, lust the most abominable, crime the most tremendous, to which the history of the world scarcely offers a parallel, and which brands the perpetrators with the execration of all succeeding generations.

The most glorious era of the Italian republics immediately preceded their downfall. Like shining lights, they perished by their own effulgence. The mutual jealousies of Florence, Pisa, Genoa, Lucca, and the numerous independent cities and states, stirred up in them a "noble and emulous rage" to excel each other in the encouragement they gave to art and letters, and the mighty works produced by their respective citizens. But the same sentiment also roused them to deadlier feuds, and the common field of national patriotism being shut up, they exhausted themselves and each other by desperately-protracted struggles and incredible sacrifices of blood and treasure. Thus they paved the way to the introduction of the foreigner and the mercenary, who completed their ruin; until, in place of the small but illustrious republics which formed a diadem of brightest gems, arose a system of petty tyrants, who plunged the country into misery and degradation. These, in turn, were swept away by the strong arm of a despotism which has never since relaxed its grasp of this loveliest country of the earth.

No influence played a more important part in bringing about this catastrophe than that of the court of Rome. By the intrigues of the Roman pontiffs the mutual jealousies of the states were exacerbated and their quarrels fomented. While these results were caused by the political actions of the popes and their advisers, the worst effects were produced upon public manners and morals by their example. The abuses which had established themselves among the Roman hierarchy were the natural consequences of long and undisturbed enjoyment by the clergy of their vast immunities and privileges. The demoralization and dissoluteness which thus existed, and which spread its poison throughout the civilized world, but especially throughout Italy, are attested to posterity by all contemporary writers.

The enormous iniquity which distinguished such men as John XXII., Sextus IV., or Alexander VI., is notorious to all. Although the character of communities is not to be inferred from the actions of exceptional prodigies, either of virtue or vice, it is evident that the system which could place monsters like these in the august positions they filled must have been rotten to the core. The worth of a Leo X. or a Clement VII. consisted in the absence of the grosser vices rather than in any positive excellence, and the encouragement given by such men to objectionable practices did more to confirm a laxity of morals than the odious and unpardonable offenses of their predecessors.

Some of the political profligacy of the court of Rome, and, through its example, of the other Italian courts, was owing to the system which had sprung up of each pope providing for his family. The term *nepote* (nephew) was in common use as expressing the relationship which existed between the pope and the individuals selected for advancement. The priests of all denominations had nephews and nieces to provide for, and the abuses covered by the term were objects of the keenest satire. In fact, Innocent VIII. thus provided for eight openly avowed sons and daughters.[1] The pseudo-avuncular obligations of Sextus IV. were also well known. Other popes, whose sins were not in this particular direction, having no sons, adopted a *bona fide* nephew, and one or two, feeling the want of ties of kindred or family relationship, actually adopted strangers. In one instance, the Donna Olimpia, a niece by marriage, and "a lady of ability and a manly spirit," took the place of a nephew in the court of Innocent X., without any imputation on the character of either pope or niece.[2]

The effect produced by this example in high places, particularly upon the clergy, and through them on the community, can be imagined. By a decree of the Church in the eleventh session of the Lateran Council it appears that the clergy were accustomed to live in a state of public concubinage, nay, more, to allow others to do so for money paid to them by permission. Dante, in one of his daring flights, compares the papal court to Babylon, and declares it a place deprived of virtue and shame. In the nineteenth canto of the Inferno, Dante, visiting hell, finds Nicholas III. there waiting the arrival of Boniface, who again is to be succeeded by Clement.

The Reformation compelled some attention to morals among the clergy, and for a time an earnest endeavor was made at a purification of the Church. This was one of the chief labors of the famous Council of Trent. That council certainly did repress the abuses among the general clergy, but the law-makers were law-breakers. They could not touch the cardinals, archbishops, or the Pope himself, and thus little radical change was effected among the chief dignitaries.[3]

There are not wanting writers who acquit the Italian national character of blame in the matter, attributing the general corruption partly to the frightful example of foreign invaders. The in-

[1] Dennistoun's Dukes of Urbino; Ranke's History of the Popes; Gibbon's Rome.

[2] Ranke, ii. Appendix.

[3] In 1849, when the Roman people opened the palace of the Inquisition, there was found in the library a department styled "Summary of Solicitations," being a record of cases in which women had been solicited to acts of criminality by their confessors in the pontifical state, and the summary is not brief.—Dwight's "Roman Republic in 1849," p. 115.

vasion of Charles VIII., himself a dissolute monarch, with the universal licentiousness of the French troops, did undoubtedly contribute largely to ruin the morals of the people at large, but, to use the words of Machiavelli, " If the papal court were removed to Switzerland, the simplest and most religious people of Europe would, in an incredibly short time, have become utterly depraved by the vicious example of the Italian priesthood."[1]

The ecclesiastics did not confine themselves to licentiousness of conduct. The clerical writers are charged with a taste for that lowest practice of debased minds, obscenity, in which particular they exceed the lay writers. Roscoe, an accomplished Italian scholar and a man not given to railing, maintains this allegation.[2] This reminds us of Pope's lines:

" Immodest words admit of no defense,
For want of decency is want of sense."

For the limited range of our present subject, history, so profuse of illustration of war, bloodshed, and the personal adventures of men noteworthy by their position or character, is exceedingly chary of materials. In the case of Italy the testimony as to the morals of men in high places is superabundant, and these and the legislative enactments of the period will furnish some of the information of which we are in search.

In the fifteenth century, Charles VIII., in his wars to gain Naples from the Spaniards, drew down unspeakable miseries upon the wretched Italians. His armies are reputed to have indulged in every excess of unbridled license and rapine; and it was during the siege of Naples that the venereal disease is said to have first made its appearance, although the particulars given of this malady in Chapter IX., under the head of France, show that syphilis existed in Naples two or three years before the siege. As generally happens with new diseases, whether from fear or ignorance of the means to control them, it was represented that the affliction was of a malignity never since known. Its frightful ravages and disgusting character impressed the minds of men with a belief that it was a new scourge, sent specially as a punishment for the debauchery and prostitution of the period, each party retorting on the other the charge of having introduced it, and styling it *Morbo-Gallico* or *Mal de Naples*, according to the nation to which they belonged. No class seems to have been exempt from it. Sextus

[1] Discorsi, i. 12.　　　　　　　　[2] Life of Leo X. Appendix.

della Rovere, nephew of Sextus IV., one of the wealthiest and most dissolute ecclesiastics of the age, was "rotten from his middle to the soles of his feet."[1]   Even the haughty and majestic Julius II. would not expose his feet to the obeisance of the faithful, because they were discolored by the Morbus Gallicus:[2]   Leo, his accomplished and munificent successor, was said to have owed his elevation to the fact that he was in such a depraved state of body as to render necessary a surgical operation in the Consistorium while the election was proceeding, the cardinals selecting the most sickly candidate for the papal tiara.[3]   An unequivocal allusion to the pontiff's pursuits is found in an honorary inscription to Leo X. on his entrance into Florence, of which he was a native.

> *Olim habuit Cypris sua tempora : tempora Mavos*
> *Olim habuit ; nunc sua tempora Pallas habet :*
> *Mars fuit ; est Pallas ; Cypra semper erit.*
> Formerly Venus reigned supreme, then Mars, now Pallas:
> Mars was, Pallas now is, Venus shall always be.

Cardinals were not ashamed to contend openly for the favors of celebrated courtesans, and Charles VIII., when on his march to Naples, was provided by Ludovico Sforza and his wife Beatrice, his liberal entertainers, with the most beautiful women that could be procured.[4]   Charles, indeed, is by some authors asserted to have been actually the first who introduced the venereal disease into Italy.

An eccentric trophy of public license is to be found in the poem of Fracastoro, a physician and accomplished writer—a really elegant production under the title of Syphilis.   The argument of it is drawn from the sufferings of Syphilus, a shepherd who has been punished by Apollo with a malignant disease for impiety.   In this work the author introduces the reader to the inner regions of the earth ; to the mines, minerals, and attendant sprites, and explains the discovery of mercury, and its beneficent and healing influences on the invalid, who, once cured, is enjoined to pay his vows to Diana.

In 1520, that turbulent and reprobate artist Benvenuto Cellini, in his autobiography (one of the most spirited representations of national manners extant) gives an account of a syphilitic disease which he contracted from a courtesan.   He says little of the mode

---

[1] Fabronius, Leo X. p. 287.
[2] Paris de Grassine, Memoirs of the Court of Julius II. p. 579.
[3] Jovius, lib. iii. p. 56.   [4] De Commines, v. ii. c. 6.

of cure, but it is evident from the above that the use of mercury was known at a very early period after public attention was generally directed to the disorder.

The excesses of this iron age were not limited to ordinary licentiousness; crimes against nature seem to have been prevalent, and are even alleged to have been a source of revenue. In a collection of papal lives which has fallen under our notice, but which is not very particular in giving its authorities,[1] we find it stated that a memorial was presented to Sextus IV. by certain individuals of the family of the Cardinal of St. Lucia for an indulgence to commit sodomy, and that the Pope wrote at the bottom of it the usual "*Fiat.*"

The case of Beatrice Cenci is better attested. Every one recollects the accumulated horrors of the story. The father, hating his children, his wife, all mankind, introduces prostitutes to his house, and debauches his daughter Beatrice by force. Through the instrumentality of a bishop she procures him to be murdered, and, with her step-mother, was executed for the crime, the Pope refusing to show any mercy. The Count Cenci had been addicted to unnatural offenses, and had thrice compounded with the papal government for his crimes by paying an enormous sum of money, and the narrator says that the acrimony of the Pope toward the wretched daughter was for having cut off a profitable source of revenue.

In Naples, the laws on the subject of prostitution were extremely severe. Previous to the thirteenth century, every procuress endeavoring to corrupt innocent females was punished, like an adulteress, by mutilation of her nose. The mother who prostituted her daughter suffered this punishment until King Frederick absolved such women as trafficked with their children from the pressure of want. The same prince, however, decreed against all who were found guilty of preparing drugs or inflammatory liquors to aid in their designs upon virtuous females, death in case of injuries resulting from their acts, and imprisonment when no serious harm was effected. These laws proved insufficient for their purpose, and toward the end of the fifteenth century profligacy ran riot in Naples. Ruffiani multiplied in its streets, procuring by force or corruption multitudes of victims to fill the taverns and brothels of the city. Penalties of extreme severity were proclaimed against them. The Ruffiani were ordered to quit the

---

[1] The Roman Pontiffs. New York, 1845.

kingdom, and prostitutes were prohibited from harboring such persons among them.   Any woman who disobeyed was condemned to be burned in the forehead with an iron, whipped in the most humiliating manner, a¹ d exiled.

Under King Roger a cha ge of seduction was never taken, but William, the successor of ¹ ¹at prince, punished with death the crime of rape.   The victim, however, was required to prove that she had shrieked aloud, and that she had preferred her complaint within eight days, or that she had been detained by force.   When once a woman had prostituted herself, she had no right to refuse to yield her person to any one.

In Naples, prostitutes, in spite of the law passed to confine brothels to particular quarters, established themselves in the most beautiful streets of the city in palatial buildings, and there, with incessant clamor, congregated a horde of thieves, profligates, and vagabonds of every kind, until the chief quarter became uninhabitable.   In 1577 they were ordered to quit the street of Catalana within eight days, under pain of the scourge for the women, the galleys for such of the proprietors as were commoners, while simple banishment was declared against the nobles.

One example of good legislation was the pragmatic law of 1470, to protect unfortunate women against the cupidity, the extortions, and the frauds of tavern-keepers and others.   Men were in the habit of going into places of amusement with single girls, contracting a heavy debt, and then leaving their victims to pay. These were then given the choice of a disgraceful whipping or an engagement in the house.   They often consented, and spent the remainder of their days in dependence on their creditors, without ability to liberate themselves.   By the new law, masters of taverns were forbidden to give credit to prostitutes for more than a certain sum, and this only to supply them with food and clothing absolutely necessary.   If they exceeded this amount they had no means of legal recovery.

The most remarkable feature in Neapolitan legislation on this subject was the establishment at an unknown, but early date, of the Court of Prostitutes.   This tribunal, which sat at Naples, had its peculiar constitution, and had jurisdiction over all cases connected with prostitution, blasphemy, and some other infamous offenses.   Toward the end of the sixteenth century it had risen to extraordinary power, and was prolific of abuses.   It practiced all kinds of exaction and violence, every species of partiality and injustice, and even presumed to promulgate edicts of its own. The judges flung into prison numbers of young girls, whom they compelled to buy their liberty with money, and sometimes even dared to seize women who, though of lax conduct, could not be included in the professional class. This was discovered, and led to a reform of the court in 1589. Its powers were strictly defined, and its form of procedure placed under regulation, while the avenues to corruption were narrowed. The institution existed for nearly a hundred years after this.

In Rome, in the eleventh century, a brothel and a church stood side by side, and five hundred years after, under the pontificate of Paul II., prostitutes were numerous. Statutes were enacted, and many precautions taken, which prove the grossness of manners at that epoch. One convicted of selling a girl to infamy was heavily fined, and if he did not pay within ten days had one foot cut off. The nobility and common people alike indulged habitually in all kinds of excess. Tortures, floggings, brandings, banishment, were inflicted on some to terrify others, but with very incomplete success. To carry off and detain a prostitute against her will was punished by amputation of the right hand, imprisonment, flogging, or exile. The rich, however, invariably bought immunity for themselves.

Among the most extraordinary acts of legislation on this subject was the bull of Clement II., who desired to endow the Church with the surplus gains of the brothel. Every person guilty of prostitution was forced, when disposing of her property, either at death or during life, to assign half of it to a convent. This regulation was easily eluded, and proved utterly inefficacious. A tribunal was also established having jurisdiction over brothels, upon which a tax was laid, continuing in existence until the middle of the sixteenth century. Efforts were made to confine this class of dwellings to a particular quarter, but without success.

In some of the Italian states, as in Lombardy, men were forbidden to give prostitutes an asylum. They were prohibited from appearing among honest citizens, and were prevented from purchasing clothes or food, and from borrowing money by the hire of their persons.

After a time, however, a system of licensed brothels, in imitation of the institutions founded at Toulouse and Montpellier, was introduced into parts of Italy, and the brothels became very numerous. There was one at Mantua, and Venice was a very sink

L

of prostitution.   In 1421, the government enlisted women in this service to guard the virtue of the other classes.   A matron was placed over them, who governed them, received their gains, and made a monthly division of profit.   The names of several women, the most notorious and beautiful of the Venetian courtesans, are preserved by Nicolo Daglioni.   A very small sum was paid them by their patrons.

The laws regulating prostitution and prostitutes seem to have had a wonderful similarity throughout Europe.   Among other enactments were those regulating clothing, which were at one time promulgated in every state.   Some of these were sumptuary, and merely prohibited the wearing of fashionable attire.   Others directed particular costumes as a badge of the prostitute's calling, and to distinguish them in public from well-conducted women. At Mantua, prostitutes, when they appeared in the streets, were ordered to cover the rest of their clothes with a short white cloak, and wear a badge on their breast.   At Bergamo the cloak was yellow ; in Parma, white ; in Milan, at first black woolen cloth, and then black silk.   If disobedient, they might be fined ; and in case of a second offense, whipped ; and any one might strip off the garment of a girl illegally attired.

In the Duchy of Asola, in Piedmont, a regulation was established that a mother could disinherit her daughter for leading a vicious life, but she lost this privilege if it was proved that she had connived at her immorality.   The father had equal authority, but with one curious limitation.   When, says the law, a father has sought to marry his daughter, and has endowed her sufficiently, if she refuses to marry and becomes a prostitute, he may cut her off ; but if he have opposed her marriage until she has reached the age of twenty-five, and she then become a libertine, he can not refuse to bequeath her his property ; and the woman, on every opportunity to marry, is bound to present herself before her father and demand his consent.   If he refused it, he was not allowed to punish her in cases where, at the age of thirty, she became a harlot.

The efforts to root out prostitution from houses and neighborhoods in Italy had, as elsewhere, the result of driving loose women to places of public resort.   The baths were regularly frequented in every city in the Peninsula (hence the use of the word *bagnio*, as expressive of a disreputable place), so that there was scarcely a bath-keeper who was not also a brothel-keeper.

In Avignon, which, in consequence of the schism of the popes, may be considered a second Rome, a statute of the Church, in 1441, interdicted to the priests and clergy the use of certain baths, notorious as brothels. The license of prostitution was soon taken away in Avignon. The residence of the popes in that city had attracted a concourse of strangers from all parts of the globe, and brothels sprung up at the doors of the churches, and close to the papal residence and bishops' palaces. They brought so much scandal on the community that an edict was passed driving prostitutes out of the city.

In endeavoring to investigate the condition of prostitution in modern Italy, our inquiries and researches have been almost profitless, from the dearth of reliable statistical information as to any part of that most interesting country. In the fine arts, and in certain departments of abstract science, the republic of letters can show numerous records of Italy's state and progress. In all that tells of the people, their condition, their relations to each other, and their rulers, the statements of writers, both native and foreign, are so contradictory, so imbued with party passions and prejudices, or so flippantly careless and inaccurate, that we must peruse them with constant suspicion. At the same time, official documents are so sparingly given to the world that it is hopeless to fall back upon them.[1]

It is customary to think and speak of Italy, like Germany, as a whole. In reality, however, a wide difference prevails among the inhabitants of Piedmont, Tuscany, and Austrian Italy, the Papal States, and Naples. Rome, though not the political capital of Italy, must be considered the capital, in virtue of her papal court, her past traditions, and her large concourse of foreigners. But even her manners scarcely give the tone to the remainder of the country.

In Rome, prostitution is tolerated, though not legally permitted. There are no statistics from which the number of prostitutes can be calculated. At one time there were said to be five thousand of these unfortunates in the city; but this estimate is only another sample of the carelessness which is to be observed in writers on this subject. Under Paul IV. there were only fifty thousand inhabitants; forty years after they had increased to one hundred thousand. Public prostitutes are now as rarely seen in

---

[1] After the occupation by the French in 1809, a collection of facts was made by the French authorities, with a view to a census, but this we have been unable to obtain.

the streets of Rome as in those of other Italian cities.   It is said, also, that there are scarcely any public brothels.[1]   There is a law that a woman guilty of adultery shall be imprisoned for three months, but Italian usages are averse to legal proceedings; the scandal is offensive to society; besides, the courts require positive proof of the offense.   With regard to seduction, the laws are equally stringent; but such cases, when brought to notice, are usually compromised by permission of the authorities, either by payment of a sum of money, or by marriage.   Syphilis is always of considerable extent in Rome, and the venereal ward in San Jacomo is always full.[2]   After the siege of Rome by the French in 1849, the disease was frightfully prevalent.

In 1798 there were thirty thousand poor, or about one fifth of the population of Rome, upon the lists of the curates of the several parishes.   Under the administration of the French, up to 1814, the proportion had been diminished to one ninth.   Since that period it has been on the increase.

There are in Rome nineteen hospitals for the treatment of the sick.   In eight public hospitals the average number of patients daily is about fourteen hundred, who cost nineteen cents each per day.   There are fourteen semi-convents where young girls are gratuitously received and educated, receiving a small dowry when they leave to marry or become nuns.   The Hospital of St. Roch is for pregnant women.[3]

The Albergo dei Poveri at Naples is the finest poor-house in Italy.   It accommodates upward of three thousand paupers of both sexes, and is provided with workshops and schools, so as to afford suitable employment and instruction.   Notwithstanding this model establishment, and numerous others, whose annual revenues amount to nearly two millions and a half of dollars, Naples is infested with a large mendicant population in addition to the numbers accommodated in the poor-houses.   The Lazaroni are a class peculiar to the place.   Many of them utterly refuse to work, and prefer to subsist on the smallest coin of the kingdom which they can gain by begging.   They bask in the sun all day, sleep on the ground or on the steps at night, and starve with the utmost complacency.   An Epicurean might find in this abnegation of the cares of life a sound practical philosophy.   That such a class is in the highest degree obnoxious to society must be ap-

---

[1] Vedical and Chirurgical Review, April, 1854.   [2] Ibid.
[3] Harper's Magazine, February, 1855, p. 326 ; Italian Life and Morals.

parent to every one. In the famous rising of Cardinal Ruffo, at the time of the French occupation in 1805, the Lazaroni perpetrated the most frightful excesses, and are said to have been relied on by the imbecile Bourbon government as their chief friends and supporters against the dangers of French Republicanism. Modern progress has drawn even Naples and the Lazaroni within its magic circle, and an accomplished traveler expresses doubts of their alleged unconquerable laziness, for he has seen them work, wear clothes, sleep at home, earn money when they had a chance, and conduct themselves very much like other people.[1] Perhaps, as with the Irish, a want of fair remuneration may be at the root of their idleness.

A singular institution of Italian society is the *Cicisbeo*, or *Cavaliere Servente*. This is a distant male relative, or friend, who invariably attends a married lady on all occasions of her appearance in public. He pays her all conceivable attentions, and performs even the most servile offices; carries her fan, her parasol, or her lapdog. We are not aware that any foreigner has been able to settle this anomaly of social life to his satisfaction. The Italians themselves sometimes maintain that there is no immorality or impropriety in the arrangement—that it is a matter of etiquette, in which the heart is in no way concerned. The husband is perfectly cognizant of it, and the appearance of the cicisbeo with the lady is more *de regle* than that of her husband. Originally, there can be very little question that the institution was of an amorous character, and the parties met privately at the Casini, where certain apartments were specially dedicated to the use of the ladies and their cavalieri.[2] With the French occupation of 1800 the custom became the subject of immoderate raillery and satire, and there is reason to believe it has been but partially revived.

In place, however, of the cicisbeo or cavaliere servente, whose services and attentions were a form of society, it is, we fear, undeniable that more intimate though less avowed relations exist between many Italian ladies and other men than their husbands. That there are numerous and admirable exceptions to the rule, if it be a rule, we freely admit; but, unless the concurrent testimony of all writers and travelers in Italy be absolutely false, and either basely slanderous or culpably careless, the marriage vow can only be regarded as a cloak for a license that is inadmissible to the unmarried woman.

[1] Rome, by a New Yorker, 1845.   [2] Sharpe's Letters from Italy, 1705.

The testimony of a profligate man is rarely to be taken against women; and though the witness be a lord and a poet, we do not know that this should make a difference were the case one of mere abuse. Coupled, however, as the inculpation is with extenuatory remarks, we think Lord Byron's observations valuable. In a letter to Mr. Murray, the celebrated London publisher (February 21, 1820), he says:

" You ask me for a volume of manners in Italy. Perhaps I am in the case to know more of them than most Englishmen. * * * * * I have lived in their houses, and in the heart of their families, sometimes merely as *Amico di Casa*, and sometimes as *Amico di Cuore* of the *Dama*, and in neither case do I feel justified in making a book of them. Their moral is not your moral; their life is not your life; you would not understand it; it is not English, nor French, nor German, which you would all understand. * * * * * I know not how to make you comprehend a people who are at once temperate and profligate, serious in their characters and buffoons in their amusements, capable of impressions and passions which are at once sudden and durable. * * * * * I should know something of the matter, having had a pretty general experience among their women, from the fisherman's wife up to the *Nobil Dama* whom I serve. * * * * * They are extremely tenacious, and jealous as furies, not permitting their lovers even to marry if they can help it, and keeping them always to them in public as in private. * * * * * The reason is, that they marry for their parents and love for themselves. They exact fidelity from a lover as a debt of honor, while they pay the husband as a tradesman. You hear a person's character, male or female, canvassed, not as depending on their conduct to their husbands or wives, but to their mistress or lover. If I wrote a quarto I don't know that I could do more than amplify what I have here noted. It is to be observed, that while they do all this, the greatest outward respect is to be paid to the husbands, not only by the ladies, but by their *serventi*, particularly if the husband serve no one himself (which is not often the case, however), so that you would often suppose them relations, the *servente* making the figure of one adopted in the family. Sometimes the ladies run a little restive, and elope, or divide, or make a scene, but this is at the starting, generally when they know no better, or when they fall in love with a foreigner, or some such anomaly, and is always reckoned unnecessary and extravagant."

As a counterpoise to these opinions of Lord Byron, it is but fair to give that of M. Valery, a traveler whose personal opportunities may have been less than in the case of the noble poet: " The morals of the Italian cities, which we still judge of from the commonplace reports of travelers of the last century, are now neither better nor worse than those of other capitals; perhaps at Naples they are even better.

The Countess Pepoli, a lady of patriotic and literary family, has written an able educational manual, in which she claims consideration for the number of "good and virtuous women" in Italy, whose existence is ignored by the prejudiced writers of extravagant diatribes. But we are afraid that the very exception, and the pains she takes to prove the temptations to which the married woman is exposed, only affirm the truth of the general charge.

Whatever allegations of veracious or exaggerated unchastity or immorality may be made against the Italians, they are generally to be laid at the door of the aristocracy and upper classes. Among the humbler Italians, the peasantry and the country poor, there is no ground for ascribing to them either greater idleness or worse morals than are to be found in other parts of Europe.

Foundling hospitals are to be met with in most great cities of Continental Europe. Among Protestants, a strong prejudice exists against these institutions. That they prevent infanticide is self-evident. Their operation as an encouragement of illicit intercourse can not be estimated without some minute inquiries into the illegitimacy of places which encourage them, and of others which are without them.

The proportion of children in the foundling hospitals of Italy is certainly large, but it is believed, on good grounds, that a considerable number of them are legitimate, and are abandoned by their parents on account of their poverty. Of the really illegitimate, there are no means of saying with accuracy (nor, as far as we know, have any attempts been made to do so) to what class of society the infants belong. Meanwhile, although there is no ground for assuming a larger proportion of illegitimate children than in northern climates, on the other hand, the publicly displayed prostitution of Italy is infinitely less.

Naples has a population of about four hundred thousand. Of fifteen thousand births there are two thousand foundlings; we can not say illegitimates, for, owing to the reasons already specified, there are no means of ascertaining the facts.

In Tuscany, in 1834, there were twelve thousand foundlings received into the various hospitals.

The Hospital of the Santo Spirito at Rome is a foundling asylum with a revenue of about fifty thousand dollars per annum.

About one in sixteen of these children is claimed by its parents;

the majority are cared for, during infancy and childhood, either in
the hospitals or with the neighboring peasantry, with whom they
are boarded at a small stipend. When of sufficient age they are
dismissed to work for themselves; but in many of the hospitals
they have some claim in after-life on occasions of distress.

We have already alluded to the wide differences of national
character in the various political divisions of Italy. The vices of
laziness, mendicancy, and their kindred failings of licentiousness
and unchastity are chiefly confined to the towns, large and small.[1]
The peasantry of Naples and of the Papal States are industrious,
temperate; and the peasant women, even those who, from the vicinity of Rome, frequent the studios of the artists as models, are
generally of unexceptionable character.[2] The mountaineers of
the Abruzzi, long infamous as banditti (a stigma affixed by the
French or other dominant powers on those who resisted their
rule), in harvest-time brave the deadly malaria of the Campagna
to earn a few liri honestly for their starving children, although in
so doing the many that never return to their mountain homes
show the risks that all have run. The corn, wine, and oil raised
in Italy, the well-supplied markets of Rome and other cities, are
evidence that the peasantry do not all eat the bread of idleness.
The Papal States contain some of the finest, richest, and best
cultivated provinces in Italy.[3] It is in the towns we must look
for the worst results of misgovernment and bad example.

CHAPTER XII.

SPAIN.

Resemblance between Spanish and Roman Laws on Prostitution.—Code of Alphonse IX.—Result of Draconian Legislation.—Ruffiani.—Court Morals.—
Brothels —Valencia.—Laws for the Regulation of Vice.—Concubines legally
recognized. — Syphilis.—Cortejo.—Reformatory Institutions at Barcelona.—
Prostitution in Spain at the Present day.—Madrid Foundling Hospital.

BETWEEN the ancient Spaniards and the Romans a most intimate connection subsisted from an early period of the Roman republic, and the laws and customs of the former bore the closest resemblance to those of the latter. This affinity continued so long

[1] History of Italy: Family Library, vol. iii.
[2] Roman Republic, 1849 ; Rome, by a New Yorker.   [3] Valery.

as the Roman empire had a name, and after the establishment of Christianity as the state religion, the ties of kindred and dependence were drawn still closer, for the Spanish kingdom has ever been the favored heritage, and its rulers the most obedient sons of Rome. Thus the maxims of the Roman civil law were early incorporated into the political system, and they still remain the chief pillars of Spanish jurisprudence. Accordingly, we find, in their legislation on prostitution, that the Spaniards, together with the general theories, adopted the specific enactments of other Latin nations.

By the code of Alphonse IX., in the twelfth century, procurers were to be condemned to "civil death." Such offenders were thus classified :

1. Men who trafficked in debauchery ; these were to be banished.

2. Keepers of houses of accommodation, who were to be fined, and their houses confiscated.

3. Brothel-keepers who hired out prostitutes, which prostitutes, if slaves, were to be manumitted ; if free, were to be dowried at the cost of the offenders, so that they might have a chance of marriage.

4. Husbands conniving at the prostitution or dishonor of their wives ; these were liable to capital punishment.

5. A class of persons styled Ruffiani (whence the modern word ruffian).

These latter were analogous to the pimp and bully of the present day, and, from the repeated and very severe laws against them, seem to have given great trouble to the authorities. They were banished, flogged, imprisoned ; in short, got rid of on any terms. Girls who supported them were publicly whipped, and the general laws upon the matter were similar to those noted in the previous chapter on Italy.

In Spain, the profligacy of public morals attained a pitch beyond all precedent, possibly owing, in some measure, to Draconian legislation. Further laws were, from time to time, passed against the Ruffiani, as preceding edicts had fallen into desuetude, and their presence and traffic was encouraged by the prostitutes. These latter were forbidden to harbor the men, and on breach of this prohibition were to be branded, publicly whipped, and banished the kingdom. Procurers, procuresses, adulteresses, and mothers who trafficked in their children's virtue, *except under pressure of extreme want*, were punished by mutilation of the nose.

In 1552 and 1566, edicts were again passed against the Ruffiani.

They were styled a highly objectionable class, dangerous to public order. On the first conviction as a ruffiano, the offender was sentenced to ten years at the galleys; for a second conviction, he received two hundred blows, and sent to the galleys for life.

Up to this time the court of Spain seems to have been almost as strongly tinctured with licentiousness as those of other nations. About the middle of the fifteenth century, Henry IV. divorced his wife, Blanche of Aragon, after a union of twelve years, the marriage being publicly declared void by the Bishop of Segovia, whose sentence was confirmed by the Archbishop of Toledo, "*por impotencia respectiva*, owing to some malign influence." Henry subsequently espoused Joanna, sister of Alphonse V., King of Portugal. The bride was accompanied by a brilliant train of maidens, and her entrance into Castile was greeted by the festivities and military pageants which belonged to the age of chivalry. In her own country Joanna had been ardently beloved; in the land of her adoption her light and lively manners gave occasion to the grossest suspicions. Scandal named the Cavalier Beltran de la Cueva as her most favored lover. He was one of the handsomest men in the kingdom. At a tournament near Madrid he maintained the superior beauty of his mistress against all comers, and displayed so much prowess in the presence of the king as induced Henry to commemorate the event by the erection of a monastery dedicated to St. John.[1] It does not appear, however, whom Beltran de la Cueva indicated as the lady of his love on this occasion.

Two anecdotes may be mentioned as characteristic of the gallantry of the times. The Archbishop of Seville concluded a superb *fête*, given in honor of the royal nuptials, by introducing on the table two vases filled with rings garnished with precious stones, to be distributed among his female guests. At a ball given on another occasion, the young queen having condescended to dance with the French embassador, the latter made a solemn vow never to dance with any other woman.

While the queen's levity laid her open to suspicion, the licentiousness of her husband was undisguised. One of Joanna's maids of honor acquired an ascendency over Henry which he did not attempt to conceal, and after the exhibition of some disgraceful scenes, the palace became divided by the factions of the hostile

[1] Prescott, History of Ferdinand and Isabella, i. 66.

fair ones. The Archbishop of Seville did not blush to espouse the cause of the paramour, who maintained a magnificence of state which rivaled royalty itself. The public were still more scandalized by Henry's sacrilegious intrusion of another of his mistresses into the post of abbess of a convent in Toledo, after the expulsion of her predecessor, a lady of irreproachable character.

These examples of corruption influenced alike the people and the clergy. The middle class imitated their superiors, and indulged in an excess of luxury equally demoralizing and ruinous. The Archbishop of St. James was hunted from his see by the indignant populace in consequence of an outrage attempted on a youthful bride as she was returning from church after the performance of the nuptial ceremony.[1]

Under the reign of Ferdinand and Isabella a total change was effected. "They both exhibited a practical wisdom in their own personal relations which always commands respect, and which, however it may have savored of worldly policy in Ferdinand, was, in his consort, founded on the purest and most exalted principles. Under such a sovereign, the court, which had been little better than a brothel in the preceding reign, became the nursery of virtue and generous ambition. Isabella watched assiduously over the nurture of the high-born damsels of the court, whom she received into the royal palace, causing them to be educated under her own eye, and endowing them with liberal portions on their marriage."[2]

Joanna, the second daughter of Ferdinand and Isabella, was unfortunate in her marriage to Philip, son of the Archduke Maximilian, and sovereign—in right of his mother—of the Low Countries. The couple embarked for Flanders in the year 1504, and soon after their arrival the inconstancy of the husband and the ungovernable sensibility of the wife occasioned some scandalous scenes. Philip was openly enamored of one of the ladies in her suite, and his injured wife, in a paroxysm of jealousy, personally assaulted her rival, and caused the beautiful locks which had excited the admiration of her fickle husband to be shorn from her head. This outrage so affected Philip that he vented his indignation against Joanna in the coarsest and most unmanly terms, and finally refused to have any farther intercourse with her.[3]

Public brothels were established in Spain, as in other countries

[1] Prescott, i. 66, *et seq.*   [2] Id. i. 227.   [3] Id. iii. 171.

of Europe, one of great extent being in existence in Valencia in the fifteenth century. It constituted a complete suburb in itself, similar to the Ghetto, or Jews' suburb of most capital cities. Indeed, from its description, it is doubtful if it was not a rogue's sanctuary, similar to the well known Alsatia in London. It was surrounded by a wall with one gate only, at which a warder was stationed. He was a public city officer, and one of his duties was to warn all comers of the risk their property ran in visiting such a place. If they wished to leave valuables in his care they could do so, and receive them on their exit. There were some hundreds of girls resident in this vast den of iniquity. To add to the disgrace of the locality, the place of public execution was at its gate

In 1486, the rents, profits and emoluments of the public brothels of Seville were assigned to Alonzo Fajardo, the master of the royal table.

In 1559, there is an enactment in Granada fixing the rents to be paid by the women for their rooms and accommodation in public brothels, and also detailing the furniture and food with which they were to be provided in return. This is similar to the minute legislation of the German cities. This public provision having been made, no person was allowed to lend these women bed-linen.

The authorities of various cities might not permit a prostitute to reside in the town without previous examination by a duly licensed physician, who was to declare, upon oath, whether the woman then was or had recently been diseased.

By some of the Spanish laws, *varraganas* (kept mistresses or concubines) seem to have been a legal institution, for men of rank were forbidden to take slave-dancers, tavern-servants, procuresses, or prostitutes as concubines. This breach of the ordinary institutions of Christianity may probably have been a compromise of Moorish and Christian usages and morals. Before the final deadly struggle which ended in the expulsion of the Moors, intermarriages were not uncommon among the two peoples. Interchange of friendship and close intimacy existed between the races, and a mutual tolerance of each other's laws and customs was maintained, except by the enthusiasts of either religion.

The Spanish jurists distinctly recognized the woman's right to recover the wages of her infamy. The scholiasts struck out various fine distinctions, for which the monkish dialecticians were so deservedly ridiculed by the free-thinkers of the eighteenth century, and these were debated and discussed with the utmost eagerness.[1] One question was whether, if the man paid beforehand, and the woman refused to complete the contract, he could compel her? The weight of opinion seemed to be that, as he contemplated an immorality, he could neither recover the money nor enforce the agreement. Another equally important point was the use to which the gains of prostitution might be lawfully applied. The legality of their gains would seem to have overridden the mode of their expenditure, but casuists thought otherwise, and, by a royal edict of Alphonse IX., it was decided that priests could not receive funds obtained from such impure sources.

By the old Spanish law prostitutes were subjected to various disabilities in matters of inheritance or testamentary disposition. As mentioned in the review of the old German customs, the Church considered it a meritorious act to marry a harlot, on the assumption that thereby a brand was saved from the burning.[2] It is related of a young man that, while being led to the scaffold, a courtesan, struck by his manly beauty and bearing, offered to marry him, whereby, in virtue of a law or usage, his life would be saved. He rejected her proposition, as existence was not worth redemption at such a price. It is added that his life was nevertheless spared, in consideration of his spirit and courage.

In 1570, by order of Philip II., the regulations in force in the principal towns of Andalusia were extended to those of Castile. By these it was enacted that a woman became a prostitute of her own free will, and that no one could compel her to continue such, even though she had incurred debts. A surgeon was directed to pay her a weekly visit at her house, and report to the deputies of the Consistory those who were diseased, in order that they might be removed to hospital. The keeper of a brothel could not receive into his house any one who had not been previously examined, nor allow any one who was diseased to remain there, under a fine of a thousand maravedis, with thirty days' imprisonment. Each room was to contain certain furniture, and the house was to be closed on holidays, during Lent, Ember Week, and on all fast days, under a punishment of a hundred stripes to each woman

---

[1] Voltaire says that these prurient questions were debated with a gusto and a minuteness of detail not found elsewhere. He instances a variety of these absurd theorems.

[2] It may be imagined, as was the case in Berlin, that this behest flowed from the irregular manner and conduct of the clergy; but some of the fathers of the Church entertained and avowed this opinion at a time when the morals of the clergy were not open to impeachment.

who received visitors, as well as to the keeper of the house. These and other orders were to be hung upon different parts of the house, under a fine (about six dollars) and eight days' imprisonment.

The subject of venereal disease in Spain has acquired some interest from a generally received opinion that its appearance was made in that country, whence it was disseminated throughout Europe. Columbus and his crew were reported to have introduced it from America, but later investigations have proved that syphilis was not known on this side of the Atlantic until imported by Europeans. Facts have been advanced in preceding pages showing its almost simultaneous appearance in Italy and Spain, and we recur to the subject now merely with reference to the theory of its American origin. A late work, *Lettere sulla Storia de Mali Venerei, di Domenice Thiene, Venezia*, 1823, enumerates some proofs on the question. The main points are : 1. That neither Columbus nor his son allude, in any way, to such a disease in the New World. 2. Among frequent notices of the disease in the twenty-five years following the discovery of America, there is no mention of its originating there, but, on the contrary, a uniform derivation of it from some other source is assigned. 3. That the disorder was known and described before the siege of Naples, and therefore could not be introduced by the Spaniards at that time. 4. That it was known in a variety of countries in 1493 and the early part of 1494 ; a rapidity of diffusion irreconcilable with its importation by Columbus in 1493. 5. That the first work professing to trace its origin in America was not published till 1517, and was the production, not of a Spaniard, but a foreigner. The question of its origin is more definitely settled by a letter of Peter Martyr, noticing the symptoms in the most unequivocal manner, and dated April 5, 1488. Some doubts have been thrown upon the accuracy of this letter, but they do not invalidate it.[1]

In Madrid, in 1522, a special hospital for venereal patients was founded by Antoine Martin, of the order of St. Jean de Dieu. In 1575 the Spaniards passed an ordinance that no female domestics under forty years of age should be taken to service by unmarried men. The tenor of this law bespeaks the evil intended to be remedied.

[1] Prescott's History of Ferdinand and Isabella, ii. 502 (note). The learned historian argues the subject at some length.

In the present day, little is done in Spain in reference to prostitution by legislation on the subject. In his memoir on the subject to the Brussels Congress, Ramon de la Segra tells us that the old edicts have gradually become obsolete, and that neither the municipal authorities or general government take any farther interest in the question. It is said that in Seville first-class houses of prostitution have a custom of retaining the services of a physician at their own expense, whose office is to attend and make examinations of the women. Cadiz is notorious for its attractive climate and its dissipations.[1]

In the last century a tone of manners prevailed in the Spanish peninsula which was materially changed by the French occupation sweeping away many of the laxities of the age. In 1780 the Italian system of an attendant upon married ladies was adopted in Spain. These were termed *Cortejos*, and it is stated that in the cities they were principally military men, but in the country the monks performed the duty. The fidelity and affection of the women were directed to their gallants, and it even was thought discreditable, without very sufficient reason, to be guilty of fickleness in this particular. Married men were even the *cortejos* of other men's wives, neglecting their own, or leaving them to follow the bent of their private inclinations. No husband was jealous, but it was etiquette for Spanish ladies to keep up an external decorum, and to abstain from marked attentions to a *cortejo* in the husband's presence, although he might be perfectly aware of his wife's infidelity, and of her lover's presence in the house.[2] A curious illustration of this extraordinary state of public manners is given in an incident that occurred in Carthagena. A gentleman one morning remarked to a friend, " Before I go to rest this night the whole city will be thrown into confusion." He occasioned this public disorder by going home an hour sooner than his usual time, whereby his wife's *cortejo* was compelled to beat a precipitate retreat. The *cortejo's* arrival at his own house produced a similar effect, which was multiplied through polite society all round the town.

[1] Byron commemorates the beauty of the women of Cadiz, and, in his description of the shipwreck, saves the mate from being eaten by his starved companions on account of

> " A small present made to him at Cadiz,
> By general subscription of the ladies."

[2] Townsend : Travels in Spain in 1786 and 1787.

By the Spanish laws, which were in many provinces especially favorable to women, they could make *ex parte* cases against their husbands of ill treatment, and if they had beaten them the punishment might be made very severe. These laws were, as may be supposed, the frequent means of flagrant injustice.

In Barcelona there was a Magdalen institution, having the double object of reforming prostitutes and of correcting women who failed in the marriage vow, or who neglected or disgraced their families. The former department was called the Casa de Galera; the latter, the Casa de Correccion. The prostitutes were partially supported at the public cost, their extra food, beyond bread and meat, being provided by their own labor, to which they were obliged to devote themselves all day. The lady culprits were supported by their relations. They were imprisoned by the sentence of a particular court, on the complaint of a member of their family, and they, as well as the prostitutes, were required to work. When deemed necessary, these offenders received personal correction. Drunkenness was one of the grounds of incarceration. The precise offenses are not mentioned by our author,[1] but the fashions and customs of nations are so distinct, that indiscretion, or even familiarity in one, might be immorality in another. A leading principle in Spanish manners is not to give offense. People may be as vicious as they please; it may be even notorious that they are so, but their manners must be outwardly correct There is little doubt the violation of this maxim was the principal cause of imprisonment.

In Barcelona there was also, in 1780, a foundling hospital liberally supported. A curious custom was observed in reference to the girls. They were led in procession when of marriageable age, and any one who took a fancy to a young woman might ask her hand, indicating his choice by throwing a handkerchief on her in public.

In the Asturias certain forms of disease appeared with excessive virulence, and were very common. Syphilis was prevalent. There was a hospital at Oviedo for its cure, but patients had considerable reluctance to apply to it. Whether incident to this prevalence of syphilis or not, we have no means of ascertaining, but leprosy was very general, and there were twenty or more large houses for its cure in the Asturias. The common itch in a highly aggravated form was also general, and often productive of parasitical vermin.

[1] Townsend.

The present state of Spanish society is the subject of the usual discrepancies between travelers, owing to their different prejudices, means of information, or opportunities of making observations. No country of Europe retains more of its original peculiarities and national habits than Spain. Under the fervid sun of Andalusia, the same rigorous observance of proprieties is hardly to be found as in the northern climate of Biscay, whose hardy sons have ever been the defenders of their rights and political privileges. Madrid, as the capital, might be thought a fair illustration of the habits and manners of the great bulk of the city populations, whose peculiarities of race have not been smoothed away by intercommunication, the traveling facilities of Spain being yet among the worst in Europe. The descendants of the Goth and the Moor are still distinct in character. A general prejudice exists as to the morality of Southern nations in Europe, and the Spanish women are by no means exempt from a full share of this unfortunate opinion. Nevertheless, a recent writer says:

"I speak my sincere opinion when I say that, with the exception of a few fashionable persons, whose lives do indeed seem to pass in one constant round of dissipations, whose time is spent in driving on the Prado, attending the theatre, the opera, or the ball-room, precisely as their compeers do in every other great city, the Spanish women are the most domestic in the world, the most devoted to the care of their children, the most truly pious, and the best *ménagères*. This latter circumstance may arise from the fact that their fortunes are rarely equal to their rank, and that a lavish expenditure would soon bring ruin upon the possessors of the most ancient names and most splendid palaces in Madrid."[1]

This opinion is confined solely to the higher classes of the city of Madrid. It expresses nothing as to the great bulk of the population, and, however gratifying the record of worth may be, we fear the eulogy must be taken *cum grano salis*.

Of the education of Spanish women, Mrs. Donn Piatt states that, by reason of the small fortunes of the nobility, the daughters of an ancient house must be made useful before they are accomplished; that the first consideration, however, is their religious education, to which, and to the preparation for confirmation—the great juvenile rite of Catholic countries—the utmost care and attention are devoted. Next after their religious tuition, the greatest pains are taken to make them accomplished housekeepers. They are taught to make their own clothes, to keep accounts, to regulate

[1] Attaché in Madrid: Appleton, 1856, p. 64.

M

their expenditure, and to attend to the most minute details of the family economy. The advantages of a good solid education are not neglected; their natural capacity and innate taste for the arts, especially as musicians and painters, rapidly develop themselves, under very moderate tuition, to acquirements of a superior character, and the productions of young women of high station are spoken of with much admiration. One trait of Spanish character that speaks loudly in favor of the women is the devotion, respect, and obedience paid by sons to their mothers long after age has relieved them from maternal tutelage.

In Madrid there is a hospital for foundlings, which are said to amount to about four thousand annually. These are actual foundlings, exposed publicly to the compassion of the charitable. It is principally served by the Sisters of Charity. The infants are intrusted to nurses, and at the age of seven they are transferred to the *Desamparados* (unprotected) college, where they receive instruction in the simpler rudiments of education, and their religious and moral training is cared for. There is also an asylum to which others are drafted to learn some practical handicraft, such as glove-making, straw-hat making, embroidery, etc., and which seems, in a great measure, a self-supporting institution.

There are three Magdalen Hospitals: St. Nicholas de Barr, founded in 1691 for women of the better class, who are banished for misconduct from the homes of their husbands and fathers; that of the *Arrepentidos*, for penitents; and that of the *Recogidos*, founded in 1637, for the correction of women sent there by their families, in order that they may be induced to return to the paths of virtue.

CHAPTER XIII.

PORTUGAL.

Conventual Life in 1780.—Depravity of Women.—Laws against Adultery and Rape.—Venereal Disease.—Illegitimacy.—Foundling Hospitals of Lisbon and Oporto.—Singular Institutions for Wives.

A WRITER on Portugal, in the year 1780, complains of the scandalous licentiousness of the monks and nuns, of whom there were no less than two hundred and fifty thousand in a population of two millions. It is said that the convent Odivelas, the harem of the monarch John V., contained three hundred women, account·

ed the most beautiful and accomplished courtesans in the kingdom. The great Marquis de Pombal suppressed many of these convents, and was the general reformer of the religious orders.

Of the effect of such an example from such quarters on the population at that time, sunk, as they were, in the most imbecile ignorance, little need be said. The women of Portugal were reputed to surpass all European females in gallantry, and their attractions were such that only one interview was necessary to complete the conquest. To this condition of common immorality, the rigor of their husbands and male relations may have contributed not a little. They are said to have been outrageously jealous, and to have made no scruple of murdering any stranger who gave them even the weakest grounds of suspicion.

In the fundamental laws of Portugal, promulgated in 1143, it is enacted that, " if a married woman commit adultery, and the husband complain to the judge, and the judge is the king, the adulterer and adulteress shall be condemned to the flames ; but if the husband retain the wife, neither party shall be punished."

In the case of a rape perpetrated on the person of a lady of rank, all the property of the ravisher went to the lady ; and in case the female were not noble, the man, without regard to his rank, was obliged to marry her.

The writer whom we have already quoted[1] speaks of the venereal disease as being, at the time he wrote (1770–1780), habitual in Portugal, and that the Portuguese not knowing how to cure it, its malignity had become so intensified that, in some cases, individuals who had contracted a peculiar form of the malady had died in a few hours, as though struck down by an active and deadly poison. This is most probably the exaggeration of popular opinion on the subject. More recent writers are chary of information, and avoid the mention of matters so offensive to ears polite.

The manners and morals of the higher ranks of society must have undergone a material change for the better in the present century, for an English nobleman (Lord Porchester, since Earl of Caernarvon) speaks in very favorable terms of the propriety, amiability, and excellence of the Portuguese ladies, which, excepting in the matter of intellectual education, left them in no wise behind the worthy of their sex in other countries of Europe.

Among the lower classes, however, it would not seem that the tone of morals had been very much amended, whether we con-

[1] Duc de Chatelet's Travels in Portugal.

sider their regard for female virtue, or their cultivation of the maternal tenderness and solicitude natural to all created beings.

In the neighborhood of Oporto, country women may be met conveying little babies to the Foundling Hospital, four or five together, in a basket. These helpless creatures are the illegitimate children of peasant girls, openly deserted in the villages, and thus forwarded by the authorities to the care of those pious strangers who undertake their nurture and preservation.[1]

In these cases, says Mr. Kingston, the females are not treated by their parents with any harshness or rigor. They are rather compassionated for their misfortune, and are only sent away from home when found obstinately persistent in a course of evil.

As may be supposed, the foundling hospitals have abundant claims on their funds. The Real Casapia, at Belem, near Lisbon, and another hospital in Lisbon attached to the Casa de Misericordia, receive together nearly three thousand children, who are brought up to different callings, and otherwise prepared for active life, as is usual in such institutions. There is a similar asylum, equally frequented, in Oporto. In this city there is also an asylum in which husbands may place their wives during their own absence from home. It often happens that ladies, on such occasions, enter the asylum of their own accord.

There is also in Oporto an establishment in the nature of a Penitentiary, in which husbands may immure their faithless wives, or even those who give grounds of suspicion. It is presumed that in the nineteenth century, even in Portugal, this must be done under color of some legal authority.

CHAPTER XIV.

ALGERIA.

Prostitution in Algiers before the Conquest.—Mezonar.—Unnatural Vices.—Tax on Prostitutes.—Decree of 1837.—Corruption.—Number of Prostitutes and Population.—Nationality of Prostitutes.—Causes of Prostitution.—Brothels.—Clandestine Prostitution.—Baths.—Dispensary.—Syphilis.—Punishment of Prostitutes.

A PAMPHLET has lately appeared in France on the subject of Prostitution in Algiers. Its author, Dr. E. A. Duchesne, has ren-

[1] Kingston, Sketches in Lusitania, 1845.

dered service by collecting a large number of important facts and statistical data.[1]

When the French conquered Algiers in 1830, they found prostitution established there, and prevailing to a large extent. So far as we are able to ascertain, it had always been a leading feature of Algerian society; travelers had noticed it in the seventeenth and eighteenth centuries. In 1830 it was estimated that, with a population of thirty thousand, Algiers contained three thousand prostitutes. We have already had occasion to notice the unreliable character of similar estimates in general, but there is no doubt that the number of lewd women at Algiers under Arab rule was inordinately large. They were mainly Moors, Arabs, and negresses. All were under the control of the chief of the native police—the Mezonar. He kept a list of them, and laid a tax amounting to about two dollars per month on each. As he paid a fixed sum to the government for the privilege of collecting this tax, it was to his interest to increase the number of prostitutes as much as possible, and he appears to have done so. He kept in his employ a number of spies, who watched women suspected of immoral habits, and denounced them whenever they were detected, in which event they were inscribed on the Mezonar's list, and became prostitutes for life. He was empowered to compel every prostitute to discharge the duties of her calling, and was frequently applied to by strangers to supply them with women. He was not allowed, however, to lease women to Christians or Jews. Twice a year the Mezonar gave a public fête, to which all the male inhabitants of Algiers were invited; the prostitutes formed the female portion of the assemblage, and the public officer profited by the increased patronage they obtained during the festivities, as well as by the sale of tickets for the entertainment.[2]

It is right also to add that the French found that other feature of Oriental manners, unnatural habits, largely developed at Algiers. The cafés, the streets, the baths, the public places were full of boys of remarkable beauty, who more than shared with the women the favor of the wealthier natives. Owing to a criminal negligence on the part of the French authorities, no systematic endeavor has ever been made to eradicate this shameful vice, which appears still to prevail to an alarming extent.

The influx of population, mainly soldiery, into a city thus

---

[1] De la Prostitution dans la Ville d'Alger depuis la conquête, par E. A. Duchesne. Paris, Bailliere, 1853.　　　　　　　　　　　　　[2] Ib. p. 64, *et seq.*

steeped in immorality, produced natural results. A few weeks after the invasion, the French general was compelled to establish a Dispensary, and to decree that all dissolute women must undergo an examination there once a week. A tax of five francs per month was laid upon prostitutes to defray the expenses of the establishment. Within less than a year, such grave abuses had crept into the collection of this tax that it was resolved to farm it out, and it was adjudged at auction to a man who agreed to pay 1860 francs per month for its proceeds. In 1832 the monthly tax was raised successively to seven $\frac{44}{100}$, and nine francs per girl, and on these rates it was farmed to one Balré, who paid $1666\frac{80}{100}$ for the privilege of collecting it. He was also entitled to levy and retain the amount of all fines imposed by the police on prostitutes, and to charge women ten francs each time they went to a fête outside the city, and five francs if the fête were within the limits. The profits of the farm were so great that in 1835 Balré was able to pay the government 2250 francs (four hundred and fifty dollars) per month.[1]

Under this system the gravest inconveniences occurred, and became so troublesome that in November, 1835, the governor promulgated a decree remodeling the regulations in force on the subject. It appears the farm system was then abandoned, and the government agents who were intrusted with the collection of the tax robbed both the prostitutes and the state shamefully.

Hence, in December, 1837, a new decree was issued by the governor, repealing all former laws and regulations, and placing the whole subject under the control of the Commissary of Police. The leading provisions of that decree were as follows:

" Every public woman who desires to prostitute herself must declare her intention beforehand to the Comptroller of Public Women, who shall enter her name in his register, and present her with a pass-book which he shall sign."

" Every girl inscribed on the register shall place in the hands of the treasurer of the Dispensary, monthly, a sum of twenty francs if she be a kept woman, and ten francs if she be not kept. The treasurer shall give her a receipt for the same, and record it in his account-book."

" The mayor shall be authorized to remit this monthly due, as well as any fines that may have been incurred, when the girl owing the same can prove by a certificate from the comptroller, the treasurer, and the physician that she is indigent."

Duchesne, p. 22, 171.

"Every girl who shall not have paid her monthly due, as well as her fines, within ten days after the visit to the Dispensary, shall undergo an imprisonment of not less than five days and not more than three months, unless she establish her indigence as aforesaid."

"Girls detained in prison shall, on the first symptoms of syphilis, be transferred to the Dispensary for treatment, after which they shall be remanded to prison to serve the remainder of the time."

"The physician of the Dispensary shall not only treat patients in that establishment, but shall pay *periodical, accidental, and all necessary visits* to the prostitutes, who are hereby subjected to such visits. He shall visit the Dispensary twice a day, from 7 to 9 A.M. and from 3 to 4 P.M. He shall enter upon his memorandum-book, and upon the pass-book of the girl, the result of all accidental or necessary visits. He shall receive a salary of two thousand francs."[1]

This law is in force at the present time, and is said to have led to great inconvenience. Police agents are accused of levying black mail on the prostitutes to an enormous extent, in the shape of fines, dues for going to balls, hush-money for escaping the visit to the Dispensary, presents to the policeman on the birth of his children, etc. The product of the tax is inordinately large, amounting, independently of fines, to one hundred and twenty francs, or twenty-four dollars per annum for each girl. Several administrators have recommended its diminution or total suppression, but it is still retained.[2]

In the year 1838, when the present law was passed, the number of women inscribed on the police register was 320, the total population of Algiers being 34,882, of whom two thirds were Africans and one third Europeans; but the mayor of the city gave it as his opinion that this figure (320) was in reality far below the truth. In 1846 measures were taken for enforcing the police regulations more strictly than before, and some care was used to procure correct statistics of population and prostitution.[3] We compile the following table from several given by Dr. Duchesne:

Year.	Registered Prostitutes (average).	POPULATION.		
		African (estimated).	European.	Total.
1847	442	25,000	42,113	67,113
1848	387	25,000	37,572	62,572
1849	395	25,000	37,572	63,072
1850	479	26,000	29,392	55,392
1851	342	......	......	55,392

To these figures, some of which are only approximative, must

[1] Duchesne, p. 31.   [2] Id. p. 172.   [3] Id. p. 54, 56.

be added the number of French soldiers in the garrison at Algiers. At times the effective force has been as large as twelve or fifteen thousand men.

Another point of interest is the nationality of the prostitutes of Algiers. It is known that the native women are loose in their morals. In many parts of the interior it is common for fathers or brothers to let out their daughters or sisters by the night or the week to strangers, and the young women themselves are only too willing to ratify a bargain which promises to gratify their unbounded sensuality. The following table gives the nationality of the registered prostitutes during the period 1846–1851.[1]

Years.	EUROPEANS.							AFRICANS.				Total.
	France	Mahon.	Italy.	Germany.	Great Britain.	Spain.	Holland.	Arabs and Moors.	Jewesses.	Mulattoes.	Negresses.	
1847	107	14	6	11	4	58	2	203	26	6	16	451
1848	78	10	5	10	3	49	...	181	28	7	16	387
1849	82	8	2	17	3	60	...	183	22	7	17	401
1850	113	8	2	20	2	57	...	248	19	7	17	493
1851	81	4	5	9	2	37	...	170	12	3	13	336

On inquiring for the causes of prostitution at Algiers, Dr. Duchesne found that they might be summed up under three heads: 1st. Poverty, mainly due to the French conquest and the wars which followed. To the present day it appears that it is not unusual for an Arab chief to relieve his wants by sending his prettiest daughter to Algiers to perform a campaign as a prostitute. 2d. The idleness in which all Arab and Moorish women are trained. It was proved that, while all the European women were capable of working at some calling or other, and did work during their stay in the hospital, not one of the native women had any idea of manual employment. A few could sing, and had at one time gained a livelihood as street-singers, but the immense majority were absolutely incapable of doing any thing for a livelihood. 3d. The Oriental idea that the woman is a chattel, to be sold or hired out by her legitimate owner, father, brother, or husband. This idea, which prevails in many savage nations, among others, many of our own Indian tribes, is, of course, the best of all entering wedges for prostitution.[2]

There are fourteen houses of prostitution at Algiers, all kept, it seems, by Europeans, and the greater part by retired prostitutes. The natives object to living under the control of a brothel-keeper. They live alone in their own rooms. Sometimes three or four of

[1] Duchesne, p. 58.   [2] Id. p. 70, et seq.

them club together and form a partnership.   Their rooms are generally shabby and ill furnished.[1]

Arab prostitutes seldom appear in the streets, and when they do, they are veiled and dressed like modest women.   They may be seen at their windows of an evening, peeping through small holes contrived for the purpose, and smoking cigarettes.   Their customers are procured by means of runners, who are mostly small boys.

As may be inferred from the amount of the tax on prostitutes, clandestine prostitution is very extensively practiced at Algiers. We have no details or even approximate estimates of the number of clandestine prostitutes, but it doubtless exceeds that of the registered women.   Many of them are attached to the garrison, and are handed from regiment to regiment, shielded from the police by being claimed as wives by some of the soldiers.   Others in like manner prevail upon some colonist to afford them a temporary home, and so elude the visit of the physician.   Dr. Duchesne had reason to believe that syphilis prevailed to an alarming extent among the secret prostitutes, and that, until the tax was removed, and they were encouraged to register themselves on the police roll, it would continue to be general and virulent.[2]

Formerly the baths were the great haunts of clandestine prostitutes.   It is known that in most eastern countries the bath is not only a sanitary necessity, but a common ally of sensuality. At Algiers, before the conquest, men and women are said to have bathed promiscuously, and frightful scenes of debauchery occurred daily.   Under French rule this has been reformed.   Men may not bathe from 6 A.M. to 6 P.M.; but Dr. Duchesne was led to believe that it was quite common for men to introduce women into the baths at night, with the connivance of the bath officials. Indeed, some of the latter appear to fill the same office to the Algerine bathers as the Roman bath servants did to the dissolute men of that day.[3]

It now remains to speak of the Dispensary at Algiers.   It was established, as has been stated, within a few days after the capture of the place.   For nearly ten years it was a scandal to the faculty and the authorities.   The wards were too small; there were not beds enough for the women; every thing was either deficient in quantity or objectionable in quality.   In 1839, orders were given for the establishment of a proper and commodious Dispensary.

[1] Duchesne, p. 132.   [2] Id. p. 144.   [3] Id. p. 148.

Three old Moorish houses were hired and divided into wards. They contain at present thirteen wards, with beds for seventy-seven patients; a bath-room, containing six baths; a hall for the visits of prostitutes; and the necessary offices, etc. The staff of the Dispensary consists of a director, treasurer (*econome*), physician, apothecary, clerk, cook, assistant apothecary, porter, five laborers, and four police agents. All the washing is done in the establish-ment. The commissariat is on the amplest scale; meat, soup, vegetables of all kinds, rice, eggs, fruit, etc., being supplied in abundance to the patients.[1]

Every morning at seven o'clock the women are visited by the physician, assisted by the apothecary. Those who are able to walk are examined in the *salle de visite*, the others in their beds. The average number of patients during the year appears to be from five hundred and fifty to six hundred. The average dura-tion of the treatment is from twenty-four to thirty-four days. The cost to the Dispensary averages from one and a half to one and three quarters franc per day for each girl (about thirty or thirty-five cents).[2]

The Dispensary physician reported to Dr. Duchesne that, so far as his observation went, syphilis was more severe on the sea-coast than in the interior; and in the months of September, October, November, and December, than at any other period of the year.[3]

Prostitutes are punished for being more than twenty-four hours behind time in visiting the Dispensary; for leaving it during treatment; for insulting the physician or other authorities; for continuing to exercise their calling after being attacked by dis-ease. The penalty is imprisonment, either in the ordinary prison or in the solitary cell. Formerly, the tread-mill was used, and in bad cases a girl's hair was cut off, and her nose slit; but these savage relics of Moorish legislation were long since abandoned. Solitary confinement is found to answer every useful purpose.[4]

[1] Duchesne, p. 152, *et seq.*   [2] Id. p. 176.   [3] Id. p. 192.   [4] Id. p. 198.

CHAPTER XV.

BELGIUM.

Hospitals and Charitable Institutions.—Foundlings.—Estimate of the Marriage Ceremony.—Regulations as to Prostitution.—Brothels.—Sanitary Ordinances.

BELGIUM takes a more prominent position in Europe than its mere extent would warrant. This influence is derived from the vigorous and effective stand made in behalf of rational freedom, and from the manner in which free institutions have been originated and maintained.

The hospitals and other eleemosynary institutions of Belgium are of a magnificent character, supported at an annual expenditure of nearly two hundred thousand dollars. Almost every town, and many of the larger villages, have hospitals for the sick, sometimes maintained at corporation expense, sometimes by private endowments. In 318 hospitals, during the four years from 1831 to 1834 (inclusive), no less than 22,180 persons were treated.[1]

Foundling hospitals are a marked feature of these charitable establishments. The turning table, which was formerly in use in all such institutions, has lately been abandoned in most of them, but still remains in use at those of Brussels and Antwerp. The total number of children annually abandoned in Belgium is estimated to exceed eight thousand out of one hundred and forty-four thousand births, a ratio of about one in eighteen. The average expense attendant upon the maintenance of each infant is about seventy-two francs.

Marriage in Belgium is, by law, simply a civil contract, requiring fifteen days' notice posted in front of the Hôtel de Ville. Notwithstanding the simplicity of this ceremonial, it is affirmed that an enormous extent of immorality and illegitimacy is to be met with, and that a virtuous servant-girl is altogether exceptional, there being scarcely one of them who has not an illegitimate child, while they maintain with the most unyielding confidence that, so long as the father is a *bon ami* (sweetheart), there is no moral turpitude in the case.

[1] W. Trollope's Belgium. Scarcely a more liberal work toward the Belgians than Mrs. Trollope's toward ourselves

Belgium is remarkable for its regulations with respect to prostitution and the spread of venereal disease. The perfections of the latter arrangements are shown in the fact that, out of an army of thirty thousand men, there were less than two hundred cases of syphilis in the year 1855.

The brothels of Brussels are of two kinds: *les maisons de debauché* and *les maisons de passe;* these are visited by *les filles éparses*, who keep their appointments there. The two classes of houses are distinguished by different-colored lanterns hung over the doors.

All classes of prostitutes are required to be examined twice a week ; those who live in brothels of the first and second class are visited by the physicians, while the very poor women of the third class, and all those who do not reside in brothels, are obliged to attend at the Dispensary. If they are punctual in their visits for four weeks in succession they are exempt from all tax; but if, on the contrary, their attendance is irregular, they can be imprisoned from one to five days. Any woman who does not live in a brothel can be examined at her own residence, provided that she pays at the Dispensary a sum amounting to about eighty-five cents. For this she receives four visits, and the physicians will continue to call upon her as long as the payments are made in advance. Thus the denizens of the aristocratic brothels are saved the inconvenience of attending at the Dispensary, as also that portion living in private lodgings who can afford to pay the fee to release themselves from going to the office as common prostitutes, while the half-starved, ill-dressed pauper of the third class must wait at the Dispensary until examined, and then return to her squalid home, where none but her companions and the police-officers are ever seen.

The medical staff of the Dispensary is composed of a superintending inspector, whose duty is to be present in the Dispensary when examinations are being made, and to visit the houses once a fortnight at least; of two medical inspectors, who, during alternate months, examine, one the women in the brothels, the other those who attend at the Dispensary. The date and result of every examination are marked on a card belonging to each woman, in the registers kept at the brothels, and in the records of the Dispensary. If a woman be found affected with syphilis or any other infectious disease, the owner of the brothel must send her immediately, in a car, to the hospital, and as soon as her cure is complete her card is handed to her, and she is at liberty to resume her calling.

CHAPTER XVI.

HAMBURG.

THE ancient legislative enactments respecting prostitution in Hamburg seem to have been of the same character, and based upon the same principles, as in other Continental cities, namely, a partial toleration of a necessary evil for the sake of preventing injurious excesses. This may be traced in the oldest extant law on the subject, dated in 1292. In the public account-books for 1350 are entries of charges which imply that public brothels were built by the corporation, though we find no satisfactory information as to whether they were managed by an appointed official as in Cologne, Strasbourg, or Avignon, or were leased by the city to an individual as in Ulm. It will be interesting to give a sketch of the regulations of prostitution in the latter city before proceeding with the investigation concerning Hamburg.

The laws of the city of Ulm in 1430, or at least that portion of them called "woman house" laws, provided that the houses should be leased, and the lessee, on becoming tenant, swore to serve the city faithfully; to prevent all foul play or concealment of suspicious goods in his house; to provide clean, healthy women, and never to keep less than fourteen. He was bound to observe a fixed dietary scale; the daily meals were to be "of the value of sixpence;" on meat days every woman was to have two dishes, soup with meat and vegetables, and a roast or boiled joint, as most convenient. On fast-days and in Lent they were to have the same number of dishes, which (out of Lent) might consist of eggs and baked meat. As a change to this, they might have herrings and eggs; or fishes (probably fresh-water fish), which they could cook for themselves, and to which the keeper must add white bread. If a woman refused the food provided, he was bound to give her something of the value of sixpence; he was also to sell them wine "when they required it." If a woman was pregnant, he was to put her out of the house. In the "woman's house" there was a chest for general purposes, and a money-box for the accounts between the host and the women. Every woman who kept company with a man at night must pay the keeper a kreutzer, the remainder of the fee being her own property. All money the women obtained in the day was to be put into the general chest; the third of this belonged to the host; the balance was paid to the women at the end of the week, less any debts they had contracted in the mean time. A woman resided in every house who made financial arrangements between inmates and visitors. If a woman received a present in addition to the stipulated fee, she was at liberty to spend it on clothes, shoes, or personal matters to which nobody could lay claim. The keeper could not supply the women with clothes, etc., without the knowledge and consent of the Master of the Beggars (a local functionary who seems to have combined the supervision of brothels, and of known vagrants and beggars). The host was required to provide, at his own cost, a cook and a cook's maid. Girls or women could, with their own consent, be apprenticed to the "women keeper" by their parents or husbands; but if one was apprenticed against her will, and she, or her friends, wished to cancel the agreement, the keeper was bound to release her without requiring the repayment of any money he might have disbursed for her. If a woman who had accumulated a guilder of her own wished to quit her sinful life, she was allowed to tender it to the keeper in discharge of all her liabilities, and must then be permitted to leave the house, wearing the clothes she wore when she entered it, or, if they were worn out, in her common "Monday clothes." A woman who desired might leave without this payment if she had nothing to give, but if subsequently detected in any other house the keeper could enforce his demands against her, the discharge not affecting his claim under such circumstances. Every Monday each woman had to contribute one penny, and the host twopence, to the money-box

to purchase tapers for the Virgin and the saints, to be offered in
the Cathedral on Sunday nights. If any of the women were sick
or could not support themselves, they were to be provided with
necessaries from the money-box, to which (for greater security)
there were two keys, one kept by the host and the other by the
Master of the Beggars. Each woman had to spin daily for the
keeper two hanks of yarn, or, in default, to pay three hellers for
each hank. On Sunday, Lady-day, and Twelfth-day, after ves-
pers, and in Passion Week, the house was not to be opened. If
the keeper broke any of these regulations the council could dismiss him. The oath taken by the Master of the Beggars required
him to visit the women-houses every quarter day; to read the
laws to the women; and to report to the council any offenses he
found existing.[1]

In Hamburg, in 1483, the calling of brothel-keeper was limited
to certain streets, apart from the ordinarily frequented thoroughfares—a rule which would imply that the authorities had discontinued building public brothels, and relinquished the business to
individuals.

In the seventeenth century a different course of action was
adopted, and, in place of toleration and limitation of brothels,
strict laws were made in reference to visiting suspected places,
and the custody of persons of bad character. The women-houses
were pulled down and the women expelled; the criminal records
contain frequent instances where the pillory or exile was inflicted
for the crime of prostitution.

In 1764, and again in 1767, the Hamburgers enacted very severe laws against offenders, under the title of "*delicta carnis*," by
which both sexes were subject to pains and penalties, but men
seem to have been allowed to clear themselves on oath. The officers of justice were directed to make domiciliary visits in search
of offenders, and the pillory, bread and water, the House of Correction, or banishment, are the penalties threatened on habitual
evil-doers.

In Germany, prostitution received a terrible impulse from the
French Revolution, when the general disruption of public obligations paved the way to unbounded private license. Probably the
licentiousness of Europe at the end of the last and commencement of the present century was more extravagant than at any
other time. The irruption of immigrants at the fall of the French

[1] Jäger's " Schwabischen Städtwesen des Mittelalters."

monarchy flooded Hamburg with Parisian morals and customs. Places of entertainment and sensual gratification arose in all directions, the homely, simple manners of the *Vaterland* were subverted, and a less rigid line of conduct took their place. In the words of a writer of the day: "Our eating-houses were metamorphosed into restaurants; our dancing-rooms into saloons; our drinking-shops into pavilions; our cellars into halls; our girls into demoiselles; in short, we were thoroughly polished up by the immoral shoal of immigrants. Quick and unrestrained strode the crowd over our pleasant streets, and modesty and respectability fled with averted faces, to the sorrow of the few good men."

The name *demoiselle* was granted to many of the common women, their places of resort being called "Ma'amselle houses." In those days the Hamburgers saw, with astonishment, houses fitted up and furnished in the style of mansions, with costly upholstery and cabinet-work.[1] Among the women were the *femmes entretennes*, who received their friends at certain hours, and whose favors were dispensed for a Louis d'or or a ducat. They frequented the first and second boxes of the German and French theatres, and drove through the public streets in handsome carriages. Some of the keepers of this class of houses had physicians in their pay, whose services were always available by the inmates. *Petits soupers* were given here, and sometimes a ball took place.

These were literally the aristocracy of prostitution. The second, third, and fourth grades resided in inferior streets or in the suburbs, differing in their attractions according to the rank which they assumed, but all equally shameless and unequivocal in their conduct and appearance.

Notwithstanding this rapid spread of prostitution, the police of the city can not justly be charged with neglect of duty, any public outrage being followed by condign punishment. At one time a whole ship-load of nymphs of the *pavé* was dispatched to the colonies; at another a raid was made on the most conspicuous houses, some of the inmates alarmed into decency of conduct, and the incorrigible publicly exhibited in the streets, decorated with inscriptions signifying their offenses. The voice of the few was powerless against the corruptions of the many. The pamphlets and papers of the time teem with the proffered services of go-betweens, and even the Hamburg ladies themselves were far from perfection, if we may credit the evidence of a fictitious petition,

---

[1] Hamburg and Altona Journal, 1805, iii. 50.

praying, among other things, that the ladies restrict the indecency of their costume, and not make such a liberal display of their charms.

It was impossible such an extravagant state of society should long exist; a reaction was inevitable; and we find, accordingly, an ordinance enacted in 1807 by the Prætor Abendroth in reference to the matter. It recognized brothel-keeping and prostitution as a calling, and permitted it under certain restrictions. A tax on the class was imposed, and means were prescribed by which a register of all persons engaged therein was to be kept, and their health and general good conduct maintained and enforced. The official justification of the tax is found in the order itself, which declares that, "for the purposes aforesaid" (police register and supervision, medical examination, maintenance in sickness, poverty, etc.), "and in order that the public shall be at no charges, each housekeeper shall, for every woman residing with him, pay two marks to the Prætor's treasury. The surplus of this treasury shall go to the Hospital."

During the French occupation in 1811, the police renewed and enforced the stringent regulations on the subject of common houses and women. The preamble of their "Instructions" (April, 1811) is worthy of notice:

"Public and personal safety require a constant inspection, as well of the public houses dedicated to debauchery, as of the women and girls who frequent the same, live therein, or dwell there from time to time. This inspection must also be extended to those places which are not expressly appointed for dwelling-houses, but which, nevertheless, must be included among the public houses, inasmuch as they serve for refuge to the women and girls who wander about the streets."

"The grounds of this inspection are two-fold. In one respect they belong to the maintenance of public order: it is needful that no one be withdrawn from the eye of the police, nor find an asylum in such houses. It is likewise expedient that the magistracy take notice of disgraceful and disorderly proceedings, or prevent those which take place too often in the town. The other grounds respect the public health. The habits of debauchery have become so general, and inspection has, for some years, become so difficult, that the most dangerous maladies have increased to an unprecedented extent. All classes of society complain, and call loudly for regulations to restrain these evils. These considerations have moved the General Police Commissary to renew, in full force, the before-enacted laws and regulations, and to order them to be enforced with rigor in the present state of affairs."

After the withdrawal of the French, the vigilance of the police authorities seems to have relaxed, if we are to judge by com-

N

plaints published at the time, in which they are accused of complicity with the unfortunates who infested the streets of Hamburg,
and are said, "by the agency of a trifling bribe, to be able to ply
their hideous trade unobstructed, and to the great annoyance of
the virtuously disposed, who, after certain hours of the evening,
are unable to pass along the streets."

In 1820, "the previously existing police regulations against
prostitutes being proved very ineffectual, insomuch that they infest the public streets and ways, not only to the offense of decency
and propriety, but to the endangerment of public order and safety," it was ordered that the regulations should be renewed, and
additional powers were given to the police to enforce the registry
of individuals coming within the scope of the law.

At this time we find some information as to the number of
prostitutes, who are stated to be about five hundred, chiefly foreigners, and their receipts from their patrons, but we have no
guide to the number of women who pursued their calling privately, which must have been large.

The civic administration of the Senator Hudtwalcker is marked
by earnest endeavors to control prostitution and restrict it within
known bounds.   Some of his views on the subject met much opposition.   He wished to close up one end of a notorious street,
and to wall up the back windows, stationing a watchman constantly at the end left open.   After great personal attention to
the subject, he published the result of his experience.[1]   His principles are those upon which the present police regulations of Hamburg are based.   He says:

"All brothel-keepers and girls should be distinctly made to understand
that their infamous and ruinous calling is only *tolerated*, not permitted, or
authorized, or even well wished.   Still less can they feel that they have
any right to compare themselves with worthy citizens as though their
calling, because an impost is levied on them, can be put on a level with
other permitted callings.   They must remember that this impost is raised
solely to defray the necessary cost of police supervision, and of the cure of
maladies brought on the common women by their own profligate course of
life."

"2. Public or private brothel-keeping to be notified to the police; the
regulations to be read over and subscribed; offenders to be punished by
bread and water, and the House of Correction.   If an uninscribed woman
have the venereal disease, the fact is *prima facie* evidence of prostitution."

[1] *Vorschriften die Bordelle und öffentlichen Madchen betreffend:* Hamburg, 1834.

"**3.** Change of residence to be notified, under penalty."

"**4.** The concession may be withdrawn by the authorities at their pleasure."

"**5.** Houses of accommodation will only be tolerated,

(*a.*) where the landlord is inscribed;

(*b.*) where a resident girl is inscribed;

(*c.*) where an inscribed girl is the party using it."

"**6.** Women from abroad, kept by single men, must obtain the police residence permission, and should pay the tax for the first class, without, however, being subject to medical visits. They have the right of the free use of the General Infirmary. Should such a girl be proved to have intercourse with several men, or, being venereal, to have infected others, she should be treated as a public woman."

7, 8, 9. Prescribe the identification of individuals subscribing, the details of their place of birth; the consent of parents when living; also, "That any brothel-keeper detaining an innocent girl on false pretenses shall be punished with fine and imprisonment, and the concession be withdrawn."

"**10.** Female servants or relatives of brothel-keepers residing with them to be over twenty-five years of age."

"**11.** No prostitute is suffered to keep children of either sex over ten years of age; even her own must be brought up elsewhere if she continues her calling."

12. Prohibits solicitation of passengers.

"**13.** No common woman to be in the streets after eleven at night without a male companion."

14. Limits the places to which prostitutes may resort.

"**15.** Young people, under twenty years, not to enter a brothel."

"**16.** No music or gaming in brothels, nor liquor-selling, except by special permission."

"**17.** Noise and uproar in brothels punishable."

"**18.** No brothel-keeper or inscribed woman to permit extortion or violence to a customer, but they may detain persons who have not paid. Thefts or foul dealing prohibited; the landlord *prima facie* responsible."

"**19.** No compulsion or violence of the women by the keeper, nor by guests with his cognizance."

"**20.** A woman wishing to return to a virtuous life at liberty to do so, notwithstanding any keeper's claims. If they disagree as to such claims, the police to settle them, but in no case has the keeper any lien on her. Nevertheless, this privilege not to be abused. If a woman returns to her evil courses, the keeper's claims on her revive, and she may even be punished. Limitation, according to the class of a woman, of the right of borrowing money."

"21. If parents or relatives will undertake the reclamation of a prostitute, the police will compel restitution of her person, irrespective of the keeper's claims, or even of the woman's own refusal."

"22. A woman changing her residence, and disputing any settlement with the keeper, can have the same rectified by the police."

"23. The women to be subjected every week to medical visitation. No woman, during menstruation, or with any malady in the sexual organs, to receive visits from a man. No woman to be approached by a man diseased, or reasonably suspected of disease. To this end, a statement of the signs of venereal disease to be furnished."

"24. The orders of the public physician are imperative, and must be strictly observed. Want of personal cleanliness increasing the virulence of syphilis, the directions of the physician on this matter to be imperatively followed."

"25. The medical officer to report the result of examination to the police, and to enter the same in a book to be kept by each woman, to be produced on demand."

"26. A woman finding herself to be venereally infected to report either to the keeper or the police; in other illness to report to the medical officer, who will direct her course of treatment at home, or, in venereal and infectious cases, at the hospital. In cases of pregnancy she is to report herself to the medical officer."

"27. A keeper punishable for the disease of a man in his house, and liable for the charges of cure."

The remaining sections relate to the collection of the tax; the penalties for violation are fine and imprisonment.

Having thus briefly sketched the progress of legislation on prostitution in Hamburg, based upon the principle that "prostitution is a necessary evil, and, as such, must be endured under strict supervision of the authorities," it seems an appropriate place to copy the following remarks of an eminent local writer:

"That brothels are an evil no one can deny; still, the arguments against the sufferance of brothels are, except as to that incontestable truth, no answer to the 'necessity,' which is the very *gist* of the thing, and which necessity is based on the uncontrollable nature of sexual intercourse, and on the circumstances of our social condition."

"The sufferance of brothels is necessary,

"1. For the repression of profligacy, of private prostitution as well as of its kindred crimes, adultery, rape, abortion, infanticide, and all kinds of illicit gratification of sexual passion. The latter cases occur very rarely with us. Of Pæderasty or Sodomy we find but few instances; and of that unnatural intercourse of women with each other, referred to by Parent-Duchatelet as common among the Parisian girls, we find no trace."

" The sufferance of brothels operates to the suppression of private prostitution, in so far as brothel-keepers and the 'inscribed' women are, for their own interest, opposed to it, and are serviceable to the police in its detection. Unquestionably, private prostitution is an incalculably greater evil than public vice."

" 2. On grounds of public policy in regard to health. It is quite erroneous to suppose that these legalized brothels contribute to the spread of syphilitic maladies. This should rather be imputed to the private prostitution which would ensue on the breaking up of the brothels, and from which that medical police supervision that now limits the spread of infection would, of course, be withdrawn. The experience of all time proves that, by means of secret prostitution, the intensity and virulence of venereal disorders have been aggravated, to the multiplication of those appalling examples familiar to every medical reader, and which cause one to shudder with horror; while numerically, disease and its consequences have been carried into every class of society. It is precisely our knowledge of these very facts which has induced the sufferance, or, rather, the regulation of these brothels."

" 3. *Suppression is* ABSOLUTELY IMPRACTICABLE, inasmuch as the evil is rooted in an unconquerable physical requirement. It would seem as if the zeal against public brothels implied that by their extinction a limitation of sexual intercourse, except in marriage, would be effected. This is erroneous, for reliable details prove that for every hundred brothel women there would be two hundred private prostitutes, and no human power could prevent this. In a great city and frequented sea-port like Hamburg, the hope of amending this would be purely chimerical."

Thus much for Hamburg legislation, and the sound arguments in its favor. We will now give some facts illustrative of the vice as it exists at the present time, using a pamphlet by Dr. LIPPERT, entitled "Prostitution in Hamburg. 1848."

It must be premised that, for the purpose, Hamburg is divided into two parts: the city proper, and the suburb of St. Paul. The latter is under a distinct municipal authority, and is the ordinary residence of seamen and those depending on a seafaring life.

For many years the police returns of the city proper would show about five hundred of the registered "common women" (*eingeschrieben Dirnen*), and one hundred registered brothels. The police regulations requiring monthly payment of the personal and house tax, and also a renewal of the permission to keep brothels at the same time, is a very convenient method of obtaining a census of the class. The following is a statement of the largest and smallest monthly number of registered women for several years:

Year 1833	. . .	Largest number, 550	. . .	Smallest number, 456
" 1834	. . .	" " 550	. . .	" " 450
" 1835	. . .	" " 481	. . .	" " 441
" 1836	. . .	" " 546	. . .	" " 473
" 1837	. . .	" " 514	. . .	" " 484
" 1844	. . .	" " 502	. . . . .	} No reports.
" 1846	. . .	" " 512	. . . . .	

These monthly reports do not show any marked variation at any particular period, the rise and fall being arbitrary. The fluctuation is not very great in the aggregate, although from November, 1834, to January, 1835, there was a decrease of 86 (or nearly one fifth), while between November, 1835, and January, 1836, there was a corresponding increase. Since that time the numbers have remained steadily at about one point.

The housekeepers' (*bordelwirth*) return does not vary to the same extent. The average is 105
But it decreased in 1844 to 90
   "   "   " 1845 " 93
   "   "   " 1846 " 96
Of these housekeepers in the last-named year (1846) there were
    Males 60
    Females . . . . 36—96
In December, 1844, there were
    Registered women 502
who were subdivided into those
    Living in registered houses 294
    Living privately . . . . 208—502
In May, 1845, there were
    Registered women 505
who were subdivided into those
    Living in registered houses 326
    Living privately . . . . .179—505
(At this period there were four registered houses without any women in them.)
In August, 1846, there were
    Registered women 512
who were subdivided into those
    Living in registered houses 334
    Living privately . . . . 178—512

These figures show that the number of those living privately is gradually diminishing, more of them being concentrated in the registered houses.

Dr. Lippert is of opinion that prostitution decreases in the summer and increases in the winter months. The statistics will certainly support this theory, but the difference is so small as scarcely to warrant its reception as a rule.

Thus the months of May and July, for five years, give a monthly
average of . . . . $499\frac{5}{10}$
and the months of November and January for the same time give
a monthly average of . . . . $501\frac{1}{10}$
showing an average increase in the winter months of . . . . $1\frac{6}{10}$
or about one third of one per cent. on the average number of prostitutes.

In reference to the classes from which the ranks of the common
women in Hamburg are recruited, Dr. Lippert states that four
fifths are from the agricultural districts of the vicinity; that they
live as house-servants, tavern-waiters, or in other callings for a
time, and then become prostitutes "as a matter of business."
Without any desire to controvert his opinion on local questions,
it may be doubted whether bad example, vicious education, ignorance of moral or religious obligations, or temptation, are not sufficient to account for their fall, aside from this sweeping denunciation, this commercial view of the question, opposed as it is to all
experience in every civilized country where any inquiries on the
subject have been made.

The private prostitutes, whether registered or unregistered, are
mainly seamstresses or others dependent upon daily labor. These
women seem to retain some natural sense of the disgrace attached
to open and avowed courtesans, and in their secrecy and quiet retain a few feminine characteristics of which the common brothel
woman is destitute.

We have no reliable detail of private unregistered prostitution,
or of mere houses of accommodation in Hamburg; but an important fact is to be found in the number of illegitimate children, and
the decrease, in proportion to the population, of the number of
marriages. The following results are taken from Neddermeyer's
"Statistics and Topography of Hamburg."

In 1799, the marriages were about 1 in 45;
From 1826 to 1835, " " " " 1 " 97;
In 1840, " " " " 1 " 100.

The proportion of illegitimate to legitimate children is about 1
to 5, the actual number of illegitimate births being as follows:

Years.	Illegitimate Births.	Years.	Illegitimate Births.	Years.	Illegitimate Births.
1826	649	1833	867	1840	754
1827	606	1834	846	1841	749
1828	723	1835	730	1842	702
1829	801	1836	807	1843	655
1830	786	1837	771	1844	797
1831	805	1838	762	1845	778
1832	926	1839	765	1846	779

The population of Hamburg was in 1826 . . 100,902
"   "   "   "   1840 . . 124,967
"   "   "   "   1846 . . 130,000 or upward was assumed as the number.

We have now to examine the physiological and pathological peculiarities of the Hamburg prostitutes.

The police regulations require that no registered woman shall be under twenty years of age; but in this they have a discretionary power, so as to keep under inspection and supervision some younger girls whom neither the work-house nor prison can reclaim, the experience of the Hamburg authorities having convinced them that such *punitive institutions are seldom successful in the work of reformation;* a truth which will, ere long, be more generally acknowledged, especially in reference to abandoned women, than it is at the present day.

The official list for 1844 shows that of the registered prostitutes there were

```
Under 20 years of age. . . . . . . . . . 16
From 20  "   to 30 years  . . . . . . 401
 "   30  "   " 40  "   . . . . . . . 74
 "   40  "   " 50  "   . . . . . . 11
                    Total . . . . . 502
```

In 1846, of women living in registered houses, there were

```
From 20 years to 30 years of age . . . . . 199
 "   30  "   " 40  "   "   . . . . . 50
 "   40  "   " 50  "   "   . . . . . 8
                    Total . . . . . 257
```

The birth-places of the 502 women reported in 1844 included most of the countries in Germany. There were from

Hamburg 108	Holland 2
Hanover 101	Russia 2
Prussia 81	France 1
Holstein 78	Total . . 502
Other parts of Germany 129	

The nativity returns for 512 women, in 1846, do not vary materially from the above, the difference in the foreign-born being that there were four, instead of five, born out of Germany. These tables show that about one in five are natives of Hamburg city and territory. Dr. Lippert notices this fact as a small proportion, and accounts for it by enumerating the difficulties of local relationship, parentage, etc., which would be opposed to the registration of native women. These circumstances favor the presumption that many of the unregistered women are city born.

The Hamburger Berg, or St. Paul's Suburb, is on the west side of Hamburg, and has already been mentioned as the abode of seamen and their dependents. Brothels were tolerated here, in deference to the wants of the inhabitants, at a time when they were strictly excluded from the city proper. The women and the houses are of a different type from those of other parts of Hamburg. All the prostitutes live in registered houses, unregistered or private traffic in this quarter being rigorously opposed by the authorities. The brothels and their inmates are in the most flourishing condition at the end of autumn, when the home voyages are completed and the sailors paid off. For a time mirth and excitement bear the sway; when the wages are all spent, things relapse into their old condition, and sometimes the keepers dismiss some of their women, the supply being in excess of the demand.

During the year 1846 the number of registered women in this district was

January	186	August	181
May	189	December	169

The 169 women registered in December were distributed among nineteen tolerated houses. In seven of these music and dancing were permitted, and they contained respectively 21, 13, 11, 19, 20, 18, 29 women, leaving only 26 women to inhabit the remaining twelve houses.

The ages of these women were

Under 20 years	27
From 20 " to 30 years	129
" 30 " " 40 "	13
Total	169

The places of birth do not vary materially from the proportions given already. Other matters relating to this particular class will be found hereafter.

In their *physique* the great majority of the registered women present no pleasing aspect. Generally taken from the rudest classes, they are coarse and unattractive in their appearance, and from the consequences of irregular indulgence and continual exposure, they soon lose the womanly characteristics they once possessed. But this is not a portrait of the whole. Among the unregistered private women may be found some of considerable beauty. The registered women who reside in private, or in first-class brothels, have some prepossessing members of their ranks, while the St. Paul suburb has few but of the roughest kind. Physical strength seems more in demand among the *habitués* of that section than a graceful form or a pretty face.

In their bodily peculiarities and diseases there is no difference between the public women of Hamburg and those of other cities. At the commencement of their career they frequently become thin and emaciated, but after a time, probably owing to their idle life and good food, regain their substance. In their phrenological development we find a marked preponderance of the animal instincts over the intellectual faculties. The effect of their mode of life will depend somewhat upon individual constitution. The teeth of women of the town are generally bad, but in Hamburg they are in excellent order—much better than the majority of the general population. Their complexion is pale, and they endeavor to remedy this by the constant use of coarse cloths, applications of eau de Cologne, and other stimulants, but very rarely by painting, except among the lowest classes. They soon lose their hair from dissipation, the use of pomatum, curling irons, etc. It is, however, in the rough, harsh voice that the most conspicuous result of their calling is shown.

We will leave, for the present, the medical portion of this inquiry, and give a sketch of their domestic or every-day life. It must be borne in mind that the police divisions are into " registered" or "unregistered," and " public" or "private" women.

The public women (*öffentlichen dirnen*) are under the special control and supervision of a police authority charged with this duty. Without his express cognizance and permission they can not be registered, or " written in" (*eingeschrieben*), nor can they have liberty to change their residence, or to be " written out" (*ausgeschrieben*). This officer is the collector of the impost upon them and upon the brothel-keeper (*bordelwirth*), which is paid over to the fund (*meretricen kasse*). We can not give the detailed application of this money, but, in general terms, it does not swell the revenues of the city, and, to avoid public scandal, is applied exclusively to the police and medical services required by the class.

The keepers and women are of three grades. It does not clearly appear whether a woman can select the class with whom she will associate. We are inclined to think the magistrates decide this point, and allot her to the one for which she seems best adapted.

In their apparel and food there exists the usual difference that may be found in all places and ranks of life. The police regulations, and the generally sober style of dress among the Hamburgers, restrict any immodest display of the person or extravagance of attire. The first-class women are generally costumed with taste and elegance, while among the lower ranks plain and serviceable garments are in demand. In most cases of the registered women residing in brothels, the keeper supplies the clothes, and very often charges extravagant prices for them. Extortionate demands in this respect are a fruitful source of complaints to the police, who moderate the bills with no very tender sympathy for the creditor. The clothes and jewelry of some of the first-class women are hired from some clothes-lender (*vermietheinnen*), but others seldom resort to this expedient, excepting for trinkets.

The food of the house-women is good and plentiful, varying according to the rate of the brothel in which they live. The old sumptuary laws are not in force, but the interest of the keeper induces him to desire a prudent popularity among his women, and to maintain the character of his house by the liberality of his entertainment both in quantity and quality. A considerable portion of their liquids is coffee, of which they are very fond. Wines and liquors are supplied by the house only on holidays, but visitors can purchase them at any time they wish. Drunkenness is comparatively rare among the better class, partly owing to the care of the keeper, but more from dread of the police supervision and consequent punishment.

In their intellectual capacity there is nothing to distinguish the prostitutes in Hamburg. Few can read, and fewer still can write. Those who can read seek their amusement in the old romances of the circulating libraries, seldom perusing that libidinous style of publications known among us as "yellow-covered literature." *En passant*, this seems the universal practice of the class, wherever any inquiries have been made. Like other ignorant persons, they are superstitious. Lippert mentions one particular omen connected with their calling: she who picks up any article which has been thrown away is sure to receive a visit from a man soon after. He does not say whether this has been verified by experience.

Their ordinary routine of life is one of useless idleness. They rise about ten and take breakfast, of which coffee is the staple. The morning is loitered away in dressing, reading novels, playing cards or dominoes, and kindred occupations. In some of the lower-class houses they dispel their *ennui* by assisting in domestic work, but this is a matter of favor which they are careful shall not become an obligation. By the middle of the day they are ready for dinner. In the afternoon they add the finishing touches to their dress, and wait the arrival of visitors. Some resort to the public lounges or dancing saloons to form or cultivate acquaintances, but the aristocracy of the order hold it more becoming to their dignity to stay at home and wait for their "friends."

In that fine and peculiar quality of modesty, which adds the crowning grace to woman's charms, even the prostitute is not wholly deficient. Some trace of the angel attribute is visible, but mostly in the private women, where a regard for the decent proprieties of life yet lingers amid the wreck of character, and to such it frequently forms the chief attraction.

Religion has an influence over some, strangely at variance with its dictates as are their lives, but a large majority are entirely destitute of any such sentiment. Occasionally, Biblical pictures may be seen in the rooms of brothels, but merely as ornaments, for they are neutralized by the contiguity of others more consonant with the place.

In their relations to the male sex there are differences between women residing in public brothels and those living privately, whether registered or unregistered. Partly from inclination, but mainly from policy on the part of the keeper, the former seldom own allegiance to any particular lover. It is true that any one who is able and willing to pay liberally can come and go as he pleases, provided he does not interfere with the girl's "business" in other profitable quarters. Not so with the private women, who frequently have particular "lovers" to whom they show much kindness, although from them they often receive but little sympathy or protection, many of these men not scrupling to exist entirely upon the earnings of a woman whom they would publicly insult if they met her away from home.

In their personal conduct toward each other the women residing in one house are constrained and envious. In the first class there is a ceremonious retention of the forms of politeness, but they are too frequently brought into personal rivalry to entertain much good feeling. In the lower classes jealousy often finds vent in reproaches or blows, and frequently a conflict ensues requiring the interposition of the host or of a neighboring police officer. Among those who live alone warm friendships are not uncommon;

much timely assistance is afforded in times of sickness or want; good offices are reciprocated; and it sometimes happens, in the delicate matter of their visitors, that a man who has been in the habit of favoring one woman will not find his attentions welcomed by others.

Their crimes and offenses include the ordinary category, but it is asserted that theft is less common in Hamburg than elsewhere, and, when it does take place, it is more frequently committed by the irregular members of the body than by the duly registered women. It will be perceived that the system of registration offers too many facilities for detection, a fact to which the unusual honesty must doubtless be ascribed. Personal quarrels and assaults, or drunkenness among the older members, consign them to the House of Detention or House of Correction. Those imprisoned from various causes generally amount to one hundred or one hundred and twenty.

The licensed brothels are supplied with inmates by females (*kupplerinnen*) whose services are recognized by the authorities. In case of any emergency, the keeper applies to one of the procuresses, and if the girl she offers suits him, the candidate is first subjected to a medical examination. Passed safely through this ordeal, she is taken to the police office and " written in" to her new keeper, who is bound to discharge certain of her debts, as the amount due his predecessor, for instance. If the medical officers report her sick, she is sent to the infirmary if she belong to Hamburg, but if a foreigner is dispatched out of the city forthwith. In cases where a woman thus applying to the authorities has not previously lived as a prostitute, she is usually exhorted by the magistrate to abandon her intention and return to the paths of virtue, a routine piece of benevolence which is usually fruitless. The ordinary police fee for registration is two marks, the physician's fee is one mark, and the agent's usual remuneration four marks.

The registered women are thus kept strictly under the eye of the police, and, whenever they are disposed to quit their wretched life, have the special protection of that body. The keepers naturally throw all possible obstacles in the way of such a determination, especially if a girl is much in debt; but, by some means, whenever a woman is under any restraint, and is consequently unable to apply personally to the police, an anonymous note finds its way to the office, and speedily effects the desired object. The authorities do not sympathize in any way with the brothel-keepers, but use all their energies to serve the women whenever any occasion offers.

The registered women are designated as "Brothel women" (*Bordell dirnen*), who live in licensed houses; as "Private women" (*für sich wohnende dirnen*) when they live by themselves, in which case their landlords are mostly mechanics, hucksters, or laundresses; and the common "Street-walkers" (*Strassen dirnen*), who ply their trade in the streets, and find shelter in the abodes of indigence and misery. These last are the lowest grade of the registered women.

Most of the brothels (*bordelle*) are in the oldest parts of the city, to which they were originally limited, but the leading houses may be found in the *Schwieger strasse*, a street of moderate traffic in a good neighborhood. Here the women are seated at the windows, conspicuously dressed up and prepared for the public eye, making themselves known to passengers by their gestures and salutations. Some of these houses accommodate as many as fourteen inmates. They are well supplied with good mahogany furniture and fine draperies, and are neat and elegant throughout. The women are generally from twenty to twenty-five years old, and are attractively dressed and decorated. The venereal disease is very rare among this class, great attention being paid to personal cleanliness, and the bath very frequently used. The men who visit this neighborhood consist of merchants, the richer public and business employes, officers, and especially the numerous commercial men who resort to Hamburg at all seasons of the year.

The denizens of the *Dammthorwall,* the *Drehbahm,* and *Ulricas strasse* lead but a dull life, as it is the custom in those localities for the women to sit at the windows all day. Their great diurnal event is the visit of the hair-dresser (*friseurian*), who, while contributing to the adornment of the person, a very serious affair, owing to the quantity of false hair required, and the necessity of making to-day's effect vary from yesterday's, also retails the latest items of interesting news or scandal. Whenever any of these women go out to walk, it is customary for the keeper to send together two who are at variance with each other, so as to establish a mutual check. The hair-dressing and walk over, the next important occurrence is dinner, after which they spend their time solely at the doors or windows.

The hours of closing in these first and second rate brothels are not so strictly enforced by the police as in the lower parts. Occasionally the women are allowed to visit the balls at the celebrated Hall of Mirrors, or other well-known dancing saloons in the vicinity.

In first-rate houses the accounts between the keeper and the women are but little understood. As already observed, some of them hire their clothes; others purchase from the landlord on credit, and he charges accordingly; but these matters trouble the women very slightly. If they leave one house to reside in another, the new keeper pays the old one's bill; if a woman abandons prostitution entirely, the host's demand is totally irrecoverable.

In the second and third rate houses the charges for board and lodging are better understood. It will average about twenty marks (five dollars) a week, washing, fire, and light being extra charges. The keeper will supply fortunate or attractive women with articles of dress to any reasonable amount, but his liberality is restricted toward those who have fewer visitors. His endeavor is to keep all in debt, and in this he is usually successful. Their ornaments are usually the property of the landlord, and form a common stock distributed among his boarders in the manner best calculated to increase or display their powers of fascination, and resumed by him at discretion.

Passing over some intermediate classes of brothels, which present no remarkable characteristics, to those in the *Gangen*, we find the lowest grade of registered houses and registered women. Most of these are drinking-shops, and the police exercise the right of determining the prices to be charged for liquors. Here may frequently be seen host, guests, and girls, drinking and frolicking together in a small back room, where scenes of gross indelicacy (to use a mild term) frequently take place. The women in this district have literally to work hard, and are generally required to perform all the domestic labor of the establishment. In winter it is a common occurrence for them to take a shovel and clear the snow and ice from the pavement in front of their domicile. Like others of their calling, they are seldom out of the landlord's debt, their board costing them from ten to fourteen marks weekly (say three to four dollars). Washing, fire, and light cost a dollar more, and the hair-dresser's charge is about fifty cents. In addition to this, they must pay the weekly medical and monthly police tax. They spend a miserably monotonous existence, seldom leaving the house for weeks or even months, except when they are required to visit the doctors or the police. Their visitors are from the roughest and most animalized of the population, and the treatment they receive is merely that of purchasable commodities, intended to supply the grosser wants of men whose lives are centred in sensuality. Like their compeers of the St. Paul Suburb, they are usually women of great strength and endurance, but soon degenerate into mere passive, passionless tools. Could it be imagined that they were of reflective habits, it would be impossible to conceive a more severe punishment than their own sense of the degradation, the total loss of all womanly feelings, exhibited in their daily existence.

The brothel-keepers, among whom are some Jews, have no striking peculiarities as a class. It has been already shown that both sexes are engaged in the hideous trade, and, despite the police regulations and restrictions, the obligations and disabilities under which they are placed, it is undoubtedly a most lucrative occupation. The rental of a registered house is usually double the ordinary charge for similar tenements. There are some keepers who own the houses in which they live. In their liabilities must be included the regulation which makes them responsible for thefts committed in their houses, and for any violence or disorder which may take place there, the penalties for which are fine, imprisonment, and loss of license. They also sustain considerable losses from the repentance of some of their inmates; but, in spite of all untoward circumstances, they contrive to make money rapidly.

The period during which they continue in *business* is uncertain, many of them continuing their houses from inclination long after they have accumulated sufficient property to retire. Of the female keepers some are young and handsome, but these do not find much favor with their women, who dread the effects of an opposition. They are rarely married, but cohabit with some man for the sake of his protection. Among these *pro tempore* husbands are some whose qualifications and previous positions render it surprising that they should consent to purchase existence from so polluted a source.

The housekeepers of the Hamburger Berg are not only under a separate municipal jurisdiction, but are in themselves a different class of people. They are mostly men, their dealings being principally with sailors, and their visitors sometimes demanding more physical strength than a woman could command to restrain them within the prescribed limits. Their houses are but indifferently furnished, and the whole arrangements are very humble and un-pretending in character. A few years ago fatal quarrels were not uncommon among their customers, but this pugnacious tendency has been materially checked by a stricter and more constant police visitation. Even now, jealousy will sometimes cause a furious contest between two of the hardy sons of Neptune. The singular fidelity of some sailors to particular women will account for this. When a man returns from a long voyage, he is desirous of paying his attentions to the female who has before shared his affections and his wages, and if he finds her under the protection of another man, the natural result is a trial of strength as to who shall be the possessor of the beauty in dispute. These tournaments, or the general fray which sometimes arises at the close of the Sunday evening dance, require to be subdued by no gentle means: hearty blows are far more effectual peace-makers than words or threats.

Some of these registered hosts have followed their calling for many years. One noble incident in connection with them must not be omitted. In the severe winter of 1846, the landlord of the "Four Lions," a brothel-keeper of twenty-four years' standing, maintained at his own cost, for some months, nearly one hundred poor families, many of them with three or four children each.

In the dance-houses there is music every evening except Sat-urday; on week-days from six to eleven, and on Sundays from four to eleven. At eleven the music is stopped, and at twelve the house is peremptorily closed. The evenings during the week are comparatively dull affairs, and male visitors are sometimes so scarce that the women are compelled to dance with each other, or sit in inglorious idleness. A scene of the wildest uproar and most uncontrolled mirth is exhibited on Sunday evenings. Every va-riety of national dance may then be seen—cachucha, reel, jig, contré-dance, waltz, and hornpipe have each their several admir-ers. Songs and shouts are heard in every conceivable dialect, and the room becomes literally "confusion worse confounded" until the hour arrives for closing.

Of the registered women living by themselves there is little to note. They are more industrious than those in brothels. Many of them have a fixed occupation, but resort to prostitution to in-crease their income. Money earned in this way is occasionally required for the common necessaries of life, but is more frequent

O

ly spent in personal gratification, in the way of fine dresses, ornaments, etc., or is appropriated to support the extravagance of some lover, who repays the generosity by a little flattering attention, or an occasional escort to some dancing saloon in the suburbs. The visitors to these women are more select than those to the courtesans hitherto described.

In the lowest ranks of prostitution, the common "street-walkers," to be met at all times and places, under all circumstances and of all ages, we find the most prolific sources of infection. A certain, though very small remnant of decency, seconded by the invaluable watchfulness of the police, secures the visitor from disease among the inmates of registered houses, but the street-walker is under no such control. Young girls scarcely more than children, old women almost grandmothers, ply their frightful trade on the "walls" around the city, and in other obscure places, where a trifling present will purchase their caresses. Their principal customers are young boys and very old men, their practices being continued under the shades of evening until the arrival of the night-watch drives them to their wretched dens.

The Hamburg police are perfectly cognizant of these proceedings, and wage perpetual war against individuals, but find it altogether impossible to suppress the class, among whom are the habitual tenants of the jail and the House of Correction. No one can differ in opinion from Dr. Lippert, who says, "In this class of women the most pernicious results of prostitution are to be found."

Private or domestic prostitution, so widely extended in every great town, exists in less proportion in Hamburg than in other capital cities of the same extent. That disgraceful union in evil occasionally met with on the Continent, in which husband and wife mutually agree to follow their inclinations or lusts untrammeled by each other, is scarcely known. The kept woman is comparatively rare. The expense attendant upon such an appendage of luxury is a serious consideration, and none but the wealthy patrician or successful business man venture on the step. It is assumed, on very good authority, that there are not fifty "mistresses" in Hamburg. Those residing there are under no police control, as in a public point of view they commit no breach of law.

Under the second head of private prostitution we find those who, having legitimate employment, increase their earnings in this manner. We have alluded already to the same class of registered women, but the greater portion keep themselves aloof from police observation as long as possible. They are composed of needle-women, laundresses, hair-dressers, shop-girls, and others, but it must not be supposed that they represent the majority of women dependent upon those occupations. The contrary is the fact; for in Hamburg, as every where else, are to be found many bright examples of chastity in the midst of poverty; of patient, persevering industry and integrity in unfavorable circumstances. Those working women who are willing to accept the price of sin are known in the streets by a peculiar gait, by their searching and inviting glances, or their treacherous but winning smile, and also by frequently walking in the same neighborhood. They are seldom seen abroad during the day, but in the afternoon, about "'change hours," they begin to resort to the streets near the *Bourse*, encountering the men as they hurry to and from the centre of business. In the evening they promenade in the vicinity of the hotels and theatres, on the *Jungfernstig*, the new walls, etc., when night helps their *incognito*, and shrouds them in a little more mystery. They are fond of attending the theatres and dancing saloons on Sundays and holidays, like the Parisian *grisette*, in company with a lover, but the sum of their enjoyment is complete if they can participate in the annual Shrove Tuesday ball and masquerade at the Apollo Saal, the Elb Pavilion, or the theatre.

Another class of private prostitutes is known to the police by the term "*Winklehuren*" (hedge w——). These are of the lower class of female operatives. Servant-girls, from their proximity to the junior members of families, often spread disease in the household of their employers. Dr. Lippert records as a medical fact that examinations have frequently shown the domestics in the highest families to be literally saturated with venereal disease, and he states his opinion that six out of every ten servant-girls who are found in the streets at night are accessible to pecuniary temptation. This ratio is very large, but as it is a local matter with which he is presumed to be well acquainted, it would be out of place to attempt either to sustain or controvert it.

All these private prostitutes resort to the houses of accommodation (*Absteigequartiere*), which exist in spite of the constant watchfulness of the police. When they are hunted up and rooted out of one place, they reappear under another guise elsewhere; a removal being facilitated by the slender nature of their equipment, which seldom consists of more than furniture for one room.

For "genteel" delinquents, they are placed where the accommodation is veiled under the French disguise of *petits soupers*, or some such flimsy artifice.

To the question, "What becomes of the prostitutes?" Hamburg offers no special reply. Under favorable circumstances, they abandon their calling, and become the wives of mechanics or small tradesmen; or they carry on some business for themselves, and strive to become reputable members of society; or they become companion to some man, and follow his fortunes, usually reverting to common prostitution. When their charms are entirely lost, and no hope remains of earning a living from their sale, they sometimes, but very rarely, become brothel-keepers; sometimes procuresses; and, more frequently, servants in the registered houses.

Some of the dancing saloons already mentioned have attained European celebrity. They stand in the same relation to common women as the exchange does to the mercantile community. Their female visitors are mostly prostitutes, a fact which deprives the scene of many fascinations existing in other cities. In the end of the last century there was no public place expressly designed for dancing, until, with the many equivocal blessings disseminated by the French Revolution, they also became an institution. The Hamburg saloons are conducted with order and quiet, and are generally closed about one o'clock in the morning. One of the most important, the Bacchus Hall, was burned down some few years since, and the authorities have, as yet, refused to grant a license for its re-erection.

As public places which in some degree facilitate prostitution, mention must be made of the common sleeping apartments locally called "deep cellars" (*tiefen kellar*). These are roomy vaults, many feet under ground, in which the poor find nightly shelter at very low prices. They are provided with beds and bedding. In the depth of poverty to which some of their customers have fallen, they can not afford to pay two schellings (about four cents) for the luxury of a bed, and these repose their weary limbs on some foul straw, or on the ground, at the charge of half a schelling. Some of these cellars are fifteen or twenty feet below the surface of the street, and it will not require a very vivid imagination to portray their horrors.

The beer and wine houses of Hamburg are tolerably free from prostitution; but a new class has lately sprung up, called "cellar-keeping" (*kellerwirthschaff*), and in these the guests are served by females in fancy costume, Swiss, Polish, or Circassian, as the case may be. Many of these contain private rooms for prostitution, and, although they are closely watched by the police, who sometimes ungallantly expel the fair foreigners and close the establishments, they still flourish, others being speedily opened else-where to fill up the gap.

From this general description of prostitutes, their habitations, and customs, we will proceed to a consideration of their condition as to health, and the extent and virulence of syphilis among them, still taking the pamphlet of Dr. Lippert for our guide.

It is generally imagined that the excessive action of the generative organs interferes with the power of procreation in common women. Dr. Lippert undertakes to controvert this opinion, with what success medical men whose professional experience has been among this class will be able to judge. He supports his views by general assertions rather than by specific facts, but refers, in corroboration, to well-known instances in which children have been born while the mothers were living in a state of open prostitution, as also to those cases where women who have abandoned the habit of promiscuous intercourse confine themselves to one man by marriage or cohabitation, and then become mothers. He attributes their sterility during prostitution to their wild and irregular life, their constant exposure to weather, etc., and argues that the powers of conception are suspended, but not destroyed thereby. He also introduces the fact that abortions are frequently produced in Hamburg by the common women themselves, or by some old crones who preside over their orgies, and are stated to have a long list of drugs applicable to this purpose, which they use in a reckless manner. The medical police are not unaware of these proceedings, but find them difficult to detect, as a woman will endeavor to avoid the stated examination by pleading excessive menstruation, or inventing some story she thinks likely to deceive, until all traces of the abortion are removed. The remarks of Dr. Lippert would lead to the belief that the *excessive use* of the female organs was more favorable to health than the disuse would be, a conclusion which most physicians will not be willing to admit. He adds, "Cancer of the womb occurred but once in my experience of eleven years at the General Infirmary, and cases of prolapsus uteri are very rare."

A disease incident to common women, *Colica scortorum* (W——'s

Colic), happens in Hamburg as elsewhere, but is attributed to exposure to the weather more than any other cause. It consists of
pain in the womb, extending across the abdomen round to the
loins, and sometimes including the whole region of the stomach.
It is frequently accompanied with gastric derangement, sickness,
or diarrhœa.

The enlargement of the clitoris, so much insisted on by some
writers, Lippert altogether doubts, except as a very exceptional
case ; nor does he admit any effect of prostitution on the rectum
unless induced by unnatural intercourse.   As a general result of
his observations, he concludes that, " apart from syphilitic affections, the generative organs of a prostitute do not usually differ
from those of a virtuous woman."

We find some returns of diseases not directly connected with
prostitution ; thus, cases of itch, which is now becoming rare,
were in

1836	 62	1844	 38
1837	 76	1845	 22
1838	 87	1846	 36
1839	 98		

Of other general maladies, including fevers, inflammation of the
lungs, liver, womb, etc., rheumatism, small-pox, piles, jaundice,
gout, dropsy, and diarrhœa, the following are reported:

1837	 62	1844	 85
1838	 90	1845	 76
1839	 100	1846	 77

Convulsions are more rare than in the female sex in general;
of hysteria there is scarcely a trace, and a few cases of epilepsy
are ascribed to the use of ardent spirits.

Delirium tremens seldom occurs.   The vigilance of the police,
and the prompt committal to prison of every prostitute found
drunk and disorderly, may account for this.   The proportion of
cases of delirium tremens was only about one in one thousand.

Mania sometimes shows itself.   Remorse may produce this, as
may a violent affection for some particular man.

Of the actual extent of venereal disease in Hamburg, or any
other city, it is impossible to speak with certainty, but the fact
that in the general hospital there it is of a very mild type is an
argument in favor of medical inspection.   Dr. Lippert says:

" The usual form is gonorrhœa, with its complications, bubo, inflammation
of the scrotum, phymosis, paraphymosis, etc.   Inflammation of the prostate

gland, and stricture, are comparatively rare. Disease of the rectum is very rare, but there are examples."

"We have excoriations and irritations of the sexual organs. The simple chancre is common; the indurated chancre not unfrequent; the phagedænic chancre is seldom met with. In general, the sores have a mild character, and heal easily with simple treatment and regular topical applications. *Herpes preputialis* is extremely general. This is a group of small pustules, quickly healing up, but as quickly breaking out again, often in regular periodical recurrence. It is found especially on men who have suffered from gonorrhœa or chancre."

"Secondary syphilis, ulcers of the neck, eruptions, syphilitic inflammation of the eyes, tumors, etc. These prevail more at some times than at others; how far the *genus epidemicum*, the weather and season, the idiosyncrasy of the person, or the intensity of the infection operate, we have yet to learn."

" *Tertiary syphilis is rare."*

"In sea-ports it is often observable that the disease takes peculiar aspects, and what may be called exotic forms are occasionally encountered. With sailors, syphilis is frequently latent or only partially cured, and is intensified by their habits and diet. Sexual intercourse with them will produce it in an exaggerated character. This is not so much the case in Hamburg, owing to the constant and prompt medical attention; still, some distinction is observable between the venereal maladies of the city women and those of the St. Paul Suburb. Among the latter the cases of a malignant type generally occur."

The negro sailor is held in very bad repute by these women, and some keepers will not allow him to enter their houses, believing that infection from a colored man is of the worst kind, and almost incurable.

The medical returns for the year 1846 give the following tables relating to the women in the St. Paul Suburb:

"In January there were 186 women, of whom 15 were sick; the diseases were

Venereal disease	9	Rheumatic fever	1
Itch	1	Catarrh of lungs	1
Colic	1	Calculus	1
Gastric fever	1	Total	15

"In May, of 189 women, 21 were sick:

Venereal disease	9	Inflammation of lungs	1
Itch	8	Spitting of blood	1
Gastric fever	2	Total	21

"In August, of 181 women, 17 were sick:

Venereal disease 13	Itch 1
Colic 2	Rheumatism 1
	Total 17

"In December, of 161 women, 18 were sick :

Venereal disease 6	Gastric fever 2
Itch 6	Disorder of digestive organs 1
Sprain 1	Cold on the chest. . . . 1
Colic 1	Total 18

This would give an average of about ten per cent. of the women of the sub-urb sick."

From the facts we have quoted, it is evident that the virulence of syphilitic affections among the registered women is unquestionably mitigated. "*Tertiary syphilis is rare;*" secondary syphilis but occasional, while primary forms have lost their malignity. "There is a marked aggravation of the disease during the summer months, when a considerable influx of strangers takes place. This was particularly observable after the great fire in 1842."

The mildness of the disease, and its easy control, can be ascribed to nothing but the weekly medical supervision. The women are visited at their own houses, and any reluctance or refusal renders them liable to punishment.

Contrasted with this state of affairs, we have the severity of syphilis among unregistered women, who conceal their disease as long as they can. Of those arrested, many are found to be diseased in an aggravated form. In the year 1845, of 138 unregistered women sent to prison, 43 had syphilis, or nearly one third of the whole. Parent-Duchatelet says this proportion is exceeded by the same class in Paris, where the infected amount to one half the illicit prostitutes.

The "*Kurhaus*" is a medical institution especially designed for bad characters who are arrested by the police, be they registered or unregistered. The General Infirmary has also a venereal ward. The police authorities contribute annually, from the amount raised by the impost on brothels and prostitutes, 5000 marks ($1500) to the funds of this infirmary. From the following facts this would seem an inadequate amount. In 1844 there were received and treated 580 females with syphilis; the total residence amounting to 30.387 days, or a *pro rata* average of 53½ days each, the stipend allowed for which service would be about *four and a half cents per day.*

The number of female cases of syphilis received into the same institution in 1843 was,

Registered women 480
Unregistered women 74
Total 554

and in 1845,

Registered women 521
Unregistered women 71
Total 592

The state of the male venereal patients proves the same general amelioration in the character of the disease. The cases, however, are worse than among the registered women, which must be ascribed to the dislike of men to enter the hospital until such a course becomes unavoidable. The numbers received were, in

1843 355
1844 335
1845 316

Some returns are given by Dr. Lippert of the amount of sickness in the garrison; but he has not stated the number of soldiers, so no comparison can be drawn from his information. The figures are as follows:

1843, Gonorrhœa 90
Chancre 67
Secondary syphilis . . . . 13—170
1844, Gonorrhœa 58
Ulcers . . . . 63—121
1845, Gonorrhœa 89
Ulcers . . . . 79—168

The treatment of syphilis adopted in the Hamburg hospital was introduced by Dr. Fricke, one of the first to apply the non-mercurial system. Ricord's practice is also followed, and Hydropathy has been tried. It would be out of place to enter into any arguments here as to the relative merits of these systems.

The mortal diseases of the Hamburg prostitutes are incidental to their course of life. Exposure to the weather, alternate extremes of want and luxury, night-watching and constant excitement, induce consumption, inflammation of the lungs, dropsy, internal and abdominal complaints; gastric, rheumatic, or nervous fevers; and these, or chronic diseases resulting from renewed venereal infection. lead to the

"Last scene of all,
That ends this strange, eventful history."

Before dismissing this subject, we will give a sketch of the

HAMBURG MAGDALEN HOSPITAL.

This institution was founded in 1821 through the exertions of the Burgomaster Abendroth and others, and was constructed on the model of a similar asylum in London. The object is to reclaim women from vice by means that can be applied only in a place expressly dedicated to the purpose.

The number of inmates is small; only twelve can be received. The business of the asylum is conducted by a committee, including two ministers, a physician, three female overseers, and a matron. The overseers are respectable married women or widows, who voluntarily undertake the duties of a sub-committee. They assume the direction of the household affairs alternately for a month each. They meet frequently at the house, assist in Divine service, and take care of the girls who are discharged. These are provided with situations or placed in business, and require to be upheld and maintained in their new character.

The chaplain assists the ladies' committee in their duties, but directs his energies particularly to the religious instruction of the inmates. Frequent meetings for prayer are held, and every half year the sacrament is administered to such as he deems duly prepared to receive it, and who have a competent knowledge of its importance and efficacy.

To be qualified for admission, the applicant must be young, and must have a desire to amend. The limited room will not allow the reception of old or worn-out women, who would flock there in crowds to obtain a shelter under which they could die in peace. When a woman's application is granted, she must go through a novitiate of four or eight weeks. During this time she works and eats with the other inmates, but sleeps alone, and is closely watched by a member of the committee. When her novitiate expires and she is fully received, she is requested to give an explicit account of her life, every particular of which is recorded. Her name is not disclosed to her companions, but she, as are all the others, is known only by a Christian name.

The women are employed in all kinds of housework, needlework. or. when practicable, in any manner which will accustom them to continued physical exertion. Their previous life having made indolence almost "second nature," this course is adopted to inculcate the necessity of industry. A strict account of the produce of their labor is kept, and a portion is set apart as a fund for their benefit.

The time of their stay is usually about two years. When they leave they give the chaplain a written promise of good conduct, and receive from him a Bible and a Prayer-book, and the sum of money accumulated for them. The results of this benevolent attempt are sufficient to encourage the laborers in the good work, and we can not but think that their endeavors must be productive of great good, based as they are upon the sound principle of receiving but a few women, and treating them as members of one family, in opposition to the general theory of such institutions, whose managers attempt to crowd in as large a number as a large building will contain, and, in the endeavor to generalize rules for reformation, lose the valuable opportunities for noticing and acting upon individual traits of character.

The particulars of the subsequent life of twenty women are given as follows:

Continued faithful to their promise 6
Removed from where they were placed 10
Relapsed into vice, only 1
Died 1
Unknown 2
Total 20

CHAPTER XVII.

PRUSSIA.

Patriarchal Government.—Ecclesiastical Legislation.—Trade Guilds.—Enactments in 1700.—Inquiry in 1717.—Enactment in 1792.—Police Order, 1795.—Census. —Increase of illicit Prostitution.—Syphilis.—Census of 1808.—Ministerial Rescript and Police Report, 1809.—Tolerated Brothels closed.—Re-enactment of the Code of 1792.—Ministerial Rescript of 1839.—Removal of Brothels.—Petitions. —Ministerial Reply.—Police Report, 1844.—Brothels closed by royal Command. —Police Embarrassment, and Correspondence with Halle and Cologne.—Local Opinions.—Public Life in Berlin.—Dancing Saloons.—Drinking Houses.—Immorality.—Increase of Syphilis.—Statistics.—Illegitimacy.—Royal Edict of 1851. —Recent Regulations.

AMONG the warlike Germans in the days of Herminius, sexual intercourse was looked upon as enervating to youth, and discred-

itable or even disgraceful to men until their valor had been proved
by deeds of arms, and their experience authorized them to assume
the duties of husbands and fathers.

In the Middle Ages, when the legislative and executive functions were vested in one individual, and the rights and obligations
of the governing power were of a paternal or patriarchal character, we find much of their law-giving directed to the preservation
of morality, the repression of extravagance, and the minute regulation of public economy. In their edicts against prostitution
this paternal spirit was visible, in conjunction with what may be
considered a due regard to the rights and interests of the law-giv-
ers, the punishments being professedly directed against a breach
of morality or a public scandal, because it was a disgrace to families, and a peril to husbands and fathers, rather than a vice in itself. The provisions tacitly sanctioned its existence; and while
they severely punished any invasion of domestic peace or infraction of marital rights, it seems to be conceded that, when no such
relationships were involved, illicit intercourse was regarded as an
allowable solace or an actual necessity for the physical requirements of unmarried men.

We learn from the German historian Fiducin ("*Diplomatischen
Beitrage zur Geschichte der Stadt Berlin*"), that the German laws
rendered it obligatory on every honorable man to espouse a virtuous maiden, and the term "*hurenkind*" (illegitimate child) was
the bitterest form of reproach. The early statutes were very severe in the punishment of immodest females, and some carried
this principle so far as to require that a woman who led an unchaste life in her father's house should be burned at the stake.
The ecclesiastical legislation moderated this severity, and crimes
against morality became sins which were expiated by public penance. The citizens of Berlin became convinced that the penances
of the Church were not sufficiently potent to counteract the evil,
the morals of the clergy themselves being frequently impeached,
and secular government was suggested in place of ecclesiastical.
This seemed especially necessary, because the canon law, which
ordained the celibacy of the priesthood, pronounced it to be a
work of mercy to marry an erring woman, in opposition to the
Berlin sheriff law (*schoffen recht*) declaring the children of such
marriages illegitimate; and persons were not wanting who held
the opinion that the work of mercy recommended by the Church
was at times advocated by the clergy as a means of covering their
own frailties.

The same writer records instances as late as the close of the sixteenth century in which adultery was punished by death, the offenders in each case being married persons. He also cites the
records of the fourteenth century to show that the same punishment was inflicted on those who acted as procurers or procuresses,
wherever family honor was encroached on.

In the sixteenth century the law required that an immodest
woman belonging to any reputable family should be publicly shorn
of her hair, and condemned to wear a linen veil; nor was any distinction made between unmarried women and widows against
whom the offense was proved.

About the same period the trade guilds enacted stringent laws
prohibiting the admission of improper characters to their public
festivals, and restraining their members from marrying women of
that class. To attain this end, any master tradesman who designed to marry was compelled to introduce his intended bride at a
meeting of the company, that all might be convinced of her discreet character and conduct, and any who married without observing this requirement were expelled the association. The
guilds inflicted the same penalties on any of their members who
had intercourse with improper characters, or who seduced a virtuous woman and subsequently married her.

A certain recognition of the existence of public women may be
traced throughout these regulations, which appear to have admitted the necessity from regard to the rigorously enforced sanctity
of the domestic circle, but, at the same time, endeavored to prevent the increase of immorality by attaching odium to its followers.

Again, turning to the pages of Fiducin, we find that, "in all the
great towns of the German Empire, the public protection of wom-
en of pleasure (*lust dirnen*) seems to have been a regular thing,"
in proof of which he says, "Did a creditor, in taking proceedings
against his debtor, find it necessary to put up at an inn, one of the
allowed items of his expenditure was a reasonable sum for the
company of a woman during his stay (*frauen geld*)." This was a
question of state etiquette in Berlin in 1410, a sum having been
officially expended in that year to retain some handsome women
to grace a public festival and banquet given to a distinguished
guest, Diedrich V. Quitzow, whose good-will the citizens desired
to cultivate.

During this period of toleration the expediency of controlling public women was unquestioned; but the first Berlin enactment of material importance to this investigation bears date in 1700, and is remarkable as clearly enunciating the principles which have been adhered to, with only a short interval, ever since. The first section declares, "By law this traffic is decidedly not permitted (*erlaubt*), but simply tolerated (*geduldet*) as a necessary evil."

Sections 2, 3, and 4 require the keeper of any house of prostitution to give notice to the commissary of the quarter when any of his women leave him, or when he receives a new one, and restrain him from keeping more women than are specified in his contract.

Sections 5 to 9 provide that a surgeon shall visit every woman once a fortnight, "for the purpose of protecting the health of revelers (*schwarmer*), as well as that of the women themselves;" that every woman shall pay him two groschen for each visit; and that, upon observing the slightest signs of disease, the surgeon shall require the housekeeper to detain the woman in her room. If the keeper neglect this order, he is made responsible for the entire costs of the illness which any visitor could prove was contracted from one of his women. If the surgeon finds the woman already so far infected that she can not be cured by cleanliness and retirement alone, he is authorized to order her removal to the Charité, "where she will be taken care of in the pavilion free of charge."

Sections 10 and 11 provide that the debts of a woman must be paid before she can remove from one house of prostitution to another, or before she can leave one house to commence another on her own account.

Section 12 enjoins that any woman who desires to quit her mode of life altogether shall be entirely discharged from any debts to the housekeeper.

The last section requires every housekeeper who has music to pay six groschen a year for the permit to his musicians, the money to be applied to the benefit of the poor-house.

The "toleration but not authorization" clause is the noticeable feature in these regulations, and indicates the policy which was then generally adopted throughout the kingdom.

In reference to the period succeeding the issue of these rules, which continued in force till 1792, we find some information in the pages of Fiducin. Thus, in 1717, an inquiry proved that the inmates of brothels, and also the secret prostitutes, were mostly the children of soldiers, who "had been brought to vice as a trade, either from the want of a proper bringing up or of a skillful handicraft." . . . . *All measures for the extermination of the evil having been found ineffectual,* " they were obliged to adopt the system of a larger toleration of common brothels, to be strictly watched over by the police, as a necessary outlet for the tendency to immorality." The number of houses of ill fame increased in proportion to the population, the influx of strangers, and the additions to the garrison made under Frederick II.; and still more so after the close of the seven years' war. In the year 1780, there were one hundred such houses in Berlin, each containing eight or nine women. They were divided into three classes; the lowest were those in which the women dressed in plain clothes, and were frequented mostly by Hamburg or Amsterdam mariners; the second class of women paraded themselves with painted faces, haunted the more retired corners of the town, had little attractive about their persons or dress, and were principally visited by mechanics and laborers; the third, and apparently the most select of the kind, was a description of coffee-house, frequented by females, who were designated "*Mamselles:*" these did not live in the houses, but used them merely as a convenient rendezvous.

In 1792 a new code of regulations appeared, the bulk of which continued in force in Berlin and other towns for many years. The rules of 1700 were too vague, made no provision for a variety of cases likely to arise, and were silent as to the question of private prostitution. Many inconveniences had arisen from these omissions, and, in consequence, a memorial was addressed to the government by the police director, Von Eisenhardt, containing suggestions for amendments to the law.

The preamble of the royal reply to this application acknowledges the attention of the police to the matter with much satisfaction; admits prostitution (*hurenanstalten*) to be " a necessary evil in a great city where many men are not in a position to marry, although of an age when the sexual instincts are at the highest, in order thereby to avoid greater disorders which are not to be restrained by any law or authority, and which take their rise from an inextinguishable natural impulse;" but expressly reiterates that it is " only to be tolerated (*zu dulden*);" and that it can not, " without impropriety and consequences injurious to morality, be established by the public laws, which do not contain any sanction whatever to common prostitution."

The sections following this preamble provide that any one who seduces a woman, or induces her to carry on a venal traffic with her person, shall be liable to one year's imprisonment in the House of Correction, and on repetition of the offense, besides doubling the punishment, shall be whipped and driven from the country; declare any man or woman who communicates the venereal disease liable for the expenses of the cure and incidental damages (*sonstigen interesse*), together with imprisonment for three months, commutable by paying a fine of one hundred dollars; prohibit taking young women from the country into houses of prostitution by any device against their will, and authorize the punishment of any man who willfully infects a common woman.

In reference to the special directions touching brothels and prostitutes, the document provides, "as a leading point, that every thing which exceeds the mere gratification of the natural passions, and tends to the advancement of debauchery, or the misuse of our toleration of a necessary evil, must be prevented;" and accordingly the women are prohibited from increasing their attractions "by painting or distinguishing attire," and also from soliciting passengers in the public streets, or at the doors or windows of their houses, "as this is not only in contravention to public morals, but especially perilous to male youth; and such means of increasing the gains of people seeking their livelihood in this manner is not to be tolerated." For similar reasons, the keepers of houses were restrained from offering wines or other strong drinks to their visitors, although it is admitted "they can not be prevented from providing refreshments," yet stimulants are forbidden, "because they are great inducements to debauchery, whereby other excesses may be caused."

The orders farther provide that no woman shall become a resident in a house of prostitution without previously appearing before the police, and obtaining permission from them; and the police are directed not to allow this permission to any female under age, unless they are satisfied that she has previously made a trade of prostitution. The section containing this stipulation is prefaced by a statement that "keepers of these houses seek especially to obtain blooming young girls, who can not be procured without infamous seduction, calculated to lead to debauchery."

In reference to precautions against infection, it provides that the prostitutes and keepers of houses shall be instructed by some competent surgeon in the signs of venereal diseases, so that they may detect it in their visitors or themselves; also that any man communicating infection to a prostitute may be sentenced to make ample compensation if the woman can identify him; and farther, that the punishment inflicted upon girls infecting their visitors shall also be inflicted on the housekeepers, "as, although they may be innocent, their being included in the punishment for an incident of their trade is for the general weal." All fines received were to accrue to the medical institutions provided for the cure of syphilis.

Again, it was deemed that "the venereal disease was much extended by common street-walkers," and no women but such as resided in the known houses, where medical visits of inspection were constantly paid, were to be tolerated, and the night-watch were instructed to arrest those common women who were in the habit of plying their trade in the streets after dark—a portion of the penalty exacted being awarded to the officers who made such arrests, "to encourage their zeal." But they were strictly cautioned against annoying innocent persons, "inasmuch as blunders in such matters create ill impressions against the authorities, and because the honor and happiness of the person might be irretrievably injured, so that it would be better to pass over a guilty person here and there, than to inculpate a single innocent one." The royal rescript concludes by directing that a strict *surveillance* be kept over the females of the garrison, many of whom are stated, in very plain language, to be of improper character.

These directions were subsequently embodied in the general statute, or law of the land (*landrecht*), and upon that the police regulations which we quote hereafter were based.

The statute formally declares procurers and procuresses liable to imprisonment for from six months to three years in the House of Correction, with "a welcome and farewell;" *Anglice*, a sound whipping when admitted, and another when discharged. In the cases of parents or guardians who may aid in or connive at the prostitution of their children or wards, the term of imprisonment is doubled, and made more severe. It requires all common women to reside in the tolerated houses "under the eye of the state," which houses are only to be permitted in populous cities, and "not elsewhere than in retired and back streets therein, the consent of the police authorities having been first obtained." And in any case where a house of prostitution was established without this consent, or in defiance of the public orders, the keeper was to be liable to one or two years' imprisonment. The police are strictly commanded to keep all tolerated houses under strict and constant *surveil-lance;* to make frequent visits in company with medical men, so as to check the progress of venereal disease; to prevent the sale of intoxicating liquors therein; to see that no woman was introduced without the knowledge and permission of the authorities, under a fine of fifty thalers, for each offense ; and, more especially, that no innocent female was, by force or deceit, compelled or induced to live therein; which latter offense imposes " a public exhibition," in the stocks or pillory, we presume, and from six to ten years' imprisonment, with "welcome and farewell," on the keeper, who was not to be allowed to keep such a house again under any circumstances.

The police are farther enjoined to see that the mistress of the house informs the authorities of the pregnancy of any woman residing in the house as soon as she is aware of it herself, but if it is concealed she (the mistress) is liable to imprisonment, especially if a secret birth takes place. The mistress is required to take charge of any woman who becomes pregnant, if there is no public institution to which she can be removed, and is at liberty to seek compensation from the father of the child, or, if he can not be found, she has a claim upon the mother. The child must be removed from the house as soon as it is weaned, and is to be cared for at the public cost if the parents have not means to do so.

If the keeper of the house, or the inmates themselves, conceal any venereal infection from the knowledge of the police, they render themselves liable to imprisonment from three months to a year, with " welcome and farewell."

If thefts, assaults, or other offenses occur in such houses, the keeper is, in all cases, liable to the injured party, who can not in any other way obtain his indemnity, and is also suspected of complicity in the offense so long as the contrary can not be substantiated; and if it is proved that he did not exert all his power to prevent such occurrences, his neglect is to be punished by fine or imprisonment.

No woman desirous of leaving a tolerated house to change her mode of life, and support herself honestly, can be retained against her inclination, and no difficulties may be thrown in the way of her doing so; nor will the master be allowed to force her to remain, even though she may be in his debt, under the penalty of the loss of his permission from the police.

Prostitutes who do not conform to the regulations and place

themselves under supervision, are to be arrested and imprisoned for three months, and, when their term of imprisonment has expired, are to be sent to the "work-houses," and detained there until they have inclination and opportunity for honorable employment. Any females, not being inmates of the tolerated houses, who had intercourse while suffering from disease, and thereby infected men, are declared liable to an imprisonment for three months.

This comprehensive legal enactment left many matters of detail to the discretion of the police, and accordingly they issued their rules. The opposition these subsequently encountered makes them important in the history of Prostitution in Berlin, and although they are in many points a mere repetition of the terms of the statute, we give them *in extenso*. They are entitled,

"PROVISIONS AGAINST THE MISLEADING OF YOUNG WOMEN INTO BROTHELS, AND FOR PREVENTION OF THE SPREAD OF VENEREAL DISEASE.

"*Preamble.* It has been brought to notice that simple young girls, especially from the smaller towns, under the craftiest pretensions to place them in good situations, have been brought to Berlin, and, without their knowledge of the fact, taken to brothels, and therein, against their will, led astray to their ruin, and to the life of a common prostitute.

" At the same time, it is matter of remark that common prostitutes, after they have been diseased, continue their practices as long as the state of their sickness permits, and thereby farther infection is extraordinarily increased and extended.

" With the express view of meeting such infamous seductions, and the highly injurious results of the before-mentioned communication of venereal disease, the following directions are brought to the cognizance and perfect information of the keepers of houses of prostitution, and of the females who make a trade of their persons.

" 1. No one can set on foot a brothel, or keep women for the purposes of prostitution, without having communicated previously with the Police Directory on the subject, and obtained their permission in writing. Whoso acts contrary to this shall, together with absolute withdrawal of his license, be liable to one or two years in the House of Correction.

" 2. Every brothel-keeper must, before taking a girl into his service, produce her before the Police Directory, and must not conclude any contract with her until the Police Director has given him written leave to do so ; whereupon, forthwith the conditions upon which the keeper and said woman have agreed are to be registered with the police, and an abstract thereof shall be given to each party, for which eight groschen are to be paid as fees. The before-mentioned brothel-keepers, to whom the Police Director's toleration is extended, must, at his order, produce the common prostitutes, and submit the same to a similar license, and the conditions must be drawn up for them in the before-mentioned manner. If a keeper omits the same, and is accused of having any woman for common use in his house for forty-eight hours without such notice, he shall pay a fine of fifty thalers, and, upon the third offense, in addition to the said fine, his trade shall be stopped, and he shall not carry on the same any more. Further, it shall be no excuse that the person in question was not there for the purpose of prostitution, inasmuch as he is enjoined to point out every female whom he receives into his house, without exception, and neglect of this shall be taken as a proof of contravention. Under penalty of the same punishment, he must give a similar notice if a common woman comes to him from another house.

" 3. Females under age, who have not, before the publication of these ordinances, notoriously abandoned themselves to common prostitution, are not to be received by any brothel-keeper, and when he produces such persons before the Police Directory the permit shall not be allowed. If he acts contrary to this prohibition, he shall be punished with two years' labor in jail.

" 4. The departure from a brothel of any woman who desires to change her mode of life, and to subsist in a respectable manner, is not to be checked or prevented. Even on account of sureties entered into or debts incurred, the keeper is not to retain any such against her will, at the risk of losing his permit, and the police are charged to give every assistance. If, however, any such person desire only to remove to another house of prostitution, this can not be done without the consent of her former keeper, until after three months' notice given, when it will be permitted upon proof of brutal treatment by the keeper, or other good and reasonable grounds shown to the police. No woman who seeks to quit a brothel for the purpose of carrying on prostitution for pay on her own account will be permitted to do so ; and if any person, having, on pretense of an honest calling, quitted a house of prostitution, shall be adjudged guilty of prostitution on her own account, she shall have four weeks at the House of Correction, with a welcome and farewell. And whereas it is known that many brothel-keepers, who treat their girls with an unbearable harshness, keep so strict a watch upon them that they can not succeed in bringing their complaints before the authorities, information shall from time to time, *ex-officio*, and without the presence of the keeper, be taken, whether the girls have any well-founded complaints to bring forward against the said keeper.

" 5. The common prostitutes in the brothels are strictly prohibited from enticing or inviting passengers in the streets, with looks or signs from the houses or windows, and the keepers are on no account to permit the same. Diligent regard to this is to be had by the police, and those who act contrary will be punished, the first time with three days, and, on a repetition of the offense, with a week's solitary coufinement, one half of the time on bread and water. The keeper who is shown to have been party to the same will suffer double punishment.

" 6. In these houses the keepers shall not supply visitors with wine, brandy, liquor, punch, or other strong drinks, or with food, but only with tea, coffee, chocolate, beer, or similar beverages ; further, it is not permitted for the visitors to bring in drink or food. For every case of contravention the keeper shall pay five thalers, or a week's detention ; on repetition, he shall be punished more severely ; if this will not suffice, the permit shall be withdrawn from the house. No brothel-keeper shall allow any guest to remain after twelve o'clock at night, nor allow any one to enter after that hour. Whoso acts contrary shall, for the first offense, pay ten thalers ; on repetition, the fine is doubled ; for the third time, the keeper shall lose his permit.

" 7. Should thefts, assaults, or other offenses take place in such houses, the keeper is in all cases liable to the injured party if he can not get his redress elsewhere. Further, the said keeper is suspected of complicity in the offense so long as the contrary is not proved, and if it appear that he did not use all possible means for the prevention of such offense, he shall be punished by fine or in person.

" 8. In case any innocent female shall, by fraud or violence, be brought into any brothel, the keeper and those who are accomplices in such infamous offense shall undergo public exhibition, and four to ten years' House of Correction, with welcome and farewell. Besides this, the permit will be withdrawn. It shall be no excuse for him to allege that he neither knew nor assisted the said seduction, inasmuch as he had no right to receive any female into his house without first giving notice thereof to the Police Directory, and receiving from them, after inquiry into the circumstances, permission to do so.

" 9. In like manner, a brothel-keeper may not, under penalty of twelve months' imprisonment, give any one (whatever his rank may be) facility to carry on criminal intercourse with any woman who has been brought into his house ; and it is absolutely forbidden for any person to bring a female to such house, and there to have any private communication with her, which shall be only with the regular women of the place, inasmuch as by section 2 no keeper is permitted to receive any woman as servant-maid, or under any pretense whatever, among his inmates, without previous notice to the police, and their assent to the same.

" 10. In order to combat the frequent infection of common prostitutes, and, if possible, prevent them from severe attacks of venereal disease, or its farther extension, and at the same time not only to restrain the rapid progress of this highly pernicious malady, but, so far as possible, entirely to root it out, the brothel-keepers and the women kept by them are bound to give their most observant attention thereto, both for their own advantage, and also for the diminution of their own misfortunes and severe punishment. To this end, the brothel-keepers are not to oppose the appointed surgeons in each quarter, so often as the same make their visits to the women at their houses ; and every woman shall be subject to these visits.   For the informa- tion of every brothel-keeper, and of the prostitutes kept by him, a copy of printed directions, prepared by competent authority, shall be given to the brothel-keeper, whereby the signs of actual infection and of the commence- ment of venereal disease may be known, and they shall be clearly instructed by the duly appointed surgeon how to form an opinion upon their own state of health, and be able to explain the same on his visits, so that thereby the detection of venereal disease at any time may be facilitated.   Furthermore, upon perceiving the symptoms whereby venereal disease is known in a man, they should abstain from carnal intercourse with him.

" 11. Should a woman suspect that she is infected, she must permit no one to have connection with her, but shall mention the same as well to her keeper as to the surgeon of the district, upon which steps shall forthwith be taken for her cure.   If she neglect this she shall be punished with detention, three months for the first time, on repetition of the offense with six months in the House of Correction, with welcome and farewell.   If the said woman, through concealment of her venereal malady, has given occasion to a wider spread thereof, she shall the first time be liable to twelve months in the House of Correction, with welcome and farewell.   In case the brothel-keeper shall know of the diseased condition of such woman, and shall not hinder her from the exercise of her trade, or shall keep her therein, he shall be liable to the same punishment, and, moreover, shall be liable to the costs and charges of cure and attendance of the man so infected by such woman, if he requires it, or if he can not pay such expenses.   For this reimbursement a brothel- keeper shall be held liable even if he did not know the diseased condition of a woman kept in his house, inasmuch as such obligation shall, for the public weal, be taken to be a risk and burden incident to the trade permitted to be carried on by him.

" 12. On the other hand, a prostitute can prosecute any one for having infected her by means of connection, and such person shall, upon the com- plaint and showing of her and the brothel-keeper, bear the expense of cure and maintenance for so a long time as, pursuant to the orders of the author- ities of the Charité, the woman may have to remain in the Charité ; and further, shall be liable to a fine of fifty thalers, or three months' imprison- ment in the House of Correction."

" 13. If any woman, before declaring her venereal disease, shall have concealed it so long that, by opinion of competent persons, she must have known the same for a considerable length of time, she shall, whether she shall or shall not have infected other persons, be liable to the same punishment as if she had infected others.

"14. Whereas, it has been the practice for the women to conceal their venereal diseases ; and whereas, they have intrusted themselves to incompetent persons for cure ; and whereas, the brothel-keepers are bound to refund to the Charité the expenses of the cure and attendance, which sometimes fall ruinously heavy upon them : it is hereby directed, for the removal of this difficulty, that a healing fund (*heilings casse*) shall be established, by means whereof the keepers and their women, on the occurrence of disease, may be relieved of the heavy expenses to which they are put, and may be assured against the destruction of their bodies and health, which ensue from the growth of this terrible disease. To this fund every brothel-keeper shall contribute a monthly sum of six groschen (twelve cents) for each woman that he keeps, and shall give in a statement of the name and place of birth of such woman ; for which, at the commencement of the following month, he shall receive an acknowledgment, and he shall recover such sum from every woman on whose account he shall have paid the same. Nevertheless, any brothel-keeper who shall have allowed more than one of these monthly payments to run into arrear with the women, shall not, on that account, be able to prevent her leaving him, if, as before ordered, she desires to change her way of life. If a woman goes from one brothel to another without the six groschen having been paid for her, the brothel-keeper to whom she goes must pay this amount in due time for her. This shall happen notwithstanding that she is bound to give notice of her removal to the police commissary of the quarter. The monthly payment of this tax is to be made to the duly appointed medical officer of the quarter, who shall pay over the whole amount of the same to the collector of the healing fund, who shall give him for the same a receipt under his own hand ; whereupon the comptroller shall compare the list of the same with the list of the brothel-keepers and women in the several districts, and shall compel defaulters to pay the outstanding tax.

"15. A perfect account is to be kept of this healing fund, and out of the same every diseased woman shall be taken to the Charité, and, without farther charges to herself or keeper, shall be maintained and thoroughly cured without being sent, as formerly directed, to the workhouse. Farther, the woman shall not intrust herself either to the visiting surgeon or to any other person for cure, but such shall take place only in the Charité.

"16. No brothel shall be tolerated in the respectably inhabited and frequented streets and squares of the city, but they shall be established at a moderate distance from the same, so that the police can watch them and speedily correct any disorder ; otherwise only in the smaller streets and thoroughfares.

"17. The matters that are ordered and prescribed in the foregoing articles to the brothel-keepers, are also to be observed by female brothel-keepers under like penalties.

" 18. Single women living by themselves for purposes of prostitution must give in their notices to the Police Directory in the same manner as the women in the brothels; must also undergo examination by the medical officers of the quarter in which they reside; must pay their six groschen a month to the healing fund, and be subject to all the directions applicable to brothel-keepers and their hired women, and to the like punishments in case of offending against the directions.

" 19. Procurers and procuresses, who make it their business to provide opportunities in their houses for criminal intercourse of men and women (whatever their condition), shall be strictly watched, and, upon conviction, shall be liable to three months' detention in the House of Correction.

" 20. The street-walkers roaming the streets after dark are not to be tolerated, but where they can be met with are to be taken into custody, and after being cured, if they are affected with venereal disease, shall be sent from six to twelve months to the House of Correction.

" 21. Whoever can not pay the fines shall receive a corresponding corporal (*am leibe*) punishment.

" 22. Informers shall receive half the fines paid in, and the remaining fines shall be collected and distributed as the reward of those who make discovery and information of any contraventions of these regulations.

" 23. In those cases mentioned in section 3, wherein, together with a breach of these regulations, a crime against the laws of the state is committed, the criminal department of the High Court will take cognizance of it, and the remedies proceed from them to the criminal deputation of the Chamber of Justice.

" 24. In order that no one who, whether as keeper or girl, makes a trade of prostitution, shall be in a position to excuse themselves on account of their ignorance of this code of regulations, a copy of them shall be given to every person at the time of registration, for which six groschen shall be paid, and carried to the reward fund for informers."

The royal rescript, the statute, and the police ordinance of 1792 are founded upon the principle that prostitution is a necessary evil, which, if unregulated, tends to demoralize all society, and inflict physical suffering on its votaries; but, as it can never be suppressed, it is tolerated in order that those who practice it may be brought under supervision and control. In furtherance of this idea, another police order was promulgated in 1795, prohibiting music and dancing at the tolerated houses, and limiting the resort of prostitutes to public places of amusement. The immediate effect of this measure was to close several coffee-houses

served by women (*mädchen tabagieen*). At the same time, the
women were classified into first, second, and third classes, and
the monthly tax graduated to one thaler (sixty-eight cents), two
thirds of a thaler, and one third of a thaler, which was appropriated to the healing fund, as directed by the regulations of 1792.
This impost was doubled at a subsequent period in consequence
of public calamities.

To enforce the police directions and collect the tax, a census of
the public prostitutes in Berlin was taken in June, 1792, when
they amounted to 311. The toleration was withdrawn from some
of these for various reasons, and the numbers were, in

July	269
August	268
September	249
October (a period of fairs and other assemblages) . .	258
And the average finally settled at about	260

in a population of 150,000.

In the exercise of the discretionary power vested in the police
of Berlin, as in most other cities of Continental Europe, they found
it necessary to extend their toleration so as to include in their supervision those private prostitutes who could not be permitted to
reside in the tolerated houses because they had not reached the
age prescribed by law, which in Prussia fixes majority at twenty-
four years; and also another class who were secretly visited at
private lodgings by those wealthy libertines whose pride would
not allow them to enter a common brothel, and whose *amours*
consequently exposed them to liabilities which the spirit of the
law justified the police in encountering. The persons (mostly
widows) with whom the private prostitutes resided were made
answerable to the police, and subjected to the same rules as the
tolerated houses.

Under the new scale of impost there were, in 1796,

6 brothels of the 1st class, with inmates	16
8 " " 2d " "	33
40 " " 3d " "	141
	——190
Private prostitutes of the 1st class	39
" " " 2d "	28
	— 67
Total	257

About this period, an epoch of general political movement, men
of the highest rank in Prussia began to doubt the propriety of tol-

erating prostitution, and orders were given, in opposition to the remonstrances of the police, to take measures which would effectually
compel brothel-keepers to close their houses. This appears to have
been the first positive attempt at absolute repression, and the police intimated that illicit prostitution would be its inevitable result.
In reply, they were directed that, if their prediction should be verified, they must pursue the vice more closely. In 1800 the number
of registered women had decreased to 246, *but it was notorious that
illicit prostitution had increased largely.* This fact was not denied by
the police. They ascribed it, very justly, to the restrictions imposed on the tolerated houses, which were now actually less than
ever, at a time when the resident population of Berlin was twenty
thousand more than at the last computation, exclusive of a large
influx of troops and foreigners. They were not supported in their
views, but were ordered, on the ground of extensive disease among
the soldiery, to "crush out" the illicit prostitution, and this order
they vainly endeavored to accomplish. An inquiry into the comparative state of the venereal disease was directed at the same
time, and the state physician reported that *there was less disease
among registered than illicit prostitutes, and inferred that a diminution
of tolerated, but strictly guarded regular brothels, was not for the public benefit.*

The year 1808, when the French army overran Europe, was a
period of general war and trouble; the police regulations fell into
abeyance, and prostitution became comparatively free and uncontrolled. The French military commanders in Berlin made complaints to the police of the lawless state of the town, particularly
specifying some of the brothels, which had become nests of gamblers, wherein robbery, duels, suicides, and other offenses were of
frequent occurrence. The results of an inspection were as follows:

50 brothels containing women	230
Private prostitutes	203—433
In addition to this, there were of notorious illicit prostitutes known to the police (60 of whom were stated to have disease in its worst forms)	400
And also reasonably suspected of prostitution	67
Making an aggregate known to the authorities of	900

There were also seventy dance-houses, which were known as
places of accommodation. The population at this time was about
150,000. The figures thus given, from an official enumeration,
are the best practical commentary upon the effects of the abandonment of a tried system of *surveillance.*

The state of affairs disclosed by this inquiry called forth a ministerial rescript, dated May 8, 1809, which we copy:

"The brothel-houses are, by reason of the great influence they have on morality and health, a very important branch of police administration. *We should desire to be satisfied whether it is more desirable to suppress or tolerate them.* In any case, it is, however, improper and injurious to license them, and thus to give them a certain sanction; still less can they be tolerated in public neighborhoods of a city. It is rather to be desired that, upon every convenient and properly occurring opportunity, they should be stamped with the well-merited brand of the deepest depravity and infamy. We have therefore commanded the Police Directory to effect the removal of all such houses into quiet, retired streets of the suburbs and liberties, and we direct you to take into consideration whether a like regulation can not be accomplished here in the city of Berlin; whereupon you will make to us a well-considered report. You are also to take into consideration what can be done to brand such places with the deepest depravity and infamy."

In obedience to this order, which had doubtless emanated direct from royalty itself, Herr Von Gruner, the head of the Berlin police, communicated a report containing his conclusions, as follows:

"1. That closing, or even limiting the brothels, would lead to very general ill health."

"2. That, in consequence of the exertions of the police, illicit prostitution had been diminished very much, and even the number of the registered women had decreased."

"3. That in 1809 there were in Berlin

```
1 first class brothel containing women  . . . . .    6
20 second   "        "        "        "  . . . . .  75
22 third    "        "        "        "  . . . . . 117—198
Private prostitutes . . . . . . . . . . . . . . .   113
        Total registered . . . . . . . . . . .     311
```

That this number might seem larger than before, but the passage of troops and the large garrison of Berlin had led to the increase, and evidently a great increase of secret prostitution and its results would have been experienced in place of the registered prostitution, had not an extension of this same registered prostitution been tolerated."

"4. That particular streets in which brothels were to be found were certainly no longer suitable places on account of the greater traffic which they had gained, and these houses might, on that account, be removed to back streets, including the *Königsmauer,* etc."

"5. That he did not know in what manner 'the brand of depravity and infamy' could be impressed on the trade of prostitution, except by directing a particular costume, differing from the clothing of respectable women."

In continuation of this report, the commissary states his opinion "that it would be dangerous to public order to keep the common houses in narrow limits, as it would bring together all the idle people, which might lead to a disturbance; that a special costume for the women would be of no use at home, and out of doors it would only give occasion for a public scandal without effecting the purpose of their reform; that, lastly, he objects to the toleration of private prostitutes, as there is no good result from their registration except their health, and the general regulation in that and other matters is much better secured in the brothels."

Among the official correspondence on this matter we find another document worthy of notice. It is a report by a sub-inspector to the superior police authorities, dated January 16, 1810.

"There are forty-four such houses of prostitution, and, compared with the population of Berlin, 180,000, that is not many. They are divided into three classes, and, together with the prostitutes living on their own account, are controlled in conformity with the regulations of February 2d, 1792. In compliance with such rules, they pay the taxes to the healing fund.

"Past negligent mismanagement has unfortunately permitted several brothels in much-frequented streets. Their removal to more retired places I find highly desirable. It is urgent that no more private women of the town should be tolerated, but rather that they should, if they can not return to good conduct, be sent into the brothel-houses, or, where they are not natives of Berlin, be sent out of the city forthwith, or otherwise be sent to the House of Industry. These women, living alone, are very perilous to morality and health, inasmuch as they can not be so perfectly controlled as in the brothels in modesty of deportment, cleanliness, and retirement; also because they are able to withhold themselves from medical inspection, and to carry on their trade when they know themselves to be suffering from venereal diseases. The lists of the prostitutes under treatment at the Charité demonstrate this. The opinion that this living alone favors a return to virtue is not supported by experience; were it even so, the disadvantages enumerated are more important than so rare and problematical a benefit.

"The question, 'whether the toleration of brothels in large cities, and their regulation by the police, so that infected females should not be permitted therein, is advisable, in order to counteract the seduction of respectable females?' can not be categorically answered in the affirmative. Still, in Berlin, it seems that brothels, if not a necessary evil, can not be momentarily abolished, but such steps must be devised as will gradually remove the evil, and make the disgrace generally noticeable. To this end, the above propositions, touching private prostitutes and removal of brothels from public streets, will be carried into effect. Express limitations of the brothels to two or three streets would give occasion to gatherings on holidays that might lead to riots and other excesses.

"A special external designation of prostitutes would only lead to uproar, without causing the women to feel the odium of their calling more than at present."

The remainder of this report is unimportant. In October, 1810, a public order was made for effectuating its recommendations.

After this event the king became impressed with an idea of the impolicy and impropriety of the "toleration" system, and a lengthy correspondence ensued between the various departments and state officials on the subject; the royal rescripts enunciating the oft-repeated opinions on the subject in general, objecting to the details of the police management, or directing reports on some particular incident of the system; the police authorities, fortified by experience as opposed to theory, adhering to the toleration practice, and demanding increased powers to restrain private prostitution, and compel all such persons to enter the public houses. The matter was brought to a close in 1814 by an order from the crown for a total closing of the tolerated brothels. The police president, Lecoq, thought it advisable to communicate with the authorities of the town of Breslau before he complied with this order, requesting some information as to the state of public morals there, it being stated that there was not a single brothel or registered prostitute to be found within its limits.

The reply from the Breslau officials was in the affirmative as to the fact. As to the results, they had consulted with the state physician and the hospital physician, and their opinion was that closing the brothels and withdrawal of toleration *had not been advantageous*, as, in spite of the police vigilance, illicit prostitution had increased since, and procuresses carried on their arts more extensively, their operations being altogether secret, and under no police control; *that the venereal disease had not decreased; that nothing counteracted it so effectually as the medical inspection of known brothels; and that its secret spread had been so great as to extend its ravages, through the instrumentality of female servants, into respectable families;* that the hospital returns proved but little, because the cases were suffered to run on or were privately cured, but these returns were given as follows:

Years.	Venereal cases in Breslau Hospital.	Illegitimate births in Breslau.	Years.	Venereal cases in Breslau Hospital.	Illegitimate births in Breslau.
1805	155	....	1810	118	382
1806	202	....	1811	98	316
1807	323	....	1812	139	282
1808	233	....	1813	159	222
1809	150	....			

The years 1806 and 1807 were those of the French invasion. In 1812 the brothels in Breslau were closed.

The general peace of 1814 diverted the energies of crowned heads and leading statesmen from matters of internal policy, and the police of Berlin were left at liberty to pursue their old plans. Then the inhabitants began to object to brothels, and to petition against those in their immediate neighborhood. This drew from the police an argumentative document, in which they fully reviewed the question, but refused the prayer of the petition.

The change of localities, alterations in the law, and other circumstances, made a re-enactment of the code of 1792 desirable, and this took place in 1829. The alterations are chiefly in minor details of no general interest, but the law against frequenting places of public amusement was made part of this police order, which declared that the presence of prostitutes at houses of public entertainment was strictly forbidden. The most material change consisted in some very minute directions for guarding against venereal disease. To this end, every brothel-keeper was required to furnish each woman in his house with a proper syringe, which she was directed to use frequently, under the orders of the medical visitors. The private prostitutes were directed to observe similar precautions, and in place of a fixed weekly inspection by a medical officer, he was ordered to make his visits at uncertain intervals.

At this time there were thirty-three brothels in Berlin. Some of the citizens renewed their petitions for a removal of a portion of them, but with no better success than before.

In 1839, the morality of the system of toleration was again questioned by those in authority, and the Minister of the Interior, in a rescript to the authorities of the Rhine provinces, alluded to the matter of prostitution, and expressed himself as strongly opposed to any system of toleration. We quote a portion of his remarks:

"As for the granting of licenses to brothels, I can not accede to it, inasmuch as the advantages to be gained are, in my opinion, illusory, and in no degree countervail the inconvenience of the state sanction thus afforded to discreditable institutions. All attempts by the police to introduce de-

cency and propriety by means of brothel regulations are idle. * * * *
Brothels are not an invention of necessity, but are simply an offshoot of
immoral luxury. (?) * * * * No one has a right to expect himself
to be protected from injury and disease while seeking the gratification of
unreasonable sexual enjoyments. * * * * The opinion that brothels are outlets for dangerous arts of seduction has never been substantiated.
* * * * Had the police ever realized the suppression of illicit prostitution by means of tolerated brothels, then, indeed, a decided opinion might
be formed as to the utility, in a sanitary point of view, of brothels."

Opinions of this nature from such a quarter, notwithstanding
their absurdity in many respects, could not be without their effect,
and induced the citizens to renew their petitions for the suppression or removal of some of the tolerated houses of prostitution.
In 1840, a ministerial order enjoined such removal. It was
promptly obeyed: some brothels were at once suppressed, and
others were removed and concentrated in a notorious spot called
the Königsmauer. The relative number of brothels and prostitutes in the years 1836 and 1844 was as follows:

1836, brothels 33	Prostitutes 200
1844, " 24	" 240

Decrease of brothels in 1844 . 9
Increase of prostitutes in 1844 40

Forty more women crowded into a less number of houses; an
average of ten prostitutes to each brothel, instead of six as before,
is but a poor commentary on enforced suppression.

The known inclination of the highest persons in the kingdom
to put down brothels speedily induced a renewal of the agitation
against them. So far as locality was in question, it was admitted
that no more suitable place could have been found. The Königsmauer was a spot shunned by decent people from old times; out
of the way, and with few inhabitants but those interested in the
traffic, there was nobody to suffer, and the whole argument virtually turned upon the moral consequences of the government regulations and their utility to the public.

Among the petitions of 1840, one had been presented "from a
number of Berlin citizens" to Prince William, the uncle of the
king, stating that these brothels were an abomination; that many
of them were splendidly fitted up, in which all means of excitement were used; that the women appeared at the windows exposed and bare-necked; in short, the memorialists said all that is
customarily said on such occasions. But they seem to have for-

gotten that the police possessed both power and inclination to suppress such grievances, or else it never occurred to these "Berlin citizens" that their assistance given to the police would have speedily checked the evils. The memorial was handed to the king himself, and he required a report upon the matter from the Director of Police. This was duly furnished, and represented,

"1. That the corruption of manners in Berlin, and in the parts of Berlin complained of, was not more extreme than in other great cities of Germany, and in like places.

"2. That in the limitation of the ineradicable vice of prostitution by her police regulations, Berlin had greatly the advantage of Vienna; for in 1840, Berlin (including the garrison) had a population of 350,000 souls, among whom there was, of course, a very large number of unmarried men. That the syphilitic cases in the Charité had been in

1838, men . . . 569	Women . . . 634	Total . . . 1209
1839, " . . 695	" . . . 738	" . . . 1433
1840, " . . . 704	" . . . 757	" . . . 1461

Assuming that one third of the venereal cases in Berlin were treated privately, this gives an average of 1 in 450, or in every four hundred and fifty men there is one syphilitic subject, whereas M. Parent-Duchatelet's calculation for Vienna is 1 in every 250."[1]

The same report continues:

"Every official will bear out my assertion that the number of brothels is in inverse proportion to illicit prostitution; that is, the fewer of the former, the more of the latter, and the greater the difficulty of dealing with them, and preventing syphilis."

In 1841 another memorial was presented, with further complaints against the same houses in the Königsmauer. This was referred to the police authorities with the brief injunction, "Make an end of the nuisances about which there are so many complaints."

The *Schulkollegium* of the province of Brandenburg now joined their influence to swell the public outcry that the few houses of prostitution on the Königsmauer were hurtful to public morals, and a bad example to youth, and, on the ground of interest in

---

[1] This calculation is not very explicitly stated. It is intended to show that syphilis is not dangerously prevalent among the general population. The police arrive at this conclusion by deducting the cases treated in the Charité (which they estimate at two thirds) from the total population, and then divide the remaining cases among the bulk of the people, to prove that only a very small proportion are exposed to venereal influence. We transcribe the statement literally, but do not consider it of much value.

their students and pupils, demanded that they be closed. The police, who had previously taken every precaution against a violation of public decency, now deputed a special inspector to give his personal attention to the locality. He reported there was no valid ground of complaint as to the outward conduct of the inhabitants, or the internal management of the houses. Thus satisfied as to the nature of the opposition, the police treated the college officials somewhat cavalierly, and recommended them to prohibit their students visiting such an out-of-the-way place: a very sensible piece of advice, and the best that could have been given under the circumstances.

According to Dr. Behrend (who has written on Prostitution in Berlin), the leading spirits of this agitation were a clergyman, and a distiller who had a brewery and spirit-store in the vicinity of the Königsmauer. The clergyman proceeded upon moral and religious grounds, and led the crusade against brothels as a public disgrace, unworthy a Christian nation. We do not learn what line of argument the distiller adopted, or whether the prohibition of liquor in houses of prostitution influenced his zeal. These agitators applied to the police with a succession of general complaints as to the luxury of the houses, the gains of the women, the bad example to the young, and other topics of a similar nature. They met with but scant favor; however, they were assured that every possible means should be used to keep the offenders within the bounds of existing rules.

The memorialists then carried their grievances to various influential people, and at length to Count Arnim, the Minister of the Interior, to whom a petition was presented, praying the entire suppression of all tolerated brothels. This petition contained all the allegations and arguments which could possibly be advanced against the places in question, augmented by much rhetorical flourish about the degradation of royal officers; the desecration of the baptismal register produced by prostitutes at the time of inscription; the insult to majesty in allowing brothels to exist in a street called Königsmauer, and many similarly weighty points. The practical knowledge of the police as to the effect of registration in checking more baneful excesses was theoretically disputed; the propositions on which the toleration system was based were denied; the defense of the plan by those cognizant of its working was entirely ruled out; so that, to a person unacquainted with both sides of the question, a sufficient *ex parte* case was presented.

Q

The ministerial reply was favorable, but not conclusive; it was to the effect that,

"1. The number of brothels is to be reduced one half, which are to be removed beyond the city walls to the most retired position possible, where annoyance to the neighbors is not to be feared.

"2. For the control of those remaining, patrols of gens d'armes are to be kept afoot, and relieved six times a day.

"3. Every third breach of the regulations, whether in small or great matters, will be followed by the closing of the house.

" Should these orders not be sufficient, the police are empowered to close all the houses, for it must be understood that brothels are not licensed, but only tolerated as necessity requires, and care for public decency permits."

The police authorities foresaw difficulties in the details of these proceedings, and asked for more explicit instructions, which were supplied.   In the second communication was this remarkable passage:

"Should a diminution in the number of brothels take place, and thereby the number of common prostitutes be affected, we shall then learn by experience whether consequences injurious to public morality and order ensue, and the decision of the main question can then be made with certainty, whether we can not advance to the entire abolition of brothels."

In following the prescribed course, and overthrowing an established system in order to furnish ministerial "experience" of the trouble it would cause, the police instituted a series of inquiries, and embodied the result in a report to the Minister of the Interior, dated July, 1844, which shows that there were

26 brothels, containing women 287
Registered private prostitutes   18
                                         Total 305

The amount received and disbursed on account of the healing fund was also reported in thalers, thus:

1841.	Received	. . 3384	Disbursed	. . . .	1027
1842.	"	. . 3393	"	. . . .	861
1843.	"	. . 3365	"	. . . .	689

It concludes with the opinion entertained by the police:

" As for the influence which the extinction of brothels may have upon the morals, safety, and health of society, the police authorities think themselves obliged, as before, to declare against the expediency of the proceeding. What should be done in case this course should be adopted is a question that requires much consideration. Meanwhile, the police are of opinion it would be highly objectionable to close the brothels before other measures are prepared in reference to prostitution."

No such measures were prepared. The king would hear no farther argument upon the matter; and, by positive "royal command," the brothels were closed and registered prostitution stopped, December 31, 1845. Berlin became (nominally) as virtuous as an edict from the throne could make it. The majority of the prostitutes were either sent to their former homes or supplied with passports for places out of the kingdom. A few were left houseless, friendless, and destitute. History does not say whether the friends of enforced continence provided for these sufferers.

This summary edict seriously embarrassed the police, especially as the state laws tolerating prostitution were unrepealed. They applied to the authorities of Halle and Cologne, where a similar measure had been enforced, and the substance of the replies received was as follows.

From Halle:

" Since the French occupation, the brothels had been put down. There had been a few persons charged with prostitution, whom the police caught *now and then*, and sent to jail, where they were cured. There were, however, very few vicious persons in Halle, and there had been no need of special provision. It was not difficult to find honest livelihood for the common women. As to syphilis, there had been no increase of cases since the last of the brothels."

The authorities of Cologne had no such pleasing tale to tell. They say,

" At the end of the French occupation, the authorities had put down all the licensed brothels, and, at the same time, made vigilant search for private prostitutes. Legal difficulties had for many years been in the way, as the laws made no provision against private prostitution, when not carried on as a trade for gain, and the technical proof was difficult. Against procurers and procuresses the law was ineffective, except in cases where the seduced female was under age. When the amendments in the law had taken place, the police had worked vigorously, and in the years 1843 and 1844, a time when illicit prostitution had enormously increased, they had presented three hundred cases of that offense.

" *As regarded syphilis, the city physician was of opinion that, in late years, the disease had increased among all classes, and had appeared in a much worse type.*

" In consequence, however, of the increased energy of the police, affairs had become under better control, and the number of private brothels had materially diminished, so that there are now but about fifteen in the city. The secret prostitution was not, however, under any control. The police found it impracticable to keep vicious persons in check, who (in default of other accommodation) committed the most depraved acts in stray vehicles or any suitable hiding-place."

The writer of this official communication added his private opinion, based upon the experience of some years, that "no effective steps could be devised to suppress prostitution: all that could be done would be to palliate it, and keep it under *surveillance.*"

These statements were not calculated to relieve the anxiety of the Berlin officials, who were pressed by the ministers to devise plans for executing the royal orders. They accordingly met, in much embarrassment, and prepared a scheme which was not acceptable to the superior powers. It was ordered, eventually, "that the women suspected of prostitution, being about 1000 or 1200 in Berlin, should be warned by the police to discontinue their practices. If found out, they were to be punished, and, after punishment, to be continued under *surveillance* until good behavior. During such period they were to be periodically examined for disease, at the police office, by medical men; the punishment to be made more severe on the repetition of the offense."

These orders, following immediately the suppression mandate, will strike every one as reaffirming the principles of the toleration system in the most important particular—the regard for public health. The police used all their energy to enforce them, but at the same time represented their fears of the consequences, namely, the spread of prostitution, the increase of disease, and a general licentiousness of habits.

It now remains to trace the effects of the suppression of registered brothels, and local authorities afford abundant and satisfactory proof that the fears of the police were realized.

The *Vossicher Zeitung* (July, 1847), says:

"Well meant but altogether erroneous is the proposition that brothels can be dispensed with in times of general intelligence and education, and that now this relic of barbarism can be done away with. Already, only two years after the closing of the brothels, this deception has been exploded, and we have bought experience at the public cost. The illicit prostitutes, who well know how to escape the hands of the police, have spread their nets of demoralization over the whole city; and against them, the old prostitution houses, which were under a purifying police control in sanitary and general matters, afforded safety and protection."

In another local paper we find:

" Prostitution, which had previously kept out of sight in dark and retired corners, now came forward boldly and openly; for it found protection and countenance in the large number of its supporters, and no police care could restrain it. The prostitutes did not merely traverse the streets and frequent the public thoroughfares to hunt their prey, thereby insulting virtuous women and putting them to the blush, they crowded the fashionable prom-enades, the concerts, the theatres, and other places of amusement, where they claimed the foremost places, and set the fashion of the hour. They were conspicuous for their brilliant toilettes, and their example was pre-eminently captivating and pernicious to the youth of both sexes."

From a work called " Berlin," by Sass, we obtain the annexed view of

PUBLIC LIFE IN BERLIN.

" No city in Germany can boast of the splendid ball-rooms of Berlin. One in particular, near the Brandenburg gate and the Parade-ground, is remarkable for its size, and presents a magnificent exterior, especially in the evening, when hundreds of lamps stream through the windows and light up the park in front. The interior is of corresponding splendor, and when the vast hall resounds with the music of the grand orchestra, and is filled with a gay crowd rustling in silks or satins, or lounging in the hall, or whirling in the giddy waltz, it is certainly a scene to intoxicate the youth who fre-quent it in search of adventure, or to drink in the poison of seductive and deceiving, although bright and fascinating eyes. Should the foreigner visit this scene on one of its gay nights, he may get a glimpse of the depths of Berlin life. Many a veil is lifted here. This splendid scene has its dark side. This is not respectable Berlin. This whirling, laughing crowd is frivolous Berlin, whether of wealth, extravagance, and folly, or of poverty, vice, and necessity. The prostitute and the swindler are on every side. Formerly the female visitors were of good repute, but gradually courtesans and women of light character slipped in, until at length no lady could be seen there. And the aforesaid foreigner, who lounges through the rooms, admiring the elegant and lovely women who surround him in charge of some highly respectable elderly person, an ' aunt,' or a ' chaperone,' or pos-sibly in company with her ' newly-married husband,' seeks to know the names and position of such evident celebrity and fashion. ' Do not you know her? Any police officer can tell you her history,' are the replies he receives. There is a class of men at this place who perform a function sin-gular to the uninitiated. These worthies are the ' husbands' of the before-mentioned ladies. They play the careless or the strict cavalier; are Blue-beards on occasion; appear or keep out of sight, according to the proprie-ties of the moment."

From the same writer we extract the following sketch of a

DANCING SALOON.

"The price of admission is ten groschen (about twenty cents), which insures a company who can pay. The male public are of all conditions, and include students, clerks, and artists, with, of course, a fair share of rogues and pickpockets. The majority of the women are prostitutes: there may be found girls of rare beauty, steeped to the lips in all the arts of iniquity. The philosopher may see life essentially in the same grade as in the last description, but in a somewhat less artificial condition. Scenes of bacchant excitement and of wildest abandonment may be witnessed here. The outward show is all mirth and happiness; pleasure unrestrained seems the business of the place. Turn the picture. The most showy of the costumes are hired; the gayety is for a living; the liberty is licentiousness. These creatures, who, all blithesome as they seem, the victims of others who fleece them of every thing they can earn, are now engaged in securing victims from whom they may wring the gains which are to pay the hire of their elegant dresses, or furnish means for further excesses, or perhaps to pay for their supper that evening. It is the fashion of the place for each *gentleman* to invite a *lady* to supper, where the quantity of wine drunk is incredible. How many a young man has to trace not merely loss of cash and health to such a place, but also loss of honor! The *ladies* who have no such agreeable partners sit apart, sullen and discontented; oftentimes they have no money to pay for their own refreshments. Pair by pair the crowd diminishes, until toward three or four o'clock, when the place is closed."

The lowest dancing-houses are the *Tanz wirthschaften*, inferior to the saloons, where (again quoting)

"The dance is carried to its wildest excess, to ear-splitting music in a pestilential atmosphere. The poor are extravagant; drunkenness and profligacy abound. Servants of both sexes, soldiers and journeymen, workwomen and prostitutes, make up the public. Here, on the most frivolous pretenses, concubinage and marriage are arranged, and from this scene of folly and vice the family is ushered to the world. The wet-nurse is met here, "the type of country simplicity," who, after a night of tumult and uproar with her lover, will go in the morning to nurse the child whose mother neglects her parental duties at the dictates of fashion. The working classes have their representatives, who drown their cares in drink, while boys and girls make up the motley party. In these assemblies there is a difference. Some are attended by citizens of the humbler classes, by working men and women; others by criminals and their paramours. In these latter resorts the excesses are of a more frightful character than in those where a show of decency restrains the grosser exhibitions; youth of both sexes are among the well-known criminals, who are habituated to smoking, drinking, and the wildest orgies, long before their frames have attained a proper development. Physiognomies which might have sprung from the most hideous fancy of poet or painter may be met with."

In an anonymous pamphlet, entitled "Prostitution in Berlin," is another hideous picture:

"In the Konigstadt there is a drinking saloon where, besides the wife of the host, there are two young girls who exceed all compeers in shamelessness and depravity. The elder betrays secondary syphilis in her voice; the younger has such noble features, is of such beauty, and is altogether of such prepossessing appearance, that the infamy of her conduct is incredible. In the evening these girls and the host are generally drunk. At one or two in the morning the place is a perfect hell, the whole company, guests, host, and girls, being mad with liquor. Some are dancing with the girls to the tinkle of a guitar, the player of which acted her part in one of the abolished brothels; others are roaring obscene songs. If the guitar-player has brought her daughter, then the tumult of the den is complete. It is never closed before four o'clock in the morning, when the girls retire to their dwellings in company with one or the other of their guests."

In reading these descriptions, it must be remembered that, under the toleration system, the police would not permit prostitutes to visit places of public amusement, nor would they allow music and dancing in the brothels.

Another part of Dr. Sass's work contains a truly horrid picture of the immorality of the city. We transcribe it, in conclusion of this branch of the subject:

PRIVATE LIFE IN BERLIN.

" . . . Let us enter the house. The first floor is inhabited by a family of distinction; husband and wife have been separated for years; he lives on one side, she on the other; both go out in public together; the proprieties are kept in view, but servants will chatter. On the second floor lives an assessor with his kept woman. When he is out of town, as the house is well aware, a doctor pays her a visit. On the other side the staircase lives a carrier, with his wife and child. The wife had not mentioned that this child was born before marriage; he found it out; of course they quarreled, and he now takes his revenge in drunkenness, blows, and abuse. We ascend to the third floor. On the right of the stairs is a teacher who has had a child by his wife's sister; the wife grieves sorely over the same. With him lodges a house-painter who ran away from his wife and three children, and now lives, with his concubine and one child, in a wretched little cupboard. On the left is a letter-carrier's family. His pay is fifteen thalers (twelve dollars) a month, but the people seem very comfortable. Their daughter has a very nice front room, well furnished, and is kept by a very wealthy merchant, a married man. Exactly opposite there is a house of accommodation, and close by there is a midwife, whose sign-board announces ' An institute for ladies of condition, where they can go through their confinement in retirement.' I can assure the reader that in this sketch of sexual and family life in Berlin I have ' nothing extenuated, nor set down aught in malice.' "

In estimating the effects of the suppression of brothels, it will be necessary to take medical testimony. In Dr. Loewe's pamphlet, " Prostitution with reference to Berlin, 1852," we find:

" In vain the Charité, after the ordinary wards were full of venereal patients, set aside other parts of the building. The patients were still poured in from the houses of detention, until, at length, the directors of the Charité refused farther admission, the consequence of which was a long and angry correspondence between them and the police. The Minister of the Interior interfered, and ordered more accommodation for the Charité. This was done, but the new wards were soon filled with venereal females ; the patients exceeded the accommodations, and at last it was found necessary to take the Cholera Lazaret for syphilitic cases. Against this arrangement the magistracy of Berlin remonstrated that the present influx of venereal patients must be regarded as the inevitable, natural consequence of the abolition of the brothels ; that this abolition had not originated with them, therefore they were not bound to provide for it."

Dr. Behrend, to whose work we have already alluded, gives much statistical information, from original documents, showing the results of suppression. He says :

" In 1839, out of 1200 women brought to punishment for begging and similar offenses, there were about 600 common unregistered prostitutes. In 1840, the period of reducing the number of brothels, there were 900 such women. In 1847, a year after their suppression, there were 1250 notorious prostitutes. Those, in the opinion of the police, constituted but a portion of those who practiced prostitution, but yet had an apparent means of living. Behind the Konigsmauer the traffic is carried on worse than formerly, while the place itself is the scene of disorder and irregularity, which used not to be under the former system. These offenses can not be punished, owing to the difficulties of technical proof which must always exist. The police have done what is possible by continually patrolling the streets, and arresting openly objectionable characters, and even those who are informed against as being diseased, but they can do no more. *The prostitution which was formerly confined within a limited district is now spread over the whole town.*"

Respecting the influence of the withdrawal of toleration upon the public health, Behrend concludes there is a greater amount of syphilis. He gives the following list of cases in the Charité:

Year 1840 . . .	Females, 757 . . .	Males, —
" 1841 . . .	" 743 . . .	" —
" 1842 . . .	" 676 . . .	" —
" 1843 . . .	" 669 . . .	" —
" 1844 . . .	" 657 . . .	" 741
" 1845 . . .	" 514 . . .	" 711
" 1846 . . .	" 627 . . .	" 813
" 1847 . . .	" 761 . . .	" 894
" 1848 . . .	" 835 . . .	" 979

He also investigated the average time each patient was under treatment, as tending to show the malignity of the disease, and reports:

Year 1844, men, $21\frac{5}{6}$ days; women, $31\frac{1}{3}$ days; both sexes, $26\frac{3}{4}$ days.
" 1845, " $26\frac{4}{9}$ " " $42\frac{5}{8}$ " " " $34\frac{1}{3}$ "
" 1846, " $30\frac{1}{2}$ " " $51\frac{1}{4}$ " " " $40\frac{1}{4}$ "
" 1847, " $34\frac{1}{2}$ " " $43\frac{3}{4}$ " " " $38\frac{3}{4}$ "
" 1848, " $33\frac{1}{3}$ " " $53\frac{1}{8}$ " " " $43\frac{1}{4}$ "

These facts are corroborated by the registers of the Military Lazaret. From returns made to the police department by Herr Lohmeyer, General Staff Physician, it appears there were in the garrison

In 1844 and 1845, 735 syphilitic cases. Of these,

    633 cases of primary syphilis required 17,916 days of attendance;
    102 " " secondary " "   4,947 " "
    735 " " " " 22,863 " "

In 1846, and the first six months of 1847, there were 618 cases:

    501 cases of primary syphilis required 17,788 days of attendance;
    117 " " secondary " "   5,213 " "
    618 " " " " 23,001 " "

Dr. Behrend states, as the results of conversations and communications with many of the medical profession, and of his own experience:

" 1. That in the last four years there are more cases of syphilis.

" 2. That, in consequence of the increased facilities for communication, the disease has spread to the small towns and villages.

" 3. That it has been introduced more frequently into private families.

" 4. That the character of the disease is more obstinate, thereby operating severely on the constitution and on future generations.

" 5. That, since the abolition of the toleration system, unnatural crimes have been much more frequently met with."

As to the influence on public morals, he contends that the abolition has produced the most injurious consequences, particularly
alluding to the desecration of matrimony.   He says:

"It is common for persons of vicious habits to arrange a marriage, for
the purpose of enabling them to avoid the police interference.   This marriage bond is broken when convenient, and other marriages are formed:
sometimes two couples will mutually exchange, and go through the ceremony."

He also made inquiries as to illegitimacy, and publishes some
voluminous tables on the subject.   From them we condense a

COMPARATIVE STATEMENT OF THE LEGITIMATE AND ILLEGITIMATE BIRTHS IN
BERLIN FROM JANUARY 1, 1838, TO MARCH 31, 1849.

Years.	Births.			Ratio of illegitimate to legitimate Births.
	Legitimate.	Illegitimate.	Total.	
1838	8,587	1196	9,783	1 in 7·2
1839	7,820	1412	9,232	1 in 5·5
1840	9,019	1487	10,506	1 in 6·
1841	9,024	1557	10,581	1 in 5·7
1842	10,269	1928	12,177	1 in 5·3
1843	10,370	1969	12,339	1 in 5·2
1844	10,958	2000	12,958	1 in 5·4
1845	11,402	2138	13,540	1 in 5·3
1846	11,717	2140	13,857	1 in 5·4
1847	11,294	2204	13,498	1 in 5·1
1848	12,113	2303	14,416	1 in 5·2
3 mos. of 1849	3,278	646	3,921	1 in 5·1

Having rapidly traced the Berlin experience of the various
methods of controlling prostitution for nearly three fourths of a
century, it only remains to say that the increased evils of illicit
prostitution, and the total inability of the police to counteract them;
the spread of the venereal disease, and its augmented virulence; the
palpable and growing licentiousness of the city; the complaints
of public journals; the investigations of scientific men; and the
memorials of the citizens generally, reached the royal ear, and
induced an ordinance in 1851, restoring the toleration system, and
entirely repealing the edict of 1845, which had produced such disastrous results.

The experiment of "crushing out" had been fairly tried.   The
king and his ministers lent all their energy and inclination to the
task, and, after six years' attempt, it was admitted to be a futile
labor, and entirely abandoned.   Berlin will have to suffer for years
from the consequences of this misdirected step, for it is an easy
matter to abandon all control, but an exceedingly difficult one to
regain it.   Now that the police are reinvested with their former
authority, they strive, by every possible means, to repair the evils

of the interregnum. Their most recent regulations are embodied in the following

DIRECTIONS FOR KEEPERS PERMITTED TO RECEIVE FEMALES ABANDONED TO PROSTITUTION INTO THEIR HOUSES.

" 1. The duties hereby imposed upon the keeper are not to be taken to relieve him from the ordinary notices to the police respecting persons taken into his house or employment.

" 2. The keeper must live on the ground floor of his house, near the outer door, in order to watch all entrance into his house, and to be ready to interfere in case of tumult or uproar therein.

" 3. The keeper has the right to refuse any person admittance into the house. For preservation of order and quiet in, and in front of his house, the keeper will have the requisite assistance from the police.

" 4. Dancing and music in the house are strictly forbidden ; billiards, cards, and other games are also forbidden, whereof the keeper is to be particularly watchful.

" 5. In order to avoid quarrels with the visitors, the keeper must affix, in each of his rooms, a list of prices of refreshment, to be previously submitted to the undersigned commission\ for approval.

" 6. The agreement which the keeper enters into with the females living in his house must be also communicated to the undersigned commission. In case of dispute as to this agreement between the keepers and the females, both are to address themselves to this commission.

" 7. Each of the females receives a printed list of directions, which she is strictly to follow. It is the duty of the keeper to make himself well acquainted with these directions, and to see that they be followed.

" 8. It is for his own interest that the keeper should keep his house in order and quiet, and should also give attention to the cleanliness and health of the female inmates. Each of these is ordered to obey him in everything relating thereto, and should any of them be contumacious, the keeper is to appeal to the police commissary, or to the undersigned commission, but he cannot himself chastise or use force with any female.

" 9. If the keeper know or suspect any female to be sick with venereal disease or itch, he must give notice to the visiting medical officer, or to the undersigned, and the person is to be kept apart until she has been examined. In default of this notice, or even of the privacy required, the keeper is liable to the same punishment as the law inflicts for being knowingly accessory to illness of other people.

" 10. If the keeper knows or suspects that any of the females are pregnant, he must give notice thereof to the visiting medical officer. Neglect of this involves the punishment of concealing pregnancy.

" 11. Every person is to be visited thrice a week by a medical officer, on appointed days and hours ; and, besides, according to the order of the commission, at hours not appointed.   These visits the keeper is to facilitate in every way.

" 12.   For these visits, indispensably requisite for the health of the female inmates, the keeper is to provide beforehand,

" (a.)   An examination chair, of an approved pattern.

" (b.)   Two or three specula.

" (c.)   Several pounds of chloride of lime.

" (d.)   For every female, besides necessary linen, her own washing apparatus, her own syringe, and two or three sponges.

" 13.   The keeper is strictly charged that he cause the women to observe decency and propriety whenever it is allowed them to walk abroad in the streets, or to take exercise in the open air for the sake of their health.   If any of these persons require to take any such necessary walk, the keeper can not refuse her, but must provide a suitable male companion, who is to take charge of her.   She is to be respectably and decently clad, is not to stand still on the streets, nor to remain out longer than is requisite for completing her business or for proper exercise.

" 14.   In case any woman manifests a fixed desire to give up her profligate mode of life, the keeper shall make no attempt to turn her from it, and can not, even on account of sureties he may be under, hinder her from carrying out her determination.   Moreover, the keeper must present the woman with apparel suitable to a woman of the serving class, in case she should be destitute of the same."

15. Provides for change of keepers.

" 16.   The keeper is expected to give all assistance to the commission in their efforts to lead such persons back to an honest livelihood ; especially so in their endeavors to suppress illicit prostitution, and to detect the sources of venereal infection."

CHAPTER XVIII.

LEIPZIG.

Population.—Registered and illicit Prostitutes.—Servants.—Kept-women.—Brothels.—Nationality of Prostitutes.—Habits.—Fairs.—Visitors.—Earnings of Prostitutes.

BUT very few remarks are necessary concerning prostitution in Leipzig, where no striking peculiarity marks the common women as a class, and the legislation is based on the ordinary German principle of toleration.

If we reckon its garrison as a part of the population of the town, the number of inhabitants will amount to about one hundred thousand, nearly one third of whom are soldiers or transient residents. It is subject to many fluctuations at various times, but the general average may be assumed at the number stated. Of the permanent residents there are about six hundred well known and professed male rogues and blacklegs; these are under the constant and vigilant *surveillance* of the police. They unquestionably exert a considerable influence on the female morality of the place, not only from their own *amours*, for which men of this character are notorious wherever located, but by the agency they frequently assume to arrange the "pleasures" of their victims and acquaintances.

It need, therefore, occasion no surprise to ascertain that, in addition to about three hundred registered prostitutes who are subject to medical and police supervision, there are about twelve hundred women who notoriously frequent the city, from the neighboring towns and villages, for purposes of prostitution, whenever a large influx of visitors makes it probable that Leipzig will be a lucrative market for them. These are not directly under any police control. To this number of fifteen hundred avowed and known prostitutes, who are to be found in the city during busy seasons of the year, must be added the class of irregular or private courtesans, mostly composed of domestics. It is estimated there are three thousand servant-girls in the city, and the habits of a large number of them leave no doubt as to the propriety of including them in this enumeration; indeed, those who have had the best opportunities for observation do not hesitate to assert that at least one third are vicious. Assuming this to be an accurate calculation, we have 2500 prostitutes, or one in every forty of the gross population, exclusive of kept mistresses, or those frail women in the more aristocratic circles of society who should properly be classed with them. In this respect we have no reason to conclude that Leipzig is either better or worse than other large cities of the present day.

There are about sixty-six common brothels in Leipzig, the majority of which are registered and closely watched by the police. They are situated in the lowest and least frequented parts of the city, and many of them present, in excess, some of the worst features of such places. To escape their annoyances as far as possible, and retain that outward show of respectability most acceptable to their visitors, many of the prostitutes have private lodgings in various parts of the town, resorting to every conceivable dis-

guise to conceal or modify their real character. Very many of
them are said to be married women, whose husbands not merely
connive at, but frequently compel this loathsome trade for the sake
of its emoluments.

The proprietors of the tolerated brothels "assume a virtue if
they have it not," and seek to disguise their houses under the
names of coffee-houses or restaurants; a course recognized by the
authorities, who do not insist upon calling such places by the vernacular designation, as is done in Hamburg or Berlin.

The women inhabiting these houses are principally natives of
Altenburg, Berlin, Dresden, or Brunswick; those from the latter
district are noted by travelers for their personal beauty. Very
few Polish women are found here. The requisite supply of women
is kept up through the agency of procuresses, as in Hamburg, who
are remunerated by the brothel-keepers in proportion to the distance they have traveled to secure recruits, or according to the
attractions of the girl, or her probable success in the establishment.

In regard to dress, manners, conduct, and the other incidents of
their calling, there is little distinction between the prostitutes of
Leipzig and those of other European cities. A late anonymous
writer gives them credit as a class for a studious, literary habit,
and names a somewhat intelligent selection of light works as those
they prefer to read, such as the writings of Fredrika Bremer, Bul-
wer, Walter Scott, Caroline Pichler, Schiller, and others. If this
statement be correct, it may be accounted for by the great local
demand for literature, books and furs being universally known as
the great staples of Leipzig, and the fact can scarcely be assumed as
indicative of any especial inclination for *belles-lettres*. Prostitution
and studious habits or reflective minds are very seldom associated.
The majority of the brothel-keepers are stated to be anti-literary
in their tastes. They keep the women plentifully supplied with
cards and dominoes, which they use more for the purpose of pre-
dicting good fortunes to their visitors and themselves than for
gambling. We have never heard that any of their liberal prog-
nostications have been verified. Apparently the same usages and
habits of life prevail among the common women of Leipzig as
among those of Paris, Hamburg, Berlin, London, or elsewhere.
Indolent from the nature of their position, envious from their relationship to their compeers, their life would seem to pass in a
routine of doing nothing with considerable zest, or of quarreling
among each other with noteworthy animation.

No material variation from the ordinary routine of sickness caused by prostitution has been discovered in Leipzig. Syphilis has its average number of victims, the intensity of the malady being diminished or aggravated as a less or greater number of strangers may happen to be in the city.

The medical and police surveillance of prostitutes in European countries being modeled almost literally from one system, as is also the strictness with which it is now enforced, it is unnecessary to say any thing of its workings in Leipzig farther than the fact that the variable and floating nature of the population, at times, makes its application a difficult task. A description of it would be only a repetition of what has already been said of Paris, Hamburg, or Berlin.

The great fairs draw a large concourse of strangers from all parts of the world to Leipzig, and its geographical position beyond the centre of Europe brings it so close to the frontiers of Turkey, Poland, the Danubian provinces, and Russia, that the scene at these meetings is perhaps more motley and curious in race, costume, and characteristics than in any other city in the world. Among so heterogeneous a mass there exist many standards of morality. The semi-barbarous habits of some of the visitors entail a large share of sorrows on the prostitutes; more, in fact, than are generally experienced by any but the very lowest grade of women in other places. When in the tolerated houses, these rude hordes abandon themselves to the grossest licentiousness, use expressions compared with which the ordinary conversation of brothels is chaste and refined, and seek to extinguish every vestige of shame or womanly feeling in their companions. If a woman ventures to remonstrate at such extravagant lewdness, the reply is, "Well, now, be silent. I have paid you, and you are mine as long as I have you." It may therefore be easily credited that during such periods no shadow of decency can be found in the common houses. Any which exists (and truth compels the admission that it is very rare during the crowded season) can only be traced among those women who have private lodgings.

The only compensation for such depravity is found in the large sums obtained by the women from their lovers, in some cases amounting to forty thalers (about thirty dollars) per week. Of this, one half always goes to the brothel-keeper as his share, and, calculating his expenses to be five thalers per week for the board and lodging of each woman, it will be seen that his profits are not inconsiderable. The sum retained by the women is spent for articles of dress, pleasure, etc. This calculation is for a time when the town is in the full tide of commercial prosperity; but if we assume the average receipts at ordinary times to be one half only, we shall be able to form a tolerably good idea of the financial result of prostitution in Leipzig.

CHAPTER XIX.

DENMARK.

Prostitution in Copenhagen. — Police Regulations. — Illegitimacy. — Brothels. — Syphilis. — Laws of Marriage and Divorce. — Infanticide. — Adultery. — New Marriage Ordinances.

PROSTITUTES are very numerous in Copenhagen. This might be expected from the mixed character of the city, at once a capital, military station, and sea-port. It has been remarked by a traveler of great experience[1] that it is very rare to see a drunken man or a street-walker in Copenhagen; all seem to have a home or a place to go to, and the general character of the Danes is that of an orderly, educated, well-conducted people.

Some of the prostitutes of Copenhagen live in a kind of hotel, where they hold public entertainments; others live in brothels; and others still have private lodgings. There is nothing remarkable enough about them to call for any particular description. They are under police regulation to some extent, and receive a sort of half permission, which is not withdrawn during good conduct. A regulation is extant which professes to limit the number of children they are allowed to bear, without becoming amenable to the law as criminals. It requires that the mother of more than two illegitimate children be fined and imprisoned. As may be readily imagined, the law is very rarely enforced, its impolicy, if rigorously applied, being self-evident, since it would operate as a direct premium for abortion.

"Formal concessions are not granted either to public prostitutes or those with whom they lodge; neither are there in Denmark brothels, in the ordinary sense of the term, as they are found in other countries."[2] So writes a Danish official. His distinction

---

[1] Laing's Denmark in 1851.
[2] Braestrup, Director of Police at Copenhagen, on Prostitution and public Health.

is too nice to be appreciated. The Copenhagen police know of the existence of such women, and put them under strict regulations, not altogether prohibitory. They control and interfere with prostitutes; they do not tolerate them—that is to say, they do not issue a regular license to them or to the brothel-keepers. Consequently, there are no recognized brothels. The house in which courtesans live is a private dwelling, so far as the police are concerned, and is only interfered with when it becomes disorderly, the keeper not being accountable for the women or their conduct.

Nevertheless, the police regulations prescribe the number of women recognized as prostitutes who may live in any house, and from their official reports, it seems that there were in Copenhagen in

1850 . . . . 201 prostitutes.
1852 198   "

In the latter year there were sixty-eight persons who were authorized to lodge from one to four women each, the total of the women permitted to live in these houses being 139, and the remaining 59 being allowed to reside in private apartments. "Care is taken that they are all treated in the general hospital, and that they shall not be treated elsewhere, unless they give a sufficient guarantee not to propagate disease, or their personal position requires certain consideration, a thing which can seldom apply to the generality of prostitutes." The meaning of this regulation is not very clear, nor is "certain consideration" an intelligible phrase; it may imply pregnancy, or it may mean influential friends. The medical officer visits all cases which the police refer to him, and makes the necessary examinations, receiving his fees from the police.

The rules for detection and suppression of syphilis in Copenhagen are very stringent. All persons under arrest are required to declare if they are then, or have been lately diseased, and are liable to punishment if they conceal or misstate the facts. A visit of inspection is made when a ship is about to go to sea. All non-commissioned officers, musicians, and soldiers are examined on entering and leaving the service, and also regularly every month during their stay in it.

To check the propagation of venereal disease, every soldier who is attacked is obliged to state the source of his infection, whereupon information of the individual is given to the police. Those who do not give early intimation of their disease are liable to

R

bread and water diet for a certain time after their cure.   In 1797, all the inhabitants of several districts were obliged to submit to an examination, ordered by the chancellor, on account of the frequency of syphilitic cases therein.

The following table, taken from Berhand's minute on Copenhagen, shows the working of the system there for seven years. The most remarkable feature is the large number who married or went to service, which would seem to indicate a more charitable feeling on the part of the Danes than is usually evinced toward these unfortunates:

Years.	Prostitutes registered.			Prostitutes abandoned their calling.							
	At commencement of the Year.	During the Year.	Total.	Went to Service.	Transferred to the commission for the Poor.	Sent to Prison.	Married.	Left the Country.	Died.	Committed Suicide.	Total.
1844	297	34	331	20	13	1	16	2	7	4	63
1845	284	43	327	14	27	–	24	4	3	–	77
1846	256	18	274	15	16	2	13	1	2	–	49
1847	241	22	263	20	17	1	17	2	4	1	62
1848	116	27	143	15	16	1	16	2	7	–	51
1849	208	19	227	17	10	1	9	–	6	1	44
1850	196	23	219	18	7	1	1	–	–	–	27

By a code of 1734, promises of marriage might be either verbal in the presence of witnesses, or written and certified by two witnesses.   Widows acting against the consent of their guardians, and women of bad repute, were excluded from the benefit of this code.   A servant pregnant by her master, her master's son, or any one domiciled in her master's house, could not plead a promise of marriage.   Corroborative testimony was sometimes required in affiliation cases, where the putative father denied his liability on oath.

Divorce was allowed on simple abandonment for seven years; desertion for three years; in case of sentence of perpetual imprisonment; of ante-nuptial impotence; of ante-nuptial venereal disease; of insanity; and of adultery.   Divorce by mutual consent might also take place, but three years' separation from bed and board was requisite as a preliminary.   The king had a prerogative of divorce, without cause shown.

Illegitimate children were to be supported by their father until two years old, according to his rank in life.   They could not inherit the paternal property, but might take the mother's.   They could be legitimatized by subsequent marriage or adoption.

Infanticide was punished by beheading, and exhibiting the head of the criminal on a spike.

Adultery is punished by law in both husband and wife. Practically it is seldom noticed.

In 1834 a new ordinance was proclaimed fixing all the minutiæ of marriage contracts, parental obligations, and the general laws of sexual intercourse. A man is a minor until eighteen, and under some degree of parental authority to twenty-five, at which age he becomes a citizen. The woman is under tutelage all her life. Guardians are assigned to widows, who control their legal powers, but a widow may choose her own guardian. The laws of divorce are similar to those of France. The practice of formal betrothal is as common in Denmark as in Northern Germany, and implies a real and binding engagement, not to be broken without cause shown, or without discredit to one or both parties. Whether this custom favors illegitimacy is still a disputed point in Denmark.

CHAPTER XX.

SWITZERLAND.

Superior Morality of the Swiss.—Customs of Neufchatel.—"Bundling."—Influence of Climate.

THIS country, from her republican form of government, and her comparative isolation from the rest of the world, presents matter of peculiar interest to the inquirer into the nature and working of social institutions. Protected, as are the Swiss, from violent contrasts of excessive wealth and extreme indigence, the moral condition of their people will compare favorably with that of most nations. The simplicity of patriarchal relations is maintained both in their national and municipal governments; and although many customs are retained which smack strongly of the despotism of the Middle Ages, they can not be said to materially check the welfare of the people. In the absence of the emulation encouraged by the constant contemplation of luxury and wealth, the wants of the population are few and easily satisfied. Their virtues, however, partake of the bold and rugged nature of their country; and while there may be little of that practical vice and immorality which are the usual accompaniments of society in most kingdoms and states, we are not prepared to assert their superiority over the rest of mankind in innate virtue.   Hardness of heart and selfishness of disposition will be found as rife in Switzerland as elsewhere; it is the manifestation only that differs.

Authors are so universally deficient of remark on the subject of prostitution, or even of ·immorality in Switzerland, that, if we may judge from their silence, nothing of the kind exists there. " The Swiss population is generally moral and well-behaved.   A drunkard is seldom seen, and illegitimate children are rare," says Bowring.[1]

In Neufchatel, which, except politically, can hardly be considered part of Switzerland, a custom exists strongly similar to one in Norway,   *   *   *   *   namely, that of associating before marriage.   This, as Washington Irving says of the "delightful practice of bundling," is sometimes productive of unfortunate results.   A lady writer says that public opinion upholds the respectability of the females if they are married time enough to legitimatize their offspring.   Instances have occurred of two couples quarreling, and a mutual interchange of lovers and sweethearts taking place, the nominal fathers adopting the early-born children.[2]

The frugal thrift of the great bulk of the Swiss population, their distribution over the country in small numbers, the absence of large masses of human beings pent up in the reeking atmosphere of cities, their constant and intimate association with their pastors, and the hope which every individual cherishes of purchasing with his savings a small patch of his beloved native soil as a patrimony, seem to discourage prostitution as a trade.   The influence of climate, also, must not be forgotten; and Mr. Chambers, in accounting for the general good conduct of the Swiss peasantry, lays much stress on their temperate habits, the use of intoxicating liquor among them being very rare indeed.

[1] Report on Switzerland to the British Parliament, 1836, by Dr. (now Sir John) Bowring.   He was sent on a Continental tour of inquiry into the condition of the working classes, in reference to the English Poor-laws.

[2] Mrs. Strutt's Switzerland, ii. 231.

RUSSIA. 261

CHAPTER XXI.

RUSSIA.

Ancient Manners.—Peter the Great.—Eudoxia.—Empress Catharine, her dissolute Conduct and Death.—Peter's Libertinism.—Anne.—Elizabeth.—Catharine
II., infamous Career and Death.—Paul.—Alexander I.—Countess Narishkin.—
Nicholas.—Court Morality.—Serfage.—Prostitution in St. Petersburg.—Excess
of Males over Females.—Marriage Customs.—Brides' Fair.—Conjugal Relations
among the Russian Nobility.—Foundling Hospital of St. Petersburg.—Illegitimacy.

THE brutality, drunkenness, and debauchery which accompany
semi-barbarism, and of which the old Russian manners had more
than a due proportion, continued to be characteristic of the people
of that country until a very recent period; while their amiability,
their plastic disposition, their highly imitative faculty in the arts,
and their capabilities of improvement, are noted by many writers.
Just emerged from savage life as a nation, they have been moulded and welded as one mass by the steady and undeviating policy
of their sovereigns, among whom we have examples of vast mental powers and towering ambition, combined with the lowest depravity and the most shameless profligacy, exemplifying in the
same individual the extremes of human nature.

Previous to Peter the Great, Russia was comparatively unknown, and in the Elizabethan age of England the Czar of Mus-
covy was considered only as a barbarian, whose subjects were far
inferior in civilization to the Tartars of the Crimea. Indeed, it
was not till the eighteenth century that the Russians were admitted
within the pale of European politics, or their power reckoned as
an element in the calculations of statesmen.

The most important, we might almost say the only lawgiver
previous to Peter the Great, was Ivan III., who reigned in the
early part of the sixteenth century. Among the laws of that period, which were all sanguinary, was one fixing the value of a female life, in case of death by misadventure, at half the life of a
man. Slavery was the institution of the state, each child being
the absolute property of its parent. The women were more en-
slaved than among the Asiatics, no law protecting them against
their husband's violence. A wife who killed her husband was to

be buried alive up to the neck, and a guard was set around her to see that no one supplied her with food or the means of ending her sufferings.[1]   Females lived in the strictest seclusion, and had no weight nor authority in the household.   Their duties were to spin, to sew, and to do menial work.

Peter I. came to the throne, as most Russian sovereigns have done, either through intrigue or usurpation.   Both before and after Peter, the will and caprice of the ruling power was paramount.   He might appoint his successor, either during life or by will, and such appointment was often set aside by a more powerful competitor.   In Peter's public life, in his aspirations for the general welfare, in his self-devotion, in his conceptions of all that was wanting to his country's elevation and greatness, and in his iron will and supernatural energy, he was a hero; in his private life, in his passions, his tastes and habits, he was on a level with the lowest of mankind.

Our object is the delineation of national characteristics, and individual propensities or delinquencies are unimportant except so far as they illustrate national character.   It has been well observed that a people's virtue or vice does not consist in the arithmetical increase or decrease of immoral actions, but in the prevailing sentiment of an age or people, which condemns or approves them.   It is in this respect that the conduct of monarchs and courtiers becomes of importance in the estimate of national manners, especially in a despotism.   The Czar of Russia is at once the religious and political leader of his people, and his personal conduct becomes the standard of their moral relations, offering encouragement and support to the good, or sanction and justification to the depraved.

Peter's first wife, Eudoxia, was a woman of virtue and merit. Neither her youth nor beauty secured the affections of her husband.   She did not escape the voice of slander.   Gleboff, her alleged lover, was impaled by Peter, who went to see him writhing in his death agonies, when the wretched man avenged himself in the only way left him: he spat in the Czar's face.   Eudoxia was subsequently sent to a nunnery at Moscow by Peter's orders, and at last took the veil under the name of Helena.

Scarcely had Peter attained the crown when he formed a connection with Catharine.   The romantic history of her origin and elevation is too well known to repeat here.   Her husband, a

---

[1] Karamsin.

Swedish dragoon, was living; and she was the mistress first of Marshal Sheremeloff, then of Mentchikoff, in whose house Peter saw her, and whence he took her. She acquired great influence over the Czar's untamed ferocity, and, to her infinite credit, this influence was always used to mitigate the fearful rigor of his punishments, and to soothe his otherwise implacably revengeful spirit. During the lifetime of her husband and of his first wife, Peter married her.

The pleasing traits of Catharine's character were obscured by the irregularity of her life. Raised, by the affection of Peter, to the imperial throne, she set an example of dissoluteness to her subjects. There is ample reason for believing that she had several intrigues during Peter's lifetime, but the case of Moens de la Croix is beyond question, and the discovery of her infidelity in this instance led to her separation from Peter and the death of her lover.

In 1724, after the campaign against the Turks, in which Catharine had accompanied the Czar, and had, by her spirit and example, kept up the courage of the army amid great difficulties and reverses, Peter determined on publicly crowning her; a ceremony very unusual in Russia, and almost tantamount to declaring her his successor.

Moens de la Croix was the young brother of Anne de la Croix, one of Peter's early mistresses. He was Catharine's chamberlain. His office brought him in close attendance on the empress, and an intimacy was established. This was for a time notorious to every one except Peter himself. At length, however, his suspicions were aroused, and, by setting spies on Catharine, he became a personal witness to her infidelity. The first explosion of his resentment was terrific, and he was on the point of executing both the empress and her paramour, but by the temperate advice of some of his friends, who counseled him to avoid a scandal, it was determined to arrest Moens on a false charge of conspiracy.

Moens and his sister were accordingly seized and confined in an apartment in the winter palace. Peter permitted nobody to approach them, and took them their food with his own hands. When they were examined as to the conspiracy, Moens, to save the empress with the public, confessed to every thing. He was accordingly condemned and beheaded. His sister was knouted and sent to Siberia.

Catharine had presented her lover with her miniature on a bracelet, which he always wore. As he walked to his death, he managed to deliver it, unperceived, to the Lutheran minister who accompanied him, with instructions to convey it back to the empress privately, which was accomplished. The Czar was a spectator of the execution, after which the head of the culprit was fixed on a stake, according to custom. To terrify Catharine the more effectually, Peter drove her round the head of her lover. Happily for her, she managed to preserve self-control during the torture of this horrid spectacle. After this the Czar only spoke to her in public.

At Peter's death, Catharine ascended the throne of Russia by virtue of a pretended dying declaration of her husband. She went through a pantomime of sorrows and tears over his body, but, as soon as she was firmly seated, she abandoned herself to pleasure and voluptuousness, and had two lovers, Prince Sapicha and Loewenwolden, at the same time. "These two rivals equally strove to please her, and alternately received proofs of her tenderness, without suffering their happiness to be marred by jealousy." The irregularity of the empress's life, and her intemperate use of ardent liquors, hastened her death, which took place in her thirty-ninth year.

Peter himself was a wretched example of conjugal infidelity and low debauchery. His associates were often of the very lowest of the populace. It is true that in his time the highest were not much removed from their inferiors in decency of manners; while the inferiors often had the advantage, if not of intellectual cultivation, at least of practical intelligence, in which Peter took delight. He spent many of his hours drinking brandy and other liquors with sailors, carpenters, and artisans, irrespective of his temporary assumption of the working man's pursuits. He consorted indiscriminately with women of all sorts and conditions. Eventually he contracted the venereal disease. From neglect, and the general depravity of his life, the disease became so aggravated that at last it proved the indirect cause of his death. He himself used to say that he had taken it from Madame Tchnertichoff, wife of the general and diplomatist of that name. Upon the fact being mentioned to her, whether casually or with *malice prepense* does not appear, she is reported to have replied very naïvely that she had not given it to him, but that he, on the contrary, had such loose habits and low associates that he had given it to her.[1]

It was in 1722 that Peter was attacked with this malady, and while suffering from it he marched into Persia, and shared the

[1] Villebois.

fatigues of the meanest soldier throughout the campaign. The heat, drought, and constant dust increased the disease frightfully, and the pains became so excruciating that he could not conceal them from his immediate attendants. Still, however, he would not consult the court physician, but directed his servant to get advice as if for some one else. He then went to the hot baths of Plonetz, and apparently recovered. But it seems the disease was not cured; it was merely palliated by this treatment, and he was obliged, on a relapse, to have recourse to the regular physicians, and for three months his life was despaired of. At last he recovered; but now, in spite of all warnings, he resumed his usual habits of life, renewed his long and severe journeys, his public works, and his general activity of mind and body, while he in nowise amended other and more injurious pursuits and practices.

On November 5, 1724, while on a journey to Finland, he stopped at the port of Lachta. There, from the shore, he saw a small vessel full of soldiers and sailors which had struck upon a shoal. Perceiving their imminent danger, he shouted to them, but the boisterous wind drowned his voice. He sprang into a skiff, pulled out to the shoal, and, having reached the vessel, jumped into the water, got her off, and landed the passengers all safe. He neglected all the precautions necessary in the then state of his health, and was seized with violent fever, and at the same time his former pangs came on with all their old force. He was taken back to St. Petersburg, where he obtained partial relief from his sufferings. He employed one of his intervals of ease in celebrating the great festival of blessing the waters of the Neva, and by his intemperance in the festivities renewed his attack, and after a period of protracted agony, died on the 28th of January, 1725.

Peter is described as having been excessively libidinous in temperament, and his coarse promiscuous amours were made the common subject of his jocularity, even in the presence of Catharine. He was even addicted to abominable depravities, which are stated by contemporary writers to have been the common practice of the Russians at that time.[1] Peter at times gave way to fits of lust, in which, like a furious beast, he regarded neither age nor sex. Unnatural vices were punished in the Russian army at this time by an express military regulation, and the crime was a standing reproach with the people, who were said to have acquired it from the Greeks of the lower empire.[2]

[1] Memoires Secrets de la Cour de Russia. Villebois.   [2] Karamsin.

Anne, the successor of Peter and Catharine, had two publicly avowed lovers—Dolgorouki and Ernest John Biren. The latter was the better known, as his influence and importance during Anne's reign were very great. Dolgorouki had become one of the deputies to announce to Anne her succession to the throne, which office he accepted, with the hope of being able to resume his former intimate relations with his future sovereign. When he entered the apartments, he found a man in mean apparel seated by the side of the princess. He ordered him to withdraw, and, upon his inattention to the order, took him by the arm to turn him out, when the empress stopped him. This unknown person was Biren, who became regent of the empire.[1]

Anne was not sunk in the same abyss of profligacy as her successor Elizabeth, nor in brutality as her ancestor Peter. She had been brought up in Courland, and had acquired some little refinement of ideas and manners. Gluttony and drunkenness were somewhat less in vogue at her court, but dissipation, ruinous gambling, and boundless extravagance were in full fashion. The whole court became a body of buffoons and jokers, and the most absurd and preposterous fashions of dress, the rudest and most boisterous romps and gambols were generally practiced. As a specimen of court manners, the practical joke played on Prince Galitzin, in which there was as much malice as fun, may be remembered.

Having given offense by changing his religion, the prince was compulsorily married to a girl of the lowest birth. A palace was built in his honor, but the material was ice, and all the furniture was composed of the same. The wedding procession, consisting of more than three hundred persons in their national costumes, who had been collected from all the provinces of Russia, passed along the streets. The newly-married couple were mounted in a pagoda on the back of an elephant. When the ball was over, the bride and bridegroom were conducted to their nuptial chamber, like the rest of the house, all of ice, and were there installed in an ice bedstead, and guards were posted at the door to prevent them escaping from the room before morning.

Anne died in 1740, and, after a short interregnum, Elizabeth, daughter of Peter I., came to the throne. She inherited all her father's vices and sensuality, but none of his great qualities. Before she became empress, Elizabeth had outraged all propriety;

[1] Karamsin, p. 424.

had openly carried on an improper intercourse with the sub-officers and soldiers of the guards who had been quartered near her dwelling. The lust and drunkenness in which she wallowed indisposed her from all longings after greatness. But there were others who needed her name, and a conspiracy being formed, she became empress in spite of herself. Her chief paramour at the time was Grunstein, sergeant in the guards, who was elevated to the rank of major-general. The other soldiers and non-commissioned officers who had been the ministers of her lewdness were made officers. These individuals frequented the common public houses, got drunk, made their way into the houses of persons of condition, and committed all sorts of depredations with impunity. When the men who could boast of the empress's favors became intolerable, they were drafted off to the army, as officers in regiments on service.

Elizabeth is said to have been privately married to Razamoffsky, as also to the well-known Chevalier d'Eon, who visited the court of Russia in the disguise of a woman, and undoubtedly enjoyed Elizabeth's favors, whatever may be the truth about her marriage to him. Elizabeth withdrew herself for whole months from business, and was drunk for days or even weeks consecutively. She had a reputation for humanity; but, although she sentenced no one to death, not less than eighty thousand of her subjects were tortured or sent to Siberia during her reign. Her extravagance was such that when she died there were in her wardrobe some fifteen thousand dresses, thousands of pairs of sleeves, and several hundred pieces of French and other silks.

Catharine II. of Russia was, like Peter, a compound of the noblest intellectual endowments, with a moral organization of unsurpassed depravity. She has usually been considered a monster of lust; but she was no less infamous for her cruelty, and for the total absence of all those qualities and feelings which form the chief grace and beauty of woman's inner life. Her favorite dining-room in the Tauric palace was adorned with pictures representing the sacking of Ohkzakoff and Ismail, in which the painter had surpassed the gloomy vision of a Carravaggio, and had depicted the assault, the carnage, the mutilation, and all the hideous details of such scenes. In these Catharine is said to have taken great delight. She hated music, and never could permit other sounds than those of drums, trumpets, and similar barbaric instruments within her hearing; and yet it is said that, in her outset in

life as Princess of Anhalt Zerbst, she had a womanly heart, delicacy of taste, and refinement of intellect;[1] that it was not till long
after her husband, Peter III., had insulted her by open neglect of
her very winning person and youthful graces, and had abandoned
her for the vulgar and ugly Princess Woronzoff, that she committed herself to the terrible career which she afterward pursued so
steadily.

The Duchesse d'Abrantes, in her memoir of Catharine, tells us
that her first lover, Soltikoff, was forced upon her as a matter of
public policy by the crafty and unscrupulous Bestujeff, the able
minister of Elizabeth, for the sake of procuring an heir to the
Grand Duke Peter. Catharine remonstrated, and threatened to
complain. "To whom will you complain?" asked the minister,
coldly. Catharine submitted, and accepted the lover thus imposed
upon her. At the time of this adultery for expediency sake,
Catharine was deeply intent upon study, with a view to qualify
herself worthily for her future destiny, disgusted as she was with
the indecencies of the Russian court!

Subsequently, it was considered expedient to remove Soltikoff.
Catharine had given birth to a child, and was not pleased with
this dismissal; but the impassible Bestujeff only sneered at her remonstrances and professions of affection for the dismissed lover,
and recommended her to choose another. This was a lesson she
was not slow to carry out. The list of her paramours was little
less numerous than that of Elizabeth.

After Catharine had caused Peter III. to be murdered, and had
ascended the throne as empress in her own right, she abandoned
herself to the fullest gratification of her passions, both royal and
personal. Besides the vulgar crowd whom she selected as the recipients of her filthy favors, the world knew, as the public and
recognized paramours, the names of Orloff, by whom she had a
son called Count Bobruski, Wassilitchikoff, Potemkin, Louskoi,
Mornonoff, and Zuboff.

These were appointed in a manner that was reduced to a system, and an etiquette was established as precise as that of naming
a state minister. When Catharine was tired of her present favorite, one of her intimate friends was commissioned to look out
for another. At other times, her notice having fallen on some
young man who pleased her fancy, she signified her wishes to some
female friend, and thereupon an entertainment was arranged at

---

[1] Duchesse d'Abrantes, p. 34.

the lady's house, which the empress honored with her presence, and thereby gained an opportunity of closer acquaintanceship with the chosen individual. He then received orders to attend at the palace, where he was introduced to the court physician, and examined as to his general health and physical condition. After this he was placed under the charge of a certain Mademoiselle Protasoff.[1] The various examinations having been successfully passed, the favorite was installed into the regular apartments of office, which were immediately contiguous to those of the empress. On the first day of his installation he received one hundred thousand rubles (about twenty-five thousand dollars) for linen, and an allowance of twelve thousand rubles per month; besides which, all his household expenses were defrayed. He was required to attend the empress wherever she went, and was not permitted to leave the palace without her permission. He might not converse familiarly with other women, and if he dined with his friends, it was imperative that the mistress of the house should be absent.

When a favorite had completed his term of service he received orders to travel, and from that moment all access to her majesty was denied. The favorites rarely rebelled against their destiny in this particular; but Potemkin and Orloff, who had far other views than those of dalliance, had the temerity to disobey the order, and succeeded in retaining power and the friendship of the empress long after their personal claims on her tenderness were at an end. On terminating the intimacy, the favorite usually received magnificent gifts. Potemkin, after he had ceased his functions as favorite, became pander to his royal mistress, thereby securing the double advantage of the favor of the empress and the patronage of the favorite, from whom he levied a handsome fee for the introduction. Potemkin and Orloff were at one period rivals, in which contest Orloff was at last defeated; but when Potemkin reached his pride of place, he became so necessary to Catharine in his higher capacity that he set up and pulled down the favorite of the hour as he pleased, and even ventured upon the most extravagant flights of insolence and personal disrespect to the empress. Orloff had been also the rival of Poniatowski, but his superior capacity and

"........ Miss Pratasoff then there
Named from her mystic office l'Eprouveuse,
A term inexplicable to the muse,
With her then, as in humble duty bound,
Juan retired."—*Byron.*

brutal energy of will made him respected and feared by Catharine long after she had ceased to like him.

The pecuniary results to the state, enormous as was the plunder, was perhaps the least of the evils sustained through this system of iniquity. The registered gifts to the twelve favorites amounted to upward of one hundred million dollars.[1] Lanskoi, who had held no political offices, and the whole of whose fortune was drawn from the flagitious profits of his post of dishonor, died, after less than four years of office, worth, in cash only, and exclusive of valuables, seven millions of rubles. Potemkin's wealth, which was accumulated from all sources of public robbery and private extortion, was fabulous. At his death he owned two hundred thousand serfs; he had whole cupboards filled with gold coin, jewels, and bank-bills; he held thirty-two orders, and his fortune was estimated at sixty million dollars.[2]

In the closing days of Catharine's reign she found a lower deep into which to plunge. When upward of sixty, she took into office, as her favorite, Zuboff, who was not quite twenty-five. She now formed the Society of the Little Hermitage. This was a picked company of wits and libertines, of both sexes, over whose scenes of debauchery and revelry the empress presided. An inner penetralia even of these orgies was established, and called the Little Society.

The pernicious influence of such an example, set for so long a period of time by a sovereign distinguished for ability, and whose reign had been rendered famous by its successful foreign enterprises, was the almost universal corruption of the Russian court and aristocracy of both sexes. The women, in imitation of her majesty, kept men, with the title and office of favorites. This was as customary as any other piece of fashion, and was recognized by husbands. Tender intrigues were unknown; strong passion was still more rare; marriage was merely an association. There was a club, called the club of natural philosophers, which was a society of men and women of the highest classes, the object of whose meetings was indiscriminate sexual intercourse. The members met to feast, and after the banquet they retired in pairs chosen by lot. This club was afterward put down by the Russian police, in common with all other secret societies. A hospital was founded by Catharine for fifty ladies affected with venereal disease. These were all to be taken care of; no question was permitted as to name

---

[1] D'Abrantes, p. 294.   [2] Id. p. 297.

or quality, and the linen of the establishment was marked with the significant word "discretion."

Catharine's end was sudden and frightful. She had grown corpulent, and her legs and body had swollen and burst. She moved about with considerable difficulty, although her imperious will would not allow her to give way in her career either of ambition or profligacy. She was at the Little Hermitage November 4, 1796, in remarkably high spirits, and even joked her buffoon, Leof Nauskin, among other things, as to his death and his fears thereupon. The next morning the dread messenger, of whose advent she had made sport, brought his orders for her. She fell into an apoplectic fit, and, after thirty-seven hours of insensibility, died unblessing and unblessed, to be succeeded by Paul, her detested son by her first lover Soltikoff.

The emperor, or as he was better known by Napoleon's sobriquet, the mad Emperor Paul, was too remarkable for his eccentricities to make himself conspicuous for his gallantries. Even in this particular he preserved his eccentricity. He neglected his wife, an amiable and handsome woman, the mother of Alexander and Nicholas, for an ugly mistress, Mademoiselle Nelidoff, and for another, Mademoiselle Lapukhin, who would not accept his addresses, but to whom he nevertheless professed the patient devotion of Don Quixote. The most noteworthy circumstance, in this connection, of Paul's life was the indirect effect of female frailty in procuring his murder. The enemies who subsequently plotted his downfall and destruction procured their return from banishment through the offices of a certain Mademoiselle Chevalier, a French actress who ruled Kutaisoff, who on his part ruled the Czar.

As we approach our own times, the description of historical characters becomes liable to the tinge of prejudice or partiality.

Alexander, the son and successor of Paul, was distinguished by the amenity of his disposition and the philosophical tone of his political theories. He was married at an early age by order of his grandmother Catharine, who in his case insisted on making him a good husband, and took numerous precautions for that purpose, all of which her example neutralized or belied. The selection made for him might, under the conditions of humble life or a free choice, have turned out happily. As it was, he preferred the society of the ladies of his court, and in particular of the Countess Narishkin, by whom he had three children. The countess proved inconstant, and all his children by her died, to Alexander's deep grief.

After the loss of these illegitimate children, the affections of Alexander were turned toward the empress, whose true worth he recognized when it was too late. She was struck with disease, and he was on a journey to Southern Russia to select a suitable spot for a residence for her, when he was seized with the fever of which he died.

If Alexander's mild character had but little influence on his subjects, the name of his successor, Nicholas, has been identified with the very existence of the Russian people, as much as any sovereign since Peter the Great. His example and expressed will have had immense effect, both for good and evil. It is almost impossible to arrive at the true character of Nicholas at the present time, for the reasons just mentioned. In his private life as husband and father, and in his public life as ruler and politician, writers are diametrically opposed to each other. Party prejudice denies him all worth, or makes him a very Socrates. Golovin and authors of the democratic school affirm, in addition to his other offenses, that Nicholas had several illegitimate children, and also "that no woman could feel herself secure from Nicholas's importunities;" while writers like Von Tietz, Jermann, and other panegyrists of the Russian court, describe Nicholas as an exemplary husband and father, a model to his subjects in his domestic relations. They allege farther, that the gross immorality which has been the chief feature of Russian society was very much discouraged, and rendered altogether unfashionable by the estimable manners of the imperial family.

Truth is rarely found in extremes. The prevalent usage among sovereigns in this century has been "to assume a virtue if they have it not," and to maintain a respectable exterior for the sake of public opinion. So politic a ruler as Nicholas was not likely to reject this. He did all that could be done to bring virtue into good repute at court. But too many little incidents are told of him to justify a belief in his perfect spotlessness. The characters of individuals, even as rulers, would be unimportant to us were it not that in Russia society is in a transition state, and shows itself plastic in the hands of an energetic emperor. "The state! I am the state!" was perfectly true in the mouth of Nicholas. By his subjects he was held in an esteem little short of idolatry, and he was, in every sense of the word, the most remarkable man in his vast dominions.

Thompson, an English traveler, who has spoken very favorably of the personal worth of the Emperor Nicholas, says of the morality of the upper classes among the Russians, "Denied the advantages of rational amusement and innocent social enjoyments, deprived of those resources which, while they dispel *ennui*, elevate the feelings, the mind resorts to sensual indulgences and to the gratification of the passions for the purpose of finding recreation and relief from the deadening pressure of despotism. Immorality and intrigue are of universal prevalence, and (in a social sense) are hardly looked upon as criminal acts, while gambling and debauchery are the natural consequences of the tedious monotony from which all seek to escape by indulging in gross and vicious excitement."

Under the system of serfage, now approaching its end, it was almost impossible that there should be such a thing as public morality in the lower classes. The Russians, both noble and serf, are false and dishonest to a proverb. Prostitution in such cases is a superfluous term: a woman had no right or opportunity to be virtuous.

The morality of St. Petersburg is undoubtedly of the lowest, and yet we have not met with any accounts of local prostitution there. It is a city of men, containing one hundred thousand more males than females.[1] Kelly says the women form only two sevenths ($\frac{2}{7}$) of the entire population, and calls it "an alarming fact." The climate is unfavorable to female beauty, and it is generally conceded that the men are handsomer than the women. The German girls have an almost exclusive reputation for good looks in St. Petersburg. By reason of the disproportion of the sexes, it is said that ladies can not venture out unattended. This is etiquette among the higher classes of all Continental Europe, and the simple fact, without the reason, would not be surprising.

The attention to minutiæ which distinguishes a despotism, and which is so remarkable a feature of Russian state craft, does not allow us to suppose there are no statistical papers on the subject of prostitution; on the contrary, it is perfectly well known that such are in existence. The secrecy which is scrupulously maintained in all public matters, and the watchful vigilance of the police over strangers, prevents them obtaining any information except on the most patent and notorious subjects. The remarks of travelers on Russian society are very vague and general, and unsupported by any of those details which could alone authenticate them.

[1] Kohl.

S

We have already alluded to the ancient Oriental seclusion of women among the Russians. This was so strict that a suitor never saw, or at least was presumed never to have seen, the face of his bride before marriage. In 1493, Ivan the Great told a German embassador who demanded his daughter in marriage for the Margrave of Baden, that Russians never showed their daughters to any one before the match was decided. Peter the Great abolished this lottery, and directed that the parties might see each other, but he still found it necessary to promulgate a strong ukase against parents compelling children to marry against their wishes.

The compromise of the ancient custom which has been brought about by this law is that the elders of the family usually precontract for the juniors: then succeeds the bridal promenade, at which the young people, if unknown to each other, are led accidentally to meet in the same walk. Having thus managed an interview, the father of the young man, if all the preliminaries have been satisfactory so far, sends to the bride's father, and a general family meeting takes place, at which the arrangements are completed, the dowry determined, and then follows the betrothal. The elect pair kneel down on a fur mat and exchange rings. The preparations for the marriage are commenced, during which time the lovers have frequent opportunities of meeting and becoming better known to each other; this is a general period of visiting and parties. On the wedding-day the bridemaids unbraid the lady's hair, and she receives her husband with flowing locks. This is a remnant of ancient Russian usage, when the greatest outrage that could be committed on a woman was to unbraid her hair. It is generally believed that among the lower orders the wife is bound to draw off her husband's boots on the wedding-day, and also that the Russian peasant beats his wife at the commencement of her married life, so as to indicate supremacy. As to the substantial observance of the latter practice modern travelers differ, although it would seem that symbolically it is still maintained.[1]

A curious exhibition takes place on Whitsunday in the Petersburg summer garden, called "The Bride's Fair." All the marriageable daughters of the Russian tradesmen turn out on that day for a promenade. The young men, in their best attire, come forth to view them. The brides expectant do not limit their dis-

---

[1] Golovin states that the whip is an article in frequent requisition in the conjugal state.

play to their charms, but second them by attractions of a more substantial character, adorning themselves with trinkets, jewels, or even now and then with silver tea-spoons, plate, and other valuables useful in housekeeping. This has been inveighed against as indicative of the prevalent indelicacy of the Russians, a sort of bride-market. Is it more reprehensible than many customs nearer home? It is now, however, falling into disuse.

The conjugal relations of the Russian nobility were extremely loose and indefensible during the time when vice was fashion, and virtue in a courtier would have been deemed condemnation of the higher powers. Then, and even down to the reign of the Emperor Nicholas, marriage was simply an affair of convenience—the husband living at Moscow or St. Petersburg, the wife in Paris or Italy; such separations frequently lasting for years.[1]

The Foundling Hospital at St. Petersburg, the *Wospitatelnoi Dom*, is the most magnificent foundation of the kind in Europe, and it pleases the authorities to give information upon its features. The endowments are enormous, owing to the munificence of successive sovereigns, who have made it a kind of state caprice. The annual expenditure exceeds five millions two hundred thousand rubles.[2] The number of children in this institution is commensurate with its wealth. Upward of twenty-five thousand are constantly enrolled on its books.

The lodge is open day and night for the reception of infants. The daily average of children brought is about twenty. The only question asked is if the child has been baptized, and by what name. If not baptized, the ceremony is performed by a priest of the Greek Church. At the time of leaving, the mother receives a ticket, the duplicate of which is placed around the child's neck. The mortality which takes place among these helpless victims of sin and misfortune is enormous. Some die in the lodge when just received; more perish during the tedious ceremonies of their baptism, which last several hours. The total number of deaths among children in the asylum and those out at nurse is probably three thousand per annum, or about one in four of the whole number committed to its charge.[3]

---

[1] Von Tietz, p. 73.

[2] Kohl. There is some difficulty in estimating the ruble from the difference in the currency of Russian silver coin. We believe this sum would be upward of a million dollars.

[3] Von Tietz says that, as regards morality, the institution does not work badly,

The children are given in care of wet nurses for about six weeks, when they are sent into the country until six years old. They are then brought back to the institution and educated in a superior manner; the girls being qualified as governesses in Russian families, and the boys as artisans in the imperial manufactories. In cases of special capacity, they receive a scientific or musicals ducation.

An incident which is said to have occurred at this institution has gone the rounds of the press. The story is, that one of the young women having given birth to an infant, and the delinquent not being discovered, the Emperor Nicholas heard of the occurrence, and made a visit of inspection. Having summoned the pupils before him, he demanded to know the guilty one, adding that, if she came forward, she should be pardoned. No one obeyed the invitation, and he was going away, with threats of disgracing the whole body, when one girl, to save her companions, came forward, threw herself at his feet, and confessed her fault. Nicholas kicked her out of the way, exclaiming that it was too late.[1]

A Lying-in Hospital is one of the appendages of this establishment. Pregnant women may enter there four weeks before their confinement, and the strictest secrecy is maintained as to their name and character. Even the omnipotent Czar respects the privileges of the place.

The institution at Moscow is on a similarly gigantic scale, and is managed after the same fashion.

The empress is the mother of the foundlings, which, be it observed, are mostly the children of such as can not or do not desire to keep their offspring. Free access, on appointed days, is permitted to the parents of the children; and, under special circumstances, the empress will permit a child to be removed from the institution, if the parents prove their means and disposition to support it properly.

Kohl, who gives us particular, and even minute accounts of the management and arrangement of the public hospitals, makes no mention whatever of the syphilitic wards. The high system of efficiency in which the military infirmaries are maintained might have encouraged a hope for more detailed information on this subject.

for there are comparatively less illegitimate births at St. Petersburgh than in most other cities, but he gives no figures to support this assertion.   [1] Golovin.

CHAPTER XXII.

SWEDEN AND NORWAY.

Comparative Morality.—Illegitimacy.—Profligacy in Stockholm.—Infanticide.—Foundling Hospitals.—Stora Barnhordst.—Laws against Prostitution.—Toleration.—Government Brothels.—Syphilis.—Marriage in Norway.

THE ancient Scandinavian peninsula, land of the Scald and the Rune, with its Vikings and Beisckers, has sent down to us many a legend of war and conquest, but few of social manners or moral relations. The high esteem in which the ancient Germans held their women, and the affinity of laws and customs between the Norsemen and the Teutons, justify us in believing that the blue-eyed maids of the Scandinavian heroes were as much respected for virtue as beloved for beauty. The eternal virgins in the Walhalla of Western mythology were not associated with the grosser pleasures with which the impure fancy of the Koran invested the houris of the Mohammedan Paradise; and the Norsemen, through their posterity, the Normans, introduced, among the other amenities of chivalry, that prominent obligation of true knighthood, "*devoir aux dames*," perhaps not the least humanizing incident of the institution.

Passing, by a long stride, at once to modern times, we find in the joint kingdom of Sweden and Norway two territories as distinct in their social condition as they are in their geographical divisions. Norway has always been remarkable for a simple and hardy population of fishermen and small farmers, elements in the highest degree favorable to virtue and independence, and their poverty and isolation from the continental interests of Europe have exempted them from politics and war. Sweden, on the other hand, though not much wealthier as a nation, has had an hereditary nobility, and the ambition and ability of some of her monarchs, especially of the great Gustavus, caused her to play a part in history wholly disproportionate to her territorial importance. If, however, the historical significance of Sweden be somewhat greater than that of the less pretentious sister kingdom, statistics do not accord to the former the same estimation, in point of morals, as they concede to the latter.

The average of illegitimate births, though not infallible, is generally accepted as a fair test of the immorality of a people. Taken by this standard, Sweden ranks lower than almost any country of Europe. But if the character of the general population be indifferent, that of Stockholm "out-Herods Herod."

In Stockholm, in 1838, there were 1137 illegitimate to 1577 legitimate; in 1839 there were 1074 illegitimate to 1492 legitimate births.

The average of illegitimate to other births in the capital and throughout the country was as follows:[1]

	1835.	1838.	1839.
In Stockholm	1 in 2·44	1 in 2·47	1 in 2·38
In other towns	1 in 6·18	1 in 6·18	1 in 6·40
In the country	1 in 20·41	1 in 20·01	1 in 20·01
Throughout the kingdom..	1 in 15·20	1 in 14·69	1 in 14·94

As regards the average of the whole kingdom, the proportion is much the same as that of England and France. What, then, must be the condition of the towns, and, in particular, of the capital?[2] The figures are such as to justify the allegation against Stockholm of being the most immoral capital in Europe, and also the presumption that the late decrease in its population, from which it is but recently recovering, is a direct consequence of the vice that stains it.

With so large an amount of illegitimacy, it is not surprising that infanticide should be of common occurrence. The penalty of this crime is death, although, from a growing aversion to capital punishment, it is generally commuted.

There are numerous foundling hospitals throughout the kingdom of Sweden; one in particular, the *Stora Barnhorst* in Stockholm, established by Gustavus Adolphus, originally intended for the children of military men of broken health and fortunes. It has been perverted from the simplicity of its original foundation, and now receives children of all comers, who pay an entrance fee of about thirty-five dollars. No questions are asked on the presentation of an infant to the asylum, and, excepting the fee, it is in no respect different from the ordinary foundling hospitals. This very fee, however, it is considered by some writers, makes all the difference, as it in some measure justifies those parents who, having adequate means, choose to release themselves of the care and

[1] Swedish Registrar-General's Reports, 1838, 1839.

[2] Baron Gall's Reiser durch Schweden, Bremen, 1838; Laing's Tour through Sweden; Baron Von Strombeck Durstellunger, 1840.

expense of their offspring, and who use this payment as a salve to their consciences, considering that they have to that extent done their duty. The Stora Barnhorst is wealthy, having an income of above one hundred and fifty thousand dollars per annum.

In 1836, prostitution was forbidden, by express enactment, throughout all Sweden, and women who had not a legally recognized occupation were liable to imprisonment as disorderly characters. The prostitute, of course, came within the category. It was asserted at the time that there was no common prostitution, but a counter statement was made by the jurist Angelot, who affirmed that every house of entertainment was a brothel, and every servant a loose woman.

This prohibitory system did not work so well as had been anticipated, and in 1837 a change was effected. A large hotel was taken by the corporation, and, after the plan of various cities in the Middle Ages, was managed by public officers. Thus a government brothel was established. Nor did this lewdness by authority have the desired effect. The brothel was filled with women, but no customers appeared. Private brothels were resorted to for a time, and were opened under regular licenses. They have now disappeared, and as the inefficient police management never succeeded in repressing illicit prostitution, even while tolerated brothels were in existence, it will surprise no one to learn that Stockholm is now one vast, seething hot-bed of private harlotry.

There are Lock Hospitals throughout Sweden, established by public funds, and kept up by direct taxation as a charge upon the municipal rates. The Stockholm Hospital for syphilis in 1832 received seven hundred and one patients, of whom one hundred and forty-eight were from the country, and the remainder from the city. The capital contained in that year 33,581 persons of both sexes above the age of fifteen, consequently *one person in every sixty-one was affected with syphilis.*

The superficial aspect of society in Sweden is certainly not such as here described. The upper classes are cultivated, polite, and observant of all the usual refinements of modern society, while to the humbler classes, excepting that intercourse is free and unrestrained among them, there is no ground for attributing any unusual departure from modesty and propriety. Neither are the laws remarkably stringent: although difficulties are thrown in the way of affiliation, they are the same in principle as those which have been adopted by the modern statute law of England.

Still, that there is such an excess of immorality can not be doubted. The official statistics of the country prove it, were any possible doubt thrown upon the statements of the many travelers, of the highest repute for correctness and reliability, who have noticed it. The latest publication upon the matter is from Bayard Taylor, who, writing from Stockholm under date May 1, 1857, says,

" I must not close this letter without saying a word about its (Stockholm's) morals. It has been called the most licentious city in Europe, and I have no doubt with the most perfect justice. Vienna may surpass it in the amount of conjugal infidelity, but certainly not in general incontinence. Very nearly half the registered births are illegitimate, to say nothing of the illegitimate children born *in* wedlock. Of the servant-girls, shop-girls, and seamstresses in the city, it is very safe to say that scarcely one out of a hundred is chaste, while, as rakish young Swedes have coolly informed me, a large proportion of girls of respectable parentage are no better. The men, of course, are much worse than the women, and even in Paris one sees fewer physical signs of excessive debauchery. Here the number of broken-down young men and blear-eyed, hoary sinners is astonishing. I have never been in any place where licentiousness was so open and avowed, and yet where the slang of a sham morality was so prevalent. There are no houses of prostitution in Stockholm, and the city would be scandalized at the idea of allowing such a thing. A few years ago two were established, and the fact was no sooner known than a virtuous mob arose and violently pulled them down. At the restaurants young blades order their dinners of the female waiters with an arm around their waists, while the old men place their hands unblushingly upon their bosoms. All the baths in Stockholm are attended by women (generally middle-aged and hideous, I must confess), who perform the usual scrubbing and shampooing with the greatest nonchalance. One does not wonder when he is told of young men who have passed safely through the ordeals of Berlin and Paris, and have come at last to Stockholm to be ruined. * * * * Which is best, a city like Stockholm, where prostitution is prohibited, or New York, where it is tacitly allowed, or Hamburg, where it is legalized ?"

We have spoken of the difference between Sweden and Norway in their moral relations. At first this is not apparent, for illegitimacy is as frequent in one as the other; but there are attendant qualifying circumstances, which go to constitute a material variation in the conclusion to be drawn from the unexplained fact. We may remark that street-walking and open prostitution are rare. Illegitimacy is of considerable extent, averaging one in five, or, in some parts, one in three of the total births. The people are betrothed by the practice of the Lutheran

Church a long time before the actual marriage. This is considered as nothing more than a wholesome check upon hasty unions in a general point of view. In Norway, however, this probationary period is extended to a limit beyond the endurance of flesh and blood. The wedding is a prodigious merry-making, and it is absolutely indispensable that the means for an extravagant hospitality should have been accumulated before the parties dare attempt the public ceremony. The profusion is so great as sometimes to dissipate a whole year's earnings. The obligation to this expense increases the delay required by the Church, and it frequently happens that the affianced cohabit before the nuptial benediction is pronounced. As the betrothal is a half-marriage, the arrangement loses part of its offensive character in the eyes of the parties themselves, and also of their neighbors. The children are legitimatized by the subsequent marriage, which takes place in by far the largest number of cases. In those occasional instances where the wedding ceremony is not duly completed, there is a particular legal act by which a child can be acknowledged. Failure of marriage under such circumstances, or failure of natural duty to offspring, is against the sentiment of the people. While these facts do not alter the actual concubinage or illegitimacy, it is easy to understand that a considerable difference exists between such conduct, however reprehensible, and those habits which may be fairly characterized as licentiousness or profligacy.

Norway is very far from being free of syphilis. Bayard Taylor says, "Bergen is, as I am informed, terribly scourged by venereal diseases. Certainly I do not remember a place where there are so few men, tall, strong, and well made as the people generally are, without some visible mark of disease or deformity. A physician of the city has recently endeavored to cure syphilis in its secondary stage by means of inoculation, having first tried the experiment upon himself, and there is now a hospital where this form of treatment is practiced upon two or three hundred patients, with the greatest success, another physician informed me. I intended to have visited it, but the sight of a few cases around the door so sickened me that I had no courage to undertake the task." We have no means of ascertaining whether the malady exists with the same virulence in the interior as on the coast. The habits of the people would seem adverse to the supposition that it does.

CHAPTER XXIII.

GREAT BRITAIN.—HISTORY TO THE TIME OF THE COMMON-WEALTH.

Aboriginal Morals and Laws.—Anglo-Saxon Legislation.—Introduction of Christianity.—St. Augustine.—Prostitution in the Ninth Century.—Court Example.—Norman Epoch.—Feudal Laws and their Influences.—Civil and Ecclesiastical Courts. — General Depravity. — Effects of Chivalry. — Fair Rosamond.—Jane Shore.—Henry VIII.—Elizabeth.—James I.

THE first references to prostitution which we find in the works of the early British annalists are so vague that it is difficult to derive from them any very definite idea as to its extent and character. Among the crude efforts at legislation there are laws to enforce chastity among women, but whether the necessity for these enactments was owing to general licentiousness or to the existence of a regular class of prostitutes does not appear.

At the period of the Roman invasion, the morals of the Britons were as low as might be expected from their nomadic habits. The population was divided into small communities of men and women, who appear to have lived promiscuously, no woman being attached to any particular man, but all cohabiting according to inclination, the carnal instinct being the feeling which regulated sexual intercourse. A sort of marriage was instituted, but with no idea that either of the parties to it should be restricted by its obligations. Its only object seemed to be to provide means for rearing the children, and to fix somewhere the responsibility of their nurture and support. A society constituted as this was can, of course, be considered scarcely a step removed from barbarism. The regulation to provide for the children was necessary to prevent depopulation; its tendency was to remove from the woman's path every obstacle to lust; over the man it exercised but very slight control.

A still farther proof of the demoralized condition of the people is found in the gross ceremonies attending these marriages. The man appeared on his wedding day dressed in all the rude trappings of the time; the woman was entirely naked. A repulsive coarseness marked their licentiousness, and the rudeness of manners was nowhere more conspicuous than in the relations existing between the sexes.

It is to be presumed that the Anglo-Saxons imported into England the laws and customs prevailing in their own country. The rules they made against adultery were frightfully severe. When a couple were detected in the commission of the offense, the woman was compelled to commit suicide, to avoid the greater tortures awaiting her if she refused. Her body was then placed on a pile of brushwood and consumed. Nor did her partner in guilt escape punishment; he was usually put to death on the spot where her ashes lay collected. These penalties would appear to be sufficiently severe, but in some instances worse were inflicted. Where the case was one of peculiar aggravation, the adulteress was hunted down by a number of infuriate demireps of her own sex, each armed with a club, a knife, or some other formidable weapon, and stabbed or beaten to death. If one party of her pursuers became weary of the sport, another took their places until the victim expired beneath the blows.

These extremely rigid ideas of the Anglo-Saxons do not seem to have been consistent, for while adultery was punished in the severe manner described, incest was not only permitted, but commonly practiced; and it was even the custom for relations to marry within the closest degrees of consanguinity.

But they were not long located in England before the more savage traits of their character were softened down, and the women soon found amusement more suitable to their sex than that of chasing their erring sisters as quarry. The marriage ceremonies also assumed a more refined and decent character, although the wife continued to be regularly purchased by her husband, and the contract was still considered a mere matter of bargain and sale. By the laws of Ethelbert marriageable women were made commodities of barter, and enactments of this character are to be found in existence long subsequent to his reign.

As the Anglo-Saxons were a hardy, vigorous race, and existed chiefly by hunting, fishing, and a rude and imperfect system of agriculture, it is not probable that prostitution existed among them to any great extent. The fatigues of the chase and field exhausted the energy of the body, and diminished the desire and capacity for sexual indulgence, and, living in small detached communities as they did, they knew nothing of the stimulating incentives of city life.

Yet that prostitutes existed, and lived by the wages of their profession, is proved by the fact that women (who were entitled by law to hold and dispose of property) bequeathed their wealth to their daughters, with the occasional stipulation that they should live chaste lives in the event of their remaining single, and not earn money by prostituting their persons.

In the reign of Canute a law was enacted by which any one found guilty of adultery was to be punished by the loss of the nose and the ears.[1] In the course of time the crime came to be punished by a fine paid to the husband of the woman. This penalty soon fell into disrepute, as it was found that some husbands and wives took advantage of it to extort fines from persons possessing more money than prudence. By a subsequent enactment the male adulterer became the property of the king, who might send him to the wars, or employ him at hard labor as he pleased. By a law of Edgar's time the adulterer of either sex was compelled to live, for three days in each week, on bread and water for seven years. This was treating the evil on physiological principles.

We can not infer any very strict condition of morals as the result of this harsh legislation. When punishment is carried to an extreme entirely disproportioned to the offense, it is as likely to fail in its object as mistaken lenity. Forgery and arson were more frequent in England when punished with death than they are at present; and although we have no statistics of the time from which we can deduce any positive conclusions, we may reasonably imagine that neither the death penalty, nor the other barbarous punishments substituted for it, exercised any very powerful influence in the diminution of the crime among our hardy progenitors. It may have taught them greater caution and dissimulation in the prosecution of their evil purposes, but it did not render them the less eager to profit by the opportunities thrown in their way.

It has been already shown that the founders of Christianity treated illicit sexual indulgence as a sin, and resorted to extreme measures for its suppression, but yet, to some extent, tolerated prostitution. Shortly after he had established himself in Britain, Augustine put some curious queries to the Pope touching the manner in which chastity among converts to the new faith should be enforced. The nature of these interrogatories and replies forbids their appearance here.[2]

[1] Spelman.

[2] Bede, lib. i. cap. 27.

That Augustine required to be instructed on such prurient details proves that he was a believer in the Jewish observances of physical ablutions and cleansing of the person being necessary to the removal of moral impurities, and that he carried his scrutiny into the morals of his flock much farther than was consistent with modesty and good sense. However much his religious teachings might have improved the manners of the people, the regulations alluded to would have exercised no very salutary or efficacious influence over them.

The lives of the early kings and rulers of Britain serve to illustrate the morals of the nation during their respective reigns, not only by exhibiting individual examples where the condition of the masses is hidden from view, but by affording us an index to that condition when it is considered that the manners of the court have, in all ages and all countries, exercised an important influence on those of the people.

Augustine converted Ethelbert, but his son Endbald deserted the Christian Church because it refused its sanction to his mother-in-law becoming his wife. It is true that he afterward divorced her, and returned to Christianity, but in this he was influenced rather by satiety than by the promptings of a reviving faith. Many of the other kings of the Heptarchy were as remarkable for the headstrong ardor of their passion as Endbald. Canulph of Wessex had, in the year 784, an intrigue with one of his female subjects, and frequently quitted his court to enjoy her society in the country. During one of these clandestine excursions he was surprised and surrounded in the night by the followers of Kynchard, a rival pretender to the throne, and murdered in the arms of his mistress.

In the ninth century prostitution seems to have been a prevailing vice throughout the country, and frequent references are made to it in the discussions of the period. In the arguments used in favor of tithes, in the time of Athelstan, it was held by some canonists that the clergy had a right to demand one tenth of the profits earned by prostitutes in the exercise of their calling. It is but right to add that the Church did not persist in enforcing this extraordinary claim.[1]

Edwy, who ascended the throne at the early age of seventeen, became involved in a controversy with the monks on the question, then first started, of the celibacy of the clergy. The celebrated

[1] Padre Paolo.

Dunstan favored the new doctrine, but Edwy opposed it. The youthful and inexperienced prince was no match for his sagacious antagonist, as he soon after discovered. On the day of his coronation, which took place soon after his marriage with his cousin Elgiva, whom he loved and resolved to wed, though she was within the degrees of consanguinity prohibited by the Church, his nobles were indulging in the pleasures of the banquet, when it was discovered that Edwy had stolen away. Dunstan and Odo, Archbishop of Canterbury, conjecturing the cause of his absence, proceeded to the private apartments of the queen, and found him in her company. They tore him from her, and dragged him back to the party. Elgiva's face was seared with a red-hot iron to destroy her beauty, and she was transported to Ireland. Her wounds being soon healed, and all trace of the injuries removed, she returned to her own country, but was met by a party the archbishop had sent to intercept her, and put to death. Thus, professedly to preserve the morals of the king, these high ecclesiastics committed crimes of far greater gravity than a marriage even between persons more nearly related than Edwy and Elgiva.

Edgar, who succeeded Edwy, was of a still more passionate and licentious disposition. He broke into a convent, and carried off one of the nuns, named Editha, who was remarkable for her beauty. In the heat of passion, he violated her person; and for the double offense of abduction and rape, the Church, according to the peculiar morality of the times, punished him by compelling him to resign his crown for the period of seven years. By a curious inconsistency, he was permitted to retain possession of Editha, who lived with him as a concubine.

Another of his mistresses he obtained by a less violent process. In passing through Andover, he accidentally met the daughter of a neighboring noble, who fascinated him by her remarkable beauty. Listening only to the suggestion of his passion, he proceeded immediately to the residence of the maiden's mother, and, informing her of the violent love with which she had inspired him, demanded that she should be permitted to share his bed that night. The mother, fearing to excite the king's anger by a refusal, resorted to a stratagem, by which she hoped to evade his wrath, and, at the same time, preserve the chastity of her daughter. She directed a handsome waiting-maid to introduce herself into the young lady's chamber, and the king was admitted after dark. When Edgar discovered the trick which had been played on him, he manifested no resentment, and the accidental partner of his bed became afterward his favorite mistress.

These were not his only amours. Elfrida, daughter of the Earl of Devonshire, was distinguished by extraordinary beauty, and the fame of her charms reached the court, although she resided in the country in strict retirement, and had never been a mile from home. Edgar, hearing of her beauty, and doubting whether her appearance justified the extravagant praise lavished on it, sent one of his trusted favorites, Earl Athelwold, to her father's residence to make a report to him on the subject. Athelwold himself, like many a similar envoy, fell in love with the young lady, and informed the king that rumor had greatly exaggerated her merits, and that she was positively ungainly. This was sufficient to allay the king's curiosity, and Athelwold shortly afterward secured the young lady's hand in marriage. He explained the matter to Edgar by remarking that it was her fortune which induced him to overlook her homely features. The king desired him to introduce her at court, and Athelwold persistently refusing, the king suspected the true state of the case. He intimated to the earl that he had determined to visit the castle where she resided, and the husband, dreading the consequences, implored his wife to conceal her beauty as much as possible. Elfrida, woman-like, did precisely the contrary, and set off her charms by the richest and most becoming toilette in her wardrobe. Edgar was so enraged at the deception practiced on him that he put the unfortunate earl to death, and married the widow.

The infusion of Danish blood does not seem to have exercised an improving influence on Anglo-Saxon manners. Judging from the following, the contrary may be inferred.

Ethelred kept a number of Danish troops in his pay, who were stationed in different parts of the country. A complaint was made to the king that the Danes had attained such a pitch of refinement, and made such an advance in luxury, that they combed their hair daily, and were guilty of other acts of personal embellishment equally reprehensible. Worse still, it was averred that the women looked with favor on these practices of the Danes, and that the latter debauched the wives and daughters of the English, and disgraced the nation.[1] It is evident that women who could thus easily be led away were only virtuous from the want of opportunity.

---

[1] Wallingford.

The legislation of this period shows that prostitution was not only tolerated, but indirectly encouraged.

If a man seduced the wife of another, he was compelled, by an early Saxon law, to pay a fine to the husband, and to procure for him another woman, whom he was to remunerate for admitting him to her bed.[1] This was not only offering a direct premium to prostitution by providing for the debauching of a woman every time another chose to be seduced, but it shows that females were in the habit of cohabiting with men for hire. The fines for adultery were graduated according to the rank of the woman. If she happened to be the wife of a nobleman, her chastity was valued at the moderate sum of six pounds sterling (about thirty dollars); while the wife of a churl brought to her husband as a salve for his injured honor about a dollar and a half. The effect of these enactments could not but exercise a demoralizing and injurious influence on the manners of the people. They reduced the estimate of female chastity to that of a cheap marketable commodity, whose loss could be repaid by a small money compensation.

By the laws of Ethelbert a man was permitted to buy a wife, provided the purchase was made openly, and many such transactions are recorded, the price being sometimes paid down in money, and sometimes in palfreys and other kinds of property. The practice, however, was soon modified, and it became necessary to obtain the consent of the bride. The husband was compelled to support and protect her, and to treat her with respect. A couple desirous of contracting marriage were formally betrothed in presence of the priest, and this practice, having something of an ecclesiastical obligation without any of its legal force, was frequently productive of the same evil consequences as in Norway at the present day. This custom of betrothal prevailed down to the time of Elizabeth.

The Normans introduced into England, if not a higher standard of morals, at least a greater refinement in vice. Their laws were moulded by the spirit of the feudal system which they imported with them. Under their sway society was divided into two classes—feudal lords and their vassals. The lord could dispose of the person and property of the vassal, limited, indeed, by certain restrictions, but still leaving so much power in his hands as to render the latter a virtual slave.

Thus, by the laws of the time, a vassal who seduced or debauch-

[1] Leges Saxonicæ.

ed his lord's wife or near relative, or who even took improper liberties with them, might be punished by the forfeiture of his land. When a baron died, the estate escheated to the king, who took immediate possession, and kept it until the heir applied to do homage for it, and pay such a fee as the king might demand. If the heir happened to be a minor, the king retained possession of the estate until he reached his majority; and when the inheritance devolved on a female, the king might give her any husband he thought proper. He often turned this privilege to account by selling the right to the hand and fortune of an heiress. Geoffrey de Mandeville paid Henry III. a sum equal to about twenty thousand dollars for permission to wed Isabel, countess of Gloucester, with the right to all her lands and revenues. Even a male heir could not select his own bride except by purchasing permission from the king, otherwise he had to accept his majesty's choice.

We have no means of estimating the amount of licentiousness arising from these arbitrary regulations, but we only require a little acquaintance with human nature to arrive at the conclusion that they must have been a prolific source of vice. The husband being selected by the king from purely mercenary or interested motives, no attention was, of course, paid to disparity of ages, or other circumstances on which the purity of the marriage-bed depends. When the inclinations are forced in this way, women, as well as men, are apt to revenge themselves on their partners by seeking illicit enjoyments. Mercenary marriages, when projected, as they are even in our day, from sordid motives on the part of parents or guardians, almost invariably lead to infidelity, and many an old dotard, who forces himself upon a girl under age, merely serves as a screen for her clandestine amours.

In the reign of Henry III., grave disputes occurred between the civil and ecclesiastical courts on the subject of bastardy. The common law deemed all children to be illegitimate who had been born before marriage. By the canon law they were held to be legitimate if the parents married subsequent to their birth.

When a dispute of inheritance arose, it was customary for the civil to issue writs to the spiritual courts, directing an inquiry to be instituted into the legitimacy of the claimants; and as the bishops always returned answers in accordance with the canon law, all persons whose parents had married at any period were legitimate. When it is considered how strongly most parents feel for the honor of their offspring, the tendency of such decisions to

T

increase prostitution becomes apparent.   It may be considered unjust to inflict disabilities on the child for the sins of the parent,
but such penalties undoubtedly have the effect of imposing a check
upon concubinage.

We have stated that the king claimed the disposal of the hands
and fortunes of heiresses: the barons claimed a still greater privilege from their tenants.   In some localities the feudal lord insisted
upon enjoying the person of one of the daughters of each tenant
who happened to be blessed with a plurality of them.   He returned her to her parents within a given time.

Every extreme is followed by a reaction in the opposite direction.   The abject condition of women, as indicated by the foregoing facts, led to the institution of chivalry, which elevated her
from the position of a slave, and the mere instrument of sensual
gratification, to that almost of a deity, thus assigning her a rank
as much above her real sphere as her former one had been beneath it.

Previous to the advent of this system, women could not appear
at any public exhibition or place of amusement unless accompanied by a band of armed retainers.   Any female encountered alone
and unprotected was liable to insult.

Chivalry, if it did not put an end to, greatly modified this state
of things.   By its rules each of its members was constituted a
champion of female virtue and honor.   No man was admitted into
the order whose valor was not above suspicion, and a word uttered by him derogatory to the *beau sexe* excluded him from its ranks.
No woman, however, was deemed worthy of knightly protection
who had not preserved her honor, it being to that quality alone
that knighthood volunteered its safeguard.   At public ceremonies,
if a woman of easy virtue ventured to take precedence of a woman
of honorable fame, she was immediately reminded of the impropriety of her conduct by some member of the order, and compelled
to retire to the rear.

This recognition of virtue had a strong tendency to promote
female chastity.   It could not put a stop to voluntary prostitution,
but it at least prevented virtuous women being necessitated to
yield their honor to force.   It held out, moreover, an attractive
premium to correct conduct among the sex by making it the object of heroic exploits, celebrated in the romantic lays of minstrels
and troubadours.   Its observances have a fantastic aspect in the
light of modern civilization, but they unquestionably exercised a

powerful corrective influence over the female character, so degraded at its commencement, while, at the same time, they elevated that of the male sex by teaching them to respect themselves.

In the wars of the period, it was against the rules of chivalry to take women prisoners. When a town was captured and entered by victorious troops, the first step taken was to make proclamation that no violence should be offered to any female. This conduct was so much at variance with the notions and habits of soldiery, that the feelings which sustained chivalry must have taken deep root in the minds of all classes to restrain the passions of the military, strengthened as they were by dissolute habits, and the absence of opportunity for their gratification during service in the field.

To such an extreme was this feeling of deferential courtesy to the sex carried, that the Normans were severely censured for their conduct at the capture of the castle of Du Guesclin, it being alleged that they disturbed the repose of the ladies. But as the tendency of every human institution is to degenerate from its original purpose, the rigid purism which marked the foundation of chivalry soon began to relax, and disorders crept in and sapped the basis of a system which was too theoretically perfect to have any extended duration.

It is difficult to ascertain the precise character of the relations which existed between the Troubadours and the mistresses to whose service they devoted themselves, and who were frequently married women. The knight Bertram happened to lose the favor of his mistress, the wife of Talleyrand de Perigord, in consequence of stories which had been related to her implicating his fidelity, and charging him with dividing his knightly attentions. He protests his innocence of these accusations in a lay as impassioned as that of a lover to the object of his adoration, and invokes a number of knightly calamities upon himself if his devotion to her be not above suspicion.

It is hardly credible that the loves of such ardent admirers was immaculate Platonism. On the other hand, the fact that husbands were rarely or never jealous of them, goes some way to refute the idea that they had a more serious character. The lords of those times were proud of the protestations of regard offered to their ladies, and rewarded the Troubadours with rich and valuable presents. The lords of our day, grown wise by experience, make a point of keeping all such interlopers at a distance.

While chivalry poised its lance in defense of the Lucretias, and

then of the Dulcineas of the day, the religious view of the commerce of the sexes was particularly ascetic.

Although the most profound devotion was paid to woman in
the abstract by the order, the Church sought to encourage perpetual celibacy, the seclusion of women, and the separation of the
sexes. The clergy were forbidden to marry, and the idea seemed
to prevail that it was impossible for men and women to mingle
without being under the influence of lascivious ideas, and ready
to carry them into practice as soon as opportunity offered. The
attempt to organize society on such a basis had an inevitable tendency to produce demoralization. Its obvious result, instead of
promoting chastity was to increase secret licentiousness and encourage prostitution.

Even the voluntary vows of knights and troubadours were, in
the end, as little observed as these ecclesiastical precepts. The
profligacy of the Troubadours became open and undisguised, and
the virtue of their mistresses naturally kept pace with their example. The knights who enlisted in the Crusades, with a large amount
of zeal and but a small share of wealth, supported their retainers
by robberies on the way, and the females who accompanied them
acted as camp followers usually do. No institution which deals
merely in external observances can restrain immorality in circumstances favorable to its development, and hence chivalry was
forced to yield before more powerful influences. That it served
its purpose in elevating the condition of woman, and in giving a
better tone to society at large, it would be unjust to deny.

Even when chivalry declined and ceased to inspire feats of
knight-errantry, we find women, instead of falling back into the
degrading position they had formerly occupied, employing themselves in intellectual pursuits, publishing books, mixing in public
controversies, distinguishing themselves in the acquisition of languages, and even taking a leading part in the political affairs of
the times.

Among the women who acquired a historical notoriety by their
position as royal mistresses, during the epoch comprised between
the Norman conquest and the reign of Henry VIII., were the Fair
Rosamond, concubine of Henry II., and Jane Shore, the mistress
of Edward IV. The misfortunes, as well as the generous qualities
of these fair sinners have thrown a sort of halo around them.

Rosamond, surnamed the Fair on account of her exquisite
beauty, was the daughter of Walter, Lord Clifford, and was edu-

cated in the nunnery of Godstow. The popular tradition concerning her is that Henry, hearing of her charms, paid her a visit, but, finding her virtue inflexible, had to exercise his authority as sovereign to compel her to yield to his wishes. He placed her in a building erected in the midst of a labyrinth at Woodstock, access to which could only be obtained by a clew of thread. Henry located her here to protect her from the jealousy of his queen Eleanor. She bore the king two sons, William Longsword, Earl of Salisbury, and Geoffrey, Bishop of Lincoln. During the king's absence in France he intrusted the keeping of Woodstock and the care of the Fair Rosamond to one Lord Thomas, who endeavored to seduce her. In revenge for the rejection of his overtures, the faithless warden conducted Queen Eleanor to her retreat, and the latter is said to have mixed a cup of poison, which her minions compelled the unfortunate Rosamond to drink. It is also alleged that the queen struck the poor girl on her lip with her clenched hand.[1] Some assert that Rosamond died a natural death in a convent at Oxford, and attribute the origin of the story of poisoning to the figure of a cup which was sculptured on her tomb. It is more probable that this effigy was placed there to commemorate the actual event. Rosamond was buried in the church of Godstow, opposite the high altar, where her remains lay undisturbed until they were ordered to be removed, with every mark of indignity, by Hugh, Bishop of Lincoln, in the year 1191. She was regarded by the people as a saint, if not a martyr, and wonderful legends were related concerning her.

Jane Shore, the celebrated concubine of Edward IV., was the wife of Matthew Shore, a goldsmith in Lombard Street, London. Edward possessed a good figure and pleasing address, and was fond of athletic sports and exercises, which he enjoyed in company with the citizens, among whom he became exceedingly popular. His popularity extended to many of the citizens' wives, and it was not considered out of the natural course of things that Mrs. Shore should be removed from Lombard Street to shine at court as the royal favorite. Historians represent her as extremely beautiful, remarkably gay in temperament, and of uncommon generosity. The king, it is said, was no less charmed with her temper and disposi-

[1] A popular ballad which narrates the particulars describes the blow as having dyed Fair Rosamond's lips

"A coral red;
Hard was the heart that gave the blow,
Soft were the lips that bled."

tion than with her person.   She never made use of her influence
over him to the prejudice of any one, and if she ever importuned
him it was in favor of the unfortunate.

After the death of Edward she attached herself to Lord Hast-
ings, and when Richard III. cut off that nobleman as an obstacle
to his schemes, she was arrested as an accomplice on the ridiculous
charge of witchcraft.   This accusation, however, terminated in a
public penance, with the loss of whatever little property she possessed.   Notwithstanding the severities exercised against her, it is
certain that she was alive in the reign of Henry VIII., when Sir
Thomas More mentions having seen her, poor and shriveled,
without the least trace of her former beauty.   Mr. Rowe, in his
tragedy of " Jane Shore," has adopted the popular story related in
the old ballad, of her perishing from hunger in a ditch where
Shoreditch now stands, but Stow assures us that that street was
thus named previous to the time of Jane Shore.

The example of none of the English kings had a greater influence
in bringing the marriage tie into disrepute than that of Henry
VIII.   An effort has been made by Mr. Fronde, in his new history of England, to redeem the character of this monarch from
some portion of the obloquy with which it is covered, but there is
no doubt that he was an unmitigated monster.   Curious to say,
during his youth and early manhood he betrayed no evidence of
the brutal passions which afterward moved him.   He was the husband of Catharine for seventeen years before his domestic conduct
incurred reproach.   At that late period of his career he conceived
a violent passion for Anne Boleyn, and, in order to get her to share
his bed, sought to divorce his wife.   From this period he seemed
to become the prey of a restless concupiscence, which sought gratification in new objects of indulgence, and his passion for the wom-
en he married and beheaded was as short-lived as it was violent.

There is reason to believe that his marriage with Anne Boleyn
was more than adulterous.   It is said Anne's mother had been
more complaisant to Henry than her duty to her husband or the
laws of morality would have sanctioned, and we have the authority
of Bishop Fisher for concluding that Anne was the result of this
illicit connection, and that, when the king expressed an intention
of marrying her, Lady Boleyn exhorted him to abandon his design, as Anne was his own daughter.   Henry was not to be deterred
by an obstacle of this sort.   He had great difficulty in procuring a
divorce, and in the mean while he and Anne had become so inti-

mate that she began to exhibit proofs of the connection which could not be concealed. A private marriage was resorted to, considerations of state rendering it prudent to keep the union secret.

Catharine was divorced through the intrumentality of Cranmer, but Henry did not long continue to repose confidence in his new bride. Soon after the marriage was made public, and she had been formally inaugurated as queen, she attended a tilting-match at Greenwich, accompanied by the king and a large concourse of spectators. The king observed her exchange amorous signals with one of the combatants, who was also one of her paramours. Henry had entertained suspicions of her connection with this man, and this proof, as he regarded it, of her infidelity aroused his jealousy. He left the scene on the instant and returned to Westminster, where he issued orders to have her immediately arrested. She was thrown into prison, and tried on the joint charges of adultery and incest. She was accused of having committed adultery with four separate members of the king's household, and of having had incestuous intercourse with her own brother, Lord Rochford. She was tried, found guilty, and executed.

Whether she committed the entire criminality laid to her charge it is impossible to say, but that the incidents of the career just described were in perfect unison with the doings of Henry and his court there is no doubt. Of the influence of such examples on the morals of the people at large, there is, unfortunately, as little question. If court manners and court styles are zealously followed, the vices that spring from them are not less assiduously improved upon.

Henry's strong sexual passions, as well as his arbitrary disposition, were bequeathed to his daughter Elizabeth. However historians may differ as to the degree of her depravity, they all agree that her right to the title of "Virgin Queen" was exceedingly ill founded. Many of her delinquencies with persons of the opposite sex were notorious, although perhaps difficult of proof. While she had not the slightest claim to beauty, she delighted in flattery, and could swallow any amount of gross and fulsome adulation. Her vanity so blinded her that she never perceived that the extravagant praises lavished on her personal attractions were merely covert satire.

It is said that Elizabeth indulged in almost indiscriminate lewdness, and that Leicester, Hatton, Essex, Mountjoy, and numerous others shared her favors. In one of the notes appended to Hume's fourth volume, the nature of Elizabeth's dealings with a large number of her favorites is set forth, the author of the statement being the Countess of Shrewsbury.

Mary, Queen of Scots, at a time when friendly relations existed between her and Elizabeth, wrote to the latter that the countess had reported that Elizabeth had given a promise of marriage to a certain courtier, but, finding the marriage inexpedient, had dispensed with the ceremony and admitted him to her bed. The countess also stated that she had been equally indulgent to Simier, the French agent, and that Hatton, another of her paramours, had spread many reports indicative of her extreme sexual passion.

The immediate successors of Elizabeth were of a different personal temperament, and did not abandon themselves to such scandalous excesses. James I. had no mistresses, and was not of a character to seek pleasure in extravagant licentiousness, but his court was not free from the scenes which had disgraced those of Henry and Elizabeth. James, being desirous of uniting the Earl of Essex with the Lady Frances Howard, daughter of the Earl of Suffolk, had the young couple betrothed, although they had not attained the age of puberty. The earl was only fourteen years of age, while Lady Frances was but thirteen, and it was deemed proper for the youth to travel until both should have arrived at the maturity necessary for the consummation of the marriage relation. After four years spent on the Continent, the earl returned to England, and found his affianced bride in the full lustre of extraordinary beauty, and of the fame which great personal charms excite. He had also the mortification to find himself repulsed when he approached her as a husband, and was met by every manifestation of dislike and contempt. He complained to her parents on the subject, and they compelled her to accompany him to the country.

Although the young countess obeyed this mandate literally, the feud between her and Essex was far from terminated: she recognized him as her husband in name only, and sedulously kept herself aloof from his society, nor could any of his endeavors overcome her repugnance. The lady persisted in her obstinacy; the husband redoubled his attentions and importunities, but, finding that she was invincible, he finally abandoned the pursuit, and separated from her.

The cause of this strange conduct on the part of the countess was the passion which she entertained for a Scotch adventurer named Robert Carr, who had found a favorable reception from the king, by whom he was created Viscount Rochester. She believed that by refusing to consummate her marriage with Essex she would not be considered by the world in the light of his wife, and she hoped to procure a divorce, which would enable her to marry Rochester.[1] As their mutual attachment was ardent, and their opportunities for being together frequent, they anticipated the probability of a marriage, and indulged their passions without waiting for the ceremony. They did not find as much trouble in procuring a divorce as they had anticipated.

The king, who had a strong partiality for Rochester, favored their views, and Essex, finding that his suit was hopeless with his wife, opposed no obstacle to the nullification of his marriage. The grounds on which the countess sued out the divorce were of rather a curious character. The chief allegation against Essex was impotency. At that time a firm faith existed in the absurd notions that there were people who possessed the power of witchcraft, enabling them, among other things, to deprive a man of his virility. It was asserted and maintained that Essex had been subjected to this influence, and was therefore incompetent to occupy the position of a married man. The divorce was secured, and Rochester and the countess experienced no farther obstacle to the gratification of their desires.

Rochester had previously consulted Overbury on the difficulties of his position, and the latter strongly advised him not to marry the countess. These facts coming to the ears of Lady Frances, she induced Rochester to have Overbury poisoned. On the discovery of the murder, Rochester and his wife were brought to trial and convicted, but the mistaken clemency of the king interposed between them and the doom they so richly merited. They passed the remainder of their days in obscurity, but as bitter enemies, and although they resided in the same house for many years, no word or message was ever exchanged between them.

[1] State Trials, i. 228.

CHAPTER XXIV.

GREAT BRITAIN.—HISTORY FROM THE COMMONWEALTH TO THE PRESENT DAY.

Puritans.—Results of Asceticism.—Excesses of the Restoration.—General Licentiousness.—Art.—Literature.—The Stage.—Nell Gwynne.—Nationality in Vice. —Sabbath at Court.—James II.—Literature of the seventeenth and eighteenth Centuries.—Lord Chesterfield.—House of Hanover.—Royal Princes.—George III.—George IV.—Influence of French Literature.—Marriage Laws.—Increase of Population.

On gaining the ascendant, the Puritans endeavored to reform the general corruption of society by cutting to the root of the disorders that afflicted it. Instead, however, of applying the knife judiciously, they excised the sound as well as the unhealthy parts. Their measures went to the extreme of killing all the affections and impulses natural to the human breast, in order to repress the excesses arising from too free an abandonment to them. Some fanatics, for instance, gravely suggested that, in order to put an end to fornication and adultery, all intercourse should be prohibited between the sexes.

In our days it is found that innocent amusements are the best safeguard against criminal indulgence, but the Puritans thought otherwise, and looked upon joyous exhilaration of any kind as almost sinful. They enforced their gloomy doctrines with a tyranny as unbending as their tenets themselves were harsh and unnatural. Theatrical entertainments, dancing, etc., were sternly placed under ban, and Puritanism presented merely a heavy and murky atmosphere, with scarcely a social star to enliven its gloomy aspect.

When the Restoration removed the oppressive weight of fanaticism from the public spirit, it rebounded as far above a healthy pitch as it had been formerly depressed below it. An immediate revolution took place in the manners and habits of the people. The theatres, which had been closed by the Puritans, were at once reopened, and the populace abandoned themselves to pleasurable excesses with an eagerness proportionate to the restraint which had been imposed on them. This license would, in time, have been checked by reflection, had not the impulse been supplied from the quarter where a repressive influence should have been exercised. The Merry Monarch and his court led the race in this national carnival, and the examples which they set only served to stimulate the public appetite for debauchery. Indeed, the court of Charles was little better than a public brothel, and the wit with which its orgies were embellished only served to increase the dangers arising from its conspicuous position, and its power over men's minds as the centre from which all rank and consideration flowed. The conduct of the courtiers was strictly modeled on that of their royal master, and their social accomplishments only imperfectly varnished over the gross features of a coarse sensuality. Women were flattered and caressed, but not respected, and the homage paid them was such as no decent woman in our time would consent to receive.

The most faithful portraiture of the manners of this epoch is to be found in its dramatic literature. The staple incidents of the pieces represented at the theatres consisted of love intrigues, seductions, and rapes. The fop of the play never elicited such hearty applause as when he recounted his exploits in the ruin of female virtue among the citizens' wives.

The theatre not only fostered lewdness by depicting it in glowing and attractive colors, but its actors spread abroad the corruption which it was their business to delineate. Their personal character corresponded, in too many instances, with the parts which they performed, and they re-enacted in private the debaucheries which they presented on the stage.

The theatre itself became a central rendezvous for immoral characters, and the place where assignations were most conveniently fixed. Lively wenches, under the pretense of selling oranges to the spectators, frequented the pit, and took their places in the front row, with their backs to the stage. It was well understood that they were as ready to sell favors as fruit, and, in fact, that they had come from the neighboring brothels for that express purpose.

Deep drinking was another characteristic feature of the times, and bacchanalian orgies were freely indulged in by all classes, from the king to the beggar, differing little in the extremes to which they were pushed. Conversation, even in what was called the best society, was disfigured by the grossest obscenity and blasphemy, and *bon ton* consisted in the extravagance to which this vicious conduct was extended.

Even the peasantry endeavored to imitate the costumes and carriage of the courtiers, and country women were to be seen in flaunting dresses cut so as to expose as much as possible of the person.

Up to this period no female had ever appeared upon the English stage; where women were introduced, their parts had been filled by boys. Neither was it customary for a monarch to show himself at a public representation of a play; but, when they were enacted for his amusement, the performance took place in some apartment of the royal palace. In Charles's reign, women for the first time appeared on the stage, and performed the parts allotted to the heroines of the drama.

The king and queen became regular frequenters of the theatre, and encouraged by their presence the *double entendre* and broad indecencies of the pieces in vogue. We may remark, parenthetically, that unmarried actresses usually adopted the title Mistress before their names, the word Miss, as then applied, signifying that she who bore it was a concubine. In modern days it is the habit to reverse this practice, as the marriage state is considered to divest the actress of half her attractions.

There were but two theatres in London at this period: the King's Theatre, where the celebrated Nell Gwynne and Mrs. Rebecca Marshall were the chief actresses, and the Duke's, where another company performed. One day the reigning favorites at the King's Theatre had a violent quarrel, and Mrs. Marshall called Nell "Lord Buckhurst's mistress." Nell contented herself with rejoining that she was but one man's mistress, though brought up in a brothel, while Mrs. Marshall bore the same relation to three or four, notwithstanding she was the daughter of a Presbyterian. Their own accounts of each other leave no doubt as to their morality.

The pieces represented in the London theatres in the time of Charles II. were, as we have before stated, filled with indecent allusions, and their interest with the public turned on the number and intensity of these prurient passages. The ladies never attended the first representation of a comedy except in masks; and when the dames of the court, with their established reputations for gallantry, were apprehensive of being seen at them, some idea may be formed of the licentious character of the pieces most in favor.

But many of these plays are still in evidence to speak for themselves. It will be seen that in the majority the plot is so framed as to admit the greatest license in libidinous allusions. The distinguishing feature of them is that the most immodest passages are put into the mouths of women, and, indeed, we know that that actress was the most successful who took the greatest liberties with the text, and most improved upon its lewdness of expression.

As a specimen of the general character of these plays, we may name "All Mistaken, or the Mad Couple," quite a favorite with the public in its day. The hero is importuned by six clamorous unfortunates whose ruin he has effected, and dunned in addition by the nurses of their illegitimate offspring for wages owing to them. The delectable superstructure of obscene dialogue which is raised on this foundation may be better imagined than described.

The usual hour at which the theatres opened their doors was four in the afternoon, and after the close of the performances the audience generally repaired to some garden or other place of public amusement. Here scenes were enacted which proved a fit sequel to those witnessed on the stage.

The orange-girls had a superior known as "Orange Moll," who occupied a position somewhat analogous to that of the modern brothel-keeper. She attended the girls to the theatre, and superintended and directed their operations there. During the *entre-actes* lewd conversations were carried on between the orange-girls and the gallants, which were interspersed with obscene jokes, and highly relished by the audience. The custom of interpellating the gay women who frequented the theatre was continued to a period comparatively recent. Every one has heard the story of Peg Plunket and the Duke of Rutland, in the days when the gods of the Dublin theatre were esteemed the most discriminating, though boisterous and rollicking audience of the three kingdoms.

Charles selected several of his mistresses from the stage, for which he had a passionate fondness. Miss Davis literally sang and danced her way into his affections. Her conquest of the king was consummated by the manner in which she sang the popular ballad "My lodging is on the cold ground." Charles thought she was deserving of warmer quarters, and raised her to his own bed. He established her in a splendid residence, and lavished on her the most extravagant gifts.

The queen at first resented the open and undisguised infidelities of the king, and publicly manifested her sense of them on one occasion by quitting the theatre when Miss Davis made her appearance on the stage; but, finding it impossible to reclaim him from his vicious propensities, she abandoned all hopes of restricting his libertinism, or even of keeping him within the bounds of conventional decency.

The Countess of Castlemaine (afterward created Duchess of Cleveland) was of a more jealous temperament than the queen, and took a more characteristic revenge on Charles for his frailties. She took another lover, and went to reside at his house, very much to the comfort of her royal patron, who had a kingly dislike of trouble.

After quarreling with Lord Buckhurst, Nell Gwynne returned to the stage, but had not long resumed her profession when it was rumored that she had made a conquest of the king. These reports were apparently contradicted by her continued appearance at the theatre, and the progress she made in her art, which could only be the result of careful study. A tragedy by Dryden was advertised, the principal character to be performed by Nell; but, before the night of its first representation arrived, it was found necessary to postpone the performance, owing to Nell's not being in a condition to appear. From this time her connection with Charles no longer remained a secret.

Nell, like her predecessors, was not long suffered to maintain uncontested her supremacy over the king's affections. When the Duchesse d'Orleans, the sister of Charles, paid a visit to the English court in 1670, she had in her train a handsome maid, who was admired for her simple and childish style of beauty. Whether instigated by the courtiers who accompanied her mistress, whose visit was a political one, or prompted by her own sagacity, she made her acquiescence in the king's desires conditional upon his executing the shameful treaty which gave France such important advantages, and rendered Charles a mere tributary to the French king. This girl, Louise de Querouaille, became the rival of Nell Gwynne, and had a child by Charles, who was created Duke of Richmond.

So scandalously public had the relations of Charles with the loose women who surrounded him become, and so flagrant and unblushing was the conduct of the latter, that the queen could no longer reside in the palace of Whitehall, and accordingly removed to Somerset House in the Strand. This feeling of indignation on the part of her majesty soon extended to the virtuously disposed part of the public. Efforts were made to apply a remedy to the disorder which threatened to corrupt the whole framework of English society. In Parliament it was proposed to levy a tax on the play-houses, which had become undisguised nests of prostitution. The debate which ensued elicited a witticism which led to serious consequences to the gentleman who uttered it. On Sir John Birkenhead's remarking that "the players were the king's servants and part of his pleasures," Sir John Coventry was imprudent enough to inquire "whether the king's pleasures lay among the men that acted or the women." For this offense to Charles he was waylaid by some of the courtiers, who slit his nose, and otherwise maltreated him.

It is impossible, however, to deny that this very license of manners rendered the king popular with a certain class of his subjects. The only exception taken by them to his conduct was the selection of a foreigner as one of his mistresses, and even this would have passed without comment but for the political consequences of the connection. It was generally understood among the people that Mademoiselle de Querouaille, or Mrs. Carwell, as she was commonly called, was an agent used for the purpose of securing the ascendency of French interests. This brought upon her the hostility of the populace, who availed themselves of every opportunity of manifesting their dislike to her.

Nell Gwynne was an English woman, a Protestant, and the idol of the town. She was known by the title of the Protestant mistress, while Mrs. Carwell went by that of the king's Popish concubine. Nell was one day insulted in her carriage at Oxford, and came very near being mobbed by the populace in mistake for Mrs. Carwell. With her usual wit and presence of mind, she put her head out of the window, and quieted the rioters by telling them that she was "the Protestant w——e."

As the literature of the times reflected the general licentiousness of manners, it was not to be expected that the arts would escape their demoralizing influence. Most of the paintings then executed were characterized by the same freedom of expression which was used on the stage. There is an old print extant of the Duchess of Portsmouth, reclining on a bank of violets, wearing no other covering than a lace robe; and in another Nell Gwynne is represented in the same semi-nude condition. It is said that this dress had belonged to the duchess, and had been much admired by the king, but that, with her usual love of mischief, Nell had purloined it, greatly to the amusement of her royal lover, and very much to the chagrin and mortification of the duchess.

The king had his own peculiar way of celebrating the Sabbath. On that day he usually collected his mistresses around him, and amused himself by toying with them and humoring their caprices. We have a picture by a contemporaneous writer of one of his Sunday evenings at Whitehall, where the court resided. It was shortly before his death. Charles sat in the centre of a group of these women, indulging in the most frivolous amusements, and apparently in high humor. At a little distance stood a page singing love-songs for the delectation of the king's mistresses, while round a gambling-table were seated a number of his courtiers, playing for stakes which sometimes ran as high as ten thousand dollars of our money.[1] The orgies of the night were kept up until daylight broke in upon the revelers. At eight o'clock the same morning the king was seized with a fit of apoplexy, and died within a week.

James II., though of a grave and stern character, was scarcely less amorous in his temperament than Charles. They differed, however, in their tastes. Charles required beauty in his mistresses; and Nell Gwynne and some of his other concubines were not only beautiful in person but possessed of intellectual graces which gilded their gross sensuality. James cared but little for personal attractions, and lavished his favors on coarse-featured and coarse-minded women. His wife was below him in rank, and he did not stoop to her for her beauty, for she was plain, if not downright ugly in her features. He soon transferred his affections to a still plainer mistress, Arabella Churchill. His strongest attachment was, however, that which he entertained for Catharine Sedley, who possessed a powerful influence over him. She was the daughter of Sir Charles Sedley, and seems to have inherited from him the strong passions and reckless disregard of public opinion by which he was distinguished. Sedley's writings were more licentious than those of any of his contemporaries. His literary talents were not of a high order, but he possessed fair conversational abilities, which made his society attractive. The extreme dissoluteness of his life and disregard of all decency provoked censure even in that age of loose morals. On one occasion, after a drunken revel with some of his profligate companions, he presented himself on the balcony of a tavern near Covent Garden in a state of complete nudity, and commenced a harangue so full of lewdness and obscenity that the crowd pelted him with stones and other missiles, and compelled him to withdraw into the house. A daughter inheriting these

---

[1] Evelyn. 4th February, 1684–5.

propensities, and brought up under the influence of this example, could not fail to become conspicuous for similar traits of character. Her person possessed none of the attributes which render women attractive. A lank, spare figure, a hollow cheek, sallow face, and an eye of glaring brightness comprised the sum total of her charms.

Charles, whose taste was more cultivated, remarked that his confessor must have recommended Catharine to his brother as a penance for his sins. She herself had the discrimination not to be insensible to the truth of this remark, and was even in the habit of boasting of her own plain looks. Her taste for finery was as great as if she possessed attractions worth setting off by its aid. James, when he formed this connection, had advanced to middle age, and it is difficult to account for the influence which she contrived to exercise over him. On his accession to the throne he promised the queen to abandon her, but his good resolutions soon gave way. Whenever the absence of his wife afforded the opportunity, Chiffinch might be seen conducting Catharine through the private passage leading to his chamber. Notwithstanding all the affected austerity of his manners, James was, in reality, but little better than his volatile brother.

At no period in the history of England, as we have just shown, had the licentiousness of the court been greater than it was during the reigns of Charles II. and James II.; only to be exceeded, perhaps, by the fearful abyss of debauchery and atheism which a few years later was beheld in the courts of Louis XV. and the Regent of France. The vigor and intellect of the early part of the reign of Louis XIV., the magnificence of his tastes, and the glory of his enterprises, stand out in powerful contrast to the doings of the imbecile, corrupt, and utterly profligate and debased court of England. The influence of this most pernicious example it is somewhat difficult to arrive at. The great body of the people, especially in the country, in those times of difficult communication, were probably but little affected by the extravagance of the restored Cavaliers, added to which there was a powerful leaven of religious feeling working through the country, which did not for some time settle down into the apathy that called for a new manifestation of Puritan feeling in the establishment of Wesleyan Methodism. In the upper classes of society, however, the core-rottenness of the courts of Charles and James was yet felt, throughout the reigns of the succeeding sovereigns, even down to the time of George III. The writings of contemporary authors, especially of the comic dra-

U

matists, "the abstract and brief chronicles of the times," are a fair type of the public morals and intelligence in all ages. At this epoch we have from these sources overwhelming evidence of the reaction which had taken place.

After the removal of the compulsory restraint of Puritan control, the nation seemed at once to have lost its reason: modesty and decency were badges of Puritan Republicanism, and therefore unsuited to loyal men, who showed their attachment to the monarchy by their abandonment of decorum and violation of every moral virtue. The productions of the favorite authors teem with coarse images, unequivocal allusions, and gross facts. Wit degenerated into blasphemy, liveliness into obscenity, metaphors into lasciviousness. The scenes that took place in the court, and which constituted its daily amusements, were disgusting to the last degree. The mere commerce of the sexes, and the libertinism of the period in that respect, were the smallest vices, and might almost be considered merely follies, but the venality and corruption were open and shameless. The courtiers cast aside the last rag of patriotic propriety, and avarice, cruelty, lust, and perjury filled the measure of wickedness. On one occasion, it is said, an infant was prematurely born in one of the rooms of the palace, and Charles, with many jocular remarks, had the body conveyed to his own closet for dissection by his own hand! An incident of such brutality, which might be frequently paralleled by others equally bad in degree, though different in fact, shows the hideous destitution of all decency with which the court must have been cursed. The pages of Rochester, Etherege, Buckingham, Congreve, Vanburgh, and Fletcher, in the close of the seventeenth, and Prior, Gay, Swift, and scores of inferior writers in the commencement of the eighteenth century, all exhibit this state of affairs, while the noble Muse even of a Dryden could stoop to earn base applause by lending her powers to the decoration of vice, and voluntarily quitting her native regions to wallow in the mire.

The vices of this period must have left an ineradicable taint behind them, when, after the full tide of iniquity had swept on, and purer waters were succeeding, we find Lord Chesterfield, a British statesman of distinguished ability and high position, thus advising his own son: "Let the great book of the world be your principal study. *Nocturna versate manu versate diurna*, which may be rendered thus: Turn over men by day and women by night: I mean only the best editions."

While, as we have already observed, there was probably a wholesome religious element in a portion of the population, which operated as an antiseptic against the rottenness of the court, it is impossible but that the capital must have been imbued with the reckless iniquity, outrageous dissoluteness, and general immorality of the higher classes. The poets, playwrights, essayists, and biographers of the age all bear traces of the effects of bad example in high places on public manners. A critic of those days says, "The accomplished gentleman of the English stage is a person that is familiar with other men's wives and indifferent to his own, and the fine lady is generally a composition of sprightliness and falsehood." A thorough disrespect for female virtue, or rather the admiration of libertinism, tainted the life's blood of the capital. And when, passing over the coarse wit of Prior, or the perverted genius of Dryden, we come to the sober and moderate writings of essayists and satirists, we find material which gives us some little insight into the lower London life of the period, and that which has more immediate interest for us in this inquiry.

In the delightful and ever youthful pages of the Spectator, there are some incidents of great pathos touching the state of those unfortunates whose condition was then, as now, one of the disgraces of civilization. One paper contains a singularly apposite remark. "I was told," says the writer (a woman of the town), "by a Roman Catholic gentleman last week, who I hope is absolved for what then passed between us, that in countries where Popery prevails, besides the advantages of licensed stews, there are larger endowments given for the *Incurabili,* I think he called them. This manner of treating poor sinners has, we think, great humanity in it; and as you, Mr. Spectator, are a person who pretends to carry your reflections upon all subjects which occur to you, I beg therefore of you to lay before the world the condition of us poor vagrants, who are really in a way of labor instead of idleness."

At another time the Spectator himself meets "a slim young girl of about seventeen, who, with a pert air, asked me if I was for a pint of wine. I could observe as exact features as ever I had seen; the whole person, in a word, of a woman exquisitely beautiful. She affected to allure me with a forced wantonness in her look and air, but I saw it checked with hunger and cold. Her eyes were wan and eager; her dress thin and tawdry; her mien genteel and childish. This strange figure gave me much anguish of heart, and, to avoid being seen with her, I went away, but could not avoid giving her a crown.   The poor thing sighed, courtesied, and with a blessing, expressed with the utmost vehemence, turned from me.   This creature is what they call *newly come upon the town.*"

The arts of the procuresses; their experiments on inexperienced country girls; their attendance at coach-offices and public places to hunt for and entrap the unwary; the regular customers they have for new wares; the mode, first of offering them to private sale, and, when the first gloss is worn off, casting them on the public market, are all as true of 1858 as of the day for which it was written.   In one case, the Spectator, being at a coach-office, overhears a lady inquiring of a young girl her parentage and character, and especially if she has been properly brought up, and has been taught her Catechism.   Desirous of seeing a lady who had so proper an idea of her duties to servants, he peeps through and sees the face of a well-known bawd, thus decoying a young girl just arrived in London.   One amusing cheat in the business of these go-betweens is complained of by a lady correspondent: for a consideration, they profess to introduce some ambitious foreigner or country gentleman to the favors of ladies of high degree, ruling toasts, leading belles, etc.   Some lady, Wilhelmina Amelia Skeggs, is foisted upon the deluded customer, who must, of course, be ignorant of the person of his inamorata, and he walks off boasting, in great self-gratulation, of his good fortune, to the great injury of an irreproachable woman's fame.[1]

It was reserved for the reign of George III. to give a favorable turn to court morals and to make virtue respectable.   The Georges I. and II. had exercised but a negative influence on their subjects.   They were merely viewed as political necessities, and held in little or no personal esteem.   Their uncouth manners, foreign mistresses, and decidedly heavy *liaisons* had no charm for either eye or fancy.   With George III. and his queen, virtue in courts became in some degree fashionable; the slough of libertinism in which Louis XV. and the Regent Orleans had plunged themselves seemed in France to have created some reaction.   Louis XVI. in Paris, and George III. in London, presented the rare spectacle to their respective subjects of two well-conducted men, whose domestic life and character were unimpeachable.   But as the sons of

---

[1] For the prose writers of those days who give lively pictures of manners and morals, the reader is referred to the pages of Fielding, Smollett, and especially De Foe. who wrote much upon low life.

George III., especially the Prince of Wales and the Duke of York, attained their majority, they were surrounded by bands of flatterers and parasites, who stimulated and encouraged the natural proneness of youth to pleasure and dissipation. The libertinism and excesses of the Stuarts again became *bon-ton*, devoid, it is true, of political debasement and national dishonor; checked also by parental disapprobation, and by the influence of public opinion. This, though very weak, was not quite powerless; and, though lenient to the errors of youth, it drew an unfavorable comparison between the reckless extravagance and dissolute tastes of the princes, and the moderate and personally estimable conduct of the king and queen.[1]

The masses of the English people were distinguished for plain good sense, and attachment to the cause of religion and morality; and although drinking, gambling, boxing, and racing were, in honor of the royal princes, fashionable amusements, and their attainment coveted and emulated by many of the rising generation, still the general sentiment of the nation at this period was condemnatory of these vices. Those inclined to charitable views of human nature found excuses in the temptations of youth, a fine person, a commanding position, and, lastly, in the infamous counsels of those who found political capital in the encouragement of these excesses, thereby promoting a division between the heir to the throne and his sovereign parent. Others there were who beheld in George IV., whether as prince or monarch, a modern Tiberius, a man of ungovernable lusts; a ruthless libertine and a debased sensualist, without any redeeming qualities. As a fact, apart from causes and political prejudices, George IV. was undoubtedly a debauchee and a man of dissolute habits;[2] but he

---

[1] "Pure, and above all reproach in her own domestic life, the queen knew how to enforce at her court the virtues, or, at the very least, the semblance of the virtues which she practiced. To no other woman, probably, had the cause of good morals in England ever owed so deep an obligation."—Lord Mahon's History of England, 1713–1782, vol. iv., p. 221, 222.

[2] It was asserted some years ago, and by many believed, that after his death a large number of prurient French prints, which were in the Custom-house of London, and designed for the private amusement of the king, were burned. The story of the prints and their deflagration may be true, but it is very questionable if they were for royal use. A number of low class London papers always attacked George IV. personally, among which the Weekly Dispatch (the "Sunday Flash" of Warren's novel of "Ten Thousand a Year") took a prominent position from the coarseness of its language and the acerbity of its animosity, assumed at a time when party feeling ran high, as an attractive bait to its readers.

was a man of liberal education, of cultivated taste, of distinguished appearance, and elegant manners. He and the Count D'Artois, brother of Louis XVI., were considered the most finished gentlemen in Europe, so far as mannerism went. These externals glossed over, and even lent a charm to, the vices of his youth; and the mysterious orgies of Carlton House were associated in the public mind with the brilliant wit of Sheridan, the manly grace of Wyndham (that *beau ideal* of an English gentleman), the vast talent of Fox, and the enchanting grace of Georgiana, Duchess of Devonshire, the bright particular star amid a galaxy of minor luminaries. The respectability belonged to the court party; the genius and fascination were ranged on the side of the Prince of Wales.

It is difficult, even at this brief lapse of time, and when so many eye-witnesses are yet surviving, to speak with any degree of confidence of the state of general public morals in England as affected by the French Revolution, and the violent Tory and Whig contests of the period. The literature which preceded and accompanied the French Revolution went the whole length of undermining and unsettling every established institution, both of politics and religion, without building up an effective substitute in place of the structure destroyed. The doctrines of moral obligation and the balance of general convenience, which, according to the Volney, Voltaire, and Rousseau school, were to supersede the effete and worn-out dogmas of the Gospel, were little known and less liked in England. At the outset of the French movements, the cause had the sympathy of the English Liberals; but afterward, when the social and political excesses of the time disgusted even its moderate British supporters, and when the deep-rooted and apparently innate antagonism of the two nations was revived by the war, the hatred and contempt of the English people for French manners, French literature, French men, French every thing, knew no bounds. Thus, while the leaven of Parisian philosophy was fermenting in the breasts of all Continental Europe, it is our opinion that its influence in England was purely of a reactionary character; and as under the last Stuarts patriotism and libertinism went hand in hand, so, in the end of the eighteenth and the commencement of the nineteenth centuries, an Englishman's love of his own country and his hatred of France were associated with a detestation of the heresies of French philosophers and patriarchs.

Of the effect produced on the morals of the people by the loose manner in which, previous to 1753, the marriage ceremony was performed, we have the evidence brought forward in the debates on Lord Hardwicke's Marriage Bill. Anterior to that time, a boy of fourteen and a girl of twelve years of age might marry against the will of their parents or guardians, without any possibility of dissolving such marriage. The law, indeed, required the publication of banns, but custom and the dispensing power had rendered them nugatory. A dispensation could be purchased for a couple of crowns, and the marriage could take place in a closet or a tavern, before two friends who acted as witnesses. But dispensations were not always necessary. There were privileged places, such as May Fair and the Fleet, where the marriage ceremony could be performed at a moment's notice, and without any inconvenient questions being asked.

Gretna Green, on the borders of Scotland, was long a famous place for runaway matches. It has been questioned how far the Scotch law of marriage was conducive to morality; but, judging from its effects upon the people themselves, it can scarcely be considered an ally of vice. This law, which has only been repealed within a few years, treated marriage as a civil contract, valid if contracted before witnesses, and required no ceremony or preparatory notice. That unions so formed were binding, admits of no possible dispute: the question has been tried in the British courts of law on every conceivable ground, and their legality has been always affirmed, but in the case of marriages at May Fair or the Fleet the same certainty did not exist. Gretna Green is the first village after passing the dividing line between England and Scotland, and owes its fame to its locality. It has doubtless been the scene of many heartless adventures, for which the actual law of the land must be held accountable.

The marriage act which came into operation in 1754, had for its object the prevention of clandestine marriages in England, but did not interfere with the law of Scotland. It sought to effect this reform by making it necessary to the validity of a marriage without license, that it should take place after the proclamation of banns on three Sundays in the parish church, before a person in orders, between single persons consenting, of sound mind, and of the age of twenty-one years, or of the age of fourteen in males and twelve in females, with the consent of parents and guardians, or without their consent in cases of widowhood. The new mar-

riage act of 1837 allows marriage, after notice to the superintendent registrars in every district, either in the public register offices
in the presence of the superintendent registrar and the registrar
of marriages, or in duly registered places of worship.

We have no statement as to the number of marriages previous
to the year 1753. All we know is, that from 1651 to 1751 the
population only increased sixteen per cent., the increase being
only one million and fourteen thousand in one hundred years.
Since the act of 1753 came into operation, the registers of marriages have been preserved in England, and show an increase of
marriages from 50,972 in the year 1756, to 63,310 in 1764. "The
rage of marrying is very prevalent," writes Lord Chesterfield in
the latter year; and again in 1767, "In short, the matrimonial
phrensy seems to rage at present, and is epidemical." After many
fluctuations, the marriages rose to seventy, eighty, ninety, and one
hundred thousand annually, and in 1851 to one hundred and fifty-
four thousand two hundred and six. Fourteen millions were added to the population, an increase of 187 per cent., or at the rate
of one per cent. annually.[1]

CHAPTER XXV.

GREAT BRITAIN.—PROSTITUTION AT THE PRESENT TIME.

Influence of the Wealthy Classes.—Devices of Procuresses.—Scene at a Railway
Station.—Organization for entrapping Women.—Seduction of Children.—Continental Traffic.—Brothel-keepers.—"Fancy Men" and "Spooneys."—Number
of Brothels in London.—Causes of Prostitution.—Sexual Desire.—Seduction.—
Over-crowded Dwellings.—Parental Example.—Poverty and Destitution.—Public Amusements.—Ill-assorted Marriages.—Love of Dress.—Juvenile Prostitution. — Factories. — Obscene Publications. — Census of 1851.—Education and
Crime.—Number of Prostitutes.—Female Population of London.—Working
Classes.—Domestic Servants.—Needlewomen.—Ages of Prostitutes.—Average
Life.—Condition of Women in London.—Charitable Institutions.—Mrs. Fry's
benevolent Labors.

THE corruption of court morals alone, and without circumstances of national weight and moment, has seldom, we take it,
affected the bulk of the population. It is nevertheless undeniable
that a lax morality, and, *à fortiori*, a system of absolute profligacy
among the wealthy classes of society, will contribute in a significant degree toward the increase of prostitution in metropolitan

[1] Census of Great Britain, 1851.

cities. It is in the service of her wealthy customers and patrons that the professional procuress is chiefly employed, and, stimulated by high gains, she plies her vile calling, and exerts all her hellish ingenuity to discover new sources of amusement and gratification for them.

In Fletcher's " Humorous Lieutenant," written in 1690, a court bawd is introduced reading her minute-book, and calling over the register of the females at her command. " Chloe, well—Chloe should fetch three hundred and fifty crowns; fifteen; good figure; daughter of a country gentleman; her virtue will bring me that sum, and then a riding-horse for her father out of it; well. The merchant's wife, she don't want money. I must find a spark of quality for her." The representation of such character is out of vogue in these days on the English stage; but, while the proprieties are observed, the omission is but a veiling of the subject. The reality exists, though unseen.

In the London *Times* of July, 1855, an incident is thus related by a correspondent: "I was standing on a railway platform at ———, with a friend waiting for a train, when two ladies came into the station. I was acquainted with one of them, the younger, well. She told me she was going to London, having been fortunate enough to get a liberal engagement as governess in the family of the lady under whose charge she then was, and who had even taken the trouble to come into the country to see her and her friends, to ascertain that *she was likely in all respects to suit.* The train coming in sight, the fares were paid, the elder lady paying both. I saw them into the carriage, and the door being closed, I bowed to them and rejoined my friend, who happened to be a London man about town. ' Well, I will say,' said he, with a laugh, ' you country gentlemen are pretty independent of public opinion. You are not ashamed of your little transactions being known!' 'What do you mean?' I asked. 'Why, I mean your talking to that girl and her duenna on an open platform.' 'Why, that is Miss ———, an intimate friend of ours.' 'Well, then, I can tell you,' said the Londoner to me, coolly, ' her friend is Madam ———, one of the most noted procuresses in London, and she has got hold of a new victim, if she is a victim, and no mistake.' I saw there was not a minute to lose; I rushed to the guard of the train, and got him to wait a moment. I then hurried to the carriage-door where the ladies were. ' Miss ———, you must get out; that person is an unfit companion for you. Madam ———, we know who you are.' That was one victim rescued, but how many are lost?"

In another case, the practices of a scoundrel named Phinn were made the subject of a public warning by the Lord Mayor of London from his judicial chair. This fellow's plan was to advertise from abroad for ladies to go to Cologne, or other places on the Rhine, to become governesses in his family, which was traveling, and whose governess had unexpectedly left them, or been taken ill, or was otherwise got rid of. The candidates were to pay their own passage to the place of rendezvous, when the appointments of the situation were to commence. In some cases in which the practices of this rascal had failed of their full effect, he had succeeded in defrauding poor women of their funds, and they had found the utmost difficulty in making their way home again.

While it is impossible to have any precognizance of the persons and circumstances among which these wretches find their prey, some cases are peculiarly within the scope of their operations. Young females who have lost their natural protectors, and are brought into contact with the world under their own guidance, are easily imposed upon by the pretended friendship of these persons, and being under a pretense of employment inveigled into their houses, are there kept until their fall is accomplished by persuasion or force. It is said that women even attend regularly at churches and Sunday-schools for the purpose of decoying female children. They first accost them, and interest them, without making any direct advances. The next time they proceed a little farther, and soon invite them to accompany them a little distance, when they lead them to a brothel. They have been known to take the children away in the presence of the teacher, who, seeing them act as acquaintances, had no suspicion of the real nature of their associations.[1]

The London Society for the Protection of Young Females have recorded instances of children of eleven years of age being entrapped by procuresses into houses of prostitution. Those who are thus decoyed are not permitted to escape, nor to go into the streets for two or three months. By that time they are supposed to be incapable of retracing their steps, or to have become reconciled to their mode of life, and are permitted to go or remain. Occasionally they are turned adrift to seek new lodgings, their places being supplied by fresh arrivals. Some of these children

[1] Dr. Ryan.

find their way home again, but the majority of them are of course irretrievably lost, and continue in the course into which they have been thus indoctrinated.

The procuresses have agents in different parts of London, whose business it is to discover young persons, servant-girls and others, who are dissatisfied with their earnings and condition in life, and who may be considered suitable subjects. The number of servants out of place, in London alone, is enormous—many thousands in number; and as "service is no inheritance," such a body constitutes a very favorable field of operations. The intermediate agents in these cases are small shop-keepers, laundresses, charwomen, and such others as from their avocations have the opportunity of becoming acquainted with young women in service. Common lodging-house-keepers too, residing in the suburbs of London, contribute their quota of assistance. Young women coming fresh from the country, and sleeping in such places for a night, receive recommendations to procuresses and brothel-keepers as servants. Intelligence-offices for hiring servants, which in London are called "Servants' Bazars," and are not under any license, are visited by these people in search of new faces.

In some cases procuresses are found to act on behalf of particular individuals only. In one case, such a woman kept a small shop, to which she invited servant-girls in the neighborhood after a little acquaintance. By her assistance, aided by liberal entertainment with wines and spirits, her employers (two men of property) were enabled to corrupt eight servant-girls in a short space of time.

A constant trade in prostitution is carried on between London and Hamburg, London and Paris, and London and the country. Three or four years ago a trial took place at the Central Criminal Court (London) of a man and woman who were engaged in the importation of females for purposes of prostitution. The prisoners were convicted. The details of the trial show that a regular organization existed. In some cases, Parisian prostitutes were hired in Paris for the London market by the ordinary agents in such contracts; in other cases, the parties in both capitals decoyed young women into their service on pretense of reputable engagements, and shipped them over to their consignees. Of course, every care is taken in these matters to keep the transaction confidential; for, although the English laws are practically most defective, still, in cases exciting any degree of notoriety, and in which the offense can be satisfactorily established by legal proof, prose-cutions do take place.

We can not close this branch of our subject better than by once again quoting from the Spectator, and giving a genuine letter, which, although written a century and a half ago, is just such a one as might, for a similar purpose, be penned at the present day. It as accurately describes the mode in which "articles of trade" in the procuress line are disposed of now as then.

"My Lord,—I having a great esteem for your honor, and a better opin-ion of you than of any of the quality, makes me acquaint you of an affair that I hope will oblige you to know. I have a niece that came to town about a fortnight ago. Her parents being lately dead, she came to me, ex-pecting to have found me in so good a condition as to set her up in a milli-ner's shop. Her father gave fourscore pounds with her for five years. Her time is out, and she is not sixteen: as pretty a gentlewoman as ever you saw; a little woman, which I know your lordship likes; well-shaped, and as fair a complexion for red and white as ever I saw. I doubt not but your lordship will be of the same opinion. She designs to go down about a month hence except I can provide for her, which I can not at present. Her father was one with whom all he had died with him, so there is four children left destitute; so, if your lordship thinks fit to make an appointment, where I shall wait on you with my niece, by a line or two, I stay for your answer, for I have no place fitted up, since I left my house, fit to entertain your honor. I told her she should go with me to see a gentleman, a very good friend of mine; so I desire you to take no notice of my letter by reason she is ignorant of the ways of the town. My lord, I desire, if you meet us, to come alone, for, upon my word and honor, you are the first that I ever men-tioned her to."

Next to procuresses in this gradation of iniquity are the brothel-keepers, who, although often procuresses, are not necessarily so. Shakspeare, who included all human existence in the sphere of his observation, says of them,

> "A bawd! a wicked bawd!
> The evil that thou causest to be done,
> That is thy means to live: do thou but think
> What 'tis to cram a maw or clothe a back
> From such a filthy vice; say to thyself,
> From their abominable and beastly touches
> I drink, I eat, array myself, and live.
> Canst thou believe thy living is a life?
> So stinkingly depending."

Many of these persons have been prostitutes themselves, and when past service in the one branch of business have naturally fallen into the other. Others, without having been such, adopt the trade from inclination or circumstances. The condition of these people and the interior of their houses are as various as the people themselves. At the west end of London there is a considerable degree of style; in the lower parts of the town they are sordid and filthy habitations, fit only for deeds of darkness. They are confined to private streets, alleys, and lanes out of the great thoroughfares. The law is usually put in operation in England against the brothel-keepers as the representatives of the whole class. As they get the chief profits of the trade, so they run all the legal risks. The indictments against them, however, are comparatively few. There is no public prosecutor in England, as with us. The police administration of the metropolis, perhaps the best organized, the most efficient and cheapest department of the public service, does not include the prevention of brothels within its duties, which are confined to the preservation of life and property. The prosecution of brothel-keepers and abolition of their establishments are usually undertaken by the parish authorities when the places are so conducted as to become a nuisance to the neighborhood; and police officers merely interfere to prevent the assemblage of prostitutes in the public streets, or the solicitation of passengers by them. Virtually this provision is little better than a dead letter, and the women evade it by walking when an officer is in sight, and thus deprive him of the only proof which would enable him to make an arrest.[1]

Some of the girls who pay exorbitant board also stipulate to give their mistresses one half of their cash receipts, which are frequently very large in the case of attractive women, amounting sometimes to one or two hundred dollars a week. The mistress is treasurer, and the prostitutes rarely succeed in receiving back what ostensibly belongs to them. The very prosecution before mentioned originated in a French girl's being cheated by the brothel-keeper. The clothing is furnished by the mistress, and for this she charges prices which absorb the entire earnings of the

---

[1] The ineffectual provisions of the law have recently engaged the attention of the inhabitants of London, and a meeting was held in January of the present year (1858) to consider the evil, and decide what steps should be taken in the premises. We shall notice in another part of this work some of the suggestions made on that occasion.

girls. She even contrives to furnish them with such a number
of showy and useless garments that she keeps them always in her
debt, and so has a lien on each to prevent her leaving as long as
she is a profitable member of the establishment. Some girls who
have been seduced have, when entering on a life of prostitution,
extensive and valuable wardrobes. The mistress runs them into
debts of her own contracting, and if they become dissatisfied with
their treatment and desire to leave, they are held for the debt.
By the common law of England, all debts incurred for an immoral
purpose are void, but this law is of little value to those who are
ignorant of its existence; besides which, the brothel-keepers have
possession of the booty, and thus effectually drive the debtor to
an adjustment of the matters in dispute.

Such of the brothel-keepers as have no lawful husbands form
intimacies with some man whom they support. In slang dialect,
there is a class of men called "spooneys," who support the wom-
en, or furnish them with funds when necessary. They set them
up in business, become responsible for their debts, and assist them
in all their difficulties. The "fancy men" are those who do nothing for them, but live at their expense. The lower class of brothel-keepers have no "spooneys," but they invariably have "fancy
men," who act as bullies, and settle by physical force any disputes
that may arise between the inmates and their visitors. These
men spend the day in taverns, and the night in the particular
brothels to which they are attached, and are frequently felons of
the deepest dye.

Some of the brothel-keepers are married women, and even mothers of families. The husbands are lazy, worthless wretches, addicted to gambling and drinking, and brutally indifferent to the
sources from which their luxuries are supplied. In some cases
the wealthier individuals have been known to send their children
to good schools away from home, and to have kept them in ignorance of their own wretched vocation. Thus sin entails its own
punishment.

The number of brothels in London has been variously estimated. The whole number of houses at the last census was three
hundred thousand and upward. Among them it was calculated,
and probably correctly, that there were five thousand brothels, including houses of assignation. The rents of these establishments
vary as much as the houses and situations (from fifteen hundred
down to one hundred dollars a year). In good neighborhoods we

should be slow to believe that landlords had any previous knowledge of the purposes to which their houses are to be applied. Independent of moral objection, such a house deteriorates the character of the property. Indeed, the clauses in leases of the great
London properties are very strict, and include all objectionable
trades as causes of forfeiture.

The owners of the houses are of all classes. The Almonry of
Westminster, once the abode of Caxton, which within these six or
eight years has been pulled down, was one of the vilest aggrega-
tions of vice and crime in existence. This was the property of
the dean and chapter of Westminster Abbey. The common law
of England, as already mentioned in the matter of dress, prohibits
the recovery of the rents of houses let for immoral purposes.
Many of the brothel-keepers themselves hire houses, furnish them,
and sublet them. It has been made a matter of reproach that
landlords should, even indirectly, derive income from such sources.
But poverty and vice are closely allied; where poverty exists,
vice will come. It is impossible for a landlord to exclude any
class of tenants in a particular neighborhood suited to them, and
those who know aught about the improvement and ventilation of
large cities, and the breaking up of bad neighborhoods, are well
aware that they are accompanied with a fearful amount of extra
misery to the very poor.

In a subsequent portion of this work we have endeavored to
analyze the causes of prostitution as it exists in the city of New
York. It may be reasonably supposed that the same reasons
would be applicable to the kindred people of Great Britain. We
give the following, mainly deduced from English writers, as indicating the sentiments of the best-informed in that kingdom as to
the sources of so deep-rooted an evil, which must be sought in a
variety of circumstances, national as well as personal.

A professional man, Mr. Tait, to whose pages we have turned
for information as to prostitution in Great Britain, classifies the
causes as natural and accidental. The natural he subdivides
into licentiousness of disposition, irritability of temper, pride and
love of dress, dishonesty and love of property, and indolence.
The accidental include seduction, ill-assorted marriages, low wages, want of employment, intemperance, poverty, defective education, bad example of parents, obscene publications, and a number
of minor causes. Without assenting to the classification, we will
accept the enumeration.

The operation of sexual desire on the female sex is a mooted question among English writers on prostitution. Whether it is latent, and never powerful enough to provoke evil courses until it is itself stimulated and roused into energy by external circumstances, or whether it be an active principle impelling the ill-regulated female mind to sacrifice self-respect and reputation in the gratification of dominant impulses, has been frequently discussed. Many consider that its influence on the inducement of prostitution is no less unsatisfactory of solution than the physiological problem, alleging that those who have followed the bent of their natural appetites would undoubtedly prefer to ascribe their lapse to other circumstances. This subject is treated more fully elsewhere, and it is needless to repeat here the views there expressed.

That sexual desire, *once aroused*, does exercise a potent influence on the female organization, can not be questioned. Self-abuse, which is a perverted indulgence of the natural instinct, is well known to English physicians as being practiced among young women to a great extent, though in a far less degree than among young men. Its frightful influences upon the latter have been the subject of the liveliest anxiety to those who have made the care of youth their profession, and this source of trouble is shared to some degree by female teachers. Such subjects seem by common consent to be banished from rational investigation by the majority of people, as if shutting one's eyes to the fact would prove its non-existence. This false delicacy is more injurious than is commonly supposed; for the unchecked indulgence in such habits is not only destructive of health, but in the highest degree inimical to the moral feeling, and directly subversive of all self-respect, leaving but one step to complete the final descent.

SEDUCTION.—The effect of undue familiarity, and too unrestrained an intercourse between the sexes, can not be exaggerated as paving the way for the last lapse from virtue. It is precisely these familiarities which, in ill-regulated minds, excite the first impulses of desire; and even where such a result does not immediately flow from too free an intercourse, it breaks down that modesty and reserve which so much enhance the beauty of woman, and constitute her best safeguard. The inclined plane by which the female who permits the first freedom glides unchecked to final ruin, though gradual, is very difficult to retrace. The unrestricted intercourse permitted, or rather encouraged between the sexes at places of public amusement much facilitates the opportunities of seduction. Prostitutes frequently, and we believe with truth, allege seduction as the first step toward their abandoned course of life, and the allegation itself should induce a sympathy for the misfortune of their present existence. Although in some cases the story can not be implicitly believed, at the same time there is no doubt that a heartless seduction is but too frequent a circumstance in such cases, and contributes its sad quota of heavy account to prostitution.

It is a general opinion that cases of (so called) seduction in England occur between employers and female servants, and that of these are vast numbers. By seduction in such circumstances is meant the inducement to do wrong by promises or other suasives, in opposition to the commonly received idea, which makes the fall the result of strong personal attachment. In a work like this we must notice the largest definitions, and can not consistently limit ourselves to the inducement customarily brought forward in law proceedings, namely, " a promise of marriage." In this sense, illegitimate children may be said to be the consequence of seduction. Certainly not all of them, however, because many persons, voluntarily and with their eyes open, enter upon cohabitation arrangements; but doubtless many are. Once seduced, of course the female becomes herself the seducer of the inexperienced.

The policy of English law, of late years, has been to compel the woman to protect herself—in the main, a wise policy. But the balance of human justice is very unevenly maintained. The male, the real delinquent, incurs no legal punishment, and but little social reprobation. Actions for seduction are very unpopular, and those brought bear but an infinitesimal proportion to the occurrence of the crime. The *onus* of proof in bastardy affiliations of course rests upon the woman. Of late years the alterations in the law have thrown great difficulties in her way by what is called the necessity of corroborative evidence, namely, some kind of admission, direct or indirect, or some overt act which will furnish oral or documentary testimony other than the woman's unsupported statement. This may be strictly expedient, but it renders the man almost irresponsible if he only play his part with knavish prudence. Lastly, popular feeling is against charges of rape: acquittal is very frequent, and the usual rebuttal is to im-

X

peach the character of the prosecutrix. The opinion of one of
England's greatest judges has passed into a proverb: "No charge
so easy to make, none so difficult to disprove." Queen Elizabeth's mode of proving her disbelief of rape is also expressive of
public opinion.

From the combination of these circumstances, it would seem
that seduction must, almost as a matter of course, lead to prostitution, inasmuch as, in ordinary English parlance, the mother of a
bastard and a prostitute are almost synonymous.

OVERCROWDED DWELLINGS.—The natural impulses of animal
instinct in both sexes seem to be implicated in the effect of crowded sleeping apartments, as met with in the habitations of the poor
both in town and country. In the latter we have the show, and
sometimes the reality, of family life and virtuous poverty. In the
towns we find abodes of poverty sometimes honest, sometimes in
closest propinquity or intimacy with vice, and there too we have
the dwelling-places of the lowest depravity and vagabondism.

Those who have not given their attention to the condition of
the poor, and the relation which their lives hold to the ordinary
habits of decency and morality, have much difficulty in compre-
hending, or even believing, statements which embody the plainest
every-day truths. It is hard to realize things as they are, if the
mind has been full of ideal pictures of things as they should be.
The Dives of society has been often reproached with his ignorance
of Lazarus. The sin lies exactly in that ignorance. As Carlyle
finely says, "The duty of Christian society is to find its work, and
to do it." Negative virtue is of no practical use to the community. But yet the ignorance is natural enough, and no easier of removal than other ignorance. It has been generally attributed to
the wealthy and upper classes of society, but it exists just the
same, differing only a little in degree, in the middle class and moderately rich members of the English social system.

The misery and inconvenience which the poor suffer from the
straitness of their domestic arrangements are beyond belief.
Grown-up girls and boys sleep in the same bed; brothers and sisters, to say nothing of less intimate relations, are in the closest
contiguity; and even strangers, who are admitted into the little
home to help in eking out the rent, are placed on the same family
footing. This momentous question to the moral well-being of the
poor has excited very lively interest in England, and has called

into active operation several philanthropic associations, which have in view the employment of capital in improving and cheapening the dwellings of the working classes.[1]

In London this system of close lodging was carried to a fearful pitch. In some places from five to thirteen persons slept in a single bed, while in the country the evil was nearly as bad, although, from the slight restraint imposed by family ties, the actual evil is positively less; though the moral contamination is of nearly the same extent, and paves the way for other relations out of doors. The facts which justify these conclusions are to be found in a variety of shapes—parliamentary reports, statistical tables, appeals from clergymen, addresses from philanthropic associations, etc., etc.[2]

The Honorable and Reverend S. O. Osborne, a clergyman well known for his philanthropic exertions in behalf of the poor, says of country life in England:

"From infancy to puberty the laborer's children sleep in the same room with his wife and himself; and whatever attempts at decency may be made, and I have seen many ingenious and most praiseworthy attempts, still there is the fact of the old and the young, married and unmarried, of both sexes, all herded together in one and the same sleeping apartment. * * * * I do

[1] General secondary questions do not come within the scope of this work, but the labors of these dwelling improvement associations are intimately connected with the subject we have now under investigation. In London, model lodging-houses for single men, single women, and married couples with their children, have been tried and found eminently successful, both as a moderate interest-paying investment, and as a very admirable arrangement for promoting the comfort and health of the working classes. The details given some two years ago, through the daily papers, on the lodgings of the poor and the very poor of New York, were frightful enough to excite the active sympathy of the benevolent capitalists of this great city. The very best philanthropy is that which teaches and enables the poor man to benefit his own condition. This principle is practically in operation all over the United States; but in great cities, the freedom of action, and the directly beneficial results of frugality and industry, are not so immediate as in country places. The attempt by the poor to improve their own dwellings in these large cities is almost hopeless, because it does not depend upon individual exertions, but on combination both of money and knowledge. The "how, when, and where" have to be found out and carried through: very small difficulties these, and easily overcome, if those who have the requisite means to carry out such a reform, and thus lend their aid to the solution of an important social problem, have an inclination commensurate with their resources.

[2] See, in particular, as regards London, Statistical Society's Reports, vol. xiii.; Reports of Metropolitan Association for improving the Habitations of the Poor; Board of Health Papers. And for the country districts, Health of Towns Reports; Report on the Employment of Women and Children in Agriculture, 1843.

not choose to put on paper the disgusting scenes that I have known to occur from the promiscuous crowding of the sexes together. *Seeing, however, to what the mind of the young female is exposed from her very childhood, I have long ceased to wonder at the otherwise seeming precocious licentiousness of conversation which may be heard in every field where many of the young are at work together.*"

Mr. A. Austin, Assistant Poor-Law Commissioner, says:

" The sleeping of boys and girls, young men and young women, in beds almost touching one another, must have the effect of breaking down the great barriers between the sexes. The accommodation for sleeping is such as necessarily to create early and illicit familiarity between the sexes."

Without entering into disgusting details, the pain of perusing which could add nothing to the value of the statements, the conclusion is indisputable that much of prostitution, if not of prostitution for hire, certainly of prostitution from corrupt and profligate motives, is engendered by the vicious habits induced by habitual proximity of the sexes in early life. The prostitutes themselves frequently assign these habits as the commencement of their career of vice, and some even admit the breach of the closest natural ties during early youth, by reason of the too great facilities thus offered.[1] The great importance of this want of decency and propriety in family life can not be overrated. The contagious nature of vice is proverbial; and it is almost impossible to imagine the power attained by ill-conditioned children, and the fatal readiness with which their sinful words and practices are propagated.

The cheap lodging-houses are a pendant to the close-packed dwellings of the poor, although they do not produce the same early pernicious results as indecency and immorality in family life. The latter prepare the way to the scenes of the common lodging-house, in which the lowest depth of vice is speedily reached. Here prostitution is habitual—a regular institution of the place. The smallest imaginable quantities of food can be purchased; adults, youths, and children of both sexes are received, and herd promiscuously together; the prices of beds are of the lowest (from three to six cents); no questions are asked, and the place is free to all. A new-comer is soon initiated, or rather forced into all the mysteries of iniquity. Obscenity and blasphemy are the staple conversation of the inmates; every indecency is openly performed; the

---

[1] Mayhew's Letters to the (London) Morning Chronicle; Mayhew's London Labor and the London Poor.

girls recite aloud their experiences of life; ten or a dozen sleep in one bed, many in a state of nudity. Indeed, the details of these places are horrible beyond description. Unmitigated vice and lustful orgies reign, unchecked by precept or example, and the point of rivalry is as to who shall excel in filth and abomination.

EXAMPLE is the next immediate cause in what may be considered the natural series. There are a few prostitutes who have children. That these latter should follow the same course is quite in the common course of events, although considerable anxiety is occasionally evinced by such women to have their children brought up to better courses. Such redemption is all but impossible. In ordinary life, however, the mind of youth is often perverted by direct evil example in the elders; and, as we have already remarked, the corruption of the human affections in their fountain-head—family life—where they ought to be sweetest and purest, is more fatally demoralizing, and more certain to insure eventual ruin than almost any other. Fathers and mothers are both wanting often enough in their duty, although it is a matter of universal faith that the influence and example of the father are of less importance than that of the mother. A bad man may have virtuous children, a bad woman hardly ever. There are cases where the mother and daughter sleep in the same bed, each with a male partner. In the city of Edinburgh there are two mothers, prostitutes, each with four daughters, prostitutes; five prostitute mothers each with three prostitute daughters, ten such with two daughters each, and twenty-four such with one daughter each, all following the practices of the mothers.[1]

Such influences brought to bear on the young are irresistible. This may perhaps account for the number of sisters who carry on prostitution. The effect of mere sisterly example would be sufficient to account for the circumstance, but the parental becomes almost a compulsion, inasmuch as the parent (in such circumstances, the mother) will not only connive at, but be the main cause of her child's ruin for her own direct profit and advantage. This, indeed, seems more accordant with our ideas of the natural tendencies of prostitutes and procuresses, than that such persons should be excessively anxious for their children's purity and moral welfare.

POVERTY is an integral part of nearly all the conditions of life

[1] Tait's Prostitution in Edinburgh.

which we have to consider as incentives to prostitution. *In some instances, more, perhaps, than may be generally credited, poverty is a direct and proximate cause of this vice.* In other words, "*women previously and otherwise virtuous do prostitute their bodies for bread.*" In most of the cases enumerated except that purely natural, but rare one, innate sexual desire, poverty is a remote cause. From the number of the human race who are under its griping, chilling pressure, poverty may be set down as a fruitful source of prostitution.

The connection of political circumstances with the phases of public morals is more intimate than the consideration of the superficial differences of the two matters would at first sight imply. But an attentive comparison of the state of public prosperity with the state of public crime will show that crime is somewhat dependent on food: the man with a well-filled stomach is no foe to order. Prostitution, as a means of supplying the cravings of hunger, is part of the same connection. It is true that in England there are poor-laws and work-houses, from and in which every destitute person, without reference to character, has a right to food and shelter. In the first place, however, the work-houses are objects of unmitigated aversion to the poorer classes. Various rules, in themselves hard, but rendered necessary by consideration for the rate-payers as well as for the beneficiaries, such as separation of husband and wife while receiving relief, separation of child and parent, etc., make the work-house system odious to the worthy and honest poor; while the strict rules, and the restraint and discipline enforced within the walls, make it still more odious to those who place their happiness in license and irregularity; added to this, in populous and poor districts, the claims upon the work-house in seasons of distress are too numerous for its capabilities. It is an awful truth that, notwithstanding the enormous revenues, nearly fifty millions of dollars per annum, collected for poor relief, and the immense establishments instituted throughout the country for the support and shelter of the distressed, sometimes the number of applicants is so great that their demands can not be met. Possibly, if these unfortunates could be distributed throughout the kingdom, so that the poverty of one spot could be balanced by the comparative prosperity of another, the fearful starvation in the midst of plenty, which is occasionally witnessed, need not occur. But in the mean while, and until the time when all the schemes and devices of modern improvement and advancement shall be finally perfected, and universal happiness attained, there is a mass of inconceivable wretchedness to be dealt with. In "Household Words" for November, 1855, Mr. Dickens gives a harrowing picture of London distress, of which he was himself an eye-witness.

It was a dark, rainy evening, and close against the wall of Whitechapel Work-house lay five bundles of rags. Mr. Dickens and his friend looked at them, and attempted to rouse them in vain. They knocked at the door, were admitted, saw the master of the work-house, and asked him if he knew there were five human beings—females—lying on the ground outside, cold and hungry. He did—at first he was annoyed—such applications were frequent—how could he meet them?—the house was full—the casual ward was full—what could he do more? When he found that Mr. Dickens's aim was inquiry, not fault-finding, he was softened. The case was certainly shocking: how was it to be met? Mr. Dickens said he had heard outside that these wretched beings had been there two nights already. It was very possible. He could not deny or affirm it. There were often more in the same plight—sometimes twenty or thirty. He (the master) was obliged to give preference to women with children. The place was full. Unable to do more, Mr. Dickens left. On getting outside, he roused one of these poor wretches. She looked up, but said nothing. He asked her if she was hungry; she merely looked an affirmative. Would she know where to get something to eat? she again assented in the same way. "Then take this, and for God's sake go and get something." She took it, made no sign of thanks—"gathered herself up and slunk away—wilted into darkness, silent and heedless of all things."

To what will not such misery as this compel suffering human nature? In times of commercial depression the police of London note an increase of street prostitution. It is said in the cities of England that the permanent prostitution of each place has a numerical relation to the means of occupation. In Edinburgh there are but few chances of employing female labor. Glasgow, Dundee, and Paisley are the seats of manufactures, and employ female labor extensively. According to Tait, the prostitution of Edinburgh far exceeds its proportion of prostitution to population as compared with the manufacturing towns.[1]

[1] These conclusions are not always reliable. Other causes may operate. If we

It seems unnecessary to multiply instances of poverty and indigence, inasmuch as the fact is most miserably indisputable: shirt-making at three cents, pantaloon-making at five or six cents—unceasing labor of fourteen hours a day bringing in only sixty or eighty cents a week, and competition even to obtain this. As the London *Times* once said, "The needle is the normal employment of every English woman; what, then, must be the condition of those tens of thousands who have nothing but that to depend upon?" Of late years, too, a still farther competition has been introduced in that ingenious invention of our country, the sewing machine.

In order to show the relation between unpaid and excessive labor and prostitution, we will instance a few cases.

One young woman said she made moleskin pantaloons (a very strong, stiff fabric) at the rate of fifteen cents per pair. She could manage twelve pairs per week when there was full employment; sometimes she could not get work. She worked from six in the morning until ten at night. With full work she could make two dollars a week, out of which she had to expend thirty-eight cents for thread and candle. On an average, in consequence of short work, she could not make more than seventy-five cents a week. Her father was dead, and she had to support her mother, who was sixty years of age. This girl endured her mode of existence for three years, till at length she agreed to live with a young man. When she made this statement she was within three months of her confinement. She felt the disgrace of her condition, to relieve her from which she said she prayed for death, and would not have gone wrong if she could have helped it.[1]

Such a case as this scarcely comes within the term prostitution, but she stated that many girls at the shop advised prostitution as a resource, and that others should do as they did, as by that means they had procured plenty to eat and clothes to wear. She gave it as her opinion that none of the thousands of girls who work at the same business earn a livelihood by their needle, but that all must and do prostitute themselves *to eke out a subsistence.*

Another woman, a case more directly in point, also said she could not earn more than seventy-five cents. She was a widow,

recollect rightly, Edinburgh is a garrison town. In factory towns, moreover, we should always expect to find a very large amount of immorality, which would somewhat displace open and avowed prostitution for hire.

[1] Mayhew's Letters to the London *Morning Chronicle.*

and had three children when her husband died. Herself and her children had to live on these seventy-five cents. She might have gone into the work-house, and been there better supported than by her labor. Had she done so, the laws of the work-house are inexorable, she would have been separated from her children. Although one child died, she was now so reduced that she could not procure food. She took to the streets for a living, and she declared that hundreds of married and single women were doing the same thing for the same reasons.

A widow who had buried all her children could not support herself. From sheer inability to do so she took to prostitution.

A remarkably fine-looking young woman, whose character for sobriety, honesty, and industry was vouched by a number of witnesses as unimpeachable, had been compelled to work at fine shirts, by which she could not earn more, on an average, than thirty-five cents a week. She had a child, and, being unwilling to go to the work-house, she was driven by indigence to the streets. Struck with remorse and shame, and for the sake of her child determined to abandon prostitution, she fasted whole days, sleeping in winter-time in sheds. Once her child's legs froze to her side, and necessity again compelled her to take to her former course. Her father had been an Independent preacher.

These circumstances, and innumerable others, will establish incontestably the intimate relation which poverty bears to prostitution. A consideration of such circumstances as the foregoing, and the every-day observation of hosts of others of a similar character which will come within the cognizance of any one who searches into human motives, must incline all but the most outrageously virtuous to judge more tenderly of the failings and errors of their fellow-creatures.

All young females engaged in sewing are liable to the same distress, and the same resource against it is, of course, open to all. The hard labor and long hours are the least part of the evil, although in that light even there would be ground for commiseration.[1] The real grievance is that the most patient and industri-

---

[1] When Mrs. Sydney Herbert instituted her Distressed Needlewoman's Society, a great deal was thought to have been accomplished in one particular branch of female labor—the millinery and dress-making business—when the leading employers had been induced to promise that the working-day should be restricted to twelve hours.—*Needlewoman's Society Report,* 1848.

ous can not, by any hours of labor, earn a sufficiency to support themselves. It is true that the work-house is the legal refuge of the poor; but the tender mercies of the work-house have passed into a proverb. The policy of the poor-laws as administered is to deter the needy from applying for relief except in very extreme cases. Hence many rules are made, and much formality is interposed, which render the legal provisions so irksome and unbearable that many fly to the nearest means of satisfying their wants rather than demand their legal rights.

DOMESTIC SERVANTS are, in respect of their removal from absolute want while in service, more happily situated than those who are thus dependent upon the needle. But they are open to influences of another kind—we mean seduction by masters and male members of the household. Where this evil begins is an exceedingly difficult question to determine. When corrupted, they become themselves, by the very opportunities they possess, ready and dangerous instruments of corruption, and contribute to disseminate the poisons of immorality and of bodily disease. We have already incidentally mentioned that this class is at times open to a great deal of poverty and distress, namely, when out of service, and at such times they are peculiarly the mark for the lures of persons who make seduction their business and profitable occupation.

The domestic servants and the sewing-women are the principal adult laborers of Great Britain, except the factory girls. In 1851 there were,

Female domestic servants, 905,165	Seamstresses	72,940
Dress-makers . . . 270,000	Stay-makers	12,969

and of these one third were under twenty years of age.

PLACES OF PUBLIC AMUSEMENT in England are few when compared with those of the Continent, and their influence must be proportionately less. On the Continent dancing saloons are a prominent feature; in England this character of entertainment is almost unknown. In London there are a few places of this sort, such, for example, as Cremorne Gardens. Mr. Tait lays some stress on the evil effects of dancing-houses in Edinburgh. We should be inclined to think the cases of misconduct traceable to these places actually few in number, though not unworthy of notice. The single females who frequent dancing-rooms, theatres, and other similar places in England, without friends or family escort, have very little virtue to risk. The country fairs are far more injurious; they are indiscriminately attended by all ages and sexes, and their effects upon the female agricultural population are often very pernicious. Greenwich Fair, a three days' scene of rollicking and junketing, was held at Easter and Whitsuntide, in the outskirts of London, but is now abolished. It had its uses a century or two ago, but recently had been attended by all the idlers of London, of both sexes, and was justly dreaded by the friends of youth. It is proverbial that more young women were debauched at Greenwich Fair (allowing for its duration) than at any other place in England.

ILL-ASSORTED MARRIAGES are decidedly a cause of prostitution. Certainly breach of the marriage vow is one thing, prostitution for hire another. In estimating the number of prostitutes in Edinburgh at eight hundred, Mr. Tait adds two hundred to them under the head of married women, which he considers accrue from ill-assorted marriages. That the marriage was ill-assorted is plainly shown by its result, and that want of congeniality and temperament is the cause of prostitution to the extent thus named we have no ground to question. He speaks of such women selling their favors generally to one lover only, occasionally to any one who will pay; although the latter forms what is commonly known as prostitution, no other construction can be put upon the former.

LOVE OF DRESS is another incident which many writers, and Mr. Tait among them, have introduced into the direct causes of prostitution. We should consider it doubtful if any woman ever positively sold her virtue for a new gown or a knot of ribbons. Of course, after the Rubicon is crossed, all subsequent steps are easy, and may be taken from any motive. The love of admiration, which, under regulation, is sometimes a commendable instinct, when uncontrolled, becomes a snare. The love of dress is a modification of this sentiment, and may help to work out the effect when other causes have overthrown the balance of the mind.

JUVENILE PROSTITUTION.—We have now arrived, in the consideration of the causes of prostitution in England, at decidedly the most painful of all the phenomena connected with this condition of human life, namely, the immense extent of juvenile depravity. We have already sketched the evils of insufficient house accommodation and its noxious effects upon the morals of the rising generation. In this connection, also, bad example is particularly

prominent; perhaps, indeed, with respect to the young, evil communications are the greatest dangers.

The work-house was formerly one great hot-bed of vice, and the
greatest license and irregularity prevailed in every department.
That children born or brought up in such a place should grow up
debased was perfectly in the expected course of things. Now,
however, under the new Poor-Laws Commission, the scene is
stripped of its more revolting accessories. The sexes do not mingle, children do not associate with adults: some modicum of education is given. The sweetest and holiest of all ties, that of family,
is yet wanting, and self-respect is totally deficient. In the absence
of these protective influences, the wonder is, not that so many
children should turn out ill, but that so many girls should turn
out well. Formerly, also, there was a system of compulsory pauper apprenticeship, and the interests of the parish apprentice out
of doors were very little looked after. This, again, has been altered, both in town and country, and the improvement is marked.

Even with all this, it is recorded in the London *Times* (June,
1848) that a correspondent, visiting one of the metropolitan work-
houses, was struck by the happy and healthy appearance of the
female children, and inquired of the master of the work-house
what became of all of them. He was informed that they were
sent out, at the age of fourteen, as servants or in other capacities,
and that *nine tenths* of them, after coming backward and forward
from their places to the work-house, eventually got corrupted and
took to the streets.

FACTORIES are made accountable by many writers for much juvenile immorality and prostitution. Factories in England are, as
most of our readers are aware, institutions materially differing in
some respects from those of our own country. In no feature is there
so wide a dissimilarity as in the character of the work-people.
The factory children of England are the offspring of the poorest
of the community, whose only heritage is pauperism, with wages
at no time too good, and often at starvation point. The miserable
earnings of the factory operatives are still farther reduced by constant strikes and contests with their employers, in which it is a
foregone conclusion that the workmen must yield. Macaulay tells
us that, two centuries ago, the employment of children in factories,
and the dependence of the parent's bread upon the children's earnings, was a notorious fact, much condemned by philanthropists.
The introduction of machinery and the value of child-labor grad-

ually aggravated all the horrors of the factory system, the enormity of which called down the indignation of the non-manufacturing community, and compelled the protective interference of Parliament. The Ten Hours' Bill, the Factory Childrens' Education regulations, appointment by government of factory commissioners and inspectors, have all contributed to ameliorate the hard lot of the factory child. The employment of very young children in factories is still to be regretted, or rather its necessity, for probably it is better they should be employed in a not very laborious occupation than left to roam the streets.

The direct influence of factory work on juvenile prostitution is insisted on by many writers; by others, some reservations have been introduced, such as, The young associate only during hours of recreation. In business hours they are generally employed in different parts of the building. They have a certain amount of education. Their parents are generally, or very often, employed in the same establishment. Assume that these children were not in the factory, where would they be, and what could they do? Are evil influences rife only in the factory? The overcrowding at home; the frequent drunkenness and debauchery of their parents and associates; the endless indigence; the frequent visits to the work-houses, are all circumstances which have been considered and argued in the case. But of the fact of juvenile prostitution and depravity in factory populations none can doubt; of its being exclusively or chiefly attributable to factory life, others are not certain.

That children who labor in factories, and thereby contribute to the family earnings and their own support, could do better in the present condition of English society, is doubtful. Mill-owners are required to devote a portion of their time to education. Sunday-schools are established; personal attention is paid by leading mill-owners to the improvement of the poor; many build good cottages (for which, by the way, they receive a good interest in the way of rent); many inspect the schools; some build school-houses and pay the teachers. The good example of benevolent mill-owners in a measure compels others, whose moral perceptions are less keen, to follow them.

We would not be supposed to argue that English cotton factories are types of the Millennium, any more than are similar institutions on this side of the Atlantic. In fact, we have a very decided opinion on the matter, but common honesty requires that the opinion of all who have investigated the subject should be fairly recorded. In submitting the various arguments adduced in favor of factory labor and its bearing on immorality, we present merely subjects for consideration.

DISEASE IN CHILDREN.—A fact of importance to public health is the disease acquired by children. In the first address issued by the London Society for the Protection of young Females, it is stated that in three of the London hospitals during the preceding eight years there had been no less than two thousand seven hundred cases of venereal disease in children between eleven and sixteen years of age.

Dr. Ryan, on the same subject, speaking from his professional experience as medical officer of several charities, mentions the shock he felt on seeing numerous cases of venereal disease in children.

Mr. Miller, of Glasgow, testifies to the same fact.

The very imperfect data which exist on this important branch of our subject will not enable one to form any sound opinion on the spread of disease from these juvenile sources. It is, however, reasonable to conclude, from the few facts, and from the very facilities afforded at their age for intercommunication between children, that the spread of disease from direct contamination, and the deterioration of health and constitution from unknown excesses, must be very great.

OBSCENE PUBLICATIONS.—Of these there are vast numbers, and the extent of juvenile contamination from this source must be very great. The Society for the Suppression of Vice, in London, reports having seized, at different periods, thousands of obscene books, copper-plates, and prints, all of which they caused to be destroyed. Within a period of three years they procured the destruction of

Blasphemous and impure books .   279   Obscene songs (on sheets).   1,495
Obscene publications 1,162   Obscene prints 10,493

and even this was but an item in the calculation.

The police of London take but little interest in this matter. The above-mentioned society is the principal agent in the repression of this infamous species of depravity. There are certain places in London in which the trade still lives and flourishes, notwithstanding the attacks made upon it. Holywell Street, in the Strand, and the vicinity of Leicester Square, are places of disgraceful notoriety in this respect. The secret is, that wherever there is a public demand, no repressive laws will ever prevent trade. The attempt at repression but makes it more profitable.

To the corruption of the youthful mind and the preparatives for prostitution these publications must contribute. It is matter of question what number of prostitutes have become such directly from this cause. The results of visitorial inspection do not show among London prostitutes, any more than elsewhere, a taste for books and prints of an obscene tendency. Their taste in literature is that which would prevail among persons of low intellectual calibre. Startling tales, romances with a plentiful spice of horrors, thrilling love-stories, highly wrought and exaggerated narratives, are their taste. In the practice of prostitution, the use of indecent or prurient prints is chiefly for the adornment of visitors' rooms in brothels.

EDUCATION.—In the relations between education and crime are found no distinctive marks whereby prostitution may be separated from any other development of vice or immorality. It is to be presumed that the same general laws which apply to the unregulated manifestation of the passions apply to those with which prostitution is chiefly implicated.

In the present generation it is generally assumed that crime is the offspring of ignorance, therefore Education! is the cry. Education has become a party watchword in England. The necessity of education, the quality and the quantity, with all the minor propositions that branch off from the main question, are, and have been for years, the subject of the hottest polemics. But recent results, evolved from statistical inquiries, would seem to call up the previous question as to the value of education at all. The present work is not the place in which to discuss the fact, or to point out a remedy, or indicate the deficiencies of a system which can suffer such a question to arise. We give the facts. From the Parliamentary reports of 1846–1848, it appears that the number of educated criminals in England was at that time more than twice, and in Scotland more than three and a half that of the uneducated:

Years.	England.		Scotland.	
	Educated.	Uneducated.	Educated.	Uneducated.
1846	16,963	7698	3155	903
1847	19,307	9050	3562	1048
1848	20,176	9671	3985	911

In calculating a percentage on certain criminal returns during the undermentioned years, the results were:

	1839.	1840	1841.	1842	1843.	1844	1845	1846.
Uneducated	33·53	33·32	33·21	32·35	31·00	29·77	30·61	30·66
Imperfectly educated..	53·48	55·57	56·67	58·32	57·60	59·28	58·34	59·51
Well educated	10·07	8·29	7·40	6·77	8·02	8·12	8·38	7·71
Superior education	0·32	0·37	0·45	0·22	0·47	0·42	0·37	0·34
Unascertained	2·60	2·45	2·27	2·34	2·91	2·41	2·30	1·78
	100·	100·	100·	100·	100·	100·	100·	100·

This table, which on its face conclusively establishes an increase in criminals imperfectly educated, and a decrease both in those who could read and write well, and those who could not read or write at all, may be, and has been made, the subject of much pseudo-philosophical remark, as proving the injury of education. In the first place, it only shows the effects of partial education, if it shows any thing. But the misfortune of statistical results is that they are relied on too implicitly, with a narrow-minded subservience to figures and facts, whereas they require to be accompanied with explanatory circumstances, which may either enhance their value up to the point of mathematical demonstration, or may so pare them away as to render them perfectly worthless. In the consideration of the above figures, all that would seem to appear is that there was an increase of education keeping pace with the increase of population, and that in the statistics of crime the increase of imperfectly educated people would be as perceptible as elsewhere. Mere reading and writing, unaccompanied by moral elevation, will not reform mankind. Alone, they will not prevent a hungry man from satisfying his hunger. The words of Cæsar apply to criminals equally as to conspirators:

> " Let me have men about me that are fat,
> Sleek-headed men, and such as sleep o'nights:
> Yon Cassius has a lean and hungry look."

Pursuing this question, and turning to the population tables of 1851, the period of the last census, we find that Middlesex was the most generally educated county, taking the signature of the marriage register as the test of education. Eighty-two per cent. signed the marriage register, yet in the list of criminality Middlesex stood third of all the counties of England. Gloucester, which was first in crime, was far from being the most ignorant. There sixty-five per cent. signed the register. The general average of the whole population by the same list is forty per cent. Here again is a qualifying circumstance. London is included in Middlesex, with its vast seething mass of human misery and corruption to swell the record of crime, while its general population is, of course, about the most intelligent of the British empire, so that in the same spot is found at once the greatest intelligence and the greatest misery. We are not aware of such qualifying circumstances in Gloucestershire.

Dr. Ryan, writing on this point, refers to the Metropolitan Police Report for 1837, by which it appears that of prostitutes arrested in that year there

Could not read or write	1773
" read and write imperfectly	1237
" " " " well	89
Had received a good education	4
Total	3103

This is a tolerably fair criterion; for although, as before said, the police only interfere with peace-breakers, and all these came under the technical term of "drunk and disorderly," still we believe the state of prostitution in London to be such that an average proportion of all classes of courtesans pass through the hands of the police during the year.

Mr. Tait, speaking of Edinburgh, confirms the view put forward as to educational influences. A large proportion of the Edinburgh prostitutes (eighty-seven per cent.) read and write. The Scottish peasantry are perhaps the best-educated in Europe, and those girls who come to Edinburgh from the country are no exception to the rule. The uneducated, Mr. Tait thinks, are city girls.

As to the religious denomination of prostitutes, for that a prostitute may have a religion we may say, in the kindly spirit of Corporal Trim, but doubtingly, "A negro has a soul, your honor." In Edinburgh they include all sects except Independents, Baptists, and Quakers. There may be those who smile at the idea of a prostitute having any belief. Of London we have no data on this point.

ILLEGITIMATE BIRTHS seem, by common consent of most writers, to be classed with details of prostitution. In France, it is said by those who profess intimate local knowledge, there is almost a prejudice against marriage, although it can be performed as a legal ceremony. We think Bayle St. John states this fact. In the poorer districts of London, the east end, for example, it is notorious that numbers live in a state of concubinage. Again: in the country, and away from the dense population of towns, a woman of immoral habits may often be found who has had two or three illegitimate children by different men with whom she has cohabited. Such a woman would most probably have been a prostitute in a town; as it is, she is no better; still, she is not a prostitute for hire. But to proceed to details.

The number of illegitimate births in every thousand births in the various counties is as follows:

Cumberland	108	Suffolk	81	York	71
Norfolk	105	Derby	81	Stafford	69
Hereford	100	Berks	79	Sussex	68
Salop	99	Leicester	79	Cambridge	66
Nottingham	91	North Wales	78	Lincoln	64
Cheshire	89	South Wales	72	Middlesex	40
Westmoreland	87				

Cumberland is a pastoral and mountainous county, with a thin-ly-settled population. Norfolk is an agricultural and grazing county, broken up into large farms. Neither county has many large towns. Stafford is a manufacturing county, with a long list of thickly-populated small towns, in which as great indigence and misery can be found as in any part of England. Middlesex contains London. Here, then, we see that illegitimacy and prostitution are not the same thing. Where there are no prostitutes there are bastards, but the women in the country are mostly employed; they are obliged to work in the fields, or in some domestic manufacture such as button-making, stocking-making, etc.

An apparent paradox may be here mentioned, although not intimately affecting these investigations. The preponderance of bastards is accompanied by a preponderance of early marriages. This has been accounted for by the theory that both are dependent on sexual instincts precociously or excessively stimulated, which seek marriage when practicable, or illicit intercourse where not.[1]

Illegitimacy is somewhat regulated by the disproportionate number of the sexes. In an excess of females there are few bastards; in an excess of males there are many. Upon this fact, unattended by qualifying circumstances, might be based an argument

[1] It would be interesting to know whether this illicit intercourse is by way of cohabitation or merely temporary. Instances are not rare of people cohabiting who allege themselves too poor to pay the marriage fees. In order to obviate this, it is customary for ministers in poor and populous parishes in England, where the circumstances of individual parishioners are not known to them, to invite all parties who are living in concubinage to come and be married free of expense. Many avail themselves of this offer.

as to the innate sexual instinct in females. It might have been expected the relations would be somewhat different, namely, an increase of prostitution with an excess of men, but an increase of bastards with an excess of women.

The number of rapes in England seems to be governed by the excess of men over women. Where the number of illegitimate children exceeds the average, rape is less frequent.

The cases of abuse of children between the ages of ten and twelve are three in every ten million of the whole population. There is some difficulty in this matter, arising from a legal technicality on the subject of age. In any case, neither of the last items of criminality is of any value, inasmuch as they include only those cases judicially investigated. Many are guilty, yet acquitted; and many more are never charged with the offense. Shame prevents parties prosecuting; or, in the case of children, the fact does not transpire, or else it is compromised.

Keeping a brothel is, as we have said, an offense at common law. We have a computation of the number of offenses of this kind based upon every ten million of the population. In Middlesex it was two hundred and ninety-six, in Lancashire one hundred and eighty-three. Both counties include the most populous towns in England. Lancashire contains Manchester and Liverpool. This fact also is of little value, owing to the peculiar administration of the law on the subject. Remote or indirect injuries to the public safety are not noticed in England. The police may be well aware of crime meditated and planned, and of the haunts of crime, but the theory of public justice is cure, not prevention.

Concealment of birth is an offense which, as it emanates from undue sexual intercourse, is generally associated with prostitution. In Hereford and other counties, the proportion of illegitimate births is eighty-eight out of every thousand born, and there were twenty-two concealments to every thousand bastards.

In four counties the illegitimate births were fifty-eight in a thousand, and the concealments thirteen in a thousand illegitimates.

In fifteen counties there were fifty-three illegitimates in every thousand births, and twenty-seven concealments to every thousand illegitimates.

With the largest proportion of illegitimates there are the fewest concealments; namely, with seventy-nine illegitimates out of a thousand births, there were only twelve concealments to a thousand illegitimates.

It is absolutely impossible to ascertain the number of prostitutes in London with any degree of certainty, and even a satisfactory approximation is exceedingly difficult; nevertheless, it is most important to attain as nearly as possible to the actual facts, because without this knowledge no adequate idea can be formed of the vast seed-bed of disease and corruption in constant action in a great capital city shedding forth and disseminating its pernicious growth on every side, through channels unknown and unsuspected.

Mr. Colquhoun, a magistrate of the British metropolis toward the close of the last century (1796), made an arbitrary enumeration, fixing the number of prostitutes in London at fifty thousand. Drs. Ryan, Campbell, Mr. Talbot, and others, carry their estimate in 1840 to eighty thousand!

Mr. Mayne (now Sir Richard Mayne), chief commissioner of the Metropolitan Police in 1840, made an estimate of the number of regular London prostitutes, which he considers were then eight thousand and upward. The seemingly irreconcilable discrepancy of these numbers is, no doubt, to be found in the loose terminology of the one party and the technicality of the other. The term "prostitute" would seem to be best applied to those unhappy females who make prostitution their sole calling, and may therefore be styled "regular" prostitutes, while the larger estimate includes all shades, both "regular" and "occasional" or "irregular," by which is understood those females with whom prostitution is auxiliary to some reputable calling.

We can not find that any reliable returns have been made on this branch of public life by the London police, although they must possess peculiar and exclusive powers of preparing them. As long back as 1837 the following rough calculation was made :

	1st Class.	2d Class	3d Class.	Total.
Well-dressed prostitutes in brothels ...	813	62	20	895
Well-dressed prostitutes walking the streets . . ..}	1460	79	73	1612
Prostitutes infesting low neighborhoods	3533	147	184	3864
	5806	288	277	6371

On this return Mr. Mayne very probably based his estimate of 1840.[1]

[1] While this work was passing through the press, we met with a recent publication by Wm. Acton, Esq., M.R.C S. of London, entitled "Prostitution considered in its Moral, Social, and Sanitary Aspects," which gives later information on this point. The Metropolitan Police estimated the number of prostitutes in London in 1841, and again in 1857, with the following results :

Mr Talbot, the secretary of the Society for the Protection of Young Females, made the subject one of special inquiry, both personally and with the aid of the local police of the different cities; and although his details are very meagre, he professes to have satisfied himself of the general accuracy of the following figures, showing the regular prostitutes in various cities.

Edinburgh 800	Leeds 700
Glasgow 1800	Manchester 700
Liverpool 2900	

All parties are, however, agreed in representing that it is impracticable to form anything like a correct estimate of " the number of female servants, milliners, and women in the upper and middle classes of society who might properly be classed with prostitutes, or of the women who frequent theatres, barracks, ships, etc."

In 1851, the police of Dublin published in their statistical returns the number of prostitutes in that city, which is the only public or official paper on the point having any appearance of system or accuracy. It is as follows:

1848 . . . . . Brothels 385	. . . . . Prostitutes 1343
1849 . . . . . " 330	. . . . . " 1344
1850 . . . . . " 272	. . . . . " 1215
1851 . . . . . " 297	. . . . . " 1170

This table shows a steady decrease in the number of these women. We are uninformed as to any local cause for this, nor do we know whether it has been balanced by an increase of " sly " or occasional prostitution.

From the preceding figures a calculation has been made of the regular prostitutes relatively to the population in the several towns. It appears to have been based on the number of inhabitants at the date of the various estimates. That of Dublin is according to the census of 1851, the remainder according to that of 1841.

	1841	1857
Well-dressed prostitutes in brothels........	2071	921
Well-dressed prostitutes walking the streets.	1994	2616
Prostitutes infesting low neighborhoods ..	5344	5063
Total	9409	8600

Mr. Acton says, " The return gives, after all, but a faint idea of the grand total of prostitution. * * * * Were there any possibility of reckoning all those in London who would come within the definition of prostitutes, I am inclined to think that the estimates of the boldest who have preceded me would be thrown into the shade."—P. 16-18.

PROPORTION OF PROSTITUTES TO POPULATION.

	Number of Prostitutes.	Proportion to Population.		
		To Males.	To Females.	To total Population.
Liverpool. ...	2900	1 to 43	1 to 45	1 to 88
Manchester ...	700	1 to 156	1 to 169	1 to 325
Leeds	700	1 to 70	1 to 75	1 to 145
Edinburgh....	800	1 to 106	1 to 130	1 to 236
Glasgow	1800	1 to 87	1 to 97	1 to 184
Dublin	1170	1 to 101	1 to 119	1 to 220
Cork [1]	350	1 to 113	1 to 134	1 to 247

The mean of the above may be taken as a fair representation of the general state of the kingdom. The qualifying circumstances to which we have already made allusion as peculiar to each city or district are, of course, neutralized by the aggregate.

For example, Liverpool is a great sea-port town, and a large number of regular prostitutes would be inevitable there. In Manchester, a large manufacturing city, with an immense pauper and factory operative population, the trade of prostitution would meet with less profitable custom; we find the proportion much smaller. Glasgow is both manufacturing and commercial; there, again, the proportion is larger. Dublin has but little commerce, but is a capital city, has a court and a large garrison. The combination of all these circumstances is found in London, and a fair estimate would be obtained by adding all the preceding proportions together, which would give a mean of about 1 in 232, and this upon the population (2,362,000) is within a fraction of ten thousand.

We have seen that Mr. Mayne in 1840 stated his opinion to be that there were about eight thousand regular prostitutes in London, qualifying that statement by a profession of total ignorance as to the irregulars who did not make prostitution their only means of living. Mr. Mayne had peculiar sources of information open to him, and it is more than probable that his opinion was well founded. From the above calculation, from the best sources available to us on this very obscure question, we are satisfied to assume ten thousand as at least a probable approximation to the number of *regular* prostitutes in London.

Mr. Mayne, in his statement on this subject, mentioned that

[1] An estimate of Cork was made in 1847 for the *Medico-Chirurgical Review*, which gave two hundred and fifty prostitutes living in eighty brothels, besides one hundred clandestine prostitutes. Their ages were stated as between sixteen and twenty years.

there were 3335 brothels. Some authors have attempted to make a calculation of the number of prostitutes on the basis of this number of houses; one has assumed three, another ten. Dr. Wardlaw has fixed upon five women per house, without, as it appears to us, any precise reason for preferring that figure. These different opinions may be thus worked out:

5 women in each house would give . . . . . 16,675 prostitutes.
4   "   "   "   (as in Dublin) would give 13,340   "
3   "   "   "   (as in Cork)   "   "   10,005   "

We have not been able to obtain Mr. Mayne's statement *ipsissimis verbis*, and failing that we may be in error, but we should be inclined to think that, in his official capacity as a magistrate, and in his personal character as a lawyer, Mr. Mayne would be apt to assign the term "brothel" indiscriminately to all houses trading in prostitution, whether houses of assignation or houses in which prostitutes habitually reside. If our reading of the word "brothels" in this sense be correct, it is clear that any attempt to enumerate on the basis of the women attached to each house would be fallacious. The expression used by the Dublin police is "houses frequented or occupied," and its ambiguity shows that the authorities there considered the word "brothel" in the sense given to it by English jurists.

How does this number of ten thousand regular prostitutes bear on the population?

In London there are, above twenty years of age,

	Male.	Female.
Bachelors	196,857	
Spinsters		246,124
Husbands	398,624	
Wives		406,266
Widowers	37,064	
Widows		110,028
Totals	632,545	762,418

Omitting fractions, the proportions would be,

On bachelors and widowers . . . . 1 in 23
  "   total male population . . . . 1 " 63
  "   "   female   "   . . . . 1 " 76
  "   aggregate population above twenty years of age 1 " 139

This would establish ten thousand as the nucleus of the prostitution system of London. Those females who come within the designation of "irregular prostitutes" are in no respect less prejudicial to the community than the "regulars." The difference is that they have some other real or nominal occupation, which they follow according to circumstances. An even moderately correct estimate of their number is little better than guess-work, and we therefore think it expedient to put our readers in possession of our own limited means of information, and take them on to a conclusion. There are so many elements to be taken into the account, and the data are so scanty, that we only consider ourselves justified in intimating an opinion rather than announcing a satisfactory conclusion.

To show the extremes to which the doctrine of possibilities may lead in this development of misery and vice, we will recur to the statement of some of the London prostitute needle-women themselves. We quote from Mayhew's letters to the Morning Chronicle:

"I now come to the second test that was adopted in order to verify my conclusions. This was the convening of such a number of needle-women and slop-workers as would enable me to arrive at a correct average as to the earnings of the class. I was particularly anxious to do this, not only with regard to the more respectable portions of the operatives, but also with reference to those who, I had been given to understand, resorted to prostitution in order to eke out their subsistence. I consulted a friend, who is well acquainted with the habits and feelings of slop-workers, as to the possibility of gathering together a number of women who would be willing to state that they had been forced to take to the streets on account of the low prices for their work.[1] He told me he was afraid, from the shame of their mode of life becoming known, it would be almost impossible to collect together a number of females who would be ready to say as much publicly. However, it was decided that at least the experiment should be made, and that every thing should be done to assure the parties of the strict privacy of the assemblage. It was arranged that this gentleman and myself should be the only male persons visible on the occasion, and that the place of meeting should be as dimly lighted as possible, so they could scarcely see or be seen by one another or by us. Cards of admission were issued privately, and, to my friend's astonishment, as many as twenty-five came on the evening named to the appointed place, intent upon making known the sorrows and sufferings that had driven them to fly to the streets, in order to get the bread which the wretched prices paid for their labor would not permit them to obtain.

"Never in all history was such a sight seen or such tales heard. There, in the dim haze of the large bare room in which they met, sat women and girls, some with babies sucking at their breasts, others in rags, and even those borrowed in order that they might come and tell their misery to the

---

[1] This may be deemed a foregone conclusion, but it was based upon previous inquiries in individual cases.

world. I have witnessed many a scene of sorrow lately ; I have heard stories that have unmanned me; but never, till last Wednesday, had I heard or seen any thing so solemn, so terrible as this. If ever eloquence was listened to, it was in the outpourings of these poor, lorn mothers' hearts for their base-born little ones, as each told her woes and struggles, and published her shame amid the convulsive sobs of others—nay, of all present. Behind a screen, removed from sight, so as not to wound the modesty of the women, who were nevertheless aware of their presence, sat two reporters from this journal, to take down *verbatim* the confessions and declarations of those assembled, and to them I am indebted for the following report of the statements made at the meeting."

Then follow a series of most heart-rending statements, all bearing all the internal evidence of truth. The letter concludes with the following sentence :

" They were unanimous in declaring that a large number of the trade—probably one fourth of the whole, or one half of those who had no husbands or parents to support them—resorted to the streets to eke out a living. Accordingly, assuming the government returns to be correct, and that there are upward of eleven thousand females under twenty living by needle and slop work,[1] the numerical amount of prostitution becomes awful to contemplate."

Thus, then, we have it in evidence that " probably " one fourth of all women engaged in sewing occupations for a livelihood are compelled to have occasional recourse to prostitution as their only and compulsory refuge from starvation.

The number of women engaged in these sewing occupations is enormous. According to the census of 1851, they constitute, indeed, the main support of the female working population throughout Great Britain, exclusive of domestic servants, laundresses, and persons employed in agricultural pursuits, and in the cotton and linen factories. The figures for the three kingdoms are as follows:

Hatters	3,500	Milliners	267,400
Straw-hat-makers	20,500	Seamstresses	72,900
Bonnet-makers	7,600	Stay-makers	12,700
Cap-makers	4,700	Stocking-makers	30,700
Furriers	1,900	Glovers	25,300
Tailors	17,600	Case-makers	31,400
Shawl-makers	3,200		

[1] We do not understand this figure. The sum of the sewing trades of London is nearly twenty times this number. Perhaps Mr. Mayhew refers only to slop-work, including the very commonest garments, both woolen and cotton, or even to that portion of the trade that have their principal abode in the particular localities visited.

In all Great Britain this class numbers 1,787,600
Of whom there are under twenty years of age . . .   458,168

We have not the details of the occupations of London, but the proportion which the population of the metropolis bears to that of Great Britain is about one ninth.   One ninth of the above aggregate would give for London about 196,500 women engaged in the sewing trades, all of whom, it may be assumed, are over fifteen.   We omit from the consideration of female trades those engaged in agricultural pursuits and factories, such occupations having comparatively few representatives in the metropolitan districts, although there are more of them than would be supposed. Laundresses are also omitted, as a very large proportion of them in and about London are, as is well known, married and middle-aged women.   But another class to which all writers assign a large amount of prostitution are domestic servants, a body most numerously represented in London.   There are in the metropolis 165,100 domestic servants, the peculiarly unprotected character of whom, as a class, may be inferred from the singular fact that to the work-house, the hospital, and the Lunatic Asylum they supply a number of inmates exceeding that of any other class.

Thus, then, are shown two very large figures, amounting together to 361,000, as the stock from which prostitutes to any extent may be procured.   Some consideration, perhaps, of the ages of prostitutes, and of other circumstances in the condition of the female population, may enable us to appreciate the state of the case without being driven to the necessity of looking on these enormous totals as incapable of reduction.

Nature would indicate the period between 15 and 45 as the age during which the trade of prostitution must be carried on. Much has been said as to the means used for decoying young children for purposes of prostitution.   Of the fact we are perfectly convinced, but should think it of little numerical importance in the aggregate body.   The influence of evil communication on the young is of infinitely greater mischief, and the extent of youthful depravity from this cause is very great among the poorer classes, and would oblige us to date the commencing age of prostitution back to twelve years.

As to the period of life at which the prostitute's career is terminated, it is contended by some of the English writers that only an infinitesimal proportion reach the age of forty-five in the exercise of their soul and health destroying trade. Mr. Tait says, " In less than one year from the commencement of their wicked career these females bear evident marks of their approaching decay, and in the course of three years very few can be recognized by their old acquaintance, if they are so fortunate as to survive that period. These remarks apply more especially to those who are above twenty years of age when they join the ranks of the victims." From the average of Edinburgh, Mr. Tait goes on to assume that " not above one in eleven survives twenty-five years of age ; and taking together those who persist in vice, and those who, after having abandoned it, die of diseases which originated from the excesses they were addicted to during its continuance, perhaps not less than a fifth or sixth of all who have embraced this course of sin die annually." Dr. Ryan seems to adopt an opinion that the average duration of life after commencing prostitution is four years.[1] Captain Miller, of Glasgow, thinks that " the average age at which women become abandoned is from fifteen to twenty, and the average duration of women continuing this vice is about five years."

The ages of patients admitted into the Lock Hospital at Edinburgh were as follows :

Under 15 years 42	From 30 years to 35 years	16
From 15 years to 20 years 662	" 35 " " 40 "	6
" 20 " " 25 " 199	Over 40 years 6	
" 25 " " 30 " 69		
Total 1000		

These figures alone would go to make out the presumption that the ages of prostitutes are between twelve and thirty, and that $\frac{861}{1000}$ are between fifteen and twenty-five. According to the above table, nine tenths of the number at twenty have disappeared at thirty, and as cases of reform and abandonment of their life are very rare, the conclusion would be that their career ends in death.[2]

[1] The reader will notice that neither Dr. Ryan, Mr. Tait, nor the views as to the duration of life expressed in the portion of this work devoted to New York, agree with those German authors who have asserted the healthfulness of prostitution. See Chapter XVI , Hamburg.

[2] At the meeting in London to which allusion has been made, Mr. Acton (late Surgeon to the Islington Dispensary and Fellow of the Royal Medical Society) said that, "in his opinion, the subject under discussion was one worth legislating for. As a surgeon, he had investigated the subject not only in London, but in Paris and other Continental capitals, and he could speak with some authority as to the statistics of prostitution, and the manner in which the women became, as it were, absorbed in the population by whom they were surrounded. *From calculations based upon the census tables, it had come out that of all the unmarried women of full age in*

The duration of prostitution being ascertained, we would find the number of women between the ages of fifteen and twenty-five. In the whole female population this is one fifth, but the very aged or the very youthful are necessarily excluded from the classes of work-women and servants; of servants, indeed, there are five and upward under twenty to three above twenty years of age. This, therefore, would indicate very little reduction of the numbers.

It is reasonable to suppose that some portion of the above are married women having husbands living, and if so, it is not an unreasonable supposition that their wives are not obliged to have recourse to prostitution: in fact, the poor creatures themselves seem to imply that immunity. The number of wives is about one third of the whole female population; of these wives about one fourth are employed in trades apart from those of their husbands. If we deduct only such a proportion from the sewing-women, it makes something when we have to deal with such enormous masses; we should strike off nearly 50,000, leaving only 150,000 sewing-women.

There is comfort, however, in the fact that, of these sewing-

the country one in every 13 or 14 were immoral. This might appear a startling announcement, but the calculation had been made upon returns, the truth of which had not been questioned. It was a popular error to suppose that these women died young, and made their exits from life in hospitals and work-houses. The fact was not so. Women of that class were all picked lives, and dissipation did not usually kill them. They led a life of prostitution for two, three, or four years, and then either married or got into some service or employment, and gradually became amalgamated with society. It was estimated that in this manner about 25 per cent. of the whole number amalgamated each year with the population."

From these remarks we may deduce the same continuance of a life of prostitution as given in the text, namely, an average of four years; but they advance another theory as to its termination, substituting reformation for death. That cases of reformation do take place, and probably to a greater extent than is generally imagined, can not be denied; but that one fourth of the total number of prostitutes abandon their sinful life every year, and become virtuous members of society, is a conclusion that American experience will not support. In England and on the European continent there may be a class of men in the lower ranks of life who do not regard virtue as a *sine qua non* in the choice of a wife; indeed, the notorious facility with which the cast-off mistresses of noblemen or gentlemen can be married to a dependent sufficiently proves this; but in this country public opinion sets strongly in the opposite direction. Here, if a woman once errs, or is even suspected of error, she is rigorously excluded from virtuous society, and, although her subsequent life may be irreproachable, the lapse is seldom forgiven. The old Roman law, "Once a prostitute, always a prostitute," is too sternly enforced on this side of the Atlantic. Mr. Acton's speech is the first intimation we have met of so very liberal a benevolence in England.

women, three fourths are known to be over twenty years of age ; and if we assume one half instead of three fourths, allowing the other fourth for the difference between twenty and twenty-five years of age, it brings our figure to seventy-five thousand.

All these deductions are, we fear, in excess ; and it must be recollected, moreover, that the above large sums by no means include all the female occupations of London,[1] but merely those classes which, either from the temptation incident to their position, or from the imperative demands of want and necessity, are, by competent authority, supposed to be peculiarly obnoxious to the risk of prostitution. If to this large number of women, which we can not assume at less than 273,000 between the ages of twelve and twenty-five, be added all the other denizens of a great city unexampled in its magnitude, embracing in itself all the peculiarities of all other cities, at once a manufacturing, a commercial, a garrison, and a capital city, and, finally, containing the largest population in the world, one such item being nearly four hundred thousand single females over twelve years of age, then, indeed, the mass of misery, wretchedness, vice, and crime there accumulated appals the mind seeking to grapple with it, and oppresses us with the apprehension that even eighty thousand, the highest estimate which has been made, is, when understood to include all contingencies, not an incredible figure.[2]

Englishmen pride themselves, and, it must be admitted, not without reason, on their numerous and admirable public charities. In this particular direction it would seem that public munificence has not been so liberally displayed as in some others. "Joy shall be in heaven over one sinner that repenteth more than over ninety and nine just persons," does not, we fear, apply to minds and hearts of earthly mould. People, in charitable as in other institutions, like to see a return for their investment ; and, not-

[1] We have calculated that there are upward of six hundred thousand women in London between fifteen and forty-five years old. The proportion of married women among these would be 370,000 and upward ; unmarried women over twenty years, and widows, about 314,000.

[2] A very singular fact in connection with the census is that there is not a single individual returned as a prostitute. This is not that the authorities do not take cognizance of crime, for there are 22,451 female prisoners in Great Britain, all of whom, however, except 1274, are returned as having some legal occupation. There are 7600 female vagrants, sleeping in barns, tents, etc., of whom 2600 are under twenty years of age.

withstanding the immense field for benevolent labor in prostitu.
tion, there is a general impression among both the public and officials that it is an irretrievably barren waste, and that it is worse
than profitless to squander money and time upon it.   The results
which have been achieved would, however, show that the exertions of philanthropy, although not producing so much fruit as
in some other quarters, have not been entirely vain.   In reference to these results, too, it must be borne in mind that the discipline of the various institutions is severe, and even repellent,
a policy ill adapted to insure a large amount of success.

The Lock Hospital is the oldest institution in London for the
benefit of lost females, and is devoted entirely to the cure of
venereal disease.   It was founded in the year 1747, and in a
century had cured 45,448 cases.

The Magdalen Hospital of London, founded in 1758, up to January, 1844, had received 6968 females.   The results were these:

Reconciled to their friends, or placed in service or other
   reputable employment 4752
Discharged at their own request 1183
     "   for improper conduct 720
Died 109
Sent to other institutions (being insane or afflicted with in-
   curable diseases) 107
Eloped 2
Remaining in the hospital 96
              Total 6968

A considerable number of the women, when discharged from
the institution, are under twenty years of age; and it is an invariable rule not to dismiss any one (unless at her own desire,
or for misconduct) without some means being provided by which
she may obtain a livelihood in an honest manner.

The Lock Asylum was founded in 1787, for the reception of
penitent female patients when discharged from the Lock Hospital; and up to March, 1837, the number of women received was
984.   The results were:

Reconciled to their friends 170
Placed in service or employment 281
Died 22
Remaining in Asylum 18
            Total 491

Of the remaining number, many had been sent to their parishes;

some had eloped, and some had been expelled for improper conduct, but of several of even of these favorable accounts had been afterward received : some of them were known to be married, and living creditably, and others were earning a living honestly. We have been unable to obtain any account of the operations of this institution since the year 1837.

The London Female Penitentiary was instituted in 1807. Of 6939 applicants, 2717 were admitted into the house. The results were :

Reconciled and restored to friends, placed in service, or
    otherwise provided for 1543
Discharged from various causes 631
    "   at their own request 350
Emigrated 47
Sent to their parishes 23
Died 28
Remaining in Penitentiary 95
                 Total 2717

The Guardian Society was established in 1812, and from that period up to 1843 had admitted 1932 wretched outcasts to partake of the advantages it offered. The results were :

Restored to their friends 533
Placed in service, or satisfactorily provided for 455
Discharged or withdrawn 843
Sent to their parishes 53
Died 17
Remaining in institution 31
                 Total 1932

Besides these institutions, others have been established with similar objects, namely, The British Penitent Female Refuge, The Female Mission, The South London Penitentiary, and one or two others. As compared with the great number of unfortunate women in London, these institutions have effected but a very small amount of good. During seventy-seven years, ending 1835, ten thousand and five females were received within the walls of four of the London asylums, of which number six thousand two hundred and sixty-two (more than three fifths) were satisfactorily provided for, and two thousand nine hundred and eighty were discharged for misconduct. Taking the whole of the institutions in London up to that time, it may be fairly estimated that fourteen or fifteen thousand prostitutes have had the opportunity of returning to a virtuous life.

Those who, like the Pharisee, content themselves with thanking

God that they are not as other men, and even as these unfortunates, are a very impracticable set to deal with, and if such there
be who read these pages, we pass them by, and pray for the better
health of their souls. The gentle spirits who, imitating a blessed
example, think it not pollution to extend their sympathy and
saving help to publicans and harlots, may, in the following lines,
written by a prostitute and found in her death-bed, see matter
for meditation, and ground for the belief that all efforts in the
cause of the sinner will not be unsuccessful. They were headed

"VERSES FOR MY TOMB-STONE, IF EVER I SHOULD HAVE ONE.

"The wretched victim of a quick decay,
　　Relieved from life, on humble bed of clay,
　　The last and only refuge for my woes,
　　A love-lost, ruined female, I repose.
　　From the sad hour I listened to his charms,
　　And fell, half forced, in the deceiver's arms,
　　To that whose awful veil hides every fault,
　　Sheltering my sufferings in this welcome vault,
　　When pampered, starved, abandoned, or in drink,
　　My thoughts were racked in striving not to think !
　　Nor could rejected conscience claim the power
　　To improve the respite of one serious hour.
　　I durst not look to what I was before ;
　　My soul shrank back, and wished to be no more.
　　Of eye undaunted, and of touch impure,
　　Old ere of age, worn out when scarce mature ;
　　Daily debased to stifle my disgust
　　Of forced enjoyment in affected lust ;
　　Covered with guilt, infection, debt, and want,
　　My home a brothel, and the streets my haunt,
　　For seven long years of infamy I've pined,
　　And fondled, loathed, and preyed upon mankind,
　　Till, the full course of sin and vice gone through,
　　My shattered fabric failed at twenty-two."

The enormous extent of this evil, its deep-rooted causes, the difficulty of combating it, either by religious arguments, legislative
provisions, or appeals to common sense and physical welfare, may
well deter the philanthropist from the attempt to purify the sta-
ble of Augeas ; but benevolence has accomplished tasks as arduous, and we can not conclude this chapter better than by a short
description of the discouragements which attended the first efforts

of Mrs. Fry in the reformation of the prostitute felons in Newgate, and of the blessed results of her indomitable perseverance and immovable faith.[1]

This admirable woman, on her first visit to Newgate, found the female side of the jail in a condition which no language can describe: "Nearly three hundred women, sent there for every gradation of crime, and some under sentence of death, were crowded together in two small wards and two cells. They all slept, as well as a crowd of children, on the floor, at times one hundred and twenty in a ward, without even a mat for bedding. Many of them were nearly naked. They were all drunk, and her ears were offended by the most terrible imprecations." The authorities of the prison, of course, advised her against going among them: *they were sure that nothing could be effected!* She, however, determined to make the trial; she went alone into what she felt was like a den of wild beasts. In vain the governor reasoned with her: "She had put her hand to the plow and was not to be turned back." In one short month, such was the effect of her merely *moral agency* and religious instruction, that she felt herself justified in inviting the lord-mayor, the sheriffs, and several of the aldermen to satisfy themselves, by personal investigation, of the result of the exertions which she herself and some few lady members of the Society of Friends, who had joined her in the good work, had effected.

Thus was conviction forced upon the obtuse intellects of corporate authorities, and hence was dated the era of Prison Reform in England.

In our own country, where the means of diffusing intelligence are unbounded, and whose reformatory system for criminals has already claimed the attention of European statesmen and philanthropists, there can be no insuperable barrier even in so difficult an undertaking as that to which our labors are directed. Paraphrasing the opinion of one of the most distinguished essayists of this century,[2] we venture to assert that "it is impossible that social abuses should be suffered to exist in this country and in this stage of society for many years after their mischief and iniquity have been made manifest to the sense of the country at large."

[1] Thomas Fowell Ruxton, on Prison Discipline.
[2] Lord Jeffrey, Edinburgh Review.

Z

CHAPTER XXVI.

GREAT BRITAIN.—SYPHILITIC DISEASES.

First Recognition in England.—Regulations of Henry VI.—Lazar Houses.—John of Gaddesden.—Queen Elizabeth's Surgeon.—Popular Opinions.—Proclamation of James IV. of Scotland.—Middlesex and London Hospitals.—Army.—Navy.—Merchant Service.—St. Bartholomew's Hospital.—Estimated Extent of Syphilis.

THE best English and French writers are of opinion that syphilis, as it exists at present, has, in some shape or another, always existed among mankind, although it was not known to science or history, in a distinct manner, until the middle of the fifteenth century.

The period at which syphilis first made its appearance in England is involved in obscurity, but we know that it began to attract attention early in the fifteenth century. The first official recognition of it found on record is a police regulation of the year 1430, during the reign of Henry VI., excluding venereal patients from the London hospitals, and requiring them to be strictly guarded at night. In the time of Henry VIII. there were six lazar houses in London for the reception of venereal patients, namely, at Knightsbridge, Hammersmith, Highgate, Kingsland, St. George's Gate, and Mile-End. These localities were doubtless fixed upon as being some distance from the city.

That the disease, however, must have been known long before the period above specified is certain, from passages which are to be found in the writings of the previous century. John of Gaddesden, who wrote in 1305, and who was a Fellow of Merton College, Oxford, thus speaks of the possibility of contracting the disease from leprous women: "Ille qui concubuit cum muliere cum qua coivit leprosas puncturas intra carnem et corium sentil et aliquando calefactiones in toto corpore."[1] Mr. Wm. Acton, upon whose pages as an English standard writer on this subject we draw largely, is of opinion that leprosy, which was formerly so common in Europe, consisted merely of what we now call secondary syphilis. Some of the Jewish observances were no doubt dictated by a scientific appreciation of the influences which predisposed the body to the effects of syphilitic virus. The practice

Rosa Anglica, Pavia, 1492.

of circumcision seems instituted with a direct view to the preservation of the chosen people from venereal contagion, to which, in a hot climate, and with the extreme deficiency of means for general cleanliness, they would be liable.

As to the type of the disease in former times, there seems no ground for believing that it was more severe than at present, while its numerical importance must have been much smaller. The following extract is from a treatise by Queen Elizabeth's surgeon:

"If I be not deceived in my opinion, I suppose the disease itself was never more rife in Naples, Italie, France, or Spain, than it is in this day in the realme of England. I may speak boldly because I speak truly ; and yet I speake it with grief of minde, that in the Hospital of St. Bartholomew, in London, there hath been cured of this disease by me and three others, within five years, to the number of one thousand and more. I speak nothing of St. Thomas's Hospital, and other houses about the citie, wherein an infinite number are daily cured. It happened very seldom in the Hospital of St. Bartholomew while I staid there, among every twenty diseased that were taken into the said house, which was most commonly on the Monday, ten of them were infected with the *lues venerea.*"[1]

It was supposed, in former ages, that syphilis was transmissible by personal communication, touching the clothes, drinking out of the same vessels, or even breathing the same air with infected persons, and accordingly we find the lower orders of people driven out into the fields to die, and physicians refusing to attend the sick for fear of infection.

Some writers, indeed, doubted this kind of contagious influence, and held that it required intercourse, or at least contact. But nobles, and especially the clergy, preferred to ascribe their maladies to misfortune rather than to licentiousness, and sought to "put down" such innovating doctrines. The consequence was that patients were shunned universally, and left to die or get well without assistance. It is not to be wondered at, therefore, that in numerous instances the disease should assume its most inveterate aspect, and hence the notices found among many old writers as to the supposed malignancy and incurability of what they were disposed to consider a newly-imported malady. That the disease, in reality, differed little from that which exists in our day, is proved by the fact that cases of the once formidable Black Lion are occasionally to be met with in the London hospitals.

[1] A brief treatise touching the cure of the disease now usually called Lues Venerea. By W. Clovves, one of her Majesty's Chirurgeons. 1569: p. 149.

Cardinal Wolsey, among other charges made against him by his enemies, was accused of whispering to the king, Henry VIII., and thereby casting his poisonous breath upon his royal grace, he (Wolsey) having at the time "the foul contagious disease" upon him. The belief as to contagion by this means is not entirely extinct, but is cherished by the laboring classes of England, many of whom entertain great prejudices on the score of health against drinking from the same vessel out of which an infected person has partaken.

In 1497, James IV. of Scotland, in consequence of the frightful prevalence of venereal disease in his kingdom, issued a proclamation banishing the infected from Edinburgh. His majesty "charges straitly all manner of persons being within the freedom of this burt, quilks are infectit, or has been infectit, uncurit with this said contagious plague, callit the grandgor devoyd, red and pass furt of this town, and compeir upon the sandis of Leith at ten hours before none; and thair sall thai have and find boatis reddie in the havin ordainit to them by the officers of this burt, reddy furneist with victuals, to have them to the Inche (Inchkeith), and thair to remain quhill God provyd for thair health." Those evading this ordinance "salle be byrnt on the cheik with the marking irne, that thai may be kennit in tym to cum."

A remnant of this barbarous system was retained in the regulations of Middlesex Hospital, London, by which an admission fee of forty shillings sterling (ten dollars) was directed to be paid by venereal patients. The reason assigned for it was, that a hospital intended for the virtuous might not be made subsidiary to purposes of vice. The regulation, however, became a nullity, and was repealed, owing principally to the fact that the work-house guardians were in the habit of paying the forty shillings and sending in pauper patients, well knowing that the cost of cure in the work-house would far exceed the admission fees.

In the London Hospital a similar regulation exists even now, but is openly evaded, however, by the house surgeon describing the disease as a cutaneous one.

The extent of this disease in Great Britain is matter of opinion alone. There are no positive data whatever upon which to form any conclusion with respect to the general population, while the hospital lists are very imperfectly kept, and it is only in the army and navy returns that we can find any real assistance.

BRITISH ARMY.

The army reports quoted extend over a period of seven years and a quarter, and enter into the details of the various venereal affections of the soldiers, amounting to the aggregate strength of 44,611 quartered in the United Kingdom. The cases admitted into hospitals were:

Syphilis Primary	1415	Gonorrhœa	2449
" Consecutive	335	Hernia Humoralis	714
Ulcer Penis non Syphiliticum	2144	Stricture Urethra	100
Bubo Simplex	844	Phymosis and Paraphymosis	27
Cachexia Syphilitica	44	Total	8072

Ratio: 181 per 1000 men, or nearly one in five in the whole number.

These returns show that the venereal disease is of much more frequent occurrence in the British than in the Belgian army.

BRITISH NAVY.

The navy reports extend over a period of seven years, and include 21,493 men, employed on home service; that is to say, on the coasts or in the ports of Great Britain. Of this number, 2880 were attacked with venereal disease. Ratio: one in seven.

BRITISH MERCHANT SERVICE.

The returns of the "Dreadnought," hospital ship for seamen of all nations, extend over a period of five years, during which 13,081 patients, laboring under surgical and medical diseases, were admitted. Out of these, 3703 came under treatment for venereal affections, showing a ratio of two in seven.

As a mode of testing these returns, we turn to the analysis of the surgical out-patients of Messrs. Lloyd and Wormald, assistant surgeons of Saint Bartholomew's, the largest of the London hospitals. These out-patients are attended gratuitously by the hospital officers:

Attended by	Venereal Cases.		
	Men.	Women and Children.	Total.
Mr. Lloyd	1009	245	1254
Mr. Wormald	986	273	1259
Total	1995	518	2513

These cases were part of a total of 5327 general patients.

This last item alone would not enable one to form any idea of the number of sufferers from this terrible scourge. There are in

London nine great hospitals, besides smaller ones, and dispensaries in every parish, or division of a large parish, and other means of gratuitous medical assistance.   Suppose the smaller medical foundations put aside, and their patients thrown into the aggregate of the great hospitals, we should have 22,617 venereal patients.   Suppose the private practice of the London army of medical men to yield only half as many more, we have 35,000 venereal patients in London only.   Without reckoning the Lock Hospital, parish doctors, barracks, and all the other institutions, one would very readily imagine that London alone furnished 50,000 venereal patients per annum.

Again, on the number of single men and widowers in London above twenty years of age (upward of a quarter of a million), the venereal cases, if in the same proportion as among soldiers and sailors, would in the same period amount to 30,000 and upward.

There is, however, another way of conjecturing the amount of disease introduced into the community by prostitution, which English writers have adopted.   The Medico-Chirurgical Review, a periodical of high standing, speaking of the extent of venereal disease and its effects on the population, says :

" There is every reason to believe that, to represent the public prostitutes of England, Wales, and Scotland, fifty thousand is an estimate too low.   We presume there will be no objection made to the assumption that, unless each of these fifty thousand prostitutes submitted to at least one act of intercourse during every twenty-four hours, she could not obtain means sufficient to support life.   The result of the evidence contained in the first report of the Constabulary force of England was that about two per cent. of the prostitutes of London were suffering under some form of venereal disease.   But yet we will descend even lower, and presume that of one hundred healthy prostitutes, if each submits to one indiscriminate sexual act in twenty-four hours, not more than one would become infected with syphilis ; an estimate which is, without doubt, far too low, yet, if admitted to be correct, the necessary consequence will be, that of the fifty thousand prostitutes, five hundred are diseased within the aforesaid twenty-four hours.

" If we next admit that a fifth of these five hundred diseased women are admitted to hospitals on the day on which disease appears, it follows there are every day on the streets four hundred diseased women.   Let it be supposed that the power of these four hundred to infect be limited to twelve days, and that of every six persons who, at the rate of one each night, have connection with these women, five become infected, it will follow that *there will be four thousand men infected every night, and, consequently, one million four hundred and sixty thousand in the year.*   Farther, as there are every night four hundred women diseased by these men, one hundred and eighty-two thousand five hundred public prostitutes will be syphilized during the year, and hence *one million, six hundred and fifty-two thousand, five hundred cases of syphilis in both sexes occur every twelve months.* If, then, the entire population had intercourse with prostitutes in an equal ratio, the gross population of Great Britain, of all ages and sexes, would, during eighteen years, have been affected with primary syphilis. Be it remembered, we do not assert that more than a million and a half of persons are attacked every year, but that that number of cases occur annually in England, Wales, and Scotland, though the same individual may be attacked more than once. Although it is evident that all the estimates used for these calculations are (we know no other word that expresses it) ridiculously low, yet we find that more than a million and a half cases of syphilis occur every year, an amount which is probably not half the actual number. How enormous, then, must be the number of children born with secondary syphilis! how immense the mortality among them! how vast an amount of public and private money expended in the cure of this disease!"

CHAPTER XXVII.

MEXICO.

Spanish Conquest.—Treatment of Female Prisoners.—Mexican Manners in 1677.—Priesthood.—Modern Society.—Fashionable Life.—Indifference of Husbands to their Wives.—General Immorality.—Offenses.—Charitable Institutions.—The Cuna, or Foundling Hospital.

THE social condition of Mexico is of importance, as it was formerly the chief seat of Spanish domination in America, and its manners and government gave the key to all the other colonies and viceroyalties which owed allegiance to the crown of Spain. Whatever the state of the native population may have been when Spanish leaders and their myrmidons burst upon them, and broke up the kingdom of the Mexican emperors, they rapidly succumbed beneath the lust, avarice, and cruelty which were ever the distinctive features of Spanish warfare and conquest in every clime and against every people. Of the enormities perpetrated by these soldiers, the history of the Mexican conquest gives us innumerable instances; but one solitary example, from Bernal de Diaz, will be enough. He tells us that when they took women prisoners, they made a division of them at night for the sake of greater peace and quietness, and that they branded them with the marks of their owners. They were thus at liberty to choose the hand-somest of the Indian women, and reserve them for their own uses. What these uses were can be easily supposed. The fate of less fa-vored female prisoners is left in doubt; they were turned over to their savage allies, to be butchered in cold blood, or otherwise dis-posed of as most convenient.

From Mexico the flood of Spanish cruelty and immorality spread itself like a stream of lava over the whole of South America. The chivalry of the soldiery soon degenerated, and the self-denial and lofty motives, darkened though they were by bigotry and cruelty in some cases, which had distinguished the priests, were lost. In-glorious ease and luxurious indolence now superseded that love of adventure and unconquerable daring which distinguished Cor-tez and Pizarro, and their comrades: no trace of the old heroic character remained save the grinding oppression and reckless sel-fishness which usually accompany ambition.

An illustration of the loosè manners which prevailed in Mexico among the clergy is to be found in the voyages of Thomas Page, a Dominican monk, who visited Mexico with some of his order on their road to the western coast of America and to Asia as mis-sionaries.

From this work, published in 1677, we learn that the writer and his companions visited the prior of Vera Cruz on their jour-ney, and, after a sumptuous dinner, adjourned, by invitation, to his cell. They found it richly tapestried and adorned with feathers of the birds of Michoacou; the walls were hung with various pic-tures of merit; rich rugs of silk covered the tables; porcelain of China filled the cupboards and sideboards, and there were vases and bowls containing preserved fruits and sweetmeats. "My companions," says he, "were scandalized by such an exhibition. The holy friar talked to us of his ancestry, of his good parts, of the influence he had with the Father Provincial, of the love the principal ladies of the place bore him, of his beautiful voice and skill in music. He took his guitar and sang us a sonnet in praise of a certain lady." Afterward, speaking of the Franciscans of Jalapa, Thomas Page says: "Their lives are so free and immodest that it might be suspected with reason that they had renounced only that which they could not obtain." After witnessing a gam-bling scene in a convent, he concludes that "the cause of so many Friars and Jesuits passing from Spain to regions so distant was libertinage rather than love of preaching the Gospel."

The same writer subsequently passes from portraiture to more general delineation, and thus depicts the body of the clergy: "It seems that all wickedness is allowable, so that the churches and clergy flourish. Nay, while the purse is open to lasciviousness, if it be also open to enrich the temple walls and roof, it is better than any holy water. . . . . . In their lifetime the Mexicans strive to excel one another in their gifts to the cloisters of nuns and friars."

"Among the benefactors was one, Alonzo Cuellar, so rich that he was reported to have a closet in his house laid with bars of gold instead of bricks. This man built a nunnery for Franciscan nuns, which cost him thirty thousand ducats, and left to it two thousand dollars yearly. And yet his life was so scandalous that commonly in the night, with two servants, he would go round the city visiting scandalous persons, and at every house letting fall a bead and tying a knot, that when he came home in the morning, he might number, by his beads, the uncivil stations he had visited that night.

"Great alms and liberality toward religious houses are coupled with great and scandalous wickedness. They wallow in the bed of riches and wealth, and make their alms the coverlet to conceal their loose and lascivious lives. . . . .

"I will not speak much of the lives of the friars and nuns of this city, but only that they enjoy there more liberty than in Europe, where they have too much, and that surely the scandals committed by them do cry up to heaven for vengeance, judgment, and destruction.

"It is ordinary for the friars to visit their devoted nuns, and to spend whole days with them, hearing their music and feeding on their sweetmeats. For this purpose they have many chambers, which they call loquatories, to talk in, with wooden bars between the nuns and them, and in these chambers are tables for the friars to dine at, and while they dine the nuns recreate them with their voices."

We need no addition to these deep shadows from the dark pencil of so vigorous a limner as worthy Thomas Page, to delineate character nearly two hundred years ago, but we can scarcely believe it equally applicable to the present day. The reign of oppression in Mexico, it is to be hoped, is approaching its end, and recent events have shown that the population is alive to some of those truths which were long ago patent to all the world except those most intimately concerned.

Of modern Mexican society, an accomplished female writer, who had the best opportunities of judging, says:

"It is long before a stranger even suspects the state of morals in this

country, for, whatever be the private conduct of individuals, the most perfect decorum prevails in outward behavior.   But indolence is the mother of
vice.   They rarely gossip to strangers about their neighbors' faults.   Habit
has rendered them tolerably indifferent as to the *liaisons* subsisting among
particular friends, and as long as a woman attends church regularly, is a
patroness of charitable institutions, and gives no scandal by her outward behavior, she may do pretty much as she pleases.   As for flirtations in public,
they are unknown."[1]

The present amiability of the Mexican ladies is admitted on all
hands, as is the genial warmth of their manner.   Some travelers,
indeed, and among them Mr. Waddy Thompson, are of opinion
that this is attributed to them as a fault, and that the reproach of
unchastity is unjustly urged against them, as there is no city in
Europe where there is less immorality.   The constant presence of
a duenna, and the house-porter, who is an appurtenance of every
household of respectability, are excellent checks on immorality.
But this would rather argue the necessity of a safeguard not found
in the female virtue of Mexico.   Besides, these appendages of rank
have lost their real meaning, and the duenna may be converted
into the convenient cloak or abettor of an intrigue, the more safe
as she is the supposed protectress of the husband's honor.   A native writer, in summing up the character of his countrymen, says
that "they are moderate in eating, but their passion for liquor is
carried to the greatest excess.   The affection which husbands
bear their wives is certainly much less than that borne by wives
to their husbands, and *it is very common for the men to love their
neighbors' wives better than their own.*"[2]   This one-sided censure
presupposes, as a necessary consequence, that the neighbors' wives
must show some reciprocity.

The general immorality of the lower classes in Mexico would
almost exclude the expectation of a system of prostitution, as we
usually understand the term.   Puebla, a manufacturing town near
Mexico, is summarily described as having a most devout female
population, and a most abandoned one; but this is matter of conduct rather than of calling.   The enumeration of offenses in the
justice list of Mexico does not tell of one prostitute, although it
contains a large number of persons guilty of "incontinence."   The
exact meaning of this offense, in its legal and technical sense, is
not given us, but we presume it relates to improper and disgusting practices.   The charge of "violation of public decency," al-

---

[1] Madame Calderon de la Barca.   [2] Clavijero.

though it may relate to mutual familiarities, will probably include both indecency and immorality.

The following table gives the number of persons arrested in the city of Mexico in 1851.

Offenses.	Males.	Females.	Total.
Drunkenness	1256	1944	3200
Affrays and wounds.................	728	246	974
Incontinence	354	403	757
Violations of public decency	311	318	629
Robbery	384	120	504
Suspicion of robbery	180	84	264
Carrying weapons	209	85	294
Picking pockets	120	25	145
False pretenses	39	17	56
Breaking prison	36	...	36
Murder	15	3	18
Total.................	3632	3245	6877

Among a population of inferior intellect, and with the excess of women always to be found in tropical countries, the character of the priesthood becomes of primary importance. On this particular, some writers are of opinion that what was written in 1677 will apply with almost equal force in the present day; a position certainly open to doubt.[1]

The lower orders of the priests and friars in Mexico are generally uneducated and frequently licentious. The most revolting spectacles of vice and immorality are exhibited by some of them. They are remarkable for the *roue* appearance they present, but they can not be considered types of the class, for the higher orders and respectable members of the priesthood are exempt from the imputation of such flagrant immorality. Even these are not blameless members of the Church. Many of them have nephews and nieces in their houses, or at least those who call them uncle, but to whom scandal ascribes a closer relationship.

Among the charitable institutions in Mexico, perhaps the most important is the *Cuna*, or Foundling Hospital. It is supported by private individuals, and the members of the society consist of the first persons in the capital, male and female. The men furnish the money; the women give their time and attention. When a child has been about a month in the hospital, it is sent with an Indian nurse to one of the adjacent villages; but if sick or feeble, it remains in the institution, under the immediate inspection of the society. These nurses are subject to a responsible person, who lives in the village and answers for their good conduct. The child

[1] Waddy Thompson, Mexico in 1846, p. 115.

is brought back to the hospital when weaned, and remains in its charge for life. Few, however, are left to grow up in the asylum; they are adopted by respectable persons, who bring them up either as servants or as their own children. In this, as in other institutions of the same character, the mothers of the children often get themselves hired as nurses. There are usually five or six hundred children in this asylum.[1]

CHAPTER XXVIII.

CENTRAL AND SOUTH AMERICA.

Low moral Condition.—San Salvador.—Guatemala.—Yucatan.—Costa Rica.—Honduras.—The Caribs.—Depravity in Peru and Chili.—"Children of the House."—Intrigue in Lima.—Infanticide.—Laxity of Morals in Brazil and Paraguay.—Foundling Hospital at Rio Janeiro.

THE whole peninsula of South America, and the states comprised in Central America, are involved in the same social system with Mexico, derived as they are by common origin from pure or mixed Spanish blood. The same political circumstances and organization have always affected the various territorial divisions, and whether we consider the semi-civilized nations of ancient Peru and its dependencies, or the savage tribes in the valleys of the Amazon and the La Plata, we find them, after the first irruption of Spanish conquerors, victims of indiscriminate oppression, insatiable avarice, and unsparing lust. South America was long considered a mere treasure-field of the Spanish monarchy, to be worked without liability to account by every adventurer who chose to encounter the hardships of foreign travel, or the perils of residence in a tropical climate and amid hostile savages.

The natives far outnumbered their masters, and the same ruthless system of depression was extended to them as to Mexico. The consequence was, that before the lapse of many generations from the Conquest, there were but two classes throughout the vast Spanish territories—masters and slaves. The natural and inevitable result of servile institutions could not long be postponed. The descendants of the conquerors rapidly degenerated, and imbecility and incapacity took the places of heroism and ability. The original hardihood and daring, which had vanquished uncounted enemies, had traversed unknown wilds, had defied every

[1] Madame Calderon de la Barca, p. 259.

danger, were lost in voluptuousness and self-indulgence. The posterity of those men who had discovered a new world, and swayed the destinies of the old by a nod or the stroke of a pen, were unable to protect themselves against the weak ministers of a worn-out despotism, or against any unscrupulous demagogue who could rally a band or roving Indians around him, and maraud the peaceable and well-disposed. A state of political degradation reigned supreme over the whole of South America, only to be paralleled by the debasement of its social condition.

In Central America, including San Salvador, Guatemala, Yucatan, Costa Rica, and Honduras, the condition of the women is very much the same as in Mexico. The statements of travelers in those little-frequented regions are very vague in reference to the subject of public morality, and give us no reliable or detailed information on the specialities which would be of service in this inquiry. In Yucatan, the ladies are said to be somewhat more domesticated than their Mexican neighbors, and to interest themselves in the management of their households and the education of their children; but still the standard of morality is not very high, if measured by United States habits and ideas.[1] In the neighboring republic of Guatemala, the free manners prevalent in the country districts of the kindred territories are usually met with;[2] but these would rather indicate low ideas of decency than any actual immorality. Difference of climate and of race would make many things tolerable, or even reputable, which our colder skies and more rigid notions would totally exclude from the observances of civilized society.

The Indian populations of South America have become so completely slaves during long years of bondage that they have lost their prominent characteristics,[3] and are but a reflex of their mas-

---

[1] Norman, Yucatan. [2] Stevens, Travels in Central America.

[3] Among the Napuals, a remnant of the ancient Aztec inhabitants, marriage seems to have been under the direction of the chiefs, and consisted in first submitting the parties to lustrations, such as washing them in a river, and afterward tying them together in the bride's house, whither the relations brought presents to the new couple.

It was customary for only the kindred to lament the death of ordinary persons, but the decease of a cazique or war-chief was signalized by a general mourning for four days. Rape was punished with death, adultery by making the offender the slave of the injured husband, "unless pardoned by the high-priest on account of past services in war." There were certain degrees of relationship within which it was unlawful to marry, and sexual intercourse in such limits was punished with death. Upon matters of this kind there existed the greatest rigor, for, says Her-

ters in the lowest state of ignorance.   The women may be generally described as of very loose morals, yet kind and gentle unless
roused by jealousy, in which case they can use the knife as promptly as their male friends.   It is said they make very affectionate
mothers.

There are a few tribes who have preserved some semblance of
nationality.   The Caribs of Honduras are a hardy and athletic
race.   Polygamy is general among them, three or four wives being a not uncommon number.   The husband is compelled to have
a separate house and plantation for each, and, if he make one a
present, he must give the others something of equal value.   He
must also divide his time among them, giving a week to each in
succession.   When a Carib takes a wife, he fells a plantation and
builds a house; the wife then takes the management, and he becomes a gentleman.   The women attend their plantations with
great care, and, in the course of twelve or fifteen months, have every description of breadstuff under cultivation.   About Christmas
they engage several creers, and freight them with produce for
Truxillo and Belize, hiring their husbands and others as sailors.
It is also the custom, when a woman can not do all the work required on her plantation, for her to engage her husband as a laborer, and pay him two dollars per week.   Industry and fore-
thought are peculiar traits of the Carib women, consequently they
easily surround themselves with necessaries and comforts.

The data bearing on the proportion of the sexes in the aggregate population, although too imperfect to be worth presenting,
yet go to show that, as in Mexico, there is a considerable preponderance of females.[1]   The disproportion in births is not so great
as in deaths; for, while the number of males and females born is
nearly equal, more of the former than the latter die annually.
There are more old women than old men, ascribable, no doubt, to
the greater sobriety of the women, drunkenness being a vice
which, under the tropics, is rapid in its consequences.   In Nica-
ragua the women number two to one of the male population.
The Department of Cuscatlan in San Salvador has an excess of
1838 women over men, and of 1709 boys over girls.

Peru and Chili, though neighboring countries, and both in the
strip of western coast between the Andes and the sea, present con-

---

rera, "he who courted or made signs to a married woman was banished."   Fornication was punished by whipping.—*Squier's Notes on Central America*, p. 346.

[1] Squier, p. 50.

siderable difference of condition. Chili is rapidly rising in political importance by means of the internal energy of the people, and the development of natural resources by native and foreign enterprise and capital.

It has been asserted by resident eye-witnesses that female virtue was at so low an ebb in Chili within a few years, that in most families, even of good standing, there were one or more children who were called "children of the house," and whose parentage was distributed generally among the ladies of the family. Nay, we have heard that the rites of hospitality sometimes included civilities in respect to the females which are usually considered as peculiar to certain Oriental nations. A rapid change for the better is, however, taking place in these usages, and even the sea-port of Valparaiso is described by Wilkes as being greatly improved from the period of his first visit, when few sailors left it without having lost both their money and health among its women.

Peru has made but little advance in its recent political changes. The government is in a state of continual anarchy. A new mine of wealth has been discovered in the guano deposits of the Chincha Islands, which has attracted great numbers of foreign vessels to its shores. But the wealth acquired from this source has done little for the people. Lima, the capital, has long been remarkable for the levity and dissipation of its inhabitants. The very dress of the ladies, which may have been originally intended to insure seclusion and privacy, has become an emblem of intrigue. It consists of a peculiar hood and petticoat, covering the wearer entirely, who, when thus in domino, is styled *tapada*, and is, by common usage, held to be secure from all impertinent interference or insult. The same term is applied to a shawl worn over the head, so as to cover the mouth and forehead. Under this concealment the wearer is known only to the most intimate friends, and ladies thus attired frequent the theatres. It is favorable to intrigue, and so perfect is the security that any place of amusement may be visited with impunity, and, even if suspected by the husband or relative, she is protected from discovery by the respect attached to the custom.

Dr. Tschudi draws a very cheerless picture of the state and prospects of Peru.[1] Its moral degradation is significantly typified in the decline of its population, which has been continually dimin-

[1] Peru; Reiseskizzen in den Jahren 1838–1842. (Peru, Sketches of Travel.) By J. J. Von Tschudi. 2 vols. St. Gallen, 1846.

ishing since the establishment of its independence. That noble land, which contained an enormous population at the time of the Conquest, numbered in 1836 less than 1,400,000 inhabitants; not so many as were formerly found in the department of Cusco alone. The deaths in Lima vary annually from 2500 to 2800 out of a population of 53,000; in the ten months from January 1st to October 31st, 1841, they were 2244, the births in that period being 1682, of which 860 were illegitimate.

" Not less remarkable than the number of illegitimate children is that of the new-born infants exposed and found dead (495). These afford the most striking proofs of the immorality which prevails in Lima, especially among the colored people. To them belong nearly two thirds of the illegitimate births, and fully four fifths of the children cast out to die. There is reason to suspect, though it can not be positively proved, that no small portion of the latter suffer a violent death by the hands of their mothers. When a dead child is picked up before the church of San Lazaro, or in the street, it is carried, without a word of inquiry, to the Pantheon ; frequently it is not even thought worth while to bury it. I have seen the vultures dragging about the sweltering carcasses of infants, and devouring them in populous streets. * * * *   On comparing the lists of births and deaths from 1826 to 1842, I satisfied myself that the annual excess of the latter over the former averages 550.

" The women of Lima are far superior to the men, both corporeally and intellectually, though their conduct in many respects is any thing but exemplary. They cling with invincible tenacity to the use of their national walking garb, the *saya y manto*, in which they take their pleasure in the streets, making keen play with the one eye they leave uncovered, and quite secure in that disguise from detection, even by the most jealous scrutiny. The veil is inviolable ; any man who should attempt to pluck off a woman's *manto* would be very severely handled by the populace. The history of their lives comprises two phases : in the full bloom of their fascinating beauty their time is divided between doing naught and naughty doings; when their charms are on the wane, they take to devotion and scandal. A young lady of Lima rises late, dresses her hair with orange or jasmine flowers, and waits for breakfast, after which she receives or pays visits. During the heat of the day she swings in a hammock or reclines on a sofa, smoking a cigar. After dinner she again pays visits, and finishes the evening either in the theatre, or the Plaza, or on the bridge. Few ladies occupy themselves with needlework or netting, though some of them possess great skill in those arts.

" The pride which the fair Limeñas take in their dainty little feet knows no bounds. Walking, sitting, or standing, swinging in the hammock or lying on the sofa, they are ever watchful to let their tiny feet be seen. Praise of their virtue, their intelligence, or their beauty, sounds not half so sweetly in their ears as encomiums bestowed on their pretty feet. They take the most scrupulous care of them, and avoid every thing that might favor their enlargement. A large foot (*pataza Inglesa*—an English foot, as they say) is an abomination to them. I once heard a beautiful European lady deservedly extolled by some fair dames of Lima, but they wound up their eulogy with these words . "*Tero que pie ! valgame Dio, sparece una lancha !* " (but what a foot! Good heavens, it is like a great boat!) and yet the foot in question would by no means have been thought large in Europe.

"The Limeñas possess, in an extraordinary degree, talents which unhappily are seldom cultivated as they should be. They have great penetration, sound judgment, and very correct views respecting the most diversified affairs of life. Like the women of Seville, they are remarkable for their quick and pointed repartees, and a Limeña is sure never to come off second best in a war of words. They possess a rare firmness of character, and a courage not generally given to their sex. In these respects they are far superior to the dastardly, vacillating men, and they have played as important a part as the latter (often one much more so) in all the political troubles of their country. Ambitious and aspiring, accustomed to conduct with ease the maziest intrigues with a presence of mind that never fails them at critical moments, passionate and bold, they mingle in the great game of politics with momentous effect, and usually turn it to their own advantage, seldom to that of the state."

Add to this picture that, though delicate, modest women are rare, actual adultery is not often committed by the sex, but that concubinage is more common, or rather, perhaps, more public than in Europe, the father being usually very fond and careful of his natural children, and a fair view is obtained of female character in Lima. The white Creoles are noted for sensuality, and some of the dances in which they indulge are of indescribable obscenity.[1]

The influx of foreign ships and seamen into Callao, the port of Lima, has brought in its train the usual accompaniments, drunkenness and debauchery. A few years ago it was almost in decay and ruin; now it swarms with drinking-shops (*pulperias*) and prostitutes, and is probably as profligate a place as any in the western hemisphere.

Passing to the Atlantic coast of South America, we find Robertson, the author of "Letters from Paraguay," writing of female Spanish society at the city of Santa Fe:

[1] Horace St. John.

A A

"I was particularly struck by the extremely free nature (to use the very gentlest expression) of the conversation which was adopted with the ladies, young and old. It was such as to make me blush at every turn, although such modesty, whenever it was observed, caused a hearty laugh."

The same author, speaking of female society in Rio, says:

"There is no society at Rio, for I can not call that society from which females are excluded. Generally speaking, the husband of a Brazilian wife is not so much her companion as her keeper. His house is the abode of jealousy and distrust, for he can not always stretch his confidence to the point of imagining fidelity in the wife of his bosom, any more than he can rely on the virtuous forbearance of the friend of his heart. His daughters are brought up in Moorish seclusion, and his wife is delivered over to the keeping of a train of sombre slaves and domestics."

It may be thought that some of these remarks are applicable to periods of time and conditions of society now happily passed away. But the poison of moral depravity, when once taken up, is not to be speedily eliminated from the system of nations more than of individuals. A very recent traveler, Mr. Stewart, testifies to the demoralization of female society in all classes.[1]

With such uniform representations of the general immorality, and of the low estimate in which female virtue is held in South America, it is not to be expected that there are any special details on the subject of our investigation. Prostitution is in some degree attendant upon a state of public feeling in which the purity of wives and daughters is held in respect—not viewed with jealousy, but with reverence. In South America, even in the present time, females mix but little in society. Their education is very limited, terminates early, and they are always under some kind of guardianship or chaperonage in public. This does not elevate the female character. Freedom and self-respect are the best protectives to virtue and honor, and the seclusion of women from general society only serves to invest them with the attraction of mystery to the libertine, while it takes away from themselves the experience and self-reliance in which they find a safeguard.

In South America generally, the character of the priesthood is unfortunately open to reprobation. In Brazil, the priests are reputed to be free livers. Nearly all of them have families, and when seen leaving the dwellings of their wives, or of the females they visit, they speak of them as their nieces or sisters. Some

[1] Stewart's Brazil and La Plata : New York, 1856.

unequivocally admit the relationship existing, and acknowledge their children.[1] The value of the priestly character, in estimating the standard of morality among a population is unquestionably great.

An enlightened native said to Mr. Ewbank, " The priesthood of this country is superlatively corrupt. It is impossible for men to be worse, or to imagine them worse. In the churches they appear respectable and devout, but their secret crimes have made this city a Sodom. There are, of course, honorable exceptions." [2]

Another, a man of unquestionable authority, said, " They are assuredly the most licentious and profligate part of the community. The exceptions are rare. Celibacy being one of their dogmas, you will find nearly the whole with families."

At Rio Janeiro there is a Foundling Hospital, established in 1582, which is a noble institution. The boys are provided for at Botofoga, and are in due time apprenticed to trades. The girls reside in the city establishment, and are taught to read, write, sew, etc. At each anniversary, bachelors in want of wives attend at the festival, and if they see girls to their liking, make themselves known. If a girl accepts such a lover, he makes his application to the managers, who inquire into his character, and, if satisfactory, the marriage takes place, and a small dowry is given from the funds of the society. In the management of the institution or the reception of infants, there is nothing peculiarly worthy notice. But if those who are averse to such institutions contrast the blessed results of saving these helpless infants from misery, and the horror of beholding their dead bodies cast on dunghills, to be devoured as carrion by obscene animals and birds of prey, as has been mentioned in the notice of Lima, they would, on such grounds, even if there were no better to be urged, suspend a hasty judgment on Foundling Hospitals.

[1] Ewbank's Brazil, p. 135.   [2] Ib. p. 141.

CHAPTER XXIX.

NORTH AMERICAN INDIANS.

Decrease of the Indian Race —Treatment of Females.—Courtship.—Stealing
Wives.—Domestic Life among the Crow Indians.—"Pine Leaf."—Female
Prisoners.—Marriage.—Conjugal Relations.—Infidelity.—Polygamy.—Di-
vorce.—Female Morality.—Intrigue and Revenge.—Decency of Outward
Life.—Effects of Contact with White Men.—Traders.

THE aboriginal inhabitants of the vast continent of America
have been variously described by different writers, one man laud-
ing them as models of chivalry and virtue, another decrying them
as the personification of meanness and vice. Hence it is only at
a recent period, comparatively speaking, that any reliable information has been obtainable on the subject. In the limited space
that can be given to a consideration of the Indian and his social
habits, we shall endeavor to reject both romance and vitupera-
tion. We do not believe him so stoically virtuous as the former
class of writers depict, nor do we think that all of the race are
so deeply sunk in depravity as the latter represent.

In addition to the authorities quoted in the progress of the
chapter, we are under obligations to Mr. Horace St. John's
article on Prostitution, incorporated by Mr. Mayhew in his
tracts on " London Labor and the London Poor."

At the time of the settlement of Jamestown and Plymouth, it
was estimated that there were about two millions of Indians scattered over this continent. They were then a brave and hardy
people who lived on the produce of the chase, varying their loca-
tions as the facilities for hunting required. When the last census
of the United States was taken, their numbers were about four
hundred thousand, exclusive of fifteen thousand in Canada and
the British possessions. This decrease has been ascribed to the
occupation of their hunting-grounds by white men, and the consequent extermination of the game upon which they depended for
subsistence ; the free use of intoxicating liquors, and the introduction of small-pox and other fatal diseases. These causes will, in
all probability, result in the entire extinction of the race. In the

small number mentioned are many half-breeds, children of white fathers and Indian mothers.

It might naturally be supposed that in the several tribes composing this people there would exist great diversity of manners, but these are found only in minor particulars. The social institutions of the North American Indians are so generally uniform as to render it possible to sketch the whole at one view.

Their occupations are still confined to the chase and the warpath. To perform a round of daily labor, even though it insured the most ample provision for his wants, would be contrary alike to the inclination and the supposed dignity of the Red Man, who will scarcely deign to follow any pursuit which does not combine enterprise and excitement. Woman, therefore, becomes the drudge and slave; upon her devolves the duty of cultivating the ground, whenever any attempt is made to assist the spontaneous efforts of Nature; she it is who must bear the load of game which her husband has killed; must carry wood and water, build huts, and make canoes. In fishing, and in reaping their scanty harvest, the man will, at times, condescend to assist her, but otherwise all the labor falls to her share. In those tribes visited by traders, her duties are still heavier; she must join in the hunt, and afterward dress and prepare the skins and furs which are to be bartered for whisky and other luxuries. To this degraded condition the women seem perfectly reconciled, and expertness at the assigned employment is a source of pride to them.

The treatment of the female sex is generally admitted to be a standard by which man's moral qualities can be estimated. It may be doubted if this rule would apply to the Indian tribes, for those who treat their females most mildly are by no means the most virtuous, nor is their deference attended by any increase of attachment. Where they aid in procuring food or luxuries for the tribe, they are held in more esteem; while in places where the chief burden of providing rests upon the men, they are treated with severity.[1]

Even when oppressed with these laborious occupations, the women have as much native vanity in respect to decoration as the sex in any part of the world; and an accurate observer remarks that, " Judging from the time a squaw often occupies in arranging her hair, or disposing her scanty dress, or painting her

[1] Lewis and Clarke's Expedition across the Rocky Mountains, vol. ii. p. 144.

round cheeks with glaring circles of vermilion, it is evident that personal ornament occupies as much of her thoughts as among fashionable women in civilized society."[1]

Courtship and marriage are differently arranged among various tribes. The predominant custom is for a man to procure a wife by purchase from her father, thus acquiring a property over which he has absolute control, and which he can barter away or dispose of in any manner he pleases. The example of Powhatan, who was chief ruler over thirty tribes in Virginia at the time of the English colonization, is a case in point. It is said that he always had a multitude of wives about him, and when he wearied of any would distribute them as presents among his principal warriors. In most cases the woman is not consulted at all, the whole transaction being a mercantile one; in others an infant female is betrothed by her father (for a consideration) to some man who requires a wife either for himself or for his son. The girl remains with her parents until the age of puberty, when the contract is completed, at which time the father often makes a present to the husband equal in value to the price originally paid for his daughter.[2]

Another mode of obtaining a wife is to steal a girl from some neighboring tribe. Captain Clarke, who crossed the Rocky Mountains in the years 1804–1806, as one of the leaders of an expedition ordered by the executive of the United States, records instances of this kind. He says, "One of the Ahnahaways had stolen a Minnetaree girl. The whole nation immediately espoused the quarrel, and one hundred and fifty of the warriors were marching down to avenge the insult. The chief took possession of the girl, and sent her by messengers to the hands of her countrymen in time to avert the threatened calamity."[3] " A young Minnetaree had carried off the daughter of a chief of the Mandans. The father went to the village and found his daughter, whom he brought home, and at the same time took possession of a horse belonging to the offender. This reprisal satisfied his vengeance."[4]

A more peaceable kind of preliminary to matrimony is for a man desiring a wife to offer a small present to the woman : if she accepts it and offers him one in return, the match is complete; or he may tell her his wishes without any introductory gift, and, if agreeable, she will reply accordingly. Others will not venture

[1] Thatcher's Indian Traits, vol. i. p. 51.
[2] Lewis and Clarke's Expedition, i. 358.   [3] Ib. i. 166.   [4] Id. ib.

to express their thoughts, but will sit quietly by a girl's side, and, if she does not remove from her seat, her assent is understood to be given.[1] Still another custom is for the lover to enter the woman's tent at night, bearing a lighted torch. If she allows it to burn, it is a sign that his attentions are not desired; but if she extinguishes it, she thus intimates that he is accepted. It will not require much knowledge of human nature to imagine the consequences of these nocturnal visits.

A recently published work, " Life and Adventures of James P. Beckwourth, New York, 1856," professes to give an accurate account of the domestic life of the Crow Indians, among whom he lived for some years, and became a chief of the tribe, who believed that he was one of themselves, and had been stolen from them in infancy. It may be necessary to say that we only quote him on points where corroborative evidence can be obtained from other sources. His character for veracity is questionable, and among the miners of California, where he is known, any extravagant tale is proverbially called " one of Jem Beckwourth's lies." His first experience of matrimony, showing that the woman's consent was not asked, but that the arrangements were made by the parents, is thus stated : " While conversing with my father, he suddenly demanded if I wanted a wife. I assented. ' Very well,' said he, ' you shall have a pretty wife and a good one.' Away he strode to the lodge of one of the greatest braves, and asked one of his daughters of him. The consent of the parent was given. He had three very pretty daughters, and the ensuing day they were brought to my father's lodge, and I was requested to take my choice. The eldest was named ' Still Water,' and I chose her. The acceptance of my wife was the completion of the ceremony, and I was a married man, as sacredly in their eyes as if the Holy Christian Church had fastened the irrevocable knot upon us."[2]

Cases are also recorded by Indian travelers wherein a custom more assimilating to civilized notions is adopted. A young man will court a girl for a length of time, using all his endeavors to cultivate her affections, and the woman, upon her part, will entertain an equal tenderness for him. Again turning to the pages of Beckwourth, we find an instance of this in the case of a woman who attracted his attention. It must not be considered that he

[1] Indian Traits, i. 104.
[2] Life and Adventures of James P. Beckwourth, p. 148.

was a victim of the romantic affliction called "first love," for he had some six or eight wives in the tribe at the time. His description is as follows:

"In connection with my Indian experience, I conceive it to be my duty to devote a few lines to one of the bravest women that ever lived, namely, 'Pine Leaf'—in Indian, *Barcheeampe*. She possessed great intellectual powers ; her features were pleasing, and her form symmetrical. She had lost a twin brother in an attack on the village, and was left to avenge his death. She was at that time twelve years of age, and solemnly vowed that she would never marry until she had killed a hundred of the enemy with her own hand. Whenever a war-party started, Pine Leaf was the first to volunteer to accompany them. . . . . . She had chosen my party to serve in. . . . . . I began to feel more than a common attachment toward her. One day, while riding leisurely along, I asked her to marry me, provided we both returned safe. She laughed and said, 'Well, I will marry you.' 'When we return ?' 'No, but when the pine leaves turn yellow.' I reflected that it would soon be winter, and regarded her promise as valid. A few days afterward it occurred to me that pine leaves do not turn yellow, and I saw I had been practiced upon. When I again spoke to her on the subject, I said, 'Pine Leaf, you promised to marry me when the pine leaves turn yellow ; it has occurred to me that they never turn yellow. Am I to understand that you never intend to marry me ?' 'Yes, I will marry you,' she said, with a coquettish smile. 'But when ?' 'When you shall find a red-headed Indian.' I saw I advanced nothing by importuning her, and I let the matter rest."[1]

It would occupy too much space to recite all the details of a long courtship, including scenes in war and chase, at the camp, or on horse-stealing excursions ; suffice it to say that the heroine accomplished her vow, and seemed convinced of the sincerity of her lover. She concluded the courtship thus :

"She then approached me, every eye being intently fixed upon her. 'Look at me,' she said. 'I know that your heart is crying for the follies of the people; but let it cry no more. I am yours, after you have so long been seeking me. I believe you love me. Our lodge shall be a happy one, and, when you depart to the happy hunting-ground, I will be already there to welcome you. This day I become your wife.'"[2]

Women will sometimes voluntarily ask men to marry them, promising to be faithful, good-tempered, and obedient. This request is seldom refused, as the marriage tie is easily dissolved if the union proves unpleasant. Tanner, who was taken prisoner by a war-party, and lived among various tribes in the northwest for

[1] Beckwourth, p. 201.　　　　　　　　　　　　　[2] Id. p. 401.

nearly thirty years, relates a case in point. The woman's endeavors to secure him as her husband commenced with an invitation to smoke with her. He acceded; but either his blood was not so warm as that coursing through Indian veins, or from some other cause, it was long before he consented to the proposed companionship, which a Red Man would have accepted on the spot. The girl pursued him, and at last, with the consent of her father, took possession of his hut while he was absent. When he returned, " he could not put the young woman to shame " by sending her back to her friends, and they became man and wife.[1]

Beckwourth also had some experience of this custom. " A little girl, who had often asked me to marry her, came to me one day, and with every importunity insisted on my accepting her as my wife. I said, ' When you are older I will talk to you about it ;' but she would not be put off. ' You are a great brave,' she said ; ' and, if I am your wife, you will paint my face when you return from the war, and I shall be proud.' The little innocent used such powerful appeals that I told her she might be my wife."[2] He lived with her until he left the Indians, and her son is now (1855) chief of the tribe.

The women taken prisoners in war are frequently married into the tribe that captured them, but never to the captors, who stand in the relation of brothers to them, and by whom they are protected from insult. A warrior who has taken a female prisoner usually makes an exchange with another who has had the same fortune, each being thus accommodated without infringing upon custom. If a man has seized more than he can dispose of in that way, he generally gives them to any man who will accept them.[3] In the same manner, a woman whose husband has been killed in battle will ask a warrior for a male prisoner, who accordingly becomes the successor of one whom he has probably slain. In these cases the man is adopted as one of the tribe, is kindly treated, and entitled to his share of all their advantages.[4]

The marriages are without ceremony of any kind ; the parties agree to live with each other as long as they can do so with mutual satisfaction, and the man conducts his bride to his hut at once, or resides with her at her father's cabin. It must not be supposed that the ordinary requirements of a married life

---

[1] Indian Traits, i. p. 114. [2] Beckwourth, p. 169.
[3] Beckwourth, p. 212. [4] Murray's British North America, vol. i. p. 115.

are systematically unheeded, for, as a general rule, the squaws are faithful to their husbands, who, upon their part, rigidly exact this fidelity, even if they do not practice it themselves.

The general description of the position of Indian women already given applies equally to their state after marriage. They continue sometimes the abject slaves, otherwise the patient servants of their husbands. While he eats the food she has cooked, and probably caught herself, she must wait in submissive silence. At all times she approaches him with the deference due to a superior being. An Indian will never evince the slightest symptom of tenderness toward his wife; this would be opposed to his idea of manly dignity; but the eagerness with which he will revenge her wrongs proves that his apparent apathy springs only from pride, or a fancied sense of decorum.[1] When Catlin proposed to paint the portrait of the wife of a Sioux chief, his offer was ridiculed, and it was considered marvelous that he should honor a woman in the same manner he had honored the warriors, as the former had never taken any scalps, never done any thing but make fires, dress skins, and other servile employments.

To infer from these facts that there is no conjugal affection among this people would be erroneous. Notwithstanding their assumed indifference, instances are not rare of strong mutual attachment. To an Indian there is nothing inconsistent with affection in his indolently walking through the forests, while his wife follows him bearing the heavy wigwam poles. Many pictures of domestic happiness are exhibited among the Indians, and the Blackfeet, Sanee, and Blood tribes strongly desire that their wives may live long and look young. Heckewelder relates a singular instance of indulgence. In 1762 there was a scarcity of food among many tribes, and during the prevalence of this famine a sick woman wished for a mess of Indian corn. Her husband rode about a hundred miles to obtain it, gave his horse in exchange for a hatful, and returned home on foot with the coveted dainty.[2]

These "lords of creation" attempt to enforce their marital rights with much severity, and, if their suspicions are excited against their wives, become very indignant, and punish them by beating, biting off the nose, dismissing them in disgrace, or even killing them. The wife of a Mandan Indian ran away from him in con-

[1] Murray's British North America, vol. i. p. 94.   [2] Indian Traits, 1. p. 136.

sequence of a quarrel. By so doing she forfeited her life, which custom would have justified the husband in taking, and he would have murdered her but for the interposition of the travelers, who "gave him a few presents, and persuaded him to take his wife home; they went off together, but by no means in a state of much apparent love." This trouble arose from jealousy.[1] In another case, a Minnetaree had much abused his wife for the same reason, and she sought refuge in the camp. Her husband followed and demanded her, and she "returned with him, as we had no authority to separate those whom even Indian rites had united."[2]

Since an Indian considers his wife as so much property, equally valuable as his horse, and for the same reason—for the labor she can perform—we can easily understand that polygamy is universally allowed, though it is not generally practiced, being confined to great chiefs and medicine-men, as the rank and file are often too poor to buy a second wife. Many follow the custom for the mere purpose of amassing wealth, but others of the stoic warriors delight in the harem for the same sensual motives as a Turk or Hindu. Among the communities that Catlin had an opportunity of visiting, it was no uncommon thing to find from six to fourteen wives in the same lodge. He mentions an instance in which a young chief of the Mandans took four wives in one day, paying a horse or two for each. These brides were from twelve to fourteen years of age. An Indian marriage at this age is far from uncommon, and, indeed, it appears that celibacy beyond the age of puberty is very rare. Some of the females are mothers before they are twelve. It is not universal for the wives to live all in one hut, some tribes requiring separate lodgings for each. This custom is in force among the Crows, and Beckwourth relates that, on returning from one of his excursions, he made a round of visits to his wives, some of whom he had not seen for months.[3]

It is not uncommon for a man to marry his wife's sister, and, indeed, the whole family of girls, on the supposition that his household will thus be rendered more harmonious.[4] For the same reason, a Cherokee will marry a mother and her daughter at one time, though he will not, upon any account, take a wife from his own kindred. Among the Oregon tribes it is strictly required that each wife should be purchased from a different family.

---

[1] Lewis and Clarke's Expedition, i. p. 135.   [2] Ib. i. p. 151.
[3] Beckwourth, p. 179.   [4] Murray's British America, i. p. 94.

So well established among Indians is the custom of polygamy, that civilization meets the greatest difficulty in opposing it, and, if ever abolished, it will overthrow their whole social system. Sir George Simpson relates an amusing anecdote of an Indian who came into the settled districts of British North America, learned to read and write, and adopted the principle of monogamy. Returning to his tribe, he endeavored to persuade them to the same course. Long and earnest were the debates on the question, and the *finale* was, instead of converting them, they reconverted him. He took a great number of wives, foreswore books, and never again appeared in the character of a social reformer. Another chief offered to renounce polygamy, he having five wives, and a large fortune in horses and cattle. Falling in love with the daughter of a gentleman in the service of the Hudson's Bay Company, he dismissed his harem, and presented himself, with great parade and confidence, to make his matrimonial proposal to the lady's family. To his extreme disgust and mortification, they rejected the honor of his distinguished alliance. He revenged himself by refilling his hut with women as quickly as possible.

If the obligation of marriage is easily contracted, divorce is effected with as little trouble. It is not often that a separation takes place, for it is held dishonorable to forsake a wife for a trifling cause, particularly if she has borne children. When it does occur, the offspring are usually permitted to decide which of the parents they will accompany, although usage gives the mother the right to take charge of them. In some instances the form of divorce is simply for the husband to bid his wife go; in others he will not take the trouble to give her notice of his discontent, but will quietly put his gun on his shoulder and move off himself.[1] There are a few instances of this being done for very slight reasons; but, in addition to the restraint of custom just mentioned, the actual value of the wife is a subject of consideration. Where a separation does take place, the man will often endeavor to renew the connection. A missionary mentions a woman who contracted a new marriage after her husband left her. He returned and claimed her. The dispute was referred to a chief, and he, either wanting a precedent or distrusting his judicial capacity, could think of no better expedient than placing the woman at an equal distance from each claimant, and then ordering the men to run,

[1] Indian Traits, i. p. 128.

promising that the one who first reached her should retain possession of the prize.[1] In some tribes divorce renders it impossible for a woman to marry again, but in others she can make a new alliance as soon as free from the old one.

It is difficult to form any opinion as to the morality of females among a people where marriages are contracted and dissolved so easily. We may safely say that they have very little idea of chastity, notwithstanding their general, although not invariable fidelity when married, which may probably be induced more by fear of consequences than sense of duty. Of prostitution for a price, as known in civilized communities, we find no trace in the Indian nations while in a normal condition; but if we assume Webster's definition, "the act of offering the body to an indiscriminate intercourse with men," it can scarcely be claimed that they are free. The predominant motive seems to be an inordinate sexual appetite, which must be gratified, if not in legitimate marriage, then by illicit intercourse. We are told that in most large assemblies of Indians there are to be seen voluptuous looking females, whose passions urge them to this; and Carver, in his " Travels in North America," says that among the Manedowessis it was a custom, when a young woman could not get a husband, for her to assemble all the leading warriors of the tribe at a feast; and, when their hunger was appeased, to retire behind a screen, and submit to the embraces of each in succession. This gained her great applause, and always insured her a husband. Though the custom is now almost obsolete, the principle still exists, and prostitution is regarded by many as the shortest road to marriage.

The birth of a bastard child entails little shame upon a girl, and that such children are not more frequent is due less to their chastity than to the means they employ to procure abortion. One of the reasons advanced for their early marriages is that the impetuosity of the girls would render it difficult to obtain a virtuous wife if the union was delayed. The confessions upon starting for war, or what is called the " war-path secret," would also favor the opinion that abstract virtue is at a low ebb. At these times every warrior is required to relate to his companions each act of illicit intercourse he has committed since the last excursion, naming his partner, and enumerating the facts attending the frailty. This obligation is enforced by the most rigid oaths known to Indian customs.[2]

[1] Murray's British America, i. 94.   [2] Beckwourth, p. 157.

This immorality is not confined to the single women, for the squaws are, at times, as ready to take part in an intrigue. Beckwourth, whose experience of Indian manners seems to have embraced every phase of life, relates his adventures in this way :

"A brave named ' Big Rain ' was elected chief of the village. He possessed a most beautiful squaw, who was the admiration of the young men, and all were plotting to win her from her lord. I determined to steal her, be the consequences what they might." Having enticed the husband to a smoking-party, he says, " I went to Big Rain's lodge, dressed and painted in the extreme of fashion, and saw the lady reclining upon her couch. She started up, saying, ' Who is here ? ' ' Hush ! it is I.' ' What do you want here ? ' ' I have come to see you, because I love you.' ' Don't you know that I am the chief's wife ? ' ' Yes, I know it, but he does not love you as I do. I can paint your face and bring you fine horses, but as long as you are the wife of Big Rain he will never paint your face. With you by my side I could bring home many scalps, Then we could often dance, and our hearts would be merry.' * * * * ' Go, now,' she pleaded, ' for if my husband should return I fear he would kill you. Go, for your own sake and for mine.' ' No, I will not go till you give me a pledge that you will be mine.' She hesitated for a moment, and then slipped a ring from her finger and placed it on mine.   All I had to do now was to watch for a favorable chance to take her away. * * * * The appointed time had arrived, and on going to the place of assignation, I found the lady true to her word—in fact, she was there first. We joined the party, and were absent about a week.   We succeeded in capturing (stealing ?) one hundred and seventeen horses, and arrived safe with them in the camp.   Meanwhile Big Rain discovered the loss of his wife. When we rode in, he took no part in the rejoicing, but ordered his wife and me to be surrounded, and, with half a dozen of his sisters, all armed with scourges, administered a most unmerciful whipping. I received it with Indian fortitude.   If I had resisted, they would have been justified in killing me ; also, if they had drawn one drop of blood, I should have been justified in taking their lives."

Without wishing to delay the progress of the narrative, we can not resist the impulse to express admiration of the Indian punishment for a seducer of married women. Could the same unromantic penalty be duly and zealously inflicted for similar transgressions, in places of more pretensions, some of the scandals of civilized life would be curtailed.   To resume :

"I sent word to the wife of Big Rain that I should go out again the next night, and should expect her company.   She returned a favorable answer, and was faithful to her promise.   On my return I received another such flogging as the first.   Two nights afterward I started on a third expedition, my new wife accompanying me, and received a third sound thrashing from her husband.   Finally, he grew furious ; but my soldiers said to him, 'You have whipped him three times, and shall whip him no more ; we will buy your claim.'   He acceded to the offer, and consented to resign all interest and title in Mrs. Big Rain for the consideration of one war-horse, ten guns, ten chief's coats of scarlet cloth, ten pairs of new leggins, and the same number of moccasins."[1]

In another case an intrigue resulted tragically.   One of the wives of a Minnetaree chief eloped with a man who had formerly been her lover.   He deserted her in a short time.   She returned to her father's hut, whither her husband traced her.   He walked deliberately into the hut, smoked quietly for a time, and then took her by the hair, led her to the door, and killed her with a single blow of his tomahawk.[2]   The caprice or generosity of the same chief gave a very different conclusion to a similar incident which occurred some time afterward.   Another of his wives eloped with a young man who was not able to support her as she wished, and both returned to the village.   She presented herself before her husband and asked his pardon.   He sent for the man, inquired if they still loved each other, and on their acknowledgment gave up his wife to her lover, made them a present of three horses, and restored them both to his favor.[3]

With the exception of some national customs, the outward life of the Indian is generally decent.   A temporary interval of wild license, corresponding to the Saturnalia of the ancients, and called the festival of dreams, is common among the Canadian tribes.   This carnival lasts fifteen days, and, laying aside all their usual gravity, they then commit every imaginable extravagance.[4]   Our authority does not say whether immorality forms a portion of this relaxation, but from the custom of other bands it is not improbable.   Lewis and Clarke mention several instances in which they

[1] Beckwourth, p. 288.				[2] Lewis and Clarke's Expedition, i. 166.
[3] Id. ib.						[4] Murray's British America, i. 125.

were present at dancing and similar festivals, and witnessed exhibitions of the most foul and revolting indecency.

Mr. Catlin records his opinion that the Old World has very little of superior morality or virtue to hold as an example to the
North American Indians. The manners of each have been described; and while it would be unjust to expect the untutored
son of the forest to display as much delicacy as his more cultivated fellow-men, it would be equally ungenerous to assert that
the white female population, as an aggregate, are governed by
the impulses which apparently sway the Indian woman.

But whatever doubts there may exist as to the immorality of
the Indian women in their natural state, all are entirely removed
as soon as they come in contact with the white race. Those in
the provinces of Nova Scotia, New Brunswick, and Canada have
rapidly learned the worst of vices. They are drunken, sensual,
and depraved. The venereal disease commits frightful ravages
among them; in fact, most of their sickness arises from excess of
one kind or another. Maclean, in his "Twenty-five years' Service in Hudson's Bay," says that the men employed by the company are reconciled to their hard employment and poor remuneration by the immorality of the women, of whom numbers are
prostitutes, selling themselves for the smallest remuneration. On
the Northwest Coast chastity is scarcely even a name. The sea
tribes are the most licentious, and at some places, where ships
touch for supplies, hundreds of women come down to the beach,
and by indecent exposures of their persons endeavor to obtain
permission to come on board. Sir George Simpson received a
visit from a chief who wanted to negotiate the loan of Lady
Simpson, and offered his squaw in temporary exchange.

Many of the traders on the Upper Missouri, from motives of
policy, connect themselves with women of the tribes. The most
beautiful girls aspire to this station, which elevates them above
their ordinary servile occupations. These engagements are not
marriages in our sense of the word; a price is paid for the girl,
and she is transferred at once to the trader's house. With equal
facility he can annul the contract, for which her father is not
sorry, as he is thus enabled to sell her over again. The tariff of
prices will range from two horses to a handful of awls: such is the
remuneration for which an Indian chief will prostitute his daughter. It must be added that occasionally the couple live perma-

nently together as man and wife, the possibility of their doing so being always supposed in the first instance.

***

CHAPTER XXX.

BARBAROUS NATIONS.[1]

Africa.—Australasia.—West Indies.—Java.—Sumatra.—Borneo.

THE relations of the sexes among uneducated races are modified by every circumstance of their position, but the natural ascendency of the strong over the weak is universally displayed, and wherever woman is allowed a social rank approaching that of man, it will be found that a degree of civilization has been attained. Many branches of the human family have advanced, more or less, beyond the utterly savage state, the love of ornament and the practice of exchange having raised them one step in the scale, while they vary as much in the characteristics of their barbarism as civilized nations do in their refinement. Waiving generalities, a better idea of their respective customs will be obtained by noticing the position of females among the different nations.

AFRICA.

Some of the most wild and savage tribes of the human family are to be found in the immense peninsula of Africa. Observation has proved that a medium state of refinement is accompanied with the least immorality, and that it is among the merest savages and the most highly-polished communities that the greatest profligacy exists. In order to present the subject clearly, we will make a geographical arrangement, and, commencing from the south, pass over the continent, till we reach the valley of the Lower Nile.

The Hottentots are a dissolute, profligate race, and have borne that character from the earliest period. It was remarked by Van Riebeck in 1655, and confirmed by Colonel Napier in 1840, the latter describing them as "proverbially unchaste." Indecency and lewdness are their characteristics; and even now, though accustomed to clothing, it is not uncommon for them to strip themselves, and dance in a lascivious manner at their festivals. The

---

[1] The principal facts in this and the following chapter are taken from Mr. Horace St. John's article on Prostitution, in Mayhew's "London Labor and the London Poor."

females prostitute themselves readily to strangers, some from inclination, others for money or a gift of finery; but we have no
means of estimating the numbers of this disreputable class. A few
of superior order are scattered among these degraded creatures,
and intelligent and well-conducted women have attracted the notice of travelers.

The pastoral Kaffirs are more moral, though more ferocious
than the Hottentots, being more addicted to arms, and less to debauch. They practice polygamy, buying their wives for so many
head of cattle. The girls undergo a probation before marriage,
during which they are kept in seclusion. As the tribe wander
from place to place, they carry their women with them, and upon
them all the domestic labor falls, even the chief's wives assisting
in grinding corn and similar work. Divorce is easy on very slight
grounds. We occasionally hear of women committing fornication,
but no professed class of prostitutes has been described. Marriage
is not held as a sacred tie, but adultery by a wife is severely punished. Natural affections appear extremely weak among the Kaffirs, and mothers have but little attachment to their children, the
sickly and feeble being sometimes abandoned to avoid the trouble
of rearing them. Mrs. Ward knew of a woman who buried alive
a sickly daughter. The little creature was but imperfectly inter-
red; it burst from the grave and ran home. A second time it
was subjected to the same torture, and again escaped. A third
attempt was made with a similar result, when its mother received
it, and it ultimately recovered. Such instances of inhumanity are
not rare. Husbands frequently drag their sick wives into a
thicket, and leave them to die. It is important to mention that,
where these people have embraced Christianity, their manners
have totally changed; polygamy has been renounced, and they
manifest an inclination to conform to the morals taught them.

Between the tropics the people are notorious for licentiousness.
Morality is a strange idea to them, nor is a man restrained by any
social law from intercourse with as many females as he pleases.
The result is, that women are regarded strictly as marketable commodities, and the commonest feelings of humanity are unknown.
On the Gold Coast husbands openly prostitute their wives for
money. In other places an adulterer pays a fine to the husband,
and many urge their wives to commit the crime for the sake of
the penalty. When Laird visited the Niger in 1832, he found
the condition of the females upon its borders most humiliating.

Polygamy was universal, and wives were reduced to slavery in their own houses. In short, the race may be described as the most idle, ignorant, and profligate in Africa. The king possessed one hundred and forty wives, one of whom was under thirteen years of age, and all had been purchased for a few muskets or a piece of cloth. Half a dozen of the fattest were known as his favorites, and one of them was said to weigh over three hundred and fifty pounds. The mother of this prince lived in his palace, and amused the court with obscene dances. Adultery by any inmate of the harem was punished with death. When a man died, one at least of his wives was expected to attend him; she was bound and thrown into the river. In another place the woman was buried alive; and in the kingdom of Fundal, when a chief died leaving fifteen wives, the king selected the ugliest to be hanged over the grave, and transferred the remaining fourteen to his own quarters.

The native of Western Africa looks upon his wife as a source of pleasure and gain, reckoning her as property to the amount she can earn. With a strange inconsistency, some of these barbarians profess a sentiment of attachment. The King of Atta told Lander that he loved him as he loved his wife. As he was a polygamist, it is to be assumed the traveler thought it a divided affection. Marriage is held as one of the common occurrences of life. When a man is old enough, he takes a wife, and goes on adding to his property until he probably owns a hundred, if he has means enough to buy them. Even under this system many women can not obtain stated husbands, as some men will not take permanent wives; but it is safe to assert that no single man lives without female intercourse, and no single woman remains chaste. A wife suspected of adultery is forced to drink a poisonous decoction, but she sometimes bribes the priest to render it harmless. Widows who have lived on bad terms with their husbands have to undergo the same ordeal. An illicit connection with the king's wife results in death to both parties, but for the wife of a chief the gift of a slave is an expiation. The price of a handsome wife is from eighteen to thirty-six dollars; a plain-looking one is worth about seven dollars. As a man's inclination varies, he often sells one wife, and buys another with the proceeds of the transaction.

In the kingdom of Dahomey, once the centre of the slave-trade, a most profligate population is found, and the traveler entering its sea-port is immediately struck with the immodesty of the women. Throughout the country the same characteristic is observable;

they are profligates from the highest to the lowest. The king is superior in brutality and filthiness (traits which seem hereditary to the throne of Dahomey) to any of his subjects. He has thousands of wives, his chiefs have hundreds, his subjects tens. The royal favorites are too sacred for the gaze of common people, who must turn aside or hide their faces if any of them are passing. Strangers are excluded from the harem, but the privileged nobility attend the king's feasts, at which his wives take a leading part in drinking rum and conducting the debauch. When the king desires to confer honor on any favorite, he chooses a wife for him, and presents her publicly. She hands her husband a cup of rum, which is a sign of union.

The King of Dahomey supports an army of several thousand amazons, who dress in male attire, do not marry, and are supposed not to have intercourse with men. These troops were long considered invincible, but a few years ago they encountered a defeat on one of their marauding expeditions, and a thousand or more were killed on the field.

As the king and his wealthy subjects have so many wives, poor people are obliged to content themselves with the company of prostitutes, who are a licensed and taxed class in Dahomey. There appears to be a band of these in every village, but their profits are often insufficient for support, and they resort to industrial occupation, hiring themselves to carry heavy burdens, etc. One traveler saw two hundred and fifty collected in a troop, and another was assailed by a crowd of women who offered to "be his wives" for a drop of rum. Many of the poorest class stroll about naked, and a gratuity, however small, will purchase their favors.

The dirty, lazy, dull people of the Fantee Coast have the same moral aspect as the subjects of Dahomey. Parents sell their children, husbands sell their wives, women sell themselves, for a trifling sum. One woman was so anxious to make a bargain of this kind that she took possession of a traveler's bed, and force was necessary to expel her. Marriage is a mere purchase, a wife costing about sixteen dollars. Women are unsalable when more than fifteen or sixteen years old. Any man committing adultery is forced to buy his paramour at her cost price.

Along the coast of Benin similar customs prevail. Public dancers act as prostitutes, and offer themselves at a small price. Every woman considers it an honor to be the king's companion, even for one night.

In Ashantee, where also polygamy prevails, adultery is common, especially among the king's wives, who are hewn to pieces if discovered. The people are profligate beyond any thing which can be conceived. A practice of unusual depravity prevails among the Kroomen, a son who inherits his father's property taking his wives also, and thus his own mother becomes his slave.

The Edeeyahs of Fernando Po offer a strong contrast to the above, treating their women with consideration, and assigning them far less than the usual amount of work. Polygamy is allowed. The first wife taken by a man must be betrothed to him at least two years before marriage, and during that time he is in a state of servitude like that of Jacob for Rachel, the girl being kept in seclusion. When she appears as a married woman, all the virgins of the tribe salute and dance round her. This custom is only observed with the first wife, the others being concubines who are governed by her. Adultery is severely punished: for the first offense both parties lose one hand; for the second, the man and his relatives are heavily fined and chastised, the woman loses the other hand, and is driven from the settlement into the woods—an exile more terrible than mutilation.

It would be but a needless repetition to pass in review all the various groups of African states. We have seen that in the west profligacy is a universal feature, and it is scarcely less so in the east. In Zulu, for example, the king has a seraglio of fifteen hundred women. The manners of the communities in the Sahara are imperfectly known, but appear to be above those in other parts of Africa, though many customs prevail which shock our ideas of decency. A chief offered Richardson his two daughters as wives. Immorality is usually a secret crime, and their general customs with regard to sexual intercourse are outwardly decent. Still the condition of the female sex is degraded, for they are regarded as materials of a man's household, and ministers to his sensuality.

Abyssinia presents various characteristics of manners. In Tajura men live with their wives for a short time, and then sell them. Parents are known to hire their daughters out as prostitutes. One chief offered his daughter as a temporary or permanent companion to a traveler, and a woman presented herself as a candidate for a similar appointment, saying, by way of recommendation, that she had already lived with five men. One strong evidence of the immorality of Tajura is the fact that syphilis affects nearly the whole population, man and woman, sultan and beggar, priests and their wives inclusive.

In Shoa the king has one wife and five hundred concubines, the latter scattered in various parts of his dominions.   He makes a present to the parents of any girl he may desire, and is usually well paid in return for the honor.   The governors of provinces and cities follow his example.   There are two kinds of marriage in Shoa: one a mere arrangement to cohabit, the other a holy ceremony.   The former is almost invariably used, the man and woman declaring before witnesses that they mean to live together. Divorces are as easily obtained, only mutual consent being neces- sary.   A wife is valued according to the amount of her property, and the owner of a hut, a field, and a bedstead is sure to get a husband.   When they quarrel and part, a division of property takes place.   Concubines are procured as well from the Christians as from Mohammedans and pagans, but the latter are forced to declare themselves converted, for Shoa is professedly a Christian kingdom.   A favorite concubine holds the same position as a married woman, and no distinction is made between legitimate and illegitimate children.   The court overflows with licentious- ness, numerous adulteries take place, and the example is followed by the people, among whom a chaste married couple is rare.   The sacerdotal class of Shoa is notoriously drunken and profligate ; in a word, the morals of the country are of the lowest description. In the Mohammedan states of the neighborhood the condition of the female sex is also degraded, and if there is less general prosti- tution, it is because every woman is the slave of some man's lust, and is closely watched by him.

In the provinces of Kordofan, south of the Nubian mountains, the sentiment of love is not altogether unknown, and men fight duels with whips of hippopotamus hide on account of a disputed mistress.   The wife is, however, a virtual slave, and is still more degraded if she prove barren, the husband then solacing himself with a concubine, who is raised to the rank of a wife if she bear a child.   The general demeanor of the girls of Kordofan is modest, and their lives are chaste, while the married women are addicted to intrigue, especially if neglected by their husbands.   In some parts of the country men consider it an honor for their wives to have intercourse with strangers, and often assist the woman to this end.   There is a class of pretty dancers who are usually prosti- tutes, and are celebrated for their successes in the latter vocation.

Marriage is arranged without the woman's consent; the man bargains for her, pays the price, and takes her home. A feast and dance sometimes celebrate the event. When a wife is ill treated she demands a divorce, and returns home, taking her female children with her. Trifles often produce these separations, an insufficient allowance of pomatum to grease her skin being a valid complaint. These remarks apply to the fixed population; the wandering tribes of Kordofan are a moral, modest race, naked, but not indecent.

A chief of the Berbers offered a late traveler his choice of two daughters for a temporary companion, both being already married. Many women there are ready to prostitute themselves for a present. A virgin may be purchased, either as a wife or a concubine, for a horse. A young Berber, who was asked why he did not marry, pointed to a colt and said, " When that is a horse I shall marry."

The condition of women in Khartum, on the upper borders of the Nile, as described in Ferdinand Werne's account of his voyage to discover the sources of the White Stream, is so degraded that it may be said with truth the female monkeys of the neighboring woods occupy a far nobler and more natural position. Farther up the river the morals are purer. The Keks are described as leading a blameless life. Marriageable girls and children are kept in seclusion, and during a considerable part of the year the women live in villages apart from the men, who possess only temporary huts, the substantial habitations of their wives being accessible to them during the rainy season. A man dare not approach the " harem village" at any other time, but some of the women occasionally creep into their husbands' huts. Polygamy is allowed, but is too costly for any but the chiefs.

Among some of the tribes on the banks of the White Nile, women sell their children, if they can do so with profit. The maidens appear naked, but married women wear an apron. All experience shame at appearing unclothed before travelers. Beyond the Mountains of the Moon Werne found a people whom he describes as chaste and decent, where unmarried men and women were kept separate.

Our information is so limited that any inquiry into the morals of Africa must be incomplete, but enough has been stated to give a fair idea of the average morality. Statistics are of course impossible, but from a description in general terms we can not hesitate to form an opinion.

AUSTRALASIA.

In this division of the earth's surface are generally included the great island of Australia, Papua or New Guinea, and some adjacent islands, comprising New Caledonia and Van Diemen's Land.   Politically and geographically the islands of New Zealand are also in this division, but there is some question as to the propriety of this distribution for ethnographical purposes.   Opinions vary as to the state of the New Zealanders.   There is much similarity between them and the inhabitants of some of the Polynesian Islands, while there are equally strong points of resemblance between them and the Australian aborigines.   The New Zealander, when discovered by Cook, was far superior to the Australian in intelligence and in the arts of life.   He inhabited a decent hut, could build a stockade fort, and lived upon cooked food.   The Australian lived in a hollow tree, could put together a temporary hut made of bark and brush, and fed upon grubs, roots, and raw flesh.   Among such a race as the Australian blacks it is needless to say that the position occupied by women was of the most degrading and brutal character.

The Australian savage does not even pay his future spouse the compliment of wooing her.   Might makes right in their case.   The woman is often betrothed by her parent or kinsman, and becomes her husband's property by sale and bargain.   If this has not been effected in the usual way, he acquires his marital privileges by an inroad on the grounds of another tribe, and then meeting a woman, he knocks her down with his *waddy* (a heavy club), and carries her to a place of security, where he makes himself master of her person by force.   This, indeed, is so usual a course of procedure, that it has given rise to a belief that the Australian rival bachelors compete for a wife by knocking her on the head, and whoever fells her bears away the belle.

The habits of the native Australians are not so observable now as they were at the commencement of the system of colonization. At first a continual intercourse was kept up between them and the settlers.   The reciprocal injuries inflicted upon each other, in which the whites were more to blame than the natives, brought about an exterminating warfare.   The black race has gradually wasted away from the settled, or rather partially settled country, while the much-diminished interior tribes have retreated, in South Australia, New South Wales, and Victoria, far into the wilderness, beyond ordinary communication with the white man.

In Van Diemen's Land the natives were almost extirpated by the constant warfare carried on between them and the settlers, convict as well as free, and the government was obliged to take the few survivors under its protection, and to establish a place of refuge for them.   They were accordingly collected, and deported to an island in Bass Straits, under the charge of a special commissioner.   But, notwithstanding the increased comforts of their condition, and their immunity from the murderous hostility of their white foes, they have languished, and, instead of the population increasing, it has gradually decreased, until, at the present time, it is believed that the numbers are under one hundred.   In Central Australia, north of the Murray, the tribes are still comparatively numerous, and in some cases warlike and hostile to settlers.

The married women among the aborigines are called "gins," and the single girls "lubbras."   The women follow their lords on their migrations and excursions, carry the loads, and do all the work.   They bear patiently and submissively the blows and ill-usage to which they are subject.   Polygamy is practiced by the more powerful men of the tribes, who appropriate to themselves such women as they choose, and cast them off at pleasure.   Now and then they sell or present a "gin" to a friend in want of such a commodity.   There is considerable disproportion between the sexes, attributable partly to continual ill-usage, partly to the habit prevalent among savage nations of destroying female infants.

At one time in the history of these colonies, the outlying stockmen and shepherds occasionally endeavored to solace their loneliness with a "lubbra" whom they had managed to decoy from her lawful owner, but the half-breeds from such unions are very rare. The natives, notwithstanding the low estimate they have of their women, are exceedingly jealous of them as property, and keep them away as much as possible from the stations.

Chastity is at all times of little account among savages, always excepting the old Celts and Teutons, who held continence in high esteem, and whose women were objects of general respect.   From the peculiar habits of the Australian aborigines themselves, it can scarcely be said that prostitution exists as an institution.   The woman has no choice in the matter.   As between the "gins" and "lubbras" and the white settlers, there is scarcely any chance for prostitution.   A woman now and then visits the towns or settlements, but always in company with her male friends.   When quite young, the girls are not more disagreeable than others of their complexion. When more advanced in years they are absolutely repulsive, and are rendered hideous by scars and other evidences of brutality. At all times both sexes are loathsome in their persons, and are clad in filthy blankets or sheep-skins, unless when they can pick up tattered remnants of European clothing.

Among the New Zealanders the state of the women was a little better than among the Australians. The amelioration was rather in degree than principle. They were subject to the same control by parents and kinsmen. They were disposed of in marriage as matter of right, and were often betrothed from infancy, in which case they were *tapu* or *taboo* to other persons than the young chief or warrior who had purchased the reversion. Cruel punishments of the women for infidelity were general, and even for minor offenses they were subject to very severe chastisement. In one case, even recently, a New Zealand woman was suspended by the heels naked, and in that position unmercifully whipped. Her sense of the outrage was so keen that she committed suicide. Licentiousness among the women was probably more rare formerly than now. Adultery was punished in both parties by death, and the family of the male offender were often involved in the punishment. Now, however, the constant visits of whalers and seafaring men, the gradual settlement of whites in the islands, and, above all, the profits and advantages derivable from illicit intercourse, cause the women to be free of their persons. Parents and even husbands are oftentimes the principal gainers by the transaction, and even negotiate the profit to be made. The marriage ceremony, too, was formerly of so easy a character that, whatever the New Zealand woman might have thought of it, no settler, and especially no seaman, would feel himself bound by the tie, and, although associations based on this weak bond were not wrong in the woman, they paved the way for less excusable relations.

The influence of civilized institutions and the presence of a regular clergy and missionaries is effecting some improvement in native morals, and many lawful marriages have taken place between the whites and the native women, the offspring of which— a fine race of half-breeds—may be met with throughout the Australian colonies. The example of the consideration in which the native women thus married are held, and the rights and social position that they acquire, is not without influence on others, and predisposes them to the same course. Among the tribes removed from the coast and withdrawn from civilized control, the ancient customs are still kept up in their integrity, and the chiefs and natives jealously resist all encroachments on their independence. Among those chiefs, even, who have been converted to a nominal Christianity, Rauperaha for instance, heathen institutions of re venge for injury, polygamy, power of life and death over their wives and followers are maintained, and the humanizing lessons of the Gospel have made but little way toward an amendment of their barbarous lives. In New Zealand it is asserted that the venereal disease is very prevalent among the natives, and from their diet and licentious habits is often fatal.

In colonial white society there are no particular incidents to characterize prostitution. At all times during the continuance of transportation, female immorality has been very prevalent. The general law so often observed as attendant upon irregularity of the sexes has been powerfully operative; besides, there have been local influences at work to deteriorate female manners. The large importations of convict women, who were always the most unruly and vicious of the felon population, and who notoriously gave more trouble and vexation to the authorities than any one else, was prejudicial to public virtue. Just, however, as, on account of these faults, women of indifferent character were lightly esteemed, so did the respectable females gain in public opinion, however poor their worldly condition. There was not much regular prostitution, although incontinence prevailed. There was a continual system of marriage going on among the convicts. When a man chose to marry, he brushed himself up, put on a clean shirt, and went to the nearest superintendent, to whom he intimated his desire for matrimony. Permission was always given. The eligibles at the station were forwarded for his inspection, and the selected one rarely refused, inasmuch as her connubial bonds relieved her, during good behavior, from the more galling bondage of the law. Some of these unions turned out more satisfactorily than might have been expected from the character of the parties, especially of the women.

South Australia and the gold colony of Victoria never were penal settlements. The deficiency of respectable young women was very much felt by the colonists, and the home government made many well-intentioned efforts to supply the want. A large number of young women went out from Great Britain, under the charge of matrons and medical officers, and, in the majority of cases, their arrival was hailed with great satisfaction. It was no unusual thing for a young man, a settler far away up the country, to come down to the government depôts at Adelaide or Melbourne on the arrival of a female emigrant ship, and then and there to pick out his partner for life.   Of course, the greater number were hired out to service by the colonists, and, in the order of events, passed from service to independence.   Parental care and precaution were exercised by the authorities over the young women thus sent abroad.   They were not allowed to hire into dram-shops or lodging-houses: the parties who hired them required to be known: they had liberty to remain at the depôt for some months if not suited, and for any length of time in case of sickness on arrival; and afterward, during good conduct, the depôt was an asylum for an indefinite length of time.   Notwithstanding all these safeguards, there was a constant supply of prostitution.   The good intentions of the emigration commissioners in London were too frequently neutralized by the depraved character of officers of the vessels in which females were sent, or by the interested conduct of the local authorities in England.   A good reputation was essential to the intending emigrant, but frequently masters of work-houses and parish officers shipped off unworthy or troublesome characters, who were better got rid of at any price.

During the gold mania, prostitution in Australia was rampant. The enormous gains and flaunting extravagance were a great temptation to young women who could not readily suit themselves with situations, and who disliked the moderate restraints of the depôt.   The persuasive arts of the procuress and brothel-keeper were not wanting.   It was a singular fact that at one time all the public vehicles were owned by brothel-keepers.   The profits of these joint callings were perfectly fabulous.   It was an every-day sight to see a party of prostitutes in the most gaudy costumes parading the streets in open carriages.   Indeed, it was generally understood to be part of their contract that they should have unlimited clothing, of the most garish colors and style, and expensive material, and also Sunday rides in open carriages.   The police authorities did what they could to check this shameful display, but they were powerless before the reckless extravagance of the miners and the influx of women.   It is believed that this excess has now toned down, and miners having taken to buying land and to marriage, order is once more resuming sway, and prostitution in the gold colonies, though not at an end, is much shorn of its public show and display.

POLYNESIA.

The principal groups of the Polynesian Islands are the Society, Friendly, Samoan, Sandwich, and Marquesas. These last have been rendered famous of late years by Mr. Hermann Melville's Typee and Omoo.

The South Sea Islands were usually depicted in the most glowing colors by early navigators. The lands were the fairest on earth's surface; the climate was unsurpassed, combining the genial warmth of the tropics with the fresh breezes of ocean; the soil spontaneously bringing forth in luxuriant abundance the loveliest and most valuable vegetable productions; and, finally, the inhabitants were fitted both in person and disposition to tenant such an Eden.

It is easy to comprehend the frame of mind which led to these descriptions. The seaman, after wandering over the pathless ocean, with only the dark waste of waters in view, might well recognize a paradise in the green hills and shady groves of the islands of the Pacific, and angels in their dusky denizens. But these pictures were eminently fallacious: the virtues of savage life disappear on close acquaintanceship. Implacable ferocity among themselves; sanguinary and exterminating warfare; cannibalism; unbounded licentiousness and its concomitants of unnatural lust and lasciviousness; debasing and horrid idolatry; infanticide; the most grinding tyranny of the strong over the weak, and of the man over the woman, who is not permitted to live in the same dwelling, eat the same food, cook at the same fire, or even use the same dish as her lord and master: these enormities are the ordinary conditions of savage life. Some local modifications may be found, but such were the main incidents in Polynesian life and character.

It is true that in the first instance the natives received the whites with all friendship, and evinced toward their visitors much hospitality and gentleness of demeanor. This is to be attributed to the wonder and reverence with which they regarded foreigners, looking on them as superior beings of another sphere, and awestruck at their wonderful powers, at the astonishing engines they wielded and managed, and at their unknown attributes. But familiarity lessened respect; some ill-advised and unjustifiable tyranny brought out the offensive points of savage character, and theft, treachery, and murder were soon practiced as freely against the whites as against each other whenever fear of consequences did not restrain them. The murder of Captain Cook and the attack on La Perouse were remarkable cases on account of the boldness of the savages, and the public loss in the death of the great navigator, but they were not isolated outrages. Many a small and feebly-manned vessel perished among the islands, and, on repeated occasions, when landings were effected, the mariners ran great risks from the uncertain despotism of the natives.

Whatever may have been their other qualities, either among themselves or in their intercourse with foreigners, licentiousness was the universal characteristic of the South Sea Islanders. It was not merely polygamy or excess among a few of the more powerful members of the community, but the ordinary habit among all classes. Chastity, whenever met with, was not a customary part of woman's life, but only an incident dependent on particular circumstances; in fact, an abnormal condition. It was associated with either marriage or betrothal. A peculiar institution of all these islanders was the *tapu* or *taboo*, a semi-religious ceremony performable either by priest or chief, whereby places, persons, or property could be rendered unapproachable by other than the lawful owner. The breach of this law has always been the greatest violation of propriety and public feeling of which a native or foreigner could be guilty. When young girls were betrothed at an early age, either to boys of corresponding years or to older persons, such females were *tabooed*. This insured chastity until they had reached a marriageable age. As this betrothal system was almost exclusively confined to chiefs, it follows that the obligation to chastity was very limited. The farther inference would be, that chastity was associated rather with property in the female than propriety in the woman.

Another institution of the South Sea Islanders was that of the *Areoi*. These were a body of men and women banded together for certain purposes, which had originally been of a religious character. They had probably been once *Obi* men, medicine-men, or wizards, as among the negroes and Indians. The custom, so often observable among heathen nations, of incorporating amusements and festivities into religious rites, had been taken up by these Areoi, and in process of time they degenerated into mere mimes or buffoons, and yet preserved to themselves by prescriptive right all the immunities and privileges otherwise accorded to priests. They traveled about from place to place, and sometimes from island to island. Their observances yet retained a trace of their religious origin, inasmuch as they commenced with a sacrifice to the gods, after which they entertained the people with theatrical performances, in which obscene songs and lascivious dances formed the chief features. They gave dialogues and recitations, in which they freely satirized all classes, not excepting the priests. They were every where gladly received, and had a right to free quarters wherever they stopped. It is said the members were usually the handsomest of both sexes, the women being the most profligate among the inhabitants. Tradition maintained that these persons had been originally incorporated by the gods, and that one of their rules was perpetual celibacy, and that they should have no descendants. This, though it might perhaps in the outset have been a prohibition intended for pure purposes, has ended in the perversion of such an intention. In their present condition, whether degenerate or not, the inhibition is not taken to exclude them from sexual intercourse and enjoyment, but from its natural consequences. Their lives were accordingly most abandoned, and abortion and infanticide were invariably practiced. Nor were their enormities confined to their own body: after their representations the wildest excesses were perpetrated in all quarters. Resistance or retaliation was impossible by the sufferer, on account of the fear these wretches excited by the mysterious powers with which they were accredited, and which were, in reality, the secret affiliations of all the bands.[1]

When performing, the Areoi painted their bodies black and their faces scarlet; they wore dresses of bright-colored plants and flowers. They were divided into several classes, named after some particular ornament; and, taking into account the subordinate members of the troops and the attendants who performed the menial offices, they must have been exceedingly numerous. Places were specially built for their reception, and for the greater convenience of their representations.[2]

Candidates for admission into their number were received by secret ceremonies akin to the mysteries of paganism. Solemnities intended to awe the vulgar were performed, and the idea of special reservation of the blessings of a future elysium to these deceivers was promulgated and believed.

---

[1] Russell's History of Polynesia, p. 75.

[2] Their institution is ascribed to Oro, the god of war. The resemblance between Areoi and Aeης, the Greek god of war, is a coincidence.

The existence of such organized societies could not but be in the highest degree subversive to all order and decency. Accordingly, when the missionaries first arrived, they found the general depravity of morals the greatest difficulty they had to encounter. Obscenity, libidinousness, and incontinence were so ingrafted into the very nature of the people that they seemed almost ineradicable. Accordingly, we find it narrated of an intelligent convert that he expressed his conviction that "the people ought to be induced to discontinue infanticide, human sacrifice, and demon worship, but that preservation of female virtue and Christian marriage would never be obtained."[1]

The Society Islands are said to have been formerly proverbial, even in Polynesia, for the licentiousness which is still remarkably prevalent among them. The missionary regulations have apparently mitigated the evils, and they have succeeded in establishing laws on the subject, which are not, however, binding upon strangers. The foreigners who come to these islands, while denouncing the conduct of the inhabitants, are too often the chief instigators to vice, and, finding themselves checked in their misconduct, they vent their disappointment on the missionaries.

The foreign influences at work in these islands are of a two-fold nature; one striving for the improvement of the natives, and the inculcation of virtuous principles, and the encouragement or enforcement of virtuous practices; the other including all the base and sordid passions and motives of seamen and whalers bent on the reckless enjoyment of the passing hour; of traders and adventurers eager in quest of gain; and among the worst specimens of runaway seamen, and even convicts from the Australian settlements. All these influences combine to check the advancement of the natives.

The beauty of the women in these islands has been much exaggerated. Commodore Wilkes says,[2] "I did not see among them a single woman whom I could call handsome. They have, indeed, a certain sleepiness about the eyes which may be fascinating to some, but I should rather ascribe the celebrity which their charms have acquired among navigators to their cheerfulness and gayety." Others, who visit them with equally cool judgment, tell us that they were disappointed in their appearance, for "there were few who could be called handsome; nevertheless, they had eminent feminine graces, their manners being affable and engaging, their step easy and graceful, their behavior free and unguarded, their temper mild, gentle, and unaffected, slow to take offense, easily pacified, seldom retaining resentment or revenge, whatever the provocation."[1]

There can be no doubt that their demeanor was winning and affable, and their conduct sportive and playful. Their industry was not very great, the few wants of the islanders being amply supplied by nature. The women prepared the poe from the bread-fruit and the ava, and, till Europeans introduced the hog, this was their usual diet, if we except the cannibal feasts of the warriors, in which the women took no part. The female occupations were weaving flowers and grasses into garlands and mats. Their chief amusement was paddling the canoe or sporting in the surf, for all the islanders took to the water, and the women were, perhaps, from the greater buoyancy of their persons, better swimmers than the men. Before the arrival of the missionaries, it was customary for the women to swim out to a ship and swarm on board, where scenes of debauchery and indecency commenced, lasting as long as the vessel lay in the harbor, and the fascination of which worked so powerfully on the excited passions of the seamen that desertions and mutiny were continually occurring.

The earliest intercourse of whites has never yet been beneficial to the untutored savage, and, had these occurrences only taken place on board the ships of foreigners, it might have been laid to the account of foreign corruption. But this was not the case. The gains derivable from the white men's visits might give profligacy a greater zest for both sexes of the natives, for indiscriminate intercourse was a time-worn institution ere yet the European came.

The South Sea Islanders are no exception to the general rule of keeping their women in a subordinate and inferior condition. A chief is sometimes *taboo*, and his women may not approach him; he may see them when he pleases; at all times the woman is in bondage. Those of the chief live in separate apartments from their master, and are not permitted to associate with him on equal terms excepting when the female is of high blood. In this case she is perfectly independent, can exercise the same powers as her husband, and in some particulars can even throw off her allegiance to him.

Polygamy was, and still is, practiced among the chiefs. Even

[1] Missionary Voyage of Ship Duff, 1796, p. 336.

C c

where missionary influences have been successful, the chiefs look upon the abolition of polygamy as a most objectionable innovation. They look back to their past liberty with regret, and can not understand why they are restricted to one wife. Polygamy could, of course, only be practiced by the powerful at the expense of the weak. Already, from various causes operating among savages there was a preponderance of males over females, rendered still more great by polygamy. This again depreciated female virtue, justifying illicit intercourse to those who lived in forced celibacy, and in its consequences came concealment and infanticide. To such an extent was illicit intercourse carried, that some writers assert that no girl ever reached the age of puberty a virgin. The nature of the marriage bond is very uncertain. The husband could get rid of the wife at pleasure. There seems to have been a slight distinction between marriage and concubinage. Most of these social institutions are extended over all the islands alike, with very few local differences. Infanticide, for example, has been practiced in most of the islands, but not invariably so. At Tutuila,[1] one of the Samoan group, it had never obtained. Circumcision was common among most of the natives.

Among the Samoans the women are treated with consideration.[2] The men do all the hard work, even to cooking, while the women perform only in-door labor, attend to the children, and prepare the food for the fire. In the Sandwich Islands there is no such chivalrous sentiment. At the arrival of the missionaries there were no marriage institutions among them. The only laws were such as to regulate somewhat their licentiousness. There were traditions to show that at some past time, before the discovery of the island, the marriage tie had been held in respect by the natives, and that the marriage ceremony had been an important one. At present, personal chastisement of the wife by her husband is not infrequent, and it is spoken of by them as a matter of course.

The relations of parents to children differed much at different periods. The Samoans seem to have been the most observant of moral obligations and natural ties. Among them it was the usage of the mothers to suckle the children for several years, and to bring them up with great care and attention, so much so that a crippled child was sometimes discreditable as evincing a degree of culpable carelessness in the mother.

[1] U. S. Exploring Expedition, vol. ii. p. 80. [2] Ib. 148.

The Society and Sandwich Islanders, whose lives were habitually dissolute, shunned all trouble which interfered with their freedom of intercourse, and children were considered especially burdensome. Infanticide prevailed to a frightful extent among them, and, as if the ordinary dissoluteness of the people had not been ample inducement to this most flagitious crime, the tyranny of the rulers invented a poll-tax, in whose operation children over ten were included. The poorer inhabitants of these blissful regions, who already felt the rod of oppression too severely, found in this an additional motive to child-murder. But in its operation it was even more cruel than infanticide, for many children who had been suffered to live were put to death as they approached the period when they would be liable to taxation. The murder was consummated sometimes by the parents, at times mercifully, and at times horribly. There were a class of persons who practiced child-murder professionally.

In the Samoan group the girls are often early betrothed, without reference to years, the girl being taboo until of marriageable age. During the intervening period the bridegroom accumulates property. The marriage festival is held with all circumstances of uproar and debauchery, and the guests stay as long as there is any thing to eat. The consummation of the marriage and the virginity of the bride are published by the proofs required in the Jewish law.

When a man in this group wishes to take a wife, he must ask the chief's consent. This obtained, he presents to the girl of his choice a basket of bread-fruit, by accepting which she accepts the donor. The husband then pays the parents a sum of money for her, according to her rank and estimation; sometimes the courtship is to the family, without consulting the girl, who is expected to conform to her parents' will in the matter.

A Samoan may repudiate his wife and marry again on certain conditions, but the woman may not leave her husband without his consent.

Adultery among the Samoans was formerly punished by death, and the marriage vow is strictly observed by them. It is considered highly discreditable for a young woman to form a connection with a native before marriage, although temporary intercourse with a foreigner is not considered objectionable. It may be that such a distinction is in compliment to the conceded superiority of the white; but the explanation of a chief would rather put the question on convenience than morality, for he objected to native young men as always hanging about the premises, and attaching themselves to the young woman, whereas the foreigner gave his presents and sailed away when the period of his stay was ended, leaving the object of his choice free again.

The Marquesas Islands have a singular institution, similar to one prevalent among the ancient Lacedæmonians. A woman has more than one husband. This has been called polyandrism, but it does not seem precisely such. A wife of a young warrior unknown to fame is honored by the advances of a more distinguished individual, by whom children may be begotten. The superior chief takes the wife and her lawful husband under his protection and into his hut.

The population of some of the districts in the Sandwich Islands is rapidly decreasing. By a register kept in Hawaii, it appears there are three deaths to one birth. This disproportion is attributed to low habit of body, the consequence of venereal disease. Syphilis was introduced into these islands by Cook's expedition, and the whole of the natives in some districts are now said to be reduced to a morbid, sickly state, many of the women being incapable of child-bearing, and but few of the children attaining maturity.

There are other concurrent causes to contribute toward this decay, among which the difference of food, and the introduction of clothing, and consequent diminution of ablution among a people who spent half their lives in the water, are not unimportant; but the district of Hanapepe, where the decrease was most rapid, was that in which the virus was first introduced, and here it is still most virulent in its action and effects.

Whatever the causes, the same effect is in powerful operation, though not to the same depopulating extent, in other places. At Waialua, in 1832, the population was 2640; in 1835 it had fallen to 2415. There had been no war nor epidemic. It was the ordinary condition of the people. Sterility and abortion are considered the most potent causes. Abortion is very common, and there are cases in which women have had six or seven, and sometimes ten in as many years, and no children.[1]

Personal and mutual abuse had been much practiced in early life among the settlers, and is a cause of sterility.

Previous to 1840, infanticide was, as we have shown, common.

[1] Wilkes, vol. iv. p. 77.

But here, as elsewhere, the marriage regulations which have been enforced by the missionaries and adopted by the converted natives are already operating in a reactionary manner against the decrease of population, and infanticide is almost unknown. The poll-tax for children over ten years of age has been repealed, and in its stead premiums are given for rearing large families of legitimate children.

It is admitted by all that licentiousness prevails extensively among the people even at present, but to a far less degree than formerly, when promiscuous intercourse was universal. Men were living with several wives, and *vice versa.* All improvement in this respect is to be ascribed to the labors of Christian missionaries. To them the Sandwich Islanders owe their moral code, and the enactment of laws respecting marriage, as well as their political institutions.

The observance of outward morality and decency of behavior has, as we have mentioned, been made compulsory in those islands in which the missionaries have permanently fixed themselves, and acquired sufficient power to make their regulations respected. They have interdicted public gatherings for the purpose of amusement, and even suppressed private games and diversions. This has been objected to as an interference with innocent recreation and pastime, and as encouraging formalism.

But the missionaries had no choice in the matter. Paganism was deeply rooted in the daily life and habits of the people. In all religious festivals, feasting, dancing, and diversion formed so prominent a part, that the only method of eradicating the attachment of the people to their heathen practices was to abolish the usages which made the worship attractive. The dances are always immodest, often lascivious and grossly indecent. They consist of little more than contortions and twistings of the limbs and body, and of throwing themselves into postures which, as they are mostly performed by females, are highly conducive to immorality.

Even among the Samoans, the dances, as performed by the women, are of the same libidinous character with the others, though the dances of the men are not indecorous.

The diseases generally prevalent are skin affections. From the delightful climate and simple diet of the people, these are not of a very severe character. The islanders have been no gainers in this respect by their intercourse with Europeans. The venereal disease has been introduced, and, from the deficiency of medical treatment, makes great ravages. Secondary syphilis is sometimes severe. At Tutuila, one of the Samoan group, it is said that venereal disease is entirely unknown, while in the other islands of the group it is very rare.

Political circumstances; the introduction of new elements into Polynesian life; the daily increasing intercourse between the islanders and foreigners, all contribute to make the alterations in the social aspects of the South Sea Islands very rapid, so that every year may work new changes. Some recent writers affect to doubt the benefits of missionary labors among the islanders, who, as they say, have been thereby diverted from their innocent and simple habits of life; in place of which, it is alleged, a harsh and hypocritical austerity has been adopted; the purity of their morals and the vigor of their constitutions have been sapped and destroyed by the contact with Europeans and Americans, and the whole result of foreign intercourse has been unmixed evil. We reject these conclusions, as savoring too strongly of party prejudice and class antipathies. The tendency of the Gospel always is to purify and elevate savage tribes. The missionaries have, perhaps, overestimated and overstated the extent of benefit accomplished by them, and the gayety and cheerfulness, so pleasing in appearance to the casual visitor, yet so deceptive in reality, may have been diminished. But the purity of savage life is a delusion, and something has been achieved if only an outward conformity to the laws and dictates of Christianity has been produced.

WEST INDIES.

A very slight notice of the West Indies will suffice, for of the savage races scarcely a vestige remains; of the negro population a general view is all that is required, and the civilized colonists retain so much of the impress of the countries whence they came as to require no special remarks. When Columbus first visited these beautiful islands, he found them inhabited by two classes of men—the savage Caribs, who delighted in war and preyed upon the weaker tribes; and the simple communities, whose pacific habits made them victims of their violent neighbors. The people were alike distinct in the treatment of women. The peaceful islanders admitted females to a participation in all the delights of their rural life, allowing them to mingle in the dance, to inherit power, and to share all their pleasures. Among the cannibal

Caribs a different fashion prevailed. The handsomest of their war-prisoners were retained as slaves, the rest were drowned. The lot of these exiles, as of the Carib women themselves, was hard enough. The nation was low and barbarous, and its women were treated accordingly, the men regarding them as an inferior race, whose degradation was only natural. A wife was her husband's slave, and all the drudgery of life fell upon her. She approached him with abject humility, and, if she ever complained of ill-usage, it was at the risk of her life; her children, however, were loved and watched with tender care.

The original inhabitants of the West Indian islands have disappeared, and are succeeded by a mixture of races, of whom the negroes claim our attention now. Among the blacks of Antigua, as an example, immorality is characteristic. Infanticide is frequently practiced, even since the Emancipation Bill was passed. The reason for this is clear. Under slavery, negroes could not contract a legal marriage; they therefore cohabited, and the union lasted as long as their affection or appetite existed. No disgrace attached to a woman who had borne children to several men. Now an idea of female virtue has been awakened, and they seek to escape the consequences of an illicit amour by destroying its offspring, upon the principle that where no tangible evidence of a crime exists, no crime has been committed.

During slavery, concubinage was general; and although many masters offered rewards to such as lived faithfully with one partner, the vice was all but universal, and a permanent engagement between a man and woman was seldom formed. Two females frequently lived with one man, one being considered his wife, and the other his mistress. When the negroes were emancipated in 1834, many were anxious to be legally married, and others put away the partners of their compulsory servitude and took new companions. Bigamy was not uncommon then, nor is it rare now, many devices being adopted to elude the stringent laws on this matter. Concubinage is less general than formerly, but the marriage covenant is by no means respected, nor is chastity much esteemed.

In St. Lucia sexual intercourse was unrestrained and almost promiscuous, and the negroes of the island are, even to this day, averse to matrimony and inclined to concubinage. In either relation they are equally faithless, the only redeeming feature being love of their children.

The same low state of morals is observable in Santa Cruz, but in Jamaica the negroes are mostly married and faithful to their engagements. Formerly the intercourse of the sexes was loose, profligate, and lewd. When the missionaries attempted to reform this, any who submitted to their teachings were ridiculed by the demoralized of their comrades. It must be admitted that Europeans have not shown any good example to the negroes, but, on the contrary, have encouraged their vices.

JAVA.

A curious system of manners now prevails in Java. Hindoos have been succeeded by Mohammedans, and they, in turn, have given place to Dutch, each having impressed some characteristic on the people. As elsewhere, the condition of the female sex will indicate the general character. The institution of marriage is universally known, if not practiced or respected, and the lot of women may be considered fortunate. They are not ill-used in any manner, and the seclusion imposed upon the more opulent is rather a withdrawal from the indiscriminate gaze of the people than that lonely secrecy exacted by jealousy in some parts of the East. The condition of the sex in Java is an exception to the habits of Asiatics. They associate with the men in all the pleasures and offices of life, eat with them, and live on terms of mutual equality. They are sometimes permitted to ascend the throne, and, in short, nowhere throughout the island are they treated with coarseness, violence, or neglect. They are willing and industrious, and are admitted to many honorable employments. Men sometimes act tyrannically in their households, but this only shows the fault of an individual, not of a class.

Polygamy and concubinage are practiced by the nobility without reference to public opinion, but are not generally adopted, being regarded as vicious luxuries. The first wife is always mistress of the household; the others are her servants, who may minister to her husband's pleasures, but do not share his rank or wealth. No man will give his daughter as second or third wife, unless to some one far superior in rank to himself; and a woman considers it dishonorable, not, in the abstract, to prostitute herself, but to form a connection with any man of humbler birth than herself.

But, though polygamy and concubinage are seldom known in Java, their absence must not be considered as implying superior morality. On the contrary, it is the most immoral country in Asia. A woman who would not condescend to be the second wife of a chief would not scruple to commit adultery with him. In general terms, both sexes are profligate and depraved, although the islanders boast the chastity of their women as a distinguishing ornament, because a married woman would shriek if a stranger attempted to kiss her before her attendants.

Divorce can be procured in Java with the utmost freedom, and is a privilege in which the women indulge themselves to a wanton degree. If a wife pays her husband a sum of money, he must leave her. He is not legally bound to accept her offer, but public opinion considers it disreputable to live with a woman who has thus signified her wishes for a separation, and he yields to general sentiment what is not exacted by law. The husband is often changed three or four times before the woman is thirty years old, and some boast the exercise of this privilege twelve times. As the means of subsistence abound, and are procured as easily by women as by men, the former are independent of the latter, and find no difficulty in living without husbands. Unfortunately for the theories of some female reformers of the present day, who imagine that such independence foreshadows the millennium of woman's rights, it must be admitted that, where the experiment has been tried, the sex are proverbially dissolute.

Among the wealthier classes the utmost immorality prevails, and in the great towns the population is debauched to the last degree. Intrigues with married women continually occur, and are prosecuted almost before the face of the husbands, who are often so tame and servile that they dare not assert their conjugal rights. Travelers have noticed flagrant instances of the looseness of Japanese manners, but one case will suffice. One of the princes, who had seduced a married woman, and was in the habit of visiting her at times when her husband, an officer in the public guard, was on duty, was surprised in her company on one occasion, the chief having returned home earlier than was expected. He knew the rank of his visitor, and discreetly coughed, so that the prince had time to escape. He then went to the chamber and flogged his wife. She complained to the prince, who was particularly desirous, at that time, to conciliate his subjects. He sent for the husband, made him many rich presents, and allowed him to select the handsomest woman in the royal household in place of the frail one who had betrayed him. The husband accepted the peace-offerings, allowed his wife to return home with him, and all the parties were satisfied.

In Java women are usually married very young, as their chastity is in danger as soon as they reach maturity. At eighteen or twenty a girl is considered to be getting old, and scarcely any are unmarried after twenty-two. Yet age does not exclude a woman from the probabilities of matrimony, for widows often procure husbands at fifty. The preliminary arrangements are made by the parents, as scandal would not allow the young people to take any part in a transaction in which they are looked upon, as the natives express it, as mere puppets. The father of the youth, having made a suitable choice, proposes to the parents of the girl. If they are willing, the betrothal is ratified by some trifling present, and visits are made, that the intended nuptials may be publicly known. Subsequently the price of the lady is arranged, varying according to the rank and circumstances of the family. Sometimes this is plainly called the "purchase-money," and sometimes by a more delicate term, the "deposit." It is considered as a settlement for the bride. The only religious feature in the marriage ceremony is an exchange of vows in the mosque. This is followed by many observances of etiquette and parade. Finally, the married couple eat from the same vessel, to testify their common fortune, or the bride washes her husband's feet in token of subjection.

The Javanese support a large class of women as public dancers. The inhabitants are passionately fond of this amusement, but no respectable woman will join in it, and all its female partisans are prostitutes; in fact, the words *dancer* and *prostitute* are synonymous in their language. A chief of high rank is not ashamed to be seen with one of these women, who figure at most large entertainments, and frequently amass enough money to induce some petty chief to marry them. So strong, however, is their ruling passion, they soon ascertain that domesticity is not their sphere, and become tired of their husbands, whom they divorce without ceremony, and coolly return to their public life. The dress in which they perform is very immodest, but they seldom descend to such obscene and degrading postures as may be witnessed in other Eastern countries.

European example has not done much for Java. The Dutch merchant has usually a native female called his housekeeper. In every city public prostitutes abound, while about the roads in the vicinity may be found others ready for hire. Their disguise as dancers is thought to conceal their profligacy.

SUMATRA.

The population of this island is divided into several tribes, slightly differing in their manners. The Rejangs, who may be supposed to represent its original inhabitants, are rude barbarians, scrupulously attentive to the show, but wanting the spirit of delicacy. They drape their women from head to foot, dread lest a virgin should expose any part of her person, and yet modesty is not a characteristic of the people in towns and villages. Those in rural districts who are not so rigid as to costume are more distinguished by decency.

The customs of Sumatra are of a peculiar character, great importance being attached to required formulas; and the ritual is more essential than the principle. It is curious to examine the intricate details of a Sumatran marriage contract, which appears to be so little understood even by the people themselves that, we are informed, one of these documents is sufficient to originate an almost endless litigation.

There are several modes of forming a marriage contract. The first is when one man agrees to pay another a certain sum in exchange for his daughter. A portion of the amount, say about five dollars, is generally held back, to keep the transaction open, and allow the girl's parents a chance to complain if she is ill used. If the husband wound her, he is liable to a fine, and in many ways his authority is controlled. But if he insists on paying the balance of the purchase-money, her parents must accept it, and then their right of interference ceases. If a father desires to get rid of a girl suffering from any infirmity, he sells her without this reservation, and she has fewer privileges in consequence.

In other cases marriage is an affair of barter, one virgin being given for another. A man having a son and a daughter will give the latter in exchange for a wife for the former; or a brother will dispose of his sister in the same way. Sometimes a girl evades these customs by eloping with a lover of her own choice. If the fugitives are overtaken on the road, they can be separated; but if they have taken refuge in any house, and the man declares his willingness to obey existing rules, his wife is secured to him. The Jewish custom of a man marrying his brother's widow is in force among the Sumatrans, and if there be no brother, she must be taken by the nearest male relative, the father excepted, who is made responsible for any balance of her purchase-money which may be due.

Adultery is not frequently committed under this system, but when it is, the husband chastises his wife himself, or else forgives the offense.   If he desire to divorce her, he may claim back the purchase-money, less twenty-five dollars, which is allowed her parents for depreciation in the woman's value.   If a man who has taken a wife is unable to pay the whole price, her friends may sue for a divorce, but then they must return all they have received from him.   The ceremony of divorce consists in cutting a ratan in two in presence of the parties and their witnesses.

Another kind of marriage is when a girl's father selects some man whom he adopts into his family, receiving a premium of about twenty dollars.   The father-in-law's family thus acquire a property in the young husband; they are answerable for his debts, claim all he earns, and have the privilege of turning him out of doors when they are tired of him.

The Malays of Sumalda have generally adopted a third kind of marriage, which they call *the free*.   In this the families approach each other on an equal level.   A small sum, about twelve dollars, is paid to the girl's parents, and an agreement is made that all property shall be common between husband and wife, and if a divorce takes place it shall be fairly divided.   The actual ceremony of marriage is simple: a feast is given, the couple join their hands, and some one pronounces them man and wife.

Where the female is an article of sale, little of what we call courtship can be expected.   It is opposed to the manners of the country, which impose strict separation of the sexes in youth; and, besides, when a man pays the price of his wife, he considers he is entitled to possession, without any question as to her predilections.   But traces of courtship may be met with.   On the very few occasions when young people are allowed to meet, such as public festivals, a degree of respect is shown to women contrasting very favorably with the observances of more civilized communities, and mutual attachments sometimes spring from these associations.   The festivals are enlivened by dances and songs. The former have been described as licentious, but an English traveler says he has often seen more immodest displays in a ball-room in his native country.   The songs are extempore, and love is the constant theme.

Polygamy is permitted, but only a few chiefs have more than one wife.   To be a second one is considered far below the dignity of a respectable woman, and a man would demand a divorce for his daughter if her husband was about to take an additional companion.

Marsden, the traveler already mentioned, says that in the country parts of Sumatra chastity is general; but the merit is lost when he adds that interest causes the parents to be watchful of their daughters, because the selling price of a virgin is far above that of a woman who has been defiled. If a case of seduction occurs, the seducer can be forced to marry the girl and pay her original price, or else give her parents the sum which they would lose by her error.

Regular prostitution is rare. In the bazars of the towns some women of this class may be found, and in the sea-ports profligacy abounds, troops of professional courtesans parading the streets. No one would estimate the morality of a country from the spectacles exhibited in maritime cities. As a general rule, the Sumatran is content to marry, and is faithful to his wife. This may proceed from temperament rather than morality, as their ideas on the latter are not very rigid. This is shown by their opinion of incest, which they regard as an infraction of conventional law, sometimes punishing it by a fine, and at other times confirming the marriage, unless it occurs within the first degree of relationship.

BORNEO.

Notwithstanding the attention which has been drawn to the island of Borneo within the last few years, it is yet but little known to the general reader. The investigations of Sir James Brooke and others have enabled us to discern many of its social features. Most of the inhabitants of Borneo are in a state of barbarism. Some wander naked in the forest, and subsist on the spontaneous productions of the earth; others cultivate the soil, dwell in villages, and trade with their neighbors. The river communities are more advanced than those who live inland, and the inhabitants of sea-ports are more educated and more profligate than any. These have been farther debased by the abominable system of piracy, which, until recently, was their occupation.

Among the Sea Dyaks, or dwellers on the coast, there is no social law to govern sexual intercourse before marriage, nor is the authority of parents recognized in the matter. The Dyak girl selects a husband for herself, and, while she remains single, incurs no disgrace by cohabiting with as many as she pleases. After marriage she is subject to more stringent rules, for, as a man is allowed only one wife, he requires her to be faithful, or in default punishes her with a severe whipping. If he is incontinent he incurs a similar penalty. Cases of adultery are not frequent, though they sometimes occur in time of war.

The ceremony of marriage is as simple as possible. The consent of the woman is first obtained, then the bride and bridegroom meet and give a feast, which completes the contract.

If a girl becomes pregnant, the father of the child must marry her, and this is a common way of securing a husband. A man and woman live together for a time, and separate if there is no prospect of a family. During this probation constancy is not considered indispensable. The fear of not becoming the father of a family, a misfortune greatly dreaded by the Dyaks, favors the loose intercourse of unmarried people. In some tribes the duties of hospitality require that if a chief is traveling he shall be furnished with a *pro tempore* female companion at every place where he sleeps.

Among the Dyaks dwelling on the hills morality is of a higher standard. Single men are obliged to sleep in a separate building, and the girls are not allowed to approach them. Marriage is contracted at a very early age, and adultery is almost unknown. Polygamy is not allowed, but some of the chiefs indulge in a concubine, for which they are generally blamed. There are certain degrees of consanguinity within which marriage is unlawful. One man shocked public feeling by marrying his granddaughter, and the people affirm that ruin and darkness have covered the face of the sun ever since that act of incest. As they marry constantly within their own tribe, the whole commonwealth is in time united by ties of blood, and to this is ascribed the insanity common among them, a conclusion warranted to some extent by the imbecile state of well-known royal families condemned to perpetual intermarriages.

It is said that many prostitutes may be found among the people of the South, but this rests on doubtful testimony, and in the Dyak language there is no word to express the vice.

The Sibnouan females are neither concealed from strangers nor shy before them. They will bathe naked in the presence of men. The unmarried people sleep promiscuously in a common room, but married couples have separate apartments. The labor of the household is allotted to females, who grind rice, carry burdens, fetch water, catch fish, and till the ground. They are not so degraded as in other barbarous nations. They eat with the men, and take part in their festivals as well as their labor.

Among the Mohammedan Malays there is more civilization and more corruption. They are polygamists, indulge in concubinage, encourage prostitutes, and ill use their wives. An English physician lately received a message from the wife of a chief appointing a secret meeting. He was punctual to the assignation, and met the lady, who asked him for a dose of arsenic to poison her husband, as he ill-treated her. Report says that the Englishman was disappointed in the nature of the interview, but firmly refused to grant her request.

The rich Malays allow their wives to keep female slaves, and the jealousy of the mistress renders their situation any thing but pleasant. They sometimes serve as concubines, in which case the law renders them free, but many refuse to avail themselves of this advantage.

We have no definite account of prostitutes in sea-port towns, but they appear to be of several classes: those who cohabit temporarily with the Malays, those who prostitute themselves indiscriminately to all comers, and those who are supported by sailors and profligate Chinese, who invariably create such a class wherever they settle. It is certain that women of this class exist in considerable numbers in Borneo.

CHAPTER XXXI.

SEMI-CIVILIZED NATIONS.

Persia.—Afghanistan.—Kashmir.—India.—Ceylon.—Ultra-Gangetic Nations.—Celebes.—China.—Japan.—Tartar Races.—Circassia.—Turkey.—Northern Africa.—Siberia.—Esquimaux.—Iceland.—Greenland.

PERSIA.

WOMEN occupy an inferior position in Persia, where they are literally the property of men. The lower classes consider them valuable for their labor, the rich regard them as instruments of pleasure. While Persian poetry and romance are devoted to the praise of female charms, the realities of every-day life prove that the sex is held in slight esteem. The wives of the Shah vegetate within the walls of a luxurious prison; and if one is ever permitted to breathe the air outside, she is paraded in solemn procession, guarded by a troup of eunuchs armed with loaded muskets, in order to drive off any curious wayfarer who might be tempted to gaze on the charms of a royal mistress.   Nor is this isolation peculiar to them; it pervades all the upper classes, and brothers are not allowed to see their sisters after a certain age.

This jealousy is not decreased by the polygamy which is common in the country.   The religious laws limit a Persian to four wives, but allow him to keep as many concubines as he can afford; and, in pursuance of this privilege, the harem of the palace is said to contain at times more than a thousand women, who need a stringent discipline to keep them in order.   They are arranged with a strict regard to precedence.   The chief favorite lives in splendor, her attire is covered with costly jewels, and she has the privilege of sitting in the royal presence.   Her inferiors are subject to much rigor, and the eunuchs preserve decorum by administering personal chastisement with the heel of a slipper on the face of a refractory woman.   They seem insensible to any degradation.   Many of them lead a pleasant, idle life, lounging for hours in the warm bath, and emerging with enervated frames to deck their pretty persons in order to render themselves attractive to the Shah.   They court his favor as much as they fear his frown, and with good reason.   The former can raise them to the summit of their ambition; the latter can condemn them to be fastened in a sack and thrown from a lofty tower.

Common usage permits a Persian to take a woman in three different ways: he may marry, purchase, or hire her.   In the first case, betrothal sometimes takes place in infancy, but it must be subsequently confirmed by the parties.   In this they seldom fail; for if a girl shows any repugnance to ratify her father's contract, he whips her until she consents, and she requires little of this kind of argument to induce compliance.   The nuptial ceremony must be witnessed by two persons, one of whom is a legal officer to attest the contract.   This is delivered to the bride, and by her carefully preserved, as it proves her title to provision in the event of widowhood or divorce.   Though a man has the right to put away his wife when he pleases, the attendant expense and scandal render it a rare proceeding.   Mohammedan jealousy farther protects the woman, as no one will willingly allow a female with whom he has lived to fall into the hands of another.   In addition to this, interest restrains a husband from using his privileges in a direct manner, as when he takes the initiative he must pay back the dowry he received with his wife. If she applies for divorce, he is free from this obligation. The advantage being thus on the man's side, a species of tyranny is frequently practiced until the woman is forced to open the suit, when he gets rid of her, but retains her property.

A Persian may purchase as many female slaves as he desires. These acquire no advantage of position by being his concubines; he may sell or otherwise dispose of them at any moment he thinks proper.

The custom of hiring wives still prevails in Persia, though strict Mohammedans abhor and condemn the practice, which was prohibited by Omar, the successor of Mohammed. In operation, it is an agreement made by a man and woman to cohabit a specified time for an agreed sum of money. The children springing from this union must be supported by the father. If the man terminate the connection prematurely, he must still pay the whole stipulated amount, and the woman is restrained from accepting any other protector until a sufficient time has elapsed to prove whether she is pregnant by the former. Although these contracts are ranked as marriages, few readers will be inclined to think them any thing but systematic prostitution.

Formerly there were numerous open and avowed prostitutes in Persia, among whom the dancing girls were conspicuous for the beauty of their persons and the melody of their voices. They had considerable sway until the time of Futteh Ali Khan, who crowded his palace with concubines, and from among them issued edicts to suppress immorality, prohibiting the dancing girls from approaching the court, and exiling them to the distant provinces. Social life was most depraved under the Sefi dynasty. Public brothels were very numerous, and largely contributed to the national revenue, no less than thirty thousand prostitutes paying an annual tax in Ispahan alone. The governors of provinces allowed similar privileges for money, and there was scarcely a town which had not one licensed brothel at least, whose inmates (also licensed and taxed) were known as *Cahbeha*, or the worthless. As soon as the shops were closed these houses were opened, and the women repaired to particular localities, where they sat in rows, closely veiled. With each company was an old harridan, whose business was to show the faces of her troop to any man desiring a companion, and to receive his payment when the selection was made. Un-

der the reigning family this system has been checked; no licenses
are now given, and prostitution has retired to secrecy. But the
vice has in no way decreased, and public brothels abound in all
the cities of Persia.

AFGHANISTAN.

Marriage in Afghanistan is a commercial transaction, the wom-
en being sold for prices varying according to circumstances. This
system is carried to such an extent that if a widow marries, the
friends of her first husband can recover from his successor the
amount originally paid for her. The necessity of purchasing a
wife renders many of the poorer classes unable to marry until
well advanced in years, in opposition to the custom of their
wealthy neighbors, among whom bridegrooms of fifteen and brides
of twelve years old are common.

The prior intercourse of the sexes is regulated by various circumstances. In crowded towns men have little opportunity of
associating with women, and there professional match-makers exist. Their functions are, in the first place, to see and report upon
any girl whom a man may wish to marry; then to ascertain if
her family would agree to the match, and, finally, to make arrangements for a public proposal. This is made by the suitor's
father, in company with a number of male friends, to the father
of the girl, while a similar deputation of females waits upon the
mother. Presents are made, the selling price determined, and the
couple are betrothed. Soon after, the parties sign a mutual contract; stipulation is made for provision for the woman if divorced;
a festival is given; the bridegroom pays for his wife, and she is
delivered at the dwelling of her future master. Similar formalities take place in the country, but, as the social intercourse is less
restricted there, marriages frequently spring from attachment, and
the negotiations are mere matters of etiquette.

A romantic lover may obtain his mistress without the consent
of her parents by tearing away her veil, cutting off a lock of her
hair, or throwing a large white cloth over her, and declaring her
his affianced bride. These proceedings do not release him from
the obligation to pay for her, which is only evaded by an elope-
ment, a serious step, considered by the girl's family as equivalent
to murder, and revenged accordingly, unless the couple secure
shelter and protection from some neighboring tribe. Sometimes
a man never sees his bride until the marriage is completed. In

certain districts where this rule nominally exists it is practically violated, secret interviews between the bride and bridegroom being tolerated, and called "the sport of the betrothed." The young man steals after dark to the house of his charmer, affecting to conceal his presence from the men, and is introduced by the mother to her daughter's room, where the couple are left till the morning undisturbed. The ordinary result of this is the anticipation of nuptial privileges, and cases have been known where the bride has borne several children before she has been formally delivered to her husband.

Polygamy is allowed, but is too expensive to be practiced by the majority of the people, although some rich men maintain a large number of concubines in addition to the four legal wives.

The social condition of females is low in Afghanistan. Among the more barbarous tribes they labor in the fields. With the poor all the drudgery of the house falls upon them, while the rich keep them secluded in the harems. The law allows a man the privilege of beating his wife, but custom is more chivalrous than the code, and considers such an act disgraceful.

Of avowed prostitutes in this region we know but little beyond the bare fact that such a class exists, and that their profligacy is materially aided by the ignorance and insipidity of the wives and concubines, when contrasted with the knowledge of the world and comparatively polished manners exhibited by courtesans, whose society is frequently sought as a relief from the monotony of home.

KASHMIR.

Unoppressed by any rigid code of etiquette, and naturally addicted to pleasure, the people of Kashmir find much of their enjoyment in female society, and from the earliest times have been noted for their love of singers and dancers. In former days the capital city was the scene of constant revels, in which morality was but a secondary consideration, and now the inhabitants relieve the continual struggle against misfortune and despotism by indulging in gross vices, and drown the sense of hopeless poverty in the gratification of animal passions. The women of this delightful valley have long been celebrated for their beauty, and are still called the flower of the Oriental race. The face is of a dark complexion, richly flushed with pink; the eyes large, almond-shaped, and overflowing with a peculiar liquid brilliance; the features regular, harmonious, and fine; the limbs and bodies are models of grace. But all writers agree that art does nothing to aid nature, and it is not unusual to see eyes unsurpassed for brightness and expression flashing from a very dirty face. Among the poorer classes filth and degradation render many women actually repulsive, notwithstanding their resplendent beauty.

Travelers always remark the dancing girls who have acquired so much renown in Kashmir. The village of Changus was at one time celebrated for a colony of these women, who excelled all others in the valley; but how its famous beauties have disappeared, and live only in the traditions of the place. The dancing girls may be divided into several classes. Among the higher may be found those who are virtuous and modest, probably to about the same extent as among actresses, opera singers, and ballet girls in civilized communities. Others frequent entertainments at the houses of rich men, or public festivals, and estimate their favors at a very high price, while the remainder are avowed harlots, prostituting themselves indiscriminately to any who desire their company. Many of these are devoted to the service of some god, whose temple is enriched from the gains of their calling.

The Watul, or Gipsy tribe of Kashmir is remarkable for many lovely women, who are taught to please the taste of the voluptuary. They sing licentious songs in an amorous tone, dance in a lascivious measure, dress in a peculiarly fascinating manner, and seduce by the very expression of their countenances. When they join a company of dancing girls, they are uniformly successful in their vocation, and have been known to amass large sums of money. Now that the valley is in its decadence, their charms find a more profitable market in other places. The bands of dancing girls are usually accompanied by sundry hideous duennas, whose conspicuous ugliness forms a striking contrast to their charge.

The Nach girls are under the surveillance of the government, which licenses their prostitution. They are actual slaves, and can not sing or dance without permission from their overseer, to whom they must resign a large portion of their earnings.

In addition to these, who may be styled poetical courtesans, there exists a swarm of prostitutes frequenting low houses in the cities or boats on the lake; but of them we have no distinct account. It is certain that they are largely visited by the more immoral of the population, and an accurate idea of their *status* may be formed from a knowledge of the fact that the traveler Moorcraft, who gave gratuitous medical advice to the poor of Serinaghur, had at one time nearly seven thousand patients on his lists, a very large number of whom were suffering from loathsome diseases induced by the grossest and most persevering profligacy. In short, there can be but little doubt that the manners of the inhabitants of this interesting and beautiful valley are corrupt to the last degree.

INDIA.

India exhibits, in its different communities, many aspects of social life, but it may be said, in general terms, that the state of woman is degraded, as she is absolutely dependent upon man, and can do nothing of her own will. She must approach her lord with reverence; is bound to him so long as he desires it, whatever his conduct may be; and if she rebel, is liable to be chastised with a rope or a cane in a cruel manner. Debarred the advantages of education, not allowed to eat with their husbands or to mix in society, women are yet not treated as abject slaves; and from the few revelations of the zenana which have been made, it may be inferred that its inmates receive considerable deference and attention.

Polygamy is permitted in India, but not encouraged by the religious law, and only sanctioned in certain cases, such as barrenness, inconstancy, or some similar cause, and then the wife's consent must be obtained before a second and subordinate wife can be added to the household.

Marriage is viewed as a religious duty by the Hindoos, only a few being exempt from the obligation. It is forbidden to purchase a wife for money; but the girls have little choice as to their destiny, being usually betrothed while young. A father has the right to dispose of his daughter until three years after the age of puberty, when she may choose a husband for herself: not many remain single till that time, as celibacy would be accounted disgraceful, and few men would marry a maiden so old. In Bengal, betrothal takes place with many rites and much ostentation. The girl-bride is taken to her future husband's house, and remains there a short time, when she returns to her parents until mature. The anxiety to dispose of a daughter as young as possible arises from the fact that her birth is regarded as inauspicious, and even as a domestic calamity, from which her parents are glad to escape.

Hence the character of the bridegroom is a secondary consideration, and marriage often results unhappily. In fact, little else
can be expected where the parties are absolutely strangers to each
other until the union is effected. The uneducated wife, without
a gleam of knowledge, amuses herself by a thousand trivial devices, such as adorning her person, curling her hair, or listening
to the gossip of her slaves. It is, nevertheless, generally admitted
that the majority of Hindoo women are faithful to their marital
vows. The severe laws against unchastity are framed more for
preserving *caste* than morals, and severely punish any woman detected in an intrigue with a man of different grade to herself.

Divorce may be easily effected by the husband, but the wife
has no corresponding power. A man who calls his wife "mother," renounces her by that act. A barren wife may be superseded
in the eighth year: she who bears only daughters, or whose children die in the birth, in the eleventh year; and one of an unkind
disposition may be divorced without any delay.

The customs that prevail in different provinces respecting wives
and their treatment may be described in a few words. In Arra-
can, when a man wants money, he pawns his wife for a certain
sum, or else sells her altogether. In the southern parts of the
peninsula polygamy is largely practiced. The Shaynagas of Ca-
nara are not allowed to take a second wife unless the first be childless. The Corannas, the Panchalura, and other tribes, permitted
polygamy and the purchase of wives. Among the Woddas every
man had as many wives as he pleased; all worked for him, and a
lazy one was divorced *sans cerémonie*. The Carruburru took no
notice of an act of adultery if the wife was a hard-working woman; otherwise she might live with any man who chose to keep
her. In Rajpootana woman holds a higher position, and exercises
considerable influence on the actions and tastes of men, for a Raj-
poot consults his wife on every important occasion. The estimation in which they are held is indicated by a national proverb,
which says, "When wives are honored the gods are pleased;
when they are dishonored the gods are offended." This district
exhibits the Hindoo women in the most favorable circumstances,
and even here they hold but a subordinate place, as must always
be the case where polygamy is tolerated. It is scarcely necessary
to review all the local peculiarities of so extended a people:
enough has been said to show the social condition of married
women. It remains to give some account of prostitution.

Some of the dancing women and musicians of Southern India were attached to every temple; a portion were reserved by the sensual Brahmins for their exclusive pleasures, and the rest hired themselves out indiscriminately. Each troop was under a chief, who regulated their performances and prices. In the temple of Tulava, near Mangalore, a curious custom existed. Any woman could dedicate herself to prostitution by eating some of the rice which had been offered to the idol, and was allowed her choice to live within or without its precincts. In the former case, she received a daily allowance of food, and her prostitution was limited to the priests; in the latter, her amours were unrestricted, but a stipulated portion of her profits must be given to the temple. In Sindh every town has a troop of dancing girls, many of whom are very handsome. Before the British conquest the vice was largely encouraged; numbers of the women acquired considerable fortunes, and their political influence was potent in the *durbars* of the debauched Amirs. An evident reform has taken place of late years.

The lascivious scenes of the southern country are not enacted, at least to the same extent, in Hindostan proper, where the interest of the English government has been directed against immorality. Toward the close of the last century an official report was made on the morals of British India. It was bad enough: much laxity prevailed in private life; receptacles for women of bad character abounded; prostitutes had a place in society, made an important figure at great entertainments, and were admitted to the zenanas to exhibit their voluptuous dances. Contrasted with former years, a great improvement is now perceptible, and the profligacy of large cities scarcely exceeds the vices of European communities. Thus Benares, with a population of 180,000, had 1764 prostitutes; and Decca, with nearly 67,000 inhabitants, had 770 prostitutes.

Apart from governmental influences, it can scarcely be denied that Europeans have contributed to the advance of vice by taking temporary companions. These *liaisons* were scarcely considered improper. The custom was to purchase girls from their mothers. Many of them were faithful and attached to their protectors, but their extravagance and propensity for gambling made them very costly adjuncts.

The religious ceremonies originated by the Brahmins were often but scenes of the wildest debauchery, rivaling the ancient Egyp-

tian festival of Bubastis, and no good would result from an extended description of dances performed by nude or semi-nude
women, of the desecration of wives by a licentious priesthood, or
of the disgusting polygamy of the Brahmins. Suffice it to say
that such customs existed, but are now yielding to more refined
observances.

The general profligacy of the country has introduced syphilis
in most parts of Hindostan. Some assert that it was carried there
after the discovery of America, but neither history nor tradition
warrants this opinion. It may be noticed that it is not called by
any Sanscrit word, but is known by a Persian appellation.

Our notice of India would be incomplete without an allusion to
the *suttee*, or burning of widows, and to infanticide. The Shas-
tres are full of recommendations to perform the first of these
shocking observances, and promise ineffable bliss to the voluntary
victim. It was carried to such an extent that fifteen thousand
women are reported to have perished in one year in Bengal. This
is doubtless an exaggeration, although the number was confessedly very large. Among the horrible details of the practice we find
that betrothed children of eight or ten years old, and women of
eighty-five, have alike been thrown into the burning pile. Fearful scenes have been witnessed on these occasions. A miserable
wretch has twice escaped from the fire and clung to the feet of a
traveler, vainly imploring him to save her; and then, naked, and
with the flesh already burned from parts of her body, has been
bound and thrown into the flames by the frantic relatives. Let
British rule in India be what it may, no man, no "Aborigines
Protection Society," can regret its spread, in conjunction with the
services rendered to our common humanity by the abolition of
the *suttee*.

Infanticide formerly prevailed to a great extent, but is now almost extirpated from British India. The crime was sanctioned
by custom, but not by religion or tradition. Its victims were
chiefly females, and their murder was in consequence of the difficulty of marrying them within the required bounds of *caste*, or of
the ruinous expenses which fashion required should be incurred
at the wedding ceremonies, rather than from any other cause. It
appears to have been the custom among the ancient dwellers on
the banks of the Indus for the father of a female child to carry it
to the market-place, and publicly demand if any one wanted a
wife. If the reply was in the affirmative, it was betrothed at once,

and carefully reared, but otherwise it was immediately killed. Wilkinson asserted twenty-five years ago that twenty thousand children were annually murdered in Malwa and Rajpootana, but by the system of rewarding parents who reared their offspring, and the gradual introduction of salutary laws, a mighty reform has been effected.

CEYLON.

Under the original institutions of the Singhalese, they never licensed public prostitution, nor made brothels of the temples, as in India. Whatever effect the Buddhist religion produced was in favor of virtue, but the character of the people is naturally sensual; profligacy among men and want of chastity among women are general characteristics, and even those who profess Christianity and acknowledge the moral law of England are not free from this stain.

In Ceylon, as, indeed, in most parts of Asia, marriage is contracted at an early age. A man "attains his majority" at sixteen, and a girl as soon as marriageable by nature is marriageable by law, at which time her parents or relatives give a feast, inviting a number of single men. Soon after, a man who may desire to marry her sends one of his friends to her parents to mention, in apparently a casual manner, that a rumor of the intended marriage of his friend and their daughter is in circulation. If this announcement meets a favorable reception, the father of the bridegroom calls, inquires the amount of the dowry, and carries the negotiation a few steps farther. Mutual visits are then exchanged, preliminaries settled, and an auspicious day fixed for the wedding, which takes place with much ceremony. The stars are consulted in every step, and should the bridegroom's horoscope differ from the bride's, his younger brother may act as his proxy at the ceremony. The whole Buddhaical ritual is a tedious succession of formalities, entails enormous expenses, and can not be followed by the poor. To those of low caste it is positively forbidden, even if they are rich enough to meet the outlay, and with these marriage is limited to a simple agreement between the parents of the young couple.

Among the Kandians polyandrism prevails to a great extent, a matron of high *caste* being sometimes the wife of eight brothers. The people justify this custom upon several grounds: among the rich, because it prevents litigation, saves property from minute subdivision, and concentrates family influence; with the poor, because it reduces expenses, and frequently where one brother could not alone maintain a wife and family, the association of several can command the means. This plurality of husbands is not necessarily confined to brothers, for a man may, with his wife's consent, introduce a stranger, who is called an "associated husband," and is entitled to all marital rights. This practice does not extend beyond the province of Kandy, although it was formerly prevalent throughout the maritime districts of the island.

Another Kandian peculiarity was a kind of marriage called "Bema," in which the husband lived at his wife's house. He received but little respect from his relations, and could be ejected at once if unpopular. There is an ancient proverb in reference to this dubious arrangement, which says that a man married according to the Bema process should only take to his bride's house a pair of sandals to protect his feet, a palm leaf to shield his head, a staff to support him if sick, and a lantern in case he should be expelled in the dark, so that he may be prepared to depart at any hour of the day or night.

In Ceylon, women frequently seek for divorces for the most trivial causes, and as separation can be attained by a mere return of the marriage gifts, it often takes place. If a child is born within nine months from this separation, the husband is required to support it for three years. If a married woman commits adultery, and the husband is a witness, he may kill her lover. When a man puts away his wife on account of an intrigue, he may disinherit her and the whole of her offspring, even if the latter were born before any crime had been committed by their mother. If he seeks a divorce from caprice, he must relinquish all his wife's property, and share with her whatever may have accumulated during their cohabitation. The Singhalese do not always exercise their privileges, but are frequently indulgent husbands, and forgive offenses which most people hold unpardonable. In proof of this, a Kandian asked the British authorities to compel the return of an unfaithful wife, pleading his love for her, and promising to forget her frailty. English jurisdiction did not extend so far as this, and the woman coolly turned her back upon her husband and accompanied her paramour, whom she soon after deserted for a third partner. Many instances of this kind have induced the native poets to produce a number of satirical effusions upon woman's inconstancy, and a traveler translates the following specimen:

" ' I've seen the adumbra-tree in flower, white plumage on the crow,
   And fishes' footsteps on the deep have traced through ebb and flow ;'
If man it is who thus asserts, his words you may believe,
   But all that woman says, distrust ; she speaks but to deceive."

To understand the first clause, it will be necessary to remember that the adumbra is a kind of fig-tree, and the natives assert that no mortal has ever seen it in bloom.

Infanticide was at one time common in Ceylon, and all female children, except the first-born, were liable to be sacrificed, especially if born under a malignant planet; but latterly the British government have denounced the crime as murder, and punished it accordingly. This has had the effect of gradually abolishing it, and the population has increased in consequence.

The social condition of the Singhalese women is not so degraded as in other parts of the East, but their moral character does not correspond. Profligacy is prevalent. Open and acknowledged prostitution is rare, excepting in the sea-port towns, and of its extent there we have no reliable particulars. Under the Kandian dynasty a common harlot had her hair and ears cut off, and was publicly whipped in a state of nudity.

ULTRA GANGETIC NATIONS.

In this division we include the immense tract lying between Hindostan and China. Although these countries present some variety of customs and degrees of progress, yet, generally speaking, their manners are uniform. In all, the condition of women is extremely low. They are held in contempt, are taught to abase themselves in their own minds, and employ their license by degrading themselves still farther. The effect of Asiatic despotism is plainly visible: every man is the king's serf, and the support of the community devolves upon the women, who, in Cochin China especially, plow, sow, reap, fell trees, build, and perform all the other offices civilization assigns to the stronger sex.

The marriage contract is a mere bargain. A man buys his wife, and may extend his purchases as far as he pleases, the first bought being usually the chief. A simple agreement before witnesses seals the union, which can be dissolved with equal facility, the only requisite in Cochin China being to break a chopstick or porcupine quill in presence of a third person. A man has also the privilege of selling his inferior wives.

The unmarried women are almost universally unchaste, and do

not incur infamy or lose the chance of marriage by prostituting themselves. Custom allows a father to yield his daughter to any visitor he may wish to honor, or to hire her for a stipulated price to any one desirous of her company, and she has no power to resist the arrangement, although she can not be married against her will.

A wife is considered sacred, more as the property of her husband than from respect to her chastity. The theory of the law is, that a man's harem can not be invaded, even by the king himself; but Asiatic absolutism was never famed for its adherence to law when personal interest was in the other scale, and there is but little exception in this case.

Adultery is punished in Siam by fine, and in Cochin China by death. In Burmah executions of females are very rare, but they are disciplined with the aid of the bamboo, husbands sometimes flogging their wives in the open streets.

Although professed prostitutes exist in large numbers throughout the region, still there are not so many as might be expected, because no single woman is required to be chaste. Little is known of their habits, peculiarities, or position, except that in Siam they are incapacitated from giving evidence before a justice. This restriction does not seem to arise from a consideration of their immorality, but from local prejudices, and the disability under which they labor is also extended to braziers and blacksmiths.

CELEBES.

Leaving the Asiatic Continent for a short time, we will now examine the condition of the inhabitants of Celebes. This island is noticed here rather than with Java, Sumatra, and Borneo, which are included in the list of barbarous nations, because it enjoys a considerable degree of civilization, and in its political and social state is far in advance of other countries of the Indian Archipelago. The idea of freedom is recognized in its public system, and its institutions have assumed a republican form.

Women are not excluded from their share in public business; and though their influence is usually indirect, their counsel is sought by the men on all important occasions. In Wajo, they are not only elected to the throne, or, rather, the presidential chair, but also often fill the great offices of state. Four out of the six councilors are frequently females.

Their domestic condition, to some extent, corresponds with their political privileges. The wife has the uncontrolled management of her household, eating with her husband, and mingling freely with the other sex on public or festival occasions. The women ride about, transact business, and even visit foreigners as they please, and their chastity is better guarded by the sense of honor and the pride of virtue, than by the jealousy of husbands or the surveillance of parents.

This is the bright side of the picture. For the reverse, we find the barbarian practice of polygamy, which is universally permitted, under certain restrictions. The most important of these is that two wives seldom inhabit the same house; each has usually a separate dwelling. The men can easily procure a divorce, and, if the wish to separate is mutual, nothing remains but to do so as quickly as possible. If the woman alone desires to be released from the matrimonial bond, she must produce a reasonable ground of complaint. Concubinage is rarely practiced, although some man may take a woman of inferior rank as a companion until he can marry a girl whose birth equals his own.

The morals of both men and women are superior to those of any other race in eastern or western Asia. Prostitution is all but unknown. The dancing girls are generally admitted to be of easy virtue, but even they preserve decorum in their manners, and dress with great decency, although their public performances are of a lascivious nature.

CHINA.

In the immense empire of China a general uniformity of manners is observable, for its civilization has been cast in a mould fashioned by despotism, and the iron discipline of its government forces all to yield. There is great reason to believe that prostitution forms no exception to the rule. We know that a remarkable system exists, that frail women abound in the Celestial Empire, and form a distinct class. We know something of the manner in which they live, and how or by whom they are encouraged, but no traveler has as yet given any lucid account of the vice and its connections, and our comparatively meagre knowledge is drawn from a multiplicity of sources.

The general condition of the female sex in China is inferior to the male, and the precepts and examples of Confucius have taught the people that the former were created for the convenience of the latter. Feminine virtue is severely guarded by the law; not for

the sake of virtue, but for the well-being of the state and the interest of the men.   But national morality, inculcated by codes, es-
says, and poems, is, in fact, a dead letter, for the Chinese rank
among the most immoral people on the earth.   The inferiority of
women is recognized in their politics, which embrace the spirit of
the Salic law.   The throne can be occupied only by a man, and
an illegitimate son is more respected than a legitimate daughter.

The paternal government of China has not failed to legislate on
the subject of marriage.   In this contract the inclinations of the
parties themselves are practically ignored; parental authority is
supreme, and it is not unusual for weddings to take place between
persons who have never seen each other before the union.   Match-
making is followed as a profession by some old women, who are
remunerated when they succeed.   When two families commence
a negotiation of this kind, all particulars are required to be fully
explained on both sides, so that no deceit can be practiced.   The
engagement is then drawn, and the amount of presents agreed on.
This contract is irrevocable.   If the friends of the girl desire to
break off the match, the one who had authority to dispose of her
receives fifty strokes of the bamboo, and the marriage proceeds.
If the bridegroom, or the friend who controls him is dissatisfied,
he receives the same punishment, and must fulfill his engagement.
If either of the parties is incontinent after betrothal, the crime is
punished as adultery.   If any deceit has been practiced, and either
person has falsely represented the party about to be married, the
offender is severely punished, and the marriage is void, even if
completed.   In spite of all precautions, such instances sometimes
occur.   It must be noticed that, though betrothal binds a woman
positively to her future husband, yet he can not force her from
her friends before the stipulated time has expired, nor can they
retain her beyond the assigned day.

Polygamy is allowed under certain restrictions.   The first wife
is usually chosen from a family equal in station to that of the husband, and acquires all the rights and privileges which belong to a
chief wife in any Asiatic country.   The man may then take as
many more women as he can afford to keep, but these are inferior
in rank to the first married, although the children have a contingent claim to the inheritance.   This position, if it brings no positive honor, brings little shame.   It is sanctioned by usage, but
was originally condemned by strict moralists, who designated the
arrangement by a word compounded of *crime* and *woman*.   It is

a position which only a poor or humble woman will consent to occupy. A national proverb says, "It is more honorable to be the wife of a poor man than the concubine of an emperor." The social rule which makes all subsequent wives subordinate to the one first married may probably have had some effect in forming this opinion.

The Chinese system is rigid as to the degrees of consanguinity between which marriage may be contracted. In ancient times the reverse of this seems to have been the rule, and tradition says that much immorality was the result. The law now prohibits all unions between persons of the same family name, and is attended with some inconvenience, because the number of proper names is small. If such a marriage is contracted, it is declared void, and the parties are punished by blows and a fine. If the couple are previously related by marriage within four degrees, the union is declared incestuous, and the offenders are punished with the bamboo, or, in extreme cases, by strangling or decapitation.

Not only are the degrees of relationship definitely specified, but the union of classes is under restriction. An officer of government must not marry into a family under his jurisdiction, or, if he does, is subject to a heavy punishment; the same being accorded to the girl's relations if they have voluntarily aided him, but they are exempt if their submission was the result of his authority. To marry a woman absconding from justice is prohibited. To forcibly wed a freeman's daughter subjects the offender to strangulation. An officer of government, or any hereditary functionary, who marries a woman of a disreputable class, receives sixty strokes of the bamboo, and the same *modicum* awaits any priest who marries at all, he being also expelled from his order. Slaves and free persons are forbidden to intermarry. Those who connive at an illegal union are considered criminals, and punished accordingly.

According to Chinese law, any one of seven specified causes are allowed to justify divorce, namely, barrenness, lasciviousness, disregard of the husband's parents, talkativeness (!), thievish propensities, an envious, suspicious temper, or inveterate infirmity. Against these the woman has three pleas, any one of which, if substantiated, will annul the husband's application. They are, that she has mourned three years for her husband's family; that the family has become rich, having been poor at the time of marriage; or, that she has no father or mother living to receive her. These are useless when she has committed adultery, in which case her husband is positively forbidden to retain her, but under other circumstances they present a check to his caprice. In cases of adultery, a man may kill both his wife and her paramour if he detect them and execute his vengeance forthwith, but he must not put her to death for any other crime. In the same connection may be mentioned a law denouncing severe penalties on any man who lends his wife or daughter. This is not an obsolete enactment against an unknown offense, for instances do sometimes occur of poor men selling their wives as concubines to their richer neighbors, while others prostitute them for gain.

From this view of the social condition of women and the laws of marriage, it is necessary to pass to a subject which has given China an unenviable notoriety, namely, the custom of infanticide. Two causes appear to have encouraged this practice: the poverty of the lower classes, and the severity of the laws respecting illicit sexual intercourse. The former is the principal cause. When the parents are so indigent as to have no hope of maintaining their children, the daughters are murdered, for a son can earn his living in a few years, and assist his parents in addition. Among this class the birth of a female is viewed as a calamity. Several methods are adopted to destroy the child. It may be drowned in warm water, its throat may be pinched, a wet cloth may be pressed over its mouth, it may be choked with rice, or it may be buried alive.

When Mr. Smith, a missionary, was in the suburbs of Canton in 1844, he made many inquiries as to the extent of infanticide. A native assured him that, within a circle of ten miles' radius, the children killed each year *would not exceed five hundred.* In Fokien province the crime was more general, and at a place called Kea King Chow there were computed to be from five to six hundred cases every month. A foundling hospital at Canton was named as preventing much of the crime, but it seems to have received only five hundred infants yearly; but a very small proportion of the births. The Chinese generally confess that infanticide is practiced throughout the empire, and is regarded as an innocent and proper expedient for lightening the pressure of poverty. It is not wholly confined to the poor; the rich resort to it to conceal their amours. The laws punish illicit intercourse with from seventy to one hundred strokes of the bamboo. If a child is born, its support devolves upon the father; but in cases where the connection has been concealed, this evidence is usually destroyed.

Prostitution prevails to a prodigious extent. "Seduction and adultery," says Williams, in his Survey of the Chinese Empire, "are comparatively infrequent, but brothels and their inmates are found every where, on land and water. One danger attending young girls walking alone is that they will be stolen for incarceration in these gates of hell." This allusion may be explained by the fact that in 1832 there were from eight to ten thousand prostitutes in and near Canton, of whom the greater portion had been stolen while children, and regularly trained for this life. Many kidnappers gained a living by stealing young girls and selling them to the brothels, and in times of want parents have been known to lead their daughters through the streets and offer them for sale. A recent visitor to Canton describes the sale of children as an every-day affair, which is looked upon as a simple mercantile transaction. Some are disposed of for concubines, but others are deliberately bartered to be brought up as prostitutes, and are transferred at once to the brothels.

Of Chinese houses of prostitution we have no particular description, but one singular feature is the brothel junks, which are moored in conspicuous stations on the Pearl River, and are distinguished by their superior decorations. Many of them are called "Flower Boats," and form whole avenues in the floating suburbs of Canton. The women lead a life of reckless extravagance, plunging into all the excitements which are offered by their mode of life to release themselves from *ennui* or reflection. Diseases are very prevalent among them, and visitors suffer severely for their temporary pleasures. They are usually congregated in troops, under the government of a man who is answerable for their conduct, or for any violation of public peace or decency. The last can scarcely be considered an offense, for the Chinese make a display of their visits to brothels. Persons pass to and from the Flower Boats without any attempt at concealment, and rich men sometimes make up a party, send to one of the junks, retain as many women as they wish, and collectively pass the time in debauch and licentiousness.

This is not the only form prostitution assumes in China. Women of the poorer classes, whose friends are not able to provide for them, are lodged in prison under the care of female warders, and these employ their prisoners in prostitution for their benefit. An incident which occurred at Shenshee a few years since reveals another phase. A young widow resided there with her mother-in-

F E

law, both being supported by the prostitution of the former.   Her charms failed, she was deserted by her visitors, and starvation seemed inevitable.   The old woman would not recognize her daughter's inability to support her, and flogged her.   The prostitute, in attempting self-defense, killed her mother.   She was convicted of the crime, but, as the victim had acted illegally in endeavoring to force her to prostitution, the sentence of the court, which had ordered her to be hewn to pieces, was commuted into decapitation.

As before remarked, it is much to be regretted that we have not more reliable information of the vice, which is acknowledged to be all but universal in China.[1]

[1] Since the preceding paragraphs were written, the operations of the Allied Powers against China, and the capture of Canton, have given some farther insight into the domestic economy of this people.   The special correspondent of the London *Times*, writing from Hong Kong, February 22, 1858, thus describes Chinese holidays:

"During the *entrée acte* all China has been exploding crackers, and Hong Kong has been celebrating its 'Isthmian games.'   Toward the close of the three days of festivity the Chinese holiday became almost exciting.   If they had kept up half as sharp a fire at Canton on the 29th of December as they did on the 14th of February, we should never have got over the walls with a less loss than 500 men.   The streets both of Canton and Hong Kong were piled with myriads of exploded cracker carcasses.   In Hong Kong, where I passed the last day of these festivities, grave men and sedate children were from morning till midnight hanging strings of these noisy things from their balconies, and perpetually renewing them as they exploded. The sing-song women, in their rich, handsome dresses, were screeching their shrill songs, and twanging their two-stringed lutes on every veranda in the Chinese quarter, while the lords of creation, assembled at a round table, were cramming the day-long repast.   The women—hired singing women of not doubtful reputation—in the intervals of their music, take their seats at the table opposite the men. They do not eat, but their business being to promote the conviviality of the feast, they challenge the men to the samshu cup, and drink with them.   It is astonishing to see what a quantity of diluted samshu these painted and brocaded she-Celestials can drink without any apparent effect.   Ever and anon one of the company retires to a couch and takes an opium pipe, and then returns and recommences his meal. I was invited to one of these feasts; the dishes were excellent, but it lasted till I loathed the sight of food.   I believe the Chinese spend fabulous sums in these entertainments; the sing-song women are often brought from distances, and are certainly chosen with some discrimination.   They are an imitation of the Chinese lady, and, as the Chinese lady has no education and no duties, the difference between the poor sing-song girl and the poor abject wife is probably not observable in appearance or manner.   The dress is particularly modest and becoming.   They all have great quantities of black hair.   If they would let it fall disheveled down their backs as the Manilla women do, they would be more picturesque, but not formal and decent, as China is, even in its wantonness.   The Chinawoman's hair is gummed and built up into a structure rather resembling a huge flat-iron, and the edifice is adorned with combs, and jewels, and flowers, arranged with a certain taste.   An embroidered blue silk tunic reaches from her chin nearly to her ankles.   Below the

JAPAN.

The recent connection established by American enterprise with the semi-fabulous empire of Japan (the Zipangi of Columbus) makes the institutions of that country more than usually interesting. From the earliest accounts of the Dutch and Jesuit writers to the present time, we know that the Japanese, like the Chinese, have attained a high degree of civilization, and among both, the vices which, in the present experience of mankind, seem the accompaniments of that improvement, have been developed in a remarkable degree.

Among savage tribes female honor is held in very little esteem; the woman is merely property. As we advance in the scale of intelligence they take higher grade, and virtue and modesty are more cherished. Our information concerning Japan is, even yet, comparatively limited, but no circumstance of its ordinary life seems more clear than that female virtue among the higher classes is much valued, and that, at the same time, there is an enormous extent of public prostitution, in which men of all ranks indulge.

The Jesuit Charleroix, Kœmpfer, Adams, and some Dutch writers, have given accounts of Japan from the sixteenth century to the present time. Like most Oriental nations, the manners and habits of the Japanese have undergone so little change, that the practices of a century ago are the fashions of to-day. The most recent traveler (for those who composed Commodore Perry's expedition can hardly be said to come under that denomination) is Captain Golownin, and he had opportunities for close observation not equaled since the times of the early writers. He was commander of the Russian sloop-of-war Diana, and visited the Japanese empire in 1811. Having paid a visit of ceremony ashore, he was induced, by the duplicity of the Japanese, who are

tunic appear the gay trowsers, wrought with gold or silver thread; the instep glancing through the thin, white silk stockings, and a very small foot (when left to nature the Chinese have beautiful feet and hands) in a rich slipper, with a tremendous white sole in form of an inverted pyramid. In these sing-song girls you see the originals of the Chinese pictures—the painted faces, the high-arched, penciled eyebrows, the small, round mouth, the rather full and slightly sensual lip, naturally or artificially of a deep vermilion, the long, slit-shaped, half closed eyes, suggestive of indolence and slyness. What the voluble and jocose conversation addressed to them by the men may mean I can not tell, but their manners are quite decent, their replies are short and reserved, and every gesture, or song, or cup of samshu seems to be regulated by a known ceremonial."

adepts in all the political arts of lying and hypocrisy, to trust himself in their hands a second time without arms or escort. The
Japanese had an old grudge to settle with the Russians on account of injuries done them by certain individuals of that nation,
and took the opportunity of rendering a *quid pro quo* by entrapping the unlucky Golownin, who was thus made prisoner. He
was treated at first with much indignity and severity; afterward
with more indulgence, but did not regain his liberty for upward
of two years.

The Japanese can marry only one wife, but have as many concubines as they please. The precise value of the distinction is
not readily appreciated, as the concubine does not lose caste by
her position. There are great facilities of divorce, and without
cause shown; but a gentleman who exercises this privilege loses
his character as a husband, and can only procure another wife or
additional concubines by paying a large price to his father-in-law.
Adultery is punished with death, either by law or at the hands
of the husband. Japanese husbands are represented as jealous,
and as keeping their wives and women in strict seclusion. This
strictness is relaxed in the cases of the middle and poorer classes,
the necessities of the household removing those artificial obligations imposed on the higher ranks by pride or fashion. But even
the women of the humbler ranks do not converse with, or even
speak to strangers, unless in the presence of their husbands.

An anecdote is told in Adams's narrative which somewhat re-
sembles that of Lucretia in Roman history, and which would imply great self-respect among the high caste of Japanese ladies.
A nobleman made dishonorable advances toward a lady of rank
during her husband's absence on a journey, and, notwithstanding
a repulse from her, seized an opportunity to gratify his passion by
violence. On the husband's return the wife treated him with reserve, and declined any explanation of her singular conduct, which,
however, she promised to afford at a banquet to be given the following day. Accordingly, during the feast, at which the author
of the outrage was present, when the guests had satisfied their appetites, the lady made her appearance. She told her husband and
his friends what had happened, denounced herself as unworthy to
live, received the caresses of her husband and relations, by whom,
however, she refused to be comforted, and then leaped from the
parapet of the house, and so killed herself. Meanwhile the criminal had escaped; but when the horror-stricken guests rushed out

to pick up the devoted wife, they found the nobleman weltering in his own blood at her side. He had ripped himself up, the ordinary way of committing suicide in Japan.

The Japanese brothels are of great splendor, and very numerously frequented, containing thirty, forty, fifty, or even a larger number of women. Every place of public entertainment or refreshment maintains prostitutes as a part of the establishment. On stopping at a tavern, it is customary for the courtesans of the house to come out, painted and bedizened, and set forth the claims of their house to the traveler's patronage, exhibiting themselves as one of the items of the bill of fare. No village, however insignificant, is without one or more houses of ill fame, and there are villages on much-frequented roads, in popular districts, the whole of whose female inhabitants are prostitutes. Two in particular, Agasaki and Goy, are thus described by Kœmpfer. The females are designated *Keise*, which literally signifies a castle turned upside down. It is uncertain whether the government licenses these places, or merely tolerates them. The former is the more probable, when it is considered that in their mythology they have a goddess analogous to the Corinthian Venus, in whose worship prostitution is a recognized part of the ceremony. Attached to the temple of this impure deity are a large number of priestesses, six hundred or upward, who all prostitute themselves to the worshipers. Notwithstanding this large force, there are constant offers to recruit the ranks by young girls.

The extent of this vice, which is universal throughout the empire, would cause it to be taken as a regular institution of Japan. Nothing is done *sub rosa*. Courtesans form part of a pleasure party; parents sell their children to brothel-keepers, or apprentice them for a time to such places, and at the expiration of their term they resume (it is said, but this is doubtful) their places in society without any stain on their reputations. Husbands make bargains for the transfer of their wives' charms, which is a legitimate charge over and above the gratuity to be accorded to the lady. Kœmpfer, in describing the prostitute quarter of Nagasaki, says it consists of very handsome houses. The poor people sell their prettiest daughters to the brothel-keepers, who bring the girls up with various accomplishments. The price of these women is regulated by law, and many of the prostitutes are enabled to abandon their calling, for their good education and agreeable manners procure them husbands, and in their married condition they are fully as good as others.

In his lifetime the brothel-keeper is said by some writers to rank with the skinner or tanner, an opprobrious calling, while others say he ranks with merchants, and his company is not deemed objectionable. This latter statement, if true, may be owing to the circumstance that he holds a government license. In Japan, as in China, the crown is the fountain of all distinction, and every government official has peculiar privileges and a distinct position in the social scale. After his death, however, the brothel-keeper is held in great disesteem. The sanctity of the burial-place, to which particular reverence attaches, would be polluted by his unholy presence, and his odious remains are denied the rite of sepulture, and are dragged in the clothes in which he died to a dunghill, there to be devoured by wild beasts and birds of prey.

Prostitution as a public institution is said to have been introduced into Japan by a certain warlike emperor or usurper, who, leading his troops from one place to another in the empire, feared lest, from want of home comforts and domestic ties, they might become disgusted and abandon his service. Accordingly, as a substitute for lawful enjoyments, he had stations for bands of prostitutes at various points, to the nearest of which he led his fatigued soldiers after his engagements.

Another statement as to the origin of this system is that, on one occasion during a revolution, the spiritual emperor having fled, attended by his foster-mother and a numerous band of female attendants, temporary nuns, the emperor and his foster-mother drowned themselves in fear of capture by the enemies; whereupon the attendant nuns, cut off from all other resource, adopted libertinism as a means of livelihood, and this gave the first public example and sanction to a reprobate state of life.

There are in Japan various religious institutions of a character similar to convents and monasteries. The vow of celibacy and chastity is one of the requisites of this state, yet, notwithstanding this vow, the monks are described as living very intemperately, seducing both women and girls, and committing other shameful enormities.[1]

Among the mendicant religious orders to which both sexes belong, the nuns are numerous. They are described as being very fine-looking women. They are generally the children of indigent parents, and good looks are essential to success in their calling, between which and prostitution there seems no difference save in

---

[1] Golownin, vol. iii. p. 52.

name. Indeed, many of these mendicant nuns go direct from the brothel to their new employment, which, combining various qualifications, is probably more lucrative.

We have been unable to find any information as to the nature or extent of venereal diseases, if any, in Japan. Of infanticide also we have no account.

Commodore Perry, in the Narrative of his Expedition, confirms the facts above stated so far as his opportunities for observation extended. Difficulties were at first thrown in the way of his seeing the Japanese women, and when he walked about the interpreters preceded him, and, under a show of doing him honor, ordered all the women into their houses. Afterward, on the commodore's remonstrance, the women were allowed to make their appearance, and their manners and looks were not by any means unpleasing. When the officers of the expedition were entertained, they sometimes waited on the party with tea, coffee, and other refreshments. Their manners were mild, their countenances were soft and pleasing, the only objectionable point about them being the abominable habit of blackening their teeth with a highly corrosive pigment partly composed of iron filings and a fermented liquor called saki, which affected the gums very offensively, and caused an appearance and odor decidedly unpleasing to the tastes of Western travelers.

The women of the working classes were engaged in hard field and out-door labor, but not to a greater extent than in densely populated countries in most parts of the world. Commodore Perry assumes that licentiousness must be prevalent in large cities, but he bears his testimony to the good conduct of the women whom the people of the expedition met while on shore.[1]

The opportunities of information and particular inquiry were, however, not very great, owing to the more important political objects of the visit, and the not very protracted stay of the squadron in Japan.

Not content with the excess of incontinence in which the Japanese as a nation indulge, they largely practice unnatural vices, and the youth of the province of Kioto, which is the peculiar appanage of the spiritual emperor, are celebrated on account of their beauty, and command a high price in this horrid traffic.

[1] Perry's Expedition, p. 462.

TARTAR RACES.

Central Asia is but little known and seldom visited. Among the most remarkable of its people are the Kirghiz Kazaks, who form a nation of shepherds. They dwell in huts, or temporary habitations of wicker-work covered with fleeces, and are a robust, hardy race, addicted to sensual enjoyments. Their manners as to the treatment of the female sex are coarse, but it is curious to re-mark that, while the men are indolent and licentious, the women are fond of exertion, for which their only recompense is to be treated as slaves.

The Kirghiz, when rich enough, eagerly avail themselves of the privilege of polygamy; indeed, this part of the Mohammedan creed is the one they have embraced with most ardor, yet few possess sufficient wealth to marry more than one wife. The price paid for a woman will range from five or six sheep among the poorer classes, to two hundred, five hundred, or even a thousand horses among the rich, to which are added different household ef-fects, and occasionally a few male or female slaves. A consider-able share of these payments is absorbed by the Mohammedan moolahs, who find a profitable source of revenue in marrying these people. They consecrate the union as soon as projected, and immediately the amount of the *kalym*, or price, has been ar-ranged between the parties, the moolah solemnly asks the parents of the bride and bridegroom, "Do you consent to the union of the children?" repeating the question three times to each, and then reading prayers for the happiness of the couple to be married. No marriage is complete till the whole of the stipulated amount is paid, but neither party can honorably retract after the first installment has been offered and accepted. From that time the bridegroom has leave to visit his bride, if he engages not to take away her chasti-ty. In cases where this liberty leads to an anticipation of the final ceremony, the unpaid portion of the *kalym* is not allowed to pro-tract the union, which is hastened as much as possible. If a man find his wife to have been incontinent before he married her, he may return her to her parents, and demand the restitution of her price, or the substitution of one of her sisters. If he actually de-tects her in the commission of adultery, he may kill her, otherwise the adulterer is fined, and the wife may be divorced or chastised.

The morals of the Kirghiz are good. Chastity in the woman is highly prized, and the sensuality of the men is served by prostitutes, who live in each camp, either in companies or in separate tents. Numbers of these women appear wherever the Russians have encampments, and virulent disease among them has tended rapidly to thin the people. The prostitutes are composed of two classes—widows and divorced women, who have no other means of subsistence, and linger out a miserable life in dirt, rags, and contempt; and a few who addict themselves to prostitution from mere licentiousness.

CIRCASSIA.

The race known as Abassians, considered the aborigines of the Caucasus, were described by Strabo as a predatory people—pirates at sea, and robbers on land. These characteristics they preserve to the present day, but otherwise they are a virtuous nation, strange to the worst vices of civilized life, and humble in their desires. Their religion permits polygamy, but as wives are costly, they are usually contented with one, who is the companion rather than the menial of her husband. The women are industrious, are allowed full liberty, and are free in their social intercourse, the veil being worn only to screen their complexions, and not for seclusion.

Their laws against immorality are stringent. An act of illicit intercourse is punished by fine or banishment. A dishonest wife is returned to her parents, and by them sold as a slave, as is also a wanton girl. Illegitimate children can not claim any relationship, and if sold as slaves or assassinated, no one is expected to redeem them in the one case, or avenge them in the other. When a man desires to divorce his wife, he must give his reasons before a council of elders, and if they are not satisfied, he must pay her parents a stated amount to recompense them for the burden thus thrown upon them. Should the woman marry again within two years, this sum is returned.

Among the Circassians themselves women are not secluded. A man will often introduce his wife and daughters to a traveler, and unmarried women are frequently seen at public assemblies. They observe one singular custom: a husband never appears abroad with his wife, and scarcely ever sees her during the day. This is in accordance with ancient habits, and is a prolongation of the marriage etiquette, which requires a man, after he has removed his bride's corset of leather, worn by all virgins, for some time to refrain from openly living with her.

Throughout the Caucasus a high state of morality is found. Open prostitution is unknown, and any girl leading a notoriously immoral life would be compelled to fly beyond the bounds of the territory, if she escaped being sold as a slave or put to death by her indignant friends. There is a general opinion that Circassians will sell their daughters to any Turk or Persian who wishes to buy them, but this is not the fact. They are particularly careful as to the position of any one who wishes to intermarry with them. Great precautions are taken to insure the happiness of the girls, and long-continued negotiations frequently lead to no result. The majority of females sold as Circassians are either children stolen from the neighboring Cossacks, or slaves procured from those Circassian traders who own allegiance to Russia.

TURKEY.

Proud, sensual, and depraved in his tastes, the Turk is too indolent to acquire even the means of gratifying his most powerful cravings. Satisfying his pride with the memory of former glories, his lust looks forward to the enjoyment of a paradise crowded with beautiful ministers of pleasure, and he passes his time in an atmosphere of Epicurean speculation, lounging on cushions and sipping coffee with a dreamy indifference to all external objects. Even the poor indulge in this idleness. They measure the amount of labor necessary to keep them from positive want, and spend the rest of their time waiting the sensual heaven promised by their prophet. In such a lethargy the most violent passions are fostered, and when these become excited the Turk can not be surpassed in brutal fury. All his fancies are gross; moral power is an incomprehensible idea, and he can conceive no authority not enforced by whip or sword.

The Turkish character thus exhibited corresponds with their estimate of the female sex. The person alone is loved; intellect in a Turkish woman is rarely developed and never prized. She finds her chief employment in decorating her person, her sole enjoyment in lounging on a pile of cushions, and admiring the elegance of her costume. Turkey is literally the empire of the senses.

Polygamy is now growing into disrepute there. Recent laws have conferred many privileges upon women in matters of property, and their comparative independence has rendered them averse to a position in which they only acquire secondary rank. Men who marry wives of equal rank to themselves frequently engage in their marriage contracts not to form a second alliance, and this stipulation is very seldom violated.

The customs of the country do not permit a man to see his wife before marriage. She may gratify her curiosity by a stealthy glance at him, but this privilege is seldom used. In consequence of the separation of the sexes, a race of professional match-makers has arisen, as in China, who realize considerable profits from their calling. Children of three or four years old are sometimes betrothed, marriage taking place about fourteen. When a wedding is contemplated, each family deputes an agent to arrange preliminaries, the terms of the contract are embodied in a legal document, and the woman is then called "a wife by writing." This is concluded some days before the actual wedding, but the interval is occupied with rejoicings and hospitality, on which the bridegroom generally expends a year's income. The union is a mere civil contract blessed by religious rites. All concubines are slaves, even in the harem of the sultan, since no free Turkish woman can occupy that position.

The morals of Turkish women are generally described as very loose. Their veils favor an intrigue, the most jealous husband passing his wife in the street without knowing her. The places of assignation are usually the Jews' shops, where they meet their lovers, but preserve their *incognito* even to them. Lady Mary Wortley Montague imagined "the number of faithful wives to be very small in a country where they have nothing to fear from a lover's indiscretion."

The dancing girls of Turkey are prostitutes by profession. Their performances are much enjoyed by all classes, and they dance as lasciviously in the harem, where they are often invited to amuse the wives and concubines, as before a party of convivialists in the kiosks. Their costume is exceedingly rich, both in color and material. During the day they resort to coffee-houses, where they attach themselves to companions whom they entertain with songs, tales, or caresses until night, when their orgies are transferred to houses belonging to their chiefs. Many of these habitations are furnished with every possible luxury.

Another form of prostitution is temporary marriage. For instance, a man on a journey will arrive in a strange city, where he desires to remain some time. He immediately bargains for a female companion, a regular agreement is drawn up, and he supports her and remunerates her friends while he remains. When he is tired of her, or wishes to leave the place, she returns to her friends, and patiently waits for another engagement of the same kind.

NORTHERN AFRICA.

A very brief notice only is required of the semi-barbarous states of Northern Africa, particularly as an account of Algeria under the French has already been given. The mass of the population are Moors, and therefore our remarks will mainly apply to them. Like the Turks, they are proud, ignorant, sensual, and depraved, and their treatment of women exactly accords with this character. They regard the female sex but as material instruments of man's gratification; and this idea is become so generally received, that the sole education of a girl is such as will render her acceptable to some gross sensualist. Intellect and sentiment are not the possessions which will recommend her: *to be attractive, she must be fat.* A girl of such bulk as to be a good load for a camel is considered a perfect beauty, and, accordingly, the mother does not train her daughter in seductive arts, but feeds her into a seductive appearance, as pigeons are fed in some parts of Italy. She is made to swallow every day a certain number of balls of paste saturated with oil, and the rod overcomes any reluctance she may have to the diet.

The Moors are extremely jealous of their enormous wives. Some have been known to kill their women before proceeding on a journey; others have forbidden them to name an animal of the masculine gender. They are entirely shut up within the walls of the harem, where they pass their time perfuming and decorating their persons, to attract the favor of their lords.

The general marriage laws of Mohammedan countries prevail in the Barbary States. Four wives and as many concubines as he pleases are the limits within which a man is confined, but few men marry more than one woman.

An extensive system of prostitution prevails in all the cities The low drinking-shops are crowded with women. The public dancers, who all belong to the sisterhood, exist in large numbers, and are very much encouraged. Their society is a favorite recreation with Moors of all classes. A man entertaining a party of friends will send for a company of dancers to amuse them. There, amid the fumes of tobacco, and sometimes of liquor (for the precepts of the Koran are disregarded on such occasions), the women practice the most degrading obscenities, and the orgies become such as no pen can describe. These prostitutes are of various classes, from the low, vulgar wretches who exist in misery, filth, and disease, to the wealthy courtesans who live in luxury and splendor.

A late traveler was introduced by a friend to a "Moorish lady." He was ushered into a spacious apartment hung with rich-colored silks. Reclining on a splendid divan, with every appliance of wealth around her, was a woman of extreme loveliness. Elegant in her manners and address, she seemed a model of feminine grace, nor did the visitor discover until after he had left her that he had been conversing with a Moorish prostitute.

SIBERIA.

The state of manners to which the population of these snowy tracts has arrived is very low. They are rude, ignorant, and gross. The condition and character of the female sex correspond with that of the male. In the perpetual migration of tribes they bear the heaviest burdens, and in their habitations the man regards his wife as a mere domestic slave, to whom it is unnecessary even to speak a kind word. There are some exceptions to this rule, especially toward the centre of the district, removed from Russia on the one hand and the sea on the other, where more equality of the sexes is observable.

A wife is generally obtained by purchase, and if a man is not rich enough to pay the sum demanded by the parents of a girl for the privilege of marrying her, he hires himself to them for a term ranging from three to ten years, according to an agreement, and his services in that time are considered equivalent to the value of his bride. These contracts are faithfully observed, the woman is invariably given up at the specified time, and the man released from his servile condition, and admitted to all the dignities and rights of a son-in-law. Where the bridegroom is in a condition to pay for his bride, the preliminary negotiations are managed by his friends and her parents; they are very quietly arranged, but the spirit of bargaining is strong on both sides. The stipulated amount must be paid before the marriage is completed; and if a man steals away his bride before he has paid the full cost, the father watches an opportunity and recaptures her, retaining her in pledge until the balance is forthcoming.

The marriage ceremonies vary in different tribes. With some

there is no feast or form of any kind; with others every marriage must take place in a newly-built hut, where no impure things can have been. The most detailed account of marriage ceremonies we can find is among the Tschuwasses. They offer a sacrifice of bread and honey to the sun on the betrothal, that he may look down with favor on the union. When the wedding-day arrives, the bride hides herself behind a screen while the guests are assembling. When the party is complete, she walks three times round the room, followed by a train of virgins bearing bread and honey. Then the bridegroom enters, removes her veil, kisses her, and they exchange rings. She is now saluted as the "betrothed girl," and is again led behind the screen, whence she emerges wearing a matron's cap. The concluding rite is for her to pull off her new husband's boots, thus promising obedience to him. In this tribe the husband can divorce his wife by merely taking her cap from her head.

Polygamy is practiced by many, though some prefer to take one wife for another as often as inclination prompts them, rather than take charge of several at the same time.

Jealousy is little known among any of the races of Siberia. Modesty is not a female characteristic, nor is chastity very highly prized. If a wife commit adultery, the husband usually exacts a fine from the paramour for invading his rights "without permission." Their barbarous manners would not induce us to expect any refined modesty. A traveler was introduced to the family of a rich man, the head of a tribe, and upon entering his low-roofed but spacious habitation, found himself in company with five or six women, wives and daughters, all entirely naked, who appeared excessively diverted at being discovered in such a state. The dancing women are as lewd as can possibly be conceived; indeed, obscene postures are the principal features of their entertainments.

A licentious intercourse between unmarried persons is almost universal. With some, religious dissensions are extremely bitter; but profligacy is more powerful, and a woman who would rigidly refuse to eat or drink with a man of some other creed, will prostitute herself to him from sheer lust. Abandoned women reside in all the towns in large numbers, and are scarcely reprobated by other classes. The education of a Siberian girl appears to be simply telling her that marriage is her destiny, and that her husband will require her to be faithful. With this view she forms acquaintances, is seduced by one and yields to another, until her profligacy becomes so notorious that no one will purchase her as a wife, and she follows, as a means of living, the habits she had resorted to for the indulgence of her vicious appetite. It is said that many prostitutes become so from this cause.

ESQUIMAUX.

The Esquimaux require but a very short notice. As a race, they are dirty, poor, and immoral. Dishonesty is a prominent characteristic, especially manifested toward any strangers coming within their reach. The lamented Kane, in his "Arctic Explorations," mentions the trouble to which he was exposed in guarding his stores from their pilfering propensities; but, after he had administered one or two lessons of chastisement, they abandoned this habit, and became of great assistance to him. He says, "There is a frankness and cordiality in their way of receiving their guests, whatever may be the infirmities of their notions of honesty;"[1] and when he parted from them on his perilous journey south, he remarks, "When trouble came to us and them, and we bent ourselves to their habits; when we looked to them to procure us fresh meat, and they found at our brig shelter during their wild bear-hunts, never were friends more true. Although numberless articles of inestimable value to them have been scattered upon the ice unwatched, they have not stolen a nail."[2]

The Esquimaux women are not absolute slaves; their duties are almost entirely domestic, and during the winter especially their life is one of ease and pleasure, so far as their notions can comprehend such advantages. Crowded inside a low hut, two or three families together, they spend their time in eating and sleeping alternately, both sexes being perfectly naked, except a small apron worn by the women as a badge of their sex. This nudity arises from the excessive heat of their cabins, which are rendered impervious to the cold outside. Dr. Kane mentions one occasion on which he was a visitor when the thermometer outside stood at 60° below zero, and inside the temperature mounted to 90°, and says, "Bursting into a profuse perspiration, I stripped like the rest, and thus, an honored guest, and in the place of honor, I fell asleep."[3]

Respecting the morality of the men or the virtue of the women little is known. Parry says that husbands frequently offer their wives to strangers for a very small sum, and also that it is not un

[1] Arctic Explorations, vol. i. p. 373.   [2] Ibid. ii. 250.   [3] Ibid. ii. 115.

common for a change of wives to be made for a short time. He
adds that in no country is prostitution carried to a greater extent,
the departure of the men on an expedition being a signal to their
wives to abandon all restraint.   Lust rules paramount, and the
children are taught to watch outside the hut, lest the husband
should return unexpectedly, and find his habitation occupied by a
stranger.   Their marriage contract is a mere social arrangement,
easily dissolved, but this is rarely done, the general custom being
for a man to chastise his wife when she displeases him.   The
usual form of matrimonial discipline consists in forcing her to lead
the reindeer while he rides at ease in the sledge.   Their laws permit any man to have two wives, and a regal perquisite of the
great chief was the privilege of having as many as he could support.[1]   These brides were not uncommonly carried off from their
parents by force, the ceremonial rite following at the convenience
of the parties.   Such attempts are sometimes resisted.   An aspirant for the favors of the daughter of a chief succeeded in conveying her to his sledge, but the father pursued with such alacri-
ty that the adventurous lover had to abandon the fair one, and
made his escape with some difficulty, leaving the equipage as
spoils to the victor.[2]

Dr. Kane is of opinion that the services of the Lutheran and
Moravian missionaries have produced a beneficial influence on the
morals of the people.   What may be called their normal religious
notions extended only to the recognition of supernatural agencies,
and to certain usages by which these could be conciliated.   Murder, incest, burial of the living, and infanticide, were not considered crimes, and these have aided exposure and disease (the small-
pox has made fearful ravages among them) to thin their numbers,
and impress them with the idea that they are so rapidly dying
out as to be able to mark their progress toward extinction within
one generation.[3]   This is more applicable to the northern tribes,
removed from the effects of civilization, among whom murder and
infanticide still exist, though not to so great an extent as formerly, while in the southern latitudes, where it was formerly unsafe
for vessels to touch upon the coast, hospitality is now the universal characteristic; and truth, self-reliance, and manly honest bearing have been inculcated with considerable success, though not
enough to render their notions of property accordant with those
of civilized nations.[4]

[1] Arctic Explorations, ii. 123.   [2] Ibid. ii. 125.   Ibid. ii. 109.   [4] Ibid. ii. 121.

ICELAND.

This country is inhabited by a serious, humble, and quiet people. Isolated from the rest of the world, they remain to this day in an almost primitive condition, and nine centuries have produced little change in their manners, language, or costume. The condition of the sexes is somewhat equal; the men divide their labors with the women, but do not oppress them. Both are alike filthy and coarse in their habits. Their hospitality assumes some singular forms. Women salute a stranger with a cordial embrace, but their dirty habits generally render him anxious to escape from their arms as quickly as possible. A missionary was upon one occasion especially scandalized. He was visiting at the house of a rich man, who treated him liberally, and upon retiring to his room at night was followed by his host's eldest daughter, who insisted upon helping him to undress and prepare for bed, declaring that it was the invariable custom of the country.

Few absolute laws regulate the intercourse of the sexes. Christianity has abolished polygamy, and public opinion holds a strong check upon illicit intercourse. With the exception of their seaports, the people may be called a moral race. The proportion of illegitimate to legitimate children is about one in every seven.

Lord Kames relates an anecdote which would stamp the Icelanders of one hundred and fifty years ago as any thing but moral. He says that in 1707 a contagious distemper had cut off nearly all the people, and, in order to repopulate the country, the King of Denmark issued a proclamation authorizing every single woman to bear six illegitimate children without losing her reputation. Report says the girls were so zealous in this patriotic work that it soon became necessary to abrogate the law.

GREENLAND.

The population of Greenland is partly composed of European colonists and partly of Esquimaux. They are a vain and indolent people, whose virtues consist in the negation of active vice. Their women occupy an inferior position. Marriage is essentially a contract for mutual convenience, dissolved when it ceases to be agreeable. It is considered etiquette for a girl, when any man demands her in marriage, to fly to the hills and hide herself, in order to be dragged home with a great show of violence by her suitor. If courted by a man she dislikes, she cuts off her hair, which is a sign of great horror, and usually rids her of her lover.

F F

The Greenlanders consider themselves the only civilized people in the world, and consequently pride themselves on decorum. They do not allow marriages within three degrees of affinity, and consider it disreputable for persons who have been educated in the same house to marry, even if no relationship exists between them. Prostitution prevails to a considerable extent, widows and divorced women almost invariably adopting it as a means of living. There are numerous habitations in the large communities which can only be considered as brothels, but the life of an abandoned woman is generally reprobated, and those following it incur the most undisguised odium of the people at large.

CHAPTER XXXII.

NEW YORK.—STATISTICS.

Schedule of Questions.—Age.—Juvenile Depravity.—Premature Old Age.—Gradual Descent.—Average Duration of a Prostitute's Life.—Nativity.—Proportion of Prostitutes from various States.—New York.—Effects of Immigration.—Foreigners.—Proportion to Population.—Proportion to Emigration.—Dangers of Ports of Departure, Emigrant Ships, and Boarding-houses.—Length of Residence in the United States.—Prostitution a Burden to Tax-payers.—Length of Residence in New York State.—Length of Residence in New York City.—Inducements to emigrate.—Labor and Remuneration in Europe.—Assistance to emigrate; its Amount, and from whom.—Education.—Neglect of Facilities in New York.—Social Condition.—Single Women.—Widows.—Early and Injudicious Marriages.—Husbands.—Children.—Illegitimate Children.—Mortality of Children.—Infanticide.—Influences to which Children are exposed.

IT is to be hoped the reader has already perused the introduction to this volume, containing a description of the *modus operandi* adopted to obtain the necessary information from the prostitutes of New York City. The following schedule of questions was prepared for this purpose, and the ensuing pages present in tabular form the answers received thereto.

" How old will you be next birth-day?

" Were you born in America? and, if so, in what state?

" How long have you resided in New York City?

" If born abroad, in what country?

" How long have you resided in the United States?

" How long have you resided in the State of New York?

" What induced you to emigrate to the United States?

" Did you receive any assistance, and, if so, from whom, and to what amount, to enable you to emigrate to the United States?

"Can you read and write?

" Are you single, married, or widowed?

" If married, is your husband living with you, or what caused the separa-tion?

" If widowed, how long has your husband been dead?

" Have you had any children?

" How many? — Boys — Girls

" Were these children born in wedlock?

" Are they living or dead?

" If living, are they with you now, or where are they?

" For what length of time have you been a prostitute?

" Have you had any disease incident to prostitution? If so, what?

" What was the cause of your becoming a prostitute?

" Is prostitution your only means of support?

" If not, what other means have you?

" What trade or calling did you follow before you became a prostitute?

" How long is it since you abandoned your trade as a means of living?

" What were your average weekly earnings at your trade?

" What business did your father follow?

" If your mother had any business independent of your father, what was it.

" Did you assist either your mother or your father in their business? If so, which of them?

" Is your father living? or how old were you when he died?

" Is your mother living? or how old were you when she died?

" Do you drink intoxicating liquors? If so, to what extent?

'Did your father drink intoxicating liquors? If so, to what extent?

" Did your mother drink intoxicating liquors? If so, to what extent?

" Were your parents " Protestants," " Catholics," or " non-professors?"

" Were you trained to any religion? If so, was it Protestant or Catholic?

" Do you profess the same religion now?

" How long since you observed any of its requirements?"

In addition to this comprehensive series, space was left for any remarks the examiner might wish to make upon other points. The queries were printed on a large sheet of paper, with suffi-cient blanks for the answers, and the officer was desired, as soon as he had obtained all the information required, to fold the sheet, and sign his name on a line left for that purpose, with the date the inquiries were made, the locality of the house in which the woman resided, and the police district in which it was comprised. It is a matter of much regret that in the burning of the Island Hospital, Blackwell's Island, on February 13th, 1858, all the sched-ules were destroyed. They contained many facts which, from want of space, are but slightly alluded to in the following pages, and would have been of material service in any measures hereafter taken to mitigate the sorrows or prevent the excesses of the abandoned women of New York.

Farther prelude is unnecessary. It only remains to give the answers as received, with such deductions as may arise from them.

Question. HOW OLD WILL YOU BE NEXT BIRTH-DAY?

Age.	Number.	Age.	Number.
15 years	2	40 years	25
16 "	17	41 "	7
17 "	62	42 "	6
18 "	143	43 "	6
19 "	258	44 "	3
20 "	268	45 "	6
21 "	206	46 "	2
22 "	176	47 "	2
23 "	153	48 "	5
24 "	96	49 "	3
25 "	97	50 "	4
26 "	75	51 "	1
27 "	53	52 "	3
28 "	58	53 "	3
29 "	49	55 "	5
30 "	44	57 "	3
31 "	18	58 "	2
32 "	16	59 "	2
33 "	29	60 "	2
34 "	15	62 "	1
35 "	19	63 "	1
36 "	23	66 "	2
37 "	11	71 "	1
38 "	9	77 "	1
39 "	7	Total	2000

The facts exhibited by this table are sufficiently palpable to render remarks almost unnecessary, but the existence of juvenile degradation is so clearly proven as to call for a few observations.

Between the ages of fifteen and twenty years are found about three eighths of the whole number embraced in this return. Between the ages of twenty-one and twenty-five years nearly three eighths more of the whole number are included, giving in the first ten years of the table three quarters of the aggregate prostitution, while the next period of five years, or from twenty-six to thirty, contains one eighth more. It is thus upon record that seven out of every eight women who came under this investigation had not yet reached thirty years of age. Beyond this standard each year snows but a few, and of these veterans the majority are those who are now keeping houses of ill fame.

Comparing this with the ages of residents in New York as given in the Census Reports, it will appear that prostitutes under twenty years of age are in excess about twenty-five per cent.; as this inquiry shows that *for every four abandoned women between the ages of twenty and thirty there are three between fifteen and twenty*, but the official classification proves that for every four women in the state between twenty and thirty years old, there are *only two* between fifteen and twenty.

While juvenile degradation is an inseparable adjunct of prostitution, premature old age is its invariable result. Take, for example, the career of a female who enters a house of prostitution at sixteen years of age. Her step is elastic, her eye bright, she is the "observed of all observers." The *habitués* of the place flock around her, gloat over her ruin while they praise her beauty, and try to drag her down to their own level of depravity while flattering her vanity. As the last spark of inherent virtue flickers and dies in her bosom, and she becomes sensible that she is indeed lost, that her anticipated happiness proves but splendid misery, she also becomes conscious that the door of reformation is practically closed against her. But this life of gay depravity can not last; her mind becomes tainted with the moral miasma in which she lives; her physical powers wane under the trials imposed upon them, and her career in a fashionable house of prostitution comes to an end; she must descend in the ladder of vice. Follow her from one step to another in her downward career. To-day you may find her in our aristocratic promenades; to-morrow she will be forced to walk in more secluded streets. To-night you may see her glittering at one of the fashionable theatres; to-morrow she will be found in some one of the infamous resorts which abound in the lower part of the city. To-day she may associate with the wealthy of the land; to-morrow none will be too low for her company. To-day she has servants to do her bidding; to-morrow she may be buried in a pauper's coffin and a nameless grave. This is no fancy sketch, but an outline of the course of many women now living as prostitutes of the lowest class in the city of New York.

Any one conversant with the subject knows that there is a well understood gradation in this life, and as soon as a woman ceases to be attractive in the higher walks, as soon as her youth and beauty fade, she must either descend in the scale *or starve.* Nor will any deny that of those who commence a life of shame in their youth under the most specious and flattering delusions, the majority are found, in a short time, plunged into the deepest misery and degradation.

Here is seen, at a glance, a reason for the large number of juvenile prostitutes. Youth is a marketable commodity, and when its charms are lost, they must be replaced. The following cases, from life, will substantiate this view. For obvious reasons, the names are suppressed.

C. B. is a native of New York, and now resides in the Eighth Police District of the city. She is twenty years old, and became a prostitute at the age of *sixteen*, through the harshness and unkind treatment of a stepmother, her own mother having died when she was an infant. Take another case from the same neighborhood. L. B. was born in Vermont; her father died while she was a child. At the age of *fifteen* she was enticed to the city, and became an inmate of a house of prostitution. She is described as an intelligent, well-educated girl, of temperate habits. One more instance from the same locality. F. W. is a native of New York City; is the child of honest, hard-working parents; has received a medium education; at *seventeen* years old was seduced under a promise of marriage, and deserted. She then embraced a life of prostitution, influenced mainly by shame, and the idea that she had no other means of subsistence.

These women are residing in that part of the city which contains the majority of the first-class houses of prostitution; they have not yet descended in the scale. The ensuing selection, taken from the Fourth Police District, the antipodes of the former locality, will forcibly exhibit the operation of this gradual deterioration.

E. S. was seduced in Rochester, N. Y., at the age of *sixteen.* She accompanied her seducer to this city, and for a season lived here in luxury. She was finally deserted, and now drags out a wretched existence in Water Street. E. C., residing in the same neighborhood, is now nineteen years of age. She was married when but a child, and, five years since, or when she was only *fourteen* years old, was driven on the town through the brutal conduct of her husband. Passing through the various gradations of the scale, she has now become a confirmed drunkard; has endured much physical suffering; and, lost to all sense of shame, will doubtless continue in her wretched career till death puts an end to her misery.

To continue this chain of evidence, the following cases have been selected from the registers of the Penitentiary Hospital (now remodeled, and called the Island Hospital), Blackwell's Island. S. A., of New Jersey, was admitted as a patient when only *fifteen* years of age, suffering from disease caused by leading a depraved life, and within six months was received and treated therein no less than four times. A. B., born in Scotland, was admitted and treated for venereal disease at *fourteen* years of age. L. A. D., born in England, was admitted at *sixteen* years of age, two years since, with similar disease, and, with only short intervals, has been an inmate of the hospital continuously from that time. M. H. was admitted at *seventeen* years of age, and endured a long and painful illness. M. J. D., after following a course of depravity for a year, was admitted at *eighteen* years of age, lingered in agony for twenty-five days, and then died, solely from the effects of a life of prostitution.

It is not necessary to pursue this subject farther, as sufficient facts have been adduced to support the assertion that youth is the grand desideratum in the inmates of houses of ill fame. Young women have been traced from the proudest resorts to the lowest haunts, and have been shown as suffering pain and sickness in a public institution, or dying there in torture. But no attempt has been made to calculate the misery produced in the respective families they had abandoned. The excruciating parental agony caused by the departure of a daughter from the paths of virtue seems more a matter for private contemplation by each reader than for any delineation here. We have witnessed the meetings of parents with their lost children; have stood beside the bed where a frail, suffering woman was yielding her last breath, and have shuddered at the awful mental agony overpowering her physical suffering. No doubt can exist that, were it possible to introduce the reader of these pages to such scenes, or even could they be adequately described in all their accumulated horrors, the cordial co-operation of all the friends of virtue and humanity would be secured in furtherance of any plan which would check this mighty torrent of vice and woe.

From the fact that youth is the grand desideratum, it is evident that a constant succession of young people will be driven into this arena, either by force or treachery. *The average duration of life among these women does not exceed four years from the beginning of their career!* There are, as in all cases, exceptions to this rule, but it is a tolerably well established fact that one fourth of the total number of abandoned women in this city die every year. Thus, by estimating the prostitutes in New York at six thousand (and this is not an exaggerated calculation, as will be proved hereafter), the appalling number of one thousand five hundred erring women are hurried to their last, long homes each year of our existence. Neglected and contemned while living, they pass from this world unnoticed and unwept. But their deaths leave vacancies which must be supplied: the inexorable demands of vice and dissipation must be gratified, and who can tell what innocent and happy family circle may next have to mourn the ruin and disgrace of one of its members? In a subsequent portion of this work it will be necessary to notice the means employed for ensnaring the innocent and unsuspecting, and to show that this is a danger which threatens all classes of the community.

Question. WERE YOU BORN IN AMERICA? IF SO, IN WHAT STATE?

State.	Number.	State.	Number.
Alabama	1	Massachusetts	71
Carolina, North	2	Missouri	1
" South	4	New Hampshire	7
Columbia, District of	1	New Jersey	69
Connecticut	42	New York	394
Delaware	1	Ohio	8
Georgia	1	Pennsylvania	77
Illinois	1	Rhode Island	18
Kentucky	2	Vermont	10
Louisiana	4	Virginia	9
Maine	24	Total born in United States	762
Maryland	15		

The number of prostitutes in New York who were born within the limits of the United States slightly exceeds three eighths of the aggregate from whom replies to these queries were obtained. They are natives of twenty-one states and one district, and may be subdivided in geographical order as follows:

1. The Eastern District, containing Maine, New Hampshire, Vermont, Massachusetts, Connecticut, and Rhode Island, contributes one hundred and seventy-two women to the prostitutes of New York City.

2. The Middle States, New York, New Jersey, Pennsylvania, District of Columbia, Delaware, Maryland, and Virginia, contribute five hundred and sixty-six women.

3. The Southern States, North Carolina, South Carolina, Georgia, Alabama, and Louisiana, contribute twelve women.

4. The Western States, Ohio, Illinois, Missouri, and Kentucky, contribute also twelve women.

On what hypothesis can these proportions be explained? Maine, on the extreme northeast, with a rocky, surge-beaten coast fronting on the wild Atlantic, with a harsh, cold climate, sends twenty-four women from her population of 580,000, while Virginia, with 1,421,000 inhabitants, contributes but nine! This difference in favor of the southern state can not be explained on the ground of distance, for the boundaries of each state are nearly equidistant from New York; nor can it be sustained by the idea that Maine has more sea-coast, as the maritime coast of the southern state is at least equal to that of the northern one, and the ordinary tendencies to immorality in sea-port towns would be equally felt in each. The case is still farther involved by the fact that in all southern cities the majority of prostitutes are from the north; and it is a well-known circumstance, that at certain periods large numbers of courtesans from New York, Boston, and other cities emigrate southward. Were the generally received opinion of the effects of a warm climate upon female organization to be adopted in this connection, not only would there be no necessity for this exodus, but the number of prostitutes received from Virginia should largely exceed those from Maine. This fact is sufficient to confirm the idea already expressed, that fraud or force is used to entrap these females. The natives of a bleak northern state are far more likely to be deceived by the artful misrepresentations of emissaries from New York than the denizens of the southern portion of our Union. The former lead a life of comparative hardship, the latter one of comparative ease. In Maine, over six thousand women, or one in every forty-six of the female population, are immured for six days in every week in a crowded factory; in Virginia, over three thousand women, or one in every one hundred and thirty-four of the female population, are similarly employed.[1] This mode of life will form a matter for subsequent consideration, so far as its tendencies to immorality are concerned.

Again: Place in contrast Rhode Island with eighteen women living by prostitution in New York, and a population of only 140,000, and Maryland with fifteen prostitutes in New York, and a population of 418,000, and a more palpable difference in favor

[1] U. S. Census. 1850.

of the southern state is apparent.   The former sends one prostitute out of every eight thousand of her inhabitants; the latter, one
out of every twenty-eight thousand.

Calculating on the basis of the respective populations, Vermont
and New Hampshire have nearly the same proportion as Maine;
Massachusetts exceeds the average; and Connecticut (*par excellence*, "the land of steady habits") has a still larger excess.   New
Jersey has the largest proportion of any state in the union, and
Pennsylvania shows about the average of Maine.   The Southern
and Western States have but few representatives.   New York, the
home state, will be noticed in due course.   The preceding facts
will supply materials for reflection, in conjunction with the question, "On what hypothesis can these proportions be explained?"

The self-evident answer to this query would seem to be that the
excess from the Eastern and Middle States arises from the employment of a much larger proportion of females in manufacturing and
sedentary occupations.   A young woman of ardent temperament
can not but feel the hardship of this position in life as compared
with her more favored sisters in other states, and when such an
idea has once obtained possession of her mind, it forms a subject
for constant thought.   Thus, when already predisposed in favor
of any change, she falls into the hands of the tempter a pliant victim.   Beyond the hardship attendant on her daily labor, the associations which are formed in factories or workshops where both
sexes are employed very frequently result disastrously for the female.   Notwithstanding all the care which may be taken on the
part of employers—and it is a subject for national pride that American manufacturers are doing far more to elevate the moral character of their employés than the same class of men in other lands—
it is morally impossible that these intimacies can be entirely suppressed, nor can their ruinous effects be prevented.   Study the
moral statistics of any of the manufacturing towns in Great Britain
or on the Continent of Europe, and the same results are presented,
but in a more alarming degree, because there the supervision is
not only weak in itself, but is frequently intrusted to improper
persons, whose interest is often in direct opposition to their duty.

A few words in respect to the State of New York.   The number of prostitutes in proportion to the population far exceeds the
ratio from any other state *except New Jersey*.   Beyond the effect
of manufactures, which operate here to a corresponding extent as
in other states, the immense maritime business of New York City,

and the constant flood of immigrants and strangers passing through it, must be taken into consideration. This constantly fills some localities with sailors, men proverbial for having "in every port a wife," and many of whom are notorious frequenters of houses of prostitution. This circumstance proves that this infernal traffic is governed by the same rules which regulate commercial transactions, namely, that the supply is in proportion to the demand. If, by any miracle, all the seamen and strangers visiting New York could be transformed into moral men, at least from one half to two thirds of the houses of ill fame would be absolutely bankrupt.

The constant flood of immigration leaves a mass of *debris* behind it, consisting, in the first place, of men idle and vicious in their own lands, who transfer their vices to the country of their adoption, and for a time after arrival here devote what means they possess to the pursuit of debauchery, and materially help to swell the torrent of immorality. Another class of immigrants are women, many of whom are sent here by charitable (?) associations or public bodies in foreign lands, as the most economical way to get rid of them. Many of these females become mothers almost as soon as they land on these shores; in fact, the probability of such an event sometimes hastens their departure. They exist here in the most squalid misery in some tenement house or hovel. Their children receive none of the advantages of education; for, as soon as they can beg, they are compelled to aid in the struggle for bread, and the most frequent result is that the boys are arrested for some petty theft, and the girls become prostitutes, thus contributing to meet the demand caused by the classes already mentioned.

But, in addition to these foreign children born by accident in our state, the proportion of prostitutes from New York is increased by the facility offered for transit from the interior to the city. Doubtless there are many courtesans from the eastern and southern districts who find their way to some of the large cities in their own part of the country, and so, on the same principle, when a woman in this state has fallen into vicious habits her natural resort is to this metropolis. In addition to the more extended market it offers for her charms, its advantages as a great central rendezvous for the nation must not be overlooked. Here a prostitute can live until her attractions wane, and hence she can easily reach any southern or other point where abandoned women are in demand. Despite of the large number of prostitutes ascertained to have been born within the bounds of New York State, it can not be conceded that we are any less moral than our neighbors in other parts of the confederation.

It is a matter for the most serious consideration, to be followed by sound and judicious action, either legislative or personal, that so large a number of American girls fall victims to this fell destroyer in a land where a good education is within the reach of every one; where industry, if properly applied in the right channels, will afford a comfortable maintenance for all; where the natural resources are sufficient to support nearly half the inhabitants of the world.

Question. WERE YOU BORN ABROAD? IF SO, IN WHAT COUNTRY?

Countries.	Numbers.	Countries.	Numbers.
Austria	2	Poland	3
Belgium	1	Prussia	6
British North America	63	Saxony	2
Denmark	1	Scotland	52
England	104	Switzerland	17
France	13	Wales	1
Germany	249	West Indies	4
Ireland	706	At Sea	13
Italy	1	Total born abroad	1238

It has been frequently remarked, and as generally believed, in the absence of any satisfactory information on the subject, that a very large majority of the prostitutes in New York are of foreign birth; but the facts already developed, with the few remarks which will be made upon the above table of nativities, go far toward falsifying that opinion. The enumeration shows that five eighths only were born abroad, the dominions of Great Britain funishing the largest proportion. The ratio in which the several parts of that kingdom supply the New World with courtesans may be stated in round numbers as follows: Ireland contributes one prostitute to every four thousand of her population; British North America, one prostitute to every seven thousand of population; Scotland, one prostitute to every sixteen thousand of population; England and Wales, one prostitute to every fifty thousand of population. Of course, this will be understood as referring to all prostitutes now living in this city, assuming the average nativities of all to be fairly represented in the replies obtained from a portion.

But these numbers, being based upon the population of the several countries, give but a very imperfect idea of the extent of vice among that portion of their people who have settled in America, and a more satisfactory comparison can be drawn from the records of emigration. Upon an examination of the arrivals in each year from the time the existing Board of Commissioners of Emigration was organized to the end of 1857 (a period of ten years), it is found that the numbers average two hundred and thirty thousand per annum, which gives a proportion of one prostitute to every two hundred and fifty emigrants. This is based upon the theory that one fourth of the abandoned women die or are otherwise removed from the city every year. To repeat this fact in plainer words: of every two hundred and fifty emigrants—men, women, and children, who land at our docks, at least one woman eventually becomes known as a prostitute.

This demoralization may be accounted for in several ways. There is frequently a protracted interval between the time when families arrive at the intended port of departure and the day on which they sail; and during this space they are exposed to all the malign influences invariably existing in large sea-port towns, which must impart vicious ideas to young people who have recently left some secluded part of the country. Take Liverpool, for instance, the port whence the largest number of emigrants come to us, and which contains one prostitute for every eighty-eight inhabitants, and the wonder will be, not that so many are contaminated, but that so many escape. When the dangers of the town are surmounted, another source of immorality is found in the steerage passage across the Atlantic. This occupies from one to three months, during which time the females are necessarily in constant communication with the other sex, and frequently exposed to scenes of indelicacy too glaring to be described here; and this in addition to the constant machinations of the abandoned and unprincipled men who are to be found, in greater or less numbers, in every ship's complement of crew and passengers. Under such circumstances, the germ implanted in the sea-port town often develops into its legitimate fruit. But when the ship has reached her haven, and the perils of the sea are passed, there are dangers to be encountered on land. The present arrangements for disembarking emigrants at Castle Garden have removed many of the most objectionable features formerly incident to their entry into the land of their adoption, yet there are many still remaining. If a family desire to travel to the interior of the country, they can do so at once; but should they remain in the city, they are exposed to the tender mercies of the emigrant boarding-house keepers, generally themselves natives of the "old country," who, having been swindled on their arrival, are both competent and willing to practice the same impositions on others. It must not be concluded that all who follow the business are worthy of this sweeping condemnation; many of them are undoubtedly honest, yet it can not be denied that others do pursue this nefarious course; and when they have drained all the resources of their customers, they turn them adrift to beg, or starve, or sin for a subsistence.

To one or the other of these causes many girls owe their ruin. Indeed, there can be no reasonable doubt that a majority of the prostitutes of foreign birth are more or less influenced thereby. In addition to these, there are other snares constantly set for strangers, to which we shall hereafter allude.

It is scarcely within the province of this section to notice measures calculated to remove the evils named. With the first, the American people have no possible means of interfering. With regard to the second, many difficulties must be encountered and overcome. The Commissioners of Emigration have taken steps to avert some of the evils, and, in consequence of their application to the present Congress, a bill has been introduced making it a penal offense for any officer or sailor on emigrant ships to have carnal intercourse with any passenger, whether with or without her consent.

The third evil named is a local question peculiarly and entirely under our own control, and, at the risk of anticipating the subject, it may be suggested that the most effectual way of obviating it would be the organization of a plan offering inducements and facilities for young women to leave the city, thus removing them from its baneful influences to a part of the country where their own labor would give them the means of a comfortable subsistence and a virtuous life. It is but poor policy to retain in New York numbers of persons who can by no possibility procure employment in an already overcrowded field of labor, and who must eventually consent to earn a precarious living by the sacrifice of virtue. It matters not through what agency their ruin is effected, whether by the oppression of a boarding-house keeper, the intrigues of an intelligence-office, or the wiles of abandoned ones of their own sex. The degradation is an indisputable fact, and the expenses to every citizen from the extra cost of police supervision, courts of justice, hospitals, and penitentiaries, would probably be enough to remove many from the city who are debauched for the want of opportunity to leave. It would be far better to try the system of prevention in the first instance, and this would probably be successful in many cases; whereas any reformatory plan is almost useless where the Rubicon has been passed.

Question. HOW LONG HAVE YOU RESIDED IN THE UNITED STATES?

Length of Residence.	Numbers.	Length of residence	Numbers.
Under 2 months	9	Under 5 years	106
" 3 "	11	" 10 "	352
" 6 "	21	10 years and upward	292
" 1 year	75	From Birth	762
" 2 years	159	Unascertained	31
" 3 "	99	Total	2000
" 4 "	83		

In intimate connection with the subject of the nativities of pros-titutes now in New York are the answers to the above inquiry. Deducting the number of native-born women, it will be found that five hundred and sixty-three, or more than forty-five per cent. of the foreigners, have resided in the United States less than five years; and of this number, one hundred and fifteen, or nearly twenty-one per cent., have resided here less than one year. These averages support, to some extent, the opinion already advanced, that a large proportion of the prostitutes in New York City were either seduced previous to leaving their port of departure, or on their passage, or very soon after their arrival here, when they com-menced forthwith a practice which forces them eventually to be-come a burden upon the tax-paying community. In a majority of cases, this must be the result of their career; the successive fall from one gradation of their wretched life to a lower finally land-ing them in the prisons or hospitals of a city toward whose ex-penses neither their pecuniary ability nor their labor have ever contributed a farthing. Their support thus falls upon the work-ing population, an argument of dollars and cents which will not be without its influence in a consideration of the numerous evils of prostitution.

The remaining fifty-five per cent., having been in the United States more than five years, are by law entitled to receive any as-sistance which their necessities may demand from local funds, but of this number there are some who have doubtless been chargea-ble to public institutions before they had completed the required term of residence, as there are unquestionably many who, in order to procure relief, make false representations as to the time of their arrival. Reasoning from well-ascertained facts, there can be little exaggeration in the estimate that from eighty to one hundred thousand dollars per annum is the amount which the citizens of New York contribute to the support of foreigners who have been less than five years in the United States. Nor can this be prevented unless the claims of suffering humanity are entirely ignored. Of course. the idea that a sick or disabled man or woman is to be left to perish can not be entertained for one moment. If they are in want or in pain, every dictate of our common nature demands that they shall be relieved. But it may be suggested to those interested in the question of local taxation to give their prompt assistance to any practicable scheme which will diminish the amount of vice, and consequently reduce the expenses resulting therefrom, such as a carefully-devised plan for shielding emigrants from corrupting influences, and forwarding the destitute to sections where labor may be obtained. Upon the moral effects of such an arrangement it is unnecessary to remark, as they are self-evident; of its successful working and eventual economy but little doubt can be entertained.

Question. HOW LONG HAVE YOU RESIDED IN NEW YORK STATE?

Length of Residence.	Numbers.	Length of Residence.	Numbers.
Under 2 months	35	Under 5 years	127
" 3 "	20	" 10 "	374
" 6 "	43	10 years and upward	433
" 1 year	132	From Birth	353
" 2 years	186	Unascertained	35
" 3 "	152	Total	2000
" 4 "	110		

Question. HOW LONG HAVE YOU RESIDED IN NEW YORK CITY?

Length of Residence.	Numbers.	Length of Residence.	Numbers.
Under 2 months	46	Under 5 years	135
" 3 "	30	" 10 "	388
" 6 "	56	10 years and upward	427
" 1 year	140	From Birth	185
" 2 years	236	Unascertained	40
" 3 "	189	Total	2000
" 4 "	128		

These tables require no comment. The attention of the reader may merely be called to the fact that three hundred and ninety-four women have been already reported as born in the State of New York, of which number three hundred and fifty-three have resided within its limits continuously from the time of their birth, and that one hundred and eighty-five, or nearly one half, were natives of New York City, and have resided therein from the day they were born. This fact alone demonstrates that the influences of metropolitan life are not very favorable to the advance of female morality.

Question. WHAT INDUCED YOU TO EMIGRATE TO THE UNITED STATES?

Reasons.	Numbers.	Reasons.	Numbers.
Came as stewardesses	2	Sent out by parents or friends	81
Ran away from home	18	Came with relatives or to	
Ill usage of parents	34	join relatives already in	
Came with their seducers	39	the United States	619
Came to improve their con-		No special cause assigned	34
dition	411	Total of foreigners	1238

This table shows that a majority of the prostitutes of foreign birth were induced to emigrate to the United States either by considerations of policy—four hundred and eleven assigning as their reason a desire to improve their condition in life—or from family connections, six hundred and nineteen having arrived with relatives and friends, or with the purpose of joining relatives and friends already in this country.

It will not be denied by any one familiar with the subject that one main reason for emigration is always found in the comparative difficulty of earning a livelihood in the place of the emigrant's nativity, and the expectation of doing better in a strange land; a conclusion sustained by the fact that a prosperous year in Europe serves to check the arrivals here, and *vice versa.* With the difficult problem of labor and remuneration in the Old World it would be out of place to interfere; but it may be remarked that, badly as many branches of female employment are paid for with us, they are still worse paid for in England. Reference to a previous chapter, treating of the causes of prostitution in that country, will at once establish this point, and the instances therein quoted of the wages paid in London will remove all surprise that this country should be a receptacle for underpaid operatives, or that the hope of realizing better wages should be sufficiently powerful to sever all ties of birth-place and home. But many of these impoverished women were actually dependent upon friends for the payment of their passage-money, and consequently arrived here almost literally penniless, with very slight prospects of obtaining work, and frequently with but one alternative, and the only one they had before coming here, which they must embrace or starve.

G G

Another class assign as a reason for expatriation the ill usage of parents, in itself a prolific cause of prostitution under any circumstances, but more especially when its effects have been to drive the girl a distance of four thousand miles from home.

From an examination of these causes alone, it is apparent that, however well qualified, physically and morally, to add their quota to the prosperity of the United States, had their exertions been properly directed, yet the circumstances under which these women emigrated were so embarrassing as to render them easy victims to those whose special business seems to be to ensnare the friendless and unfortunate.

This branch of inquiry may be continued by a reference to the following table, giving a summary of answers to the

Question, DID YOU RECEIVE ANY ASSISTANCE, AND IF SO, TO WHAT AMOUNT, TO ENABLE YOU TO EMIGRATE TO THE UNITED STATES?

Amount of Assistance	Numbers.	Amount of Assistance.	Numbers.
Paid their own expenses .	262	Received assistance . } $110 each,	1
Rec'd assistance, amount not specified . . . }	618	" " 120 "	3
Rec'd assistance, $20 each,	89	" " 140 "	2
" " 25 "	94	" " 150 "	3
" " 30 "	43	" " 175 "	1
" " 35 "	15	" " 180 "	2
" " 40 "	24	" " 200 "	5
" " 45 "	6	" " 220 "	1
" " 50 "	28	" " 250 "	2
" " 55 "	3	" " 300 "	4
" " 60 "	12	" " 400 "	1
" " 65 "	2	" " 600 "	1
" " 70 "	2	Totals . . .	976 262
" " 75 "	2		—- 976
" " 100 "	12	Total of foreign-born prostitutes	1238

It appears that only two hundred and sixty-two, or about one fifth of the total number, paid their own passage-money, the remainder having received pecuniary assistance toward that object ranging from an unspecified amount, which, in all probability, was not more than the positive expenses of the voyage, to six hundred dollars. It will be observed that the majority did not receive more than forty dollars each, eight hundred and eighty-three of those assisted stating that such help did not exceed that sum. This certainly was but a very inadequate amount to pay the expenses of an outfit and a voyage across the Atlantic, and then to support a person in a strange land until employment could be secured; particnlarly if she was but one of a family each member of which had the same imperative necessity for work as herself. These remarks may be thought inconsistent with the statements published in 1856 of the amount of money brought to this country by immigrants; but it may be suggested that, although these reports gave a correct statement of the sum in the possession of all the passengers by a certain vessel, they are altogether silent as to the numbers who were destitute. They merely proved what has been universally conceded within the last three or four years, namely, that among the immigrants arriving are many with considerable cash means. But it does not require much reflection to convince any one that when a family bring available funds with them, they will leave New York as quickly as possible in search of some locality where their money may be advantageously employed. This is still more likely, as the fact of their being possessed of capital proves them to have practiced habits of industry and economy at home, which would scarcely abandon them when they reached the New World. The aggregated facts as to property do not touch isolated cases of poverty, the most dangerous to this community, because individuals who are forced to remain in the city from want of means to leave it not only swell its long list of paupers, but are in circumstances which may materially influence them to become prostitutes, and have the spur of necessity to urge them forward in this or any other course which may offer a respite from starvation.

The following table corroborates this theory; it consists of replies to the other part of the same

Question. DID YOU RECEIVE ANY ASSISTANCE, AND IF SO, FROM WHOM, TO ENABLE YOU TO EMIGRATE TO THE UNITED STATES?

By whom assisted.	Numbers	
Paid their own expenses		262
By relatives or friends	805	
By money remitted by relatives or friends in the U. S.	100	
Stole money from their friends	34	
By seducers	28	
By public authorities	9	
Totals	976	262
		976
Total of foreign-born prostitutes		1238

As a general rule, the parties by whom assistance was rendered were not likely to advance any amount beyond what was absolutely required. Even this amount would perhaps be reduced before the termination of the voyage, if it should prove a protracted one, and the provisions of the passengers be exhausted, as there are on board every ship persons who are willing to sell articles of food at prices ranging from three to six times their value, and who are equally ready to supply demands for brandy or tobacco also. On a review of the responses given to the three questions which have been under consideration in this section, it appears that the opinions expressed are legitimate deductions from the premises. They may be thus recapitulated: The majority of those immigrants who subsequently become prostitutes in New York were almost destitute in their own country; they arrive here with little or no means of support; their poverty renders them peculiarly liable to yield to temptation, if, indeed, many of them have not previously fallen. Thus, if we do not receive them as prostitutes when they reach our shores, we receive them in a condition immediately to become such for the sake of subsistence.

Question. CAN YOU READ AND WRITE?

Degree of Education.	Numbers.
Can read and write well	714
Can read and write imperfectly	546
Can read only	219
Uneducated	521
Total	2000

Seven hundred and fourteen of the women who were examined in New York City say that they can read and write *well*. This must not be regarded as proof that they have received a superior, or even a medium education, but is a phrase which may be interpreted to mean that they can read a page of printed matter without much trouble, and can sign their names, although truth compels the admission that their writing is very often a species of penmanship extremely difficult to decipher. Beyond such acquirements as these, very few, scarcely one in each five hundred, have progressed. Five hundred and forty-six can read and write *imperfectly*, a grade of education which may be defined as midway between the amount of knowledge already described and a state of total ignorance; enough, in fact, to relieve them from the suspicion of being altogether illiterate, which is the sole advantage they can claim over the two hundred and nineteen who can *read only*, or the five hundred and twenty-one who confess that they *can neither read nor write*. As a whole, there is little doubt that the prostitutes in New York believe, "where ignorance is bliss, "tis folly to be wise." These remarks are made from observations upon this class during a long hospital experience.

But, seriously, such a state of ignorance is most deplorable. To give an idea of the facilities for acquiring education in the various countries from which these prostitutes reach us, the following statement from the United States Census for 1850[1] is submitted:

The ratio of persons receiving education is as follows:

United States, 1 to every 5 of total population.
Denmark, 1 " " 5 " " "
Sweden, 1 " " 6 " " "
Prussia, 1 " " 6 " " "
Norway, 1 " " 7 " " "
Great Britain, 1 " " 8 " " "
France, 1 " " 10 " " "
Austria, 1 " " 13 " " "
Holland, 1 " " 14 " " "
Ireland, 1 " " 14 " " "

The following is a fair average estimate of the acquirements of native and foreign-born prostitutes:

Degree of Education.	Natives.	Foreigners.
Can read and write well . . .	25 per cent.	10 per cent.
" " " " imperfectly .	50 " "	50 " "
Uneducated	25 " "	40 " "
	100	100

The average of educational facilities in the United States is as one to five; in European countries it is one to ten. In other words, every one in this country has twice the opportunities for education compared with those born in the Old World: opportunities which, in the cases of these women at least, have not been improved to their full extent. Of those who claim to be well educated, the United States show more than the average. In the class imperfectly educated, foreigners show one half of their number, and the superior advantages in this country only produce exactly the same proportion. The proportion of those uneducated is not much more favorable in natives than in foreigners. Some allowances must be made, however, in this calculation, for the fact that many children of foreign birth arrive here at an early age, and gain such education as they possess in American institutions; but even this will but slightly affect the disproportion alluded to. But no possible modification of the facts can be conceived sufficient to excuse the negligence of the parents or friends of one fourth of the native-born prostitutes in this city at the present

Compendium of U. S. Census, 1850, p. 148.

day, when education may be obtained literally "without money and without price."

Sectarian bigotry must be held responsible for much of this offense. "If our children can not be educated as we please, they shall not be educated at all. If they must not read the books we wish, they shall never learn the alphabet," is, in effect, if not in words, the language of thousands in this country to-day. What are the results of this cruel policy? The children go forth into the world: the boys, to earn a precarious living by the sweat of their brow; the girls, condemned to the most servile work in any family where their stupidity may find a shelter, until they meet with some man of their own mental calibre, whom they marry, and forthwith bring up their unfortunate children in the same manner in which they themselves were reared. This is the brightest view of the future of ignorant children; the darker shades are depicted in the annals of vice and crime—may be seen daily in our prisons, hospitals, poor-houses, and pauper burying-grounds.

The picture is not overdrawn; nor will the reply so common in this generation, "These are the children of foreigners," serve to exonerate the parents; for even if all the uneducated native women who have answered these questions were born of foreign parentage, a fact which must be proved before it is admitted, but which we are not inclined to concede, yet they were born on our soil, where public schools were open to receive them, and their intelligence would enhance the credit of the land in the same proportion that their ignorance diminishes it. A love of their adopted country, its institutions and its fame, is not too much to ask of parents who derive their maintenance from its resources. It is a libel upon the parental instinct (it can not be called feeling) to allow any child in the United States to arrive at years of maturity without acquiring a good plain, solid education. Fathers or mothers who pursue such a course as this would consider themselves unjustly accused if told they were training their daughters to become prostitutes, but such is the fact. It is scarcely possible to imagine any thing so likely to lead a woman from the paths of rectitude as ignorance, coupled with the conviction that such ignorance is an insurmountable barrier to her progress in life; it drives her to intoxication to drown her reflections, and from intoxication to prostitution the transition is easy and almost certain.

Here, then, are a number of young women thrown into society every year without the least education; untrained for good, and only fit for evil. Ignorant of their duties to themselves or to the world; with sensibilities callous because they have never been cultivated; with faculties on a level with the inferior animals from the same cause, they are expected to succeed in life! It would be as consistent to take a man who had never seen a steam-engine, and give him the control of a locomotive and a train of cars without anticipating an accident, as it is to presume in this day of knowledge that an uneducated man or woman can ever become a respectable and useful member of society.

Could our liberal facilities for education be duly improved, much would be done to prevent the vice of prostitution. No classical or extraordinary tuition is required to accomplish this end; merely common sense rightly cultivated, and conscience enlightened and developed, so as to appreciate the difference between right and wrong, will do much to aid a woman to pass unscathed through trials which constantly ruin the ignorant.

The question has sometimes arisen whether it should not be made compulsory on parents to educate their children. The present is not the place to discuss that subject, but the following statistics will show to what extent the duty is neglected.

The United States Census for 1850 reports:

Population of New York City 515,547
Proportion of population between the ages of five and
    fifteen years 101,006
Children attending school 76,685
Percentage of children attending school . . . . 75$\frac{9}{10}$

The New York State Census for 1855 reports:

Population of New York City. 629,904
Proportion of population between the ages of five and fif-
    teen years 116,627

No returns are made of the numbers attending schools, and these must be sought from other sources. The report of the Board of Education for 1856 states the average daily attendance at the ward or public schools to be 44,598. The same document gives data from which the attendance at religious, corporate, or other public schools can be calculated, but says nothing of private schools. An approximate estimate of the latter can, however, be made with the help of the United States Census. In 1850, the proportions were about one private to every twelve public scholars, and since that period there has probably been but little change in the ratio.

From these facts the subjoined may be assumed a reasonably correct statement:

Average attendance at public schools 44,598
Allowance of twenty per cent. for absentees, whose names
  are on the school registers, but who attend irregularly . 8,920
Corporate schools receiving state assistance 7,517
    "   " without " " . (estimated) 10,000
Private schools . . . . " 6,000
    Total children attending school 77,035

This would give a school attendance of sixty-six per cent. of the population between the ages of five and fifteen years, or ten per cent. less than in 1850.

That the proportionate numbers receiving education are diminishing is susceptible of proof from one fact. In 1856, the pupils in the public schools were 347 more than in 1855. During the last fifteen years the population of the city has increased more than twenty thousand per annum, and of this increase about one fifth (or four thousand) are between the ages of five and fifteen. It follows that in 1856 there were four thousand additional children in New York as compared with 1855, but there were only 347 additional attendants at the public schools. Admitting that other schools received the same increase of pupils—an admission more liberal than facts would warrant—the education of seven hundred only would be provided for, leaving three thousand three hundred destitute of instruction.

In the course of the year 1856, the attention of the Board of Education was directed to the large number of children not attending any school, and upon the basis of a partial census of the city they were assumed to amount to sixty thousand. This was conceded to be an over-estimate. The figures given above would make the number 39,594, which may very likely be nearer the truth; but even this may be in excess, and, to allow for all possible contingencies, we will place it at thirty thousand. Even this is an alarming statement: the suggestion that of all the children in our city nearly twenty-seven per cent. are growing up in a state of perfect ignorance, presents so many frightful considerations that the mind revolts at the bare possibility. But the facts will not permit any other construction. If this criminal neglect be continued, it must produce fatal consequences to society, and the view of impending results would almost sanction a compulsory education.[1]

[1] Compendium of United States Census, 1850, p. 142, etc.; Census of the State

Question. ARE YOU SINGLE, MARRIED, OR WIDOWED?

Condition.	Numbers
Single	1216
Married	490
Widowed	294
Total	2000

The civil condition of the prostitutes in New York City fur-nishes matter of serious consideration in view of the slight restraints which the ordinarily received rules of society place upon the passions, and the utter inefficiency of such regulations to counteract the influences tending to female degradation; influences, in fact, which they very frequently augment rather than check. In the cases of many females now under notice, marriage was invested not only with the sanctions of a civil contract between the parties, as recognized by our state laws, but, according to the tenets of the Roman Catholic Church, was regarded as one of the seven holy sacraments which it is deemed an act of sacrilege to violate. Yet, in the face of these ordinances, the civil contract is broken, the sacrament is profaned in one fourth of the total number of cases, or four hundred and ninety out of two thousand which are now under notice. It would be out of place to enter here on any disquisition respecting the duties of the married state; regarded in its abuses as provocative of prostitution it is noticed hereafter. Enjoined by the precepts of Holy Writ, supported by the sentiment of the world, and respected by all virtuous men, marriage is an institution which needs no argument to enforce its claims to the most rigid observance.

That this sacred compact is too frequently violated by one or other of the contracting parties is proved by almost daily experience either in courts of law or by intercourse with the world. Conflicting testimony sometimes renders it doubtful to whom the blame ought to be imputed, but there can be no uncertainty whatever as to the opinions entertained by society at large in such cases. If the husband has been guilty of a breach of his conjugal duties, he reads the whole of the evidence, graphically reported, with occasional embellishments, in the columns of the daily papers, flatters himself that he is acquiring notoriety, is congratulated by friends of his own predilections on his success, and in a short time is fully reinstated in his former social position. On the contrary, if the weight of evidence is against the wife, the whole artillery of the world's scorn is leveled at her head. She is driven from society, crushed by the proudly virtuous frowns of her own sex and the contemptuous sneers of the other. Dishonored and despised, she is too often left with no means of existence but indiscriminate prostitution, the temptation to such degradation being aggravated by the consciousness of her previous infidelity and its results. There is no possibility of salvation for her. The moral world has resolved she shall not repent, and the least attempt on her part to atone for an error over which she mourns with all the intensity of her nature is sternly resisted by the virtuous indignation of society, which erects an impassable barrier between herself and her hopes of reformation.

Of the prostitutes in New York, one thousand two hundred and sixteen have never been married. Their sin is the less because they have not to answer for broken vows, nor have they any outraged confidence on which to brood, but to endure only the sin and odium attached to their present condition. Two hundred and ninety-five prostitutes are widowed. In their cases death has put an end to the marital contract, and, thus left free to act for themselves, they stand in nearly the same condition as single women.

An investigation of the nativities of these women shows that about one third each of the single and married prostitutes are natives of the United States, and of widows about one half were born in this country.

The question may arise as to the causes to be assigned for the depravity of married women, and for the large proportion of widows in the ranks of the abandoned. It would certainly appear that one of the principal, if not *the* principal cause which can be specified is the very early age at which such marriages are contracted. Young people yield to the impulse of a moment, acknowledge the charms of a person they meet in a ball-room or public assembly, and are married with a very imperfect knowledge of each other's character, with but little reflection on the probable result of the alliance, and with but a slight appreciation of the obligations they are contracting. It was a wise regulation, whether regarded physically or morally, which fixed the earliest period of marriage in ancient Germany at twenty-five years, and declared the union invalid if the parties had not reached that time of life : nor would the morality of New York suffer if a similar restriction was the rule instead of the exception here. The annexed cases, selected at random from the replies received, are submitted in support of this opinion.

E. C., now nineteen years of age, is a married woman, who has been separated from her husband five years, and must therefore have been married when less than fourteen years old. C. W., now twenty-one years of age, has been a widow for five years, and was married at fifteen. A. S. was married at sixteen, and E. R. at fifteen. C. C., now twenty-eight years old, has been a widow more than twelve years. C. G., aged twenty-four, has been a widow seven years. Both these women were under sixteen when married. The list might be extended almost indefinitely.

The following inquiry, as a continuation of the same branch of the subject, is embodied in this section.

Question. IF MARRIED, IS YOUR HUSBAND LIVING WITH YOU, OR WHAT CAUSED THE SEPARATION?

Causes.	Numbers.
Living together	**71**
Ill-usage of husbands	103
Desertion of "	60
" " " to live with other women	43
Intemperance	45
Husbands went to sea	39
" refused to support them	29
Infidelity	25
No cause assigned	75
Totals	419 71
	— 419
Aggregate of married women	490

The most striking and painful fact in these answers is revealed in the first line of the table, which contains an announcement so disgraceful to humanity that, but for the positive evidence adduced by the figures, it would be scarcely credited, namely, that of four hundred and ninety married women now living as prostitutes, seventy-one (more than one seventh) are cohabiting with their husbands. It can not be controverted that such cohabitation necessarily implies a knowledge of the wife's degradation, and a participation in the wages of her shame. Nor will any argument, however plausible, succeed in removing from the public mind the conviction that the man is far the more guilty party of the two, and he can not escape the suspicion that he was the primary agent in leading his wife to prostitution, or, in legal parlance

he was "an accessory before the fact." While such a consideration will not exonerate the woman from her offenses, it may be
justly pleaded in extenuation; although it will not prove her
guiltless, it will sink him to the lowest depths of disgrace.

The conduct of husbands is alleged in a majority of the cases
as the cause of separation; two hundred and thirty-five out of
four hundred and nineteen women give the following causes:

Husbands refused to support their wives 29
"   deserted their wives 60
"   "   "   " to live with other women 43
Ill-usage of husbands 103
   Total 235

The cases wherein "intemperance," "infidelity," or "no cause
assigned" were replied, are vague, and may be construed to attach
blame to either, or both.

Sufficient has been proved to show that in many cases prostitution among married women is the result of circumstances which
must have exercised a very powerful influence over them. The
refusal of a husband to support his wife, his desertion of her, or an
act of adultery with another woman, are each occurrences which
must operate injuriously upon the mind of any female, and, by
the keen torture such outrages inflict on the sensitiveness of her
nature, must drive her into a course of dissipation. Many wom-
en thus circumstanced have actually confessed that they made
the first false step while smarting from injuries inflicted by their
natural protectors, with the idea of being revenged upon their
brutal or faithless companions for their unkindness. Morality
will argue, and very truly, that this is no excuse for crime; but
much allowance must be made for the extreme nature of the
provocation, and the fact that most of these women are uneducated, and have not sufficient mental or moral illumination to reason correctly upon the nature and consequences of their voluntary debauchery, or even to curb the violence of their passions.

"Ill-usage of husbands," a crime particularly rife in England,
and apparently fast becoming naturalized here, also stands as a
prominent cause of vice, and is one which can not be too pointed-
ly condemned. It strikes at the root of the social fabric, and must
invariably be denounced both on account of its enormity as an offense, and of its almost inevitable consequences to the woman, a
sense of degradation, too often followed by the sacrifice of rectitude as the only means to escape such brutal tyranny. Without

advocating capital punishment, it may be allowable to suggest the query whether our city would not be benefited if all such unmanly offenders against propriety were to be tried by a jury of married women, and hanged without benefit of clergy.

The following table will conclude this section:

Question. IF WIDOWED, HOW LONG HAS YOUR HUSBAND BEEN DEAD?

Length of Time.	Numbers.	Length of Time.	Numbers.
Under 6 weeks	2	Under 5 years	24
" 3 months	6	" 6 "	21
" 6 "	8	" 7 "	17
" 7 "	1	" 8 "	18
" 8 "	2	" 9 "	16
" 1 year	22	" 10 "	13
" 2 years	30	10 years and upward	32
" 3 "	38	Time not specified	11
" 4 "	33	Total	294

It will be perceived that nineteen prostitutes have been widows less than one year, twenty-two for one year, thirty for two years, and so throughout the scale. The table presents but little necessity for observation, the principal conclusion to be drawn from it being that the majority of this class are driven to a course of vice from the destitution ensuing on the husband's death. It has been shown that a large number of them are very young, and it can be scarcely necessary to repeat that any young woman in a state of poverty will be surrounded with temptations she can with difficulty resist. Much as this state of society may be deplored, its existence can not be denied.

Question. HAVE YOU HAD ANY CHILDREN?

Condition of Women.	Replies.		Total of Women.
	Yes.	No.	
Single	357	859	1216
Married	357	133	490
Widowed	233	61	294
Totals	947	1053	2000

The women who reply to this question in the affirmative are

Single women	357, or 30 per cent.	
Married "	357, " 73 "	
Widows "	233, " 79 "	

In continuation of this subject is the

Question, IF YOU HAVE HAD CHILDREN, HOW MANY?

Number of Women.	Condition of Women.	Number of Children Born.
357	Single women	490
357	Married women	791
233	Widows	636
947	Women were mothers of	1917

The replies give the total number of children borne by each class: thus the single women have given birth to four hundred and ninety-one children, the married women to seven hundred and ninety-one children, and the widows to six hundred and thirty-six children. The following tables exhibit the same facts in a more extended form, showing the number of children which each woman has borne, and specifying the sex.

Question. IF YOU HAVE HAD CHILDREN, HOW MANY?

REPLIES OF SINGLE WOMEN.

Number of Women.		Borne by each.			Totals.			
		Boys.	Girls.	Abortions.	Boys.	Girls.	Abortions.	Aggregate.
1	Mother.	8	2		8	2		10
2	Mothers.	3	3		6	6		12
2	"	2	3		4	6		10
1	Mother.	1	4		1	4		5
1	"	3	2		3	2		5
1	"	1	3		1	3		4
1	"	4			4			4
1	"	3	1		3	1		4
5	Mothers.	2	1		10	5		15
6	"	1	2		6	12		18
3	"	3			9			9
2	"		3			6		6
33	"	1	1		33	33		66
4	"		2			8		8
17	"	2			34			34
150	"	1			150			150
99	"		1			99		99
27	"			1			27	27
1	Mother.			4			4	4
357					272	187	31	490

REPLIES OF MARRIED WOMEN.

Number of Women.		Borne by each.			Totals.			
		Boys.	Girls.	Abortions.	Boys.	Girls.	Abortions.	Aggregate.
1	Mother.	7	8		7	8		15
2	Mothers.	7	7		14	14		28
1	Mother.	7	6		7	6		13
1	"	8	4		8	4		12
1	"	6	6		6	6		12
1	"	4	6		4	6		10
1	"	5	4		5	4		9
2	Mothers.	4	4		8	8		16
2	"	3	4		6	8		14
1	Mother.	7			7			7
1	"	2	4		2	4		6
6	Mothers.	4	2		24	12		36

Number of Women.		Borne by each.			Totals.			
		Boys.	Girls.	Abortions.	Boys.	Girls.	Abortions.	Aggregate.
3	Mothers.	2	3		6	9		15
7	"	3	2		21	14		35
5	"	4	1		20	5		25
3	"	4			12			12
8	"	2	2		16	16		32
7	"	3	1		21	7		28
5	"		3			15		15
11	"	3			33			33
11	"	1	2		11	22		33
23	"	2	1		46	23		69
4	"	1	1		4	4		8
28	"		2			56		56
28	"	2			56			56
74	"		1			74		74
115	"	1			115			115
4	"			1			4	4
1	Mother.			3			3	3
357					459	325	7	791

REPLIES OF WIDOWS.

Number of Women.		Borne by each.			Totals.			
		Boys.	Girls.	Abortions.	Boys.	Girls.	Abortions.	Aggregate.
1	Mother.	6	4		6	4		10
3	Mothers.	5	4		15	12		27
2	"	6	3		12	6		18
1	Mother.	6	2		6	2		8
6	Mothers.	3	4		18	24		42
1	Mother.	5	3		5	3		8
4	Mothers.	3	3		12	12		24
1	Mother.	5	1		5	1		6
1	"	2	4		2	4		6
1	"	4	2		4	2		6
9	Mothers.	3	2		27	18		45
5	"	2	3		10	15		25
2	"	4	1		8	2		10
1	Mother.	1	4		1	4		5
1	"	5			5			5
3	Mothers.	4			12			12
9	"	2	2		18	18		36
4	"	1	3		4	12		16
1	Mother.	3	1		3	1		4
4	Mothers.		3			12		12
10	"	3			30			30
14	"	2	1		28	14		42
11	"	1	2		11	22		33
20	"	2			40			40
47	"	1	1		47	47		94
30	"		1			30		30
40	"	1			40			40
1	Mother.			2			2	2
233					369	265	2	636

Commencing with the offspring of single women, it will be seen that one was the mother of ten children, eight boys and two girls. Two women gave birth to six children each. Four gave birth to five children each. Three gave birth to four children each. Sixteen gave birth to three children each. Fifty-four gave birth to two children each. Two hundred and forty-nine gave birth to one child each. Twenty-seven have suffered abortion once, and one has suffered in the same manner four times. The corresponding tables for married women and widows express similar facts in the same form. It is not necessary to quote them, as the figures give all the required information. The results may be recapitulated thus:

	Boys.	Girls.	Abortions.	Totals.
357 single women bore	272	187	31	490
357 married " "	459	325	7	791
233 widows bore	369	265	2	636
947	1100	777	40	1917

Excess of male over female births, 223.
Ratio of excess upon the total number born, $11\frac{6}{10}$ per cent.

The next point claiming attention is the number of illegitimate children resulting from prostitution, based upon answers to the

Question, WERE THESE CHILDREN BORN IN WEDLOCK?

Legitimate children of married women	469
" " " widows	358
Total legitimate	827
Illegitimate children of single women	490
" " " married "	322
" " " widows	279
Total illegitimate	1090
Aggregate.	1917

The whole of the children borne by single women are, of course, illegitimate. Of the children of married women over forty per cent., and of the children of widows forty-four per cent. are illegitimate. Taking the total number of children of the three classes, and calculating upon this broad basis, it will appear that 1090 illegitimate children were born, giving an average of fifty-seven per cent.; or, to speak in plain terms, of every hundred children borne by women who are now prostitutes, forty-three were born before the mothers (married women or widows) had embraced this course of life, and the remaining fifty-seven were the fruit of promiscuous intercourse, liable physically to inherit the diseases of the mother, morally to endure the disgrace attached to their birth, and very probably to be reared in the midst of blasphemy, obscenity, and vice, to follow in the footsteps of their parents, and perpetuate the sin to which they owe their origin.

The excessive mortality among this class of children is developed in the following replies to the

Question, ARE THESE CHILDREN LIVING OR DEAD?

Living children of single women 133
" " " married " 334
" " " widows 265
    Total living 732
Dead children of single women 357
" " " married " 457
" " " widows 371
    Total dead 1185
    Aggregate 1917

The ratio of mortality will be as follows:

Children of single women . . . . 73 per cent.
" " married " . . . . 58 " "
" " widows . . . . 59 " "
    Average on the total number . . . . 62 " "

or more than six deaths for every ten children born. The average infantile mortality of New York City for three years is,

Under 1 year of age 8499
From 1 " to 2 years 3259
" 2 " to 5 " 2578
    Total . . . . 14,336[1]

The population between those ages in 1855 was 77,568.[2] This
would give a mortality of 18½ per cent., or about 1¾ to every ten
children under five years of age. It is not exceeding the bounds
of probability to assume that the greater part of the children of
prostitutes die before they reach the age of five years, which will
give a *pro rata* mortality among that class of nearly *four times the
average ratio of New York City.* This calculation must be taken
in connection with the cases of abortion produced by extraneous
means, not admitted in the replies to the interrogatories, and
which will probably never be known. It is impossible to doubt
that these are far more frequent than recorded in the tables.

Under the heads of "Premature Births" and "Still-born" the
following numbers are reported.[3]

Years	Premature Births.	Still-born.	Total.
1854	. . 435	. . 1615	. . 2050
1855	. . 374	. . 1564	. . 1938
1856	. . 387	. . 1556	. . 1943
	1196	4735	5931

The births during the same period were:

[1] New York City Inspector's Reports, 1854, 1855, 1856.
[2] New York State Census, 1855, p. 38.
[3] New York City Inspector's Reports, 1854, 1855, 1856.

1854	17,979
1855	14,145
1856	16,199
Total	48,323

This would show a proportion of 12½ per cent., or one to every eight of all the children born in New York City. It is not to be taken for granted that all these are the result of improper conduct, although unquestionably many are so. Applying the same ratio to the children of prostitutes, and calculating the 1917 births in these tables as extending over a period of five years, would give forty-eight cases each year; but multiplying the average by four (the proportion of deaths from natural causes), we shall find the appalling number of one hundred and ninety-two cases each year—an array of infantile mortality presenting features which place it almost on a level with the infanticide of some Eastern nations. Were it possible to form any definite idea of the abortions actually procured, and which are suspected, on reasonable grounds, to amount to a very considerable number, the amount would be startling. The sacrifice of infant life, attribute it to what cause you may, is one of the most deplorable results of prostitution, and urgently demands active interference.

The attention of the American Medical Association has been drawn to this subject, and from a "Report on Infant Mortality in large Cities, by D. Meredith Reese, M.D., LL.D., etc.," published in their Transactions, we extract: "The causes of mortality among children of tender age are, in a multitude of cases, to be found only by extending our inquiries to their *intra-uterine* life, and the physiological state of the parents, but especially the sanitary condition of the mothers, their hygienic and moral habits and circumstances.[1] * * * Celibacy should be required of all syphilitic persons of either sex."[2] It will at once occur to the mind of the reader that enforced celibacy would not affect the maternity of prostitutes. They are liable to give birth to children, and, as their physiological condition is such as to preclude the possibility of their children being healthy, the only way to check infant mortality in this class is to deal with the mothers, and adopt means, if not to prevent their infection, at least to limit the ravages of disease as much as possible. This point is discussed more fully in the chapter on Remedial Measures. To men tainted with

[1] Report on Infant Mortality in large Cities, by D. Meredith Reese, M.D., LL.D., p. 8.   [2] Ib. p. 13.

syphilis the same course of reasoning would apply. If debarred from marriage, the sexual appetite would drive them to commerce with prostitutes, and their illegitimate children swell the total of mortality. The health of parents must be protected before we can hope for healthy children.

Dr. Reese's very able pamphlet contains some remarks upon abortionism, and its extent, thus: "The ghastly crime of abortionism has become a murderous trade in many of our large cities, tolerated, connived at, and even protected by corrupt civil authorities. These murderers—for such they are—are well known to the police authorities: their names, residence, and even their guilty customers are no secret. Would that it were only the profligate, or even the unfortunate of their sex, whose guilty fear or shame thus seeks to hide the evidence of illicit amours."[1] That prostitution largely contributes to this crime can not be doubted, but to what extent must remain unknown, from the secrecy which surrounds it. The revolting cases which appear at intervals in the daily papers are but a mere fraction of the total.

Question. ARE THESE CHILDREN LIVING WITH YOU, OR WHERE ARE THEY?

		Numbers.	
Children living with the mothers		73	
" boarding at the expense of mothers	. .	247	
" " with mothers' relatives	. . .	140	
" supporting themselves		129	
" living with the fathers		59	
" in public or charitable institutions	. . .	36	
" adopted by families		20	
" unascertained ·		28	
Totals		659	73
		73	
Aggregate of children . .		732	

This table shows the social influences to which the survivors of this ill-fated band of children are exposed. There are seventy-three stated to be living with their mothers, and, so far as they are concerned, no reasonable person can entertain any hopes as to their future morality. Born in the abodes of vice, their dwelling is in an atmosphere of squalid misery or sordid guilt; they never have a glimpse of a better life; they are marked from their cradles for a career of degradation; they can fall no lower, for they stand already on the lowest level. Such as these are de-

[1] Report on Infant Mortality in large Cities, by D. Meredith Reese, M.D.,LL.D., p. 9.

nominated "dangerous classes" by the French authorities, and from their ranks are obtained many of the inmates of prisons and brothels. The children stated to be with their fathers, fifty-nine in number, it may be concluded were born before the mother's fall from virtue, and are decidedly the most fortunate of any coming under notice, while those living with the parents or relatives of the mother, amounting to one hundred and forty, or boarding at the mother's expense, of whom there are two hundred and forty-seven, stand less chance of contamination than if actually residing within the domains of vice. Those living in public or charitable institutions exhibit one cause of taxation upon the general body of the citizens, and show that, indirectly, every man in New York is compelled to contribute toward the maintenance of vice or its offspring. A visit to the public institutions on Blackwell's and Randall's Islands will prove that this is but one item of the expenses which prostitution inflicts upon the community.

CHAPTER XXXIII.
NEW YORK.—STATISTICS.

Continuance of Prostitution.—Average in Paris and New York.—Dangers of Prostitution.—Disease.—Causes of Prostitution.—Inclination.—Destitution.—Seduction.—Intemperance.—Ill-treatment.—Duties of Parents, Husbands, and Relatives.—Influence of Prostitutes.—Intelligence Offices.—Boarding-schools.—Obscene Literature.

Question. FOR WHAT LENGTH OF TIME HAVE YOU BEEN A PROS-TITUTE?

Time.	Numbers.	Time.	Numbers.	Time.	Numbers.
1 month	71	6 years	87	20 years	4
2 months	49	7 "	56	21 "	2
3 "	76	8 "	69	22 "	1
4 "	62	9 "	32	23 "	2
5 "	51	10 "	26	24 "	2
6 "	126	11 "	8	25 "	1
7 "	129	12 "	14	27 "	1
8 "	17	13 "	6	29 "	1
9 "	21	14 "	7	30 "	1
10 "	32	15 "	9	32 "	1
1 year	325	16 "	13	34 "	1
2 years	55	17 "	3	35 "	1
3 "	245	18 "	4	Unascertained	53
4 "	203	19 "	8	Total	2000
5 "	125				

It has already been stated that the average duration of the life of a prostitute does not exceed four years from the commencement of her career. This is one year beyond the estimated duration as given by some English writers, but very far below the average, as ascertained in Paris, in which city, at the time M. Parent-Duchatelet instituted his elaborate system of investigation, he found in the gross number of 3517 prostitutes, two hundred and forty-two who had led that life for upward of fourteen years, and six hundred and forty-one who had continued their course upward of ten years. What a contrast to the table given above! In Paris, 6⅘ per cent. had survived the horrors of courtesan life for fourteen years; in New York, only 2¼ per cent. have reached the same period. In Paris, 17½ per cent. existed; in New York, 3¾ per cent. exist after ten years of exposure; or, in other words, where seven exist in Paris, only three have survived in New York, or where seventeen exist in Paris, only four survive in New York. It can not be asserted that Paris is a more healthy city than New York, and this difference must arise from the fact that, while judicious arrangements are *enforced* in the former, a similar policy has not been recognized in the latter. If this relative mortality were the only fact known on this matter, the economy of human life would be an irresistible argument in favor of measures of supervision judiciously conceived and promptly executed.

In the city of New York, six hundred and thirty-four women, more than thirty-one per cent., have been on the town less than one year, and three hundred and twenty-five, or more than seventeen per cent., for a space of time ranging from one to two years. Here, then, is one half of the total number, the experience of the remainder extending through various periods up to thirty-five years. With reference to those who assign such an extent of duration, it may be remarked, as was done in considering the question of age, that they are, with scarcely a solitary exception, those who, having been prostitutes in their younger days, are now engaged in brothel-keeping, and are thus exempted from many dangers attending the ordinary life of a harlot. If the same rule had been observed here in their cases as was done in the inquiries at Paris, namely, to exclude them from the list of prostitutes, the relative mortality given above would have shown still more unfavorably for New York.

It may be asked, What peculiar dangers attend the life of a prostitute in this city? There is a frightful physical malady to which all are liable, and which will be alluded to under its proper head. There are other dangers to which prostitutes, in a greater or less degree, are exposed. It is not necessary to remind the reader that at intervals the public is shocked by accounts in our daily papers of cowardly and outrageous assaults upon these unfortunate women, perpetrated by ruffians of the other sex. Sometimes it is an onslaught made by a party of men, for little or no provocation, on a number of females; or it may be an attack of a paramour on his victim. To this latter description of ill-treatment common women are peculiarly liable; for, beyond their habits of promiscuous intercourse, almost every one of them, particularly those in the middle or lower classes, has attached herself to some indolent fellow who acts as her protector ("bully" or "lover" is the common designation) when she becomes involved in any difficulty with strangers, but who exercises an arbitrary and brutal control over her at other times. In many cases, singular as it may appear, an actual love is felt by the woman for "her man." In others it is a mere arrangement for mutual convenience, the man taking her part in all quarrels, and the woman providing funds to maintain him in idleness. The intemperate habits of the prostitutes also tend materially to shorten their lives.

In addition to physical dangers must be considered the mental anguish they undergo, which inevitably preys upon the constitution. To this even the most depraved of them are at times subject. In the earlier stages of their career is an agonizing memory of the past; thoughts of home; regrets for the position they have lost. As they proceed in their course they suffer from an anticipation of the future; the grave, a nameless, pauper grave, yawns before them; thoughts of the inevitable eternity intrude; and a past of shame, a present of anguish, a future of dread, are the subjects of thought indulged by many who would never be suspected by the gay world of entertaining a serious reflection. It may be said, in the words of Byron,

> "But in an instant o'er her soul
> Winters of memory seem to roll,
> And gather in that drop of time
> A life of pain, an age of crime."

The period for their nocturnal revelry returns, and, though with a breaking heart, they must deck themselves with tawdry finery, and forcing a smile upon their faces, resume a loathsome trade to earn their daily food. With such torments, physical and mental, can long life be expected as their lot? Can any human frame withstand these incessant attacks for a lengthened period? It would not be at all surprising if the ratio of mortality among prostitutes were greater than it is.

Question. HAVE YOU HAD ANY DISEASE INCIDENT TO PROSTITU-TION? IF SO, WHAT?

Disease.	Attacks.	Numbers.
Gonorrhœa	1 Attack	153
"	2 Attacks	53
"	3 "	44
Gonorrhœa and syphilis		36
Syphilis	1 Attack	395
"	2 Attacks	81
"	3 "	38
"	4 "	12
"	5 "	4
"	6 "	4
"	8 "	1
Total attacked		821

The nature and effects of venereal disease have been already so fully specified in notices of the various systems adopted for its prevention, given in the preceding pages of this work, that it would be a needless repetition to dwell upon them here. It is sufficient, for the present purpose, to call attention to the fact that more than two fifths of the total number of prostitutes examined during the investigation CONFESS that they have suffered from syphilis or gonorrhœa. The probability is that the real number far exceeds this average; that, alarming as is the confession, the actual facts are much worse. This opinion is based upon the re-sults of professional experience, and a knowledge of the difficulty which exists in obtaining any voluntary reliable statement on the subject.

Even assuming that the answers obtained are correct, they in-dicate ample cause for the perpetuation of the disease, and its in-troduction into almost every branch of society. One half of the total number who confess that they have suffered or are suffering from this disease, state that they have been so afflicted once only. In other forms of sickness which admit of a perfect cure this would be no cause for alarm, but in this instance it is a mooted point among medical writers whether the syphilitic taint can ever be eradicated from the system where it has been implanted, and the arguments on each side are urged with great ability. With-out presuming to pass an opinion on the question, or expressing any doubt of the correctness of those learned men who think it possible to remove the taint from the body, it is policy to urge, in this case, the views of their opponents that it can not be eradicated. Upon this ground every citizen is competent to determine for himself the amount of public mischief resulting daily from a mass of prostitutes, two out of every five of whom are *confessedly* diseased.

Question. WHAT WAS THE CAUSE OF YOUR BECOMING A PROSTITUTE?

Causes.	Numbers.
Inclination	513
Destitution	525
Seduced and abandoned	258
Drink, and the desire to drink	181
Ill-treatment of parents, relatives, or husbands	164
As an easy life	124
Bad company	84
Persuaded by prostitutes	71
Too idle to work	29
Violated	27
Seduced on board emigrant ships	16
" in emigrant boarding houses	8
Total	2000

This question is probably the most important of the series, as the replies lay open to a considerable extent those hidden springs of evil which have hitherto been known only from their results. First in order stands the reply "Inclination," which can only be understood as meaning a voluntary resort to prostitution in order to gratify the sexual passions. Five hundred and thirteen women, more than one fourth of the gross number, give this as their reason. If their representations were borne out by facts, it would make the task of grappling with the vice a most arduous one, and afford very slight grounds to hope for any amelioration; but it is imagined that the circumstances which induced the ruin of most of those who gave the answer will prove that, if a positive inclination to vice was the proximate cause of the fall, it was but the result of other and controlling influences. In itself such an answer would imply an innate depravity, a want of true womanly feeling, which is actually incredible. The force of desire can neither be denied nor disputed, but still in the bosoms of most females that force exists in a slumbering state until aroused by some outside influences. No woman can understand its power until some positive cause of excitement exists. What is sufficient to awaken the dormant passion is a question that admits innumerable answers. Acquaintance with the opposite sex, particularly if extended so far as to become a reciprocal affection, will tend to this; so will the companionship of females who have yielded to its power; and so will the excitement of intoxication. But it must be repeated, and most decidedly, that without these or some other equally stimulating cause, the full force of sexual desire is seldom known to a virtuous woman. In the male sex nature has provided a more susceptible organization than in females, apparently with the beneficent design of repressing those evils which must result from mutual appetite equally felt by both. In other words, man is the *aggressive* animal, so far as sexual desire is involved. Were it otherwise, and the passions in both sexes equal, illegitimacy and prostitution would be far more rife in our midst than at present.

Some few of the cases in which the reply " Inclination" was given are herewith submitted, with the explanation which accompanied each return. C. M.: while virtuous, this girl had visited dance-houses, where she became acquainted with prostitutes, who persuaded her that they led an easy, merry life; her inclination was the result of female persuasion. E. C. left her husband, and became a prostitute willingly, in order to obtain intoxicating liquors which had been refused her at home. E. R. was deserted by her husband because she drank to excess, and became a prostitute in order to obtain liquor. In this and the preceding case, inclination was the result solely of intemperance. A. J. willingly sacrificed her virtue to a man she loved. C. L.: her inclination was swayed by the advice of women already on the town. J. J. continued this course from inclination after having been seduced by her lover. S. C.: this girl's inclination arose from a love of liquor. Enough has been quoted to prove that, in many of the cases, what is called willing prostitution is the sequel of some communication or circumstances which undermine the principles of virtue and arouse the latent passions.

Destitution is assigned as a reason in five hundred and twenty-five cases. In many of these it is unquestionably true that positive, actual want, the apparent and dreaded approach of starvation, was the real cause of degradation. The following instances of this imperative necessity will appeal to the understanding and the heart more forcibly than any arguments that could be used. As in all the selections already made, or that may be made hereafter, these cases are taken indiscriminately from the replies received, and might be indefinitely extended.

During the progress of this investigation in one of the lower wards of the city, attention was drawn to a pale but interesting-looking girl, about seventeen years of age, from whose replies the following narrative is condensed, retaining her own words as nearly as possible.

"I have been leading this life from about the middle of last January (1856). It was absolute want that drove me to it. My sister, who was about three years older than I am, lived with me. She was deformed and a cripple from a fall she had while a child, and could not do any hard work. She could do a little sewing, and when we both were able to get work we could just make a living. When the heavy snow-storm came our work stopped, and we were in want of food and coals. One very cold morning, just after I had been to the store, the landlord's agent called for some rent we owed, and told us that, if we could not pay it, we should have to move. The agent was a kind man, and gave us a little money to buy some coals. We did not know what we were to do, and were both crying about it, when the woman who keeps this house (where she was then living) came in and brought some sewing for us to do that day. She said that she had been recommended to us by a woman who lived in the same house, but I found out since that she had watched me, and only said this for an excuse. When the work was done I brought it home here. I had heard of such places before, but had never been inside one. I was very cold, and she made me sit down by the fire, and began to talk to me, saying how much better off I should be if I would come and live with her. I told her I could not leave my sister, who was the only relation I had, and could not help herself; but she said I should be able to help my sister, and that she would find some light sewing for her to do, so that she should not want. She talked a good deal more, and I felt inclined to do as she wanted me, but then I thought how wicked it would be, and at last I told her I would think about it. When I got home and saw my sister so sick as she was, and wanting many little things that we had no money to buy, and no friends to help us to, my heart almost broke. However, I said nothing to her then. I laid awake all night thinking, and in the morning I made up my mind to come here. I told her what I was going to do, and she begged me not, but my mind was made up. She said it would be sin, and I told her that I should have to answer for that, and that I was forced to do it because there was no other way to keep myself and help her. and I knew she could not work much for herself, and I was sure she would not live a day if we were turned into the streets. She tried all she could to persuade me not, but I was determined, and so I came here. I hated the thoughts of such a life, and my only reason for coming was that I might help her. I thought that, if I had been alone, I would sooner have starved, but I could not bear to see her suffering. She only lived a few weeks after I came here. I broke her heart. I do not like the life. I would do almost any thing to get out of it; but, now that I have *once done wrong*, I can not get any one to give me work, and I must stop here unless I wish to be starved to death."

This plain and affecting narrative needs no comment. It reveals the history of many an unfortunate woman in this city, and while it must appeal to every sensitive heart, it argues most forcibly for some intervention in such cases. The following statements of other women who have suffered and fallen in a similar manner will show that the preceding is not an isolated case. M. M., a widow with one child, earned $1 50 per week as a tailoress. J. Y., a servant, was taken sick while in a situation, spent all her money, and could get no employment when she recovered. M. T. (quoting her own words) "had no work, no money, and no home." S. F., a widow with three children, could earn two dollars weekly at cap-making, but could not obtain steady employment even at those prices. M. F. had been out of place for some time, and had no money. L. H. earned from two to three dollars per week as tailoress, but had been out of employment for some time. L. C. G.: the examining officer reports in this case, "This girl (a tailoress) is a stranger, without any relations. She received a dollar and a half a week, which would not maintain her." M. C., a servant, was receiving five dollars a month. She sent all her earnings to her mother, and soon after lost her situation, when she had no means to support herself. M. S., also a servant, received *one dollar a month wages.* A. B. landed in Baltimore from Germany, and was robbed of all her money the very day she reached the shore. M. F., a shirt-maker, earned one dollar a week. E. M. G.: the captain of police in the district where this woman resides says, "This girl struggled hard with the world before she became a prostitute, sleeping in station-houses at night, and living on bread and water during the day." He adds: "In my experience of three years, I have known *over fifty cases* whose history would be similar to hers, and who are now prostitutes."

These details give some insight into the under-current of city life. The most prominent fact is that a large number of females.

both operatives and domestics, earn so small wages that a temporary cessation of their business, or being a short time out of a situation, is sufficient to reduce them to absolute distress. Provi-
dent habits are useless in their cases; for, much as they may feel
the necessity, *they have nothing to save*, and the very day that they
encounter a reverse sees them penniless. The struggle a virtuous girl will wage against fate in such circumstances may be conceived: it is a literal battle for life, and in the result life is too oft-
en preserved only by the sacrifice of virtue.

"Seduced and abandoned." Two hundred and fifty-eight wom-
en make this reply. These numbers give but a faint idea of the
actual total that should be recorded under the designation, as
many who are included in other classes should doubtless have
been returned in this. It has already been shown that under the
answer "Inclination" are comprised the responses of many who
were the victims of seduction before such inclination existed, and
there can be no question that among those who assign "Drink,
and the desire to drink" as the cause of their becoming prostitutes, may be found many whose first departure from the rules
of sobriety was actuated by a desire to drive from their mem-
ories all recollections of their seducers' falsehoods. Of the number who were persuaded by women, themselves already fallen, to
become public courtesans, it is but reasonable to conclude that
many had previously yielded their honor to some lover under
false protestations of attachment and fidelity.

It is needless to resort to argument to prove that seduction is a
vast social wrong, involving in its consequences not only the entire loss of female character, but also totally destroying the consciousness of integrity on the part of the male sex. It matters not
under what circumstances the crime may be perpetrated, none can
be found that will exonerate the active offender from the imputation of fraud and treachery. A woman's heart longs for a reciprocal affection, and, to insure this, she will occasionally yield her
honor to her lover's importunities, but only when her attachment
has become so concentrated upon its object as to invest him with
every attribute of perfection, to find in every word he utters and
every action he performs but some token of his devotion to her.
Love is then literally a passion, an idolatry, and its power is universally acknowledged.

But this passion can not be the growth of an hour. Its devel-
opments are gradual. From the first stage of mere acquaintance,

it ripens progressively under the influence of tender words and solemn vows, frequently sincere, but often simulated, until the woman owns to herself and admits to her lover that she regards him with affection Such an acknowledgment, virtually placing her future life in his custody, should inspire him with the high resolve to protect her name and fame, to justify the confidence she has reposed. But not unfrequently is it made the medium for dishonorable exactions, and for a momentary gratification, valueless to him except as a proof of her fervent adoration, and fatal in its consequences to her, he tramples on the priceless jewel of her honor, confidingly surrendered to this love and truth.

It should be remembered that, in order to accomplish this base end, he must have resorted to base means; must either have professed a love he did not feel, or have allowed his affection to cool as he approached its consummation. Pure and sincere attachment would effectually prevent the lover from performing any act which could possibly compromise the woman he adores. None but an unmitigated ruffian can calmly and deliberately wrong an unsuspecting female who has acknowledged a tender sentiment toward him, thus placing herself so entirely in his power. The crime of seduction can be viewed only as a mean and atrocious perjury, and strangely callous must he be whose conscience in after life does not pursue him with scorpion stings and fiery tortures.

But how account for the participation of the female in the crime? Simply by viewing it as an idolatry of devotion which is willing to surrender all to the demands of him she worships; to the intensity of her affections, which absorbs all other considerations; to a perfect insanity of love, excited and sustained by a supposed equal devotion to herself. As soon as this conviction of a mutual love possesses her mind, as soon as her heart responds to its magic touch, she lives in a new atmosphere; her individuality is lost; her thoughts revert only to her lover. Devoted to the promotion of his happiness, she thinks not of her own; and only when it is too late does she awake from the spell that lures her to destruction. In such a case as this, a woman does not merit the contempt with which her conduct is visited. She has sinned from weakness, not from vice; she has been made the victim of her own unbounded love, her heart's richest and purest affections.

Moralists say that all human passions should be held in check by reason and virtue, and none can deny the truthfulness of the assertion. But while they apply the sentiment to the weaker party, who is the sufferer, would it not be advisable to recommend the same restraining influences to him who is the inflictor? No woman possessed of the smallest share of decency or the slightest appreciation of virtue would voluntarily surrender herself without some powerful motive, not pre-existent in herself, but imparted by her destroyer. Well aware of the world's opinion, she would not recklessly defy it, and precipitate herself into an abyss of degradation and shame unless some overruling influence had urged her forward. This motive and this influence, it is believed, may be uniformly traced to her weak but truly feminine dependence upon another's vows. Naturally unsuspicious herself, she can not believe that the being whom she has almost deified can be aught but good, and noble, and trustworthy. Sincere in her own professions, she believes there is equal sincerity in his protestations. Willing to sacrifice all to him, she feels implicitly assured that he will protect her from harm. Thus there can be little doubt that, in most cases of seduction, female virtue is trustingly surrendered to the specious arguments and false promises of dishonorable men.[1]

[1] Since these pages were prepared for the press, a work has been reprinted in New York, called "A Woman's Thoughts upon Women, by the Author of 'John Halifax, Gentleman," which contains many passages pertinent to this inquiry. The high reputation of its author (Miss Mulock), not only for literary ability, but for practical benevolence and womanly charity, will be sufficient apology for submitting some of her remarks to the reader in the shape of notes. It is satisfactory to know that many sentiments advanced herein are such as Miss Mulock has advocated on the other side of the Atlantic. On the subject of seduction, she remarks:

"I think it can not be doubted that even the loss of personal chastity does not indicate total corruption, or entail permanent degradation; that after it, and in spite of it, many estimable and womanly qualities may be found existing, not only in our picturesque *Nell Gwynnes* and *Peg Woffingtons*, but our poor every-day sinners: the servant obliged to be dismissed without a character and with a baby; the seamstress quitting starvation for elegant infamy; the illiterate village lass, who thinks it so grand to be made a lady of—so much better to be a rich man's mistress than a working man's ill-used wife, or, rather, slave.

"Till we allow that no one sin, not even this sin, necessarily corrupts the entire character, we shall scarcely be able to judge it with that fairness which gives hopes of our remedying it, or trying to lessen, in ever so minute a degree, by our individual dealing with any individual case that comes in our way, the enormous aggregate of misery that it entails. This it behooves us to do, even on selfish grounds, for it touches us closer than many of us are aware—ay, in our own hearths and homes; in the sons and brothers that we have to send out to struggle in a world of which we at the fireside know absolutely nothing: if we marry, in the fathers we give to our innocent children, the servants we trust their infancy to, and the influences to which we are obliged to expose them daily and hourly, unless we

The every-day experiences of life are amply sufficient to justify this opinion, for it is a fact that these specious arguments and false promises are continually resorted to by many men for the express purposes of seduction; and, nefarious as these cases confessedly are, still they form common incidents in the lives of some who claim to be what the world calls respectable! Men who, in the ordinary relations of life, would scruple to defraud their neighbors of a dollar, do not hesitate to rob a confiding woman of her chastity. They who, in a business point of view, would regard obtaining goods under false pretenses as an act to be visited with all the severity of the law, hesitate not to obtain by even viler fraud the surrender of woman's virtue to their fiendish lust. Is there no inconsistency in the social laws which condemn a swindler to the state prison *for his offenses*, and condemn a woman to perpetual infamy *for her wrongs?* Undoubtedly there are cases where the woman is the seducer, but these are so rare as to be hardly worth mentioning.

Seduction is a social wrong. Its entire consequences are not comprised in the injury inflicted on the woman, or the sense of perfidy oppressing the conscience of the man. Beyond the fact that she is, in the ordinary language of the day, ruined, the victim has endured an attack upon her principles which must materially affect her future life. The world may not know of her transgression, and, in consequence, public obloquy may not be added to her burden; but she is too painfully conscious of her fall, and every thought of her lacerated and bleeding heart is embittered with a sense of man's wrong and outrage. Memory points to the many bright passages in their acquaintance, and says, these shone but to ensnare you; to the many tokens of endearment received from her betrayer, and says, these were but so many arguments to effect your ruin; to the many vows he breathed, and says, these were but perjury; to the many smiles with which she was greeted, and says, these were but so many hypocritical devices. She remembers the thrill of joy with which her heart so gayly bounded when he first told her she was beloved, and she contrasts her

were to bring them up in a sort of domestic Happy Valley, which their first effort would be to get out of as fast as ever they could. And supposing we are saved from all this; that our position is one peculiarly exempt from evil; that if pollution in any form comes nigh us, we sweep it hastily and noiselessly away from our doors, and think we are right and safe—alas! we forget that a refuse-heap outside her gate may breed a plague even in a queen's palace."—*A Woman's Thoughts upon Women* (New York ed.), p. 261.

ecstasy then with her agonies now. She remembers, with detestation, the caresses he was wont to bestow. But, above all, she
remembers, and her blood boils with indignation as the thought is
forced upon her, that by these means he has wrought her shame.
She has learned in the school of sorrow that man's promises of
fidelity are valueless; and her future life, whether spent in sorrow and repentance for the past, or in a wild, impetuous career of
subsequent vice, will be indelibly marked with the remembrance
of his treachery. It can not be a matter of surprise that, with this
feeling of injustice and insult burning at her heart, her career
should be one in which she becomes the aggressor, and man the
victim; for it is a certain fact that in this desire of revenge upon
the sex for the falsehood of one will be found a cause of the increase of prostitution.

The probabilities of a decrease in the crime of seduction are
very slight, so long as the present public sentiment prevails;
while the seducer is allowed to go unpunished, and the full measure of retribution is directed against his victim; while the offender escapes, but the offended is condemned. Unprincipled men,
ready to take advantage of woman's trustful nature, abound, and
they pursue their diabolical course unmolested. Legal enactments
can scarcely ever reach them, although sometimes a poor man
without friends or money is indicted and convicted. The remedy
must be left to the world at large. When our domestic relations
are such that a man known to be guilty of this crime can obtain
no admission into the family circle; when the virtuous and respectable members of the community agree that no such man
shall be welcomed to their society; when worth and honor assert
their supremacy over wealth and boldness, there may be hopes of
a reformation, but not till then.

The following cases will exhibit some of the results of seduction: M. C., a native of Pennsylvania, seventeen years of age, was
induced to run away from home with her lover, who promised to
marry her as soon as they reached Philadelphia. Instead of keeping his word, he deserted her. She was afraid to go home, and had
no means of living except by prostitution, which she practiced for
eight months in Philadelphia, and then came to New York to reside. Her father, a physician, died when she was about ten years
old, and her mother subsequently married a hotel-keeper, in whose
house the girl was reared, and to the associations of which she
probably, to some extent, owes her fall from virtue.

In one of the most aristocratic houses of prostitution in New York was found the daughter of a merchant, a man of large property, residing in one of the Southern states. She was a beautiful girl, had received a superior education, spoke several languages fluently, and seemed keenly sensible of her degradation. Two years before this time she had been on a visit to some relations in Europe, and on her return voyage in one of her father's vessels, she was seduced by the captain, and became pregnant. He solemnly asserted that he would marry her as soon as they reached their port, but the ship had no sooner arrived than he left her. The poor girl's parents would not receive her back into their family, and she came to New York and prostituted herself for support.

A. B., the child of respectable parents in Germany, was seduced in her native place by a man to whom she was attached. He promised to marry her if she would accompany him to the United States. She obtained the permission and necessary funds from her parents, and two days after they landed in New York her seducer deserted her, carrying off all the money she had brought from home. H. P., a school-girl, sixteen years of age, was seduced by a married man who now visits her occasionally. C. A. was seduced in New Jersey, brought to New York, and deserted among strangers. M. R. was seduced by her employer, a married man. A. W. was seduced while at school in Troy, N. Y., and was ashamed to return to her parents. L. H. followed a lover from England who had promised to marry her. When she arrived in New York he seduced and diseased her, and then she discovered that he was a married man. There is no necessity to multiply these cases.

"Drink and the desire to drink." We will alter an old saying, and render it, "When a woman *drinks* she is lost." It will be conceded that the habit of intoxication in woman, if not an indication of the existence of actual depravity or vice, is a sure precursor of it, for drunkenness and debauchery are inseparable companions, one almost invariably following the other. In some cases a woman living in service becomes a drunkard; she forms acquaintances among the depraved of her own sex, and willingly joins their ranks. Married women acquire the habit of drinking, and forsake their husbands and families to gratify not so much their sexual appetite as their passion for liquor. Young women are often persuaded to take one or two glasses of liquor, and then their ruin may be soon expected. Others are induced to drink spirits in which a narcotic has been infused to render them insensible to their ruin. In short, it is scarcely possible to enumerate the many temptations which can be employed when intoxicating drinks are used as the agent.

"Ill-treatment of parents, husbands, or relatives" is a prolific cause of prostitution, one hundred and sixty-four women assigning it as a reason for their fall. In consideration of their important relations to society, it may be well to inquire, What are the duties of parents, husbands, and relatives?

In all countries where the obligations of the marriage contract are recognized, one of its most stringent requirements is found in the necessity to provide for the children of such union. This is acknowledged as a moral duty on account of the relationship between parents and children; it is recognized as a religious duty because specially enjoined in Holy Writ, and it is regarded as a civil duty because the future welfare of any community must depend upon the training of its future citizens.

As to the moral duty, what arguments would be effectual to prove to a hard-hearted parent the necessity of bestowing a kindly education upon his child? Surely nature itself would supply all the necessary reasons. The still, small voice of conscience will whisper to him, I have been the instrument of bringing this child into the world, and I am therefore responsible for its welfare. And even plain, old-fashioned common sense (despised as it is since a certain philosophy has come into fashion) would say, I am the father of a child, and it is my interest to do the best I can for it.

The religious duties are abundantly enforced in the Scriptures. These, while requiring in explicit terms the obedience of children to their parents, and annexing to such commandment the only promise which the Decalogue contains, are equally plain in specifying the duties of parents. These points are acknowledged by all sects and parties; and commentators or preachers, however much they may differ on questions of theology, or articles of faith, or rules of Church government, are unanimous upon the extent of parental obligation.

The civil duties are important for the reason already assigned. Children will be our successors in this arena, as we have succeeded the patriot fathers who achieved our independence, and made us the people that we are. The principles enunciated by every shot fired during the Revolutionary war have descended to us, but we are only trustees for their safe transmission to the next generation, and we shall be recreant to our duty, false to the memory of our ancestors, and traitors to our country, if we allow our children to assume the responsibilities that will naturally devolve upon them without due preparation for the sacred trust.

Having thus briefly alluded to the duties of parents, it remains to give some information as to the manner in which such obligations are performed, selected from the returns received in the progress of this investigation.

L. M., a very well educated girl: "I was seduced at eighteen years of age, and *forced* to leave home to hide my disgrace." Admitting that this girl had been led into an error, the plain duty of her parents, in every point of view, was to endeavor to reform her instead of driving her from home. Human nature, in its most favorable condition, is fallible; all are liable to error; but as all hope for forgiveness, so should they forgive. This is the doctrine of the sublime prayer taught by our Savior to his apostles; this is the duty of humanity. "The bruised reed He will not break," is a Divine promise from which poor finite man might draw a valuable lesson.

E. B.: "My parents wanted me to marry an old man, and I refused. I had a very unhappy home afterward." This case was directly in conflict with the dictates of nature. She had formed an attachment for a man who would, in all human probability, have made her a good husband, and caused her to remain a virtuous member of society; but her parents wanted her to marry an old man, and, in consequence of refusal, treated her with unkindness. She has now, poor girl, to answer for her sin of incontinence, but who can tell what other offenses would have been laid to her charge had she married as desired by her parents? How many awful deeds recorded in the annals of criminal jurisprudence have been produced by ill-assorted marriages! How many outrages, how much bloodshed, owe their origin to such a cause! Parents who, for their own selfish purposes, would drive a daughter into a marriage repugnant to her feelings, deserve the severest condemnation. So far from performing their duty in the matter, they are acting in diametrical opposition to it.

C. B.: "My stepmother ill-used me." The stepmother in this case stands in the place of the natural parent. In assuming the duties, she assumes all the responsibilities of the relation, and is equally guilty as if this girl were her own child. Women's feelings, in a normal state, are generally kind, gentle, and forgiving; but when they are perverted, she becomes more inveterate than man. So it was in this instance.

E. G.: "My mother ill-treated me and drove me from home. My father was very kind, but he died when I was seven years old." A similar case to the preceding in the perversion of feminine feelings, coupled with the melancholy fact that the girl's father, who had always used her kindly, died when she was a child. It would be natural to conclude that all the affections of a widow would concentrate upon her children, but the reverse of this is too frequently found to be true, and as soon as the husband to whom her vows were pledged is laid in the grave, and the children are deprived of his protecting hand, her love is alienated from them. A mother's duties to her offspring are increased by her husband's death, but she neglects them, and does violence to the maternal instinct.

M. B.: "I support my mother." It may possibly be objected that this case does not come within the scope of this section, as showing no positive neglect of parental duty, but, by implication, it is decidedly entitled to a place in the catalogue. It is, unfortunately for the sake of morality, but one of many similar instances which have been encountered, and some of which will be noticed in due course. The self-evident conclusion is, that if this mother had properly trained her daughter in early life, she would not now have to endure the agony arising from the knowledge that every morsel of food she eats, every article of clothing she wears, is purchased with the proceeds of her child's shame. It is difficult to imagine any position more disgusting than this—any circumstance more horrible than that of a mother quietly depending for existence upon the prostitution of a daughter, with the certainty that the inevitable result of such a vicious course of life will drive the child of her affection to a premature grave and a dreadful eternity.

J. C.: "My father accused me of being a prostitute when I was innocent. He would give me no clothes to wear. My mother was a confirmed drunkard, and used to be away from home most of the time." Here we have a combination of horrors scarcely equaled in the field of romance. The unjust accusations of the father, and his conduct in not supplying his child with the actual necessaries of life, joined with the drunkenness of the mother, present such an accumulation of cruelty and vice that it would have been a miracle had the girl remained virtuous. It is to be presumed that no one will claim for this couple the performance of any one of the duties enjoined by their position.

S. S.: "I had no work, and went home. My father was a drunkard, and ill-treated me and the rest of the family." Here is a specimen of a father's cruelty. His daughter is out of employment, and has no home but with her parents, and he, maddened with liquor, abuses her for flying to her natural protectors. Where was she to expect aid and comfort but from the authors of her being, and how was such expectation realized? She was forced to resort to prostitution as a means of living.

C. R.: "My parents are rich. They would not let me live at home, because I had been seduced." In this case there was no excuse for parental unkindness. Blessed with an ample supply of this world's treasures, they could calmly see their daughter exposed to want and penury. Living in the enjoyment of opulence themselves, they could doom her to earn a miserable subsistence by a life of shame. Satisfied with their own lot, and complacently surveying the comforts which surrounded them, they condemned her to a course of infamy in which no enjoyment could be found to cheer her path; where every day must add fresh tortures to her lot, every hour sink her yet lower in the social scale. Why? Because an indiscretion or a crime—call it which you please—had made her a fitting object for their kindness; because her own act had placed her in a position where she felt her disgrace, and asked their sympathy and aid to retrace her steps. Can there be a more pitiable object than a woman who has sacrificed her virtue to the importunity, the entreaties, or the vows of her lover, when she reflects upon her conduct? The delirium of love is past, but the overwhelming sense of shame is left; she feels that a momentary act has blasted her future life; she knows that the world will condemn her, and the only resource she has is an appeal to her parents. If they kindly take her by the hand, in all probability the evil will extend no farther, and she may regain her position in life. If they refuse their sympathy, they practically drive her to a course of vice, for there is no other road open to her. Who, then, is responsible for her after-career but those who have the power to preserve her from farther guilt and shame?

J. A.: "I am the eldest of a large family. My father is a

drunkard, and would not support his children. I have supported my parents, brothers, and sisters for the last five years." This is an example of an outrageous social crime which can not be contemplated without horror; the parents of a family, with their remaining children, relying for subsistence upon the aid furnished from the sinful earnings of the first-born! In this instance the economy of nature is reversed. The filial affection which leads a child to support her aged and infirm parents can be understood and appreciated, but it is impossible to reprobate too severely the conduct of a man whose own actions have reduced him to poverty, and who then encourages his daughter to lead a life of prostitution that he may revel on money produced by a course of debauchery which he was mainly instrumental in producing.

A. B.: "My lover seduced and diseased me while I was working in a factory. I went home, and my parents turned me out." Neither loss of character nor physical suffering were sufficient punishment for this poor girl, only eighteen years of age; nor could the probability of a future moral life induce her parents to pardon the first offense. They had sent her to work amid associations which were almost certain to cause her ruin. This, of itself, is a sufficient ground for their condemnation, for they were in comfortable circumstances, and could not plead poverty as an excuse; and when this ruin was accomplished, they added to their former crime by refusing a shelter to the sufferer.

These cases are taken from actual facts. The words included in inverted commas are, as nearly as possible, those used by the women when being questioned. As to the truth of the statements, we hesitate not to believe them *all* to be substantially correct. They are not a fiftieth part of the instances in which similar disclosures have been made, but they are sufficient for the purpose of argument, and to prove that the assertions made in other places rest upon a solid foundation, and are not mere fancies of the brain. It would certainly be much more to the credit of society if their authenticity were not so indisputable.

The foregoing examples strongly suggest and justify a farther consideration of the duties of parents. While these include the obligation to furnish a child with food and clothing, they do not stop at that point. It would be erroneous, indeed, for any father to imagine he had fulfilled all the requirements of his position when he gave a child enough to eat and to wear. He would attend to the wants of his cattle in the same way, but there is something more to be done in the case of his children. He must so treat them as to induce, on their part, a sentiment of gratitude. Children are proverbially keen-sighted, and they seem to have a natural faculty for logic, so far as they themselves are concerned. They can very soon discriminate whether a parent is doing barely just as much as the laws of the country and the voice of public opinion require, or whether he is acting toward them with true paternal affection. In the former case they become selfish, and practice all their little arts to obtain as many advantages that the law allows them as possible, without entertaining any feelings of respect or affection toward their parents, because they know that such obligations can not be evaded without censure. In the latter case their gratitude and affection forms a return for the kindness bestowed. They immediately perceive that they are loved, and, as a natural consequence, endeavor to manifest love in return, by acting in a manner most pleasing to their parents. By simply encouraging this sentiment, children can be moulded much as the father wishes, whereas, by destroying it, he loses one of the most effective aids to his government. There are so many different ways by which this affection for children can be manifested, and they are all so simple and so certainly effective, that it is scarcely possible to conceive how any man or woman of the most ordinary intelligence can overlook them.

In addition to providing for the personal wants of his family, their education claims a large portion of the parents' care. Not only the mere tuition imparted in schools, but a careful training at home, as preliminary to their conflict with the world, is required. It is the instruction and advice given in the quiet of the domestic circle that exercises the most powerful influence, most effectually shapes the destiny of the future man or woman. No person is justified in delaying the performance of this duty. So soon as a child can talk and walk, so soon is this guidance necessary. It would be an interesting and important matter of investigation to ascertain, if possible, the time of life at which children become influenced by the temptations which surround them. The result would show a much earlier age than is generally supposed. A boy, when playing with his companions, overhears an improper expression from one of them. His mind retains it, and it may prove the germ from which habits of profanity subsequently spring. A girl may notice an improper action, which will rest upon her memory, and produce sad fruit hereafter. Thus the ed-

ucation of children for the ordinary duties of life can not be commenced too soon.   If delayed, the probabilities are that, when you
attempt to cultivate the soil in after years, you will find it already
choked with weeds, which require more time and trouble to eradicate than would the inculcation of proper principles in early life.
A lady remarked upon one occasion, in presence of an eminent
preacher, that she thought children should not be trained to any
religious exercises until they had arrived at an age when they
could fully understand such subjects.   The reply of the aged minister is appropriate to the present subject.   He said, "Madam, if
you do not implant good doctrines in your children's minds before that time, the devil will fill them with mischievous ones."

A somewhat prevalent error in the training of children must
not be passed unnoticed, namely, excessive rigidity.   This practice is common in many well-meaning but unthinking families
professing Christianity.   Every thing is conducted with as much
mathematical precision as if they were demonstrating a problem
in Euclid.   Such a system is open to very grave objections, from
the numerous cases in which it has proved prejudicial to the
child's best interests.   It acts precisely like the spring of a watch,
which you can retain in a fixed position by a mechanical contriv-
ance, but which resumes its elasticity and power the moment the
pressure is removed.   Children's minds are elastic also; you can
confine them within any circle you please by the exercise of parental authority, but in a large proportion of cases the end sought
to be attained is surely defeated.   Many justly blame this cause
for the mishaps of their future lives.   It presents virtue and religion in a repulsive aspect, picturing them only as connected with
asceticism, not recognizing the beauty and happiness which are
their chief attractions.   Thus is engendered in the minds of children an intuitive dislike for what they are taught to consider as a
bondage.   It is not uncommon to hear men describe the way in
which their youthful Sabbaths were spent, and attribute to the
irksome monotony of that day's discipline their subsequent dis-
taste for even a few hours' confinement in church.   This strictness, like ambition, "overleaps itself," and extinguishes the spirit
it is designed to foster.   The proper way to educate children for
lives of usefulness, honor, and happiness, the most effective plan to
reach the desired end, is to cultivate their affections and reason,
instead of repressing the one and fettering the other by stringent
applications of arbitrary rule.

But no man or woman can educate children properly unless their precepts are confirmed by example. Talk to your son as long as you please upon the advantages of temperance, and then let him see you in a state of intoxication the next day, and all your labor will be fruitless. Enlarge, in the presence of your daughter, upon the value of integrity, and then allow her to hear you utter a falsehood, and she will contrast the theory and practice, and conclude that the former is worthless. Parents must educate themselves before they can hope to instruct their children, and must lead a life in conformity with the principles they teach, if they expect any beneficial results from their endeavors.

Before leaving this part of the subject another matter may be mentioned, namely, the necessity of winning the confidence of children. Their hearts pine for sympathy. If they are in trouble, encourage them to reveal their perplexities to you; sigh with them when they are sad, and rejoice with them when they are happy. A girl who has been in the habit of imparting all her childish sorrows to her mother, and has there found a heart which would beat in unison with her own, will not withhold her confidence as she grows in years. Remember that children, while a blessing to their parents, are also a responsibility. You have the power to train them for good or evil; you can win their trust, or inspire them with distrust; you can make them useful members of society, or render them nuisances to the community; to you their destiny is confided to a great extent, and from you will be required an account of the stewardship.

The length to which these observations have been extended can be justified by the importance of the subject, and the conviction that a more careful fulfillment of parental duties would go very far toward diminishing prostitution. Every man must admit it to be his duty to aid in effecting this desirable consummation; and while it would be Utopian to imagine that the vice can be eradicated by family influences, it is reasonable to conclude that its extent may be materially curtailed.

Great as are the duties and responsibilities of a father, they are equaled by those devolving upon a husband. He has to provide for the welfare of his wife besides caring for the interests of his children. When he marries he vows to remain faithful to the woman of his choice, to "love, honor, and cherish her" so long as they both shall live. This is an implied oath, if not audibly expressed in all circumstances, and any violation of it is neither more nor less than perjury. Of course, the obligation is a mutual one; the wife is bound by the same ties, and in as stringent a form as the husband. It can not be said that every case of prostitution in a married woman is the result of her husband's misconduct, but it is notorious that many women are induced or compelled by such misconduct to abandon a life of virtue. All married prostitutes can not be exonerated from the charge of guilt, yet the facts which will be hereafter quoted prove that many were driven to a life of shame by those who had solemnly sworn to protect and cherish them.

The violation of any known duty is a positive crime against society, but it becomes increased in magnitude when it involves more than one person in the offense. It is then the cause of a second transgression, and sophistry would vainly attempt to prove that the man who committed the first and caused the commission of the second offense was not morally responsible for both. Descending from generalities, it may be truly asserted that the man whose conduct to his wife is such as to lead her to vicious practices is guilty in both respects. Here are some few cases in point.

C. C.: "My husband deserted me and four children. I had no means to live." In this case the husband violated the law of God in forcibly rending the matrimonial bond, and violated the laws of his country by leaving his wife and children as burdens on society. For the former of these offenses he must answer at the bar of Infinite Justice; for the latter he is liable to punishment in this world. "Then why not punish him?" asks some one. For the very simple reason that he could not be found. In this day the law does not assume the latitude claimed by the Spanish Inquisition, and sentence a man to punishment without giving him an opportunity to plead his cause. A woman in a state of destitution, with four hungry children looking to her for bread, has neither time nor means to pursue a delinquent husband. Her present necessities require her immediate attention, and so he escapes the penalty the laws have awarded, and can live (although it may be with an uneasy conscience) in some other place, and probably repeat there the iniquities he has practiced here. The custom of deserting wives and children would receive a severe check were it possible in every instance to enforce the legal provisions respecting abandonment.

J. S.: "My husband committed adultery. I caught him with another woman, and then he left me." This individual's turpitude was enhanced by his boldness. He seems to have recklessly defied all consequences, to have been entirely callous to any sense of shame, and, when detected in his adulterous intercourse, he adds desertion to his offense. He regarded not the feelings of her whom in early life he had won to his side by vows of affection; he outraged the laws of decency, and trampled upon the statutes of his country. His wife's agony may be conceived, although words would be faint to express it, and the mental sufferings she must have endured before she abandoned herself to indiscriminate prostitution as a means of living will not aggravate her offense.

A. G.: " My husband eloped with another woman. I support the child." Here the husband was morally as guilty as in the previous case, but without the disgusting bravado which characterized that. He had, however, another claim which should have secured his fidelity, namely, an infant child; but this tie was powerless to restrain him. Fascinated by the charms of another, forgetting all the rights of his wife, all the obligations of paternity, and all the requirements of morality, he basely abandoned those dependent on him, and forced the wife, whose virtue he was bound to protect, into a career of vice to support his child.

A. B.: " My husband accused me of infidelity, which was not true. I only lived with him five months. I was pregnant by him, and after my child was born I went on the town to support it." The first idea derived from this statement would be that five months of matrimonial life had been sufficient to change this husband from a devoted lover to a revengeful tyrant, who would not scruple to resort to a groundless accusation to effect his purpose. In this short space of time he conveniently forgot the promises he had made, repudiated the bonds in which his own act had placed him, and, to accomplish a separation from his wife, did not hesitate to bear false witness against her, placing her in a position from which she could extricate herself only by performing a logical impossibility, namely, by proving a negative. Nor could the probable destiny of his unborn child influence his determination. It mattered not to him whether the infant first saw the light in a den of infamy, nor whether his unkindness killed it before it was born, so that he could desert his wife. Neither did it make any difference to him whether she starved to death or maintained her existence by the most loathsome means. He was satiated with possession, and neither the voice of nature nor the dictates of conscience could arrest his purpose. The result was precisely what might have been expected: she became a prostitute rather than starve and let her child starve.

R. B.: "My husband brought me here (a house of ill fame). I did not know what kind of a place it was. He lives with me, and I follow prostitution." Another variety of unnatural conduct. The wife in this case was a very good-looking young woman, not exceeding eighteen years of age; the husband held a respectable and well-paid employment, and was in possession of ample means to support her. By false representations he induced her, within three months after marriage, to board in a fashionable house of prostitution. She soon discovered its character, but eventually succumbed to his orders, and became guilty. He resides with her, and is supported by her. What language can be used adequately to denounce such a cold-blooded piece of treachery on the part of a wretch claiming to be human?

L. W.: "I came to this city, from Illinois, with my husband. When we got here he deserted me. I have two children dependent on me." This man brought his wife from a distant state to a strange city, where she had no friends nor relatives to advise and assist her, and there abandoned her, with two helpless children, to the mercy of the world. Had he left her where she had been living previously, it is possible she might have found sufficient friends to assist her until she was able to support herself; but with a refinement of cruelty he transferred her to a place where she was unknown, and then effected his escape. The entire circumstances favor the supposed existence of a determination to abandon her as soon as they arrived in New York, where he could act thus with more safety than in her native place.

C. H.: "I was married when I was seventeen years old, and have had three children. The two boys are living now; the girl is dead. My oldest boy is nearly five years old, and the other one is eighteen months. My husband is a sailor. We lived very comfortably till my last child was born, and then he began to drink very hard, and did not support me, and I have not seen him or heard any thing about him for six months. After he left me I tried to keep my children by washing or going out to day's work, but I could not earn enough. I never could earn more than two or three dollars a week when I had work, which was not always. My father and mother died when I was a child. I had nobody to help me, and could not support my children, so I came to this place. My boys are now living in the city, and I support them with what I earn by prostitution. It was only to keep them that I came here." These were the words used by an honest, sorrowful looking woman encountered, in the course of this investigation, in the fourth police district of the city. No reasonable doubt can be entertained of the truth of the story; the manner in which she told it plainly indicated that she was narrating facts. Some inquiries were made respecting her of the keeper of the house, and he (for it was a man) stated that he knew her story to be correct. He had at first employed her as a servant because he wished to help her, but the wages he could pay were insufficient to support her children, and she eventually prostituted herself because she could earn more at this horrible calling, and was thus enabled to discharge her maternal duty. But at what a sacrifice was this obtained! In order to feed her helpless offspring she was forced to yield her honor; to prevent them suffering from the pains of hunger, she voluntarily chose to endure the pangs of a guilty conscience; to prolong their lives she periled her own. And at the time when this alternative was forced upon her, the husband was lavishing his money for intoxicating liquor. If she sinned—and this fact can not be denied, however charity may view it—it was the non-performance of his duty that urged, nay, positively forced her to sin. She must endure the punishment of her offenses, but, after reading her simple, heart-rending statement, let casuists decide what amount of condemnation will rest upon the man whose desertion compelled her to violate the law of chastity in order to support his children.

E. W.: "My husband had another wife when I married him. I left him when I found this out. I was pregnant by him, and had no other way to live than by prostitution." In point of law, this is not a married woman, the existence of the former wife rendering the second union invalid; but this is no excuse for the man's conduct; in fact, it materially aggravates his guilt. In the first place, he deserts a woman whom he was legally bound to support, leaving her to battle her way through life, to resist the temptations which would be sure to assail her, careless whether she lived or died, and heedless whether she retained her character or sank into vice; and then, with the greatest *nonchalance*, goes through the ceremony of marriage with another woman. It is easy to imagine the feelings of the latter when she discovered the fraud which had been practiced to secure her hand, and the indignation which caused her to leave him immediately, notwithstanding her condition; nor will it require much stretch of fancy to picture the mental suffering she endured, her agony during the hour of nature's trial, before she consented to earn a precarious living as a prostitute. Such cases are of frequent occurrence, and even the probability of a criminal indictment is insufficient to deter some men. No punishment could be too severe for such offenses, even considering them without any reference to this particular instance, because they pervert one of our most solemn contracts, and destroy all confidence in the security of the marriage tie.

C. H.: "My husband was a drunkard, and beat me." How much of misery and crime is contained in these few words! Either of the vices practiced by this fellow is enough to make a woman wretched; the combination is sufficient to drive her mad. She would doubtless sit and ponder during the long and weary night hours when he was carousing with his drunken companions, and would contrast her present wretched state with the happiness of early days. Her thoughts would revert to the time he won her love, to the day on which he brought her to his home a bride, and then she would cast her eyes around the room, now robbed of almost every thing portable to supply his insane appetite for liquor, and a heavy sigh would burst from her heart. But still she would continue her sad reminiscences, and think of the kindness he displayed then, and of his brutal ferocity now— would remember his considerate tenderness and compare it with his maniac fury. And then something would whisper to her, "Why do you endure it?" and her woman's nature would be aroused, resistance would take the place of submission, and she would leave her home and him who had desecrated it, and immolate herself upon the altar of vice, a victim to her husband's drunkenness and cruelty.

C. N.: "My husband left me because I was sickly and could not do hard work." This woman's husband may be pictured as a lazy, worthless fellow; probably one who married not to secure a helpmate and a partner, but to obtain a slave. Her health would not allow her to perform as much drudgery as he expected; the speculation did not turn out as well as he had anticipated, and he left her destitute, to starve or sin, as she thought fit.

P. T.: "My husband was intemperate, and turned out to be a thief. He was sent to prison." Still another victim of a drunken husband, but he carried his vicious habits to a point where the laws of his country would reach him. Had he merely deserted his wife, nobody would have thought it his business to arrest him, but he stole some person's property, and all the enginery of the law was forthwith arrayed against him. In the one instance, his conduct condemns his wife to shame in this world and perhaps perdition in the next, and the good-tempered public looks quietly on and says nothing. In the other case, he defrauds his neighbor of some dollars and cents, and the indignant community demands his condign punishment! What conclusion can be drawn from these facts? Honor, character, and life are ruined, and the offender escapes: money is stolen, and he is punished! Is money more valuable than the character and life of woman?

It requires no argument to prove that when the care of a child is assumed by its relatives, the parental obligations also devolve upon them; nor can there be any difference of opinion as to the duty of relations to assist, to the utmost of their power, any children whom death or other circumstances may have deprived of their natural protectors. Were not these principles generally recognized, all large cities would be crowded with destitute orphans. The beneficial results often arising from such guardianships argue very strongly in their favor; but still the imperative duty is frequently evaded, or acknowledged and made the opportunity for an exhibition of tyranny which naturally tends to the encouragement of vice. Take the following cases in illustration:

J. F.: "I support my aunt." In this case the duties of the aunt were not merely evaded, but she adds to her neglect a positive approval of the girl's abandoned life, by voluntarily receiving a portion of her earnings. What species of education she bestowed upon her niece may be inferred from its results. Such disclosures are almost too disgusting to be criticised.

S. B.: "My parents were dead. I came to this country with an uncle and aunt, who ill-used me from the time I landed till I ran away." The death of her parents should have been a passport to the affection of the relatives to whose charge she was intrusted, but, instead of producing such an effect, they brought her to a strange land, and practiced a succession of cruelties, until she could endure them no longer. It is more than probable that this was a plan intended to drive her from their home. They neither acknowledged their duty to supply the places of the father and mother she had lost, nor did they recognize the force of relationship, which, at least, should have protected her from positive unkindness. Nor did they possess any of those feelings of sympathy which every well-disposed person must entertain toward an orphan. They could not have been unaware of the probability of her falling into bad company and vicious habits if she left their care, but no regard for her happiness or character seems to have entered into their calculations, which may have been somewhat in this form: She is an expense to us, so we will contrive to drive her away; if she can make her living honestly, so much the better; if she turns out a prostitute, that is her own concern. It was not solely "*her own concern,*" but it involved them also in its consequences, through their agency in its accomplishment, and, morally speaking, they are as liable for her ruin as if they had actually, and not indirectly, caused it.

The following cases closely resemble each other, and are presented in conjunction:

A. D.: "My parents were dead. I lived with my uncle, who treated me very unkindly."

L. S.: "My parents died when I was young. I lived with an uncle and aunt, who used me ill." The deprivation of each of these unfortunate women in the death of their parents, a loss almost incalculable in its results, placed them under the guardianship of those who alike neglected their duties and rendered the trust a medium for unkindness to the orphans. It seems surprising that the memory of a deceased brother or sister can not secure even ordinary care for their children. It can not be expected that the surviving relatives would exhibit the same amount of affection as would have been shown by the parents, but disappointment must be experienced if they make no pretensions to kindness. The dictates of nature are violated when harshness takes the place of sympathy, and destitution is considered a sufficient warrant for deliberate and continuous ill-treatment. Such conduct renders a girl reckless and misanthropic, and will drive her to seek, in unhallowed love, the affection her guardians have refused.

L. M.: "I was taken by my sister-in-law to a house of prostitution, and there violated." It is not often such a case of barbarity is found in civilized life, nor indeed in less polished communities, as this forcible violation of a young girl through the aid and connivance of her sister-in-law. The mind recoils, with disgust, from the instances of rape so frequently occurring, but this case is so peculiarly aggravated that it can not be contemplated without a feeling of shame for the depravity of human nature. In the one case, the brutal passions of a man are displayed in a brutal manner; in the other, the same cause exists to a similar extent, coupled with the blackest perfidy of a female relative. To such a shameless violation of the laws of consanguinity, such an outrageous conspiracy between a vile man and a monster of a woman, the sister must have been induced to lend her aid by some means best known to herself. It is quite impossible to imagine she possessed a single spark of virtue; on the contrary, she must have sunk, long before this occurrence, to the lowest depths of vice, or she never would have been an instrument in such an infernal scheme. The consideration she received is, of course, known only to the parties themselves, but it would give a farther insight to her character if the reader could be informed of the estimate set by a sister-in-law upon an orphan's virtue. The result of the outrage is, no doubt, exactly what the criminals anticipated. The victim knew that her character was ruined, that she had no alternative but prostitution, and, while the guilty pair who literally forced her to sin can congratulate each other on the success of their machinations, she must endure the penalty in a life of crime and misery.

G. H.: "I was detected and exposed by my brother." This girl, who had yielded to the entreaties of a man whom "she loved, not wisely, but too well," may assign her subsequent career of vice to the conduct of her brother. He must have been sadly deficient in all kindly feeling thus to parade his sister's dishonor, and also possessed of a very limited knowledge of human nature, or a large amount of malevolence. It can scarcely be imagined that he acted from ignorance, as he must have been certain that such an exposure would most probably induce his sister to continue an intercourse which was publicly known, and therefore could not augment her disgrace; nor can it be conceived that a malicious desire to blast her character governed his conduct. But, whatever his motive, the result was the same. She was forced to a life of prostitution, from which she might have been rescued had kind and affectionate means been employed, instead of the cruel and heedless course which was adopted.

C. W.: "My parents died when I was young. I was brought up by relatives who went to California when I was sixteen years old, and left me destitute. I had no trade." There is no allegation that this girl's relatives used her unkindly during the time she lived with them, but they deserted her, in a helpless condition, at the very time when she most needed their guardianship. They

K K

could not have been ignorant of the many temptations to which a young woman, without protectors or means of livelihood, is exposed in New York, and yet they removed to a distance, and left her to meet these trials alone. A girl whom they had reared from infancy, and for whom they must have entertained considerable affection, they tamely abandoned to an almost certain fate far worse than death. To say the least, it was a most inconsiderate step, and has resulted very disastrously.

E. R.: "My husband deserted me to live with another woman; my parents were dead; I went to my brother's house, and he turned me out." Fraternal unkindness farther exemplified! An orphan sister, deserted by her husband, asked from her brother the shelter of his roof, and he drove her from the house! Such conduct would have been barbarous if even a stranger had made the appeal; in the present instance, it exhibits a cruelty which can not be too severely reprobated.

C. B.: "My parents were dead. I was out of place. I had no relations but an uncle, who would not give me any shelter unless I paid him for it. I went on the town to get money to pay for my lodgings." This uncle's name ought to be handed down to posterity as a synonym of hard-hearted selfishness, and as indicating another manner in which money can be made. His miserly propensities must have been very strongly developed when he refused a shelter to his destitute niece unless she paid for it. It certainly did not matter to him how or where she obtained the means, and doubtless his equanimity was not disturbed when he ascertained that the money she paid him was the price of her shame. The coin was as bright in his hand, as useful to him to hoard or to spend, as if it had been her honest earning. Probably he would have been excessively annoyed (it is the characteristic of such men) if any plain-spoken person had told him that he was the means of making this girl a prostitute; but can it be denied that such was the fact, when he received some portion of the money earned by his niece's prostitution before he would allow her to sleep in his house?

L. S.: "My sister ill-treated me because I had no work." Here a sister seems to have regarded money as the chief good. The applicant was out of employment, in itself enough to enlist one's sympathies; she was in want, which should have been an additional reason for kindness; and yet, for these causes, a sister ill-treated her.

In thus endeavoring to show the several duties of parents, husbands, and relatives to those dependent females who are liable to be exposed at any moment to temptations leading from the path of virtue, cases have been exhibited in which a departure from the universally recognized obligations of these classes has added recruits to the ranks of prostitution. In these remarks, the endeavor has been to advance nothing resting on a theory; to advocate nothing unless supported by facts or acknowledged by common sense; to exonerate no one from blame when circumstances demanded a censure, and to condemn none in favor of whom there could be an existing doubt.

The recorded extracts, giving an insight beyond the scene of public view, exhibiting the secret machinery of the family circle, can not be contemplated without a mingled feeling of sorrow and shame. Sorrow, that so many females who might have been useful members of society have been forced into the ranks of sin; and shame, that the instruments in these proceedings were those who should have exerted every power to prevent such a result.

Cases have now been presented to the reader where a sorrowing, heart-broken girl has been denied the opportunity of repentance, and driven from a father's home; where another has been expelled from the family circle because she would not consent to an ill-assorted marriage; where stepfathers and stepmothers have violated their duties, and despised the obligations they had voluntarily assumed; where a mother's ill-treatment has driven her daughter to ruin; where parents were living and reveling upon the wages of their children's dishonor; where false accusations and unkind treatment were resorted to, and, from their natural effects, drove a girl from home and virtue; where drunkenness and debauchery made home a hell upon earth; where parents in affluent circumstances have driven a child from their home; where prostitution was willingly embraced as an escape from parental tyranny.

Again: Instances have been cited where husbands have deserted their wives and children; where the marital vow has been broken in the most glaring manner, and the crime followed by deliberate abandonment; where the wife's affections have been slighted, and her love relinquished for the purchased caresses of another woman; where a charge of infidelity has been made against a wife without cause; where a husband has deliberately brought his wife to a house of prostitution, and is now leading an idle, worthless life upon her earnings; where another husband brought his wife to a strange city in order to desert her and her children; where the solemn contract of marriage has been perverted; where a drunken husband has raised his hand against the woman he had sworn to protect; where a wife's sickness and incapacity for labor was made a reason for her husband's desertion; where a man's insane thirst for intoxicating liquor has forced a woman to prostitution for a maintenance; where the husband has been committed to prison for theft.

Farther: Cases have been given where an aunt lives upon the proceeds of a niece's prostitution; where uncles and aunts have systematically ill-used their orphan relatives; where a sister-in-law procured and assisted at the violation of a child; where a brother's unkindness forced his sister to continue a life of shame; where relatives to whom an orphan child was intrusted abandoned her when she most needed their care; where a brother refused an asylum to a deserted and suffering sister; where an uncle forced a girl to prostitute herself for money to pay him for her lodgings.

As already stated, these cases are all facts, collected in the course of this investigation, and are believed to be substantially correct. With such disclosures as these, can any one be surprised at the continued spread of prostitution? The family circle is one of the sources whence it emanates; so is the matrimonial bond; and so are the different branches of consanguinity. When fathers, husbands, and relatives thus forget their duties, and lend their influence to swell the tide of vice, it is no matter of surprise that strangers should be found ready and eager to contribute their share to the polluted current.

But the evil is not incurable, if public opinion can be enlisted on the side of public morals, and parents are satisfied, by unmistakable demonstrations, that the voice of an indignant people will be raised against them if practices similar to those narrated continue to occur. Husbands, too, must be convinced that any infraction of their marriage vows will expose them to popular odium; and if they have contracted an ill-assorted, hasty alliance, the responsibility must be borne by themselves. The contracts they voluntarily made must be fulfilled. Relatives also must be warned that the performance of their duties will be rigidly required. There is no deficiency of legislation on this subject; all that is wanted is determination to enforce existing laws; and when this is done, some of the main causes of prostitution will be removed.

To resume the analysis of the table of replies: Seventy-one women were persuaded by prostitutes to embrace a life of depravity. One of the most common modes by which this end is accomplished is to inveigle a girl into some house of prostitution as a servant, and this is frequently done through the medium of an intelligence office.

Most of the inhabitants of New York are acquainted with the arrangements and routine of business in those offices, but they may be described as a matter of information to others. Imagine a large room, generally a basement, in some leading thoroughfare. Upon entering from the street you will observe two doors, marked respectively "ENTRANCE FOR EMPLOYERS" and "ENTRANCE FOR SERVANTS." Passing through the first, you approach a desk, where the proprietor or his clerk is seated with his register books before him. You make known your wish to engage a servant, specifying her duties and the wages you are willing to pay. This is registered with your name and address, the fee is paid, and you are invited to walk into the other department, and ascertain whether any of the throng who are waiting there will suit your purpose. If successful in the search, it is merely necessary to inform the book-keeper that you are suited, and to take your servant home with you; but if you do not succeed, a woman will be sent to the registered address, and the office-keeper will continue to send until you are satisfied.

Servants who wish to obtain situations register their wants and pay a fee. If there are no places likely to suit them on the list of employers, they have permission to remain in the waiting-room until an applicant appears. In these waiting-rooms may be found a crowd of expectants varying from twenty to one hundred, according to the business transacted by the office.

In theory this arrangement is a very good one; in practice it is frequently abused. A respectable housekeeper who wishes to engage a servant will find but little trouble in doing so, and any person wishing to make the office a medium for securing females for improper purposes will seldom be disappointed. It is rarely that the proprietors notice the arrangements made; they merely act as brokers, and make known the wants of each party, and do not interfere with the character of either unless it is so notoriously bad as to force them to notice it for their own sake. So long as the employer and servant agree, the office-keeper is contented.

The following facts illustrate the manner in which young women are sometimes entrapped. A respectably-dressed man went into an intelligence office, and represented himself as a storekeeper residing some twenty miles from New York. He wished to hire a girl as seamstress and chambermaid, who must go home with him the same afternoon. Glancing around the waiting-room, he soon saw one of sufficiently attractive appearance, to whom he made the proposition. The wages he offered were liberal, the work was described as light, and the woman made an arrangement to accompany him forthwith. He told her that he had a little business to transact before he could leave the city, but that she could wait for him at his sister's until the cars were ready to start. She had but slight knowledge of the temptations of New York, and went with him to a brothel, the keeper of which he stated to be his sister. Here she remained for some hours waiting his return. The "sister" expressed her surprise at his absence, but concluded that his business had detained him, and, with apparently a kindly feeling, told the girl that she would be welcome to sleep there that night. Her suspicions were lulled by the seeming respectability of the persons, and she remained. In the course of the evening the character of the house became evident, and then the proprietress offered to engage her as a servant, solemnly promising that she should not be exposed to any insult. Almost a total stranger in the city, and destitute of money, she consented. A very few days in such a hot-bed of vice was sufficient to deaden her sense of right and wrong, and within a fortnight she was enrolled as a prostitute.

Keepers of houses sometimes visit these offices themselves, but generally some unknown agent is employed, or, at times, one of the prostitutes is plainly dressed, and sent to register her name as wishing a situation, so as to be able to obtain admission to the waiting-room. There she enters into conversation with the other women, whom she uses all the art she possesses to induce to visit her employer, and very frequently with the same result as in the case just narrated.

There exists among many prostitutes a fiendish desire to reduce the virtuous of their own sex to a similar degradation with themselves. Since they can not elevate their own characters, they strive to debase those of others. To accomplish this, they spare neither trouble nor misrepresentation. One system in which they are commonly employed may be noted, although the mode is similar to the case of the servant-girl just given. A man had resolved to ruin a woman who placed implicit confidence in his sincerity, and admitted that she loved him. He found that her modesty and good sense were proof against his persuasive powers, and he finally resorted to stratagem, and invited her to walk with him to visit some relations. He took her to a brothel, introduced its keeper (who had already been instructed in her part) as his aunt, and one or two of the inmates represented her daughters. The deception was maintained for a time; family matters were discussed, and refreshments introduced. A glass of drugged wine was handed to the victim, and as soon as its effects were visible the villainous deed was effected. Such machinations as this show that not only are many of these prostitutes dangerous to society from their open and avowed life of crime, but also from the influences they exert to deceive the honest of their own sex.

Allusion has been already made to the numerous dangers which surround young women during their passage to this country on crowded emigrant ships, or after their arrival in the equally crowded emigrant boarding-houses, and it is needless to repeat them in this section; but an incomplete statement of the causes of prostitution would be presented if the injurious effects of some of our fashionable boarding-schools were suffered to pass without notice. Startling as such an assertion may appear, it is no more strange than true. A system of education, the prominent design of which is to impart a knowledge of the (so-called) modern accomplishments to the almost total exclusion of moral training; to make the pupils present the most dazzling appearance in society, regardless of their real interests and duties, does, in some cases, lead to unhappy results. Filial affection, or early training, or innate virtue, enable many to overcome these temptations, but others succumb to them. One case, in particular, it is desirable to record, although several of a similar nature were met with.

A girl, eighteen years of age, born in Louisiana, of highly respectable parents, was induced to elope from a boarding-school in the vicinity of New Orleans with a man who accorded with her romantic ideal of a lover. No marriage vows ever passed between them; she trusted him as the heroine of a modern novel would have done, and he deceived her, as all modern rakes deceive their victims. She lived with him for a considerable time. When he deserted her, she was left almost destitute. She was afraid to return to her parents, knowing that they were acquainted with the life she had been leading, and she had no other means of support than open and avowed prostitution.   These features of her history should present a warning to both parents and daughters of the dangers attending a superficial and improper system of education.

Of course it must not be inferred that all schools are open to such objections.   In the numerous institutions of the kind scattered throughout the land, the majority are worthy of every confidence.   Instances like this are probably exceptions to the rule, but still, what has been pernicious in one case may be in another; and the education of young women, forming, as it does, their character for life, should be conducted, as far as possible, so as to secure their safety, honor, and usefulness.   In a subsequent chapter, this superficial education will be farther noticed.

One of the *real* improvements of modern times is the introduction of physiology as a branch of education in our schools.   Yet it is to be regretted that the knowledge communicated to youth upon a subject so important is still extremely limited.   Indeed, such is the present state of public opinion, that any text-book or teacher that should impart thorough instruction in regard to all the organs and functions of the human body, would be considered entirely unfit for use or duty.   Notwithstanding this, the young of both sexes do become informed upon the subjects of marriage, procreation, and maternity.   And how?   By force of natural curiosity and injurious association.   It is the imperative duty of parents to rightly inform their children concerning the things which they must inevitably know.   In consequence of their neglect of this duty, both boys and girls are left to find out all they can about the mysteries of their being from ignorant servants or corrupt companions.   Let fathers teach their sons, and mothers their daughters, at the earliest practicable age, all that their future well-being makes it necessary for them to know.   The information thus acquired will be invested with a sacredness and delicacy entirely wanting when obtained from unreliable and pernicious sources.

Thus would many of the injurious influences incident to the present secrecy upon such subjects be avoided.   Of the evil habits and practices common among youth, physicians are well cognizant, and many a parent has had to mourn their sad results in the premature death or dethroned reason of children who, with proper physical training, might have been their pride and joy.

Next to the responsibility of parents in this matter is that of teachers, who, with all judiciousness and delicacy, should supply

the deficiencies of ignorant or incapable parents in the physiological education of all committed to their care.

And here a word in regard to the bad effects of, so called, classical studies. Are they not oftentimes acquired at the risk of
outraged delicacy or undermined moral principles? Mythology,
in particular, introduces our youth to courtesans who are described
as goddesses, and goddesses who are but courtesans in disguise.
Poetry and history as frequently have for their themes the ecsta-
sies of illicit love as the innocent joys of pure affection. Shall
these branches of study be totally ignored? By no means; but
let their harmless flowers and wholesome fruit alone be culled for
youthful minds, to the utter exclusion of all poisonous ones, however beautiful.

This lack of information has resulted in another evil in the impetus it has given to the sale of obscene books and prints. Recent legal proceedings have checked this nefarious trade, but it
still exists. Boys and young men may be found loitering at all
hours round hotels, steam-boat docks, rail-road depôts, and other
public places, ostensibly selling newspapers or pamphlets, but secretly offering vile, lecherous publications to those who are likely
to be customers. They generally select young and inexperienced
persons for two reasons. In the first place, these are the most
probable purchasers, and will submit to the most extortion; and,
in the second, they can be more easily imposed upon. The venders have a trick which they frequently perform, and which can
scarcely be regretted. In a small bound volume they insert about
half a dozen highly-colored obscene plates, which are cut to fit
the size of the printed page. Having fixed upon a victim, they
cautiously draw his attention to the pictures by rapidly turning
over the leaves, but do not allow him to take the book into his
hands, although they give him a good opportunity to note its
binding. He never dreams that the plates are loose, and feels
sure that in buying the book he buys the pictures also. When
the price is agreed upon, the salesman hints that, as he is watched,
the customer had better turn his back for a moment while taking
the money from his pocket-book, and in this interval he slips the
plates from between the leaves and conceals them. The next
moment the parties are again face to face, the price is handed
over, and the book he had seen before is handed to the purchaser
under a renewed caution, and is carefully pocketed. The book-
seller leaves, and at the first opportunity the prize is covertly

drawn forth to be examined more minutely, and the unwary one finds that he has paid several dollars for some few printed pages, without pictures, which would have been dear at as many cents.

Despite all precautions, there is every reason to believe that the manufacture of these obscene books is largely carried on in this city. It is needless to remind any resident of the large seizures made in New York during the last two years, or to particularize the stock condemned. More caution is observed now, and the post-office is made the vehicle for distribution. Circulars are issued which describe the publications and their prices, modes of transmitting money are indicated, and the advertiser plainly says that he will not allow any personal interviews on account of the dangers which surround the traffic. By using an indefinite number of *aliases*, and often changing the address to which letters are sent, he succeeds in eluding the vigilance of the police, and secures many remittances.

Not less dangerous than the directly obscene publications is a class of voluptuous novels which is rapidly circulating. Some are translations from the French; but one man, now living in England, has written and published more disgustingly minute works, under the guise of honest fiction, than ever emanated from the Parisian presses. He writes in a strain eminently calculated to excite the passions, but so carefully guarded as to avoid absolute obscenity, and embellishes his works with wood-cuts which approach lasciviousness as nearly as possible without being indictable. It is to be regretted that publishers have been found, in this and other cities, who are willing to use their imprints on the title-pages of his trash, and sell works which can not but be productive of the worst consequences. Those who have seen much of the cheap pamphlets, or "yellow-covered" literature offered in New York, will have no difficulty in recalling the name of the author alluded to, and those who are ignorant of it would only be injured by its disclosure. There can be but one opinion as to the share obscene and voluptuous books have in ruining the character of the young, and they may justly be considered as causes, indirect it may be, of prostitution.

Some of the sources of prostitution have been thus examined. To expose them all would require a volume; but it is hoped that sufficient has been developed to induce observation and inquiry, and prompt action in the premises.

CHAPTER XXXIV.

NEW YORK.—STATISTICS.

Means of Support.—Occupation.—Treatment of Domestics.—Needlewomen.—Weekly Earnings.—Female Labor in France.—Competition.—Opportunity for Employment in the Country.—Effects of Female Occupations.—Temptations of Seamstresses.—Indiscriminate Employment of both Sexes in Shops.—Factory Life.—Business of the Fathers of Prostitutes.—Mothers' Business.—Assistance to Parents.—Death of Parents.—Intoxication.—Drinking Habits of Prostitutes. —Delirium Tremens.—Liquor Sold in Houses of Prostitution.—Parental Influences.—Religion of Parents and Prostitutes.—Amiable Feelings.—Kindness and Fidelity to each other.

Question. IS PROSTITUTION YOUR ONLY MEANS OF SUPPORT?

Resources	Numbers.
Dependent solely upon prostitution	1698
Have other means of support	302
Total	2000

No surprise will be excited by the fact indicated above, that seventeen of every twenty women examined in New York reply to this question in the affirmative, for it is almost impossible to conceive that any honest occupation can be associated with vice of such character. The small minority who have other means consists principally of women who work at their trades or occupations at intervals, or who receive some slight payment for assisting in the ordinary work, or for sewing, in the houses of ill fame where they reside. It is difficult to believe women working as domestics in brothels are virtuous themselves; on the contrary, it is a well-known fact that they are, in every sense of the word, prostitutes; the only difference being that they work a portion of the time, while the "boarders" do not work at all.

Those who follow an employment at intervals are mostly women whose trades are uncertain, and who are liable at certain seasons of the year to be without employment. Then real necessity forces them on the town until a return of business provides them with work. They are more to be pitied than blamed.

There is another class not entirely dependent on prostitution. It consists mostly of German girls, who receive from five to six dollars per month as dancers in the public ball-rooms. In the first ward of New York there are several of these establishments, and the Captain of Police in that district has attached some interesting memoranda to his returns, from which is gleaned the following information respecting these places and their inhabitants. It is submitted to the reader, in order that he may draw his own conclusions as to the virtue of the dancers.

"These dance-houses are generally kept by Germans, who consider dancing a proper and legitimate business. They are in general very quiet. The girls employed to dance do not consider themselves prostitutes, because the proprietors will not allow them to be known as such. Each girl receives monthly from five to six dollars and her board, and almost every one of them hires a room in the neighborhood for the purpose of prostitution. I have classed them all as prostitutes, because, in addition to the previous fact, I know that the majority of them have lived as such. Very few of these girls are excessive drinkers. Although the regulations of the ball-room require them to drink after each dance with their partners, yet the proprietor has always a bottle of water slightly colored with port wine, from which they drink, and he charges the partner the same price as for liquor."

Alluding to the keeper of one of these places, the same officer says:

"The proprietress of this house is a German woman over seventy years of age. She established the house over eighteen years since, to my certain knowledge. Her husband had just then arrived from Germany with their four children. They were not worth one hundred dollars at that time. The man died three years ago, and by his will directed forty thousand dollars to be divided among his children. The widow is possessed of an equal amount in her own name."

Question. WHAT TRADE OR CALLING DID YOU FOLLOW BEFORE YOU BECAME A PROSTITUTE?

Occupations.	Numbers	Occupations.	Numbers.
Artist	1	Shoe-binders	16
Nurse in Bellevue Hospital, N. Y.	1	Vest-makers	21
School-teachers	3	Cap-makers	24
Fruit-hawkers	4	Book-folders	27
Paper-box-makers	5	Factory girls	37
Tobacco-packers	7	Housekeepers	39
Attended stores or bars	8	Milliners	41
Attended school	8	Seamstresses	59
Embroiderers	8	Tailoresses	105
Fur-sewers	8	Dress-makers	121
Hat-trimmers	8	Servants	933
Umbrella-makers	8	Lived with parents or friends	499
Flower-makers	9	Total	2000

Wherever the social condition of **woman has been** considered, one fact has always been painfully apparent, namely, the difficulties which surround her in any attempt to procure employment beyond the beaten track of needlework or domestic service. Numerous light or sedentary employments now pursued by men might with much greater propriety be confided to women, but custom seems to have fixed an arbitrary law which can not be altered. If a lady enters a dry goods store, she is waited upon by some stalwart young man, whose energy and muscle would be far more useful in tilling the ground, or in some other out-door employment. If she wishes to make a purchase of jewelry, she is served by the same class of attendants. Why should not females have this branch of employment at their command? It would in a majority of cases be more consonant with the feelings of the purchasers, and consequently more to the interest of store-keepers. It would open an honorable field of exertion to the women, and improve the condition of the men who now monopolize such employments, by forcing them to obtain work suitable to their sex and strength, and driving from the crowded cities into the open country some whose effeminacy is fast bringing them to positive idleness and ruin.

Many people are prepared to frown upon any attempt to improve the social condition of dependent women. They regard it as a part of that myth which they call opposition to constituted authorities, without any reference to the consideration which should form the basis of all society, namely, ensuring the greatest amount of good to the greatest number. Others who are opposed to any amelioration sustain their views by a libel upon woman, and upon her Almighty Creator. They assert that she has not sufficient intellect for any thing beyond routine employment, or blame her because she has received only such an imperfect education as the world has thought proper to award her, and thus has not had an opportunity to cultivate her faculties. It is not necessary to point to the productions and achievements of women even in our own days, omitting all mention of what has been done heretofore, to expose the fallacy of this proposition. The facts are patent to the world. With special reference to the subject in hand it may be asserted, unhesitatingly and without fear of contradiction, that were there more avenues of employment open to females there would be a corresponding decrease in prostitution, and many of those who are now ranked with the daughters of shame would be happy and virtuous members of the community.

In the list of occupations pursued by the women who are now prostitutes in New York, a most lamentable monotony is visible. Domestic service and sewing are the two principal resources. From the gross number of two thousand deduct those who lived with their parents or friends, children attending school, domestic servants, and housekeepers, amounting in the aggregate to 1322, and there is a balance of 678, nearly six hundred of whom depend upon needles and thread for an existence. In the total number reported there are *only four, or exactly one in every five hundred*, who relied for support upon any occupation requiring mental culture, that is, one artist and three school-teachers. This fact in itself sustains the theories that mental cultivation and sufficient employment are restrictions to the spread of prostitution.

If women are compelled to undergo merely the slavery of life, no moral advancement can ever be expected from them. If every approach to remunerative employment is systematically closed against them, nothing but degradation can ensue, and the moralist who shuddered with horror at the bare possibility of a woman being allowed to earn a competent living in a respectable manner will ejaculate, "What awful depravity exists in the female sex!" He and others of his class drive a woman to starvation by refusing to give her employment, and then condemn her for maintaining a wretched existence at the price of virtue.

But to notice more particularly the employments which the

¹ Miss Mulock remarks on female occupations: "Equality of sexes is not in the nature of things. One only 'right' we have to assert in common with mankind, and that is as much in our hands as theirs—the right of having something to do." —*A Woman's Thoughts upon Women* (New York ed.), p. 13.

"The Father of all has never put one man or one woman into this world without giving each something to do there."—Ibid., p. 19.

"This fact remains patent to any person of common sense and experience, that in the present day one half of our women are obliged to take care of themselves, obliged to look solely to themselves for maintenance, position, occupation, amusement, reputation, life."—Ibid., p. 29.

"Is society to draw up a code of regulations as to what is proper for us to do, and what not?"—Ibid., p. 31.

"The world is slowly discovering that women are capable for far more crafts than was supposed, if only they are properly educated for them; that they are good accountants, shop-keepers, drapers' assistants, telegraph clerks, watch-makers; and doubtless would be better if the ordinary training which almost every young man has a chance of getting were thought equally indispensable to young women."— Ibid., p. 76.

courtesans of New York have followed. The domestic servants amount to 931. No modern fashion has yet been introduced to deprive females of this sphere of labor, but so progressive is the age that even that may be accomplished within a few years, and the advertising columns of the newspapers teem with announcements of some newly-invented "scrubbing-machine." The space will not permit any extended remarks on this employment, but, while allowing that many employers treat their servants as human beings gifted with the same sensibilities and feelings as themselves, it must be regretted that there are others who use them in a manner which would bring a blush to the cheek of a southern slave-driver. With such mistresses the incapacity of servants is a constant theme, nor do they ever ask themselves if they have learned the science of governing. Assuming that they themselves are right, they conclude that the "help" is, of course, wrong. Is it any wonder that girls are driven to intoxication and disgrace by this conduct? Another reason which forces servant-girls to prostitution is the excessive number who are constantly out of employment, estimated at one fourth of those resident in the city, an evil which would be diminished were there more opportunities for female labor.

What is the position of the needle-woman? Far worse than that of the servant. The latter has a home and food in addition to her wages; the former must lodge and keep herself out of earnings which do not much exceed in amount the servant's pay. The labor by which this miserable pittance is earned, so truthfully depicted in the universally known "Song of the Shirt," is distressing and enervating to a degree. Working from early dawn till late at night, with trembling fingers, aching head, and very often an empty stomach, the poor seamstress ruins her health to obtain a spare and insufficient living. There is no variety in her employment; it is the same endless round of stitches, varied only by a wearisome journey once or twice a week to the store whence she receives her work, and where the probabilities are that a portion of her scanty wages will be deducted for some alleged deficiency in the work. She has no redress, but must submit or be discharged.

Nor is the position of a milliner or dress-maker much superior to this. She has a room provided for her in the employer's establishment, and there she must remain so long as the inexorable demands of fashion, or the necessity of preparing bonnets or dresses for some special occasion require.   It matters not if she faint from exhaustion and fatigue ; Mrs. ——— wants her ball-dress to-mor. row, and the poor slave (we use this word advisedly) must labor as if her eternal salvation rested on her nimble fingers.   But the gay robe which is to deck the form of beauty is completed; the hour of release has come at last; and, as at night the wearied girl walks feebly through the almost deserted streets, she meets some of the frail of her own sex, bedecked in finery, with countenances beaming from the effects of their potations, and the thought flash. es across her mind, "They are better off than I am."   Her human nature can scarcely repress such an exclamation, which is too oft. en but the precursor of her own ruin.

Paper-box-makers, tobacco-packers, and book-folders are no bet. ter off.   They must work in crowded shops, must inhale each other's breath during the whole day (for such work-shops are not the best ventilated buildings in New York, generally speaking), and receive, as their remuneration, barely sufficient to find them food, clothes, and shelter.

It is needless to pursue this subject.   Enough has surely been advanced to demonstrate the necessity of a more extended field of female labor.

Question. HOW LONG IS IT SINCE YOU ABANDONED YOUR TRADE AS A MEANS OF LIVING?

Length of Time.	Numbers.	Length of Time.	Numbers.
3 months	174	5 years	117
6 "	151	10 "	90
1 year	273	12 " and upward	16
2 years	254	Not abandoned	296
3 "	147	Unascertained	378
4 "	104	Total	2000

A very few words will suffice on this table, as the remarks which would arise from it have been already made in reference to other questions.   In most instances the occupation is abandoned as soon as the first false step is taken, unless in those cases of des titution where a previous want of employment renders prostitu tion necessary as the only means of living.   Of course, as before observed, a life of prostitution must be incompatible with any de. scription of honest employment, and, in those cases where a wom. an has followed any trade or occupation after she had yielded to promiscuous intercourse, it will generally be found that her mo. tive was to deceive the world as to her own pursuits, or else to satisfy her conscience that she was not entirely depraved.

Question. WHAT WERE YOUR AVERAGE WEEKLY EARNINGS AT YOUR TRADE?

Average Earnings.	Numbers.	Average Earnings.	Numbers.
1 dollar	534	7 dollars	8
2 dollars	336	8 "	5
3 "	230	20 "	1
4 "	127	50 "	1
5 "	68	Unascertained	663
6 "	27	Total.	2000

This question is of equal importance with that referring to the number of employments available for females, and the replies quoted above will give as many reasons for prostitution as in the former case. From the work of a French author on this subject the following is condensed as indicative of the hardships and insufficient remuneration of women employed in factories in France:

"Women are employed principally in the manufacture of cotton, silk, and wool. The preparation of cotton presents two dangerous features, in the 'beating' and 'dressing,' *which are performed solely by women.* In the manufacture of silk there are also two processes dangerous to life, and *these are performed by women.* The woolen manufacture has no real danger but in the 'carding,' and *all the carders are women.* Of these mortal occupations there is not one that will afford the workwoman a sufficient maintenance, the average wages being from sixteen to twenty-five sous per day, subject to the fluctuations of trade."[1]

Commenting upon these facts, the Westminster Review says,

"We took some pains to ascertain the relative wages of men and women employed in the same trades (in England), and almost in every instance it appeared that for the same work, performed in the same time, they received one third less, sometimes one half less than men, without any inferiority of skill being alleged. One master gravely said that he "*paid women less because they ate less.*"[2]

In a subsequent chapter of this volume will be found some particulars of the wages paid in manufacturing districts of the United States, and the same disparity between male and female operatives will be noticed.

M. Parent-Duchatelet assigns insufficient wages as one of the principal causes of prostitution in Paris. He says,

"What are the earnings of our laundresses, our seamstresses, our milliners? Compare the wages of the most skillful with those

[1] Histoire Morale des Femmes. Par M. Ernest Legouvé. Paris, 1849.
[2] Westminster Review (London), July, 1850. American edition, vol. xxx. No. 2.

of the more ordinary and moderately able, and we shall see if it be possible for these latter to procure even the strict necessaries of life; and if we farther compare the price of their work with that of their dishonor, we shall cease to be surprised that so great a number should fall into improprieties thus made almost inevitable."[1]

This low rate of wages is defended upon the plea of competition. A manufacturer practically says, "If one man or woman will do my work for five per cent. less than another, I must employ him or her unless I am prepared to carry on my business at a positive loss; for if I do not give them work, my neighbor will." Valid as this reason may be in the old countries, where the supply of labor far exceeds the demand, it is invalid in America, where there is a constant demand for workers. Our cities are overcrowded; remove some of their inhabitants to the country. In our cities work can not be obtained; in the country both male and female laborers are urgently required. In cities an unemployed woman is exposed to innumerable temptations; in the country she need never be unemployed, and consequently would escape such dangers. The difference between the New and Old worlds is simply that in the former the cities are overcrowded, but the country is free; in the latter, both cities and country are full to repletion.

In the city of New York one fourth part of the domestic servants are constantly out of employment; remove them, and, while the wants of the community will be amply supplied, the market value of a faithful servant would increase to a living rate. Send away a number of needle-women, reducing the supply of labor to meet the actual demand; tailors, shirt-makers, and dress-makers must employ seamstresses, and in such cases they could not obtain them without paying remunerative wages. The prices of our wearing apparel would probably be advanced five per cent., with a saving of fifteen per cent. taxation in the reduced expenses of police, judiciary, prisons, hospitals, and charitable institutions.

The experience of the winter of 1857–8 has proved that but very slight difficulties attend this plan when efficiently carried out, and to the "Children's Aid Society" and the other benevolent organizations, which have shown not only the possibility, but the success of the system, all praise is due. No man entering upon a farm in the West requires any argument to convince him that his

[1] De la Prostitution dans la Ville de Paris, vol. i. p. 96.

property will increase in value as it is cultivated, and many will gladly advance the sum necessary to pay the expenses of a servant's journey out. As fast as men are sent to fell the timber or break the prairie, the farmer's necessities force him to engage women for the increasing work of his house and dairy, and to supply the places of those who obtain husbands in their new home. When the tide of emigration to the Australian colonies commenced, nearly the whole of those who left England were single men, and in a few months the cry was ringing from one end of the island to the other: "Send us female help, send us wives." A benevolent woman, resident in the colony, repeated the demand, and subsequently lent the aid of her powerful talents to it. She made a voyage to England, and there influenced public opinion to such an extent that the British government yielded to the outside pressure, and many ship-loads of well-recommended, healthy, and virtuous women were sent out at the national expense to supply the want. The subsequent advancement of the colony has proved that the measure was a judicious one, nor can the abuses to which it became subject detract from its merits.

Similar plans with respect to destitute children have been practiced in New York for several years, and their subsequent extension to meet the wants of adult females has been limited only by the means of the projectors. If the necessity and prospective benefit of this emigration were known and appreciated, the required funds could be raised without any difficulty. The citizens of New York are never dilatory in responding to calls upon their benevolence in aid of any practicable and judicious scheme of philanthropy, and, under the management of an energetic business committee, arrangements could be made which would render the movement self-supporting within a few years.

The competition which keeps wages at starvation point is aggravated by a notion entertained by many native women, and by some foreigners who have been long in the country, that domestic service is ungenteel. This idea drives them to needlework to maintain their respectability, and thus, while service is abandoned, the ranks of seamstresses are augmented. By decreasing the number to be employed, and consequently advancing their wages and insuring better treatment from their employers, the servant's life would be divested of many of its objections, and old-fashioned house-work would once more be deemed respectable. This consummation rests more with mistresses than servants.

The former give tone to the manners of the latter. It can not be denied that many young women date their ruin from unkind or unwomanly treatment by their mistresses, who have given a free rein to their caprices, confident that if a girl left them they could soon supply her place. This confidence would be shaken if a housekeeper knew that servants were less plentiful, and her own interest would induce her to use well those who suited her. Such a conclusion would be an important step toward reducing prostitution, and elevating the character of the masses.[1]

It can not be expected that this vice will decrease in New York when five hundred and thirty-four, out of a total of two thousand, earn only one dollar weekly. No economist, however closely he may calculate, will pretend that fourteen cents a day will supply any woman with lodging, food, and clothes. She who should attempt to exist on such a sum would starve to death in less than a month, and yet it is a notorious fact that many are expected to support themselves upon it. How such expectations are realized, and the sad manner in which the deficiency is made up, are amply shown by the result of this and similar investigations, here and elsewhere.

Thus far manufacturers have been blamed for the depression of wages, but is not the consumer equally open to censure? He purchases an article of dress from A, because it is a trifle cheaper than in B's store. The cost of the raw material is the same to each, and each uses the same quantity in every article; but if A can find customers for three times the amount of goods which B can sell, on account of the saving he effects through paying lower wages, it is scarcely in human nature, decidedly not in commercial nature, to be expected that he will refuse the opportunity. He flatters himself that competition forces him to make the reduction, and as the public do not denounce his action, but flock to his store so long as his price continues lower than his neighbor's, he concludes that his customers should bear the blame. Nor are his conclusions false. The public sanction a system which enforces starvation or crime, and, for the sake of saving a few cents, add their influence to swell the ranks of prostitutes, and condemn many a poor woman to eternal ruin.[2]

[1] "The root of all improvement must be the mistress's own conviction, religious and sincere, of the truth that she and her servants share one common womanhood, with aims, hopes, and interests distinctly defined, and pursued with equal eagerness; with a life here meant as a school for the next life; with an immortal soul." —*A Woman's Thoughts upon Women* (New York ed.), p. 130.

[2] "Neither labor nor material can possibly be got 'cheaply,' that is, below it

Before leaving the question of employment, the effects of different branches of female occupation, as inducing or favoring immorality, must be noticed. Apart from the low rate of wages paid to women, thus causing destitution which forces them to vice, the associations of most of the few trades they are in the habit of pursuing are prejudicial to virtue. The trade of tailoress or seamstress may be cited as a case in point. One mode in which this business is conducted between employer and employed is as follows: The woman leaves either a cash deposit or the guarantee of some responsible person at the store, and receives a certain amount of materials to be made up by a specified time: when she returns the manufactured goods she is paid, and has more work given her to make up. This may seem a very simple course, and so it is, but one feature in it gives rather a sinister aspect. The person who delivers the materials, receives the work, and pronounces on its execution, is almost invariably a man, and upon his decision rests the question whether the operative shall be paid her full wages, or whether any portion of her miserable earnings shall be deducted because the work is not done to his satisfaction. In many cases he wields a power the determinations of which amount to this: "Shall I have any food to-day, or shall I starve?"

It is reasonable to conclude that hardly any thing short of positive want can force a girl to undertake this labor at its present price, and it is reasonable to imagine that her necessities will force her to use every means to accomplish her task in a satisfactory manner. If she finds that a smile bestowed upon her employer or his clerk will aid her in the struggle for bread, she will not present herself with a scowling face; or if a kind entreaty will be the means of procuring her a dinner as a favor, she will not expose herself to hunger by demanding it as a right. In this there is no moral or actual wrong, but there are instances where lubricity has exacted farther concessions, and the sacrifice of a woman's virtue been required as an equivalent for the privilege of sewing at almost nominal prices. If this is conceded, the victim may be assured of the best work and the most favors until her seducer becomes satiated with possession, when means will easily be found to displace her for some new favorite. If the outrageous request

average acknowledged cost, without *somebody being cheated:* consequently, these devotees to cheapness are, very frequently, little better than genteel swindlers."— *A Woman's Thoughts upon Women* (New York ed.), p. 72.

is denied, she will get no more work from that shop, and may seek other employment with almost a certainty of meeting the same indignity elsewhere. That this is a frequent occurrence, unfortunately, can not be denied: that it exercises much influence on public prostitution can not be doubted.

The employment of females in various trades in this city, in the pursuit of which they are forced into constant communication with male operatives has a disastrous effect upon their characters. The daily routine goes very far toward weakening that modesty and reserve which are the best protectives against the seducer, and renders them liable to temptation in many shapes. A girl frequently forms an attachment to a man working in the same shop, believing it to be a mutual one, and only finds out her mistake when she has yielded to his persuasions and is deserted. Or women contract acquaintance for the sake of having an escort on their holiday recreations, or because some other woman has done so, or as the mere gratification of an idle fancy; but all tend in the same direction, and aid to undermine principles and jeopardize character.

In this connection only city employments have been mentioned, but the same reasoning may be applied with greater force to factory life in any of our manufacturing districts. There the operatives of both sexes in one mill may sometimes be counted by hundreds, and their large numbers cause a more frequent and constant communication than in smaller workshops. It has been urged in support of the superior morality of such places, that the very nature of the employment requires the most constant attention to be paid to it, and precludes the possibility of any idle time. We freely concede to the apologists all the advantages they claim, and admit that during the time—say ten hours daily—when the machinery is running, neither males nor females can abandon their respective positions; but, unfortunately for the force of the argument, the motion is not a perpetual one. A steam-engine or a water-wheel can run for a week or a month without complaining of fatigue, but human machines become exhausted after a few hours' consecutive labor. Machinery can receive the necessary attention and supplies without arresting its progress, but men and women must sometimes cease work in order to eat and drink.

Granting, then, that during actual working hours a young woman can not leave her post, yet the mind is free, and the range of thought, when locomotion is denied her, will often turn to the hardships of her position. Busy as may be her hands, her brain is disengaged, and while her mechanical duties are adroitly performed, the mental faculties will be in full exercise, and for these she has ample scope. Dissatisfied with her close confinement in the factory, weary of the dreadful monotony which makes to-day but a repetition of yesterday and a sure type of to-morrow, she is happy, when the bell rings the signal to leave work, to escape from the building, and renew outside its walls an acquaintance she has formed before; and too frequently the persuasions and promises of her lover will induce her to seek, in some less guarded position, the independence for which she longs. It may be taken as a general rule that any confinement or restraint which is irksome to human nature must result injuriously.

Domestic servants are not exempt from temptation when employed in large establishments where both sexes are engaged, and many a poor girl ascribes her ruin to the associations formed in places of this description.

Thus far it has been supposed that man is the chief agent in the propagation of vice, nor is there any apparent reason to recede from that position. The numerous cases of seduction under false promises and subsequent desertion; of seduction by married men; of violations of helpless and unprotected females, are abundantly sufficient to prove this, much as it may be regretted for the credit of the stronger sex, and also to vindicate the opinion that employing males and females under one roof, in different branches of the same business, has a strong tendency to promote prostitution. Sometimes, however, it is true that woman, lost and abandoned herself, lends her aid to drag her fellow-women down to perdition. In many of the stores and workshops in our city, in every factory throughout the country, such are to be found, and their insidious influence is quickly felt. By false representations and elaborate coloring, they work upon the minds of the simple, or inflame the passions of the ambitious, but in either case their object is the same, and in it they frequently succeed.

Question. WHAT BUSINESS DID YOUR FATHER FOLLOW?

Fathers' business.	Numbers.	Fathers' business.	Numbers.
Architects	4	Bakers	21
Auctioneer	1	Builders	11
Agents	5	Book-keepers	3
Butchers	47	Boatmen	7
Blacksmiths	63	Brothel-keeper	1
Barbers	2	Bankers	2

Fathers' business.	Numbers.	Fathers' business.	Numbers.
Carpenters	139	Men of Property	5
Carmen	26	Naval Officers	31
Coopers	19	Overseers	5
Clerks	32	Peddlers	5
Coachmen	10	Policemen	15
Clergymen	6	Painters	16
Coach-makers	9	Printers	3
Cabinet-makers	16	Planters	5
Diver	1	Pavers	4
Drover	1	Physicians and Surgeons	19
Dyers	3	Plumbers	2
Engineers	18	Pawnbrokers	2
Engraver	1	Ship-carpenters	23
Farmers	440	Sailors	35
Fishermen	6	Shoe-makers	48
Grocers	14	Stage-drivers	4
Gilders	2	Store-keepers	37
Gardeners	10	Stone-cutters	20
Glass-blowers	2	School-teachers	14
Hotel and Tavern keepers	36	Silversmiths	3
Hatters	13	Soldiers	38
Jewelers	10	Sail-makers	4
Laborers	259	Saddlers	14
Liquor-dealers	22	Servants	4
Lawyers	13	Surveyor	1
Lumber-merchants	7	Tailors	35
Livery-stable-keepers	5	Traders	11
Millers	20	Tanners and Curriers	7
Masons	82	Tinsmiths	2
Merchants	37	Weavers	20
Moulders	3	Wheelwright	1
Manufacturers	24	Unascertained	106
Musicians	8	Total	2000

This table shows that almost all classes of society are exposed to the influences which result in prostitution, from the children of men of property, bankers, merchants, and professional men, down to the families of mechanics and laborers. The numerous and varied occupations of the fathers of those women who answered the question renders any classification of them almost impossible. A majority of the parents were either mechanics or laborers, men who earned the daily food for themselves and families by manual labor, and whose resources would be governed by the ordinary fluctuations of trade.

In following the proportion of natives and foreigners as exhibited in previous tables, it must be remembered that about five eighths of these fathers were residents of other countries than the United States when those daughters were born whose replies form the bases of these statistics, and it is scarcely necessary to say that labor is nowhere so well remunerated as with us. The average wages, for instance, of a first-class mechanic in England or Ireland seldom exceed, and, indeed, rarely amount to, nine dollars per week, and an ordinary laborer is very well paid if he receives half that sum. This estimate refers to large cities, where the expenses of maintaining a family are as heavy as in New York, and it indicates poverty, which has already been proved to be one of the main causes of female depravity.

If the investigation is pursued into the rural districts of Great Britain, the wages of mechanics and laborers will be found lower than they are in large cities, without any material reduction in the necessary expenditure except in the item of house-rent. The pitiful amounts paid to agricultural laborers (often only twenty-five cents a day) will surprise any one who is not fully acquainted with the hardships endured by this unfortunate class, and the state of destitution in which they are compelled to *exist* (it can not, with any propriety, be called *living*), and to rear their families.

More than one half of the foreigners are from Ireland, and no person acquainted with the social history of that unhappy country need be told of the want and deprivation endured by its peasantry, of their useless efforts to benefit themselves, or of the ruin, starvation, and disease with which they are so frequently afflicted. To constitute a farmer in Ireland, a man must hire an acre or two of land, for which he pays a heavy rent, as two or sometimes three "middle-men" have to obtain their profits before the landlord receives his share. In this field he plants as many potatoes as can be crowded into it; and in his hut or cabin he keeps a pig or some fowls, regularly domesticated as members of the family, and receiving more attention than the children. From the sale of the pig the rent has to be obtained, and from the proceeds of the poultry, with the potatoes, all their wants have to be supplied. Thus, with the potatoes he raises for almost his sole means of support, with peat from some bog in the neighborhood to furnish him with fuel, he lives until the impoverished soil refuses to yield its annual crop, or yields it in a diseased and poisonous state, when fever and starvation come to fill his cup of misery, and render him dependent upon charity for an existence. And this in a land peculiarly rich in all that is necessary to make its people a great and happy nation.

This has been known as the state of Ireland for many years, and in this condition it unquestionably was when the women who here are now prostitutes were born there. Whether the severe lessons taught by the last famine, the more enlightened and liberal policy which has governed England, since that terrible calamity, in its legislation for the sister island, the introduction of Anglo-Saxon capital and enterprise, and the large exodus of the natives of the soil, have been of advantage to the country, it is difficult to determine in the face of the conflicting testimony furnished respectively by English and Irish partisans. It seems reasonable to conclude that an improvement must have taken place under these circumstances. But this is not the place to argue the political questions so often agitated there and elsewhere; it is enough for the purpose of this work to show the poverty of twenty years ago, and the vice resulting from it now, and to remind the reader that because of the lamentable manner in which the Irish have suffered in their own country, we must be taxed in New York for the support in hospitals, alms-houses, and prisons, of the women whose poverty compelled their crime.

Question. IF YOUR MOTHER HAD ANY BUSINESS INDEPENDENT OF YOUR FATHER, WHAT WAS IT?

Mothers' business.	Numbers.	Mothers' business.	Numbers.
No independent business	1880	Bakers	4
Dress-makers	35	Hat-trimmers	3
Tailoresses	26	Milliners	3
Seamstresses	12	Artificial Flower-maker	1
Store-keepers	9	Music teacher	1
Boarding-house-keepers	7	Nurse	1
Servants	6	Umbrella-maker	1
Vest-makers	6	House-cleaner	1
Laundresses	4	Total	2000

Only one hundred and twenty of two thousand women answer that their mothers had any business independent of their fathers, and they were mostly of the same ill-paid class as those alluded to in the portion referring to the occupations of the women themselves. The exceptions were, boarding-house, store, and bakery-keepers, amounting to twenty only, the remaining one hundred being servants or needle-women. The fact that even this number found it necessary to augment the income of their families by their own exertions is another evidence of poverty.

Question. DID YOU ASSIST EITHER YOUR FATHER OR MOTHER IN THEIR BUSINESS? IF SO, WHICH OF THEM?

Assisted.   Numbers.

Assisted neither parent 1515
  "   both parents 149
  "   mothers 306
  "   fathers 30

       Totals 485 1515
                                  485

      Aggregate 2000

To this question, thirty women reply that they were in the habit of assisting their fathers, three hundred and six say they assisted their mothers, and one hundred and forty-nine assisted both parents. The two latter answers, embracing four hundred and fifty-five cases, must be construed to mean such assistance in the ordinary work of a family as usually falls to the lot of children. The residue say that they never assisted either father or mother, or, in other words, that they were brought up in habits of idleness, which can scarcely have forsaken them in after-life, and probably had some considerable agency in their fall.

Question. IS YOUR FATHER LIVING, OR HOW OLD WAS YOU WHEN HE DIED?

Age at fathers' death.   Numbers.

  Fathers living 651
Under 5 years 289
From 5 " to 10 years 208
  " 10 " to 15 " 252
  " 15 " to 20 " 389
Unascertained 211

     Totals 1349 651
                               1349

    Aggregate 2000

Question. IS YOUR MOTHER LIVING, OR HOW OLD WAS YOU WHEN SHE DIED?

  Mothers living 766
Under 5 years 268
From 5 " to 10 years 195
  " 10 " to 15 " 277
  " 15 " to 20 " 281
Unascertained 213

     Totals 1234 766
                               1234

    Aggregate 2000

From the preceding tables, it appears that more than half of these women are orphans, 1349 of them have lost their fathers, and 1234 were deprived of their mothers. In both cases, the ages of the children at the death of their parents are in nearly the same ratio; thus, two hundred and eighty-nine father, and two hundred and sixty-eight mothers died when their children were under five years of age; two hundred and eight fathers and one hundred and ninety-five mothers died when their children were under ten years of age; two hundred and fifty-two fathers and two hundred and seventy-seven mothers died when their children were under fifteen years of age. The average of the deaths of either parent will therefore be, when the children were

Under 5 years of age 279
From 5 " to 10 years 202
"   10 " to 15 "   265

and the aggregate result that 1479 parents died before their daughters had reached the age at which a female most needs aid and advice.

At any time and under any circumstances the thought of death is dispiriting. The idea of rending all earthly ties; of bursting asunder bonds which have formed for years a part of our very existence, of leaving the world with its joys and pleasures, its cares and griefs, for the "undiscovered bourne," is appalling in contemplation; more appalling still when the family circle is invaded, and a father whom we have revered, or a mother whom we have loved, is taken from us.

The death of a father is a sad calamity for his children; the hand that has nourished and protected them, that has toiled for their support, is cold in the grave; their earthly support is gone. But a more grievous affliction still is the death of a mother. It is she to whom the children look in all their infant sufferings; it is her ear that is ever open to their sorrows; it is her bosom on which they are pillowed in sickness; her care which guides their steps in infancy; her love which warns them of the dangers that menace them in after life. Bereft of a mother's watchful tenderness, they are comparatively alone in the world, and many of their sorrows must be dated from that event.

The answers to these questions are full of material for mournful reflection, and strongly indicate the increased responsibilities of surviving relatives toward the orphans. This point has been already so strongly insisted upon that it would be a needless reiteration to argue its necessity.

Question. DO YOU DRINK INTOXICATING LIQUOR? IF SO, TO WHAT EXTENT?

Extent.	Numbers.	
Do not drink liquor		359
Drink moderately	647	
" intemperately	754	
Habitual drunkards	240	
Totals	1641	359
		1641
Aggregate		2000

It may be assumed as an almost invariable rule, that courtesans in all countries are in the habit of using alcoholic stimulants to a greater or less degree, in order to maintain that artificial state of excitement which is indispensably necessary to their calling. One of the class in London said to Mr. Mayhew, when he was making the inquiries alluded to in the chapters upon English prostitution, *"No girls* COULD *lead the life we do without gin;"* and drinking is undoubtedly universal among abandoned women. Even according to the most favorable view of the replies to the query now under consideration, and admitting them to be strictly correct, it will be found that five sixths of the total number confess they are in the habit of using intoxicating liquors. But with the knowledge of facts already ascertained in other cases, the inquirer will be compelled to believe that this is not the whole truth, for it is almost certain that the three hundred and fifty-nine who claim to be total abstinents indulge themselves in occasional potations. In prosecuting investigations like the present, there are many difficulties to encounter. A woman who is found residing in a house of ill fame will scarcely attempt to deny that she is a prostitute, although even this has been done in some cases, yet she will equivocate upon other matters. The facts of her birth, family, and life will probably be given correctly, because there exists no motive for concealment; but the answers to any questions which she deems degrading, such as relate, for example, to her habits or the state of her health, must be received with some considerable allowance, and compared with well-ascertained facts.

Among the more aristocratic prostitutes it is considered a disgrace to be absolutely intoxicated, and the keeper of a first-class house would scarcely retain a boarder who was addicted to habitual inebriety. Still, the most fastidious are ready and eager to sell champagne, or what passes for it, to any visitor of liberal disposition, and will generally condescend to assist him to drink it, of course inviting all the ladies to participate. In the lower grades it is not deemed disreputable to be inebriated, but the proprietors, knowing intoxication would interfere with their business, interdict it until late at night, when "the mirth and fun grows fast and furious," and when visitors, women, proprietors, bar-keepers, and servants frequently all contrive to be drunk, and close the night with a general saturnalia. The following morning, every thing is changed. The proprietor takes his stand behind the bar, and tenders the inmates, as they appear, their "bitters," namely a bumper of raw spirits. The visitors depart about their business, and the women await, with all the patience they can command, the result of another day's campaign, anxiously watching for any contingency which may arise likely to bring them another glass of liquor. Even in this case they are narrowly watched, and as soon as the depression from the previous night's debauch has been overcome, they must either take "temperance drinks," or colored water, when any stray customer invites them to the bar. *Our decided impression is that not one per cent. of the prostitutes in New York practice their calling without partaking of intoxicating drinks.*

The effects of this habit are well known. In the first instance the woman drinks but little, probably just enough to cause a slight artificial excitement, and bring a color to her cheeks. After a time the proportion must be increased as the effect upon the system is diminished, until the finale is a habit of confirmed and constant drinking. As a general rule, the horrible consequences then become apparent. The whole frame is relaxed, and every movement of the limbs is a motion of uncertainty; the brain is impaired; the reasoning faculties are destroyed; the powers of the stomach and digestive organs are weakened, and an attack of delirium tremens is the *ultimatum*, usually cured, if cured at all, at the public expense in a hospital or prison.

A work of fiction, published some ten years ago, gives the following truthful account of the effects of drunkenness on prostitutes, by one of whom the words are supposed to be used:

"I must have drink. Such as live like me could not bear life without drink. It's the only thing to keep us from suicide. If we did not drink we could not stand the memory of what we have been, and the thought of what we are, for a day. If I go without food and without shelter, I must have my dram. Oh! what awful nights I have had in prison for want of it." She glared round with terrified eyes as if dreading to see some supernatural creature near her, and then continued: "It is dreadful to see them. There they go round and round my bed the whole night through. My mother carrying my baby, and sister Mary, and all looking at me with their sad stony eyes. Oh! it is terrible. They don't turn back either, but pass behind the head of the bed, and I feel their eyes on me every where. If I creep under the clothes I still see them, and, what is worse, they see me. *I must have drink. I can not pass to-night without a dram. I dare not.*"[1]

Although this is an imaginary picture its counterpart can be seen at almost any time in the hospitals under the charge of the Governors of the Alms House on Blackwell's Island, New York City, where large numbers of such cases are constantly treated. In 1854, in the Penitentiary Hospital alone, more than fourteen hundred persons received medical assistance for delirium tremens and other maladies arising from excess in drinking. This fact induced the remarks in the report for that year, that the "cases actually treated here during the last year were directly caused by the lowest and foulest kinds of dissipation and vice, a fact which speaks trumpet-tongued in favor of shutting up 'grog shops,' and shows the absolute necessity of adopting some plan whereby the enormous amount of prostitution now among us shall be decreased."[2] Since then an alteration in the law has sentenced drunken persons to an incarceration in the City Prison, and the number sent to Blackwell's Island has diminished, but not to the extent which would be supposed, as, during 1857, the hospitals thereon afforded relief to seven hundred and ninety-one inebriates.

The fearful havoc upon the constitution is produced as well by the quality as the quantity of the liquors consumed. Let any man not thoroughly informed on these subjects taste a glass of the compounds retailed at these places, and he will be immediately convinced that it would be quite as judicious an act to swallow the same quantity of camphene or sulphuric acid if diluted, sweetened, and colored. The various liquors, gin, rum, brandy, whisky, or wine, having nothing in common with the genuine articles of commerce but the name, are so many varieties of the cheapest and most poisonous "raw spirits" that the markets afford, and are manufactured in this city in large quantities to meet the demands arising from such places. Instances have been known where liquors subsequently sold in houses of ill fame as pure French

[1] Mary Barton, by Mrs. Gaskell, vol. i., p. 258 (London edition.)
[2] Report of the Resident Physician, Blackwell's Island, to the Governors of the Alms House, 1854, p. 26.

brandy have been furnished by wholesale dealers at prices ranging from thirty-six to fifty cents a gallon.   There may be exceptions; some few brothels of the higher rank may sell what is called "good liquor," but they are very rare indeed.   Is it any
matter of surprise that drunkenness, or, more properly speaking,
stupefaction and insensibility are so rife; that so many constitutions are ruined and so many characters destroyed when agencies
like these are tolerated?

Question. DID YOUR FATHER DRINK INTOXICATING LIQUORS?
IF SO, TO WHAT EXTENT?

Fathers' habits.		Numbers.
Did not drink liquor	. .	548
Drank moderately	636	
" intemperately	596	
Unascertained	220	
Totals	1452	548
		—— 1452
Aggregate		2000

Question. DID YOUR MOTHER DRINK INTOXICATING LIQUORS?
IF SO, TO WHAT EXTENT?

Mothers' habits		Numbers.
Did not drink liquor	. .	875
Drank moderately	574	
" intemperately	347	
Unascertained	204	
Totals	1125	875
		—— 1125
Aggregate		2000

How much of the intemperate habits of these women must be
traced to the influence of the parent's example?   One thousand
four hundred and fifty-two fathers; one thousand one hundred
and twenty-five mothers, are represented as having been addicted
to the use of liquors in various degrees, the moderate in both cases
exceeding the intemperate drinkers.   And yet even moderate
drinking, when pursued by parents in the presence of, or to the
knowledge of children, is a practice open to the gravest censure.
In the mind of a child any action is deemed right if performed by
a father or mother.   As the children advance in years parental
customs are followed, and, in such a case as this, probably the
single glass of beer or wine of the father lays the foundation of
intemperance in the children.   Without undertaking to argue the
question of the absolute necessity for a total abstinence from all
liquors under all circumstances, the proposition may be seriously

submitted that the effect of this personal example upon children is satisfactorily ascertained, from many different sources, to be prejudicial to their best interests, and a natural deduction therefore is that it is the duty of parents to abstain.

Instances are upon record where both fathers and mothers, in the temporary insanity of intoxication, have turned their daughters from home into the streets, and that, too, in cases where not even the remotest grounds existed for any suspicion of improper conduct on the part of these children. Occurrences like this are sufficient to enforce the necessity of temperance on the part of parents, in view of the fearful responsibility which rests upon them.

Question. WERE YOUR PARENTS PROTESTANTS, CATHOLICS, OR NON-PROFESSORS?

Religion.	Numbers.
Protestants	960
Roman Catholics	977
Non-professors	63
Total	2000

Question. WERE YOU TRAINED TO ANY RELIGION? IF SO, WAS IT PROTESTANT OR CATHOLIC?

Religion.	Numbers.
Protestant	972
Roman Catholic	977
No religious training	51
Total	2000

Question. DO YOU PROFESS THE SAME RELIGION NOW?

Profession.	Numbers.
Profess religion as educated	1909
Non-professors	91
Total	2000

Question. HOW LONG IS IT SINCE YOU HAVE OBSERVED ANY OF ITS REQUIREMENTS?

Time.	Numbers.	Time.	Numbers.
1 year and under . .	861	From 7 years to 8 years .	42
From 1 " to 2 years . .	310	" 8 " " 9 " .	20
" 2 " " 3 " . .	226	" 9 " " 10 " .	36
" 3 " " 4 " . .	135	" 10 " " 12 " .	20
" 4 " " 5 " . .	106	Unascertained	130
" 5 " " 6 " . .	72	Totals	2000
" 6 " " 7 " . .	42		

It certainly seems a very incongruous association to connect religion and prostitution; to place in juxtaposition the most noble aspirations of which the mind is capable, and the lowest degradation to which the body can descend. But such a contrast is not without its moral. It is not too great a stretch of imagination to suppose that of those unfortunate women who subsequently lost their position in society, some had the advantages of an early Christian education; were taught to believe in and reverence the Inspired Writings; were taught that there is a God who judgeth the world, and that there exists for all a future state. Reflecting upon this, and considering how deplorably such have fallen from the observance of precepts inculcated in the days of childhood, all persons will feel the necessity of watchfulness and care that the same fate does not befall themselves or their connections. The facts may teach another lesson. It may be presumed that some of these women were trained in the rigid and austere manner animadverted upon in the remarks on the causes of prostitution, and that their present career is but the recoil from that unnatural restraint. Such conclusion would afford a solemn warning to all who have charge of the education of children to choose the happy mean between the extremes of careless laxity and excessive harshness. Either course is alike fatal to the welfare of their trust, and must end in disappointment and sorrow.

If it were consistent with propriety, it would not be possible to make any comparison between the results of Protestant and Roman Catholic teachings, because of the nearly equal number in each case. In the table exhibiting the religions professed by the parents there are seventeen more Roman Catholics than Protestants; in the table of the religions professed by the prostitutes themselves there are five more Roman Catholics than Protestants. The relative value of the two creeds as rules of life can not therefore be made the subject of argument from such data. So far as our duties to the Almighty, to our fellow-men, and to ourselves—so far as the obligations to virtue and morality are concerned, the adherents of both parties are agreed, and in the investigation of the intricate social problem of female depravity it matters but little whether a majority of the pitiable subjects of the inquiry were educated in the tenets of the Church of Rome or in the doctrines of the Reformation. If the articles of faith of either Church are honestly observed by those who professedly believe in them, they will be effective in preventing immorality; but when this observance is confined to words, and not exemplified by actions, neither the simple rituals of Protestantism nor the more elaborate and artistically arranged ceremonials of Roman Catholicism can be of any avail. Neither, if our lives accord not with our profession, will it make an iota of difference in our future destiny whether we have bowed the knee in a temple devoted to Roman Catholic service before the image of a crucified Savior, and endeavored to train our thoughts to a contemplation of his mercy and beneficence, or have knelt in a Protestant Church, and there joined in the public confession that we are sinners.

The facts exhibited in the tables show that 1937 women had parents who were professedly members of one or the other of these communions; that 1949 women out of 2000 were taught to believe in the necessity of some religion, and that 1909 of these women still assert their confidence in the creed in which they were educated.

It can not be expected that, living in the constant practice of that which their consciences must teach them is sinful, these women would have continued to observe the outward form of religion. By comparing the table upon this point with the one framed from the replies to the question, "For what length of time have you been a prostitute?" it will be observed that 1674 admit they have been prostitutes for six years and upward, and 1710 confess they have neglected to observe the requirements of religion for the same space of time; a coincidence which leads us charitably to suppose that the crime and the omission are nearly parallel, so far as dates are concerned, and that hypocritical professions of religion do not rank among prostitutes' offenses.

But even with their neglect of the outward requirements of faith, and while in the actual commission of known and acknowledged sin, they still preserve many traits which are much to their credit. They possess one of the chief virtues belonging to the female character, which never seems to become extinct or materially impaired; namely, kindness to each other when sick or destitute, and indeed to all who are in suffering or distress. This has attracted the attention, and called forth the admiration, of every one who has been thrown into contact with them. A very touching instance of these amiable feelings occurred some years ago, and is narrated in the Westminster Review for July, 1850. A poor girl, who was rapidly sinking into a decline, after a short but impetuous course of infamy, had no means of support but from the continued exercise of her calling. With a mixture of kindness and conscientiousness which may well surprise us under the circumstances, her companions in degradation resolved among

themselves that, as they said, "at least she should not be com
pelled to die in sin," and contributed from their own sad earnings
a sufficient sum to enable her to pass her few remaining days in
comfort and repentance.

This is far from being an exceptional case.   An extended hospital experience has brought under our personal observation many
acts of real sympathy and kindness toward each other among the
prostitute class.   If one of their number is discharged, and is un-
provided with suitable clothing, they will club their scanty resources to supply her needs, frequently contributing articles they
really want themselves.   In any case of serious sickness, where
prompt attention is required, they form most reliable nurses, and
will cheerfully sacrifice their own rest at any time to minister to
the sufferer, performing their duties with the utmost care and
tenderness.   Their fidelity to each other is strongly marked.   It
is literally impossible, in any case where a breach of discipline has
occurred, to find a woman who will bear witness against any of
her companions, and neither threats nor promises are sufficiently
potent to extract the desired information.

These traits are not submitted with any intention of offering
them as an equivalent to the morality which has been violated,
but merely to prove that hearts which can conceive and execute
such kindly purposes can not be entirely lost to the sense of virtue or the claims of benevolence.   Truly they are but as an atom
in the balance, but, like an oasis in the desert, they show that all
is not arid and sterile.

CHAPTER XXXV.

NEW YORK.—PROSTITUTES AND HOUSES OF PROSTITUTION.

First Class, or "Parlor Houses."—Luxury.—Semi-refinement.—Rate of Board.—
Dress. — Money.—Lavish Extravagance. — Instance of Economy.—Means of
Amusement.—House-keepers.—Rents.—Estimated Receipts.—Management of
Houses.—Assumed Respectability.—Consequences of Exactions from Prostitutes.
—Affection for Lovers.—Second Class Houses.—Street-walkers.—Drunkenness.
—Syphilitic Infection.—Third Class Houses.—Germans.—Sailors.—Ball-rooms.
—Intoxication.—Fourth Class Houses.—Repulsive Features.—Visitors.—Action
of the Police.—First Class Houses of Assignation.—Secrecy and Exclusiveness.
—Keepers.—Arrangements.—Visitors.—Origin of some Houses of Assignation.
—Prevalence of Intrigue.—Foreign Manners.—Effects of Travel.—Dress.—Sec-
ond Class Houses.—Visitors.—Prostitutes.—Arrangements.—Wine and Liquor.
—Third Class Houses.—Kept Mistresses.—Sewing and Shop Girls.—Disease.—
Fourth Class Houses.—"Panel Houses."

IT will not be out of place here to say somewhat concerning the
manner of life among prostitutes; how they occupy the time, and
what facilities they possess for mental or bodily recreation. The
domestic life of a number of women whose every action is contrary to all the rules of virtue, who are living in the constant violation of the law, with a daily subsistence contributed by those
whose folly or passions make them visitors to their abode, can not
but possess considerable interest to all who have followed thus far
in this painful task. In entering upon the subject, the endeavor
will be to give such particulars as will enable the reader to form
satisfactory conclusions, without recording what would merely
minister to a prurient curiosity. The object is to give information as explicitly as possible without offending the most sensitive
delicacy, wounding the most refined feelings, or unnecessarily
parading these poor women before the public eye. The subject
is invested with such an array of real and palpable horrors as to
render unnecessary any endeavor to excite undue emotion by
penetrating the mysteries of the saturnalia.

There is a wide diversity among the various grades of prostitutes in New York. The first class are those who reside in what
are technically called "Parlor Houses." These very seldom leave
their abodes, unless for the purpose of making purchases of dress,
jewelry, or articles of toilette, or taking an afternoon promenade on

the fashionable side of Broadway, excepting when they accompany their lovers or visitors in a ride, or to some public place of amusement. These utterly repudiate the name of " street-walkers," and very seldom perform any act in public which would expose them to reprobation, or attract the attention of the police. They assume to be, and are, in fact, the most respectable of their class, if any respectability can be associated with so vicious a course. Being almost invariably young and handsome, and always very well dressed, they pass through the streets without their real character being suspected by the uninitiated.

The houses in which this class of courtesans reside are furnished with a lavish display of luxury, scarcely in accordance with the dictates of good taste however, and mostly exhibiting a quantity of magnificent furniture crowded together without taste or judgment for the sake of ostentation. The most costly cabinet and upholstery work is freely employed in their decoration, particularly in the rooms used as reception parlors. Large mirrors adorn the walls, which are frequently handsomely frescoed and gilt. Paintings and engravings in rich frames, vases and statuettes, add their charms. Carpets of luxurious softness cover the floors, while sofas, ottomans, and easy chairs abound. Music has its representative in a beautiful pianoforte, upon which some professed player is paid a liberal salary to perform. Even the bed-chambers, passages, halls, and stairways are furnished in a similar style. In such an abode as this probably dwell from three to ten prostitutes, each paying weekly for her board from ten to sixteen dollars, exclusive of extras, which will be noticed hereafter. Their active life comprises about twelve or fourteen hours daily, ranging from noon to midnight or early morning. Their visitors are mostly of what may be called the aristocratic class; young, middle aged, and even old men of property, of all callings and professions; any one who can command a liberal supply of money is welcome, but without this indispensable requisite his company is not sought or appreciated.

None of the disgusting practices common in houses of a lower grade are met with here. There is no palpable obscenity, and but little that can outrage propriety. Of course there is a perfect freedom of manner between prostitutes and visitors, but so far as the public eye can penetrate, the requirements of common decency are not openly violated. Profanity, as may naturally be expected, exists to some extent; it is an almost invariable accompaniment of prostitution, but even that is divested of its grossness, and is not of frequent occurrence. There is no bar-room or public drinking place in the house, but it is a general custom for each visitor to invite his *pro tempore* inamorata and her companions to take champagne with him, which is supplied by the keeper of the place at the charge of three dollars a bottle. As remarked in the preceding chapter, excessive drunkenness is rare, both prostitutes and keepers trying to suppress it, because an intoxicated man would be likely to give them trouble, damage their furniture, and injure the reputation of the house. By means of a small aperture in the front door, covered by a wrought-iron lattice-work, the candidates for admission can be examined before entrance is given, and the door is kept closed against any person who is likely to prove an annoyance.

As a natural consequence of their position, the women exert all their powers of fascination, by adopting the latest and most superb fashions in dress, and by a very tasteful arrangement of their hair, for which purpose a hair dresser visits them every day, charging each woman two or three dollars a week for his assistance. Besides these they practice a thousand other artifices, unknown to mere lookers on, in order to secure the favor of their visitors.

About three fourths of the courtesans of this grade are natives of the United States, and mostly from New England or the Middle States. Some of them are very well educated; accomplished musicians and artists are sometimes found among them, while others aspire to literature. With the greater number much elegance and refinement of manner, or a close observance of what may be called the conventionalities of life, is seen. Their income is large, but so are their expenses. It is no exaggeration to state that their individual receipts very seldom fall short of fifty dollars per week. From this amount deduct the sum charged for their board, an additional fee which they pay the proprietress for every visitor they entertain, the expenses of hair-dressing, perfumery, etc., the cost of their washing, which is all done at their own charge, away from the house, and must be considerable, and the remainder will give their expenditure for dress. All are not equally extravagant. Some seem to consider prostitution a business, and act upon the idea of saving as much money as possible. In one case a woman asserted that she had seven thousand dollars in the bank, which she had accumulated by prostitution in a few years, and her statement was confirmed by the captain of police

for the district. The economical ones are generally shrewd, calculating "down-Easters," who argue that if they can save enough
during the zenith of their charms to support them when their attractions fail, or to help them establish a house of this description
on their own account, they are only doing their duty. Others
have dependent relatives whom they support, or illegitimate children whom they maintain and educate, frequently appropriating
considerable sums for these purposes. In nearly all of them,
kindness toward the unfortunate of their own sex and grade is a
striking trait. Much as they may quarrel among each other when
all are alike in health, let one be visited with sickness, or overcome by misfortune, and, as a general rule, their envy or jealousy
is forgotten, and they freely contribute to her support.

Their means of amusement are limited. When they have no
visitors they generally indulge in a luxurious indolence. For
any useful employment, such as even sewing or fancy needle
work, they have but little inclination, and their general refuge
from *ennui* is found in reading novels. These are not, as would
be generally supposed, works of lascivious character; to these
they seem to have an objection, most probably because their own
experience has proved the fallacies of the highly-colored descriptions of the delights of love which abound in such productions.
To one source of recreation they are extremely partial, namely,
driving in carriages some few miles out of town, and they frequently persuade their visitors to indulge them in these rural excursions. They are well acquainted with the most pleasant drives,
and know exactly where to find quiet and retired hotels where all
the delicacies of the season can be served in the most approved
style. If they can not induce their friends to gratify them in this
manner, they will endeavor to secure an invitation to take lunch-
eon or oysters at some fashionable saloon. Dress, gay life, and
excitement seem necessary to their existence.

And amid all this array of luxurious homes, of splendid dresses,
of comparative affluence, the question arises, Are they happy?
A moment's consideration will prompt the answer that they can
not be. Continued indulgence in their course of life tends to
obliterate the sense of degradation, and makes their career almost
second nature, but even the most confirmed must at times reflect.
The memory of what they have been, the thought of what they
are, the dread of what they must be, haunt their minds; conscience will make itself heard. Many a poor girl dressed in silks

or satins, gleaming with jewelry, and receiving with a gay smile the lavish compliments of her "friend," is mentally racked with a keen appreciation of her true position. She knows that the world condemns her, and her own heart admits the justice of the verdict. She knows that he who is so ostentatiously parading his admiration regards her but as a purchased instrument to minister to his gratification. She feels that she is, emphatically, alone in the world, and her merry laugh but ill conceals a breaking heart.

These houses are generally kept by middle-aged women who have themselves passed through the initiatory course of a prostitute's life. In some cases they own the real estate and furniture. In others they hire or lease the house, paying an exorbitant rent (often to some wealthy man who considers himself a respectable member of society), and provide their own furniture; in other cases they rent both house and furniture. *In one house in this city the enormous sum of nine thousand one hundred* (9100) *dollars is, or was at the time of examination, paid annually for rent and use of furniture,* the owner being a woman who formerly kept the place, but who is now living in the enjoyment of a large income in one of the Italian cities.

The following extracts from information obtained on this subject will give a very good idea of the facts:

E. M. pays $1300 per year for rent and use of furniture, which is owned by a woman who formerly kept the house.

M. S. pays $1000 per year rent, and owns the furniture.

M. L. owns the house and furniture, estimated to be worth $15,000.

M. A. T. pays $700 per year rent, and owns furniture valued at $5000.

J. G. pays $700 per year rent, and owns furniture valued at $3000.

E. T. owns the real estate and furniture, valued at $30,000.

C. G. pays $1800 per year rent, and owns furniture valued at $6000.

M. C. K. pays $3900 per year for rent and use of furniture.

C. E. pays $1400 per annum rent, and owns furniture valued at $6000.

M. B. owns the house and furniture, valued at $15,000.

J. B. pays $560 per year rent, and owns furniture valued at $2000.

E. B. pays $1000 per year rent, and owns furniture valued at $3000.

M. M. owns house and furniture, valued at $15,000.

C. C. pays $850 per year rent, and owns furniture valued at $8000.

M. M. pays $750 per year rent, and owns furniture valued at $2000.

M. G. pays $625 per year rent, and owns furniture valued at $1000.

V. N. pays $1300 per year rent, and owns furniture valued at $3000.

C. E. pays $1400 per year rent, and owns furniture valued at $6000.

L. C. pays $1000 per year rent, and owns furniture valued at $2000.

A. T. pays $1000 per year rent, and owns furniture valued at $3000.

The financial effects of the system of prostitution will furnish a theme for some remarks hereafter. These facts are quoted now to explain the expenses connected with first-class houses. Of course, where such outlays are incurred the receipts must correspond. The following statement will exhibit the *minimum* weekly receipts in a house where ten boarders reside :

Board for ten women, at $16 00 per week each $160 00
Fees for visitors, say one each day to each woman ($1 00 each)   70 00
Profit from sale of one basket of Champagne each day (weekly) . 168 00
Total $398 00

This estimate does not reach the daily average of visitors, and a more correct statement would be:

Board for ten women, at $16 00 per week each $160 00
Fees for visitors, say two each day to each woman ($1 00 each)   140 00
Profit from sale of two baskets of Champagne each day (weekly)   336 00
Total $616 00

Taking the mean of these two calculations will give receipts exceeding twenty-six thousand dollars per year, or five hundred dollars weekly. The cost of maintaining these luxurious establishments, in addition to the rent, is considerable, but still there is a very large excess. This is satisfactorily proved by the fact that the women who own the houses in which they conduct their traffic have, almost without exception, purchased them *since* they commenced housekeeping, and also that many of them own considerable personal property in addition to the real estate. One woman is positively affirmed to be worth over one hundred thousand dollars, many are reported as worth sums ranging from fifty thousand downward, and many more are reputed to be rich, but no special amount mentioned.

The management of many of the houses is confided to a housekeeper, acting for the principal, who is rarely visible unless specially called for, and under this housekeeper are a number of servants, varying from three to seven, according to the size of the house and the number of boarders it accommodates. These servants are almost invariably colored women, and no difficulty is ever experienced in obtaining a full complement. Their wages are liberal, their perquisites considerable, and their work light. A neat and well-arranged breakfast is prepared for the "lady boarders" about eleven or twelve o'clock, and their dinner is served about five or six o'clock. As a general rule these are the only meals supplied them in the course of the day. If they re-

quire any thing more they send out for it, or persuade their visitors to escort them to some saloon.

The proprietors of this class of houses assume to be respectable
women when they are away from the scenes of their business.
An anecdote, and a true one, has been related of one of them
who, on a recent visit to Newport, so effectually carried out her
disguise as to receive the escort of a reverend gentleman, a D.D.
of this city, to the dinner-table and elsewhere, with his family, he
thinking her a most amiable and deeply afflicted widow. Some
of them have private residences up town, in the quiet respectable
streets, and come to their houses of prostitution every forenoon,
returning at night. A portion of them profess to be religious,
frequently attending some place of worship the better to preserve
their mask. Naturally benevolent, as are all women, they contribute liberally to charitable objects, and freely relieve any indigent persons who may ask their assistance. Even in political
matters they have some weight, their resources and connections
proving valuable to some aspirant for local distinction who has
promised them that he will, if elected, use all his influence to
protect them from annoyance.

Toward the miserable women whose vice is the source of their
wealth, these proprietors act as interest dictates. A girl who has
not the tact or disposition to attract visitors is seldom treated with
much consideration, while one who is successful receives more
favors, but favors, generally speaking, of a nature to render her
subservient to their wishes; such as the loan of money to purchase new and fashionable articles of dress, a short credit for her
board, or some equivalent which will place her under an obligation, and render it difficult for her to leave the house. They are
actuated in this by a desire to retain an attractive girl; for, in addition to the actual cash payments she makes, she also possesses
the power of inducing her visitors to be liberal in their orders for
wine, and the profit from its sale, about two hundred per cent., is
an important source of revenue.

The excessive demands made upon the earnings of prostitutes
by these women has been productive of a serious social evil.
Many unfortunate girls can not appreciate the advantages of leading a vicious life for the benefit of a landlady, and in self-defense
have hired apartments in some private house, so as to secure their
earnings for themselves. This is generally arranged so that two
of them engage a suite of rooms, say a parlor and two bed-rooms,

representing themselves as virtuous women, governesses or seam-stresses, and frequently as the wives of sailors or of men who are in California or some other distant land. Here they either board themselves or resort to some saloon, and to this lodging, or to the house of assignation, which will be noticed in due course, they introduce their visitors. It is a fact more than suspected that many prostitutes are living in this manner in our city. It is needless to enlarge upon the injurious effects likely to result therefrom.

Before leaving this branch of the subject, there is another char-acteristic of keepers of these houses which must be noticed, name-ly, an exaggerated affection for some man to whom they are pas-sionately attached. Some few of them are professedly living with their husbands, but this is an exception to the ordinary rule. Generally speaking, they are the mistresses of some persons upon whom they lavish all their tenderness, and for whose gratification they willingly incur any amount of expense. Some of these indi-viduals are men upon town, gamblers, or rowdies of the higher class, whose noblest aspirations are satisfied by a liberal supply of money. They will readily ignore all social virtues for the same consideration. It is related as a fact concerning a celebrated brothel-keeper in the city, that when she was residing in the inte-rior of the State, some years since, she became desperately enam-ored of a young man whose friends discovered the connection. They removed him to the far West. Undaunted by the dangers and difficulties which surrounded her, she followed him, and dur-ing her journey through the large towns had many offers of pro-tection from men acquainted with her antecedents. True to her affection, she refused them all, and traced her lover to the forests. Here she remained with him, living in a log hut, deprived of many of the necessaries and all of the comforts and elegances of life, for three years. At least, infidelity to her love can not be charged against this woman, and is it not a natural conclusion that a heart so sincere and devoted in its attachment could have been led to a more virtuous course had a different social feeling existed toward her and her former transgressions?

As a general rule, the keepers of these first-class houses will not permit the boarders to have the men whom they style their "lovers" residing with them, although they allow them to visit; a constant residence is considered as likely to engross too much of the girl's time to the neglect of the interest of the proprietress.

We come now to the second grade of prostitutes and houses of prostitution. Many of the women of this rank are those who made their *début* in first-class houses, but left them when their charms began to fade. To some extent, they endeavor to carry out the same rules of conduct which governed them while there, and, generally speaking, the management of some portion of the houses of this grade assimilates very much with the former, the same privacy being observed, though in a less expensive manner. In others a marked difference is perceptible, and these will now claim attention.

A longer continuance in the habits of prostitution, and the association with a less aristocratic class of visitors, has diminished the refinement of the women and imparted to them coarser manners. There is not the same desire to " assume a virtue, if they have it not," or the same ambition to make vice seem unlike itself. Degradation has had its effect upon them, and now that they are reduced to a humbler sphere they feel more of the world's pressure, and become more daring and reckless in their conduct. Many of the street-walkers and women frequenting theatres are of this class, and any one who has ever come in contact with them would have found no difficulty in at once assigning their true position. It is right to say here, that many of the managers of our best theatres have abolished the third tier, so called, and if any improper woman visits them she must do so under the assumed garb of respectability, and conduct herself accordingly.

Other women in this grade, or rather this section of the second grade, commenced their life of vice in it, and as the natural tendency of prostitution is to depress instead of elevating its followers, they have very little chance of ever rising beyond their present rank, although such instances do occasionally happen, the keeper of a first-class house sometimes consenting to receive a boarder from a lower rank, if she has only recently commenced prostitution and is sufficiently prepossessing in manners and appearance for this exaltation. A great number of foreign-born women are found in this class, victims of emigrant boarding-houses, or of seduction on board ship during their passage to this country.

The houses are generally conducted in a similar manner to those of the first class, with this distinction, that what is costly luxury in the one is replaced by tawdry finery in the other, and for expensive mirrors and valuable paintings they substitute cheaper ornamentation. Their reception-rooms are of much infe rior finish. They also furnish wine and brandy to customers who wish for them. Drunkenness is more general, both with the pros titutes and their visitors, and the most revolting scenes are not uncommon. Profanity is indulged in to a considerable extent, and in some places seems the vernacular language. The attempts at fascination made by the women are more excessive, and fre quently vulgar to a degree which, while it excites a smile, also inspires disgust. The general charge for board here will be from six to ten dollars a week, rarely reaching the latter figure.

When evening approaches, if there is little or no company in the house, the girls resort to the streets, dressed in their most at tractive finery, in the expectation of finding some man whom they can induce to accompany them home. They are seldom unsuc cessful in this search, and very frequently repeat it several times in the course of the evening. Others of them visit the third tier of such theatres as will admit them, and there exert their charms to secure conquest. Intercourse with these women is attended with considerable danger, professional experience having shown many of them to be infected with syphilis, while numbers are con nected with dishonest men who would not scruple to rob a stran ger, if any opportunity offered for the purpose, such opportunity being not unfrequently afforded by some arrangement of the woman herself.

In such places vice presents comparatively few attractions, and yet these houses are numerously visited, principally by travelers, clerks from stores, the higher class of mechanics, etc., some of whom will spend in an evening the earnings of a week.

The women who preside over these brothels are usually of the strong-minded, and frequently of the strong-handed order, the lat ter being those who can by their own strength suppress any riot that may occur without calling in aid from the police, and gener ally calculate to preserve a moderate decorum in their establish ments. Their profits are very large, derived not merely from the board money and extras paid by the women, but also from the wines and liquors they sell. They do not endeavor to screen their own character, as do those of the upper class, but openly acknowledge what they are, and do not hesitate to give their personal attention to the business of the place. Anxious to accu mulate money as rapidly as possible, they are not very particular about the means they employ, and although they would not allow any positive act of dishonesty to be performed toward a visitor while he was in the house, on account of the trouble to which it might subsequently expose them, yet they would scarcely consider it their duty to warn him against the proceedings of the men who live as "lovers" with the prostitutes under their roofs. The virtue of these keepers is certainly not of a very rigid order, and their favored lovers are universally selected from among men of the same character as themselves.

The meals provided for boarders are served at about the same hours as in the fashionable houses, but they lack that neatness and arrangement which a good cook would give, the domestic matters being mostly confided to inexperienced servants, and frequently to some old prostitutes who are retained at nominal wages to do as much work as they can, and in their own style.

It has been already stated that some of the second-class houses of prostitution are conducted in a similar manner to those of the first, and therefore no attempt has been made to give any detailed account of them, which would be a mere repetition of what has been once described. The lower class have been taken as illustrating the second grade, and consequently the account must not be taken as a sweeping condemnation of the whole.

The next, or third grade of prostitutes and houses of prostitution may be found very fully developed in the first police district, among the Germans; in the fourth district, where sailors mostly resort; and also in the third, fifth, sixth, and fourteenth districts. A majority of the women in these districts are of foreign birth, the largest proportion being Irish and German. Although rated as third-class houses, some of them are equal in all respects, and sometimes superior in many, to houses of the second class. Most of the women are young, and many of them are very good-looking, while the houses, particularly those kept by Germans, are in general conducted very quietly. Even in those places resorted to by sailors, the principal part of any noise which may occur is caused by the boisterous mirth and practical jokes of the visitors themselves. The houses are, in every sense of the word, "public" places of prostitution, and neither women nor keepers seek to disguise the fact in any manner, the general argument seeming to be, "We live by prostitution, no matter who knows it."

There are many distinctive features in the several districts, but the first and the fourth will be fair average types of the whole, and these we will notice briefly, commencing with the German houses in the first district.

Here drinking is openly carried on, although seldom to such an extent as to cause absolute intoxication. There is a public bar-room opening directly from the street, where can be obtained la-ger beer and German wines, as well as the usual liquors sold in porter-houses. This is the reception-room of the establishment, and a stranger in the city, who might walk in to get a glass of lager beer, without knowing the character of the place, or being aware of the signification of the crimson and white curtains fes-tooned over the windows, would find himself followed to the bar by some German girl, who would ask him in broken English if he would "treat her." If he feels inclined to gaze around him and study human nature in this phase, he sees that the room is very clean; a common sofa, one or two settees, and a number of chairs are ranged round the walls; there is a small table with some German newspapers upon it; a piano, upon which the pro-prietor or his bar-keeper at intervals performs a national melody; and a few prints or engravings complete its furniture. Two or three girls are in different parts of the room engaged in knitting or sewing; for German girls, whether virtuous or prostitute, seem to have a horror of idleness, and even in such a place as this are seldom seen without their work. Every thing bears an unmis-takable Teutonic appearance; from the heavily-mustached pro-prietor, or the recently-imported bar-keeper, to the mistress, or madame as she is generally called, and the women themselves, all plainly tell their origin. He is surprised at the entire absence of all those noisy elements generally considered inseparable from a low-class house of prostitution. He can sit there and smoke his cigar in as much peace as at any hotel in the city; and if he once tells a woman he does not wish to have any conversation with her, he will scarcely be annoyed again, unless he makes the first ad-vances. If he thinks proper to enter into conversation with the proprietor, he will be certain of a courteous reply, and will fre-quently find him an intelligent and communicative man. Finally, concluding to resist the temptations around him, he leaves the place in the most perfect security, and without the least fear of being insulted.

The majority of the girls here have recently arrived in the United States. Some have embraced this course of life from absolute poverty and friendlessness; some have followed it in their own country; others have been the victims of seduction; and with some the ruling motive seems to have been a desire to speak and be spoken to in their native tongue. Their pecuniary arrangement with the proprietor, for there is almost invariably a man at the head of each establishment, is that they shall give him one half of all the money they receive, for which he provides them with board and lodging. They are not generally intemperate women, the light German wines being their principal beverage, and although they frequently indulge in profanity, yet, as it is in their national language, it is unintelligible to those who understand only English, and the annoyance is consequently restricted. They are generally honest; in fact, it is the testimony of those best qualified to judge, that there is very seldom much disturbance, and very rarely any dishonesty practiced in this class of brothels. It can not be said that literally there is not much noise, for any one who has been in a room where two or three Germans of each sex were talking and gesticulating with their characteristic earnestness will be of opinion that they talked quite loud enough; but by *disturbance* is to be understood quarreling or fighting, which sometimes occurs, but not very frequently.

As before remarked, a man and his wife are mostly the keepers of such houses. The man, sometimes with a lad for his assistant, attends to the bar-room, and takes charge of the money, the wife does the cooking and general house-work, and the girls attend to their own rooms. By this division of labor the work is generally done to the satisfaction of all parties, and, the expenses being light, a considerable profit is made. There are mostly three or four girls in each house, seldom exceeding that number, and the rule among house-keepers is to consider any girl an unprofitable acquisition who does not pay them about ten dollars a week. Their rents are low, because they have but little room. The basement of an ordinary-sized house is generally the extent of their accommodation; the front part of this forms the bar-room, and the remainder is partitioned into very small bed-rooms.

There is another feature connected with German prostitution, and exhibited in the same neighborhood, which has already received a cursory notice on a former page, namely, their dancing-saloons. Saltatory amusements are carried on, more or less, in all their houses of prostitution, but in these saloons it is considered a respectable business enterprise, although the morality of the es-

N N

tablishments is, at least, questionable. The ball-room is a large, open apartment devoid of all furniture excepting chairs or benches round the walls; the musical arrangements generally comprise a piano and violin, and the dances are national waltzes and polkas. No charge is made for admission, and the bar is the only source of revenue. The "orchestra" occasionally appeal to the charitable for assistance, and the call is mostly responded to in a liberal manner. The business commences in the evening, and is invariably discontinued at midnight. The places are frequented by very few but Germans, and order is well maintained.

Leaving the Germans of the first district, the reader's attention will now be asked to the brothels of the fourth police district. Here the principal part of the women are of Irish parentage; some few are natives of the United States. The greater part of the visitors are sailors. When a succession of storms which have driven homeward-bound vessels off the coast is followed by a fair wind, so as to allow them to enter the harbor in large numbers, these houses are crowded, and for a few days, or while the sailors' wages last, a very extensive business is carried on. The bar-room, as in the case of the German houses, is the reception-room, and here may be seen at almost any hour of the day a number of weather-beaten sailors, verifying the truth of the old proverb, which says they resemble two distinct animals in earning and spending their money. It matters not who it may be, but any one who enters the room is almost sure to be asked to take a drink immediately, and if he remains, in less than five minutes somebody else will ask him to take another. A sailor with cash in his pocket has a decided antipathy to drinking alone, and generally invites every one in the room, male and female, to partake with him. By such a course he very soon gets intoxicated, when the girl whom he has honored with his special attention convoys him to bed, and leaves him there to sleep himself sober.

In these houses less neatness is observable than in those just noticed, but they have entirely a different class of customers. A German, in the midst of his pleasures, likes to see every thing neat and orderly about him; a sailor is not particular, so that his pleasures are unobstructed. A curious observer, also, does not meet with the same civility: if he comes to spend money he is welcome; if not, the landlord does not care about his company. Considerable card-playing is practiced; not what may be termed gambling, but for amusement, the stakes being seldom more than intoxicating drinks for the players. There is less noisy rowdyism than might be expected, since the men who generally cause such disturbances lack the courage to impose upon a crowd of hard-fisted sailors, who are always able and willing to take their own part, and resent any interference. Still, occasional quarrels occur among the visitors themselves, frequently resulting in a pitched battle. The landlord is then called for, and his knowledge of his customers enables him speedily to discover the aggressor, who always happens to be the man that has the least money, and he is forthwith pushed into the street without any ceremony, as a kind of peace-offering to the rest of the company.

The landlord is a character in his way. He is a man who has been to sea himself, for no one else would be deemed fit to keep a house where sailors resort, and is usually a large, powerful man. By the freemasonry of the craft, and by freely joining his visitors whenever they ask him to drink, and occasionally treating them in return, he is sure of their custom until their wages are all spent and they are obliged to go to sea again.

The women in these houses use liquor very freely, but they are not permitted to get drunk in the daytime. If the landlord observes any symptom of intoxication he gives them water, instead of gin, the next time they are asked to drink, as he knows very well his prospects for business would be injured unless the girls were kept sufficiently sober to be on the watch for contingencies, or, as he phrases it, "to look out for chances."

In some of these houses it is the rule that all the money received by the girls is to be given to the landlord, who provides them with clothing and necessaries, but in others a fixed rate of board—six or eight dollars a week—is paid, and the women retain the surplus. In either case it is a very profitable business, particularly where many girls are kept. In one house that we visited, in the fourth district, the keeper informed us that his expenses amounted to about one hundred and fifty dollars weekly, and of course some estimate can be made from this as to the amount of business he transacted.

The dancing-saloons in this neighborhood are not conducted on the platonic principles of the Germans. They are, in fact, so many accessories to prostitution, and many scenes there witnessed will not permit description. The women residing in the house are there, dressed in the most tawdry finery they can command, many of them assuming the bloomer costume. The band consists of a violin, a banjo, and a tambourine, and whatever is wanting in musical ability is adequately supplied by vigorous execution. The bar is very liberally patronized, and before midnight drunkenness is the rule and sobriety the exception.

Passing now to the fourth grade of this vice, we find prostitution in a most repulsive form; the women themselves diseased and dirty, the houses redolent of bad rum. The prostitutes are the refuse of the other classes who have fallen through the successive gradations on account of disease and drunkenness, or they are some of those children of iniquity who, born in scenes of vice and squalid misery, know nothing of a virtuous or happy course of life. Destiny seems from their birth to have intended them for vagrants, and has planted them so low in the moral scale that they can scarcely hope to rise.

It would be useless to attempt a specification of the localities of these houses; any one who has been through the purlieus of New York City must have observed some of them, and it will be quite sufficient to glance at a few of their peculiarities. They are generally kept by an old prostitute, who gathers around her some of the most debased of her class, takes a cheap basement wherever she can obtain possession of one suited to her purpose, erects a small bar furnished with three or four bottles of the commonest liquor she can procure, partitions off one or two small hovels of bedrooms, and forthwith begins housekeeping. Her arrangements are about as extensive as her preparations. She seldom professes to board the girls, generally making a charge for every visitor they entertain, and giving them the privilege of cooking any thing they want. These dens are largely patronized by the vilest of the male sex; the petty thieves who hang around the public markets, stealing from the wagons, or who haunt the doors of grocery stores and abstract whatever they can reach; as they find them convenient places of concealment, and can frequently dispose of their booty by means of the women. Another class of visitors consists of the lowest order of rowdies, who assume a free license to perpetrate any mischief they please, because there is no one to interfere with them. A fatal case of this nature, which occurred but a few months since, will be fresh in the recollection of all citizens.

It is dangerous for a stranger to enter a place of this description, for if he does not get his pocket picked by the one, he will most probably be assaulted by the other class of visitors. Upon such establishments the police are compelled to keep a watchful eye, and although they have no power to enter them except some actual necessity calls for their services, yet they frequently induce a neighbor to make a complaint against the keepers for maintaining a disorderly house, and then, duly armed with a warrant, they enter, and arrest every one found on the premises. The *finale* of such an experiment at housekeeping as this is very frequently a commitment for vagrancy to Blackwell's Island. The character of the place will be a sufficient proof that syphilis abounds there, and its dangers must be added to those already enumerated.

The divisions thus made are presumed to be accurate as far as the distinctive characters of the various grades are concerned, but the lines of demarkation are of course arbitrary. Any attempt to classify so large a social evil must, from its very nature, be incomplete, and in this case farther experience or a more extended inquiry would very probably warrant an alteration in the arrangement. But there is another class of whom a few words must be said, namely, those truly wretched beings, the outcasts of the outcasts. In many cases destitute of home or shelter, diseased, starving, and afflicted with an insatiable thirst for ardent spirits, they present most ghastly and heart-rending spectacles, retaining scarcely any vestiges of humanity. These wretched beings can be found clustered round the bars of liquor-stores in low neighborhoods, begging for the price of a glass of gin. Much of their time is spent in the prisons on Blackwell's Island, from which they are no sooner released than they return to their old haunts and habits. They can scarcely be called prostitutes, for their aspect is so disgustingly hideous that all feminine characteristics are blotted out, and thoroughly sensual and animalized must he be who could accept their favors. They are, in every sense of the word, outcasts; compelled, for the short time they may be in the city—and this is seldom more than a few days at once—to eke out a wretched existence by stealing or begging; frequently so miserable that they gladly hail the day on which they are returned to prison. They present subjects for mournful consideration, and the reflection that they are experiencing the degradation to which every prostitute in the city is rapidly tending, should be a powerful argument in favor of any remedial measures which can be devised to ameliorate the condition of the frail women of New York, and prevent them from falling so far below humanity.

HOUSES OF ASSIGNATION.

Every resident of New York is aware of the existence of houses used especially as places for the meeting of the sexes with a view to illicit intercourse; but so carefully have all particulars respecting them been concealed from the public gaze, that very little more than this mere fact is generally known, particularly with reference to those of a higher grade. Secrecy is necessary to their continuance, and essential for the maintenance of the social position of their patrons.

The most exclusive are generally situated in the quietest and most respectable portion of the city. They are fitted up neatly, and even luxuriously, but without any extravagant or gaudy display. Their arrangements, of course, do not require reception or sitting rooms, and the whole care bestowed upon them is lavished on the bed-chambers, the appointments of which contain every possible comfort and convenience.

The keepers of this class of houses are generally very shrewd, quiet, cautious women, who never seek to penetrate into any engagements made by their visitors, who never know any person that enters their house, and from whom it is impossible to obtain information by any means. In fact, it has been said that the keepers and servants around these places have neither eyes, ears, nor tongues. Money is confessedly their object, and, as they receive liberal pay, self-interest dictates quietness, because if they adopted any other course, their houses would inevitably become known to the public, which would be an effectual barrier against visitors, and result in an entire loss of their customers. Consequently, if a liberal bribe could ever induce treachery, their shrewdness enables them to discern that such an act would at once and forever close their establishments.

It will be readily understood that, as the intrinsic value of these houses as places for meeting depends upon the secrecy and selectness with which they are operated, in order to carry out this principle fully, arrangements are made with much precision. Two parties are not allowed to meet casually in the halls or staircases. The keeper maintains a strict watch, in order that ingress and egress may be free and uninterrupted, and there can be little doubt that the desire to make money on her side, and the fascination of illicit passion on the part of her visitors, conjointly tend to insure more actual secrecy than could be obtained by any system of oaths or discipline. In some of the most exclusive, the system is carried to such an extreme that no accommodation will be afforded to parties unless the gentleman has been previously introduced to the proprietress, and his character for secrecy and integrity vouched for by some person with whom she is acquainted. This rule is adopted to prevent the possibility of the house becoming known as a place of assignation to any one who might use his knowledge to the prejudice of the keeper or her visitors.

No public women reside in these houses, nor would they be admitted under any pretext, as such a course would attract attention and defeat the purposes contemplated. Many of them are open for months without the knowledge of the neighbors or of the police of the district, as visitors very rarely enter or leave together, and to prevent any delay the outer door is generally kept unlocked, so that persons pass immediately into the hall, where a second door, with a bell attached, is generally found.

The business of these houses is done mainly during the promenade hours of Broadway, say from eleven or twelve to four or five o'clock. The visitors are confined to the upper walks of life, the men being of all sorts of business, and the women exclusively from our fashionable society. If the mysterious "personal" advertisements in the daily papers could be understood by the outside world, it would be seen that appointments are not unfrequently made through their agency. Arrangements for a meeting are generally made with the keepers in advance, and at the designated time the parties arrive from different directions and proceed direct to the room which has been already selected. If they wish it they can obtain wine or refreshments by ringing a bell in their apartment.

A majority of the females who visit these places can scarcely be called prostitutes, notwithstanding their undeniable fall from virtue. They sin but with one individual, and that, in many cases, from positive affection, and in others from the desire of sexual gratification. Whatever may be the motive, it does not concern the keeper of the house, whose only business is to receive the rent of her room, which ranges from two or three dollars upward to any amount that policy or the desire to insure secrecy may dictate. Doubtless very few of the visitors regard money in their negotiations. Females are very frequently closely veiled when they enter the house, so that their features can not be recognized, as has been illustrated in trials for divorce in this city, especially if the prior arrangements for the meeting have been made by the gentlemen. If, on the other hand, the lady takes the preliminary steps, she can scarcely be unknown to the proprietress, in whose keeping she consequently places her character.

The unsuspecting moral men of New York will scarcely credit these facts, but men of the world know that such meetings and places for meeting are not uncommon. It may be objected that the exposure of these mysteries imparts information which may lead the uninitiated into similar practices. It is believed that the information here given is not sufficiently definite for this end, and, certainly, nothing could be farther from the design of this work than to aid an immoral purpose. But it is a duty to record the general facts, in order that our citizens may be aware of the dangers that abound on every side; and particularly is it necessary because many of the female visitors are married women, who take advantage of the absence of their husbands at business.

A question will arise: " Who are the women that keep these houses?" That they can not have lived as common prostitutes, or been the keepers of houses of prostitution, is evident. In the first place, the acquaintances they would have made in either of those avocations would preclude the possibility of their maintaining the inviolable secrecy necessary in a house of assignation; and, again, no female would enter a place of this description, the keeper of which would be likely to betray her. It is apprehended that some of these houses originate in the following manner; in fact, we know of more than one that did commence so:

A female engaged in an intrigue which she can not carry out at her own residence, and desiring a place of security for her meetings, has an acquaintance with some shrewd woman, possibly one who works for her as seamstress, or in some other capacity, whom she makes partially a confidant. She tells her that she is desirous of seeing a gentleman, whom, for some particular reason, she can not invite to her house, and asks if she will accommodate her with a room in which the interview can take place. It is not likely that a person who felt under any obligation to her employer would refuse such a request, especially for so simple a purpose as a short conversation. The meeting accordingly takes place, and a handsome present is made her. It is frequently repeated, until she becomes suspicious, and finally satisfied that these interviews are for the purpose of sexual intercourse. By this time it has become a question of *policy* with her. She argues that if she refuses to extend any future accommodation she will lose not only a considerable income from the presents, but also all employment from the lady. She knows that by allowing such meetings she realizes considerably more than she can procure by her daily labor, and self-interest is generally strong enough to overcome her scruples. She goes on extending her accommodations, and enlarging the circle of her visitors, until she becomes mistress of a select house of assignation, which will be always liberally patronized so long as her power of maintaining the requisite secrecy remains unimpeached. Some of these women are from distant cities; entire strangers in New York, except to their immediate customers. If they are widows who have children, these are invariably educated away from home. From the privacy observed it is very difficult to estimate their receipts, which must be large. They sometimes degenerate into keepers of houses of public prostitution, and then become dangerous members of society, on account of the secrets which have been intrusted to them.

Probably some of our ultra-fashionable citizens might be enabled to give more particulars of these houses than are here collected. What has been stated is gathered from authentic sources, and may command implicit belief. Indeed, so trustworthy is the authority that it may be confidently asserted that even Fifth Avenue and Union Square are not exempt from these resorts.

Such houses must be regarded as the connecting link between the licentious excesses of the capitals of Europe and this city of the New World. They are dangerous from their secrecy and exclusiveness. As yet they are rare; and it speaks well for the morals of our upper classes that they are so. It shows that the majority of people in the higher walks of life are untainted. But the course of deterioration has commenced. Will not American good sense and American morality check this base imitation of a foreign custom?

The recently avowed sentiments, or rather the resuscitation of sentiments which were proclaimed years ago respecting the obligations of marriage and the theory of "free love," have doubtless increased the patrons of houses of assignation among our fashionable novel-reading people, or weak romantic heads made giddy by the sudden acquisition of wealth. For the last fifteen years a loose code of morals has been promulgated among us, the foreign apostles of which—many of them pretending to nobility, but being in truth mere adventurers—have visited us, and by them and through their influence many intrigues have originated. A spice

of romance in the American character has induced many to join
this movement in search of adventure, while a portion of our
female society are ardent admirers of every thing foreign, be it a
lord or a lace veil, and these delight in an intrigue because it is
an exotic.

The facilities of communication with Europe are now so great
that American travel on that continent is largely on the increase,
and perhaps there are at this time in the cities of continental
Europe more representatives of our society than of any other
nation.   Many of our people go there with the laudable desire to
improve their minds by general culture, or for the study of particular branches of science or art, but it is to be regretted that
some come back to our shores with ideas calculated to be any
thing but beneficial to their native country in a social or moral
point of view.   The sons of our staid and "solid men" go to the
capital of the French empire to study medicine.   Apart from the
impropriety of this course when there are the same facilities for
study here, where a few seconds of lightning intercourse will place
them in immediate communication with their friends, instead of
their being separated four thousand miles from parents and guardians, does the end justify the means?   What course do these
young men frequently pursue?   Unable to speak the language
intelligibly, they resort to the acquaintance of a *grisette*, in order
to study in her company.   The language they acquire by this
means is, at best, a vulgar *patois;* but they also obtain a knowledge of intrigue entirely incompatible with the simplicity and
purity of our republican institutions—a species of male and female
diplomacy foreign to the character of our people.

Young ladies, too, when they return from a foreign tour, are
more fascinated with the charms and successes of the favored mistress of some European prince or potentate than benefited by the
useful solid lessons of travel.   With them, as with the others, it
is all superficiality.   Superficial when they started, superficial
while traveling, they are still more superficial when they return.
There are always weak-minded people in this country who will
ape foreign manners, and to this cause must be assigned the
gradual approximation of our fashionable society to the vices of
the European capitals, their ladylike and gentlemanlike frailties,
their genteel peccadilloes and affectations.   The effects of foreign
travel upon such persons can not but be injurious.   It demands a
clear head and a sound heart to decide between the vicious fri-

volities and the positive good submitted to their notice, and with the class mentioned it requires but little judgment to know which will first attract them. They must see Lord A—— or Count B——, no matter what valuable opportunities for instruction they miss. They must become *au fait* in the observances of courts and the manners of courtiers, no matter what else they leave undone.

As remedial measures for another evil are elsewhere spoken of, this may be an appropriate place to suggest for profound consideration whether it would not be a wise policy to adopt some preventive system for this evil. We might establish a phrenological and psychological bureau, armed with full powers to examine all persons desiring to travel, so as to ascertain whether they may safely make the grand tour, and have sufficient strength of intellect and firmness of principle to resist the vitiating influences and examples which will surround them there, so that they may return only with a knowledge of the good and valuable lessons taught!

But the evils of foreign manners and customs are not imported solely by the traveling class of our own community. The political turmoils of Europe, in the last eight or ten years, have thrown among us numerous *refugees* who have been reared in the hot-beds of intrigue, and who, styling themselves *artistes*, depend upon our unexampled prosperity, the increase of our wealth, the improvement of our country, and our known predilections for foreigners, to enable them to make a living, and also to establish the same state of morals and manners existing in the cities whence they came. The United States are now the great harvest-field for art, which, with science, music, and poetry, aids to improve the mind. At the same time these bring with them an excessive devotion to fashion, both in dress and manners, as the low-necked dress and the lascivious waltz, which are so decidedly positive degenerations from our normal state that none but the most superficial will ever copy.

That we are rapidly introducing many of the most absurd follies and worst vices of Europe is a patent fact. Almost every one can specify acts now tolerated in respectable families which, so far from being permitted fifteen years ago, would have been thought by our plain common-sense parents amply sufficient to warrant the exclusion of the offender from the domestic circle; and it is an equally conspicuous fact that our social morality is deteriorating in a direct ratio to the introduction of these habits.

Every day makes the system of New York more like that of the most depraved capitals of continental Europe, and it remains for the good innate sense of the bulk of the American people to say how much farther we shall proceed in this frivolous, intriguing, and despicable manner of living; or whether they will not strive to perpetuate the stern morality of the Puritan fathers, our great moral safeguard so far, and thus put an effectual barrier against the inroads of a torrent which must undermine our whole social fabric, and finally crush us beneath the ruins.

The second class of assignation-houses are, to a great extent, private, but not so rigidly exclusive as the others. Their furniture is of the same luxurious style, but of a more gaudy character. Generally the same routine is observed in regard to entrance as in those of the first class. The principal portion of the females who resort to them are married women, most of whom are from the upper classes, whose sexual passions are not gratified elsewhere, or who resort to this means to obtain more money to expend in dress; kept mistresses, residing with their lovers as husband and wife in hotels or boarding-houses, whose attachment is not strong enough to keep them faithful to one man; occasionally the best class of serving-women, or shop-women, or females whose occupations, such as milliners, artificial florists, etc., lead them into contact with the fashionable classes. It is told on good authority that there are husbands cognizant of the fact that their wives visit such places, and who live wholly or in part upon money earned in this way. These cases are not supposed to be numerous, but it is to be hoped, for the credit of our national character, that the number will become still smaller. A few prostitutes of the upper grades sometimes visit this class of houses; they are known to the keeper, and she encourages them for the following reason: An habitué of the place will make an appointment to visit it at a specified time, and he tells the keeper he would wish to meet a female there. At the appointed day his wishes are gratified, the keeper having acted as negotiator with one of the girls mentioned. More wine is consumed in these houses than in the strictly select ones, probably from the different class who frequent them.

The third-class houses of assignation are not situated in such select parts of the city as are the other two classes. Some of them are managed with much privacy and seclusion, while others are simply houses of public prostitution on a large scale. Their principal female patrons are those prostitutes who have rebelled against the exorbitant charges made by keepers of fashionable houses, and shop-girls who resort to prostitution to augment their income. Many of these live some distance up town, and any one who is journeying downward in the after part of the day may see numbers of them going to these places in the cars and stages. This is another imitation of the French and English systems. Very little disguise is attempted about these third-class houses. Each has a parlor or reception-room, where a man can have a bottle of wine, and one or two of the girls named will join him. Of course many couples visit there, but a large number of men go alone, knowing that there are always women in the house. Fast young men about town are in the habit of keeping their mistresses at these houses, as more economical than boarding with them at hotels. Considerable disease is propagated in such places, a contingency from which the first and second classes are almost entirely exempt. Business is generally over here in three or four hours, commencing in the dusk of the evening; but it is unquestionably a source of considerable revenue to the keeper, particularly in those cases where she acts as procuress, since, in addition to the rent of the room which the man pays, she always receives a *present* from the woman.

There is another or fourth class of assignation-houses to which the commonest portion of street-walkers take their company, and these may be emphatically described by an old saying, "Cheap and nasty." Dirty and insufficient accommodations are the equivalents for low prices, and such places are, in the general estimation of connoiseurs, very *low* and despicable. Notwithstanding this they thrive and multiply, from which it may safely be inferred that they are profitable in a business point of view, repulsive as they may be in their features and arrangements. Some of them are ingeniously arranged with a view to robbery, and are called "panel-houses." The plan adopted is somewhat as follows: Some man, generally a countryman not very well informed in the tricks of the metropolis, meets with a prostitute, and agrees to accompany her to an assignation-house. She is in league with the "panel thieves," and therefore introduces her victim to one of their rooms. The apartment seldom contains more furniture than a bed and a chair or lounge, with the floor covered with a thick carpet. To make "assurance doubly sure," the man himself locks the door by which he enters, and, when undressing, naturally throws his clothes upon the chair or lounge. The bedstead is placed so that the feet come toward the only *apparent* door in the room, with one side against the wall, and the head and other side hung with curtains, which the woman carefully draws as soon as the man lies down by her side. At the head of the bed, and of course concealed by the drapery from any one occupying it, is another door, which forms the secret entrance. It is so adroitly arranged, and so neatly covered with paper the same as the walls, that no one would suspect its existence. The hinges and fastening on the outside are oiled, so that no noise can be perceived when it is opened, and the operator steals with cat-like step over the carpet, and quietly examines the clothes without alarming the unsuspecting stranger. The thief completes his inspection, appropriates as much as he thinks proper, and the temporary occupant of the apartment resumes his clothes and prepares to leave. If his suspicions are excited by the circumstance that his wallet looks less plethoric than it did, and an examination reveals that some of its contents are missing, he knows not how to account for it. He is perfectly certain that no one has entered that room while he was there, and if he has "visited" much before meeting the girl, he concludes that he must have lost some of his money in his career, and that the only way is to take the loss contentedly, and avoid New York fascinations in future. Sometimes the loser has not enough philosophy for this, and if he can be certain that his money was right when he entered the room, will call in the police, and thus expose the secret arrangements of the establishment. This is comparatively a rare case, as most men would rather submit to a pecuniary loss than encounter the trouble and exposure attending a criminal prosecution, and the knowledge of this reluctance enables the "panel thieves" to pursue their operations almost with impunity.

CHAPTER XXXVI.

NEW YORK.—EXTENT, EFFECTS, AND COST OF PROSTITUTION.

Number of Public Prostitutes.—Opinion of Chief of Police in 1856.—Effects on Prostitution of Commercial Panic of 1857.—Extravagant Surmises.—Police Investigation of May, 1858.—Private Prostitutes.—Aggregate Prostitution.—Visitors from the Suburbs of New York.—Strangers.—Proportion of Prostitutes to Population.—Syphilis.—Danger of Infection.—Increase of Venereal Disease.—Statistics of Cases treated in ISLAND HOSPITAL, BLACKWELL'S ISLAND.—Primary Syphilis and its Indications.—Cases of Venereal Disease in Public Institutions. —Alms-house. — Work-house. — Penitentiary. — Bellevue Hospital. — Nursery Hospital, Randall's Island.—Emigrants' Hospital, Ward's Island.—New York City Hospital.—Dispensaries.—Medical Colleges.—King's County Hospital.— Brooklyn City Hospital.—Seamen's Retreat, Staten Island.—Summary of Cases treated in Public Institutions.—Private Treatment.—Advertisers.—Patent Medicines.—Drug-stores.—Aggregate of Venereal Disease.—Probabilities of Infection.—Cost of Prostitution.—Capital invested in Houses of Prostitution and Assignation, Dancing-saloons, etc.—Income of Prostitutes.—Individual Expenses of Visitors.—Medical Expenses.—Vagrancy and Pauper Expenses.—Police and Judiciary Expenses.—Correspondence with leading Cities of the United States. —Estimated Prostitution throughout the Union.—Remarks on "Tait's *Prostitution in Edinburgh.*"—Unfounded Estimates.—National Statistics of Population, Births, Education, Occupation, Wages, Pauperism, Crime, Breweries and Distilleries, and Nativities.

THE preceding chapters have given a statistical and descriptive account of prostitution in New York. Before considering what measures can be best applied for the amelioration of its accompanying evils, it will be necessary to ascertain the extent of the system, and this inquiry must include the number of abandoned women in the city, and the amount of venereal infection propagated through their agency.

It has been assumed in these pages that the two thousand women whose replies form the basis of the statistical tables, represent about one third of the aggregate prostitution of New York. This is allowing an increase of twenty per cent. during the winter of 1857-8, in consequence of the commercial panic of last autumn, and the resulting paralysis of trade, and suffering of the laboring community.

In the progress of this investigation it was deemed advisable to consult those whose acquaintance with the details of city life would entitle their opinions to confidence, as to the actual number of prostitutes within our limits; and in addition to much information obtained privately, the following correspondence took place with the then Chief of Police:

(Copy.)

"Resident Physician's Office, Blackwell's Island,
New York, September 1, 1856.

"GEORGE W. MATSELL, Esq., Chief of Police:

"DEAR SIR, – During the last twenty years various estimates have been made by different persons, foreigners and natives, interested and not interested, as to the number of prostitutes in the city of New York. It is generally supposed that they reach the large number of twenty-five or thirty thousand. You, sir, have been at the head of the police department of the city for the past fifteen years, while previous to that time you acted, if I mistake not, as one of the police justices of the city. I presume, therefore, that you have a considerable knowledge of prostitution as it exists here, and consequently can give a very correct opinion as to the number of prostitutes in New York City.

"You will greatly oblige me if, at your earliest leisure, and in any form most convenient to yourself, you will state what you believe to be the total number of prostitutes now in the city.

"It is proper to add that, with your permission, I intend to publish this letter, with your answer, in the report on Prostitution which I am preparing, and shall soon have the honor to lay before the public.

"Yours respectfully,   WILLIAM W. SANGER,
"Resident Physician, Blackwell's Island."

(Reply.)

"Office of the Chief of Police, New York, Dec. 12, 1856.

"Doctor WILLIAM W. SANGER:

"DEAR SIR,—I received your letter asking me to express in writing my estimate of the whole number of known public prostitutes in the city of New York. In the absence of any law compelling the registering of public prostitutes, it would be very difficult to testify with accuracy to the exact number of such persons in the city. I have no hesitancy in stating that, in my opinion, they do not number over five thousand persons, if indeed they reach so high a figure. Having been engaged in public life for many years, my opinion is based on the observations made by me from time to time, and from various official reports made to me.

"You are at liberty to make such use of this answer to your interrogatory as you may deem proper.   Very respectfully yours,

"GEO. W. MATSELL, Chief of Police."

This communication, in addition to the facts gleaned from other sources, was amply sufficient to warrant the conclusion that the known public prostitutes in New York did not exceed five thousand in number at the close of the year 1856. Then ensued the summer, with its artificial inflation—that false prosperity which excites unbounded hopes and stimulates to measureless extravagance, followed by the revulsion and panic of the fall and winter. Trade was literally dead: operatives, never too well paid, were threatened with starvation; females, particularly, felt the rigid pressure of the times. In many families the embarrassments of the fathers compelled a reduction of the servants employed, and a large number of domestics were added to the aggregate of that class already out of situations. The occupations of the army of seamstresses, dress-makers, milliners, and tailoresses were suspended, and their struggles for bread were merged in the general cry for labor. It was, in short, a trying time alike for the sufferers and the observers. But one resort seemed available; the poor workless, houseless, foodless woman must have recourse to prostitution as a means of preserving life.

As usual in any time of great excitement, surmise ran actually wild as to the extent of the consequences, and extravagant theories abounded; one gentleman actually stating in a public meeting that a thousand virtuous girls were becoming prostitutes every week through sheer starvation! An assertion so appalling as this is its own refutation. It assumes that one woman in every hundred of the female population of New York City, between the ages of fifteen and thirty years, became a prostitute every week; and therefore, during the six months of fall and winter, twenty-six thousand women, one fourth of the inhabitants of the ages named, one in every four of all the women under middle age, would have been forced into vice! The practice of "jumping at conclusions" upon serious matters like this is much to be reprehended. An exaggerated statement made in the fervor of enthusiasm, while advocating a benevolent object, must always recoil to the injury of the cause it is intended to promote. It will be necessary only to consider for a moment the financial condition of New York to be convinced that such an increase of prostitution was impossible. It can not be denied that the number of abandoned women is regulated by the demand; or that the only inducement which could lead virtuous girls to the course alleged must have been the necessity to earn money for subsistence. But this necessity to earn money was felt as strongly by men as by women. The revulsion for a time left a large portion of the community without resources. Merchants, manufacturers, and store-

O o

keepers found their receipts inadequate to meet their expenditures. Commercial *employés*, book-keepers, clerks, salesmen, and agents were discharged. Mechanics in every branch were without work, and consequently without wages. Merchants from other parts of the country had no money to meet their liabilities or make fresh purchases, and therefore did not visit the city as usual. These causes combined to reduce the business of houses of prostitution, and instead of large accessions to the ranks of courtesans, many of this very class were forced to seek a refuge in the public charitable institutions. Hence arose the increase in the denizens of Blackwell's Island, where hospital, alms-house, work-house, and penitentiary were alike over-crowded. Some of the places vacated by these recipients of eleemosynary aid were doubtless filled by new recruits; but the supposition that a thousand were added every week would imply a change in the whole *corps* every six weeks, or a change nearly five times completed during the fall and winter.

That female virtue was yielded in many instances can not, unfortunately, be doubted, but the sufferers did not become public prostitutes. Poor creatures! they surrendered themselves unwillingly to some temporary acquaintance, probably in gratitude for assistance already rendered, or anticipating aid to be afforded. There is something truly melancholy in the consideration that bread had to be purchased at such a price; that the only alternative lay between voluntary dishonor and killing indigence. It is but charity to conclude that the woman who thus acted, if her subsequent course was not a continuous life of abandonment, was impelled by the stern necessity of the times rather than induced by a laxity of moral feeling. Unchaste as she must be admitted, she can scarcely be deemed a prostitute in the ordinary acceptation of the word.

It would be foolish to deny all increase of prostitution since the date of the correspondence just transcribed. The population of New York is now some thirty or forty thousand more than at that time, and female degradation has extended as a natural consequence. Relying upon the estimate of five thousand as correct at the time made, the subsequent augmentation of inhabitants would suppose an addition of about three hundred prostitutes, but to take the widest scope, and assume that the debasement required by hunger degenerated into a habit of confirmed vice, it may be admitted that the number of abandoned women in New York has increased from five thousand in 1856 to six thousand in 1858. This is a very liberal estimate, and the total assigned is certainly not too small. How much it may be in excess can not be said with precision, but in an argument of this nature it is safer to err in the direction of overstating an evil than to be lulled into false security by too flattering a representation.

The known public prostitutes of New York are thus presumed to amount to six thousand at the present day. But to this number exceptions might be taken. To secure farther accuracy, additional evidence was sought. In the month of May, 1858, the assistance of the Board of Metropolitan Police Commissioners was requested, and, under the direction of its president (General JAMES W. NYE), to whom our acknowledgments are respectfully tendered for his courtesy and aid, a list of queries was submitted to the Inspector of each Police precinct. Below is a copy of the circular, with a synopsis of the replies.

(Copy.)
" Office of the Metropolitan Police Commissioners, ⎱
New York, May 1, 1858. ⎰

" Inspector ———— ———— : — Police Precinct.

" SIR,—You will please report to this office as early as possible on the questions given below. Let your answers be full and explicit, to the best of your knowledge and belief. Space is left below each query for the insertion of your replies, and you will therefore write them on this sheet, and return it without delay.

" 1. How many houses of prostitution, from the most public to the most private, are there in your police district ?

" 2. How many houses of assignation are there in your district ?

" 3. How many dancing-saloons, liquor and lager-beer stores, are there in your district, where prostitutes are in the habit of assembling, in addition to the known houses of prostitution ?

" 4. How many prostitutes do you suppose reside in your district ?"

SYNOPSIS OF REPLIES.

Pre-cincts.	Reported by	Houses of Prostitution.	Houses of Assignation.	Dancing-saloons, Liquor or Lager-beer Stores, where Prostitutes assemble.	Estimated Number of Prostitutes.
1	Inspector James Silvey........	22	...	3	76
2	" Hart B. Weed......	1	...	1	2
3	" J. A. P. Hopkins..	9	...	...	26
4	" Morris De Camp ..	35	13	8	750
5	" Henry Hutchings..	63	7	46	420
6	Acting Inspector Lush	52	6	12	228
7	Inspector John Cameron.....	6	...	4	100
8	" C. S. Turnbull......	43	15	...	300
9	" Jacob L. Sebring..	...	...	...	50
10	" T. C. Davis	26	1	4	100
11	" Peter Squires.......	...	...	12	50
12	" Galen P. Porter ...	...	...	...	...
13	" Thomas Steers.....	15	4	8	150
14	" J. J. Williamson...	39	5	...	125
15	" G. W. Dilks	5	19	7	175
16	" Samuel Carpenter.	6	4	10	500
17	" J. W. Hartt.........	20	3	6	150
18	" Theron R. Bennett	1	...	3	250
19	" James Bryan	5	1	2	30
20	" F. M. Curry	15	1	5	250
21	" Francis Speight....	15	10	6	75
22	" James E. Coulter..	...	...	14	50
	Totals............	378	89	151	3857

Upon some of the reports are notes, which may be extracted.

Inspector Silvey, 1st district, says, in answer to question 4, "There are *to my knowledge* seventy-six common prostitutes living in this precinct."

Inspector De Camp, 4th district, says, in answer to question 4: "350 who reside in houses of prostitution, 150 kept mistresses, 150 who reside in the ward, and prostitute themselves in this and other wards, and probably 100 occasional prostitutes."

Inspector Hutchings, 5th district, in answer to question 3, classifies the resorts as

Dancing-rooms 2
Saloons and cigar-stores 31
Lager-beer-stores 13
                                        ——
                                        46

and, in answer to question 4, subdivides the prostitutes into

Whites 360
Blacks 60
                                      ——
                                      420

Acting Inspector Lush, 6th district, says, in answer to question 4: "One hundred and seventy-eight known prostitutes whose names we have; supposed to be *at least* fifty more residing in the district."

Inspector Cameron, 7th district, in answer to question 3, classifies the resorts into

Lager-beer-stores 3
Cigar-store 1
                                          ‾
                                          4

and, in answer to question 4, says: "Can give no reliable information; probably one hundred."

Inspector Sebring, 9th district, says, in answer to question 1, "This precinct does not contain any houses of prostitution that I am aware of;" and in reply to question 4: "Scattered through the precinct there are *probably* fifty."

Inspector Squires, 11th district, says, in answer to question 1: "None, properly speaking. There are many low drinking places where dissipated persons of both sexes often meet, and where, no doubt, prostitution is sometimes practiced, but no regular houses of that character." To question 3: "There are about a dozen lager-beer-saloons where Dutch girls of loose character assemble and dance at night. They do not remain long in the same place, but when driven from one place they locate in another." To question 4: "I presume there are fifty young women and married women, some of whom pass for respectable persons, who are in the habit of going across to the eighth, fifteenth, and other disreputable wards for purposes of prostitution, and some of the lowest of these are even said to visit the fifth ward, but I have never been able to ascertain this fact positively."

Inspector Porter, 12th district says, "This precinct, comprising all that portion of the island north of 86th street, is not infested with any of the evils enumerated in the within questions."

Inspector Williamson, 14th district, says, in answer to question 4, "I should *suppose* about 125."

Inspector Carpenter, 16th district, says, in answer to question 4, "It is generally conceded by those of us who presume to know that there are in this precinct at least five hundred prostitutes, of all ages, nations, grades, and colors."

Inspector Hartt, 17th district, says, in answer to question 4, "This being a hard question to answer, the answer must be taken as entirely guess-work: supposed to be about one hundred and fifty."

Inspector Curry, 20th district, says, in answer to question 4: "Probably two or three hundred, but this is mere guess-work. We know there are a great many; some of them very young."

Those reports from which no extracts have been made consist

simply of figures without any remarks, and are given fully in the synopsis. It will be observed that all the officers quoted give the number of prostitutes more as a conjecture than a certainty; and although their avocations would lead them to know most of the disreputable women in their several districts, none of them assume to be so thoroughly informed as to be enabled to answer positively. To the numbers they give must be added the floating prostitute population of station-houses, city and district prisons, hospitals, work-house, alms-house, and penitentiary, which varies from one thousand to two thousand, and may be taken at an average of one thousand five hundred. This, with those known to the police, makes a total of 5357, and the balance of six hundred and forty-three (643), required to raise the number to six thousand (6000), is but a moderate allowance for those who have escaped the eyes of the officers when taking the census. As before remarked, it is better to overestimate than underestimate the abandoned women of the city.

But to this number are to be added those whose calling is so effectually disguised as to prevent its being known—those who practice prostitution in addition to some legitimate occupation, and those who resort to illicit pleasures for the indulgence of their passions. To obtain information on these points some supplementary questions were addressed to the captains of police at the commencement of this investigation in 1856, and their replies are now submitted.

The first inquiry was, "How many houses of assignation are there in your district?" It was known when this interrogatory was propounded that the secrecy maintained in these places would in some instances baffle the keenness, not often at fault, of our shrewdest police officers, and no surprise was felt when their replies indicated that only seventy-four (74) of these houses were known to them. Reliable information from other sources led to the conviction that this was understated. The investigation of May, 1858, fixes the number at eighty-nine (89), which is also too low; and we shall be perfectly justified in estimating the number of houses of assignation in New York at one hundred (100).

The next question was, "What, to the best of your belief, are the average number of visitors to such houses every twenty-four hours?" The replies gave an average of six couples to each house every day, or an aggregate of six hundred women every twenty-four hours. This was followed by the query, "Are all the females who visit these houses of assignation known public prostitutes? If not, of what class do you suppose or know them to be?" From the replies it was found that about two fifths were known as prostitutes, the remainder being sewing or shop girls, kept mistresses, widows, and some married women.

Again: "State your opinion as to how many kept mistresses there are in your district?" In the twenty-two districts two hundred and sixty-eight (268) were ascertained, and the presumption was that there were more. The number may be safely taken at four hundred. The next question was, "How many women, to the best of your belief, and that you have not previously examined, are there in your district that obtain a livelihood in whole or in part by prostitution?" To this the numbers are stated (upon belief, for the nature of the question precludes any positive information) as about four hundred. "Can you form an opinion as to how many women in your district, who are not impelled by necessity, prostitute themselves to gratify their passions?" No definite answers were obtained to this, the general suppositions ranging from one third to one fourth of those who were not recognized as public prostitutes. "To what extent, in your opinion, is prostitution carried on in the tenant houses in your district?" It is generally admitted that there is some, but no calculation can be made with any accuracy. Many of what may be called private prostitutes live in this class of houses, but their visitors would be taken to houses of assignation, where the numbers are included in the estimate given. "It is believed that there are many women who follow prostitution living in nearly all the respectable portions of the city. They (singly or in couples) hire a suite of rooms, and under the garb of honest labor, sewing, etc., pass as respectable among those living near them. It is also known that such as these are the great frequenters of houses of assignation. How many such women (to the best of your belief) are there in your district?" The officers reply that they have ascertained that there are about two hundred, but they believe there are many more.

Thus much for the information we have been enabled to collect. There are six hundred women who visit these houses of assignation every day, of whom two fifths are known as public prostitutes, and the remainder are of other classes. It may be assumed that the known prostitutes visit such houses at least once every twenty-four hours, which leaves over three hundred visits daily for the others. Kept mistresses or married women who resort there for the gratification of their passions probably amount to one hundred per day. It can scarcely be supposed that such visit houses of assignation more than once a week as a general rule, while the others, sewing or shop girls, etc., who resort there to augment their income, would probably take this step two or three times per week, which would bring their number to about four hundred. It thus appears that a very fair estimate of the total number of frail women who are now in New York may be stated as follows:

Known public prostitutes 6000
Women who visit houses of assignation for sexual gratification . . 1260
Women who visit houses of assignation to augment their income　. 400
One half the number of kept mistresses, assuming the other half to
　be included in those who visit houses of assignation 200
　　　　　　　　　Total 7860

It will be seen that, to arrive at this conclusion, all are included who are suspected to be lost to virtue, although of the number who visit houses of assignation for sexual gratification many are guiltless of promiscuous intercourse.

This total number falls very far short of the estimates made at different times by various persons, that there are from twenty to thirty thousand prostitutes in New York City! Such rash conclusions, hastily formed in the excitement of the moment—sometimes influenced by the fact that "the wish is father to the thought"—must give place to the results of a careful and searching investigation made for this special purpose. The *modus operandi* of examination in the city rendered it incumbent on those having it in charge to approximate to the facts, and is itself a sufficient guarantee of correctness.[1]

If it were possible to parade the six thousand known public prostitutes in one procession, they would make a much larger demonstration than the mere printed words "six thousand" suggest to the reader. It requires a man who is in the habit of seeing large congregations of persons to comprehend at a glance the aggregate implied in this statement. Place this number of women in line, side by side, and if each was allowed only twenty-four inches of room, they would extend two miles and four hundred

---

[1] On a former page the results of a police investigation of the number of prostitutes in London in the year 1857 is given. It will be remembered that only 8600 common women were reported, in a population of nearly 2,500,000. The inquiries in New York and London would alike lead to the opinion that the extent of the vice is generally ovverrated.

and eighty yards. Let them march up Broadway in single file, and allow each woman thirty-six inches (and that is as little room as possible, considering the required space for locomotion), and they would reach from the City Hall to Fortieth Street. Or, let them all ride in the ordinary city stages, which carry twelve passengers each, and it would be necessary to charter five hundred omnibuses for their conveyance. These simple illustrations will make the extent of the vice plain to many who could form but an inadequate idea from the mere figures.

Yet the estimate will probably appear low to those residents of the city who have been accustomed to believe New York reeking with prostitution in every hole and corner, while it will seem excessively large to readers residing in the country. For the information of the latter it may be remarked, that vicious as Manhattan Island unquestionably is, much as there may be in it to need reform, in this matter of prostitution it must not bear all the blame of these six thousand women, for although they certainly reside in it, a very large number of their visitors do not dwell there. Brooklyn, the villages on Long Island, Fort Hamilton, New Utrecht, Flushing, and others; Jersey City, Hoboken, Hudson, Staten Island, Morrisania, Fordham, etc., contain numbers of people who transact their daily business in New York, but reside in those places. In very few of these localities are any prostitutes to be found, nor would they be encouraged therein while New York is so close at hand and so easy of access. Again, the strangers flocking into this city from all parts of the world average from five to twenty thousand and upward every day, and they must relieve it of some part of this obloquy.

The population of New York at the last census (1855) was officially stated to be (in round numbers) 630,000, and the proportionate increase for three years to the present time will bring it very near 700,000. If illicit intercourse here were carried on only by permanent residents, its proportion of public prostitutes would be one to every one hundred and seventeen (117) of the inhabitants; but the calculation must include the denizens of the places already enumerated, and, adding 500,000 for them and the number of strangers constantly visiting the city, we have a total of 1,200,000 persons; making the proportion of prostitutes only one in every two hundred, including men, women, and children. It is desirable, however, to ascertain what proportion courtesans bear to the classes who patronize them, and the census shows that males above the age of fifteen form about thirty-two per cent. of the population. A wider range might have been taken, as it is notorious that many boys under fifteen years old, especially among the lower classes, practice the vice; but assuming that to be the standard, there is one prostitute to every sixty-four adult males, certainly not a large proportion in a commercial and maritime city. It is impossible to form any idea of the proportion of male inhabitants and visitors who encourage houses of prostitution. Marriage is not always a check to indiscriminate intercourse, and professions of religion are often violated for illicit gratification. Still there are a vast number whom these obligations bind, and, if they could be exactly ascertained, this would make a corresponding difference in the proportions.

As the case now is, New York City stands somewhat in the position of a seduced woman, and has to endure all the odium attached to the number of prostitutes residing within her limits; while her neighbors and strangers who largely participate in the offense are like seducers, and escape all censure, self-righteously saying, "How virtuous is our town (or village) compared with that sink of iniquity, New York." It has been already stated what the effect would be if all visitors to New York were moral men, and, although the remark need not be repeated, its appositeness is apparent.

From the prostitutes within our borders emanates the plague of syphilis, and when the number of abandoned women is considered in conjunction with the certainty that each of them is liable at any moment to contract and extend the malady; when the probabilities of such extension are viewed in connection with the acknowledged fact that each prostitute in New York receives from one to ten visitors every day (instances are known where the maximum exceeds and sometimes doubles the highest number here given), there can be no reasonable doubt of the danger of infection, nor any surprise that the average life of prostitutes is only four years.

The actual extent of venereal disease must be the first point of inquiry, and here the records of public institutions are of great service. The hospitals on Blackwell's Island, under the charge of the Governors of the Alms-house, present the largest array of cases, the principal part of which were treated in the Penitentiary (now Island) Hospital. The number of these cases was in

| 1854 | . . . . . . | 1541 | 1856 | . . . . . . | 1639 |
| 1855 | . . . . . . | 1579 | 1857 | . . . . . . | 2090 |

Upon these facts the writer of these pages remarked in his annual report to the Board of Governors for 1856:

"The ratio of venereal disease on the gross number of patients treated in
1854 was . . . . $37\frac{4}{10}$ per cent.
The ratio of the same disease in 1855 was . . . . . $58\frac{7}{10}$ "
Showing an increase in the year 1855 of . . . . . . $21\frac{3}{10}$ "
The ratio of venereal disease on the gross number of patients
treated during 1856 was . . . . $73\frac{1}{10}$ "
Showing an increase in 1856, as compared with 1855, of . $14\frac{4}{10}$ "
Or an increase, as compared with 1854, of . . . . . $35\frac{7}{10}$ "

This steady increase, $21\frac{3}{10}$ per cent. in one year, and $14\frac{4}{10}$ per cent. in the next, or $35\frac{7}{10}$ per cent. within two years, may be considered an incontrovertible proof of the progress of this malady in the city of New York. The fact that the people regard the Penitentiary Hospital as a *dernier resort*, an institution to which nothing but the direst necessity will compel them to apply, justifies the conclusion that the cases treated are but a fraction of the disease existing, and its increase here may be taken as a sure indication of a corresponding or larger increase among the general population."[1]

Again, on the same subject in 1857:

"In my last report I took the opportunity to submit to your Honorable Board facts proving the increase of venereal disease, and I then gave the ratio of that malady on the gross number of patients treated as $73\frac{1}{10}$ per cent. In the year 1857 the ratio was $65\frac{2}{10}$ per cent.; but this reduction of $7\frac{9}{10}$ per cent. must be considered in connection with the fact that other diseases, much beyond the general average, have been treated in the last year, so that a larger number of venereal cases will yet show a smaller percentage. The cases of phthisis pulmonalis (consumption), which have advanced from 58 in 1856 to 159 in 1857, sufficiently explain that the decrease of venereal affections is apparent and not real."[2]

An investigation beyond the statistics upon which these remarks were based, and including the Penitentiary Hospital, Almshouse, Work-house and Penitentiary, had shown that of the total number admitted to these several institutions $59\frac{1}{2}$ per cent. had suffered or were suffering from venereal disease at the time the inquiry was made. Of this proportion 45 per cent. of the total were suffering *directly* at the time of investigation, and 19 per cent.

[1] Report of Resident Physician, Blackwell's Island, to the Governors of the Almshouse, New York, for 1856, p. 40. [2] Ibid., 1857, p. 26.

were suffering *indirectly*, or, in non-professional language, were laboring under diseases more or less consequent on the syphilitic taint.

The following detailed statistics of venereal disease treated in the Penitentiary Hospital for four years ending December 31, 1857, will be found to embrace many subjects which have been alluded to in these pages.

	1854	1855	1856	1857.
Total number of patients treated	4058	2657	2083	3158
Cases of primary syphilis	606	660	650	882
" of secondary and other forms of syphilis .	935	919	989	1208
Total of syphilitic diseases	1541	1579	1639	2090
NATIVITIES :				
Natives of United States	410	489	531	673
Foreigners	1131	1090	1108	1417
	1541	1579	1639	2090
AGES :				
Under 16 years	65	72	77	68
From 16 " to 20 years	481	457	472	593
" 21 " to 25 "	490	481	494	631
" 26 " to 30 "	314	304	311	423
" 31 " to 40 "	128	151	165	190
" 41 " to 50 "	42	99	101	157
" 51 " and upward	21	15	19	28
	1541	1579	1639	2090
EDUCATION :				
Good	175	227	231	175
Imperfect	787	794	830	1161
Uneducated	579	558	578	754
	1541	1579	1639	2090
From the total number of venereal patients under treatment	1541	1579	1639	2090
Deduct those discharged each year	1253	1316	1389	1710
Leaving to add to the next year's account . . .	288	263	250	380
Of the numbers discharged the following is the **RESULT OF TREATMENT :**				
Cured	874	1051	1201	1491
Relieved	370	263	183	213
Not relieved	7	...	...	1
Died	2	2	5	5
	1253	1316	1389	1710
DURATION OF TREATMENT :				
5 days and under	13	16	17	83
6 " to 10 days	57	36	68	102
11 " to 20 "	80	59	81	131
21 " to 30 "	154	121	137	187
1 month to 2 months	293	333	453	528

	1854.	1855.	1856.	1857
2 months to 3 months	304	443	340	328
3 " to 4 "	220	245	207	260
4 " and upward	132	63	86	91
	1253	1316	1389	1710

Some few remarks may be made on the subject of primary syphilis. The proportion of the cases of this malady to the gross number of patients treated was in

1854 . . . $14\frac{9}{10}$ per cent.	1856 . . . $31\frac{2}{10}$ per cent.
1855 . . . $25\frac{2}{10}$ "	1857 . . . $27\frac{9}{10}$ "

By the term "primary syphilis," non-professional readers will understand the commencement of the disease, or symptoms which are the direct consequence of an impure connection, in contradistinction to "secondary syphilis," which is the comparatively remote result of infection; never appearing until after the primary symptoms are well developed, and frequently not until all traces of them are removed. He will thus see that every case of primary syphilis is in itself a proof of recent intercourse with a diseased person. These cases, then, have increased from 15 per cent. in 1854 to $31\frac{1}{4}$ per cent. in 1856, and 28 per cent. in 1857. The remarks recently quoted explain how 882 cases in 1857 make a smaller percentage than 650 in 1856. The fact of this increase compels us to but one conclusion, and that is a very important and suggestive one, namely, that *commerce with prostitutes in* 1857 *was attended with nearly twice the risk of infection incurred in* 1854; *and, of course, the health of abandoned women has deteriorated in the same proportion.* This is not said with any wish on the part of the writer to be considered an alarmist. The facts are those which have come under his personal observation: the inference is but a plain and natural deduction.

But the Hospital, although the chief, is not the only institution on Blackwell's Island where patients are treated for venereal disease. The Alms-house, Work-house, and Penitentiary have each a share of sufferers from this malady, to what extent will be shown by the annexed table:

	1854.	1855.	1856.	1857.
Alms-house	33	173	85	52
Work-house	65	31	5	56
Penitentiary		176	234	430

Bellevue Hospital, New York City, also under charge of the Governors of the Alms-house, is not professedly available to venereal cases. By a report from the Medical Board of that institution, which will be found in the next chapter, it is seen that they estimate "not far from 10 per cent. of the inmates of Bellevue Hospital are admitted for affections which have their origin remotely in venereal disease." These data are sufficient to fix the numbers thus treated as follows:

Year.	Total number of patients.	10 per cent. for venereal cases.	Year.	Total number of patients.	10 per cent. for venereal cases.
1854	. . 7033	703	1856	. . 6392	639
1855	. . 6697	670	1857	. . 7676	768

In regard to the Nursery Hospital on Randall's Island, it is stated by Dr. H. N. Whittlesey, the Resident Physician, that "nine tenths of all diseases treated in this hospital during the past five years have been of constitutional origin, and for the most part hereditary. The exact proportion which hereditary syphilis bears to this sum of constitutional depravity can not be stated with accuracy." It is an estimate far within the bounds of probability to assume that one half of the diseases referred to by Dr. Whittlesey are complicated with or by syphilitic taint, and the numbers in the Nursery Hospital will therefore stand as follows:

Year.	Total number of patients.	50 per cent. for venereal cases.	Year.	Total number of patients.	50 per cent. for venereal cases.
1854	. . 2199	1100	1856	. . 1275	638
1855	. . 2310	1155	1857	. . 1469	734

Following the institutions in charge of the Governors of the Alms-house is the New York State Emigrants' Hospital on Ward's Island, New York City, under the direction of the Commissioners of Emigration, in the reports whereof the following cases of venereal disease are noted:

1853	 657		1856	 511
1854	 732		1857	 559
1855	 856			

The New York Hospital, Broadway, next claims attention. The reports for the under-mentioned years give the number of venereal cases as follows:

1852	 478		1856	 372
1853	 338		1857	 405

These embrace the principal public hospitals of New York. There are other institutions, such as St. Luke's Hospital, St. Vincent's Hospital, the Jews' Hospital, etc., but they are of recent origin, and their practice will not form an element in this calculation.

The dispensaries of the city relieve yearly a large amount of sickness. In the New York Dispensary, Centre Street, the cases of venereal disease are reported as follows:

1855 1154
1856 1393
1857 1580

This gives an average of about three per cent. of all the patients treated.

The Northern Dispensary, Waverley Place, does not publish any detailed report of the diseases treated, and to make an estimate it will be necessary to assume that the proportion is the same as in the New York Dispensary, namely, three per cent By this rule the following results are obtained:

Year.	Total number of patients.	3 per cent. for ven. cases.	Year.	Total number of patients.	3 per cent. for ven. cases.
1850	19,615	588	1855	12,378	371
1851	20,680	620	1856	11,797	354
1852	21,941	658	1857	10,895	327
1854	14,075	422			

The Eastern Dispensary, Ludlow Street, does not give any detailed report of the diseases treated, and the same approximation will be made as previously:

Year.	Total number of patients.	3 per cent. for ven. cases.
1855	25,612	768
1856	21,017	630

To the Demilt Dispensary, Second Avenue, the same system of approximation will be applied:

Year.	Total number of patients.	3 per cent. for ven. cases.	Year.	Total number of patients.	3 per cent. for ven. cases.
1852–3	2,197	66	1855–6	20,004	600
1853–4	9,006	270	1856–7	20,684	620
1854–5	14,034	421	1857–8	26,785	803

The Northwestern Dispensary, Eighth Avenue, subjected to the same rule gives

Year.	Total number of patients.	3 per cent. for ven. cases.
1854	9,264	277
1855	11,581	347
1856	11,477	344

Cases of venereal disease are treated in the Clinical Lectures at the three medical colleges of New York City. From the New York University Medical College the following report of patients has been obtained. It is undoubtedly much too low an estimate.

1855 47
1856 53
1857 69

and assuming that the practice of the others is of the same extent, we have as the venereal cases treated in the three colleges:

1855 141
1856 159
1857 207

As many of the patrons of New York houses of ill fame reside out of the city, some further information must be sought beyond our own limits. Without professing to inquire into the public health in all the suburbs previously enumerated, it will be sufficient to take the reports of the superintendents of the poor of King's County to ascertain what amount of syphilitic infection has been treated at the public cost in Brooklyn and its environs. The reports of Doctor Thomas Turner, Resident Physician of the King's County Hospital, show the following cases:

1853 165
1855 362
1857 311

or about ten per cent. on the total number treated.

In the Brooklyn City Hospital the cases of venereal disease received and treated were in

1854	 158	1857 186
1855	 173	1858 (to May 1) . . 65
1856	 160	

It has been already stated that sailors are great patrons of prostitutes, and to obtain any true statement of venereal disease among them, some estimate respecting this class must be made. For this purpose the reports of Dr. T. Clarkson Moffatt, Physician-in-chief of the "Seaman's Retreat," Staten Island, New York, are available. The number of cases treated in the several years is here given:

1854	 657	1857 365
1855	 473	1858 (to April 1). · 82
1856	 355	

This is nearly twenty-four per cent. on the gross number treated.

This concludes the published reports of charitable institutions, and the question next arises, What amount of syphilis is treated by physicians in private practice? It is impossible to obtain any reliable data upon this head. The Medical Board of Bellevue Hospital, composed of some of the leading members of the profession in the city, state that they "are unable to say what proportion of the practice among regular and qualified physicians in this city is derived from the treatment of venereal diseases, but they know it is large, and that many receive more from this source than from all other sources together."

There are also a very large number of advertising pretenders who offer their services for the treatment of secret diseases; and many drug-stores whose main business is derived from a similar source; together with an infinity of patent medicines announced and sold as specifics for all venereal maladies. Upon the simple commercial principle of supply and demand these are so many proofs of the extent of the evil they profess to relieve. Should the number of cases of venereal disease treated in private practice by qualified physicians and by advertisers, added to the number of patients who supply themselves with patent or other medicines from drug-stores, be regarded as equal to the aggregate of those treated in public institutions, the estimate could not be deemed extravagant.

The design is now to ascertain how much venereal disease exists in New York at the present time, and to do this it will be necessary to recapitulate the information already given. The cases below are those treated in 1857:

Institutions.	Cases.
Penitentiary Hospital, Blackwell's Island	2090
Alms-house, Blackwell's Island	52
Work-house, Blackwell's Island	56
Penitentiary, Blackwell's Island	430
Bellevue Hospital, New York	768
Nursery Hospital, Randall's Island	734
New York State Emigrants' Hospital, Ward's Island	559
New York Hospital, Broadway	405
New York Dispensary, Centre Street	1580
Northern Dispensary, Waverley Place	327
Eastern Dispensary, Ludlow Street	630
Demilt Dispensary, Second Avenue	803
Northwestern Dispensary, Eighth Avenue	344
Medical Colleges	207
King's County Hospital, Flatbush, Long Island	311
Brooklyn City Hospital, Brooklyn, Long Island	186
Seaman's Retreat, Staten Island	365
Total	9847

Medical men, and those acquainted with the internal arrangements of public institutions, need not be reminded that the general system of record in hospitals includes only what may be called the prominent malady. Thus, if a man were admitted with a broken limb, it would be registered as a fracture; and if the same man were suffering indirectly from syphilis at the same time, no entry would be made thereof, although the physician rendered him every professional assistance toward its cure. It is

P P

estimated that in this manner a large number of the cases of venereal disease treated in all public institutions, except such as make a specialty of those maladies, is never recorded elsewhere than on the private case-books of the attending physicians.   More particularly is this the rule in institutions supported wholly or in part by voluntary contributions.   Their benevolent directors have not yet outlived the prejudice which formerly held it almost as disgraceful to treat as to contract syphilis.   Some of the spirit which drove the unhappy men and women so afflicted from civilized life to perish in the fields or woods, as in London, Edinburgh, and Paris, during the fifteenth and sixteenth centuries, and at a later period drew from the Papal government a bull recognizing the affliction as a direct punishment from the Almighty for the sin of incontinence, still survives in the present generation.   The trustees of more than one of the dispensaries in New York have directed their medical officers not to prescribe for such complaints, and a hospital in a sister city, which receives a yearly grant from public funds, has in its printed rules and regulations : " No person having ' Gonorrhœa' or ' Syphilis' shall be admitted as a charity patient."   Some remarks are made hereafter upon this course, and the facts are mentioned now to explain why many cases of venereal disease never appear upon the reports of institutions where patients are treated.

Practically such prohibitions are a dead letter.   No physician of a public institution, applied to by a poor wretch suffering from syphilis, could pass him by without attempting to relieve, let the orders of the board of trustees be what they may.   His mission is simply to apply the aid of science and skill to the alleviation of any ailment which may be presented to his notice, and his appreciation of the responsibility of his office is too keen to allow him to refuse the prayer of such an applicant.   Hence arises the circumstance that the case is treated under some other name.

If then the cases recorded are but two thirds of the aggregate, the numbers stand thus :

Cases recorded in public institutions . . .	9847
Cases not recorded	4923
Total . ·	14770

cases in the year 1857 in public institutions.

The difficulty of forming an opinion as to the extent of venereal disease treated in private practice has been already mentioned.   In the absence of all information, collateral circumstances form the only guide to a conclusion. The amount is unquestionably very large; so large that, if its full magnitude could be discovered and announced, every reader must be astonished. The first consideration to support this view may be found in the army of advertising empirics who make it a source of revenue. Each of these men must have numerous patients; he could not keep up his business without them. Any practical advertiser knows that to insert an announcement of some twenty or thirty lines every day in at least two daily papers, to repeat the same in weekly journals, and, in addition to this, to post handbills on the corner of every street, and employ men or boys to deliver them to passengers at steam-boat docks, ferry landings, and rail-road depôts, can not be done without a considerable outlay, whatever its prospective advantages may be. No one supposes these charlatans to be actuated by pure disinterested benevolence. They crowd the columns of our journals, and insult us with their printed announcements in the public thoroughfares, simply because "it pays." These means obtain them customers, and whenever this result ceases the announcements will be discontinued. While they appear there is positive proof that their issuers are gathering patronage.

The number of patent medicines always in the market for the cure of secret diseases, and which the vendors announce "can be sent any distance securely packed, and safe from observation," affords a corroboration. They are made and sold as a business speculation. When their reputation diminishes, and the public become doubtful if all the virtues of the *materia medica* are comprised in a single bottle of "Red Drop," or "Unfortunate's Friend," the manufacture will soon stop, and the inventors will resort to some other employment for their capital. The extent to which advertising empirics and patent medicines are flourishing is an undeniable proof of the prevalence of the maladies they professedly relieve.

The legitimate business of drug-stores affords another link in the chain of evidence. Beyond the regular nostrums, almost every druggist in the city sells large quantities of medicine for the cure of venereal disease. Sometimes a man will candidly tell the storekeeper that he has contracted disease, and ask him to make up something to cure it. At other times a prescription, which has been efficacious in a former attack, will be presented, or the sufferer has taken counsel among his friends and companions, and obtained some infallible recipe from one of them. In short, there are so many different means taken by persons who have contracted disease that it is impossible to enumerate the various methods in which the aid of the drug-store may be invoked.

There are many traditional recipes which can be used withouf the necessity of purchasing ingredients of a druggist. One favorite remedy among the lower classes is "Pine Knot Bitters." Bottles of this preparation are kept for sale in liquor stores, particu larly in those neighborhoods where prostitutes "most do congregate."

Another reason may be submitted why a large amount of venereal disease must be treated privately. Many of the victims are men who move in a respectable sphere of society, and have probably been led to the act which resulted so disastrously in a moment of uncontrollable passion. Their social position would be irreparably damaged should they enter a public hospital, and the desire to retain their *status* forces them to secrecy, even if the natural repugnance of every man to the former course did not exist. It is vain to deny that, while medical institutions designed for the public good are so managed as to inflict a disgrace upon their inmates, their benefits are circumscribed, and will never be accepted by any but the poor unfortunates who have no other means of obtaining relief. In the case of syphilis this is particularly to be regretted from the nature of the disease. Every day it is neglected it becomes in a tenfold degree more aggravated, and entails proportionate misery in after life.

If it be assumed that the private cases of venereal disease equal in number those treated in public institutions, an aggregate is obtained of more than 29,500 cases every year. If the former are double the number of the latter, the sum will be over 44,000 cases per annum. Either of these conjectures is below the truth, and we are satisfied, from professional experience and inquiry, that there is no exaggeration in estimating the number of patients treated privately every year for *lues venerea* as at least quadruple the cases receiving assistance in hospitals and charitable establishments. *The result is the enormous sum of seventy-four thousand cases every year!* If each person suffered only one attack each year, this would represent one sixth of the total population above fifteen years of age. But many persons, especially among abandoned women and profligate men, are infected several times in the course of twelve months, and any attempt to say what proportion of individuals are represented in these 74,000 cases would be mere speculation without a particle of conclusive evidence to support it.

Notwithstanding the magnitude of the result, a very brief consideration will show that it is not extravagant. In addition to the arguments already advanced in this chapter, the reader will recollect that in a previous section it has been shown that two out of every five prostitutes in New York *confessed the syphilitic taint*. Supposing a girl relinquishes her calling as soon as she becomes aware of being diseased, several days may have elapsed before she discovered her condition, and during that interval she must have infected every man who had intercourse with her. To take the most liberal view, it may be conceded that the portion who acknowledged infection were not all suffering from the primary or communicable form; many of them had doubtless recovered from that; but if only one half were so suffering, and each of these infected only one man, the result would be 365,000 men diseased every year.

This is not an exaggerated estimate. As was said when alluding to the prostitutes who admitted their contamination, there can be no possible suspicion that they would acknowledge sickness if they could avoid doing so, and consequently the sick are certainly not overrated. It may be objected that the numbers who owned disease were spread over a considerable space of time, but this can be met with the fact that the inquiry which produced this result was in progress simultaneously in all parts of the city. At the farthest it did not extend three months from the time of commencement to completion, and the natural presumption would be that, as during that time the health of the women was neither better nor worse than in any other three months of any year, the same proportion of diseased women could be found whenever an investigation was made; in other words, that two out of five prostitutes in New York are diseased.

The calculation that of these diseased women one half only are affected in a manner which renders them liable to infect their paramours is also a liberal one. Syphilis, when manifested in its secondary stage in the shape of sores, eruptions, and blotches upon the face or person, is so disgusting that no prostitute thus disfigured could retain her place in any brothel, unless it was one of the very lowest grade, because her appearance would immediately repel all visitors. In its primary or local form it is of course concealed from her customers, and may be so concealed for a considerable length of time. These facts borne in mind, is it not almost too liberal an estimate to assume that one half who admit syphilis are suffering in the secondary or palpable form?

This line of argument, supported by the facts given, is perfectly justifiable, view it in what light you may, and proves that the estimate of 74,000 cases of venereal disease annually is much too small.

Another course of reasoning may be adopted. The time occupied in taking the census is stated at three months. This included all the needful preliminary measures, the instructions to examiners, the conferences with police captains, etc; and the final proceedings, such as arranging and writing out reports. Allow one third of the time for these introductory and concluding adjuncts, and it will leave about sixty days, including Sundays, or fifty-two working days devoted to the actual inquiry. The inquiry resulted in the discovery of syphilis in such a proportion of women as would amount to an aggregate of two thousand on the total number of public prostitutes. Suppose the disease of two thousand women equally distributed over the fifty-two days; or, in other words, that an average number were infected and confessed it every day, and the result is thirty-eight women diseased every twenty-four hours. We wish to make this argument as plain as possible, and the reader will pardon what may appear needless repetition. If this disease existed in each woman for four days before she was conscious of it, or it became so troublesome as to force her from her calling, and during this interval of four days each woman had intercourse with only one man per day, over fifty thousand men would be exposed to the risk, almost the certainty of contracting infection in the course of the year. As the *Medico-Chirurgical Review* said, in the course of a similar argument upon syphilis in London, this estimate is "ridiculously small." In the first place, a majority of the women would not abandon their calling in four days after infection, but would continue it as long as they could possibly submit to the suffering involved. Every resident of New York will remember the excitement caused in the spring of the year 1855 by the arrest of a large number of prostitutes in the public streets, their committal to Blackwell's Island, and their subsequent discharge on writs of *habeas corpus*, on account of informality in the proceedings; but it is not generally known that of those arrested at that time a very large proportion, certainly more than one half, were suffering from syphilis in its primary form, and many of them in its most inveterate stage. We make this assertion from our own knowledge, the result of a professional examination, and mention the circumstance now to prove that women will not abandon their calling when they know themselves diseased, so long as they can possibly continue it. If the estimate had been made that each woman continued prostitution for eight days instead of four days after she was infected, it would have been a closer approximation to the truth, and it would have shown over *one hundred thousand* (100,000) men exposed to infection every year.

Again : The supposition that a prostitute submits to but one act of prostitution every day is "ridiculously small." No woman could pay her board, dress, and live in the expensive manner common among the class upon the money she would receive from one visitor daily; even two visitors is a very low estimate, and four is very far from an unreasonably large one.

But suppositions might be multiplied, and the argument extended almost *ad infinitum.* One more calculation shall be submitted, and then the reader can form his own conclusion upon the question whether the theory of seventy-four thousand cases of venereal disease in New York every year has not been supported by a mass of evidence far more weighty than can ordinarily be adduced to establish a controverted point.

It shall be assumed that the thirty-eight women infected every day continue their calling for six days after the appearance of venereal disease, and during such six days one half of them shall submit to one, and the other half to two sexual acts daily. Then, in the course of a year, one hundred and twenty-five thousand men would be exposed to contamination. To this add the number of women infected, which, at thirty-eight daily, would amount to nearly thirteen thousand in the year, and a total of one hundred and thirty-eight thousand will be presented, or nearly double the number assumed as a basis for remark. It is needless to advance farther reasons in support of the soundness of that opinion.

Next in order will be the consideration of the amount of money prostitution costs the public. The amount of capital invested in houses of ill fame, and the outlay consequent thereupon presents a total which can not but surprise all who have not deeply re-

flected upon the ramifications of the evil. The police investigation of May, 1858, quoted a few pages back, gives the total number of houses of prostitution as 378, and the worth of property
thus employed can be ascertained with a tolerable degree of accuracy from information obtained, in many cases, by actual inquiry.
The value of real estate where it was owned by the keepers of
these houses has been already given in some instances, and in
others the rent may be assumed equivalent to ten per cent. per
annum upon the cost of the property, which is certainly not an
undue valuation. Dividing the total number of houses into four
classes the estimate stands as follows:

80 houses of the first class are estimated, from actual inquiry,
   to be worth, including real estate and furniture, $13,800
   each, or a total of $1,104,000
100 houses of the second class are estimated at twenty-five per
   cent. less than those of the first class, namely, $10,350 for
   each, or a total of 1,035,000
120 houses of the third class at $5000 each 600,000
78 houses of the fourth class at $1000 each 78,000
378 houses of prostitution are estimated worth $2,817,000
   Add for houses of assignation :
25 houses of the first class at $12,000 each 300,000
25   "   second   "   9,000   " 225.000
35   "   third   "   5,000   " 175,000
15   "   fourth   "   3,000   " 45,000
100   Total for houses of prostitution and assignation . . . $3,562,000
In addition to this are 151 dancing-saloons, liquor and lager-
   beer stores, mainly dependent upon the custom of prostitutes and their companions. Any place in which it is possible to carry on either of these businesses must be worth
   $200 a year rent, which would give a value of $2000 each,
   or a total of 302,000
The necessary stock, fixtures, and implements can not be
   worth less, on an average, than $100 in each place: this
   gives a total of 15,100
and an aggregate capital of $3,879,100

invested in the business of prostitution. That this is not an extravagant estimate will be admitted by any real estate owner or
person acquainted with the value of property in the city ; espe
cially if he takes into consideration the location of many of the
houses, and calculates how much more the adjacent lands and
buildings would be worth if these resorts of vice and infamy were
removed.

On a scale correspondingly large is the amount of money actually spent upon prostitutes. The weekly income of each woman

can not be less than ten dollars. Many pay much more than that sum for their board alone, and in first-class houses it is not uncommon for a prostitute to realize as much as thirty or fifty dollars, or upward, in a week. But if the income is taken at the lowest point, the aggregate receipts of six thousand courtesans amount to $60,000 per week, or $3,120,000 per year.

Every visitor to a house of prostitution expends more or less money for wines and liquors therein. In some cases this outlay will be larger than the cash remuneration given to the women, but other men are not so lavish in their hospitality; and it is fair to assume that such expenditures amount to two thirds of the previous item—a weekly total of $40,000, or $2,080,000 spent for intoxicating drinks in houses of prostitution every year.

In describing the customers of houses of assignation, it has already been remarked that in the first class many of the female visitors take that step, not for gain, but impelled by affection or sexual desire. They would spurn the idea of being paid for their company; but the houses at which their intrigues are consummated being luxuriously furnished, and conducted by women of known discretion and secrecy, have a high tariff of prices as one of their features. Visitors must pay as much there for accommodation as the rent of a room and compensation to a female would amount to in places of less pretension. It is assumed that 4200 visits are paid to houses of assignation every week, and for the foregoing reason estimating them to cost the men the same in every instance, and fixing that cost at three dollars for each visit, this item will amount to $12,600 per week, or $655,200 per year.

The consumption of wine and liquor is small in houses of assignation, as compared with houses of prostitution. It may probably amount to $5000 per week, or $260,000 per year.

The income of the dancing-saloons, liquor, and lager-beer stores, frequented and mainly supported by prostitutes and their friends, can not be less than $30 per week for each house, and as there are 151 establishments of that description, the aggregate of money disbursed in them will be $4530 per week, or $235,560 per year.

These sums exhibit the outlay for the pleasures of prostitution: the ensuing items give its penalties. Of the inmates of the Island (late the Penitentiary) Hospital, in 1857, over 65 per cent. were afflicted with venereal disease. The total expense of that institution for the year was $35,000, and the *pro rata* amount for syphilitic patients would be $22,750 during the year, or $438 per week.

Bellevue Hospital cost to maintain it during 1857, $70,000 in round numbers. The Medical Board say that ten per cent. of its inmates are treated for diseases originating in the syphilitic taint, and this proportion of the expenses being chargeable to prostitution amounts to $7000 per year, or $135 per week.

The Nursery Hospital on Randall's Island cost the city of New York $17,000 for maintenance during 1857. One half its infant patients are treated for diseases resulting from venereal infection, and $8,500 per year, or $163 per week, is the quota of expense caused by this vice and its sequel.

The number of cases of venereal disease treated in the New York State Emigrants' Hospital on Ward's Island was 6½ per cent. of the total relieved on that island. The expenses for 1857 were $109,000, and the share chargeable to prostitution will be $7075 per year, or $136 per week.

In the New York City Hospital, Broadway, 14 per cent. of the patients during 1857 were treated for venereal disease. The cost of maintenance for that year was $59,000, and the share caused by prostitution was $8260 per year, or $159 per week.

The cases treated in dispensary practice have been averaged at three per cent. throughout the city. The yearly expenses of those charities are as follows:

New York Dispensary	. . $9100	Demilt Dispensary . . .	$5300
Northern Dispensary	. . 3550	Northwestern Dispensary .	2630
Eastern Dispensary .	. . 3700	Total	$24,280

and the proportion chargeable to syphilis must be $728 per year, or $14 per week.

Very little expense is incurred by the medical colleges in the cases of syphilis treated at their clinical lectures, as the relief is generally confined to a prescription or a slight operation, and if medicine is supplied in a few cases the amount is so small that in a calculation of this sort it is not worth notice.

The expenses of the King's County Hospital, Long Island, for 1857, amounted to $75,300. About ten per cent. of the patients treated were venereal sufferers, and the cost for them amounts to $7530 per year, or $145 per week.

In the Brooklyn City Hospital the proportion of venereal patients is twenty-seven per cent. of the aggregate. The total annual expenses are $17,200, and the amount incurred on account of this disease is therefore $4644 per year, or $89 per week.

In the Seaman's Retreat, Staten Island, New York, twenty-four

per cent. of the inmates suffer from venereal disease. The expenses during the year 1857 were $43,500, of which $10,540 per
year, or $203 per week, must be considered the proportion ren-
dered necessary by syphilis.

To ascertain the amount expended for private medical assistance it will be necessary to recapitulate the outlay of the public
institutions mentioned.

Institutions.	Yearly Outlay.	Weekly Outlay.
Island Hospital, Blackwell's Island . . .	$22750	$438
Bellevue Hospital, New York	7000	135
Nursery Hospital, Randall's Island . . .	8500	163
Emigrants' Hospital, Ward's Island . .	7075	136
City Hospital, New York	8260	159
Dispensaries	728	14
King's County Hospital, Long Island . .	7530	145
Brooklyn City Hospital, Long Island . .	4644	89
Seaman's Retreat, Staten Island	10540	203
Total	77027	1482

These totals must be multiplied by four, and the product will
show the amount paid for private medical assistance as $5928
weekly, or $308,108 yearly. This is calculated on too liberal a
scale, for no one believes that an individual requiring professional
aid can obtain it so economically in private life as in a public institution; nor would even the fact that in the latter case the patients
are boarded and supplied with all necessaries more than counter-
balance the sums which must be paid for individual medical attendance. The desire not needlessly to exaggerate facts which
are sufficiently comprehensive without such a procedure is the
only reason that induces so low an estimate.

But there are yet other items of expenditure which must be
noticed before the long array is completed. Foremost of these is
the cost for support of abandoned women in the Work-house and
Penitentiary on Blackwell's Island. The proportion of females
committed to the Work-house during 1857 was three fifths of the
total commitments. It is not asserted that all these were prostitutes, but it is certain that the larger part were unchaste, and for
argument's sake we will take the ratio as two abandoned to one
virtuous woman, the latter representing the class whom poverty,
sickness, or friendlessness may have driven to accept a shelter in
the institution. The expenses of the Work-house for the year
amounted to $76,000, and the share of cost incurred on behalf of
prostitutes would therefore be $30,400 per year, or $585 per
week.

The females sentenced to the Penitentiary from courts of criminal jurisdiction during 1857 amount to twenty-seven per cent. of the total number incarcerated. It will violate no probability to assume that all these women were prostitutes; there may be exceptions to the rule, but so rare are they as not to invalidate the principle. The Penitentiary was supported during 1857 at an outlay to the tax-payers of nearly $89,000, and the proportion chargeable to prostitutes, at the ratio given above, is $24,030 per year, or $462 per week.

A farther portion of the expenses of the Work-house and Penitentiary might very plausibly be included in the list; namely, the share incurred by the maintenance of those men who owe their imprisonment either to crimes committed at the instigation of common women, or for the sake of supporting them; or to a course of idleness and dissipation resulting from the companionship of prostitutes. To pursue this subject in all its *minutiæ* would lead to the conclusion that nearly every male prisoner owes his confinement, less or more remotely, to one or the other of these causes, and hence it could be argued that all the expenses of male imprisonment should be taken into this account. On the other hand, such a course could be opposed with the plea that crimes which send men to Blackwell's Island are only indirect results of the system under discussion, and to recognize them would force the recognition of many other indirect consequences daily occurring elsewhere. Strictly speaking, the position is scarcely demonstrable enough to form an arithmetical calculation, but its moral certainty is so far acknowledged as to make it a serious matter of reflection in connection with the attendant evils of prostitution.

To resume: About fifty-five per cent. of the population of the Alms-houses, Blackwell's Island, are females. Some of these are old decrepit women whom it would be impossible to consider as prostitutes; others are virtuous women whose poverty has driven them there; but many are broken down prostitutes who have lost whatever of attraction they once possessed, and with ruined health and debilitated constitutions it is impossible for them to exist even in the lowest brothels. They make the Alms-house their last resting-place, and there await the final summons which shall close their career of sin and misery. Yet another class in this institution is composed of women with young children. Some claim to be respectable married women, while others are known as disreputable characters; but the former have little to support their pretensions except their own assertion, and collateral testimony sometimes invalidates that. It is not an uncharitable conclusion, that at least one half of the female inmates of the Alms-house owe their dependence upon charity to their own prostitution. The support of the Alms-house in 1857 cost the city of New York $63,000, and the proportion resulting from prostitution, on the above data, is $15,750 per year, or $303 per week.

The children on Randall's Island may be classified according to the rule already adopted in reference to disease in the nursery hospital there; namely, to assume that one half owe, if not their existence, certainly their support from public funds to causes that originated in vice. The nursery, exclusive of the hospital, cost during last year $60,000, one half of which must, in accordance with the previous estimate, be charged to prostitution; namely, $30,000 per year, or $577 per week.

The final charge arises from the police and judiciary expenses of the city of New York, of which it is believed that ten per cent. is caused by prostitution and its concomitant crimes and sufferings. The aggregate forms a large amount, and will be rather a surmise than an assertion. The maintenance of police-officers and station-houses, of police-justices and their court-rooms, of the city judge and recorder, with their respective courts, of the city and district prisons, and numerous contingent expenses, can not be less than two million dollars a year. The percentage chargeable to prostitution will therefore be $200,000 per year, or $4000 per week.

Thus much for preliminary explanations. It will now be possible to present the reader with a tabular statement of the weekly and yearly cost of the system of prostitution existing in the metropolis of the New World. Those who have followed us through this argument, and noted the facts upon which every calculation is based, will bear witness that nothing has been exaggerated, that no dollar is debited to the vice without strong presumptive evidence to support such charge, and that the endeavor has been throughout rather to underestimate than exceed the bounds of strict probability. Upon this ground the attention of the public is earnestly requested to the first exposition ever attempted of the amount paid by citizens of and visitors to New York for illicit sexual gratification.

RECAPITULATION.

Expenditure.	Weekly outlay.	Yearly outlay.
INDIVIDUAL EXPENSES:		
Paid to prostitutes	$60,000	$3,120,000
Spent for wine and liquor by visitors . .	40,000	2,080,000
Paid by visitors to houses of assignation .	12,600	655,200
Spent for wine and liquor by visitors to houses of assignation	5,000	260,000
Spent in dancing-saloons, liquor and lager-beer stores frequented by prostitutes and their friends	4,530	235,560
MEDICAL EXPENSES:		
Island Hospital, Blackwell's Island . . .	438	22,750
Bellevue " New York	135	7,000
Nursery " Randall's Island . . .	163	8,500
Emigrants' Hospital, Ward's Island . .	136	7,075
New York City Hospital, New York . .	159	8,260
Dispensaries		728
King's County Hospital, Long Island . .	145	7,530
Brooklyn City " " . .	89	4,644
Seamen's Retreat, Staten Island	203	10,540
Private medical assistance	5,928	308,108
VAGRANCY AND PAUPER EXPENSES:		
Work-house, Blackwell's Island	585	30,400
Penitentiary " "	462	24,030
Alms-house " "	303	15,750
Nursery, Randall's Island	577	30,000
POLICE AND JUDICIARY EXPENSES:		
Proportion of aggregate	4,000	200,000
Totals	$135,467	$7,036,075

The footings of the columns show the total expense to be

Weekly $135,467
Yearly $7,036,075

over SEVEN MILLIONS of dollars! or nearly as much as the annual municipal expenditure of New York City.

Comment upon these figures would be superfluous. They present the monetary effects of prostitution in a convincing point of view, and will prepare the reader for an attentive perusal of the suggested remedial measures which form the subject of the next chapter. The American mind is said to be proverbially open to argument based upon dollars and cents. Without giving an unqualified assent to the proposition, we may be permitted to hope that financial considerations, combined with the claims of benevolence and humanity, the appeals of virtue and morality, the demands of public health, and the future physical well-being of the community at large, will exercise that influence on the public mind which is necessary to the accomplishment of any valuable prac‑ tical result from the present investigation.

Before leaving the subject of the extent of prostitution it may be appropriate to remark that it was considered advisable to as‑ certain the prevalence of the vice in some of the leading cities of the United States, and, in order to do this effectually, a circular letter was addressed to the Mayors of

Albany, New York,	Mobile, Alabama,
Baltimore, Maryland,	*Newark*, New Jersey,
Boston, Massachusetts,	*New Haven*, Connecticut,
Brooklyn, New York,	New Orleans, Louisiana,
Buffalo, New York,	*Norfolk*, Virginia,
Charleston, South Carolina,	*Philadelphia*, Pennsylvania,
Chicago, Illinois,	*Pittsburgh*, Pennsylvania,
Cincinnati, Ohio,	Portland, Maine,
Detroit, Michigan,	Richmond, Virginia,
Hartford, Connecticut,	*Savannah*, Georgia,
Louisville, Kentucky,	St. Louis, Missouri,
Memphis, Tennessee,	Washington, District Columbia.

(The names printed in *italics* are those of cities from which re‑ plies were received.)

The circular forwarded was as follows:

(Copy.)

"Mayor's Office, New York City, Sept. 1, 1856.

"To His Honor the Mayor of the City of ———:

"Dear Sir,—Below you will receive from Dr. Sanger a note containing a few questions concerning Prostitution and Prostitutes in your city, which I shall feel obliged if you will have the kindness to answer.

"Very truly yours, Fernando Wood, Mayor New York City."

"Dear Sir,—During the past six months, with the aid of His Honor, Mayor Wood, of this city, and the police force at his command, I have been collecting materials for a report on Prostitution, as it exists in New York at the present time. I inclose you a list of questions that have been asked all the women examined here.[1] Of course I do not expect that you will or can give answers to these questions from the prostitutes in your city, but I would wish to have your replies to the following queries:

"1. How many houses of prostitution are there in your city?

"2. How many houses of assignation are there in your city?

"3. How many public prostitutes are there in your city?

"4. How many private prostitutes are there in your city?

[1] The list of questions inclosed was a printed copy of the interrogatories used in New York, and already given in these pages.

" 5. How many kept mistresses are there in your city?

" 6. What is the present population of your city?

" Of course these questions can be answered to you, by your chief of police and officers, only as to the best of their knowledge; but, as a general thing, shrewd police-officers will be able to give correct answers to them. I do *not* wish names, only the round numbers in each class.

" I shall do myself the honor to forward you a copy of the report when completed, and shall be glad to receive your replies to the above queries by the 30th of this month. You will please direct your answer to

  " Yours respectfully, WILLIAM W. SANGER,

   " Resident Physician, Blackwell's Island, New York City."

The following are the replies received:

BUFFALO, N. Y.

(Copy.)

" Mayor's Office, Buffalo, October 2, 1856.

" DEAR SIR,—I received your circular of the 1st of September, asking that certain questions concerning houses of prostitution, prostitutes, etc., might be answered.

" I immediately directed our chief to collect the necessary information through the police, and I have just received his report: I here inclose the answers.

" To show how far the report can be relied on for accuracy, I here copy from his report: 'The captains inform me that they experienced much difficulty in their endeavors to make a correct report and answer to the several questions proposed; they, however, believe that the returns, so far at least as the number of houses and public prostitutes is concerned, are very near correct.'

" Any farther information you may desire I will cheerfully give, so far as I am able. I am respectfully yours, F. P. STEVENS, Mayor."

(Inclosure.)

" Houses of Prostitution . .	87	Private Prostitutes	81
" of Assignation . .	37	Kept Mistresses	31
Public Prostitutes	272	Population	75,000."

LOUISVILLE, KY.

(Copy.)

" Police Office, Louisville, Ky., December 26, 1856.

" Hon. JOHN BARBER, MAYOR:

" DEAR SIR,—Below I give a statement of such matters as called for by Dr. Wm. W. Sanger, Resident Physician of Blackwell's Island, New York City, which I think you will find correct, or as near as can be arrived at from the facilities afforded. Hoping that it will prove satisfactory to the doctor, and that it will *many tales unfold,* I remain respectfully yours,

   " JAS. KIRKPATRICK, Chief of Police.

"Houses of Prostitution	. . . 79	Kept mistresses	60
" " Assignation	. . . 39	Population of city (sup-	
Public prostitutes	 214	posed to be)	70,000
Private "	 93		

"I am now preparing to take the census for 1857."

NEWARK, N. J.

(Copy.)

"Newark, N. J., October 4, 1856.

"WM. W. SANGER, M. D. :

"DEAR SIR,—I can not make any excuse for not answering your letter of inquiry that will justify me. (Yours of September 1st was unfortunately mislaid.)

"Our population in 1855 was 55,000 by census.

"We have no houses of ill fame in our city; none of assignation; there are no public prostitutes.

"It may appear strange to you that the above should be the case, but there is good reason for it. From the best information that I can get there are perhaps fifty private prostitutes in this city, composed of girls living at service or as seamstresses, but who conduct themselves so as not to be known. Our city is so near to New York that as soon as a girl turns out she makes her way to it, where associations and congenial amusements make it more agreeable. It is rather singular, but so soon as it becomes known that a girl is loose, she is marked and followed in the streets by half-grown boys hooting at and really forcing her to leave town. Occasionally it is made known to the police that a couple of girls staid a night or two at some boarding-house, when they are arrested as vagrants, or warned off, and they are gone.

"New York being so much greater field for them, they are the least of our troubles. Truly and respectfully yours, H. J. POINIER, Mayor."

NEW HAVEN, CONN.

(Copy.)

"New Haven, September 18, 1856.

"Dr. WM. W. SANGER :

"DEAR SIR,—Herewith I hand you the report of our chief of police in answer to your inquiries relative to prostitution in this city.

"Your obedient servant, P. S. GALPIN, Mayor."

(Inclosure.)

"TO HIS HONOR THE MAYOR OF THE CITY OF NEW HAVEN :

"SIR,—I have had the communication addressed to you by Wm. W. Sanger, Resident Physician, Blackwell's Island, New York, in regard to prostitutes and prostitution in the city of New Haven, under consideration, and beg leave to report :

Q Q

" That the answers to the questions propounded are given in a general manner, with near approximation to exactness without pretending to be minutely accurate.

" And to the first question, namely, 'How many houses of prostitution are there in the city?' I answer, That the number now known as such to the police is *ten*, and that these are only such (some of them) occasionally; and that none of them would be so called in New York, being inconsiderable, in poor, out-of-the-way houses, and conducted with great secrecy, and are constantly liable to the penalties of a law peculiar to Connecticut, which punishes *reputation*, rendering it impossible for them to gain strength and become permanent.

" And to the second inquiry, 'How many houses of assignation are there in the city?' I answer, There are known to be *six*, and others suspected; but these all are not such proper, but are connected with some business, as eating-houses, hotels, dance-houses, etc.

" And to the third inquiry, 'How many public prostitutes are there in the city?' There are known by name, ninety-three, all well known.

" And to the fourth inquiry, 'How many private prostitutes are there in the city?' I answer, That there are thirty, with many married women; and, indeed, this class is mostly composed of married women.

" And to the fifth question, 'How many kept mistresses are there in the city?' the answer is, That the number is not known, but is small, and no one instance is certainly known to us.

" The population of the city is thirty-two thousand.

" All which is respectfully submitted.   JOHN C. HAYDEN,
                                        " Chief of Police City of New Haven.
"Dated at New Haven, September 16, 1856."

NORFOLK, VA.

(Copy.)

" Mayor's Office, Norfolk, Va., Sept. 15, 1856.

" DEAR SIR,—Yours of 1st instant was duly received, and in reply would state that I have endeavored to be as accurate as possible in my replies to your several interrogatories, namely,

" 1. How many houses of prostitution in your city?

" Answer. About forty.

" 2. How many houses of assignation in your city?

" Answer. None as such; there being no places, so far as I can learn, used as meeting-places.

" 3. How many public prostitutes are there in your city?

" Answer. About one hundred and fifty.

" 4. How many private prostitutes are there in your city?

" Answer. About fifty.

" 5. How many kept mistresses are there in your city?

"Answer. About six or eight.

" 6. What is the present population of your city?

" Answer. About eighteen thousand.

" I would, in connection with the above, state that about twenty-five of the forty houses are used almost exclusively by sailors and seafaring men, and are sometimes improperly called ' Sailor Boarding-houses,' especially the most decent of them.

" Any other information I can give you I will most cheerfully do, should you desire any.

"I am very respectfully yours,   F. F. FERGUSON,

" Mayor City of Norfolk, Virginia.

"To Dr. WM. W. SANGER, Resident Physician, Blackwell's Island, New York."

PHILADELPHIA, Pa.

(Copy.)

" Office of the Mayor of the City of Philadelphia, Sept. 8, 1856.

" DEAR SIR,—As near as we can arrive at the facts (of course no great reliance can be placed on this general answer) the following are the figures:

1. Houses of prostitution	. 130	3. Public Prostitutes	. . 475
2. Houses of assignation	. 50	4. Private "	. . 105

6. (Say) six hundred thousand population.

" Our city has one hundred and twenty-nine (129) square miles of police jurisdiction, and six hundred and fifty (650) policemen besides officers. You will therefore make some allowances for the want of time to enable me more fully to state answers to your questions.

" The answers given are from estimates made by the lieutenants of police of their own districts.

"Respectfully,   RICHARD VAUX, Mayor of Philadelphia.

"To WM. W. SANGER, M. D., Resident Physician, Blackwell's Island."

PITTSBURGH, PA.

(Copy.)

" Mayor's Office, Pittsburgh, Sept. 18, 1856.

" WM. W. SANGER, M. D. :

" DEAR SIR,—Your favor of the 1st instant came to hand a few days ago, requesting answers to the following questions:

" 1. How many houses of prostitution are there in our city?

" Answer. Nineteen.

" 2. How many houses of assignation?

" Answer. Nine.

" 3. How many public prostitutes?

" Answer. Seventy-seven.

" 4. How many private prostitutes?

" Answer. Thirty-seven.

" 5. How many kept mistresses?

" Answer. Sixteen.

" 6. What is your population?

" Answer. Seventy-five thousand seven hundred and fifty (75,750).

" The above is arrived at from the personal knowledge of some of our police-officers; no doubt the number is much greater.

" At the last census our population of the city proper was over sixty thousand (60,000). The population at that time of Pittsburgh, Alleghany, and the suburbs of Pittsburgh, was nearly one hundred thousand.

" Respectfully, your obedient servant, WM. BINGHAM, Mayor."

SAVANNAH, GA.

(Copy.)

" Mayor's Office, City of Savannah, Ga., Sept., 18, 1856.

" WM. W. SANGER, Resident Physician, }
Blackwell's Island, New York City : }

" DEAR SIR,—In this city there are fifteen houses of prostitution, three assignation-houses, ninety-three white, and one hundred and five colored prostitutes. In the winter season the number is greatly increased by supplies from New York City.

" I can not answer what number of private prostitutes or kept mistresses there are here.

" Our present population is about twenty-six thousand.

" Very truly yours, EDWARD C. ANDERSON, Mayor."

These replies may be condensed as follows:

Cities.	Reported by	Houses of Prostitution.	Houses of Assignation.	Public Prostitutes.	Private Prostitutes.	Kept Mistresses.	Total of abandoned Women.	Population.
Buffalo	Mayor Stevens.....	87	37	272	81	31	384	75,000
Louisville.....	" Barber......	79	39	214	93	60	367	70,000
Newark.......	" Poinier	...	...	...	50	...	50	55,000
New Haven..	" Galpin......	10	6	93	30	...	123	32,000
Norfolk	" Ferguson ..	40	...	150	50	8	208	18,000
Philadelphia.	" Vaux	130	50	475	...	105	580	600,000
Pittsburgh....	" Bingham ..	19	9	77	37	16	130	75,750
Savannah	" Anderson..	15	3	198	...	...	198	26,000

It has already been stated, on the authority of the state census of 1855, that the adult male population of New York City form nearly one third of the total inhabitants, and the same rule may be applied to these cities to ascertain the comparative number of prostitutes and their customers. The proportions stand as follows:

New York, on the resident population of the city proper, has

	1 prostitute to every 40 men.
but including the suburbs . . 1	" " " 64 "
Buffalo has 1	" " " 65 "
Louisville has 1	" " " 64 "
Newark has 1	" " " 366 "
New Haven has 1	" " " 87 "
Norfolk has 1	" " " 29 "
Philadelphia has 1	" " " 344 "
Pittsburgh has 1	" " " 192 "
Savannah has. 1	" " " 44 "

It can scarcely be doubted that the worthy mayors of Newark, Philadelphia, and Pittsburg have been misinformed as to the extent of the vice in their respective cities. Respecting Newark, for instance, the writer was recently informed that prostitution was not so rare as Mayor Poinier's letter would imply, but that prostitutes and known houses of prostitution were to be found scattered over the city, and that the fact was notorious to nearly every resident. This information was received from a gentleman himself an inhabitant of Newark. There is no doubt that much of the vice of Newark finds a home in New York, as the mayor says, but it is equally certain that it is not all expatriated.

The mayor of Philadelphia is particularly wide of the mark. There may not be as many public prostitutes there as in New York, but it is proverbial, and is as widely known as is Philadelphia itself, that its streets abound in houses of assignation and private houses of prostitution.

Pittsburgh is situated at the head of navigation on the Ohio River, at the confluence of the Alleghany and Monongahela Rivers, both navigable. She has canals, rail-roads, and large manufactories, and, if closely examined, would probably show a larger proportion of prostitutes than above reported.

Norfolk is the largest naval depôt in this country, and its population can not be held responsible for all the prostitution within its limits. In both Norfolk and Savannah we presume that the larger portion of the abandoned women at the time the census was taken were colored people, whose virtue is always at a discount under the most favorable circumstances, and to which a seaport is always fatal.

But another calculation may be made upon the assumption that the males who have commerce with prostitutes form only one fourth of the population, and the proportions resulting from that are as follows:

New York, on the resident population of the city proper, has
1 prostitute to every 30 men.

but including the suburbs . . 1	"	"	"	50	"
Buffalo has 1	"	"	"	49	"
Louisville has 1	"	"	"	48	"
Newark has 1	"	"	"	275	"
New Haven has 1	"	"	"	65	"
Norfolk has 1	"	"	"	23	"
Philadelphia has 1	"	"	"	258	"
Pittsburgh has 1	"	"	"	144	"
Savannah has . . . . . .¹ . 1	"	"	"	33	"

To arrive at an average we will omit the calculation of the pro
portion of prostitutes to the population of New York City proper,
it having been shown already that the responsibility of much of
it must rest upon the suburbs and upon visitors, and also omit
Newark, Philadelphia, and Pittsburg, because the reports from
those cities are palpably underrated.   This done, the mean of the
two estimates stands thus:

New York 1	prostitute	to every	57	men.	
Buffalo 1	"	"	"	.57	"
Louisville 1	"	"	"	56	"
New Haven 1	"	"	"	76	"
Norfolk 1	"	"	"	26	"
Savannah 1	"	"	"	39	"
and the mean of the whole is . . . 1	"	"	"	52	"

This mean may be fairly assumed as the proportion existing in
all the large cities of the Union, and the farther assumption that
the men who visit houses of prostitution form one fourth of the
total population will give a basis upon which the total number
of the Prostitutes in the United States may be estimated with
some accuracy.   The calculation can not, of course, be claimed as
absolutely correct, as that would be an impossibility, but is submitted as a probability on which the reader can form his own
conclusion.

The population of the United States in 1858 was estimated by
Professor De Bow, when preparing the compendium of the census
of 1850, and his calculation at that time was that by the present
year it would amount to 29,242,139 persons, which may be taken
in round numbers 29,000,000.   From this must be deducted
3,500,000 slaves, which will leave the free inhabitants 25,500,000,
and the proportion of adult males to this number is 6,375,000.
It may next be assumed that one half of these men live in country places or small cities where prostitution does not exist, the
other moiety being inhabitants of cities with a population of twen-

ty thousand or upward; and upon the basis already proved of one prostitute to every fifty-two men, the result would be a total of 61,298 prostitutes. The whole area of the United States is 2,936,166 square miles, and if all the prostitutes therein were equally divided over this surface, there would be one for every forty-seven square miles, or if they were walking in continuous line, thirty-six inches from each other, they would make a column nearly thirty-five miles long. If the inhabitants of large cities were only one third, the number of prostitutes would be 41,058. These suggestions are, of course, mere matters for consideration, and are not given as definite facts.

Allusions have already been made to many exaggerated opinions as to the extent of prostitution in New York City, and it may be well to notice in this place some passages in a work entitled " An inquiry into the extent, causes, and consequences of Prostitution in Edinburgh, by William Tait, Surgeon : 2d edition, 1842." The author starts with the impression that the capital of Scotland is the most moral city on the face of the earth, and after fixing the number of public prostitutes in Edinburgh at eight hundred, or one to every eighty of the adult male population, remarks:

" In London there is one for every sixty, and in Paris one for every fifteen. Edinburgh is thus about twenty-five per cent. better than London, while the latter is about seventy per cent. better than Paris." (Happy Edinburgh!) " And what is to be said of the chief city of the United States of America, of the independent, liberal, religious, and enlightened inhabitants of New York? It will scarcely be credited that that city furnishes a prostitute for every six or seven of its adult male population! Alas! for the religion and morality of the country that affords such a demonstration of its depravity. It was not surpassed even by the metropolis of France during the heat and fervor of the Revolution, when libertinism reigned triumphant, and the laws of God and man were alike set at defiance."—Page 6.

This picture is any thing but flattering to our national pride; but it loses very much of its effect because it is contrary to the truth. It will, however, satisfy our readers that Mr. Tait was misinformed, and they may feel a slight gratification in the conclusion that his pathetic lament for the religion and morality of their country was unnecessary. On page 8 of the same work we find:

" After stating that there were upward of ten thousand abandoned women in the city of New York, the Rev. Mr. M'Dowall

chaplain to the New York Magdalen Asylum, goes on to say:
' Besides these, we have the clearest evidence that there are hundreds of private harlots and kept mistresses, many of whom keep
up a show of industry as domestics, seamstresses, nurses, etc., in
the most respectable families, and throng the houses of assignation every night. Although we have no means of ascertaining
the number of these, yet enough has been learned from the facts
already developed to convince us that the aggregate is alarmingly
great, perhaps little behind the proportion of the city of London,
whose police report asserts, on the authority of accurate researches, that the number of private prostitutes in that city is fully equal
to the number of public harlots.' "

In this passage Mr. Tait shifts the responsibility of his figures
to the shoulders of the Rev. Mr. M'Dowall, who is represented as
declaring the number of public prostitutes in New York sixteen
years ago to be ten thousand, and assuming the private prostitutes
to amount to the same number, making an aggregate nearly three
times as large as an actual and searching inquiry has found at the
present time. During the last sixteen years vice has not decreased in New York, but has steadily increased, and yet the
most diligent search can discover in 1858 only 7860 public and
private prostitutes, instead of the twenty thousand mentioned in
the publication under notice! We imagine it to be an imperative
duty to be tolerably well acquainted with a social evil before attempting to write upon it, and although Mr. Tait's book can not,
by any possibility, injure our city, on account of the palpable misrepresentations it contains, we allude to it to show the opinion
entertained of New York and its vices on the other side of the
Atlantic. Were an apology necessary for the present work, such
statements as these would be amply sufficient.

Mr. Tait loses no opportunity to hurl a sly dart at New York.
Thus (on page 38), after quoting the words of the Rev. Mr.
M'Dowall as to the character of an abandoned woman in New
York, he (Mr. Tait) continues:

" He says nothing of the state of religious feeling among the
prostitutes there; and if we are to regard his statement of the
number of prostitutes as strictly correct, it may very well be questioned whether any considerable number of the inhabitants of
that city are under the influence of sincere religious feeling."

Some of our New York City readers may probably recollect
that the publication of Mr. M'Dowall's "Inquiry" produced very

considerable excitement here at the time, and opinions were freely expressed that he was either very ignorant on matters of that
nature, or intentionally colored his statements, and was in either
case entirely unfitted for the task he had assumed.

Mr. Tait assumes the population of Edinburgh at about two
hundred thousand, the number of public prostitutes at eight hundred, and of private prostitutes at nearly twelve hundred, or a total
of two thousand abandoned women.   This gives one prostitute to
every thirty-two adult males, if we adopt his system of calculation; or one prostitute to every twenty-five adult males, if we
adopt the system of calculation which has been applied to the
United States in the present work.   From his own figures, then,
it can be seen, that although New York City is so awfully irre-
ligious, it has less prostitution than pious Edinburgh.

Again : on page 189, while speaking of the demoralizing effects
of theatrical representations, Mr. Tait says :

" In the report of the House of Refuge in New York, it is stated
that one hundred and fifty boys and girls, out of six hundred and
ninety, are guilty of theft and impurity to get a seat in the theatre." He does not mark this as a quotation, nor does he state
the report from which it was extracted.   As he has printed it, it
must be supposed correct, although we must confess we can not
see very clearly what connection exists between the New York
House of Refuge and prostitution considering the ages of children
generally admitted to that institution; and while we have very
little doubt that many of the inmates thereof have committed
theft for the reason he assigns, we are rather dubious as to the
acts of impurity alluded to, except in a very few exceptional cases.

Farther: on page 194, Mr. Tait quotes "The address of the
Rev. Mr. M'Dowall on prostitution in America" as follows:

" At the very hour in the morning, afternoon, and evening of
every Lord's day when the people of God assemble for religious
worship, then, in a special manner, do the children of the wicked
one meet in troops at harlots' houses.   On the Sabbath days the
rooms are so filled with visitors that there is no place for them to
sit down, and on that account many are refused admission at the
doors." These palpable exaggerations require no contradiction.
They show, however, the extremes of misrepresentation to which
an enthusiastic and incompetent writer may be led.

Inclined to exaggeration as Mr. Tait has been proved to be, he
yet protests (in page 251) against some opinions upon infanticide

by prostitutes in New York, advanced by his informant, the Rev. Mr. M'Dowall, and quotes the opinion of Parent-Duchatelet to prove that mothers are generally very fond of their children. This fact warrants the conclusion that his other opinions upon social morals in New York are entirely derived from Mr. M'Dowall, who is shown to be any thing but a credible witness. His reliance upon such a source is much to be regretted as materially impairing the value and truthfulness of his otherwise interesting and useful volume.

The following extracts from the "Compendium of the Seventh Census of the United States, 1850," will be interesting, from their relation to various points which have been discussed in the progress of this work. They have all a more or less direct bearing upon the subject of prostitution, and the condensation of them here will give readers an opportunity of verifying many of the previous remarks.

The estimated population of the Union at the present time (1858) has been already given as 29,242,139 persons (including slaves). The proportion of females to males at each census from 1790 to 1850 is stated as follows:[1]

	1790.	1800.	1810.	1820.	1830.	1840.	1850.
Males.......	100·	100·	100·	100·	100·	100·	100·
Females ...	96·4	95·3	96·2	96·8	96·4	95·6	95·

This relates only to the free population. In enumerating slaves no distinction of sex was made earlier than the year 1820. The ratio of male and female slaves since that date is as follows:[2]

	1820.	1830.	1840.	1850.
Males	100·	100·	100·	100·
Females	95·19	98·36	99·55	99·95

From these tables it appears that the males in the free population and the females in the slave population have been steadily increasing, but with no determined ratio of progression.

Taking the total of free and slave population since the census of 1820, the excess of males is stated thus:[3]

	1820.	1830.	1840.	1850.
Males................	4,898,127	6,529,696	8,688,532	11,837,661
Females	4,740,004	6,336,324	8,380,921	11,354,215
Excess of males..	158,123	193,372	307,611	483,446

It will be seen from this that in 1850 the males were in excess at the rate of 2·08 per cent., and by applying the same rule to the

[1] Compendium of Seventh Census, p. 49.   [2] Ibid. p. 87.   [3] Ibid. p. 101.

population of 1858 a fair estimate of the relative number of each sex at the present time may be made as follows:

Males (1858) 14,925,188
Females 14,316,951
Excess of males 608,237
Total estimated population . 29,242,139

In the several geographical divisions of the Union the proportion of white males to white females is thus shown:[1]

New England States (Maine, New Hampshire, Vermont, Massachusetts, Rhode Island, and Connecticut), 100·87 females to 100 males.

Middle States (New York, New Jersey, Pennsylvania, Delaware, Maryland, and District of Columbia), 97·70 females to 100 males.

Southern States (Virginia, North Carolina, South Carolina, Georgia, and Florida), 98·54 females to 100 males.

Southwestern States (Alabama, Mississippi, Louisiana, Texas, Arkansas, and Tennessee), 91·66 females to 100 males.

Northwestern States (Kentucky, Missouri, Illinois, Indiana, Ohio, Michigan, Wisconsin, and Iowa), 92·11 females to 100 males.

California and Territories, 36·73 females to 100 males.

Two facts are developed in this statement. In the New England States females are in excess of males. From this district comes the majority of all the native-born prostitutes who find their home in New York City. In the Northwestern States, to which it has been proposed to remove some of the surplus female labor of New York, the males are in excess, and any women sent there would aid in restoring the equilibrium of the sexes.

The following table gives the relative percentage of each sex at different ages, and also the number of females to each hundred males:[2]

Ages.	Percentage of Males.	Percentage of Females.	Females to each 100 Males.
Under 5 years...................	14·68	14·95	96·76
From 5 years to 10 years	13·69	13·98	97·03
" 10 " 15 "	12·23	12·35	96·00
" 15 " 20 "	10·39	11·42	104·46
" 20 " 30 "	18·64	18·46	94·08
" 30 " 40 "	12·85	11·84	87·55
" 40 " 50 "	8·38	7·86	89·09
" 50 " 60 "	4·97	4·83	92·15
" 60 " 70 "	2·64	2·69	96·88
" 70 " 80 "	1·11	1·18	101·01
" 80 " 90 "	·31	·36	110·11
" 90 " 100 "	·04	·05	123·16
" 100 years upward......			120·45
Ages unknown	·07	·03	44·09
	100·	100·	95·

[1] Compendium of Seventh Census, p. 49.   [2] Ibid. p. 57.

Experience has proved that the age at which female virtue is exposed to the most temptations, or at least the age at which the greater part of the prostitutes in New York have embraced their wretched calling, is from fifteen to twenty years, and the table above shows that at those periods females are in excess over males nearly 4½ per cent. Is it to be supposed that the numerical predominance is the cause of the temptations; or may it not rather be concluded that both are co-existent, and equally contribute to the sad result; or even would not temptation be more aggravated, because concentrated, if, at that critical period of life, males and females were in equal numbers?

The following table gives the relative ages of the whole population without distinction of sex, but compares the white, free colored, and slave classes:

Ages.	Percentage of white Population.[1]	Percentage of free colored Population.[2]	Percentage of slave Population.[3]
Under 5 years of age.............	14·81	14·00	16·87
From 5 years to 10 years......	13·83	13·36	14·95
" 10 " " 15 "	12·28	12·04	13·61
" 15 " " 20 "	10·89	10·08	11·15
" 20 " " 30 "	18·55	17·85	17·86
" 30 " " 40 "	12·36	12·71	11·04
" 40 " " 50 "	8·13	8·73	6·86
" 50 " " 60 "	4·90	5·60	3·96
" 60 " and upward.....	4·20	5·56	3·68
Ages unknown	·05	·07	·02
	100·	100·	100·

BIRTHS.

The ratio of births is in the[4]

United States . .	1 birth to every 36 persons, or 2·75 per cent.	
Great Britain . . 1	" " 31 " 3·22 "
France 1	" " 35 " 2·86 "
Russia 1	" " 36 " 2·75 "
Prussia and Austria 1	" " 26 " 3·87 "

EDUCATION.

The importance of education and its influence upon the social problem of prostitution is a sufficient apology for the following extracts, in addition to what has been said already on the subject.

There are in the United States

239 colleges with an annual income of .	$1,964,428
80,978 public schools	9,529,542
6,085 academies and private schools . . .	4,644,214
87,302 educational institutions which cost .	$16,138,184

[1] Compendium of Seventh Census, p. 94.   [2] Ibid. p. 69.
[3] Ibid. p. 91.   [4] Ibid p. 104.

These institutions are attended by 3,644,928 scholars.[1]

There are in the United States

Natives 858,306
Foreigners 195,114
Total 1,053,420

persons above twenty years of age who can not read or write. This number is subdivided thus:[2]

	White.	Free colored.	Total.
Males	389,664	40,722	430,386
Females....................	573,234	49,800	623,034
Total...........	962,894	90,522	1,053,420

This shows a remarkable preponderance of uneducated women. The percentage of children attending school in the United States, calculated on all between the ages of five and fifteen years is

Natives . . . . 80·81 per cent.[3]
Foreigners . . . . 51·73 "

a proof of the fact intimated already that foreign parents do not endeavor to avail themselves of the facilities provided for the education of their children.

The illiterate of the population are thus minutely analyzed:[4]

White illiterate to total white . . . . 4·92 per cent.
Free colored illiterate to total free colored . . . . . 20·83 "
Native white and free colored illiterate to total native white and free colored . . . . 4·85 "
Foreign white and free colored illiterate to total foreign white and free colored . . . . 8·24 "
Native illiterate white and free colored to total of both (native) over 20 years of age . . . . 10·35 "
Foreign illiterate white and free colored to total of both (foreign) over 20 years of age . . . . 14·48 "
Foreign illiterate over twenty years of age . . 195·114
Foreign illiterate to total foreign over 20 years of age, supposing the illiterate to be all white . . . . 14·51 "

Following the geographical sections we obtain the following results:[5]

Sections.	Percentage of Pupils to the white Population.	Percentage of Pupils to the white and free colored Population.	Percentage of illiterate to white Population.
New England States.	25·90	25·71	1·88
Middle States.........	21·79	21·02	3·16
Southern States.......	14·52	13·92	9·22
Southwestern States.	16·32	16·10	8·45
Northwestern States.	21·72	21·51	5·03

[1] Compendium of Seventh Census, p. 141, 142.　　[2] Ibid. p. 145.
[3] Ibid. p. 150.　　　　[4] Ibid. p. 152.　　　　[5] Ibid. p. 152, 153.

Sections.	Percentage of illiterate to Natives.	Percentage of illiterate to Natives over 20 Years of age.	Percentage of illiterate to Foreigners.	Percentage of illiterate to Foreigners over 20 Years of age.	Percentage of illiterate to free Colored.
New England States	·26	·42	14·63	24·39	8·45
Middle States	1·84	3·00	9·55	15·92	22·42
Southern States......	9·30	20·30	5·28	8·80	21·20
Southwestern States	8·41	16·63	9·12	15·20	18·54
Northwestern States	4·97	9·92	4·63	7·72	21·44
California and Territories................ }	17·50	21·63	14·13	23·51	12·47

OCCUPATIONS.

In the tables of occupations the only class noticed is the white and free colored male population over fifteen years of age, no returns of female employment being given. As interesting to the general reader, although not in immediate connection with the subject, the following is given:[1]

Occupations.	Ratio per cent. to the total employed.
Commerce, trade, manufactures, mechanic arts, and mining .	29·72
Agriculture	44·69
Labor (not agricultural)	18·50
Army	·10
Sea and river navigation	2·17
Law, Medicine, and Divinity	1·76
Other pursuits requiring education	1·78
Government civil service	·46
Domestic service	·41
Other occupations	·41
	100·00

A similar but more elaborate statement of the occupations of the people of Great Britain was published in the British census for 1841, and is reprinted by Professor De Bow in his compendium.[2]

Occupations.	Percentage to total Males.	Percentage to total Females.	Percentage to total Population.
Commerce, trade, and manufactures...........	26·24	7·12	16·52
Agriculture	15·33	·84	7·96
Labor (not agricultural)	6·99	1·21	4·05
Army..	1·42	.....	·70
Navy and merchant seamen, boatmen, &c....	2·35	.....	1·17
Clerical, legal, and medical professions.......	·66	·02	·34
Other pursuits requiring education	1·17	·36	·76
Government and municipal civil service.......	·43	·02	·22
Domestic servants	2·78	9·48	6·18
Persons of independent means	1·47	3·88	2·69
Pensioners, paupers, lunatics, and prisoners..	1·11	1·01	1·06
Unoccupied (including women and children)..	40·05	76·06	58·35
	100·	100·	100·

[1] Compendium of Seventh Census, p. 128.   [2] Ibid. p. 130.

WAGES.

In introducing this subject, Professor De Bow remarks, "The money price of wages, unless the price of other articles be known, gives but an unsatisfactory idea of the condition of the laboring classes at different periods and in different countries." In the following tables of the rates of remuneration in 1850 this difficulty will scarcely exist, so far as New York is concerned at least. The large number of domestic servants who have been added to our population since that year precludes the possibility of any considerable advance in the rate of wages, and, as every reader has an idea of what a woman's necessary expenses must be, each will be enabled to decide for himself whether the compensation is sufficient, or whether society at large would not be benefited were some of the surplus domestic servants removed to other localities, and thus, by increasing the demand, augment the wages. The following was the average weekly wages (with board) of a domestic servant in the year 1850 :[1]

States.	Wages	States.	Wages.
Alabama	$1 41	Missouri	$1 17
Arkansas	1 67	New Hampshire	1 27
California	13 00	New Jersey	0 97
Columbia (District of)	1 31	New York	1 05
Connecticut	1 36	North Carolina	0 87
Delaware	0 84	Ohio	0 96
Florida	1 83	Pennsylvania	0 80
Georgia	1 52	Rhode Island	1 42
Illinois	1 14	South Carolina	1 42
Indiana	0 90	Tennessee	1 00
Iowa	1 07	Texas	2 00
Kentucky	1 09	Vermont	1 19
Louisiana	2 57	Virginia	0 96
Maine	1 09	Wisconsin	1 27
Maryland	0 89	Territories. { Minnesota	2 25
Massachusetts	1 48	New Mexico	0 78
Michigan	1 10	Oregon	10 00
Mississippi	1 52	Utah	1 46

The following is a table of the monthly wages in factories in the different states. It is, of course, exclusive of board and lodging. Looking at the amount received by female operatives, will any one feel surprised that they should abandon the incessant and poorly paid employment?

[1] Compendium of Seventh Census, p. 164.

WAGES PER MONTH (WITHOUT BOARD).

States.	Cotton.		Wool.		Pig Iron.		Iron Castings.		Wrought Iron.		Fisheries.	
	M.	F.	M.	F.	M.	F.	M.	F.	M.	F.	M.	F.
	$ c.	$ c.	$ c.	$ c.	$ c.	$ c.	$ c.	$ c.	$ c.	$ c.	$ c.	$ c.
Alabama ...	11 71	7 98	...	...	17 60	...	30 05	...	15 29	...	...	...
Arkansas...	14 61	5 88	...	...	...	...	...	...	...	...	...	...
California..	...	...	...	...	...	...	23 33	...	...	...	...	...
D. of Col....	14 02	8 00	30 00	...	...	...	27 05	...	...	...	...	...
Connecticut	19 08	11 80	24 12	12 86	26 80	...	27 02	8 00	31 59	...	20 81	...
Delaware...	15 31	11 58	18 79	17 33	...	...	23 36	...	25 53	...	...	...
Florida......	32 14	5 00	...	...	...	...	...	...	...	...	17 58	8 40
Georgia.....	14 57	7 39	27 47	14 10	17 44	5 00	27 43	...	11 35	5 00	...	...
Illinois			22 00	12 52	22 06	...	28 50	...	...	...	...	...
Indiana.....	13 02	6 77	21 81	11 05	26 00	...	25 74	...	27 45	4 00	...	...
Iowa..........	...	...	11 14	...	...	...	32 35	...	...	...	...	...
Kentucky...	14 95	9 36	15 30	11 11	20 23	4 70	24 89	4 15	32 06	...	...	...
Louisiana ..	...	...	...	...	...	...	35 60	...	...	...	...	...
Maine	29 35	12 15	22 57	11 77	22 00	...	29 00	5 00	...	...	19 12	...
Maryland ..	15 42	9 48	18 60	11 89	20 14	...	27 50	...	24 31	...	...	...
Massach'sts	22 90	13 60	22 95	14 22	27 50	...	30 90	...	29 46	12 79	15 70	...
Michigan...	...	...	21 65	11 47	35 00	...	28 68	...	...	...	22 43	...
Mississippi .	14 21	5 94	...	...	...	...	37 91	...	...	...	...	...
Missouri	10 93	10 00	32 00	6 50	24 28	...	19 63	...	30 00	...	...	...
N. Hamp...	26 00	13 47	22 86	14 53	18 00	...	33 05	...	31 34	...	10 00	...
New Jersey	17 98	9 56	25 22	8 60	21 20	...	24 00	...	27 31	13 34	...	...
New York..	18 32	9 68	19 97	11 76	25 00	...	27 49	...	28 91	...	20 35	...
N. Carolina	11 65	6 13	18 00	7 00	8 00	4 00	23 46	...	10 43	4 78	23 64	11 77
Ohio	16 59	9 42	20 14	10 90	24 48	...	27 32	...	29 58	...	19 07	...
Pennsylv'a.	17 85	9 91	19 23	10 41	21 65	5 11	27 55	6 00	28 31	6 57	...	...
Rho. Island	18 60	12 95	20 70	15 18	...	...	29 63	...	57 85	...	34 00	...
S. Carolina	13 94	8 30	...	...	...	...	13 59	4 00	...	...	...	...
Tennessee..	10 94	6 42	17 66	6 00	12 81	5 11	17 96	4 50	15 20	5 00	...	...
Texas	...	...	20 00	20 00	...	...	43 43	...	...	...	...	...
Vermont....	15 53	12 65	24 46	11 81	22 08	...	28 27	...	32 08	...	...	...
Virginia	10 18	6 98	18 17	9 91	12 76	6 86	19 91	9 44	25 41	...	21 70	...
Wisconsin..	...	...	22 48	...	30 00	...	26 73	...	...	...	21 50	...

The number of hands employed in these manufactures is as follows:[1]

Manufactures.	Men employed.	Men's average Wages per Month.	Women employed.	Women's average Wages per Month.
Cotton...............	33,150	$16 79	59,136	$9 24
Wool	22,678	21 49	16,574	11 86
Pig-iron	20,298	21 68	150	5 13
Iron castings	23,541	27 38	48	5 87
Wrought iron......	16,110	27 02	138	7 35
Fisheries............	20,704	20 49	429	10 08
Total employed	136,481		76,475	

PAUPERISM.

From tables relating to pauperism in the United States we learn that in the year ending June 1, 1850, when our population was 23,191,876, there were supported (in whole or in part) at public expense:[2]

[1] Compendium of Seventh Census, p. 180–184.   [2] Ibid. p. 163.

Natives 66,434
Foreigners 68,538
Total 134,972

The cost of such support was $2,954,806. This is much less than the outlay in England, where, in the year 1848, there was expended £6,180,764 sterling (or over thirty million dollars), the population being 17,521,956.[1]

CRIME.

There were confined in the various state prisons throughout the Union on June 1, 1850:[2]

White males 4643
" females 115
Total whites . . . . —— 4758
Colored males 801
" females 87
Total colored . . . . —— 888
Aggregate 5646

Of these there were

Native whites 3259
" colored 866
Total natives . . . . —— 4125
Foreign whites 1499
" colored 22
Total foreign . . . . —— 1521
Aggregate 5646

INTEMPERANCE.

It need not be repeated that habits of intemperance and prostitution are closely allied. The following figures give the statistics of the breweries and distilleries in the United States:[3]

The total number of these establishments is 1217
In which is invested a capital of $8,507,574

They employ 6140 hands, and consume during the year,

Barley	. .	3,787,195 bushels.	Apples	. .	526,840 bushels.
Corn	. . .	11,067,761 "	Hops	. . .	1,294 tons.
Rye	. . .	2,143,927 "	Molasses	.	61,675 hogsheads.
Oats	. .	56,607 "			

Their yearly production is,

Ale, 1,179,495 barrels, or . . . . . 42,471,820 gallons.
Whisky, etc. . . . . 41,364,224 "
Rum . . . . 6,500,500 "
Total . . . . 90,336,544 "

[1] Compendium of Seventh Census, p. 162 (note). [2] Ibid. p. 166. [3] Ibid. p. 182.

If these stimulants were used in the United States, exclusive of export or import, the average allowance for each man, woman, and child in the community would be nearly four gallons per year. The figures show how much we produce, but will not aid the inquiry as to how much is consumed.

NATIVITIES.

The words " Natives" and " Foreigners" have been so frequently used in the course of this investigation, that the official census returns as to their relative numbers can not but be interesting.[1]

Of the white population of the United States there were

Born in the state in which they are now living . . 67·02 per cent.
"   "   United States, but not in the state in which they are now living . . . . . . 21·35 "
       Total of natives . . . . 88·37 "
Born in foreign countries . . . . 11·46 "
Unknown nativities . . . . ·17 "
                    100 "

Thus of every hundred white inhabitants of the United States, eighty-eight were natives of the soil.

Of the free colored inhabitants there were[2]

Natives . . . . 98·59 per cent.
Foreigners . . . . ·94 "
Unknown nativities . . . . ·47 "
                100

The slave population are (for all practical purposes) entirely native.

[1] Compendium of Seventh Census, p. 61.   [2] Ibid. p. 79.

CHAPTER XXXVII.

NEW YORK.—REMEDIAL MEASURES.

Effects of Prohibition.—Required Change of Policy.—Governmental Obligations. —Prostitution augmented by Seclusion.—Impossibility of benevolent Assistance. —Necessity of sanitary Regulations.—Yellow Fever.—Effect of remedial Measures in Paris.—Syphilitic Infection not a local Question.—Present Measures to check Syphilis.—ISLAND HOSPITAL, BLACKWELL'S ISLAND.—Mode of Admission. —Vagrancy Commitment "on Confession," and its Action on Blackwell's Island.—Pecuniary Results.—Moral Effects.—Perpetuation of Disease.—Inadequacy of Present Arrangements.—Discharges.—Writs of *Habeas Corpus* and *Certiorari*, how obtained, and their Effects.—Public Responsibility.—Proposed medical and police Surveillance.—Requirements.—*Hospital Arrangements to be entirely separated from punitive Institutions.* — Medical Visitation. — Power to place diseased Women under Treatment and *detain them till cured.*—Refutation of Objections.—Quack Advertisers.—Constitution of Medical Bureau.—Duties of Examiners.—License System.—Probable Effects of Surveillance.—Expenses of the proposed Plan.—Agitation in England.—The London *Times* on Prostitution.—Objections considered.—Report from MEDICAL BOARD OF BELLEVUE HOSPITAL on Prostitution and Syphilis.—Report from RESIDENT PHYSICIAN, RANDALL'S ISLAND, on Constitutional Syphilis.—Reliability of Statistics.—Resumé of substantiated Facts.

HAVING traced the causes and delineated the extent and effects of the evil of prostitution as it exists in New York at the present time, an evident duty is to inquire what measures can be devised to stay the march of this desolating plague in its ravages on the health and morals of the public. This is a problem the solution of which has for centuries interested philanthropists and statesmen in different countries. They commenced with the theory that vice could be suppressed by statutory enactments, and the crushing-out process was vigorously tried under various auspices, until experience demonstrated that it virtually increased and aggravated the evil it was intended to suppress. At subsequent periods, however, different measures have been adopted with different results.

It will be necessary, in the first place, to consider the effect of stringent prohibitory measures. The records given in the previous chapters of this work show what these have attempted, and they also show at the same time the uselessness of endeavoring to eradicate prostitution by compulsory legislation. The lash, the dungeon, the rack, and the stake have each been tried, and all have proved equally powerless to accomplish the object. Admitting that, in religion, morals, or politics, it is impossible to force concurrence in any particular sentiment, while a kindly persuasive plan may lead to its adoption; admitting that all attempts to compel prostitutes to be virtuous have notoriously failed; has not the time arrived for a change of policy? If, in direct ratio to the stringency of prohibitory measures, the vice sought to be exterminated has steadily increased, does not reason suggest the expediency of resorting to other measures for its suppression?

It has been said that "History is philosophy teaching by example," and, if such instruction is well considered, none can fail to see therein an unanswerable argument against excessive severity in this matter. The several statutes proscribing prostitution have been detailed, and their specific results given, as gathered from the experience of various countries. At the time these laws were in force, it is hardly probable that their authors regarded them as unsusceptible of improvement; and the question now arises for decision, in this age of general progress, is it not our duty to try the effect of some other line of action in this country?

In common with other nations, we have passed laws intended to crush out prostitution; have made vigorous protests (on paper) against its existence; and there our labors have ended. The experience acquired in this course of legislation only demonstrates that such laws can not be enforced so as to produce the desired effect. But why are they still retained on the statute books? Is it not an opprobrium upon our national character to allow them to exist, if they are never to be enforced? If they are powerless for good, effective only to increase the plague they were designed to check, why not expunge them at once, and substitute others more practicable and more useful in their stead? A candid acknowledgment of error, whether by an individual or a community, is always a creditable and graceful act. It shows that experience has dictated a wiser course; that reflection and experiment have condemned the former plan.

It is not to be supposed that any system of laws will entirely eradicate prostitution; history, social arrangements, and physiology alike forbid any such utopian idea. But will not a more enlightened policy do much toward diminishing it? Many of the present generation can recollect the time when it was considered right and proper to imprison an insolvent debtor; but this idea is now wisely repudiated by society, and no one will assert that the effect of the change has been to place any additional difficulties in the way of collecting legal claims. Capital punishment has been abolished in many cases, and yet it is a well-known fact that crime has diminished where this experiment has been tried. This is more particularly the case in England, where forgery, which was punished with death, is comparatively rare since the amelioration of the law. A general conviction is becoming prevalent that the most effectual way to deal with criminals is to attempt to raise them above what they were, in contradistinction to the old plan of sinking them lower.[1] It is now freely acknowledged that the elevating, instead of the depressing process, is consonant both with the spirit of our republican institutions and with humanizing policy. Even if American society is not yet prepared to take a course directly the reverse of its present prohibitory practice, prudence dictates the adoption of some medium rule by which prostitution can be kept in check without being encouraged or allowed, as in the Prussian laws, which expressly declare that the vice is "tolerated but not permitted."

Government should be patriarchal in its character, and exercise an effective but parental supervision over all its subjects. This is the living principle which gives vitality and strength to any organization, and no satisfactory government can exist if it is absent. Now, in regard to prostitutes, admitting that they have erred, still, the people, who constitute the government in this country, are

[1] "That for a single offense, however grave, a whole life should be blasted, is a doctrine repugnant even to Nature's own dealings in the visible world. There her voice clearly says, 'Let all these wonderful powers of vital renewal have free play; let the foul flesh slough itself away; lop off the gangrened limb; enter into life, maimed if it must be,' but never until the last moment of total dissolution does she say, 'Thou shalt not enter into life at all.'

"Therefore, once let a woman feel that 'while there is life there is hope,' dependent on the only one condition that she shall *sin no more*, and what a future you open to her! what a weight you lift off from her poor miserable spirit, which might otherwise be crushed down to the lowest deep, to that which is far worse than any bodily pollution, ineradicable corruption of soul."—*A Woman's Thoughts upon Women* (New York ed.), p. 269.

"It may often be noticed the less virtuous people are, the more they shrink away from the slightest whiff of the odor of unsanctity. The good are ever the most charitable, the pure are the most brave. I believe there are hundreds and thousands of Englishwomen who would willingly throw the shelter of their stainless repute around any poor creature who came to them and said honestly, 'I have sinned, help me that I may sin no more.' But the unfortunates will not believe this. They are like the poor Indians, who think it necessary to pacify the evil principle by a greater worship than that which they offer to the Good Spirit, because, they say, the Bad Spirit is the stronger."—Ibid. p. 272.

concerned in the matter, and their mutual obligations, their policy, and their pecuniary interests require that these wandering members of the body corporate should have a reasonable opportunity for reformation. Which will give this opportunity most effectually—to crush them under the weight of their own misdeeds, or to adopt a liberal course likely to induce them to abandon their depraved habits? One of the secrets which bound the soldiers of the empire to the standard of Napoleon through all his battles and vicissitudes was the knowledge that France regarded them as her children, and would not fail to protect and support them. The words "I am a Roman citizen" derived their magic power from the fact that the Roman Empire treated all her citizens as sons, and watched over their interests with parental care. The recent outburst of popular enthusiasm in our own country when the commander[1] of an American national vessel rescued a citizen from threatened outrage in a foreign land, was an emphatic recognition of the principle. Can we now consistently refuse to apply the rule to all who need our kindly care?[2]

It may be considered a bold assertion, that our present mode of dealing with prostitution is calculated to widely extend its preva-

[1] Captain Ingraham.

[2] "Surely the consciousness of lost innocence must be the most awful punishment to any woman, and from it no kindness, no sympathy, no concealment of shame, or even restoration to good repute, can entirely free her. She must bear her burden, lighter or heavier as it may seem at different times, and she must bear it to the day of her death. I think this fact alone is enough to make a chaste woman's first feeling toward an unchaste that of unqualified, unmitigated pity.

"Allowing the pity, what is the next thing to be done? Surely there must be some light beyond that of mere compassion to guide her in her after-conduct toward them. Where shall we find this light? In the world and its ordinary code of social morality, suited to social conscience? I fear not. The general opinion, even among good men, seems to be that this great question is a very sad thing, but a sort of unconquerable necessity; there is no use in talking about it, and, indeed, the less it is talked of the better. Good women are much of the same mind. The laxer-principled of both sexes treat the matter with philosophical indifference, or with the kind of laugh that makes the blood boil in any truly virtuous heart.

"I believe there is no other light on this difficult question than that given by the New Testament. There, clear and plain, and every where repeated, shines the doctrine that for every crime, being repented of and forsaken, there is forgiveness with Heaven, and if with Heaven there ought to be with men.

"When you shut the door of hope on any human soul you may at once give up all chance of its reformation. As well bid a man eat without food, see without light, or breathe without air, as bid him mend his ways, while at the same time you tell him that, however he amends, he will be in just the same position, the same hopelessly degraded, unpardoned, miserable sinner."—*A Woman's Thoughts upon Women* (New York ed.), p. 266.

lence, yet the historical facts already given are sufficient to prove its truth without further argument. The existing rule of treatment, instead of suppressing the vice, merely drives it into seclusion—a result far different from the design, and infinitely increasing its power. To those secret haunts of prostitution resort the lowest and most depraved of the male sex, with the full knowledge that a fundamental law of our commonwealth considers every house a castle, into which no officer can enter unless armed with a special legal authority, or called in to suppress an outrage. The result of such seclusion is to confirm the vicious habits of the prostitutes, and frequently to lead them to the commission of other and more heinous offenses.

Again: Secrecy further augments prostitution by preventing the approach of those benevolent individuals who would feel a pleasure in advising and directing the daughters of misery for their real good. Philanthropists have organized Prison Associations and Magdalen Asylums to bear upon prostitution, but they can only reach it in its lowest grades, when the females become inmates of public institutions from destitution and disease. Reformers can not come near the fountain-head, and they are consequently now as far from the consummation of their praiseworthy intentions as when they commenced their labors; because prohibitory measures force prostitutes to take shelter in seclusion, and it is only when women are consigned to our hospitals, work-houses, and penitentiaries that they become accessible. By this time they are so far sunk in depravity as to afford very slender hope of reformation. This is more especially true of Magdalen Asylums. There is indeed a "field white unto the harvest" for benevolent exertions in the most secluded haunts of prostitution, if they could only be made accessible. Sympathy is worthily bestowed upon the sick or dying women transferred from public institutions to charitable organizations. To alleviate the sorrows of their final sufferings, to soothe the agony of the hour of death, to divest of its terrors the passage from this world to the dread future, is a work in which the heart of any Christian must rejoice. But it is only a part of the duties contemplated by such asylums. While their projectors gladly administer the consolations of our holy religion to an expiring Magdalen, they also seek an opportunity to direct erring women to the paths of virtue during the life that still remains to them; to guide them to a path in which they can retrace the false steps already taken, and become useful members of society. This opportunity for exertion is denied under the system which drives vice into seclusion.

Turning now from considering the operation of repressive laws, we notice the importance of sanitary and quarantine regulations. One of the first cares of a good government is to preserve and promote the public health. An illustration of this position occurred in the summer of 1856, when fears were entertained that the city would be visited by a frightful epidemic fever. The public voice declared through the newspapers that the most rigorous and careful sanitary measures were needed, and the cleaning of streets, the removal of nuisances, the purification of tenant-houses, and many other measures of the same kind, were loudly called for, and adopted as far as possible, while the quarantine regulations of the harbor were strictly enforced. In view of this danger, so dreadful and apparently so imminent, the united voice of public opinion sanctioned the very course advocated here; namely, the adoption of remedial, or, more properly speaking, preventive measures. Venereal poison is as destructive, although not so suddenly fatal, as yellow fever, and every motive of philanthropy and economy urges the necessity of effective means for its counteraction.

Since remedial or preventive measures have been adopted in Paris the number of cases of disease and the virulence of its form have materially abated. This fact is asserted not merely on our own personal knowledge, but also from the corroborative testimony of physicians who have had recent opportunities of investigating the subject in that capital. The diminution can be easily explained by a comparison of the laws and regulations applicable to prostitution. We in New York, by our stringent prohibition, drive the vice into seclusion, and deprive ourselves of the means of watching either its progress or results; while our French contemporaries insist that it shall be at all times open to the *surveillance* of properly appointed persons.

The extent of syphilitic infection in New York has been portrayed in the preceding chapter, but the danger of contamination must not be viewed as a merely local question. From its commercial importance, its mercantile marine, its centralization of railroads and canals, and its facilities for river navigation, this city is now the great point of arrival and departure of travelers and emigrants from and to all parts of the Union. Foreigners reach here in large numbers every day, intending to travel to other states. If they remain in the city a few days only, they are exposed to its temptations, and may contract disease which, by their agency, will be perpetuated in the district they have selected as their future home. Returned adventurers from the Pacific shores come here to find the readiest transit to their several destinations. They are exposed to the same temptations, with a probability of the same result. Merchants and store-keepers visit this commercial emporium to obtain supplies of goods, and they are exposed to the same fascinations and the same contingencies. The sailors in port are similarly liable. In short, it is scarcely possible to imagine the extent over which the syphilitic poison originating in the proud and wealthy city of New York may be spread, nor would it be an error to describe the Empire City as a hot-bed where, from the nature of its laws on prostitution, syphilis may be cultivated and disseminated.

Possessed, then, of indubitable proofs of the existence of syphilis, and the knowledge that its range is more widely extended every day, gathering additional malignity in its progress, the next point is to inquire what measures have been adopted to check its ravages. These have hitherto been found totally inadequate, because based upon an erroneous theory, namely, the idea of suppression. The principal public or free hospital where the venereal disease is *confessedly* treated is the Penitentiary Hospital on Blackwell's Island, now known as the Island Hospital. To obtain the benefit of medical treatment therein, it is necessary that the patient should have been sentenced from the Court of Sessions to the Penitentiary for the commission of some crime; or committed to the Work-house by a police justice for vagrancy, drunkenness, or disorderly conduct. From this fact it will be seen that there is, strictly speaking, no "free" hospital for such diseases, as the only one intended for their treatment will or can receive none but those sentenced for an infraction of the laws.

Still the necessity for professional assistance compels many, both males and females, to submit to the degradation of a police commitment. Unfortunate women, or laboring men, find that they are suffering from infection. Possibly they have no money, or probably they have exhausted their funds in payments to charlatans, and so resort for aid and advice to some one of the public dispensaries. Unless the case is a slight one, the medical officers there advise them to resort to hospital treatment, to procure which the poor sufferers are furnished with a certificate of their state, and directed to apply to a police justice. They follow this advice, and in nine cases out of ten the magistrate's only remark is, "Do you want me to send you to the Hospital?" The answer, of course, is in the affirmative, and he forthwith signs a printed commitment to the Penitentiary or Work-house for a time named therein, and ranging from one to six months at the discretion of the magistrate. The following is a copy of one of these documents:

"*City and County of New York, ss.*

"By —— ——, ESQUIRE, one of the Police Justices in and for the City and County of New York.

"To the Constables and Policemen of the said City, and every of them, and to the Warden of the Penitentiary of the City and County of New York:

"THESE ARE IN THE NAME OF THE PEOPLE OF THE STATE OF NEW YORK, to command you, the said Constables and Policemen, to convey to the said PENITENTIARY the body of —— ——, who stands charged before me with being a VAGRANT, viz., being without the means of supporting —— self, and having contracted an INFECTIOUS DISEASE IN THE PRACTICE OF DEBAUCHERY, viz., the venereal disease, requiring charitable aid to restore —— to health, whereof —he is convicted of record on confession, the record of which conviction has been made and filed in the office of the Clerk of the Court of Sessions of the City and County aforesaid, and it appearing to me that the said —— —— is an improper person to be sent to the Alms-house, you, the said Warden, are hereby commanded to receive into your custody, in the said PENITENTIARY, the body of the said —— ——, and —— safely keep for the space of —— month—, or until —he shall be thence delivered by due course of law.

"Given under my hand and seal, this —— day of ——, in the year of our Lord one thousand eight hundred and fifty——.

"—— ——, Police Justice."

This is technically called a commitment "on confession," and its effects are precisely the same as they would be if the individual had been convicted of any tangible act of vagrancy. He is in law and in fact a prisoner for the space of time named in the commitment; he must wear the prison garb, and submit to the prison discipline, until the expiration of his sentence. It is well known to the justices that a penal commitment like the above will immediately secure the sufferer the medical attention his case requires, but they have no power to send any one direct to the Hospital.

And here an inquiry will naturally suggest itself, What does, or what should a magistrate know about committing a sick person, and how can he decide the time such invalid shall remain under treatment? A self-evident conclusion will be that the whole process is an absurd one at the best, and its requirements a hardship on magistrates already overburdened with legitimate duties.

The reader's attention is requested to the pecuniary effects of this plan. To illustrate: Suppose the case of a man committed for six months. He is suffering from some form of venereal disease, and in this state is received at the Penitentiary or Work-house, where his clothes are taken from him, the institution costume supplied, and the particulars of his name, age, nativity, occupation, etc., are registered with an abstract of the commitment by virtue of which he is detained. He is then subjected to medical examination and transferred to the Hospital. In this institution he remains until cured, if that end is attained before the expiration of his sentence, and is then re-transferred to the Penitentiary or Work-house. The average time required for the successful treatment of the disease named, in the Blackwell's Island Hospital, will not probably exceed *two* months, and often a much shorter period is sufficient. But the man has been committed for *six* months, and for the unexpired *four* months of his incarceration he has to be fed, clothed, and lodged at the expense of the Alms-house Department. The labor he can perform will never amount in value to the actual cost of his support, so that he is maintained four months *in accordance with law* at a positive cost to the tax-payers of the city, because they have already supported him for two months in the Hospital. In the aggregate of cases during a year these costs amount to a very large sum. Need any farther argument be adduced to show the palpable absurdity of the system?

A few words upon the moral effect of this local system upon prostitution in New York, premising that being a prostitute is acknowledged by all as a degradation; while a vagrancy commitment to the Work-house or Penitentiary is a positive disgrace. The system is a portion of the crushing-out plan already mentioned, and it says, in effect, " We (the people of New York City) will give you an opportunity to be cured of your loathsome and destructive malady, but only upon the condition that you become the inmate of a penal institution. We know that you can not be cured unless you accept our terms, and we will make those terms as hard and repulsive to human nature as ingenuity can devise." It has been a medical axiom that no two poisons can exist in the system at one and the same time; but the citizens of New York have been experimenting for some years to ascertain whether two moral poisons can not be coexistent in the same person, by adding farther and unnecessary disgrace to the vice of prostitution—thus widening the gulf between the sinner and her possible return to virtue.

The impolicy of making syphilis a reason for imprisonment, except so far as curative measures actually require it, must be apparent to all, were it merely from the fact that it deters many who are suffering from embracing the opportunity of cure until they are absolutely compelled to do so. How excessively wrong is this principle in a hygienic point of view must be evident; a directly contrary course, making the hospital attractive instead of repulsive, would be the true policy, and would be the most economical in its results. Nor is it justice to the medical departments of our public institutions to clog their labors with a proviso which prevents their aid being sought until the last extremity, when it can only exert a palliative and not a curative agency. If syphilis could be reached in its primary stages, their task would be much less difficult and their services much more effectual; whereas little or nothing can be accomplished when official regulations keep away the patients until the disease becomes constitutional, and the mischief is done. As in morals, so is it in medicine. Any evil, to be treated with success, must be encountered in its first stage, and if our regulations preclude this opportunity, but slight hopes can be entertained of any good results. Under a more liberal system, the physician and the philanthropist could combine their efforts. The former would not have to encounter disease inveterately fixed on a broken-down constitution; the latter would not find his benevolent designs frustrated by a lengthened career of depravity now become habitual.

The effect of the provision which offers medical aid to prisoners only is, that every woman of the town will try all possible means to dispense with the treatment. It is only when she has actually fallen to the lowest deep of her class, when one step more will plunge her into a bottomless abyss of helpless and hopeless woe, that she will voluntarily accept the proffered aid. She will endure torture from her maladies, or rely upon the assistance of empirics, and submit to all their extortions, rather than become a prisoner. But when every resource is exhausted, and her physical torments plainly tell her that she must obtain medical relief or die, then she submits. Once in the hospital, she is relieved, after a period of protracted sickness, and leaves it to return to her old haunts, because she can go nowhere else, the law having affixed the additional disgrace of imprisonment upon her former bad character. Sociality is a characteristic of human nature, and if these women can not gain admission to any company but that of the vicious and abandoned, they prefer that to solitude. Returned once more to her former associates, the time soon comes when farther medical assistance is needed, and thus she alternates for a few months or years between prison, hospital, and brothel, till death puts an end to her sufferings, and a nameless grave in Potters' Field receives the remains of one whom charitable measures, properly applied, might possibly have made a useful member of society.

The sense of shame which follows a single deviation from the paths of virtue drives many women to prostitution. Why add to the existing sense of shame another infamy when she unfortunately contracts disease? Can we consistently blame her if she becomes callous, when every legal provision directly tends to indurate her sensibilities? The misconduct of parents toward children has been shown as one of the causes of prostitution. The father or mother drives from the paternal roof the child who has committed but a single error. Then, under the pressure of hunger, she inevitably sins more deeply, becomes diseased, applies to the public for relief, and is sentenced to imprisonment! The first mistake, that of the parents, makes her vicious: the second mistake, incarceration, confirms her in vice. We denounce such ill-treatment in the parents, while practically we ourselves, as the natural guardians of all who need assistance, are doing precisely the same thing. Where, then, is our consistency? If it is right for us, a body corporate, to practice such cruel oppression, is it not equally justifiable for each member of the body to act in the same manner in his individual capacity? Of course, what is right for the multitude must be right for the individual, and our own conduct convicts us of inconsistency. We have no warrant to condemn parents for single acts which we perform collectively; or, if we are right in censuring them, we are wrong in performing the same acts ourselves: if they are reprehensible, we also are culpable.

This system, with all its absurdity, its prejudicial effect on public health, and its obvious tendency to immorality, is not adequate to stay the destroying scourge; on the contrary, it is likely to extend its ravages.   If a prostitute, arrested and committed to Blackwell's Island for drunkenness or any disorderly conduct, is found to be diseased, or if she commits herself knowing that she is infected, she is immediately placed under medical charge.   She will probably remain contentedly in the hospital until the worst symptoms of the disease are subdued: by this time the discipline of the institution has become irksome to her.   She communicates with the brothel-keeper with whom she formerly boarded, or with some "lover" or acquaintance, who sues out a writ of *certiorari* or *habeas corpus*, which instantly effects her discharge.   She now returns to her former haunts, half-cured, again to aid in disseminating disease, farther to undermine her own constitution, and to infect men who will in turn become a charge upon the tax-payers, or by their agency cause others to become thus liable.   The instance of wholesale release mentioned in the previous chapter will recur to the mind of the reader.

The experience of almost every day confirms these statements. It is well known that there are those who hang around the various police courts expressly to attend to such business, and who make a large income from this source, exclusive of other matters pertaining to prostitution in which they occasionally exert their abilities.   The vagrancy commitments by which women are "sent up" are generally insufficient, and there is no legal power to detain them, and force them to submit to the treatment they so much require.   It has been asserted by legal men of high standing that nearly the whole of the commitments issued by police justices are defective, and that there exists in law no impediment to the immediate discharge of every prostitute now on Blackwell's Island. The public can readily perceive the necessary inefficiency of these institutions so far as the prevention of venereal disease is concerned.

The facility with which prostitutes committed to Blackwell's Island can obtain their discharge may be attributed to want of care in making out the commitments.   A recent statute (1854) prescribes the form in which these should be made, requiring the recital of admitted or substantiated facts, and the filing of a copy of the original in the office of the clerk of the Court of Sessions. These requirements are not observed, and the reason assigned by magistrates is, that their own time, and the time of their clerks, is so fully occupied by the press of business before them that they can not proceed as minutely as the act directs. This confirms the view already expressed of the impolicy and impropriety of placing such onerous and extra-judicial duties upon the justices. But as they would be liable to be sued for false imprisonment if they committed under this act without observing all its requirements, they issue their commitments in the old form required by the Revised Statutes, and are sheltered thereby from ulterior consequences. These commitments direct the persons to be confined in the Penitentiary, but the local arrangements of Blackwell's Island require them to be sent to the Work-house, and unless this transfer is actually made in each case by the Governors of the Alms-house—for they can not deputize their power—it is a *waiver* of the right of custody, and consequently entitles the prisoner so transferred to a discharge. It has been claimed that the Work-house is a part of the Penitentiary, but this point has been overruled, because the statute establishing the Work-house plainly shows a contrary intent.

A prisoner is entitled to a discharge on another ground, namely, because the commitment has not been filed as directed; or, on another ground, that the commitment does not recite the evidence by which the fact of vagrancy was proved. A final ground of discharge, which is never pressed till all the minor technicalities have failed, is that the whole proceeding is illegal because the statute of 1854 has not been complied with.

On these grounds a writ of *certiorari* or *habeas corpus* is sued out, the preliminary steps being a petition from the prisoner or his friend, setting forth that he is illegally detained, an affidavit of verification, and a certificate of the clerk of the Court of Sessions that the commitment has not been filed in his office. Upon the presentation of these documents, the judge to whom application is made issues the required writ, and specifies the time at which it shall be returnable. The action of the two writs is similar, excepting that a writ of *habeas corpus* requires the production of the prisoner before the judge in addition to a return of the cause of detention, while a writ of *certiorari* only requires a return of the cause of detention. The return is made by the person having custody of the prisoner, and consists of a copy of the commitment under which he is held; and, from the already-stated informality of these documents, it will be apparent there can be no legal ground for his detention. The judge is strictly prohibited from entertaining any question beyond the legality of the papers; with the moral aspect of the question he can not interfere, and as the commitments are generally informal he has no alternative but to discharge the prisoner.

Application for these writs must be made in the name of an attorney, but such name is often used by an agent who transacts the business, and divides the fee with his principal.

From this sketch it will be evident that, if the prescribed form were observed in these commitments, frequent discharges would be avoided, or there would be so many difficulties to surmount that they would be very rarely attempted.

Does no responsibility rest upon the public, and on our lawmakers, for negligence in this matter? Without conceding that a vagrancy commitment is likely to reform a prostitute (in fact, the weight of evidence is against the possibility of its doing so), the case stands thus: the Legislature has provided a mode of relief which was deemed effectual at the time, but this mode is evaded, or can not be observed, by those upon whom its administration devolves. The public have long known the existence of these difficulties, but have never interfered to give us a better act. By their refusal to interfere they stand in the position of aiders and abettors in this neglect, or, worse than neglect, the actual propagation of a dreadful disease. Had public opinion been concentrated upon this matter, an inquiry would long ago have shown the fallacy of our present system, and suggested the required amendments. This has not been done; but public remissness in no way diminishes public responsibility.

This doctrine of public accountability may be profitably examined for a few moments in connection with the general aspect of prostitution. Few will deny that the mass of the people are answerable for many of its evils. They are cognizant of the existence of vice in the aggregate, if not in detail; they can understand its effects, and are not ignorant of the principal causes which lead to it; yet they make no effort to remove existing causes or to prevent future evils. They practically treat women as an inferior race of beings, and can not even give a poor seamstress employment without saying, in fact if not in words, "You can not be trusted to make this unless a man examines every button hole, and inspects every row of stitching, to see that you are not defrauding us." The only way to secure confidence is to bestow confidence; but if a person is treated in a manner likely to destroy self-respect, the inevitable result will be a recklessness as to his or her own character. Despised without a cause; treated in mere business matters as imbeciles, or children, or thieves, it is not surprising that women become careless as to their future life, and, smarting under the injustice of their position, too frequently degenerate into the wretched beings who infest our streets and pollute the atmosphere with their deadly infection.

The public, then, are responsible for this prostitution, because they have never bestowed any attention upon it. It is one of the gravest and most difficult of social problems, involving the interests of every man in the community, and yet the most stupid indifference has been shown respecting it. The subject has been canvassed by medical men on account of its sad effects upon the physical organization; its extent has been known to judicial and police authorities from its social and civil results; but the great body of the public have hitherto decided that they know nothing, and want to know nothing about it. They admit its existence, being too evident to be denied; but so far they have taken no steps to ascertain its source or stay its progress, because it was a matter with which they were afraid to interfere, and now the deplorable consequences accruing from it must be laid to their charge.

It can not be denied that there are many difficulties attending any investigation of this vice; that many well-meaning but timid people entertain the opinion that it is one of those gangrenous ulcers upon society which can not be alluded to except in whispers; that more harm would result from instituting inquiries than if it were allowed to exist and fester on unnoticed.[1] This apathy,

[1] "We have no right, mercifully constituted with less temptation to evil than men, to shrink with sanctimonious ultra-delicacy from the barest mention of things we must know to exist. If we do not know it, our ignorance is at once both helpless and dangerous; narrows our judgment, exposes us to a thousand painful mistakes, and greatly limits our powers of usefulness."—*A Woman's Thoughts upon Women* (New York edition), p. 255.

"No single woman who takes any thought of what is going on around her, no mistress or mother who requires constantly servants for her house and nursemaids for her children, can or dare blind herself to the fact. Better face truth at once in all its bareness than be swaddled up forever in the folds of a silken falsehood."—Ib., p. 259.

"Many of us will not investigate this subject because they are afraid: afraid not so much of being, as being thought to be, especially by the other sex, incorrect, indelicate, unfeminine; of being supposed to know more than they ought to know, or than the present refinement of society—a good and beautiful thing when real—concludes that they do know.

which has heretofore been the policy, has made prostitution the monster evil which it now is, and upon those who have advocated, or may advocate, a continuance of the same course of silence and inaction the sufferers from the vice may justly charge their destruction. The "masterly inactivity" of the statesman is unquestionably justifiable in any case where passive resistance will overcome an evil, but in dealing with prostitution a diametrically opposite method must be pursued. It requires an active aggression upon all old prejudices; an explosion of still older theories; a vigorous commencement of a new course.

It has been shown elsewhere that the public are responsible for prostitution, because they persist in excluding women from many kinds of employment for which they are fitted; while for work in those occupations which are open to them they receive an entirely inadequate remuneration. It has also been shown that the community are equally responsible on account of their non-interference with known and acknowledged evils. Another reason why accountability can not be evaded may be designated; namely, the carelessness, or, more properly, heartlessness, with which the character of woman is treated. Let there be but a breath of suspicion against her fair fame, no matter from what vile source it may emanate, and the energies of man seem directed toward her destruction. "She is down, keep her down!" is the almost universal cry, and this malignant process is continued until the victim is positively forced into a life of undisguised immorality. The sacred decision, "Let him that is without sin among you cast the first stone," is entirely forgotten, and the most violent in their denunciations are frequently those who are the most blameworthy themselves.

The whole force of the world's opinion has been directed, not to the censure of actually guilty parties who induced the crime, but to the poor wronged sufferer. She, who is too frequently the victim of falsehood and deceit, or the slave of an absolute necessity, must expiate her fault by submitting to a constant succession of indignities and annoyances. He, whose conduct has made her

"Oh! women, women! why have you not more faith in yourselves, in that strong, inner purity, which alone can make a woman brave! which, if she knows herself to be clean in heart and desire, in body and soul, loving cleanness for its own sake, and not for the credit that it brings, will give her a freedom of action, and a fearlessness of consequences, which are to her a greater safeguard than any external decorum. To be, and not to seem, is the amulet of her innocence."—Ib., p. 261.

what she is, escapes all censure. But some moralist will ask, "How would you have us treat such women?" Treat them, sir, as human beings, actuated by the same passions as yourself; as susceptible beings, keenly sensitive of reproach; as injured beings, who have a claim upon your kindness; as outraged beings, who have a demand upon your justice. Lead them into a path by which they can escape from danger; protect the innocent from the snares which environ them on every side. And when this is done, pour the vials of your hottest wrath on those of your own sex whose machinations have blighted some of God's fairest created beings.

Public responsibility must be understood in its broadest and most literal sense, as meaning the individual accountability of every member of the community. The time has not yet arrived, unfortunately, when this matter can be left in the hands of corporations or legislatures. Their constituents must be aroused to consideration of its importance before any satisfactory action can or will be taken by them; and it is to the thinking men of the age that these pages are addressed, in the full confidence that so soon as their sympathies are enlisted public action will follow.

To this end an endeavor has been made to show the injurious effects of prohibition, disappointing expectation as a means of decreasing syphilis, or of curtailing the limits of prostitution; the necessity which exists for effectual preventive measures; and the inefficient, or worse than inefficient, nature of the local arrangements of New York to accomplish this desideratum. Thus the way for a consideration of the remedial process has been opened, and now with such evidence as he has before him the reader may be asked, in all sincerity, if he does not seriously believe that *it would be a prudent step, instead of trying to extirpate the evil, to place prostitutes and prostitution under the surveillance of a medical bureau in the Police Department?* Extirpation never has been, never can be accomplished in any community; repression and restriction, as proposed, have been tried and have proved successful.

Assuming an affirmative answer to this question, and it is difficult to imagine it otherwise if the facts are dispassionately considered, attention is respectfully requested to the manner in which the change could be effected.

To meet the exigencies of the case there are required

(1.) A suitable hospital for the treatment of venereal disease;

(2.) A legally authorized medical visitation of all known houses of prostitution, with full power to order the immediate removal of any woman found to be infected to the designated hospital;

(3.) The power to detain infected persons under treatment until they are cured, a term of time which none but medical men can decide.

By a suitable hospital is meant an institution devoted to the treatment of such diseases, like the special hospitals of Paris and other Continental cities, and entirely removed from all connection with any punitive establishment. The rules proposed for the government of the Island Hospital, when its name was changed from Penitentiary Hospital, do not, by any means, meet the urgent requirements of the case. The Penitentiary, its officers and inmates, must be entirely shut out from the desired hospital, and no prison-warden or keeper of criminals must have any jurisdiction within its walls or over its grounds. Inmates of hospitals have too long endured the stupid interference of non-medical men, and it is time that medical law exclusively was considered in the direction and management of buildings devoted to medical purposes. This is especially necessary in a syphilitic hospital, on account of the character of its patients. *No amount of imprisonment as a punishment ever yet reformed a prostitute, and it never will; all intercourse with prisoners, be it ever so transient, has but confirmed women in vice.*

The tendency of imprisonment is directly contrary to any reformation, confirming previous habits instead of rooting them out. The instinctive dread of incarceration has prevented many from availing themselves of the medical advantages offered them, particularly among the better and higher grades of frail women. We want a hospital exclusively for the treatment of syphilis, with the power to place and keep there all women so diseased until cured. Matters of detail can be arranged in such a manner as to admit of a proper classification, based upon the degree of moral turpitude belonging to each. Payment could and should be required from all who possess the means, for expenses actually incurred, and this would contribute a considerable sum to meet the expenditures of the institution. Among these women, as a body, there exists an excessive amount of pride. Those of the upper class will not associate with any of a lower rank, and, in fact, look upon them in very much the same manner that moralists regard the whole body. To be enabled to reach them at all, a liberal management must be adopted. But will not this be deferring to vice because it is dressed in silks or satins? asks some one. Most decidedly not. Let the arrangements be what they might, such a hospital as described would afford no encouragement to vice, for in it all must submit to the same course of treatment, varied only in the minor accessories which surround it.

Even if the arrangements were exposed to an objection like the above, the end would justify the means. The city of New York contains, at this day, venereal infection sufficient to contaminate all the male population of the United States in a very short space of time. It has been proved from official and medical statistics that this malady is rapidly on the increase, and a paramount question is, how to be relieved of the incubus. Rigorous prohibitory measures will not effect this; they only make the matter worse. Punitive hospitals will not effect this; they have been tried and found wanting. Free institutions would, in all probability, succeed in accomplishing far more than any other measure our citizens have ever tried. The question is one, if not absolutely of life, certainly of healthy existence, and its inestimable importance must over-ride all doubts and difficulties. In view of the dangers surrounding our rising generation, even supposing the men and women of the present day exempt from them, it would be perfectly inexcusable to refuse any available plan because some one of its features might not please all tastes. Adopt an arrangement similar to that suggested, and if any crudities are discovered they can be readily cured as experience points them out. The plan is not presented as a perfect one, but merely as an outline sketch of what is necessary.

A regular medical visitation of all prostitutes is an essential part of the scheme, and its organization should be a matter of serious consideration. The Parisian plan already submitted might form a very good basis; and an arrangement which throws the whole system of prostitution open to an effective police supervision, and the establishment of a medical bureau in connection therewith for professional purposes, is suggested as most desirable. This medical visitation, conducted by physicians to be connected with the Police Department, and sustained by the power of that body, should be confided to men of recognized skill and known integrity. To insure public confidence, so essentially necessary in the inception of any social innovation, it would be necessary that the agents upon whom its execution devolved should be men of tried probity and acknowledged reputation, both professional and personal. The slightest symptom of disease should be sufficient evidence to warrant the immediate removal of any woman to the syphilitic hospital. The residence of any woman, be it temporary or permanent, in a known house of prostitution must subject her to a medical examination, as it would afford a very strong presumption that she was there for immoral purposes.

The propriety of a medical examination of prostitutes at certain intervals can not be doubted, and, in fact, it is practically admitted at the present time by some few of the brothel-keepers in the city. These pay a physician a liberal salary to visit their boarders every few days for the express purpose of carrying out the plan suggested now; resorting to treatment whenever he finds it necessary. Some of the most aristocratic houses of prostitution are thus attended, but the system is in use more especially among those natives of Continental Europe who are now keeping houses of ill fame in New York, and who, in bringing to the New World many of the customs of the old, have thus testified to the benefit of the regulations enforced there.

But although such visiting physician may pronounce a girl infected, the world has no security that she will not continue her avocation; and in order to remove all doubt upon this question she should be instantly removed to an institution where she can not possibly propagate the malady. This must be done under conjoint medical and police authority. Among prostitutes of the lower grades systematic visitation is more imperatively necessary. They will not place themselves under medical treatment unless they are compelled, but until their disease assumes a character that prevents the possibility of farther concealment from their visitors, they continue to ply their loathsome and destructive trade. The summit of ambition with them is to keep their liberty; so long as they can earn enough to provide themselves a shelter, and feed their ravenous appetite for intoxicating liquor, they are content to submit to the pains and ravages of syphilis, alike heedless of their own sufferings and the injuries they inflict on others. We have had cases under our own professional treatment where women have actually persevered in this course for many weeks after they had become aware they were diseased, solely for the reasons indicated.

It may be objected that such a plan would offer a premium to lewdness by circumscribing the dangers of infection; but this argument can have little weight, as it is scarcely possible that promiscuous sexual intercourse can be carried on much more extensively than it is at present. The vice seems to have reached its culminating point. Experience proves that in all ages of the world there have been many men whose passions were so violent and so ill regulated that they would attain their gratification at any risk, even though that risk included the probability of venereal infection. As in games of hazard every player hopes to be a winner, so in carnal indulgences every man flatters himself that, because some gratify their lusts unscathed for a long series of years, so may he; that as hitherto he has escaped disease in his unhallowed amours, he may continue equally fortunate to the end of his career. This is confessedly a poor dependence, but it is the reliance of hundreds and thousands of the followers of her whose "house is the way to hell."

Diseases of a syphilitic nature are viewed by some persons as special punishments for special sins, and hence they argue that it would be an interference with the order of Providence to attempt to eradicate them. The discussion of a theological question would be altogether out of place in these pages, but the supposition may be met by a parallel case. Delirium tremens is the result of an excessive use of intoxicating liquors, and may justly be considered a special punishment for that offense; but did any body ever know a case in which those who object to the treatment of syphilis extended a single obstacle to the case of a drunkard? If it is right to adopt curative measures in one case, why exclude them in the other? But even supposing that the treatment of syphilis is open to this objection so far as the guilty parties are concerned, shall their descendants be involved in suffering because the parents sinned? If a rigorous medical examination offers additional inducements to prostitution by reducing the probabilities of disease, it also guarantees that helpless wives and unborn children shall not be included in its list of victims. Go to the thousands of married women now childless or suffering from abortion; ask their opinion. Go to the thousands of disappointed husbands whose hopes of offspring have been blighted in consequence of their own youthful dissipation; ask their opinion, and see what the answers would be. Go and ask the diseased children on Randall's Island, and in their emaciated frames read their testimony. The evidence thus obtained would prove unanswerable arguments in favor of the plan proposed.

It can not be imagined that forcing diseased women to submit to a specific routine of treatment in a special hospital involves any undue interference with their personal liberty. The right to commit a wrong, be it social, moral, or physical, never can exist; the slightest reflection upon such a proposition will at once prove it untenable. The spread of venereal disease is a positive wrong, and, therefore, a woman who is suffering from it, and is certain or likely to propagate it, is as legitimate an object for compulsory treatment as would be a maniac whom we should find roaming through the streets of the city, or a person afflicted with small-pox, yellow fever, or any other contagious or infectious malady. If either of these cases were to come before any member of the community, he would not for one moment regard it an infringement of personal liberty to place the subject under proper care and restraint. On the contrary, he would think of the danger to which he and his family were exposed, and, flinging theory to the winds, would immediately urge prompt and practical measures. This is all that is asked respecting prostitution. Let the public be once thoroughly convinced of the extent and danger of syphilitic infection, and there would be but few objectors to these suggestions. Among that few, the principal portion doubtless would be the advertising empirics whose disgusting announcements occupy so much space in the columns of our daily journals. That they derive a large income from this source is indisputable, and it is equally certain that if the recommendations now made were adopted they would find their "occupation gone." Speaking in all candor, the health, decency, and good morals of the city would be better cared for in their absence than it now is, with all the combinations of their "extraordinary success," "unequaled experience," and "unparalleled facilities." In a financial view, the money they extort (we refrain from using a harsher term) from their credulous patients could be far better applied than in contributing to their wealth.

Farther: Such an institution and organization as has been described would be useless did it not possess the absolute power to retain every patient under treatment until cured. Whatever modification of principle or mode of action may be ultimately adopted (and, sooner or later, *something must be done*), this is an indispensable requisite. One half the danger of venereal infection arises from imperfectly cured cases. Under the existing system, as already explained, writs can be issued at an almost nominal cost to remove any, or all of the prostitutes now under medical treatment on Blackwell's Island ; and such an abuse of a valuable privilege on account of mere technical errors must be fatal to the success of any remedial project. It would be as reasonable for a lawyer to petition the courts to order a vessel detained in Quarantine by the Board of Health because she was infected with yellow fever to be brought to her wharf in this city, and there to have permission to disseminate the disease on board, as it is for the same individual to apply for a writ of *certiorari*, the effect of which is to take an abandoned woman reeking with disease from an institution where she is under treatment, and allow her to extend the venereal poison to every one who may have intercourse with her. This must not be understood as indicating a wish to curtail the constitutional privileges attached to writs of *habeas corpus* or *certiorari*, but merely their applicability to cases like the supposed one. How can the evil be prevented? Simply by making any legislative enactment on the subject so plain that it can not be misunderstood or evaded. No lawyer would find any difficulty in drafting a short act giving the Police Department the power, based upon an affidavit made by a member of their own medical bureau, to remove any diseased woman to a proper hospital, and *retain her there until cured*.

It may appear to a casual observer that this detention would be of the same nature as the imprisonment required by the existing mode, but a little thought will point out a wide difference. Now, we force a woman to become an inmate of a penitentiary, and add disgrace to her disease by assuming her to have been guilty of crime. Then, we should require her to become an inmate of the Hospital, with no additional disgrace but that arising from the fact that she had contracted syphilis by vicious habits. In the one case, we make her the companion of some of the vilest wretches on the face of the earth; in the other, she would have no associates but those of her own class.

The Medical Bureau to whom these reforms should be intrusted, although connected with the Police Department, would require to be an independent body so far as professional duties are concerned. Its connection would be necessary, because there would be many cases requiring the intervention of the civil power; and its isolation would be equally important, because much would depend on the discretion of the examiners, and many contingencies might arise where a strict line of routine duty would defeat the object in view. They would be literally a "detective corps," and with a known amount of duty before them must be left to choose their own method of performing it. Any definite arrangements or positive orders from a non-medical board would only embarrass their action, for medical and non-medical executives always clash when they aim at one common object.

Of course a leading requirement in their instructions must be that their examinations be rigid and thorough. No half-way measures in this respect could meet the absolute demands of the case, or satisfy the expectations of the community. It must be plainly understood by the world that the Medical Bureau was required to perform its whole duty, uncompromisingly and fearlessly; and that its members were men who would not evade the responsibility. In their investigations many cases would occur where their services would be valuable to society, beyond the pale of professional duty. It is not to be expected that they would become evangelists, but they could be the willing and efficient coadjutors of those who delight to bear the Gospel to these poor degraded beings; and even while listening to a recital of bodily sufferings, instances would arise where the acts of the good Samaritan would be required at their hands. They would be the depositaries of many a narrative of wrong and outrage, of sorrow and suffering, and it is not unreasonable to believe that of the histories poured into their ears some would indicate a channel by which the lost one might be restored to home and friends and virtue, or point to some chord in the mind which would give a responsive sound when touched by the hand of pity.[1]

[1] "Reformatories, Magdalene Institutions, and the like, are admirable in their way, but there are numberless cases in which individual judgment and help alone are possible. It is this, the train of thought which shall result in act, and which I desire to suggest to individual minds, in the hope of arousing that imperceptibly small influence of the many, which forms the strongest lever of universal opinion.

"All I can do—all, I fear, that any one can do by mere speech, is to impress upon every woman, and chiefly upon those who, reared innocently in safe homes, view the wicked world without somewhat like gazers at a show or spectators at a battle, shocked, wondering, perhaps pitying a little, but not understanding at all, that repentance is possible. Also, that once having returned to a chaste life, a woman's former life should never be 'cast up' against her; that she should be allowed to resume, if not her pristine position, at least one that is full of usefulness, pleasantness, and respect, a respect the amount of which must be determined by her own daily conduct. She should be judged solely by what she is now, and not by what she has been. That judgment may be, ought to be stern and fixed as justice itself with regard to her present, and even her past so far as concerns the crime committed; but it ought never to take the law into its own hands toward the criminal, who may long since have become less a criminal than a sufferer. Virtue degrades

The adoption of these suggestions would be, at least, a step in the right direction, and lay the foundation of a system which can be gradually enlarged until it embraces regulations as to registry, management of houses of ill fame, etc., to the same extent as is now done in Europe.

And here a few words relative to the licensing system may not be inappropriate. The propriety of granting licenses, and thus making vice a sort of revenue, is open to grave objections, but on the other hand acknowledged social evils have, ere this, been made to contribute to the public funds. Witness the dealing in ardent spirits. The city does now, and has for years derived a considerable income from licenses to sell liquors. A great number of wise and good men contend that the sale or use of intoxicating beverages is not only an unmitigated evil, but even criminal; they have entertained and publicly declared these sentiments for years, but still the license system is continued. It may be a question for decision whether prostitution is not as liable for taxation as drunkenness, and if both were equally taxed whether, as a body, we should be more responsible for the results of one or the other. *En passant*, it may be noticed that an annual tax of one per cent. upon the property engaged in the business of prostitution, and a similar assessment upon the revenue of houses of ill fame, would amount to over one hundred thousand dollars.

The plan here shadowed forth would not be likely to extend prostitution, but on the contrary there is very little doubt but it would check it. Even if it did not, the community would reap an advantage in the sanitary reform it would enforce. In low neighborhoods many of the brothels are as dangerous to public health on account of their crowded and excessively filthy state, as are the syphilized inmates themselves. Such places would legitimately come within the province of the medical inspectors, and their reports thereon to the police executive would insure immediate attention.

Public morals would be advanced by such visitations. These houses, or a great number of them, are the resort of all species of dishonest characters who would unquestionably abandon them, at

herself, and loses every vestige of her power, when her dealings with vice sink into a mere matter of individual opinion, personal dislike, or selfish fear of harm. For all offenses, punishment, retributive and inevitable, must come; but punishment is one thing, revenge is another. One only, who is Omniscient as well as Omnipotent, can declare, 'Vengeance is Mine.' "—*A Woman's Thoughts upon Women* (New York ed.), p. 275.

least as places of residence, if they knew they were at any moment liable to a domiciliary visit. Again, almost every person
has in his remembrance some female who left home and could not
be found, because securely secreted in some one of these houses of
prostitution ; at least it is not uncommon to read of such cases in
the daily papers, accompanied with an account of the unsuccessful
search of her friends and the police. Occurrences like this could
not take place if all known houses of bad repute were under the
surveillance of the Medical Police Department.

Nor is it unreasonable to hope that prostitution would be diminished. It has flourished of late years in seclusion, but our
plan would render privacy impossible. Seclusion has attracted
many unfortunate women, whom shame, or a dread of exposure,
would have deterred, had they known that houses of ill fame were
always open to the visits of the police, or that every few days a
physician would make a tour of inspection, and a personal examination, to which they must submit. Generally speaking, these
women have a dread of falling into the hands of a doctor, and in
present circumstances they know that a medical examination is
optional with themselves, until they become so sick as to render
it unavoidable. But if their miserable life were burdened with
the additional annoyance of a compulsory medical treatment it is
probable that a considerable check might be imposed thereon.

Public decency would be advanced by such visitations. To effectually perform their duties the Medical Bureau and the General Police Department would find it necessary to make themselves personally acquainted with these women, and to keep a
register of all houses where prostitution was carried on. Now,
the prohibition which has driven it into secrecy has also rendered
it difficult to determine who are frail. Prostitutes are found in
hotels, fashionable restaurants, steam-boat excursions, watering-
places, and suburban retreats. They visit balls and other public
entertainments ; sometimes by sufferance, but more frequently because they are not known. It is needless to say how virtuous
women can be annoyed and insulted by such companionship, or
to what extent prostitutes can use their influence in miscellaneous
society. If the police were personally acquainted with these wom-
en, they could act in the same manner as on the Continent of Europe, namely, touch them upon the shoulder and quietly give
them a hint to leave. Or another reform could easily be introduced—the confinement of all prostitutes to particular localities in

the city, so as to limit their influence. This would be tantamount to the ancient regulations prescribing their dress or some distinctive mark; and to the present arrangements in Europe, where the houses are distinguished by some specified peculiarity. It would also prevent the depreciation of property which takes place in any neighborhood where a brothel is established.

Public decency would be served in another manner. It is a most humiliating admission, that New York is fast approaching to the condition of certain foreign cities, where unnatural practices first led to the contemplation and adoption of these or similar remedial measures. In our case, *they are known to the authorities*, but are so revolting that they never have been, and never can be, made public. Of course, such an organization would take special cognizance of these detestable abominations.

Objections to the expense of the plan may be raised, and it can not be denied that it will be large, yet it will be a matter of economy to incur it, even at the risk of increasing taxation, which *it will not do*. Recollect that every year, as the virulence of syphilis was abated, the cause of the expense would diminish, and that in a direct ratio to the energy displayed in the examination would be the progressive reduction of expenditure. It has already been indicated how some of the inmates of a syphilitic hospital, from whom hitherto nothing has been received, could be made to contribute their quota of the cost. Now, the public bear all the expenses, either as assessments or as private payments in individual attacks. The magnitude of the latter item has been already estimated, and were it possible to calculate in addition the value of lost time, the injury to business, and the deterioration of the constitution, the total in one year would be far more than sufficient to carry out the whole of this plan for double the time.

It would also be economy to incur the outlay on account of the benefits to succeeding generations. Syphilis is not confined in its effects to the life-time of the men or women who contract it, but is entailed on their descendants. These, provided they survive its baneful effects during infancy, are mentally and physically unfitted for business or the active pursuits of life, and, consequently, are frequently indebted for the means of sustenance to their friends or to public institutions. If the liability to that disease among parents can be removed, no fears need be entertained about their children.

We are not so sanguine as to imagine that all the good effects above enumerated could be accomplished *instanter*. It would be a work of time, but the sooner it is commenced the better for all the interests involved. Many persons will say, "Oh! these evils do not concern us; these diseases will never injure us or ours; why should we trouble ourselves, and give our money, time, and attention to such matters?" Stop, reader! *While human passion exists, and while the means of gratifying it can be obtained, you and yours can and will, nay, do now suffer from it, directly or indirectly.* The first question for any citizen to ask himself is, Can prostitution be abolished; can it be crushed out? If this be answered in the negative, as it must be, then the next question brings him to the point sought to be attained in these pages, namely, the means that shall be taken to circumscribe and diminish its consequent diseases and evils.

This question has latterly been attracting some attention in England, and plans to mitigate the evil have been publicly discussed. The chief grounds of complaint, or at least those brought most prominently forward, were the assembling of prostitutes in the streets, the annoyance they caused to passengers, and the disorderly character of "night-houses." This term is applied in London to those public houses, supper-rooms, wine and cigar saloons, etc., which are situated near the theatres and places of public entertainment, and, being permitted to remain open all night, become resorts for prostitutes. A public meeting for consultation upon these evils was held in London in January last (1858), and the remarks made by some of the speakers are so much in accordance with the general tenor of this work as to be worth extracting. In justice to the writer it must be premised that the preceding part of this chapter was penned twelve months before the report of this meeting was made public.

The chairman observed "that he was glad to see so general an interest elicited on this subject, and that he hoped it would lead to some practical result. It would, in fact, be impossible to aggravate the evil, for neither in Paris, Berlin, New York, nor even in the cities of Asia, was there such a public exhibition of profligacy."

The following resolutions were submitted and adopted:

" *Resolved,* That a deputation do wait as early as possible upon Sir George Grey, for the purpose of most respectfully but earnestly representing to her majesty's government the necessity of effectual measures being taken to put down the open exhibition of street prostitution, which in various parts of the metropolis, particularly in the important thoroughfares of the Haymarket,

Coventry Street, Regent Street, Portland Place, and other adjacent localities, is carried on with a disregard of public decency and to an extent tolerated in no other capital or city of the civilized world.

" That such deputation be instructed to urge upon her majesty's government the following measures, whereby it is believed that the evil complained of may be effectually controlled :

" Firstly, the enforcement, upon a systematic plan and by means of a department of the police specially appointed and instructed for that purpose, of the provisions of the 2d and 3d of Victoria, cap. 47, in reference to street prostitution, which provisions have in certain localities been heretofore carried out with the best effect, and in others have been ineffectual only because acted upon partially, and not upon any uniform system.

" And, secondly, the passing an act for licensing and placing under proper regulations, as to supervision and hours of closing, all houses of entertainment, or for the supply of refreshments, intended to be opened to the public. after a certain fixed hour, it being matter of public notoriety that the houses of this description popularly known as night-houses have, by becoming the places of resort of crowds of prostitutes and other idle and disorderly persons at all hours of the night, greatly contributed to the present disgraceful exhibition of street prostitution.

" That the attention of the government be also directed to the number of foreign prostitutes systematically imported into this country, and to the means of controlling this evil."

The substance of one of the addresses made on the subject was as follows :

The speaker " begged to remind the meeting that a change had already been effected through the action of the police in the aspect of the Haymarket and Regent Street, heretofore so much complained of. The sense that the public eye was upon their class had caused a corresponding amendment in the dress and demeanor of the females frequenting those streets ; and the objects of this association were, so far, in good train. Strongly oppressive, or, as some delicately said, repressive measures could only be carried out by an extent of police interference inconsistent with the prejudices of English people, who were indisposed to deny a large extent of personal freedom to persons of even the most disorderly classes who had not absolutely forfeited their civil rights. If the association went the length of advocating that the act of prostitution should involve such forfeiture, and the entire riddance of London streets from the presence of prostitutes, they would soon find their hands over full. Unless they thought it possible to exterminate the vice altogether, they would find that its wholesale clearance from the streets would necessitate registration, licensing, and confinement in certain authorized quarters or streets, as prevailed abroad ; but such restrictions would entail a more ample recognition and legalization than had hitherto obtained, and so ample, indeed, as to be very distasteful to what was called the religious public. It would be obviously unjust to exempt from pressure the ladylike prosperous harlot, while a miserable, vulgar, painted outcast was consignable, because she stood out from the picture somewhat broadly, to the police cell and the bridewell. The meeting must be aware that there was already abroad among the lower half million of Londoners an impression that the police was already strict enough—and that this opinion was shared by numbers of intelligent men, neither paupers nor criminals. They must remember that many a gentleman of character had passed a night in a police cell for interfering in the defense of prostitutes against the police. And this sentiment would deepen very dangerously if the police pressure were put on double, or, as some would have it, tenfold. The very policemen, too —men sprung from the same class of society as those female offenders— were as likely as any one else to be fainthearted in the work of relieving the eyes and ears of gentility from the presence of those whose situation they were not slow to trace to the schemes and desires of the genteel class. He did not think that the power of discrimination could be safely intrusted to the ill-paid constables of the Metropolitan Police, and the association of certain rate-payers with the police as witnesses, as hinted at by one of the delegates, would soon, if established, fall into desuetude. With the view of checking the evil in a satisfactory manner, he would recommend the institution of a special service of street orderlies or regulators in uniform, a well-paid, superior, temperate, and discreet class of men, if possible, whose functions should be to observe, not to spy upon all prostitutes, especially those of the street-walking order, and whose circulation, as opposed to loitering and haunting particular spots, they should insist upon. They should work, not by threats, but by entreaty, advice, suggestion; but in case of contumacy, should have the right to call in the regular force. He believed that the right of entry and inspection of all places of ill fame should be vested in the Home Secretary and his delegates, and this would be attained least oppressively by a proper system of licensing. Forced concentration would not be tolerated here; but concentration was valuable, as bringing immorality more under control. Parochial crusades, though *prima facie* a public blessing, had often the effect of spreading corruption. It was recollected at Cambridge that when a certain proctor made very frequent descents upon the hamlet of Barnwall, where much of the parasitical vices of that University had taken root, the people in question, far from cure or conversion, merely extended their radius into more rural villages. These were so soon corrupted that representations were addressed to the University by the parochial clergy, praying that the plague of Barnwall should be confined to its old bounds, and not let loose upon their simpler parishes. It was notorious that the same kind of thing followed on a very large scale the expulsion of prostitutes from Brussels, and it could not be supposed that the attempt to strangle the growth of immorality by broadcasting its seeds, which was found impracticable under the powerful discipline of the English University and the Belgian capital, could answer among this enormous, and when roused, unmanageable population. The evicted of Norton Street, in the parish of All Souls, had settled quietly down in the next parish. Incompressible as water, the vice had but shifted its ground, and from a really moral point of view, more harm than good had accrued from the change."

These remarks do not call for any amplification. A few days after the meeting a leading article appeared in the London *Times*. It must be remembered that for many years the settled policy of the conductors of that journal has been to make it rather the exponent than the leader of public opinion, and the importance generally attached to it arises from a knowledge of this fact. We give the article almost entire.

"There is a very disagreeable subject which we are compelled to bring, although most reluctantly, before the notice of the public, because it has become necessary to bring public opinion to bear upon it. Many clergymen and gentlemen are now associating themselves together for the purpose of dealing in some degree with the notorious evil of street prostitution. It is our earnest desire to give them all the support in our power, so long as they confine themselves to reasonable measures of discouragement and repression. Let us not nourish any visionary expectations; it would be simply idle to suppose that the evil against which we are now directing our efforts, can be put down by the strong hand of power. It is with moral as with physical disease—there is no use in looking for an entirely satisfactory result from the treatment of symptoms; there may be alleviation, there may be diminution of the disorder, but there will be no perfect cure. *Whatever tends to raise the standard of public morality will also tend to diminish prostitution.* In such a case we are dealing with two parties: the tempter, let us say, and the tempted; with the man and with the woman. It is probably with the first of the two that we should principally concern ourselves if we would bring about any serious result. It is on the sacred action of family life, with the thousand influences it brings to bear upon the minds and conduct of men, that we must chiefly depend if we would see any notable diminution in the numbers of those unfortunate creatures who now parade our streets. Let it be once understood that even among a man's fellows and associates immorality is a thing to be ashamed of, and at least we should get rid of the contagion of vice. Time was, and the time is not a very remote one, when a British gentleman—we speak of all three home divisions of the empire—would nightly stagger or be carried up to his bed fuddled, if not absolutely drunk. A man who should thus expose himself in our own days would be set down as a beast, and his society would be avoided by

all who set store on their own good name.   In this respect there has been
a palpable improvement in the manners of the age.   Surely public opinion
can be brought to bear against one vice as well as another.   The time
may come when a man may shrink from presenting himself in the sacred circle of his mother, his sisters, and his other female relatives, reeking
from secret immorality.   Conscience can turn on a bull's eye as well as a
policeman, and the culprit may stand self-convicted, although no one has
been there to convict him save himself.

"The influences, however, of which we speak are of slow growth, and can
not be much quickened by the hand of power.   It has become necessary
to deal at once with certain results.   Now we say it with much shame,
that in no capital city of Europe is there daily and nightly such a shameless display of prostitution as in London.   At Paris, at Vienna, at Berlin,
as every one knows, there is plenty of vice; but, at least, it is not allowed
to parade the streets, to tempt the weak, to offend and disgust all rightly-
thinking persons.   If any one would see the evil of which we speak in its
full development, let him pass along the Haymarket and its neighborhood
at night, when the night-houses and the oyster-shops are open.   It is not
an easy matter to make your way along without molestation.   In Regent
Street, in the Strand, in Fleet Street, the same nuisance, but in a less degree, prevails.   Now we are well aware that, if all the unfortunate creatures
who parade these localities were swept away to-morrow, if the night-houses
and oyster-shops were closed by the police, we should not have really suppressed immorality.   We should, however, have removed the evil from the
sight of those who are disgusted and annoyed by its display; and, still
more, we should have removed it from the sight of those who, probably, had
they not been tempted by the sight of these opportunities, would not have
fallen.

"Now, as one practical measure for the discouragement of prostitution, all
these night-houses and others might be placed under the surveillance of the
police.   Licenses for opening them and keeping them open might be given
only in the cases of persons who offered some guarantees of their respectability.   They might be compelled to close at certain hours; in point of
fact, the community could tolerate well-nigh any degree of inconvenience
inflicted upon their frequenters.   In two other analogous cases similar evils
have been dealt with in this way, and with the happiest results: we speak
of gaming-houses and betting-offices.   It is quite certain that persons who
are firmly resolved to play and to bet will effect their purpose even now, but
at least the sum of the evils resulting from these two vices has been greatly
diminished since the community has resolved to withdraw from them its
recognition.   England should not grant her *exequatur* to prostitution.   This
is one thing which might be tried; another would be to give increased
force to clauses which, as we believe, already exist in police acts, by which

the police are empowered to stop the solicitation and gathering together of prostitutes in the public streets. In such a case we must trample down definitions and exceptional cases with an elephant's foot, and go straight for results. The rule in all such cases is to give the power, and to leave it in the discretion of the authorities only to employ it on proper occasions. We have ample guarantees nowadays that such discretion can not be abused.

"Here, then, are two things which may be done without opening any visionary trenches. The police may be directed to deal with prostitutes as they do with mendicants, and the centres of pollution may be brought under proper regulation.

"We know well enough that in such a capital as London it is hopeless to expect that vice of this description can be expunged altogether from the catalogue of our national sins, but at least let as many difficulties as possible be thrown in its way. Again: the benevolent persons who have taken it in hand to deal with this monstrous evil assert that the introduction of foreign prostitutes, or, what is still worse, of girls yet uncontaminated, for the purposes of prostitution, might be discouraged much more than it is, perhaps well-nigh totally prevented. Undoubtedly England does not desire free trade in prostitution. Preventive measures upon this subject are surrounded with difficulties; but that is no reason for despair, but one for additional exertion. Very numerous and influential meetings have been held upon this subject, and we augur well of their success. There was no display of ultra-Puritanic rigor, no attempt to deal with impossibilities. The speakers in the main contended that the public exhibition of prostitution might be successfully dealt with, even if the vice were beyond their reach. Our streets, at least, can be purged of the public scandal, the disgraceful night-houses may be deprived of their powers of corruption, the keepers of brothels may be brought under the lash of the law, and the importation of foreign prostitutes may be diminished, if not put down altogether, if the public will take the subject up in earnest. Such were the principal points on which the speakers insisted; at least their views deserve a trial."

This plan is calculated to restrict prostitution by placing it under *surveillance*. It requires no additional licensing system, as every public house, wine-shop, or cigar-shop in London, whether kept open at day or night, whether of a respectable or immoral class, requires a license under the excise laws. The proposals just quoted urge that the permission to keep these places of entertainment should be limited, and "given only in the cases of persons who offered some guarantees of their respectability." It will be necessary for the reader to bear in mind that "night-houses" are not houses of prostitution, but merely resorts for prostitutes, as already mentioned, as, in default of this, a natural construction would be that the *Times* proposed to license brothels. The two are as distinct as possible, and it would be as consistent to style some of the fashionable oyster-saloons and restaurants of New York houses of ill fame because abandoned women resort to them, as to class the "night-houses" of London in that catalogue. They are simply places for public refreshment in the neighborhoods of theatres, markets, etc., which are permitted to continue open all night in deference to a supposed public requirement, and though, from the character of their visitants, they can not be considered schools of morality or decency, yet no prostitution takes place in them. The interests of the proprietors guard against this, as it would immediately cause the licenses to be revoked, and consequently close the place entirely.

By placing the resorts of London prostitutes under this restriction much would be gained, so far as the public decency of the streets and the transit of passengers are concerned, but no possible check would be imposed on the ravages of disease. The proposition at the meeting to license the brothels would do this, but, as was anticipated by the speaker, "it would be very distasteful to the religious public," and the act of recognition would be immediately construed as an act of approval, or at least of sanction. That it would not merit this censure must be evident. The only approval or sanction given to the vice would, in fact, consist in saying to the keepers of houses of ill fame: We shall not attempt to close your doors, for we know that would be impossible, but we shall claim the right of entry at any moment to watch your proceedings.

It has ever been an unquestioned policy to choose the least of two evils when you must take one, and if the British government should ever license brothels, they will certainly adopt the theory. To the population of London less danger would inure from this toleration than from the unknown, unwatched courtesans who haunt their streets. Many an apparently respectable man will follow a woman into a house of prostitution when it is conducted quietly and furtively, who would hesitate before he accompanied her into a known and licensed brothel, while many a stranger who may date his physical ruin, and possibly the loss of character and honor, from the hour when he entered a private house ot prostitution, would be saved many a bitter memory had an official recognition of its true character met him on its threshold, and intimated that it was the resort of the abandoned and vicious. In London, as in New York, we do not believe that illicit sexual intercourse can be carried to any greater extent than it is now; so no danger of an increase of vice need be apprehended there from any measures calculated to remove some of the ulterior and fatal effects of dissipation.

In contrast to the public display of immorality in the streets of London, is the following description of prostitution in Paris. It is extracted from the foreign correspondence of a New York journal:

"Paris, Thursday, May 27, 1858.

"In a late letter on the subject of the 'turning-boxes' of the Foundling Hospitals I spoke of the repugnance of Protestant communities to any official compromise with one sin in order even to destroy a greater; for, that the secret reception of illegitimate children by the state does contribute enormously to the extinction of the crime of infanticide, while it does not generally increase the number of these unfortunate children, is too well shown by statistics to remain longer a question for discussion. But we have another and a more striking example of this repugnance to a collusion with one evil in order to smother out another and a greater in the want of legislation in Protestant countries on the subject of prostitution.

"For many months, as you know, the municipality officers, the church-wardens, and the journals of London have been excited over this very question of prostitution; and no wonder. One need but to leave Paris and fall suddenly in the streets of London at an advanced hour of the evening to comprehend the excitement of its citizens on this subject. To the Frenchman, crossing the Channel is like crossing the River Styx; he falls suddenly into a pandemonium of street disorder and drunken licentiousness for which he is not prepared. He recalls Mery's terrible picture in 'Nezim,' and does not find it overdrawn. He sees nothing like this in his own city, and he is surprised beyond measure, for he has been taught to believe in the Puritanism of Protestant countries.

"When an American or an Englishman, habituated to the revolting night-scenes of New York or London, first arrives in Paris, he is astonished at the absolute absence of similar scenes in our streets. He has, perhaps, arrived here with the impression—most foreigners do—that prostitution, and revelry, and drunken debauchery stalk forth in the day and render hideous the night. But he forgets that he has arrived in a city where there are laws and a police to execute them—in a city where refinement and the proprieties of life are carried to their extreme perfection, and where such license and debauchery as prevails in English and American cities would be an absolute contradiction to the spirit and habits of the people. The reader will please observe that I do not speak of the morals of the people, but of their ideas of decorum and of the proprieties of life; of what is due to decency and an ordinary respect for appearances.

"This extreme attention to appearances is, in fact, one of the principal attractions of a residence in Paris. The city is not only maintained free of inanimate filth, but of animate filth as well; at least, you are not forced to see it if you do not wish to. In London no lady dare walk out unattended after 8 o'clock in the evening, and after 11 o'clock she will have her eyes and ears insulted, no matter how well attended, while in Paris she may remain in the streets to any hour of the night, and neither have her eyes offended nor her ears insulted.

"How is this happy result accomplished? In 1851 the official register of the police of Paris showed 4300 public girls on its books; the number now may be stated at 5000. These girls and the houses in which they live are subjected to a series of stringent laws which renders them innoxious and inoffensive to the community, the police adopting the principle that since it is impossible to suppress the evil, it should be rendered as inoffensive to the public eye and to the public salubrity as possible. All these houses are obliged to be closed at 11 o'clock precisely. The girls are obliged to remain in the house, and the windows are always covered with blinds, night and day. A few girls are permitted, here and there, to walk up and down, in front of their door, from 7 to 11 o'clock precisely, but it is against the law to accost the passers-by. The houses are visited once a week by a medical and an ordinary inspector—real inspectors, appointed by government, and not humbugging ward politicians.

"Another class of girls, and much the larger class, are those who frequent the public balls, concerts, and theatres—girls who live alone in public lodging-houses, and who, for the most part, are not enrolled on the police-books nor submitted to the ordinary sanitary regulations. But this class are no more permitted than the rest, either in the street or at their favorite evening resorts, to accost people for purposes of commerce. The streets and the public balls are full of policemen in citizen's dress, whose business it is to detect such girls as violate the law in regard to addressing people, and to put their names on the police-books, thus requiring them to take out a license, and to submit to all the police regulations on the new class to which they have entered. As a girl regards herself as forever lost when her name is once placed on the police-book, and as she never knows when an officer's eye may be upon her, she takes good care to violate as rarely as possible this law prohibiting solicitations in public. This class are always elegantly dressed; it is notorious even that they are the first to initiate and to propagate those very fashions which make the tour of the world as the latest Paris modes. Many of them are reserved and elegant in their manners, and require a punctiliousness of etiquette which would not be out of place in the most aristocratic saloon. But one of the great aids to the Paris police in the maintenance of public decency in this class, is the fact that they do not use strong drinks; a drunken public woman is never seen. As liquor is the greatest debaser of mankind, this one fact strikes out a marked line of distinction between this class here and in England and the United States. The great majority do not lose their self-respect, and they take good care of their health, hoping later on to reform and get married. This is here the rule, whereas in England and the United States they throw themselves away as rapidly as possible.

"It is thus that the fashionable promenades of Paris, the public balls, and the gardens even, may be frequented by ladies and children at all hours of the evening and night without once seeing any of those offensive movements of public women so common in the streets of English and American cities. Contrast this state of things with that of London. Let the reader, if he has ever lived there, recall to mind the Strand, the Haymarket, Piccadilly, Leicester Square, and Regent Street—the fashionable business quarters of the city. One hesitates to enter upon a description of such a scene. It refreshes his historical recollections of the decadence of Rome; his name should be PLATO to look upon such sights. The streets swarm with drunken and foul-spoken young girls—often mere children; and when I say swarm, I mean that you have to push your way to get through them. Is it then strange that the citizens of London should feel scandalized at this state of things, or that its journals or its church-wardens should seek to find a remedy for the nuisance? They will think of every thing else before they arrive at the simple, *effective*, and beautifully working Paris system, because they are a Protestant people and must not compromise with a sin. It must be left to find its own level. Honorable citizens must consent to allow their sons, often their families, to come in contact with these demoralizing, stony-hearted horrors of the streets; they must suffer individually and as a community from the vile tendencies of street prostitution, because they hesitate to legalize it and to give it over to the care of the police. To see the finest evening promenades of a Protestant and Christian city given up exclusively to the unutterable shames and horrors of street-prostitution is a problem in the catalogue of inconsistencies which Catholic and infidel France can not fathom. In France the law acts on the principle that for a public woman to be seen in the street is an insult to public taste, and hence, when it is necessary for these girls to be conveyed to prison, to the Hospital, or to the dispensary of the Prefecture of Police, they are mounted in close carriages constructed for the purpose; or when by hazard they are obliged to take a public *fiacre* they are required to keep the blinds down. You may say what you please about the surface-morality of the French, but their respect for the public eye does honor to their civilization, and their law on this evil would be well adopted elsewhere. There is no truer principle in civil government than that the moral sores of society should be hidden as much as possible from the public view, for it is now too late in the day to combat the maxim long ago put in print by Pope, that vice is propagated by a familiarity with it.   The French law may be culpable in permitting masked balls and the keeping of concubines, but these are affairs that belong to the interior, which the public need not see if they do not wish to; the important distinction is, that the French law does not compel an honest father of a family, in returning from church or theatre, to push his way through mobs of drunken lewd women, who salute his children's ears with language they ought never to hear.

" In one of its last articles on the general subject of prostitution, the London *Times* makes some judicious remarks which are completely verified in the same class in Paris.   Thus the *Times* declares that the proper method of diminishing the number of these unfortunates (for to think of eradicating the evil is an illusion) is not by missionary efforts directed to them, but rather to their poor parents; for these poor girls were raised in sin, and *never made a fall.*   The same thing holds good here.   Ninety-five hundredths of all the public women of Paris are born and raised in filthiness of mind and body; at the age of ten, twelve, and fourteen years they are already prostitutes and thieves, and when they get their first silk dress, their first fine toilet, earned in their shameful profession, they take a step higher in the scale of morality; for then they cease to steal, they acquire a certain degree of pride in their conduct, they are more respectful and decently behaved.   So that, paradoxical as it may seem, the immense majority of the public women of Paris, instead of making a fall, have actually been promoted in the scale of morality.   But all these women know nothing else than the life in which they have been raised; they are fit for nothing else, they are incorrigibly averse to all the moral suasion that can be addressed to them, and the real remedy is an enlightenment of the parents of such children, a general improvement in the moral tone of the lowest classes.   In fine, if it is an evil which can not be eradicated, if the children of beggars, and ragpickers, and *concièrges* will fall into evil-doing, it is right to protect society at least from the public demonstration of their vile occupation by the passage of effective police laws."

As an indication that the sentiments advanced in this chapter are entertained by others of the medical profession, and as endorsing our views to a considerable extent, the reader's attention is requested to the annexed report adopted at a special meeting of the Medical Board of Bellevue Hospital, New York, in reply to interrogatories addressed to them by Isaac Townsend, Esq., President of the Board of Governors of the Alms-house (by whose direction they are embodied in this work); and also to a report from H. N. Whittelsey, M. D., Resident Physician of the Nursery Hospital, Randall's Island. on the same subject.

(Copy.)

" *Report of the Medical Board of Bellevue Hospital in reply to Interrogatories of* ISAAC TOWNSEND, *Esq., President of the Board of Governors
of the Alms-house, upon Constitutional Syphilis.*

"Office of the Governors of the Alms-house, Rotunda, Park,
New York, August 24, 1855.

"TO THE MEDICAL BOARD, BELLEVUE HOSPITAL:

"GENTLEMEN, —I am led to believe that a large number of the inmates of
Bellevue Hospital are affected with syphilis in some of its many forms, and
believing that the Governors of the Alms-house are called upon to take
measures to remove, as far as possible, the cause of this great malady, to
dry up the sources of an evil which prevails so extensively, saps the health
and taxes the wealth of the city, etc., largely ; and believing farther that, if
the vice can not be stayed, humanity as well as policy would suggest that
the dangers which surround it can be lessened, I propose a few interrogatories tending toward the accomplishment of this great object, desiring your
views upon them in reply as early as 1st of October.

" 1. What percentage of the total number of patients admitted to Bellevue Hospital suffer directly or indirectly from syphilis ?

" 2. Are there not patients admitted to Bellevue Hospital whose diseases are attributable to the taint of syphilis ; and have not many of the
inmates been forced to place themselves under treatment therein, and thus
become dependent on the city, from being unfitted in body and mind for the
ordinary duties of life in consequence of syphilitic diseases ?

" 3. Are not the children of parents thus affected unhealthy ?

" 4. What means, in your opinion, could be adopted to eradicate or lessen the disease in the city ?

"By giving the above queries your earliest attention, you will greatly
oblige your very obedient servant,   ISAAC TOWNSEND, President."

" At a special meeting of the Medical Board of Bellevue Hospital, held
December 18, 1855, the following report, in answer to a letter from Isaac
Townsend, Esq., President of the Board of Governors of the Alms-house,
dated August 24, 1855, touching the subjects of syphilis and prostitution,
was read by Doctor Alonzo Clark, Chairman of the Committee appointed
by the Medical Board to consider and reply to said letter.

"On motion, the report was accepted, and ordered for transmission to
the President of the Board of Governors, after having received the signa-
tures of the President and Secretary.

"JOHN T. METCALFE, M. D., Secretary *pro tem.* to the
Medical Board of Bellevue Hospital.

"New York. December, 1855."

"REPORT ON PROSTITUTION AND SYPHILIS.

"To Isaac Townsend, Esq., President of the Board }
of Governors of the Alms-house.   }

"In answer to your inquiries, the Medical Board of Bellevue Hospital respectfully reply,

"That they caused a census of the Hospital to be taken on the 24th October last, for the purpose of ascertaining what proportion of the patients had suffered from venereal diseases. From that enumeration they learn that out of 477 persons then under medical and surgical treatment, 142, or about one third, had been so affected. In the several divisions of the house the numbers are as follows, viz. :

"Of   72 females on the surgical side, 17, or 1 in 4·24.

"Of 130 females on the medical side, 17, or 1 in 8 nearly.

"Of 118 males on the medical side, 45, or 1 in 2·6.

"Of 127 males on the surgical side, 63, or 1 in 2.

So that out of 245 males then under treatment, 108, or 1 in 2·27, had had some form of venereal disease; and among 202 females, 34, or 1 in 6, had been similarly affected.

"Of the whole number who confessed that they had had affections of this class, 106 had had syphilis, and 36 had had gonorrhœa.

"Of the 106 who had had syphilis, 53, or just one half, were still laboring under the influence of the poison with which they had been inoculated, in many instances, years before.

"As almost all these patients were admitted for other diseases, or with affections which the physician alone would recognize as the remote effects of syphilis, it is perhaps fair to assume that they represent, with some exaggeration, the class of society from which they come.

"The Board has been favored with the census of the New York Hospital (Broadway), taken for the purpose of ascertaining the proportion of syphilitic cases among the patients of that institution; from which it appears that the whole number of patients on the 8th of December was 233, and that 99 of that number had had venereal disease, and 37 were then under treatment for the same affections recently contracted. Counting the old cases alone, most of which were admitted, probably, for other diseases, this proportion considerably exceeds that above recorded for Bellevue Hospital, it being as high as 1 in 2·35. It is proper, however, in this connection to state that the returns for Bellevue Hospital are believed to be incomplete. They are based in a considerable degree on the confessions of the patients; and it is known that many, especially among the women, have denied any contamination, when facts, subsequently developed, have shown that their statements were not true.

"Is it to be believed, then, that one in three, or even one in four, of that large class of our population whose circumstances compel them to seek the occasional aid of medical charities, are tainted with venereal poison? This the Medical Board do not think they are authorized to state. But the facts here cited, and others within their reach, justify them in saying that venereal diseases prevail to an alarming extent among the poor of the city. The large number of women sent by the police courts to be treated for these diseases at the Penitentiary Hospital would alone be sufficient evidence of this. Yet such persons constitute but a small proportion of those who, even among the poor, suffer from these disorders. Dispensary physicians, and those in private practice, can show a much longer list of the victims of impure intercourse.

"But the disease is not confined to this class. The advertisements which crowd the newspapers, introduced by men who ' confine their practice to one class of disease, in which' they ' have treated twenty thousand cases,' more or less, demonstrate how large is the company of irregulars who live and grow rich on the harvest of these grapes of Sodom. And yet their long list of ' unfortunates' would disclose but a fraction of the evil among those who are able to pay for medical services. The Medical Board are unable to state what proportion of the income of regular and qualified physicians in this city, is derived from the treatment of venereal diseases, but they know it is large, and that many who never advertise their skill receive more from this source than from all other sources together. They believe that there is no one among the unavoidable diseases, however prevalent, for the treatment of which the well-to-do citizens of New York pay one half so much as they pay to be relieved from the consequences of their illicit pleasures.

"The city bills of mortality give little information regarding the frequency of venereal affections. *Lues Venerea* keeps its place in the tables, and counts its score or two of deaths annually. Although this class of disorders is not frequently fatal, except among children, it is credited with only a fraction of the work it actually performs. The physician does not feel called upon, in his return of the causes of death, to brand his patient's memory with disgrace, or to record an accusation against near relatives. During infancy the real disease is buried under such terms as Marasmus, Atrophia, Infantile Debility, or Inflammation, while in adults, Inflammation of the Throat, Phagedæna, Ulceration, Scrofula, and the like, take the responsibility of the death.

"These affections are strictly what the advertisers denominate them, ' private diseases'—a leprosy which the ' unfortunate' always strives to conceal, and, so long as it spares his speech and countenance, usually succeeds in concealing. The physician is his only confidant, and the physician refers all to the class of ' innocent secrets,' which are not to be revealed. The public, therefore, know little of the prevalence of such diseases, and still less of the fearful ravages they are capable of making.

" Still, as has been just said, syphilis is not often the immediate cause of death in adults. After its first local effects are over—and these, though generally mild, are sometimes frightful—the poison lingers in the system ready to break out on any provocation in some one of its many disgusting manifestations, often deforming and branding its victim, threatening life and making it a burden, and yet refusing the poor consolation of a grave. Like the vulture which fed on the entrails of the too amorous Tityus, it tortures and consumes, but is slow to destroy, and often its visible brand, like the scarlet badge once worn by the adulteress, proclaims a lasting disgrace. The protracted suffering of mind and body produced by this class of distempers, the ever-changing and often loathsome form of their secondary accidents, and the almost irradicable character of the poison, seem almost to justify an old opinion, sanctioned by a papal bull as late as 1826, that these diseases are an avenging plague, appointed by Heaven as a special punishment for a special sin.

" The relentless character of syphilitic diseases stands out in painful relief in its transmission from parent to offspring. Here it is, indeed, that the children's teeth are set on edge, because the fathers have eaten sour grapes. The contaminated husband or wife is left through years of childlessness or of successive bereavements to mourn over early follies, and to repent when repentance is fruitless. The syphilitic man or woman can hardly become the parent of a healthy child.

" A young man has imbibed the contagion ; it has become constitutional. After a few weeks, or months perhaps, of treatment, the visible signs of the disease no longer torment him. He has contracted a matrimonial alliance, and soon marries a healthy and virtuous woman. He flatters himself that he is cured. A few months suffice to give him painful proof of his error, for then his growing hopes of paternity are suddenly blasted. Instead of the child of his hopes he sees a shriveled and leprous corpse. This is but the first in a series of similar misfortunes. He has poisoned the fruit of his loins, and again and again, and still again, it falls withered and dead. At length nature seems to have triumphed over this foe to domestic happiness, and the parents' hearts are gladdened by the sight of a living child. Their joy is short-lived. The child is feeble and sickly, and in a few days or weeks another death is added to the penance list of the humbled and grieving father.

"This mournful story will need no essential changes in the narration, should the poison of impure intercourse, legitimate or illicit, linger in the veins of the mother.

" A child of such a connection may be born in apparent health, but before six months have passed, some one of the numerous forms of infantile syphilis will be likely to appear and threaten its life. In the contest which follows between disease and the treatment, the physician is commonly victorious, but the contest is in many cases protracted, and often it is to be renewed again and again. And after all, it is not believed that children thus tainted at their birth often grow up and acquire that degree of health and vigor which is popularly ascribed to a *good constitution*.

"These are facts familiar to physicians practicing in large towns. But the history of inherited syphilis is not complete. If, in the case just recited, the wife escape contamination from her husband and her unborn child, yet the sad consequences of that husband's folly are not yet exhausted. That tainted child, now a sickly nursling at her breast, has a venom in its ulcerated lips which can inoculate the mother with its own loathsome poison, while it draws its sustenance from the sacred fountain of infantile life. But this is not all. These little innocents sometimes spread their disease through the whole circle of those who bestow on them their care and kindness. The contagion spreads through the use of the same spoon, the same linen, and even by that highest token of affection, a kiss. It has been known that a single diseased child has contaminated its mother, a hired nurse, and, through that nurse, the nurse's child, and, in addition to these, the husband's mother and the mother's sister. Such are sometimes the weighty consequences of a single error.

" PREVENTION.

" That the great source of the venereal poison is prostitution, requires no argument. The first question, then, to be answered, is, Can prostitution be prevented? In answering this question, it is necessary to remember that the history of the world demonstrates the existence of this vice in all ages, and among all nations, since the day its first pages were written. The appetite which incites it has always been stronger than moral restraints—stronger than the law. No rigor of punishment, no violence of public denunciation; neither exile, nor the dungeon, nor yet the disgusting malady with which nature punishes the practice has ever effected its extermination, even for a single year. Great as this evil has always been, it can not be denied that in our own time some of the accidents of what is called *the progress of society* tend, at least in large towns, greatly to increase it. The expenses of living are every where the great obstacle to early marriages, whether such expenses be positively necessary or be demanded by the social position of the individual, the fashion of his class, and therefore become relatively necessary. Wherever these expenses increase more rapidly than the rewards of labor, marriage becomes impossible for a constantly increasing number, or can only be purchased at the price of social position. But abstinence from marriage does not abolish or moderate the natural appetites. The great law of nature on which the existence of the race depends is not abrogated by any artificial state of society. Moral or religious principles will restrain its operations in some; human laws in some; the fear of consequences in some; yet there always have been, and probably always will be, many of both sexes who are not restrained by any of these considerations. These have sustained, and probably will continue to sustain, not only prostitution but houses of prostitution, in the face of every human law. Suppressed in one form, it immediately assumes another. Again pursued, it retreats to hiding-places where darkness and secrecy protect it from the pursuer.

" Severe penalties have heretofore only increased the evils of prostitution. If a hundred women are consigned to prison for this vice to-day, before a month has elapsed a hundred more have taken their places, and the hundred, though punished, are not reformed. Impelled by a love of their profession, or some by the passion to emulate the more fortunate of their sex in the finery of dress (a passion which first occasioned their fall), many by want, and all by a sense that they are outcasts, they are no sooner liberated than they return with new zeal to the life from which they have been detained only by force. Severe laws compel secrecy; they can do no more. When prostitution is criminal, disease, if known to others, is a practical conviction. Under such circumstances the contaminated will be slow to confess disease, and so subject themselves to punishment. Yet their passions and their necessities alike forbid even temporary abstinence. They spread disease without limit.

" Under this fact lies an important thought. Were it no more disgraceful to contract syphilis than it is to have fever and ague, the diseased would seek early relief, which is nearly equivalent to certain relief, and the disorder would soon be confined to the pitiable few who have lost in drunkenness and misery the instinctive dread of all that is foul and disgusting in personal disease. Prostitution, it is true, would then be restored to its old Roman dignity, yet *venereal disease could then be reached, and all but eradicated.* But a respectable syphilis does not belong to our age and nation. It lost caste in the beginning, and its exploits in modern times have not been of a character to win it friends. The supposition aims only to show, by contrast, the evils of well-intended, but probably injudicious legislation. Regarding pains and penalties: if the whip, confiscation, and banishment, in the hands of Charlemagne and St. Louis, aided by a right good will and all the powers of a military despotism, could not suppress prostitution, or even prevent the opening of houses of prostitution; if penal laws in Europe, from the days of these earnest princes until now, have utterly failed of their object, as they notoriously have, it is fair to ask how much more can prohibitory laws accomplish in a country where the right of private judgment and personal liberty in speech and action are the very foundation of the body politic? They have hitherto been ineffectual. In spite of such laws, the vice is increasing. *In consequence of such laws, its most enormous physical evil is extending its baleful influence through every rank and circle of soci-*

ety. It is still emphatically the plague of the poor; it still brings sorrow and misery to the firesides of the affluent and titled.

"A utopian view of the perfectibility of man might look for the remedy to this evil in universal early marriages, in domestic happiness, and in a universal moral sense which will compel men and women to keep their marriage vows. But, taking man as he is, we find the tides of society set with constantly increasing strength against early marriages; that domestic happiness is not synonymous with marriage, whether early or late; and that the moral sense which should teach all men to observe even their solemn promises would be miraculous. For these things the law has done all that has been thought wise to attempt, probably all that it can do.

"But it may be asked, If government has the power to relieve society of the vice of drunkenness, why despair of its power regarding prostitution? In reply it may be asked if the drunkard himself is ever cured of his vicious appetite by penalties? The statute despairs of this. It even recognizes its inability to prevent the sale of intoxicating drinks while they exist; it therefore claims the right to seize and destroy them. Can it seize on and destroy the inborn passion which fills and supports houses of prostitution? Then it can not do for the one what it hopes to do for the other.

"Again: the suppression of slavery and the slave-trade have been cited in this connection as illustrating the power of law. In trespass, theft, violence, or fraud, some one is wronged; and those who have been injured seek to bring the offender to justice. Here there is no aggrieved person. All who are in interest are so in interest that they deprecate the interference of all law, except what they claim to believe is the law of Nature.

"But is there no hope in the societies of moral reform? For the suppression, or even checking of the general vice, none whatever. The association in New York deserves much praise for its zealous benevolence. They have brought back some of these erring women to the paths of virtue, but they have done no more to stop the current of prostitution than he could do to dry up the current of the Hudson who dips water with a bucket. In truth it may be said that the paths of virtue have been found to be slippery places for some that would be thought converts. Wisdom's ways have been found too peaceful for these daughters of excitement. This is said in no spirit of disparagement to the efforts of the society. They may well be proud of what they have done. But it is said to show how little the kindest and the best can do to reclaim those who have once fallen from virtue and honor.

"Let the great fact, then, be well understood, that prohibitory measures have always failed, and, from the nature of the case, must forever fail to suppress prostitution.

"Let this additional fact, illustrated in the foregoing remark, be well considered, that penalties do not reform the offender, but that they enforce secrecy in the offense, and silence regarding its consequences, which is a chief cause of the present wide diffusion of the venereal poison.

"What, then, is the proper province of legislation in this important matter?

"The wise lawgiver does not attempt impossibilities. He knows that laws which experience has demonstrated can not be enforced, teach disrespect and disobedience to all law. He knows that human passions can not be changed by human legislation. He knows that, if he attempt the impossible greater in the control of vice, he is certain to neglect the possible and important less. He knows that the river will not cease to flow at his command. If it overflows and desolates, he raises its banks and dikes in the flood to prevent a general inundation. For hundreds of years the governments of Europe have tried in vain to dry up the sources of prostitution; with the opening of the present century they began to dike in the river and prevent avoidable mischief. For a long time we too have had laws against prostitution, which, with every proper effort on the part of those in authority, have proved as useless as those who live by this illicit traffic could desire—as mischievous in spreading disease as the quack advertiser could wish. Is it not time, then, to inquire whether we have not attempted too much; whether, if we attempt less, we shall not accomplish more? May we not be able to limit and control what we have not the power to prevent? If we can not do all that a large benevolence might wish to accomplish, in the name of humanity is it not our duty to do what is useful and practicable —all that is possible?

"While the Medical Board are persuaded that by a change of policy, such as is suggested by the facts and reasons herewith submitted, much can be done to limit and control prostitution, and much more toward the eradication of venereal diseases, they are not yet prepared to offer the details of a plan by which they hope these important ends can be attained. With the assistance of the Board of Governors, they are now in correspondence with the medical officers of many of the larger cities of Europe, where restrictive measures have replaced prohibitory. When they have obtained the information which they hope this correspondence will furnish, they will ask leave to submit a supplementary report.

"JOHN W. FRANCIS, M. D., President.

"JOHN T. METCALFE, M. D., Secretary pro tem.

"NOTE.—It is believed that not far from ten per cent. of the inmates of Bellevue Hospital are admitted for affections which have their origin remotely in venereal disease. A certain form of rheumatism, certain inflammations of the throat, eyes, bones, and joints; stricture and cutaneous eruptions are the most common diseases of this class. What proportion, if any, of those who suffer from scrofula and scrofulous inflammations, from consumption and other chronic diseases, owe their present illness to a constitutional syphilitic vice, inherited or acquired, there are no means of determining satisfactorily."

(Copy.)

" *Report of Doctor* H. N. WHITTELSEY, *Resident Physician of Randall's Island, in answer to certain queries of* ISAAC TOWNSEND, *Esq., Governor of the Alms-house, upon Constitutional Syphilis:*

" New York, November 28, 1855.

" DEAR SIR,—From repeated conversations with you, I am led to believe that many diseases incidental to the children on Randall's Island may properly be traced to parents who are affected with constitutional syphilis. Please give me your views as to the following questions as early as 10th December.

" 1. Among the children under your care, to what extent does inherited syphilis exist?

" 2. Under what form does constitutional syphilis present itself, and what diseases are attributable to its taint?

" 3. Are not the children of parents thus affected unhealthy, scrofulous, subject to diseases of the eye, joints, etc.?

" Very respectfully,   ISAAC TOWNSEND, Governor A. H.

" Doctor H. N. WHITTELSEY, Resident Physician, R. I."

" Randall's Island, Dec. 24, 1855.

" ISAAC TOWNSEND, Esq., President of the Board }
  of Governors of the Alms-house. }

" DEAR SIR,—In regard to the interrogatories contained in your note of a recent date on the subject of hereditary syphilis, I have the honor to reply:

" 1. Regarding its prevalence. It is a matter of record that nine tenths of all diseases treated in this hospital during the past five years have been of constitutional origin, and for the most part hereditary. These diseases assume a variety of forms, and involve nearly every structure of the body, terminating in cachexia, marasmus, phagedæna, etc., etc. The exact proportion which hereditary syphilis bears to this sum of constitutional depravity can not be stated with accuracy for the following reasons:

U u

" Children are admitted to this institution between two and fifteen years of age, thus throwing out of the category infantile syphilis in all its forms; and except in few cases, showing none of its specific characteristics, having been modified by appropriate treatment, but manifests itself by general constitutional depravity, and determines a great variety of diseases, embracing nearly every form of skin disease, affection of the mucous membranes and their dependencies, diseases of the eye and ear, of the bones, especially of joints, etc., proving the prolific and lamentable source of many of the diseases incident to children of the class presented in this institution. Making, then, due allowance for its masked form, in which the consequences of inherited syphilis appear in this institution, together with the absence of the previous history both of patients and parents, it is believed an approximate estimate may be made of the part which this malady bears to the sum of constitutional disease. From the foregoing facts, and from careful observation during the past few years in this branch of the Alms-house Department, it appears that human degradation is the source of the stream of pollution supplying this hospital with disease ; and farther, that of all the vices which make up the sum total of depravity, both moral and physical, prostitution and its consequences furnish the larger proportion.

" Here we have the sad picture presented of a large number of children doomed to an early grave, or to breathe out their miserable existence bearing a loathsome disease, carrying the penalties of vice of which they themselves are innocent, being a generation contaminated, and capable only of contaminating in turn.

" In the above sketch I have confined my statement to syphilis as manifested in the Nursery Hospital, where the average number of cases of disease treated is about two thousand. From this field is excluded every variety of the disease except the one, viz., constitutional syphilis affecting children after having been modified by treatment in the infant.

" H. N. WHITTELSEY, M. D."

It has been stated already that the information obtained in the course of this investigation is, to a very great degree, undoubtedly reliable; but a few words more in reference to the same subject will not be out of place, if we consider the importance such information assumes when it is made the basis of serious deduction. These women were examined singly and alone, and a person who has been engaged for a number of years in any particular inquiry is able, by his experience, to judge whether his informants are speaking the truth in their replies. For this, among other reasons, we are satisfied that in almost every case there was no deception practiced, but that the answers obtained were true in all essential points. Another evidence of correctness is the degree of congruity that characterized the greater part of the replies. Farther than this: a reference to the questions themselves (as reprinted in chapter XXXII.) will show that they were so arranged that falsehoods would be easily detected unless very carefully contrived before the time of examination, of which those examined had no notice, and consequently no opportunity for fraud or deception could possibly exist.

It is not denied that there were many difficulties to be encountered, although the mode of operation was simple. It may be briefly described as follows. The captain of each police district (and oftentimes the writer with him) explained his object to the keeper of the house, assuring her that there was no intention to annoy, harass, or expose her; and, particularly, that no prosecutions should be based upon any information thus collected. This latter promise was supported by a letter from a high legal functionary addressed to the Mayor and Police Department, assuring them that the particulars they collected should not be used in any manner prejudicial to the women themselves, as it was believed that a collection of the necessary information required by such a work as the present would be productive of good to the city. When satisfied upon the subject of prosecution, they were told that the real motive was to obtain correct particulars of prostitution without exposing individual cases, so as to enable the public to judge of its extent, and assist them in forming an opinion as to the necessity of arrangements which would ultimately become protective to our citizens at large, as well as to housekeepers and courtesans, and many of the housekeepers expressed a hope that the design might be accomplished. Their interests, therefore, led them to speak the truth. In short, from the precautions taken, and from the result itself, very little doubt can be entertained as to the authenticity of the principal part of the replies on all essential points; and upon this consideration these replies have been made the basis of the description and remarks upon PROSTITUTION IN NEW YORK.

The task is completed, and the reader's attention may be invited to the various facts substantiated, as embodied in the following

RECAPITULATION.

There are six thousand public prostitutes in New York.

The majority of these are from fifteen to twenty-five years old.

Three eighths of them were born in the United States.

Many of those born abroad came here poor, to improve their condition.

Education is at a very low standard with them.

One fifth of them are married women.

One half of them have given birth to children, and more than one half of these children are illegitimate.

The ratio of mortality among children of prostitutes is four times greater than the ordinary ratio among children in New York.

Many of these children are living in the abodes of vice and obscenity.

The majority of these women have been prostitutes for less than four years.

The average duration of a prostitute's life is only four years.

Nearly one half of the prostitutes in New York admit that they are or have been sufferers from syphilis.

Seduction; destitution; ill treatment by parents, husbands, or relatives; intemperance; and bad company, are the main causes of prostitution.

Women in this city have not sufficient means of employment.

Their employment is inadequately remunerated.

The associations of many employments are prejudicial to morality.

Six sevenths of the prostitutes drink intoxicating liquors to a greater or less extent.

Parental influences induced habits of intoxication.

A professed respect for religion is common among them.

A capital of nearly *four millions of dollars* is invested in the business of prostitution.

The annual expenditure on account of prostitution is more than *seven millions of dollars.*

Prohibitory measures have signally failed to suppress or check prostitution.

A necessity exists for some action.

Motives of policy require a change in the mode of procedure.

APPENDIX.

Estimated Number of Prostitutes.—Growth of the City Attended with Increase of Vice.—Official Figures and Views.—Effects of Attempted Suppression.— Prostitution and the Public Health.—Syphilis in the Hospitals.—The St. Louis Experiment.—Its Wholesome Effects.—Why the Law was Repealed.— Divided Public Sentiment as to Recognizing and Regulating Prostitution.

THE investigation of the subject of public prostitution in the city of New York, the results of which are given in the preceding pages, was brought to a close in 1858. The population of the city at that time was about 700,000, and Dr. Sanger placed the number of public prostitutes at 6,000, or one in every 117 inhabitants. According to the last State census (1892) the population of the city was about 1,800,000, and, if the increase of prostitution has kept pace with the city's growth, the number of those constituting the appalling roll of vice at the present time should be, in round numbers, 15,500. But these figures, startling as they are, would seem to fall far short of the calculations of many intelligent investigators of the subject, who place the number as high as 25,000 and even 30,000. The latter was the figure given by a high police official about a year ago. The sensational estimate, tacitly accepted by the committee of the State Senate during its late inquiry, putting the number at 50,000, bears on its face the mark of exaggeration, as it would show one prostitute in every 36 inhabitants, including men, women, and children.

An attempt, at the present time, to make such an enumeration of the prostitutes of the city as was made by Dr. Sanger in 1858 would, for several reasons, prove quite futile. Even were the police authorities disposed to contribute their aid to the undertaking, they would be powerless to perform the work intelligently, since recent events with which the reader is familiar have resulted in driving very many of these prostitutes into hiding. In short, open prostitution and the existence of recognized houses of prostitution, as in 1858, are now officially denied by the police as a body, whatever views on the subject may be individually entertained by them. Superintendent Byrnes has only to say : " There is no record of these people kept in this department."

If we accept 30,000 as a reasonable estimate of the number of prostitutes and 1,800,000 as the resident population of the city, we have a showing of one prostitute in about every 55 inhabitants. But those constituting the resident population of New York are by no means the only patrons of New York's prostitutes. The floating population of the city, always large, and made up chiefly of the male sex, away from home and home influences, contributes, no doubt, more largely than any other element to the support of these women. The outlying cities and larger towns, where there are few or no public prostitutes, are also all tributary to New York in this respect, just as they contribute nightly to the attendance at our theatres; and in view of these facts it would probably be no exaggeration to say that the 30,000 prostitutes of New York are maintained by a population of 4,000,000 or even 5,000,000 instead of 1,800,000. When we consider the close proximity to the metropolis, to its theatres, its churches, its shops, as well as its haunts of vice, of such cities as Brooklyn and Newark, it speaks little or nothing for the superior virtue of these communities that they are not infested with public courtesans as New York is. The hundreds of thousands who, while claiming to be residents of these outlying cities and towns, daily come to the metropolis to transact their business, must necessarily contribute thousands who also spend nights of dissipation here. They are, moreover, quite as well acquainted with the ways and byways of the city as are the residents of our up-town wards. Nor is this surrounding population less a contributor to, than it is a patron of, the prostitution of New York. The woman whose fall from virtue occurs in the smaller town naturally seeks the larger city in which to lead a life of sin; and it not infrequently occurs that, while practising her calling here, she is still known to and patronized by her former townspeople who were her associates when a virtuous girl. Thus the vicious class of a very large population outside of New York becomes directly a charge upon this city, swelling the number of inmates first of our fashionable haunts of vice. then of our dives, of our reformatories, our asylums, our hospitals, and, at last, our potter's field.

That the increase of prostitution has even outstripped the continuous growth of New York in the last quarter of a century there can be little doubt. Such a disproportionate increase of vice and the vicious classes would seem to attend the growth of all cities. Definite data shows this to have been the case in London, Paris, Berlin, and other European capitals. There are periods, also, that seem to be peculiarly prolific of prostitution. The police official to whom we have already referred, and whose opinions are based upon long experience and observation, expresses the view that during the years of our late civil war there was a very marked increase of prostitution, not only in New York, but throughout the country. Periods of business depression, also, would seem to be marked by like results; and the same authority is of the opinion that in the past two years, despite all efforts to suppress public prostitution, there has been an almost unprecedented addition to the ranks of those who either covertly or openly seek to exist by the practice of this vice. That such should be the case will appear when we come to consider the causes which lead women to prostitution. Chief among these causes, as Dr. Sanger found it in 1858, as we find it to-day, and will, no doubt, find it to the end, is poverty, " the stern necessity to live." [1] The fact that women are perhaps better paid to-day than they were when Dr. Sanger made his inquiry, and that new avenues of employment have been opened to them, cannot be regarded as affecting the matter to any marked extent, when we consider the vast and constantly increasing number of the unemployed and dependant.

The last quarter of a century has witnessed great changes in New York—changes in the types and character of its population as well as a numerical increase—and could Dr. Sanger revisit to-day the scenes of his former labors he would witness a metamorphosis of the city in respect to not only its geography and inhabitants, but in the location, number, and character of those constituting its vicious and dangerous classes. He would dis

[1] Dr. F. R. Sturgis, whose observation has been very large both in this country and abroad, expresses the opinion that love of dress is even a more common cause of woman's fall than poverty.

cover new causes and sources of vice, if, indeed, he did not
discover new vices. Where he met the Irish, German, and
Anglo-American, he would find to-day the Italian, the Russian
Jew, and the Chinese. The influx of these latter in the last
few years, while contributing very slightly to the ranks of
public prostitution, has introduced vices peculiar to these races,
and, through habits of uncleanliness and lax morals, done much
to generate and scatter infections incident to illicit sexual indulgence. The statistics of the City Dispensary, to which we will
have occasion to refer later on, convey some idea of the vice and
disease which exist among and infect the large class who pop-
ulate the overcrowded tenement districts of the city. When
we consider that venereal disease is the direct offspring of
uncleanliness, this condition of things, this fearful menace to the
public health, cannot be wondered at. Dr. R. W. Taylor,[1] consulting surgeon of the City Hospital, and whose long experience in
the treatment of contagions incident to vice is probably not
exceeded by that of any member of his profession, did not hesitate to express to the writer the startling opinion that the
large majority of those who have come under his care and attention in the last few years have come not from the houses of
prostitution nor the street-walking class nor those contaminated
by public prostitutes, but from the overcrowded tenements in
the foreign quarters of the city. We will endeavor, before concluding this chapter, to consider the wisdom of legislation looking to the enrollment and regulation of New York's 30,000
public courtesans, and, in view of the facts just stated, it would
seem that more effective and rigorous tenement-house and factory laws are equally essential as sanitary measures. A startling discovery made by the writer, in his investigation of the
vice and disease existing in a single block on the east side of the
city, was the extreme youth of a majority of the women or girls
infected. A mere child of fourteen years, in one tenement, having
contracted disease, communicated it directly to eleven others
living under the same roof. This would seem to suggest

[1] Dr. Taylor has, in various capacities, been connected with the City Hospital since 1860, and, during this long period, his practice has been largely confined to the venereal wards of the institution. He is, therefore, an authority on
this subject. There are in the City Hospital, at present, three male and three
female wards, six in all, in which patients suffering from venereal diseases
only are admitted

almost promiscuous intercourse among the occupants of the building.

That there has been a fearful increase of juvenile vice in the last few years cannot be questioned. Dr. Sanger found among the inmates of public houses of prostitution many who had not reached fifteen years of age. Yet he probably knew nothing of that modern creature of depravity, to whom we can refer only in the vernacular of the day, the "chippy." To some extent these children correspond to the "flower girls" of Paris, and here, as there, their patrons would seem more frequently to be those libertines who are far advanced in years as well as in sin.

Probably the average life of a prostitute is neither more nor less than it was at the date of Dr. Sanger's investigation, for there has been no marked change in the habits of these women, certainly no improvement. The use of intoxicating liquors, an almost invariable accompaniment of prostitution, has certainly not diminished, if, indeed, it has not increased among them. The elder Dr. Gross, of Philadelphia, writing about twenty years after Dr. Sanger, says of the prostitute in this respect: "Her life is generally a short one, often not exceeding three, four, or, at most, five years. Steeped as she commonly is in misery, poverty, and degradation, she soon seeks consolation in hard drink, and finally sinks under the combined influence of syphilitic poison and alcoholic stimulation." [1]

From time to time, since the earliest history of human government, efforts have been made to suppress prostitution. The utter failure of such efforts in every instance has been shown by Dr. Sanger and numerous other writers; and, as the passions of man and the frailty of woman remain unchanged, there is no reason why the arm of the law or moral influences should be more potent in accomplishing enforced virtue and chastity in the nineteenth than they were in the tenth or the fifth century. On the contrary it may be asserted that the advance which mankind has made in civilization and intelligence has, on the one hand, swept away superstitions which once gave to the Church a power it no longer possesses, while,

---

[1] "Syphilis in its Relation to the Public Health," being a paper read by S. D. Gross, M.D., LL.D., before the American Medical Association at its meeting in Detroit, June 3, 1874.

on the other hand, it has been productive of a vastly enlarged spirit of personal liberty which is too quick to defy the enforcement of sumptuary measures. There are ample laws against prostitution, both human and divine; but all attempts to rigidly enforce them, whether dictated by considerations of public policy or sentiments of religious duty, have signally failed whenever or wherever they have been made.

New York has, within the past year, witnessed such an effort, inaugurated and led by a clergyman of much intelligence and great courage, and backed by the thoroughly aroused moral sentiment of the community, regardless of sect or creed; and yet the writer ventures the opinion that there is no well-informed observer of the movement or its results who will assert that prostitution in this city has decreased or that there is one less prostitute among us than there was a year ago. If such there be, he has only to consult the records of New York's hospitals and infirmaries, where the statistics of diseases incident to prostitution attest the existence of prostitution, to find a most emphatic refutation of any claim to increased virtue among us. There has been no exodus of prostitutes from the city, and if, in any instance, a woman of this class has fled beyond the jurisdiction of courts or a legally constituted investigating committee, her flight has been prompted not by the fact of her being a prostitute or the keeper of a house of prostitution, but because she might become an involuntary witness to questionable transactions, not with her patrons, but with those charged with enforcing the laws against her business and her class.

It is claimed that notorious houses of prostitution have been closed, and that prostitutes have been driven out of certain neighborhoods which were hitherto their haunts. If this be so, and these women have not left the city, where are they? Or, to use the language of a physician who has a large private practice among them, we might rather ask, "Where are they not?" The testimony of real estate and renting agents who have on their lists apartments and flats in the upper wards of the city, on streets and in neighborhoods heretofore regarded as respectable, would no doubt supply an answer to this question. In January last a city journal,[1] under the cap-

[1] The Morning Advertiser.

tion of " What Shall We Do with the Outcasts?" published several communications from these agents, all of whom admitted having had numerous applications for apartments from women they thought to be prostitutes, and whom, on this account, they refused to do business with. But that these women have experienced much difficulty in securing quarters somewhere, and generally beyond the more thoroughly policed quarters of the city, following the flow of population farther and farther uptown, and insidiously penetrating even aristocratic neighborhoods, would not seem to be borne out by the facts of the case. If there has been any decrease of public prostitution, which is perhaps a debatable proposition, it has logically resulted in an increase of clandestine prostitution, which is invariably a more dangerous phase of vice, whether regarded from a moral or sanitary standpoint.

That there is more or less clandestine prostitution in all cities, and even in the smaller towns, cannot be questioned, and this leads us to inquire, what is clandestine in contradistinction to public prostitution? The query is not so simple a one to answer as it may seem, and involves an inquiry into what constitutes prostitution. Where both parties to the act have more or less regard for their reputations, and seek to conceal their sin from the knowledge of the world, the woman, if she may be called a prostitute, is only such clandestinely. If, in such a case, the woman sells her favors for a consideration of money or other valuables, she comes, no doubt, within the accepted meaning of the term prostitute. If the man is regardful of his reputation, and, though the woman is lost to shame, seeks the gratification of his passion outside of the common brothel, as, for instance, in a house of assignation or a hotel, where he may even register the woman as his wife, the act on the woman's part is prostitution clandestinely practised. Where both man and woman are thoroughly depraved and lost to shame they may, nevertheless, for various reasons, consummate the vicious act clandestinely. When the reckless and shameless woman finds a customer (or a victim) she rarely experiences any difficulty in finding a safe place into which to conduct him, whatever his fears of scandal or exposure may be.

There has, no doubt, been a marked change in the character of assignation houses in New York within the past few years; not that they have become any less in number, however. Those houses, presided over by women, and in many instances known to the initiated only, have to a great extent been supplanted by a certain class of so-called " hotels," conducted by men and open to all comers. The recent raiding of several of these places by the police has brought them into notice and made public the methods on which they are conducted. About the only claim to their being hotels rests upon the fact that a hotel register is kept in them. Upon this the male customer is required to enter his supposed name, with the addenda "and wife," before he and his female companion are assigned a room. Of course the name he inscribes in no way concerns or interests the recipient of his money, and its being entered is nothing more than a form, or rather a " blind," for the protection of the place. That the name written (perhaps in a disguised hand) is that bestowed upon the man at the baptismal font, rarely occurs. That these places are hotels only in name, and in fact are really assignation houses, is sufficiently attested by the facts that their patrons seldom if ever have baggage, even so much as a satchel containing a night-robe, and that the rooms are occupied in turn by numerous couples during a single night. That these places are further equipped for mischief can be found in the fact that attached to most of them is a licensed bar from which intoxicants can be readily ordered to the rooms. But here we wish to do full justice to the Excise Department of the city by stating that in almost every instance where these establishments have been detected and raided by the police, the license to sell liquor on the premises has been promptly revoked. And perhaps this is the severest penalty that could be imposed on the proprietors.

That clandestine prostitution, or at least illicit intercourse of the sexes, is also carried on to a greater or less extent in even the best and most exclusive of our hotels, is a fact that we refer to only because it serves to show how extremely difficult it is to control this vice or erect barriers, legal or other, that will keep it within channels where virtue and respectability are least apt to come in contact with it. When these channels are dammed and the overflow follows, what neighborhood, what class can escape the inundation? There is, no doubt, a constant effort made on the part of those conducting the respectable hotels to exclude persons of bad or even questionable reputations, of either sex, but no precaution in this matter can prevent at least occasional imposition. The most scrutinizing hotel clerk, who is generally a good judge of human nature, will admit that he has often been deceived. Of the couple well dressed and of proper deportment, he has no warrant to demand a marriage certificate. Indeed, he would do so at his personal peril in some cases, and in any instance a mistake would be not only embarrassing, but expensive. Those availing themselves of this fact generally understand full well the disadvantage the hotel clerk labors under. The well dressed country swain, over attentive to his pretty and susceptible wife, would be more apt to raise in the clerk's mind a suspicion than would the nonchalant city *roué* who, having often rehearsed, knows full well how to play his deceptive part. There is happily this to say, however, that those who impose upon the proprietor or the clerk of the respectable hotel generally so demean themselves that they come and go without their true character being discovered, and so no scandal is created and no real harm is accomplished.

In considering prostitution, either public or clandestine, in its relation to public health, we approach the subject in its most serious and important aspect; and, fortunately, in this case we are provided with somewhat more definite data and a much fuller expression of opinion than we have been able to secure from those persons who have had to do with the evil merely as instruments of our defective laws. But even here the non-existence of reliable statistics, outside of a very few institutions, the closing of their doors against sufferers from venereal afflictions by many of our hospitals, in short, the inclination of the public to close its eyes against the existence of the evil and its direful ravages, physical as well as moral, sadly confront us. If even sufficient data to arouse the public understanding and the public conscience to an appreciation of what unregulated prostitution and the unchecked spreading of the infections resulting from this evil can be given, we will feel that our labor in this direction will not have been in vain. To quote again from Dr. Gross:

"It would be a matter of deep interest, and, in a practical point of view, of the greatest possible value, if we could ascertain, even approximately, the extent of syphilis in our cities and larger towns ; but for

such a decision there are, unfortunately, little data. It may, however, be
assumed that it is of gigantic proportions ; that it exists in many of the
best and noblest families of the land ; that since the establishment of
railway travel it has penetrated every rural district ; and that it is
poisoning, and slowly, but surely, undermining, the very fountains of life
in every direction, sowing the seeds of death among our people, and
gradually deteriorating the national health."

Dr. Gross estimated, at the date of his paper, that there was
in the United States one person infected with the syphilitic
virus in every 20 of our population. This, at the present time
(1895), estimating our population in round numbers at
70,000,000, would show the startling number of 3,500,000
syphilitics. In 1874, Dr. F. R. Sturgis read before the American Public Health Association an interesting paper,[1] in which
he estimated that out of a population of 942,292 persons, 50,450
were suffering from syphilis in New York City. And he
observes: "I believe this number to be under, rather than
above, the true amount." But "even this," he continues,
"represents only the civil population." The report of the
Mercantile Marine of New York City shows a still worse state
of things. During 1872 and 1873 the total number of patients
treated was 24,645, and of this number 3,779 were due to
syphilis. If all the venereal cases are considered in the above
sets of figures the number becomes still larger—for New York
City, 61,705 ; for the Mercantile Marine, 4,170.

In giving these figures of Dr. Sturgis, we may remark that
they are the most complete and authentic that have been compiled since Dr. Sanger's investigation, and they afford us a basis
of estimating with approximate accuracy, at least, the amount
of venereal and syphilis prevailing in this city at the present
time. Dr. Sturgis expressed to the writer the opinion that
these diseases have certainly not decreased in later years, but
have fully kept pace with the city's growth and the attendant
growth of prostitution. The population of New York has at
least doubled since the date of Dr. Sturgis's enumerations, therefore it is reasonable to conclude that instead of 50,000 there are
100,000 persons among us to-day who are suffering from syphilis.

In 1893, Dr. Prince A. Morrow, Chairman of the Board of

[1] "The Relations of Syphilis to Public Health." By Frederic R. Sturgis,
M.D., Clinical Lecturer upon Venereal Diseases in the University of the City
of New York, Surgeon to Charity Hospital, etc.

Surgeons of the Charity Hospital, Blackwell's Island, contributed to medical literature an exhaustive treatise, in three large volumes, upon the ailments resulting from vice.[1] From a paper contributed to the second volume of this work by Dr. Samuel F. Armstrong,[2] we quote, under the heading of "Statics [of syphilis] in the General Hospitals," the following:

Here our research is confronted by the fact that general hospitals, as a rule, take but few patients suffering from syphilis ; the illogical position being maintained that such patients are affected by a disease that has been acquired in consequence of their own viciousness, and that, as a hospital cannot afford relief to all that apply, therefore these cases are best refused. Thus, in the reports of the Massachusetts General Hospital for the years 1879 to 1887 inclusive, it may be found that from four to twelve per cent. of the total number of persons refused admission were suffering from syphilis. The annual reports of St. Luke's Hospital, New York City, show the number of cases of men and women suffering from syphilis that were treated in that institution, as well as the diseases from which those refused admission were suffering. From Table I. it may be seen that from three to fifteen times as many syphilitic patients were refused treatment as were treated for that disease; and from this hospital, here cited because its reports happened to be most convenient, we may judge the action of most, if not of all, similar institutions.

TABLE I.

PER CENT. OF SYPHILITIC PATIENTS TREATED AND REFUSED TREATMENT, ST. LUKE'S HOSPITAL.

Year.	1881	1882	1883	1884	1885	1886	1887	1888	1889	1890
Per cent. of Syphilitic Patients treated.....	0.8	0.7	0.9	1.0	1.2	1.1	0.8	1.3	1.3	1.8
Per cent. of Syphilitic Patients among those refused....	6.0	4.8	4.8	15.4	18.0	4.0	4.4	5.0	5.4	4.5

From the statistics of the United States Marine Hospital Service for the decade 1881 to 1890 inclusive, it may be learned that in a number of patients, ranging from thirty-two to fifty thousand a year, the number of cases of primary syphilis varies from three to five and one-tenth to fifteen per cent., while the percentage of deaths due to syphilis to the total mortality varies from one to two and three-tenths per cent. When these

[1] "A System of Genito-Urinary Diseases, Syphilology, and Dermatology," edited by P. A. Morrow, M.D., Clinical Professor of Genito-Urinary Diseases, formerly Lecturer on Dermatology in the University of the City of New York, etc.

[2] Samuel Treat Armstrong, M.D., Ph.D., Visiting Physician to Harlem Hospital, ex-passed Assistant Surgeon United States Marine Hospital, Chairman of Section on Public Health, New York Academy of Medicine. etc.

statistics are further analyzed, a difference is found between the frequency with which these forms of syphilis occur in hospital and in dispensary patients. In the former class the percentage of primary syphilis varies from one to three, while among dispensary patients it varies from one and one-tenth to two and two-tenths per cent.; and secondary syphilis in the former class varies from four and five-tenths to six and four-tenths per cent., while in the latter class it varies from seven and two-tenths to eight and six-tenths per cent. The average annual percentage of cases of primary syphilis among hospital patients is 1.94, and among dispensary patients it is 1.58; the average annual percentage of cases of secondary syphilis in the former class is 5.29, in the latter 7.77. Notwithstanding the wide variation in the number of patients treated annually, an inspection shows the close relationship sustained between the percentage of cases of primary and secondary syphilis.

In 1881, 9.7 per cent. of the total patients treated were suffering from syphilitic diseases; in 1882, 8.8 per cent.; in 1883, 8.2 per cent.; in 1884 and 1885, about 7.6 per cent.; in 1886, 8.3 per cent.; in 1887, 1888, and 1889, about 9.2 per cent.; and in 1890, 8.4 per cent. In other words, among a number of thousands of patients coming from a class of society supposed to be particularly susceptible to venereal diseases, less than ten per cent. of the total number of patients treated were suffering from the various forms of syphilis. These percentages show no tendency to an increase or to a decrease of the disease during successive years, and their range or variation is so moderate that the mean and probable error of each year is about one per cent. Another factor that is to be considered is, that there is absolutely no more restriction imposed upon these men than there is upon the members of the community at large.

We are indebted to Warden Robert Roberts of the Charity Hospital for the following table showing the number of persons suffering from venereal disease who were sent to that institution by the Commissioners of Charities and Correction during the five years from 1890 to 1894, inclusive:

Month.	1890	1891	1892	1893	1894
January	119	120	121	92	74
February	116	94	113	78	54
March	130	94	109	76	89
April	131	93	88	55	99
May	127	102	95	68	113
June	125	127	116	88	115
July	150	140	112	104	122
August	147	126	141	163	156
September	152	118	127	164	131
October	138	105	96	66	113
November	140	137	123	113	108
December	133	152	121	111	92
Total	1,608	1,408	1,362	1,178	1,266

These figures may admit of some explanation. The steady decrease in the number of persons treated from 1890 to and including 1894, can possibly be accounted for upon the theory that several of the city hospitals have somewhat relaxed their former rule of wholly excluding those suffering from venereal diseases. It is upon this theory that Dr. Taylor accounts for these figures. Not that the fact carries with it any great significance, but it will be noted that the number treated for venereal disease in this hospital in 1894, covering the period when a spasmodic effort to enforce the laws against prostitution was being made, shows a considerable increase as compared with the preceding year, 1893.

The number of venereal patients treated in the New York Dispensary during the first three months of the current year likewise shows an increase when compared with the corresponding period of the preceding year. These are the figures:

First three months of 1894 769
    "   "   "   " 1895 823
        Increase   46

And we may add, in this connection, that about ten per cent of those treated in these periods were suffering from syphilis.

The following interrogations, which are substantially the same as those submitted to Dr. Sanger by Isaac Townsend, Esq., in 1858, when the latter was president of the "Board of Governors of the Almshouse of the City and County of New York,"[1] were submitted by the writer to Dr. Prince A. Morrow, Chairman of the Board of Surgeons of the City Hospital, and to Dr. Frederic R. Sturgis, and Dr. R. W. Taylor, also of the medical staff of that institution:

1. What proportion of the inmates of the institution under your medical charge are, in your opinion, directly or indirectly suffering from syphilis?

2. Are, or are not, the number of such inmates on the increase?

3. Do not patients in the different institutions often leave before the disease is cured, so that they are liable to infect other persons after their departure?

4. Are not the offspring of parents affected with constitutional syphilis

[1] In 1860 the present Board of Commissioners of Public Charities and Correction succeeded the Governors of the Almshouse in its charge of the va grant and pauper institutions of the city and county of New York.

44

subject to many diseases of like character which cause them to become a charge upon the city for long periods of time and often for life ?

5. What are your views in reference to the best means of checking and decreasing this disease; and what plan, in your opinion, could be adopted to relieve New York City of the enormous amount of misery and expense caused by syphilis ?

To these interrogatories were added the following also:

6. Is it your opinion that there has been a marked abatement of diseases incident to prostitution within the past twenty-five years ?

7. Have more recent methods of treating venereal diseases resulted in lessening the transmission of such diseases to the offspring of those contaminated ?

8. Do you believe that the closing of houses of prostitution and the scattering of the inmates of such houses into less public places to ply their calling is calculated to increase or diminish disease among them ?

Dr. Morrow has kindly given the following replies to all but the first two questions (referring for answers to these to the books of the hospital):

3. Yes; the duration of the stay of such patients in the hospital being entirely voluntary, they often leave before they are cured, when the disease is actively contagious and susceptible of hereditary transmission.

4. The effect of hereditary syphilis is manifest in the production of numerous diseased states or conditions which seriously impair the vitality of the child, and which may be termed *para-syphilitic* affections. Prominent among these may be mentioned certain organic and dystrophic troubles, arrest of development (physical and mental), hydrocephalus, rickets, epilepsy, infantile paralysis, tabes, etc.

5. No system or plan of checking the spread of syphilis can be devised into which the *regulation of prostitution* does not enter as the principal and most essential factor. I am not prepared to formulate my views as to the best means of regulating prostitution.

6. I think not; on the contrary, there has been an increase.

7. No; while it is generally conceded that syphilitics are less liable to transmit their disease when under the full influence of active specific treatment, practically this condition is seldom complied with, especially among the ignorant lower classes.

8. A careful investigation into the sources of syphilis would seem to show that clandestine or private prostitution is responsible for more cases of the disease than public houses of prostitution, where commercial interest prompts the proprietress of the establishment to protect her patrons as far as possible from danger of contagion.

In response to the above inquiries Dr. Sturgis has given his views quite freely and fully in the following communication addressed to the writer:

New York, *April* 27, 1895.

My Dear Sir :

In reply to the list of questions which you have submitted to me, with regard to the subject of prostitution as affecting the public health, before answering your questions categorically, allow me to state that, of course, the answers given are based upon opinion and belief, and cannot be considered as absolutely correct without an opportunity of consulting statistics and figures bearing upon the several points contained in your communication.

In answer to the first question, "What proportion of the inmates of institutions under your medical charge, are, in your opinion, directly or indirectly suffering from syphilis ?" I would reply that, in the wards devoted to venereal diseases which are under my professional supervision, I should say that certainly from fifty per cent. to sixty-five per cent. of the cases were syphilitic. In a paper which I read some years ago before the American Public Health Association, I collated the cases which occurred in the New York Dispensary, and in the Charity Hospital, as it was then called, on Blackwell's Island, and the proportion of syphilis to all venereal cases was forty-one per cent.

Query 2. Are or are not the number of such inmates steadily on the increase ?

That question I cannot answer without having the statistics of the hospitals at my disposal. I should say, however, that while there might be no actual increase as regards the hospital itself, the proportion of venereal diseases to the total population is slowly but steadily increasing.

Query 3. Do not patients in the different institutions often leave before the disease is cured, so that they are liable to infect other persons after their departure ?

Yes. It is certainly very unfortunate that syphilitic or venereal subjects cannot be retained until the surgeon decides that they at least are no longer objects of dangerous contamination to those about them. Formerly patients were self-committed ; that is to say, upon application at the central office of the institution, they were obliged to become as "self-committed criminals." That gave the surgeon the right to retain them as long as he thought it necessary to complete the cure or, at any rate, if not a cure, to retain them until the dangerous and contagious period had passed. That wise rule has been abolished, and patients can come and go from the venereal divisions as they do from other divisions of the hospital.

Query 4. Are not the offspring of parents affected with constitutional syphilis subject to many diseases of like character, which cause them to become a charge upon the city for long periods of time, and often for life ?

Probably not ; for, fortunately, most of the offspring of parents affected with syphilis, and this is especially true where both parents are diseased, die within the first six months of their extra-uterine life. Where the male parent only is infected and the mother escapes infection, the children in a very large proportion of cases, and I myself personally think in all cases, do not show any signs of disease, and are, to all intents and purposes, as healthy as the average child. If the mortality among syphilitic children were not so great, they would possibly become a charge upon the city charities.

Query 5. What are your views in reference to the best means of checking this disease ; and what plan, in your opinion, could be adopted to relieve New York City of the enormous amount of misery and expense caused by syphilis ?

A good-sized volume could be written in answer to this question. Stated briefly, proper supervision (both medical and police). Proper control, if honestly and conscientiously carried out, would, in my opinion, decidedly check the increase of the disease, and probably decrease not only its virulence, but its frequency. As to the plan, I must decline to commit myself to any special one, as it is impossible, in the present condition of municipal politics, to even hope that such a thing would be conscientiously and thoroughly carried out. Irrespective of the question of official blackmail which is always in these cases possible, and which a recent investigation in this city has shown to be more than possible, the sentiment of the Anglo-Saxon race, whether wise or foolish, is strongly against the question of official supervision and control of this evil. In this we appear to follow the example of the ostrich, which remarkable bird is said to bury its head in the sand, and, inasmuch as it sees nothing, believes that nothing sees it. Although a self-evident fact that such things as harlots and syphilis exist, we declare that nothing shall be done to check or control them. In sanctified circles such control, I understand, is considered a compromise with sin.

Query 6. Is it your opinion that there has been any marked abatement of disease incident to prostitution within the past twenty-five years ?

Again the absence of statistics prevents me from making a categorical reply to this question. Judging from my own experience and that of others, I should say decidedly that it had not.

Query 7. Have more recent methods of treating venereal diseases resulted in lessening the transmission of such disease to the offspring of those contaminated ?

My opinion is that they have, in lessening the intensity of the disease, diminished the chances of transmission to the fœtus in utero, either indirectly through the father, if we believe in that mode of transmission, or directly through the medium of the mother.

Query 8. Do you believe that the closing of houses of prostitution and scattering the inmates of such houses into less public places to ply their calling, is calculated to increase or diminish disease among them ?

I know such action is calculated to increase venereal diseases among public women, inasmuch as the majority of them are careless of their health and somewhat careless in their habits. The seasoned woman, who has passed her novitiate in prostitution, who appreciates the fact that her bread and butter depends upon her sexual health, and who knows that disease of her genital organs means loss of custom, loss of money, and perhaps destitution, is a careful woman, and, looking at it in a purely sexual light, is the best of all women to have connection with. But the young harlot knows little about the question of her sexual health, and appreciates still less the importance of looking after herself until disease has overtaken her, and then, either through ignorance, or perhaps from dire necessity, plies her trade till pain and misery force her to stop, and, in the meantime, she has been the cause of numerous infections, not only to her male companions, but to the innocent wives and children at home. Now, I urge the plea of proper regulation, entirely apart from the sentimental side. Medical men can not and do not look upon disease as a divine punishment, and I do not see how any sensible person can hold that view without having his belief in the goodness and kindness of God severely shaken. It is purely a matter of sanitation; and I believe that a proper control would tend to diminish venereal diseases. Failure of the system in foreign cities, where it has been introduced, is due to the fact that the supervision has not been properly carried out and the control has not been stringent. In instances where thoroughness and knowledge are directed towards the extinction of this disease, I believe it is as capable of amelioration and of limitation as is its no less terrible, if more decent, congener, the small-pox.

I trust I have answered the questions you have put to me satisfactorily, and I remain, with expressions of respect,

Yours very faithfully,

F. R. STURGIS.

Dr. Taylor, while substantially agreeing with Drs. Morrow and Sturgis in the views expressed by them, is of the opinion that not only a larger percentage of venereal disease and syphilis comes from clandestine than from public or open prostitution, but that a still larger percentage than from either of these is contributed by a class composed of those who are not recognized as prostitutes, and who, therefore, could not be reached by any scheme of regulation or control. A thoroughly enforced system of sanitary visitation and inspection of those females who could be enrolled by the police would, in his opinion, be conducive to the public health, and result, in some measure at least, in lessening the existence and spread of venereal disease and syphilis, and should, therefore, be adopted; but that this should be followed by supplementary legislation, which should, if possible, reach the tenement house, the factory, and all establishments where females in large numbers are employed on small salaries.

The view which Dr. Taylor entertains of accomplishing this latter result is, however, a very gloomy one.

Volumes have been written upon the scourge of syphilis, and volumes more might still be written without exhausting the terrible subject. We have quoted quite sufficiently from those who are eminent as syphilologists, and there is probably no physician, however circumscribed his practice or observation, who cannot testify to the ravages of the disorder. Can the disease be controlled? Can its ravages be circumscribed or lessened? The writer, adopting the language of Dr. Morrow, believes that " the regulation of prostitution, and the control of syphilis are but convertible terms."

No one can read the concluding pages of Dr. Sanger's work without discovering that he was an earnest advocate of the regulation of prostitution by legislative enactment, of a thorough system of enrollment, licensing, and sanitary inspection. It is sad to reflect that, practically, the only experiment in that direction on this side of the water was made in a Western city about the time of his death, which occurred in 1872. A law, drafted upon the lines of that in operation in Paris, was enacted by the Missouri legislature, the object of which was to regulate and bring under control prostitution in the city of St. Louis. For about a year only this law remained upon the statute books of the State—a very short period, and yet sufficiently long to test, in a measure, its operation and effect. Its repeal, to quote the language of a St. Louis journalist in a recently published communication,* " was the result, not of any failure of the measure to accomplish the wholesome ends for which it was enacted, but it was in obedience to a morbid sentiment, begotten of absolute ignorance of the subject." The writer adds: " There was not a vote from any member representing a city constituency favorable to the repeal of the law, and not a vote expressive of the sentiment of a country constituency against it. The incidents attending the event were dramatic. Throughout the State there was a moral uprising against what was regarded as the licensing of vice, and the lobbies of both branches of the legislature were taken complete possession of by the clergy of the various denominations and earnest co-workers of the other sex. A petition, praying for

*" The Missouri Social Evil Law."—*Morning Advertiser*, January 12, 1895.

the repeal of the obnoxious law, signed by more than one hundred thousand good people, was presented. The document was cumbersome. A wheelbarrow decorated with white ribbons, and accompanied by a group of innocent young girls attired in spotless white gowns, was brought into service, and on it the gigantic and emphatic protest against the licensing of vice was wheeled up to the clerk's desk to be read. Courageous, indeed, would have been the country member who would have voted otherwise than he did. There were, of course, counter-petitions from the cities, and conspicuous among the signers of these latter were members of the medical profession. Indeed, I am sure the law received the almost unanimous endorsement of the doctors of medicine, as it received quite as unanimously the condemnation of the doctors of divinity.

The provisions of the St. Louis law were substantially as follows: All prostitutes publicly plying their avocation were registered. These were divided into three classes—the inmates of houses, the occupants of rooms outside of such houses, and those known as "kept women," or mistresses. There was no distinction whatever between these classes. In the eye of the law the "kept woman" was quite as much a prostitute and subject to the provisions of the law as her less fortunate sister of the common disorderly house. No registered woman was permitted to change her abode without first giving notice to the authorities, so that her whereabouts was constantly known.

Many of the more vicious and corrupting practices of the business were absolutely prohibited and practically suppressed. Soliciting, either on the street or from windows or doors of houses of prostitution, was severely punished, a second offense generally resulting in a deportation of the offender from the city as a vagrant. No carriage or public conveyance was permitted to stop or stand in front of a house. No "red lamp of sin" was tolerated; in short, no light of a color calculated to attract the attention of a passerby was allowed in hallway or parlor. The front doors of all houses were kept unlocked, thus admitting at all hours not only the patron, but the police as well. In fact, every barrier between the authorities and this vicious class was, as far as possible, removed.

The city was divided into three districts, both in respect to sanitary and police regulation. A physician of recognized standing was placed in charge of each of these districts, whose duty it was to compel a weekly medical inspection of each and all of the registered unfortunates. A nominal fee was collected weekly from the inmates of houses and rooms, and a larger fee from the proprietors of houses. The money thus collected went indirectly back, to a great extent, to those contributing it, as it was largely devoted to the maintenance of a hospital, open at all times to the members of this unfortunate class.

Referring to this hospital, the writer from whom we have just quoted observes : " If ever these rarely reclaimable women were brought directly under effective moral influences, it was when inmates of this well-regulated sanitary institution, where not only the best medical attention was afforded them, but every moral influence cast about them calculated to induce reformation."

Again this apparently well-informed writer says : " The law had been in operation but a short time when its salutary effects were clearly discernible. Primarily, the evil itself was lessened, many of the worst members of a bad class preferring to leave the community sooner than to subject themselves to the requirements of the new law. But of more consequence and value to the city was the marked decrease of physical ailments invariably attendant upon this vice." And this latter statement would seem to have been attested by many of the leading physicians of the city. The *Missouri Medical Record*,[1] in an editorial printed a few weeks after the repeal of the law, stated that " the system had operated most beneficially in the interests of the community as well as the welfare of the prostitute," adding that "many of the inmates of the hospital, influenced by the ministrations of good men and noble women, had been seeking the ' purer and better way,' and had become so fully aware of the physical advantages arising out of the law, that not a few of them voluntarily subjected themselves to inspection at their own expense, after the abrogation of the law."

Even prior to the enactment and repeal of the St. Louis law another short-lived experiment was made in the same direction, in a much smaller city, and under very different conditions. It is well worth referring to, however, as the results accomplished bear out all that was claimed for the St. Louis system.

---

[1] *Missouri Medical Record*, May 15, 1874.

At the eighth annual meeting of the American Public Health Association, held in New Orleans, in November, 1880, Dr. A. L. Gihon, Medical Director of the United States Navy, as chairman of a committee appointed the preceding year to investigate the prevalence of venereal diseases and suggest some practical plan of prevention, submitted a very interesting report, in which occurs the following: "Colonel Fletcher, of the Surgeon-General's Office of the United States Army, writes to your committee:

"In 1863, while I was on duty in Nashville, the question of the periodical examination of prostitutes, as a protection to the troops stationed at or passing through that city, was referred to another medical officer and myself. We drew up regulations for the purpose, and for nearly three years the women were examined, at first every two weeks, but subsequently every ten days.

"I believe this was the first occasion of any systematic inspection of prostitutes attempted in the United States. Its results may be briefly stated thus:

"1. The amount of venereal disease was markedly lessened, so much so that its occurrence came to be looked upon (absurdly, of course) as an imputation on the care of the examining surgeon.

"2. The women, who were at first rebellious, became quite reconciled to the system. I have known them to come to the hospital voluntarily, desiring to be examined for suspected disease.

"3. It was self-supporting, the fees paying the expenses of the hospital."

The committee from whose report we have quoted the above recommended that a law should be enacted that would make it a criminal offense to knowingly communicate, directly or indirectly, or to be instrumental in communicating, a contagious disease, such as small-pox, scarlatina, or venereal diseases, and giving to boards of health, and to State and municipal health officials under their control, the same power of preventing, detecting, suppressing, and gratuitously treating venereal diseases that they now possess in the case of small-pox or other contagious diseases.

Since the publication of Dr. Sanger's work the law known as the "Contagious Diseases Act" has been tried and abandoned in Great Britain. The arguments advanced by members of the medical profession as well as laymen, both favorable to and against this law, would fill volumes, and many of the latter were based upon morbid ideas of morality. Perhaps the strongest argument put forward (if it is an argument) by those favoring the abrogation of the measure was that its provisions were carelessly and indifferently enforced. The same assertion has been advanced against the system as it exists in Paris, Berlin, and elsewhere. But neglect, inefficiency, or dishonesty among those charged with executing a law cannot logically stand as arguments against the law.

The great majority of the members of the medical profession who have given the subject attention, would seem to earnestly favor some system of regulation and inspection as the only means of checking and controlling syphilis. This profession has strong allies also among laymen who are not blinded by prejudice. Were the effects of the scourge of syphilis to end with the guilty, were the innocent exempt, we might, perhaps, accept the argument of the moralist that "those who sin should suffer." But when we bear in mind that the unoffending offspring of erring parents are also sufferers, justice and humanity demand, for them at least, succor and protection. After giving the statistics that we have elsewhere presented, Dr. Gross adds: "Can we wonder at the enormous rate of infantile mortality in our larger cities? Like apples which rot upon the tree before they are ripe, the children of these infected persons drop dead from their mother's womb; or, if they are born alive, they are sure to perish soon after birth."

That there has been no abatement of venereal diseases since the date of Dr. Sanger's investigation, but that they have steadily increased with the growth of the country, and the corresponding increase of prostitution, may be inferred from the figures we have been able to present as to New York City.

Shall we as a people, as a nation, or a State, still close our eyes, and ostrich-like bury our heads, that we may not see the vice and disease that are working such mischief, such havoc among us; or will we by legislation attempt at least to lessen the evil and its ravages and keep them within bound? To quote again from Dr. Gross:

"When a pestilence, as, for example, small-pox or cholera, breaks out in a community, and threatens to decimate its population, every man's fears are at once aroused, and steps taken to counteract its progress; every citizen is upon the alert. and every newspaper is urgent in its appeals for help ; but here is a disease (syphilis), a thousand times worse than the most deadly epidemic, doing its work slowly, and, as it were, in disguise and darkness, ruining entire families, destroying many of our best men and women, and laying the foundation of untold misery, wretchedness, and woe, not unfrequently extending through several generations, and literally poisoning the very fountains of life."

Many arguments have been advanced by the metropolitan press favorable to local self-government for our larger cities, and possibly none stronger could be put forward than that through local legislation, uninfluenced by rural ignorance and prejudice, and unobstructed by rural interference, some system might be devised by which prostitution in New York City and in the larger cities of other States could be brought under such surveillance and control as would greatly lessen its ghastly consequences, DISEASE and DEATH.

ACKNOWLEDGMENTS.

For numerous courtesies and much assistance in the preparation of the appendix and notes to this volume, the writer desires to express his grateful acknowledgments to those members of the medical profession whose names appear in the work, and also to Dr. C. W. Cutler, Physician-in-chief, and Dr. M. J. Echeverria, in charge of the Genito-Urinary department of the New York Dispensary; Mr. G. F. Britton, Secretary of the Commission of Charities and Correction ; Mr. John S. Brownne, Resident Librarian of the Academy of Medicine; and to Mr. Robert Roberts, Warden of the City Hospital, Blackwell's Island.

INDEX.

THE END.